Forensic Social Work

Tina Maschi, PhD, LCSW, ACSW, is an associate professor at the Fordham University Graduate School of Social Service where she teaches research, practice, and human rights and social justice. She has over 30 years of clinical social work and research experience in juvenile and criminal justice settings and community mental health settings. Dr. Maschi was a 2010 recipient of the Hartford Geriatric Social Work Faculty Scholars Program Award and a 2009 recipient of the Council on Social Work Education's Faculty Scholar's Award for the research project Promising Practices in Social Work Research Education. Her research and practice interests focus on human rights and social justice, forensic social work practice, cumulative trauma, resilience and well-being, justice-involved aging people, and community-based research and evaluation.

George S. Leibowitz, PhD, LICSW, is a professor at Stony Brook University, School of Social Welfare in New York, where he teaches courses in mental health, trauma, substance abuse, and clinical practice. He is a licensed clinical social worker and was listed with the state of Colorado as a sex offense–specific treatment provider and evaluator. Dr. Leibowitz provides training and consultation to several agencies nationwide involving risk of sexual harm cases. His research agenda includes developing etiological models of sexual aggression, trauma-informed practices with families and incarcerated populations, restorative justice, and assessment and interventions with juveniles who present with sexually harmful behavior. He has published articles in journals such as *Trauma and Dissociation, Criminal Justice and Behavior,* and *Journal of Child Sexual Abuse.*

Forensic Social Work

Psychosocial and Legal Issues Across Diverse Populations and Settings

Second Edition

Tina Maschi, PhD, LCSW, ACSW
George S. Leibowitz, PhD, LICSW
Editors

SPRINGER PUBLISHING COMPANY
NEW YORK

Springer Publishing Company, LLC
11 West 42nd Street
New York, NY 10036
www.springerpub.com

Acquisitions Editor: Debra Riegert
Compositor: Exeter Premedia Services Private Ltd.

ISBN: 978-0-8261-2066-3
ebook ISBN: 978-0-8261-2067-0

Instructor's Materials: Qualified instructors may request supplements by e-mailing textbook@springerpub.com:
Instructor's Media Resources: 978-0-8261-3554-4
Instructor's Sample Syllabus: 978-0-8261-3552-0
Instructor's PowerPoints: 978-0-8261-2224-7
Instructor's Assessments and Evaluations: 978-0-8261-3553-7

18 19 20 21 / 6 5 4 3

The author and the publisher of this Work have made every effort to use sources believed to be reliable to provide information that is accurate and compatible with the standards generally accepted at the time of publication. The author and publisher shall not be liable for any special, consequential, or exemplary damages resulting, in whole or in part, from the readers' use of, or reliance on, the information contained in this book. The publisher has no responsibility for the persistence or accuracy of URLs for external or third-party Internet websites referred to in this publication and does not guarantee that any content on such websites is, or will remain, accurate or appropriate.

Library of Congress Cataloging-in-Publication Data

Names: Maschi, Tina, editor. | Leibowitz, George S., editor.
Title: Forensic social work: psychosocial and legal issues across diverse
  populations and settings / editors, Tina Maschi, PhD, LCSW, ACSW; George
  S. Leibowitz, PhD, LICSW.
Description: Second edition. | New York, NY: Springer Publishing Company,
  LLC, [2018] | Includes bibliographical references and index.
Identifiers: LCCN 2017012272 | ISBN 9780826120663 | ISBN 9780826120670 (e-book)
Subjects: LCSH: Social workers—Legal status, laws, etc.—United States. |
  Evidence, Expert—United States. | Social legislation—United States.
Classification: LCC KF3721 .F67 2018 | DDC 363.25—dc23
LC record available at https://lccn.loc.gov/2017012272

Contact us to receive discount rates on bulk purchases.
We can also customize our books to meet your needs.
For more information please contact: sales@springerpub.com

Printed in the United States of America by McNaughton & Gunn.

Contents

PART III. Core Skills: Practice, Research and Evaluation, Policy, and Advocacy

Contributors

Chapter Authors

Rosemary Barbera, PhD, MSS, is associate professor of Social Work at La Salle University, Philadelphia, Pennsylvania. She has been working in human rights since the 1980s in the United States and Latin America. Her areas of practice and research include human rights, surviving torture, community rebuilding after human rights violations, the role memory plays in postdictatorship society, community resilience after disaster, and social work in Latin America.

Carolyn Bradley, PhD, is associate professor of Social Work at Monmouth University, West Long Branch, New Jersey where she teaches primarily in the clinical concentration. Currently, she serves as the Master's in Social Work (MSW) program director. Prior to teaching at Monmouth University, Dr. Bradley was employed for 25 years as a school social worker and a substance awareness coordinator in a large, suburban New Jersey public school district.

Carolyn Brouard is a psychology major at Centenary University, Hackettstown, New Jersey, scheduled to graduate in 2018. She has coauthored one publication and several conference presentations.

Patricia Brownell, PhD, is associate professor emeritus of the Fordham University Graduate School of Social Service, New York. Dr. Brownell served as president of the National Committee for the Prevention of Elder Abuse (NCPEA) in 2016.

Karen Bullock, PhD, LCSW, is professor in the Department of Social Work at North Carolina State University, Raleigh, North Carolina. She has 20 years of clinical experience in health and hospital settings. Her research focuses primarily on cultural competence in health care service delivery.

Gale Burford, PhD, MSW, is emeritus professor of Social Work at the University of Vermont, Burlington, Vermont, and Distinguished Visiting Scholar of Restorative Justice at the Vermont Law School in South Royalton, Vermont.

Kelli Canada, PhD, LCSW, is assistant professor in the School of Social Work at the University of Missouri, Columbia, Missouri. She has 15 years of practice and research experience with adults with serious mental illness and people who encounter the criminal justice system.

Wesley T. Church II, PhD, is the director and J. Franklin Bayhi Endowed Professor in the School of Social Work at Louisiana State University, Baton Rouge, Louisiana. He has over 20 years of experience in the juvenile and criminal justice fields.

Carol L. Cleaveland, PhD, is associate professor at George Mason University, Fairfax, Virginia. She has been researching Latino immigration since 2004.

Frank J. Corigliano, PhD, is a clinical psychologist and director of Supportive Televisiting Services at the United Social Services, Inc. of the New York Society for Ethical Culture. Dr. Corigliano provides training, consultation, and thought leadership to support individuals and organizations in leveraging technology to address clinical and social issues such as telemedicine or televisiting programs.

Kelsey Denison-Vesel, BA, just finished her undergraduate psychology degree at Centenary University, Hackettstown, New Jersey and is applying to graduate school. She has coauthored two publications and several conference presentations.

Ida Dickie, PhD, is associate professor in the School of Professional Psychology at Spalding University Louisville, Kentucky. She has 20 years of experience conducting research and clinical intervention with justice-involved populations.

Karen J. Dunn, MSW, LSW, is adjunct professor at Monmouth University, West Long Branch, New Jersey for the past 8 years. She is also a school social worker on the child study team at Ocean Township High School, Ocean Township, New Jersey with experience in substance abuse, mental health, and perinatal addictions.

Danielle Easter, MSW, LCSW, is a veteran justice outreach (VJO) specialist with the Department of Veteran Affairs (VA) working at the Truman VA in Columbia, Missouri. She has worked as a social worker with individuals involved in the criminal justice system for over 10 years.

Joy Swanson Ernst, PhD, MSW, is associate dean for academic affairs at the Wayne State University School of Social Work, Detroit, Michigan.

David Fitzpatrick, PhD, is a teaching assistant professor in the Department of Social Work, North Carolina State University, Raleigh, North Carolina. He earned a PhD in counseling and counselor education from North Carolina State University and master's degrees in clinical and substance abuse counseling and rehabilitation counseling from East Carolina University.

Sandy Gibson, PhD, LCSW, is associate professor in the Department of Counselor Education at the College of New Jersey, Ewing, New Jersey. She served as a study director for a research institute for 7 years and has taught graduate counseling and social work research for 12 years.

Melissa D. Grady, PhD, MSW, LICSW, is associate professor at the National Catholic School of Social Service at Catholic University in Washington, DC. She is chairperson of the Clinical Concentration and teaches courses on clinical theory and practice, research, and human development and psychopathology. In addition, she maintains a clinical practice and conducts research on sexual violence.

Jodi Hall, MSW, EdD, is assistant professor and director of Field Education at North Carolina State University Department of Social Work, Raleigh, North Carolina. She earned her Doctorate of Education from North Carolina State and master's degree in social work from the University of North Carolina at Chapel Hill.

R. Anna Hayward-Everson, PhD, MSW, is associate professor at Stony Brook University School of Social Welfare, Stony Brook, New York. Dr. Hayward's research focuses on children and families living in poverty with a focus on father involvement and parental incarceration. Dr. Hayward currently serves as the principal investigator on the evaluation of the federally funded Suffolk County Fatherhood Initiative where she is examining the impact of fatherhood and relationship-focused intervention on low-income fathers.

Kirk James, DSW, is professor at the Silver School of Social Work at New York University. His work focuses on mass incarceration, trauma, modalities of healing, and human rights.

Mary Lou Killian, PhD, is a nonprofit administrator with over 30 years of experience in clinical and macro social work. She has taught sociology, political science, and social work at the undergraduate and graduate levels.

Eileen Klein, PhD, LCSW, MS, is associate professor in the Department of Social Work at Ramapo College, Mahwah, New Jersey. She has over 25 years of experience as an administrator in public mental health prior to teaching full time.

George S. Leibowitz, PhD, LICSW, is professor at Stony Brook University, School of Social Welfare in Stony Brook, New York. His research agenda includes understanding the developmental pathways to criminal and juvenile justice involvement and sexually harmful behavior among adolescents.

Jill Levenson, PhD, LCSW, is associate professor of Social Work at Barry University in Miami, Florida. She also provides clinical services to perpetrators and survivors of interpersonal violence and sexual assault.

Rebecca Linn-Walton, PhD, LCSW, is the director of Planning, Research, and Evaluation at a nonprofit in New York City. She provides planning for evidence-based practice usage in mandated and voluntary programs for youth and adults, research support and publications, and evaluation of existing programs. She is on the adjunct faculty at Fordham University in New York, and has a research background in clinical interventions with justice-involved individuals with mental illness or substance abuse diagnoses. Her focus is on reducing stigma and increasing empathic, recovery-oriented services for justice-involved individuals.

Shreya Mandal, JD, LCSW, is the owner of One World Mitigation & Forensic Services in New York. She has over 13 years of experience in mitigation and forensic social work in capital defense, criminal defense, and immigration defense.

Tina Maschi, PhD, LCSW, ACSW, is associate professor at the Fordham University Graduate School of Social Service in New York and founder and director of the Justia Agenda, which hosts global forensic research and advocacy projects, such as Aging in the Criminal Justice System. She has over 30 years of experience in practice, research, and advocacy in criminal justice settings and with forensic populations.

Carl Mazza, DSW, LMSW, is associate professor and chair of the Social Work Department at Lehman College of the City University of New York. He has over 35 years of experience with incarcerated people and their families, exonerees, and child welfare.

David Axlyn McLeod, PhD, MSW, is the graduate program coordinator and an assistant professor with the University of Oklahoma Anne and Henry Zarrow School of Social Work, Norman, Oklahoma. A former police detective and clinical forensic social worker, his research focuses on forensic psychopathology, with specific attention to differential experiences of trauma and relational violence across the life span.

Marie Mele, PhD, is assistant professor in the Department of Criminal Justice at Monmouth University, West Long Branch, New Jersey. She is a former victim advocate with research and teaching interests in intimate partner violence and repeat victimization.

Nancy J. Mezey, PhD, is professor of Sociology and associate dean of Academic and Faculty Affairs at Monmouth University, West Long Branch, New Jersey. Her research focuses on the sociological formation, experiences, and impact of diverse family forms.

Keith Morgen, PhD, LPC, ACS, is associate professor of Psychology & Counseling at Centenary University, Hackettstown, New Jersey. He also has a part-time counseling practice at Discovery Psychotherapy & Wellness Centers (Morristown, NJ).

Alissa Nowak, BA, is a recent psychology graduate of Centenary University, Hackettstown, New Jersey.

Joan Pennell, PhD, MSW, is the founding director of the Center for Family and Community Engagement and professor of Social Work at North Carolina State University, Raleigh, North Carolina.

Tam Perry, PhD, MSSW, MA, is assistant professor at Wayne State University School of Social Work, Detroit, Michigan. She researches the intersection between housing and health for older adults.

Clark Peters, PhD, JD, MSW, is associate professor in the School of Social Work at the University of Missouri. His research and teaching focus on youths and young adults in state care, as well as the intersection of human services and law.

David S. Prescott, LICSW, has authored and edited 14 books and numerous articles and chapters in the area of assessing and treating abuse and trauma. He is a past president of the Association for the Treatment of Sexual Abusers.

Joanne Rees, PhD, is assistant professor in the Department of Social Work, School of Health Professions at Long Island University (LIU) Brooklyn New York. She teaches in both the BASW and MSW programs, and is the coordinator of the Forensic Social Work and Child & Family Welfare Advanced Concentrations.

Susan P. Robbins, PhD, LCSW, is professor at the University of Houston Graduate College of Social Work. She is a clinical and forensic social worker.

Vanessa Rorai, MSW, conducted community-based research on housing issues in Detroit while completing her MSW. She is now a Community Outreach Specialist at the Institute of Gerontology at Wayne State University, Detroit, Michigan.

Claudia Sanford, BFA, is a tenant organizer and Volunteers in Service to America (VISTA) supervisor at the United Community Housing Coalition (UCHC), Detroit, Michigan. In her 10 years with UCHC she has also been a program manager/supervisor assisting tenants at risk of homelessness with finance, education, and job support.

Jaclyn Smith is a psychology major at Centenary University, Hackettstown, New Jersey scheduled to graduate in 2018. She has coauthored one publication and several conference presentations.

Anne Sparks, PhD, holds the position of assistant professor at the University of Rio Grande in southeastern Ohio and teaches courses in social work, sociology, and service learning. Her areas of expertise include cultural diversity, women's issues, low-income families, and financial literacy.

Sandra Turner, PhD, ACSW, is associate professor at Fordham University Graduate School of Social Service in New York. She is the director of the Institute for Women and Girls at Fordham.

Katherine van Wormer, PhD, MSSW, is professor of Social Work at the University of Northern Iowa and the author or coauthor of over 20 books including *The Maid Narratives: Black Domestics and White Families in the Jim Crow South* (LSU Press).

Abigail Voelkner, BA, just finished her undergraduate degree in psychology at Centenary University, Hackettstown, New Jersey and is a counseling graduate student at Lehigh University in Bethlehem, Pennsylvania. She has coauthored two publications and several conference presentations.

Johannes Wheeldon, PhD, LLM, is adjunct professor at Norwich University, Northfield, Vermont, with more than 15 years of experience managing evaluation and juvenile justice projects for the American Bar Association, the Open Society Foundations, and the World Bank. He has published four books and more than 25 peer review papers on aspects of criminal justice, restorative justice, and organizational change.

Voices From The Field Contributors

Melissa Elder, MSW, is the coordinator at the Kids' HOPE Program at the Oklahoma City Family Justice Center.

Claire Gilligan, PsyD, is a forensic psychologist with Vermont Forensic Assessment, PLLC.

April Harvin, LCSW, is a licensed clinical social worker with over 20 years of direct service and administrative experience working with youth and families in a variety of social service settings. Ms. Harvin has worked with justice-involved youth in foster care, housing, employment, and mental health settings. She knows that a thorough knowledge of and engagement with systems is necessary to this work.

Tammy Leombruno, LCMHC, is a licensed clinical mental health counselor with 25 years of experience in the field of sexual abuse and trauma. She specializes in the assessment and treatment of young children and adolescents with sexual behavior problems, and provides advanced training and consultation to various child-serving agencies on best practice interventions with this population.

Victoria Marini, PhD, is a forensic psychologist with Vermont Forensic Assessment, PLLC.

Gia N. Marshall, LCSW, is a licensed clinical social worker at the North Carolina Correctional Institution for Women in Raleigh, North Carolina.

Romarie McCue, BA, is director, Suffolk County Fatherhood Initiative (SCFI), a program of Retreat, Inc. in Long Island, New York. Romarie has over 12 years of experience in community-based programs serving individuals affected by HIV/AIDS, substance abuse, and incarceration.

Deana "Dee" McDonald, BS, has over 20 years of experience working as a social worker in the Kentucky Cabinet for Health and Family Services. Prior to becoming a circuit court judge in both the juvenile and family divisions, she worked as a prosecutor for over 10 years. She currently serves as a judge in Louisville, Kentucky, using her interdisciplinary perspective daily.

Dierdra Oretade-Branch, MSW, LCSW, is a licensed clinical social worker at the Department of Justice, Federal Bureau of Prisons, Federal Medical Center in Butner, North Carolina.

Diane Pfaff, MSW, LISW-S, is the community services manager for the Alcohol, Drug Addiction and Mental Health Services Board of Athens, Hocking, and Vinton Counties in Ohio. She received her MSW degree in 2002 from Ohio University and has experience working in the field of aging and long-term care.

Paula Price, LCSW-C, is an adult protective services investigator for the Washington County (Maryland) Department of Social Services.

Eileen Price-Farbman, is a social work student at Fordham University of Social Sciences in New York. She has over 15 years of experience working in the area of intimate partner violence as a private and group counselor as well as with teen programs. She currently has an internship at the New York Society for Ethical Culture in the Supportive Televisiting Program helping incarcerated parents engage with their children in the community.

Judith L. F. Rhodes, PhD, LMSW, is the program manager at YEP Village—Youth Empowerment Program in Baton Rouge, Louisiana.

Susan Robinson, LICSW, is a licensed clinical social worker with over 23 years of clinical experience specializing in trauma and sexual offending behavior. She provides services to youth with sexually harmful behavior, women involved in the criminal justice system, and adolescent and adult survivors of trauma.

Joetta Shepherd, MSW, LCSW, is the director of the Safe Relationships Division at Family Services, Inc., Winston-Salem, North Carolina. She has over 30 years of experience working within the domestic violence field.

Julie Smyth, LMSW, has spent the past 5 years working in public defense settings in both Philadelphia and New York City. She was a supervising social worker at The Bronx Defenders in New York and now works as a mitigation specialist and sentencing advocate in private practice.

Michele Sneed, BSW, MSW, LGSW, is an assistant professor of social work at the College of St. Scholastica, Duluth, Minnesota.

Michael Todd, LCSW, has 36 years of experience in the field of psychiatric social work. He served as director of Social Work at South Beach Psychiatric Center, Miami, Florida, from 2011 to 2016 and was the chairperson of the Hospital Forensic Committee for over 22 years. Currently, he is the director of Social Services at East Mountain Hospital, Belle Mead, New Jersey.

Louise Vandenbosch, MS, is a registered social worker and accredited family mediator based in London, Ontario, Canada, and owner of Wesbrook Mediation Services. She has been working with families in a variety of settings for over 30 years in the areas of adult mental health, children's mental health, adult and children's developmental services, system navigation of services, community social work, and alternative dispute resolution.

Jeff Yungman, MSW, LISW-CP, MPH, JD, is the clinical director of Crisis Ministries and director of the Crisis Ministries Justice Project, Charlestown, South Carolina.

Keila Zapata-Kelly, MSW, CASAC-T, is the administrator of Continuing Education and Social Work Licensure at the Graduate School of Social Service at Fordham University, Manhattan Campus.

Preface

We are thrilled to offer this second edition of *Forensic Social Work: Psychosocial and Legal Issues Across Diverse Populations and Settings*. Since the 2009 publication of the first edition, the recognition of the need for a specialized and integrated workforce in the field of forensic social work has grown. Both nationally and abroad, the growing public awareness of bias and discrimination and the disproportionate involvement of minority populations, especially based on race, class, and gender, have affected the social work profession with a call to fulfill its long-forgotten mission to respond and advocate for justice reform and health and public safety.

Forensic social workers practice far and wide where issues of justice and fairness are found. As we emphasize throughout the book on the diversity of populations and settings, social workers would best serve their clients by adding a forensic or legal lens to their practice. The diversity of settings with forensic clients include social services agencies, schools, hospitals, substance abuse and mental health programs, child welfare agencies, and courts and prisons throughout the world.

Regardless of the location of practice, to be the most effective forensic practitioners, social workers must share common professional needs. We need to have the integrated forensic knowledge, values, and skills of practice, research, advocacy, and collaboration to assist individuals, families, organizations, and communities who may be struggling with an array of problems, especially human rights, social justice, and legal issues that include human rights violations (e.g., trauma and abuse), unjust policies, and lack of legal protections. In the changing world of integrated health and behavioral health services, it has become a further imperative to work collaboratively with professionals and other key stakeholders, especially the clients most affected by these issues, to respond to a mixture of financial, psychological, emotional, social, and legal concerns.

This book targets the important and emerging practice specialization of forensic social work, a practice specialization that speaks to the heart, head, and hands (i.e., knowledge, values, and skills) of social work using a human rights and social justice approach integrated with a forensic lens. Consistent with the first edition, we define *forensic social work* to include not only a narrow group of people who are victims or convicted of crimes and subsequently involved in the juvenile justice and criminal justice settings, but broadly all the individuals and families involved with family and social services, education, child welfare, mental health, and behavioral health or other programs in which they are affected by human rights and social justice issues, or federal and state laws and policies. Examples include social workers advocating for legal protection for undocumented workers, those assisting individuals and families in need as they apply for entitlements such as Medicare or Social Security disability benefits, and those providing mental health treatment to inmates with special needs in a correctional setting.

Goals of the Book

Overall, this new edition prepares students and professionals to practice at the intersection of human rights, social work, public health, and the legal system in order to tackle contemporary social problems, including health disparities and mass incarceration. Many forensic populations, such as racial and ethnic minorities, at-risk youth, the elderly, veterans, immigrants, lesbian, gay, bisexual, transgender, and queer (LGBTQ) individuals, people with disabilities, or those living in poverty or communities of violence, often lack access to quality services and political, civil, social, economic, and cultural justice.

Practitioners who read this book will learn and apply a human rights legal framework and social justice and empowerment theories to guide multilevel prevention, assessment, and interventions with historically underserved individuals, families, and communities. They also are exposed to innovative practice, research, and advocacy solutions that address the psychosocial determinants of health, well-being, and justice. After reading this book, individuals will increase their knowledge, values, and skills for collaborative and integrated forensic practice with diverse populations in diverse practice settings, such as health care, social service, and legal settings, including protective services, the courts, and corrections. The book can be used with advanced year content, professional continuing social work, or interprofessional education credits and infuses clinical, macropractice and leadership, and research and evaluation skills.

Special or vulnerable populations and salient human rights practice, research, and advocacy issues addressed in the second edition include:

- Children, adolescents, and family (including children of incarcerated parents)
- Racial and ethnic minorities
- Women
- Immigrants and refugees
- Undocumented workers
- Veterans
- Older people
- HIV/AIDS patients
- LGBTQ individuals
- People living in poverty
- People who are homeless
- People with mental health and substance use issues
- People with serious and terminal illnesses
- People with serious offense histories
- Trauma survivors and victims of crimes
- Prisoners
- Others

These individuals and groups are highlighted because of the higher likelihood that they will experience health and justice disparities.

In general, this book fills a critical gap in the knowledge, values, and skills for human rights and social justice–focused social work education and training. According to the 2015 Council on Social Work Education (CSWE) accreditation standards (see Table P.1), generalist and specialized knowledge values and skills of engagement, assessment, intervention, evaluation, research, policy practice, interprofessional practice, legal knowledge, and advocacy that advance human rights and social justice are essential for social workers while they balance

TABLE P.1   Forensic Lens With Nine Core Competencies

1. Demonstrate Ethical and Professional Behavior
2. Engage Diversity and Difference in Practice
3. Advance Human Rights and Social, Economic, and Environmental Justice
4. Engage in Practice-Informed Research and Research-Informed Practice
5. Engage in Policy Practice
6. Engage With Individuals, Families, Organizations, and Communities
7. Assess Individuals, Families, Organizations, and Communities
8. Intervene With Individuals, Families, Organizations, and Communities
9. Evaluate Practice With Individuals, Families, Organizations, and Communities

Source: CSWE EPAs (2015).

the dual goals of public health and public safety. Yet the implications of legal issues are rarely addressed or integrated in social work education in a meaningful and practical way. This book addresses this perceived oversight. Readers of the book will become more confident and competent in integrating sociolegal knowledge, values, and skills, especially with forensic practice, research, advocacy, and collaboration across diverse populations and settings.

New to This Edition

Changes to the new edition include:

- Incorporation of the 2015 CSWE Educational Policies and Accreditation Standards (EPAs) as outlined in Table P.1
- Application of a human rights and social justice approach to forensic populations and settings, and integration of micro, mezzo, and macro skills (e.g., research, practice, and advocacy)
- An expanded pedagogical program, now with chapter competencies and objectives, theoretical knowledge, and detailed coverage of core themes and strategies of forensic practice and forensic skills
- Updated case studies and Voices From the Field of social work and allied professionals, making this text ideal for social work, psychology, legal, public health, and other allied professionals
- Additional pedagogical tools, including end-of-chapter summaries, exercises, and web-based resources, as well as instructor PowerPoints, sample syllabi, and psychosocial assessment and other tools
- An array of interdisciplinary emerging and seasoned scholars and practitioners from diverse disciplines, such as social work, psychology, criminal justice, and the law, as featured authors
- Expanded and updated chapters from the first edition that include the history of forensic social work, child welfare, juvenile justice, immigration, and victim advocacy
- An updated section (Part II) that now includes new chapters emphasizing race and the criminal justice system using a mass incarceration lens, health care and persons with disabilities and serious illnesses, housing and persons who are homeless, adult protective services and older people, and veterans
- A new section (Part III) that features updated chapters on core forensic skills, including evidence-based assessment and intervention, motivational and forensic interviewing, expert testimony, family engagement, restorative justice theory and practice, empowerment practice, case- and policy-level advocacy, interdisciplinary collaboration, technology, and supportive televisiting

Intended Audience

The intended audience for this book includes social work and other interdisciplinary students, such as psychology students, Juris Doctor/MSW students, and criminal justice majors at the bachelor's and master's level. It is largely intended as an advanced-year elective but also can be used in foundation-level courses that target diverse populations and settings. This book also is relevant for continuing education programs and professionals who want to expand their practice skills to include the intersection of practice and the law or legal issues.

Organization and Content

Forensic Social Work is structured so that the reader can make the most of its content. It is divided into three parts that move from the broad discussion of the conceptual and historical foundation of forensic social work to specific populations and settings, as well as core forensic social work skills. Part I, A Human Rights and Social Justice Approach to Forensic Practice, prepares the reader with a definition of collaborative forensic social work practice. Assuming a human rights and social justice systems approach, we define this specialty practice area to include all practice fields that operate in some way in the sociolegal environment. These fields range from health, social, and mental health services to the juvenile and criminal justice systems and can involve individuals, families, organizations, and communities. Readers are guided on a journey through the conceptual and historical foundation of forensic social work from its roots in human rights and social justice. It reviews the social work profession's charity and corrections movements to its current manifestation as the work of professional clinicians, researchers, and policy advocates. The use of a human rights and social justice systems approach helps readers visualize their practice within a holistic and integrated environment. A comprehensive description of human rights and the law, social work, and ethics and the law, along with a review of civil and criminal law, helps readers understand and infuse the legal issues and procedures that affect client populations and professional practice.

In Part II, Systems of Care and Forensic Practice, readers are introduced to diverse populations and settings affected in some way by human rights, social justice, and the legal system. In this section, readers learn what it means to use forensic integrated practice that involves practice, research, advocacy, and collaborative knowledge, values, and skills within diverse issues and settings, such as family and social services, education, child welfare, behavioral health, veteran's services, adult protective services, juvenile justice, criminal justice, and immigration justice sectors of care. In the complementary Voices From the Field supplementary readings, readers also have the opportunity to hear from seasoned practitioners and experts about the types of clients or practice issues they may encounter in a specific system of care.

Part III, entitled Core Skills: Practice, Research and Evaluation, Policy, and Advocacy, highlights the majority of core skills that forensic social workers commonly use. The skills include the use of forensic-oriented risk assessments and evidence-based practices, motivational interviewing, forensic interviewing, expert testimony, restorative justice theory, and practice. We also highlight core forensic skills using empowerment practices, family engagement interventions, mental health and recovery skills, interdisciplinary and intersectoral collaboration, forensic research and evaluation, case- and policy-level advocacy, and the use of technology advances with families at risk of or involved in the criminal justice system.

After reading this book, social workers will be better positioned to use a forensic lens to engage, assess, prevent, and intervene with individuals, families, organizations, and communities across various fields of practice. They will also be better prepared to integrate forensic specialized knowledge, values, and skills in practice, research, advocacy, and interdisciplinary and intersectoral collaboration with a variety of key stakeholders.

Learning Tools

As previously noted, this new edition also includes expanded learning tools. These tools include chapter objectives based on the 2015 CSWE EPAs, end-of-chapter exercises, and chapter summaries and conclusions. They also include Voices From the Field: perspectives of forensic social workers in diverse settings that give readers a realistic look at what it is like to work in diverse forensic settings with diverse populations.

Instructor's Resources

Additional resources found on the Springer Publishing website for the book benefit instructors and students. Instructors will find chapter PowerPoint presentations, sample syllabi, and other resources such as a sample biopsychosocial assessment, case studies, and more.

Students and professionals who read this book are offered the gift of an early lifelong learning process in the specialized field of forensic social work practice with a variety of populations across a wide range of practice settings. It is our recommendation to accept this gift and be sure to pass it along!

Reference

Council on Social Work Education. (2015). *2015 educational policy and accreditation standards.* Retrieved from https://www.cswe.org/getattachment/Accreditation/Accreditation-Process/2015-EPAS/2015EPAS_Web_FINAL.pdf.aspx

Acknowledgments

There are many people who helped shape this book idea into a reality. We are most indebted to the individuals, families, and community members who shared their experiences. Special thanks are extended to the Springer staff for editorial words of wisdom and to Diane Richer for all of her assistance with preparation of this manuscript. We also thank our friends, colleagues, and family members for embarking on this collaborative adventure with us. We hope you know who you are!

Forensic Social Work

PART I

A HUMAN RIGHTS AND SOCIAL JUSTICE APPROACH TO FORENSIC PRACTICE

CHAPTER 1

Conceptual and Historical Overview of Forensic Social Work

Tina Maschi

George S. Leibowitz

Mary Lou Killian

CHAPTER OBJECTIVES

The major objectives of this chapter are to:

- Describe a forensic practice framework using a human rights and social justice systems approach.
- Articulate the definition and theme-based strategies that distinguish forensic social work from social work practice as usual.
- Review the history of forensic social work, especially as it relates to the United States.

CHAPTER COMPETENCIES HIGHLIGHTED

- Competency 3: Advance Human Rights and Social, Economic, and Environmental Justice
- Competency 5: Engage in Policy Practice

Section One: Central Concepts and Theme-Based Strategies in Forensic Social Work

Social work has been an enduring and dynamic force, and its presence has helped improve individual and societal conditions. Born out of early-20th-century efforts of charity workers or "friendly visitors," social work has grown from being a loose-knit group of community volunteers who were "doing good" to an internationally recognized profession endowed with the responsibility of providing social welfare services and advocating for social change (Addams, 1910; Ehrenreich; 1985; Richmond, 1917). However, contemporary social work practice finds itself in a complex and interactive global society fraught with social problems, and has arrived at a critical crossroad in which advancing the mission of social work involves equipping practitioners with additional skills.

Today, social workers are called on more than ever to navigate the legal system, collaborating from within the system to create lasting social change. Madden (2003) stressed the point: "If the social work profession is to be in control of its future, it must become committed to the role of exerting influence on the legal system through education, advocacy and proactive legal policy development" (pp. 3–4).

In contemporary social work discourse, scholars and practitioners have advanced the *Grand Challenges* (Uehara et al., 2013) to promote dialogue and policy reform about a range of social justice issues, including health disparities, mass incarceration, the interrelationship between substance use and incarceration, unemployment and education, and racial and ethnic inequalities in the juvenile and criminal justice systems (Poe-Yamagata & Jones, 2000). The mission of the Grand Challenges is to "galvanize social workers' collective contribution to the quality of life and promotion of an equitable society in the 21st century" (Uehara et al., 2013), relying on social innovation to increase health and well-being among vulnerable populations, which are broadly a concern for forensic social workers. Additionally, social workers are compelled to be data driven and apply the empirical literature and the evidence from scientific research to address the most pressing social problems (Maschi & Youdin, 2012) (For more information see http://aaswsw.org/wp-content/uploads/2013/12/Intro_ Context_GCSW.pdf or *From Mass Incarceration to Smart Decarceration. American Academy of Social Work & Social Welfare* at http://aaswsw.org/wp-content/uploads/2015/03/From-Mass-Incarceration-to-Decarceration-3.24.15.pdf).

To this end, this book frames forensic social work and collaboration through the lens of central guiding conceptual models of social work practice: a human rights, social justice and person-in-environment perspective along with social systems theory. We propose an integrated theoretical perspective that we refer to as a human rights and social justice systems (HR-SJS) approach. This perspective is useful for visualizing practice with clients influenced by a combination of social and legal issues. Figure 1.1 presents a conceptual diagram of the HR-SJS approach to forensic practice.

The HR-SJS approach, described in more detail in Section Two of this chapter, helps to visualize forensic social work practice in any practice setting. As illustrated, social workers working with individuals and families involved in the service systems are affected by social issues as well as laws, legal issues, and policies. As the arrows indicate, social workers can be involved with clients sequentially or concurrently, and be affected by civil law (e.g., going through a divorce, death of a loved one, sexual harassment on the job) or criminal law (e.g., victim of a violent crime, arrested for a nonserious or serious criminal offense).

The specialization of forensic social work is an ideal vehicle for navigating the sociolegal environment that goes beyond social work practice as usual. It is an integrative practice model that incorporates social work ethics, generalist and specialist practice, and the

Figure 1.1 A Conceptual Model of a HR-SJS Approach to Forensic Practice

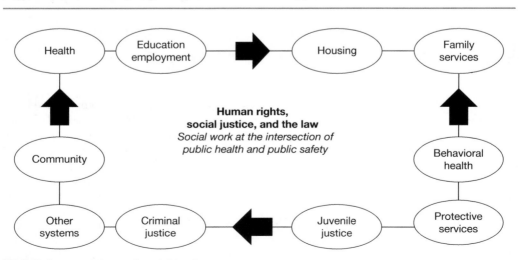

HR-SJS, human rights and social justice systems.

knowledge and skills of research, as well as the nature of evidence, law, policy practice, and interdisciplinary or interprofessional and intersectoral collaboration. In fact, a commitment to practice that involves psychosocial and legal interventions is consistent with the historic two-pronged integrated approach to social work practice.

The Two-Pronged Approach to Social Work Practice

Social work has long used a two-pronged approach to facilitate change: (a) assisting individuals and families to improve functioning, and (b) combating unjust and unfair community and societal conditions through strategies of social reform (Bartlett, 1958; see Figure 1.2). These strategies are explained in the mission statement of the National Association of Social Workers' (NASW) *Code of Ethics* (1996) in which a historic and defining feature of the social work profession is "individual well-being in a social context and the well-being of society" (NASW, 1996). Central to the social work mission is consideration of the "environmental forces that create, contribute, and address problems in living" (NASW).

Figure 1.2 A Two-Pronged Approach to Practice in the Sociolegal Environment That Influences Forensic Social Workers' Activities Across the Fields of Practice

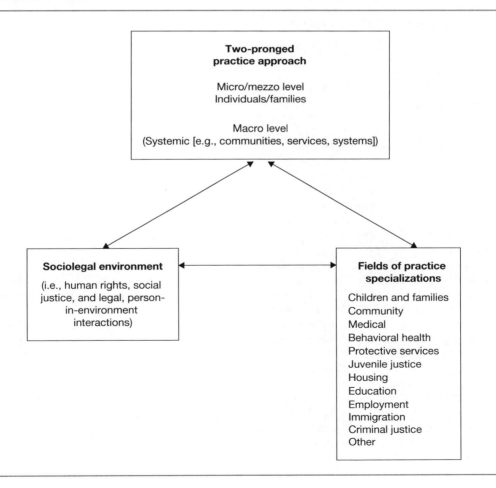

The two-pronged approach also is echoed in the Social Work Dictionary's definition of social work. It is defined as an "applied science of helping people achieve an effective level of psychosocial functioning and effecting societal changes to enhance the well-being of all people" (Barker, 2003). Consequently, social work practitioners target their interventions at the micro level (e.g., individuals), the mezzo level (e.g., families and groups), and/or the macro level (e.g., institutions, organizations, cultures and communities, and society) (Zastrow & Kirst-Ashman, 2012). Miley, O'Meila, and DuBois (2012) outlined four major goals for practice addressing multilevel assessment and intervention strategies. These four goals are:

1. enhancing people's individual functioning, problem-solving, and coping abilities;
2. linking clients to needed resources;
3. working to develop and improve the social service–delivery network;
4. promoting social justice through the development of social policy.

It is interesting that the seemingly opposite roles of helper and advocate have both unified the profession (a common person-in-environment perspective) and divided it (should the primary target of change be the individual or the environment? Bartlett, 1970). In social work literature, the environment is commonly referred to as the "social environment." We argue that expanding the definition of a "social environment" to include the ever present "justice environment" is necessary for achieving the best possible positive outcomes consistent with the dual mission of social work to enhance empowerment and individual, family, and community well-being.

Advancing a HR-SJS Perspective for Forensic Practice

Applying a Human Rights Framework

Applying a human rights framework to the laws, policies, and practices with forensic populations and settings can be used to assess the extent to which these laws meet basic human rights principles. In particular, the principles of a human rights framework can provide assessment guidelines for developing or evaluating existing public health and criminal justice laws or policies, such as U.S. compassionate and geriatric release laws. The underlying values/principles of a human rights framework include dignity and respect for all persons, and the indivisible and interlocking holistic relationship of all human rights in civil, political, economic, social, and cultural domains (United Nations [UN], 1948). Additional principles include participation (especially with key stakeholder input on legal decision making), nondiscrimination (i.e., laws and practices in which individuals are not discriminated against based on differences, such as age, race, gender, and legal history), transparency, and accountability (especially for government transparency and accountability with their citizens; Maschi, 2016).

The Universal Declaration of Human Rights (UDHR) also is an instrument that provides assistance with determining the most salient human rights issues affected. Ratified in 1948 as a response to the atrocities of World War II, 48 countries, including the United States, voted in favor of the UDHR (UN, 1948). It provides the philosophical underpinnings and relevant articles to guide policy and practice responses to the aging and seriously and terminally ill in prison. The UDHR preamble underscores the norm of "respect for the inherent dignity and equal and inalienable rights" of *all human beings.* This is of fundamental importance to crafting the treatment and release of the aging and seriously ill persons in prison.

Using a case example of aging and seriously ill people in prison, there are several UDHR articles that are important to consider when providing a rationale and response to the aging and seriously ill population in prison. For example, Article 3 states, "Everyone has the right to life, liberty, and the security of person." Article 5 states, "No one shall be subjected to torture or to cruel, inhuman or degrading treatment or punishment." Article 6 states, "Everyone has the right to recognition everywhere as a person before the law." Article 8 states "Everyone has the right to an effective remedy by the competent national tribunals for acts violating the fundamental rights granted him by the constitution or by law," and Article 25 states, "Everyone has the right to a standard of living adequate for the health and well-being of himself and of his family, including food and clothing" (UN, 1948).

The Social and Justice Environments

The social environment is often viewed as the place in which person-in-environment interactions occur (Zastrow & Kirst-Ashman, 2012). However, although the social environment is commonly viewed as omnipresent, the justice environment that is informed by human rights is equally present. The justice environment consists of individuals, families, and communities seeking fairness, equality, freedom from oppression, and the balance of power, as well as the laws, policies, and legal system that affect the social environment (Barker, 2003).

The presence of justice, if not explicitly stated, is implicit in the descriptions of the social environment as usual. The social environment may range from an individual's interactions with social or organizational settings (e.g., home, school, society, work, agency, and neighborhood), social systems (e.g., individuals, groups, families, friends, work groups, and communities), attributes of society (e.g., laws and social norms and rules), social institutions (e.g., health care, social welfare, education, juvenile and criminal justice, and governmental systems), to social forces (e.g., political, economic, cultural, environmental, and ideological forces; Zastrow & Kirst-Ashman, 2012). Although person-in-environment interactions describe social settings and interactions, it also suggests justice situations (e.g., denied employment because of a disability or history of incarceration) or settings (e.g., involvement in juvenile and criminal justice settings) and justice-oriented interactions (e.g., associating with delinquent peers, being arrested by the police for driving while intoxicated, being a victim of a bias or hate crime, or losing one's home to eminent domain).

Envisioning Forensic Practice in a Sociolegal Environment

Most clients are affected by some type of legal issue, such as divorce, custody of children, accessing civil rights, death and inheritance, or being convicted of a felony (Madden & Wayne, 2003; Saltzman & Furman, 1999; Schroeder, 1997). In the United States, it is critical that social workers be aware of how our federal legal system operates. The U.S. legal system is made up of different branches, levels, and types of government. Laws range from the federal level—governing the entire United States—to individual state laws, as well as local ordinances and regulations from municipalities, counties, and quasi-public agencies (Saltzman & Furman, 1999). Madden (2003) argued that law, with its legal rules and mandates, should be viewed as a mechanism that frames social work practice.

A HR-SJS Perspective

We propose a social justice systems (SJS) perspective that conceptualizes the interaction of persons within a "social justice" environment. The core social work value of social justice is a central aspect of this perspective. Barker (2003) defined social justice as "an ideal condition in which all societal members have the same rights, protection, opportunities, obligations, and social benefits." The sociolegal environment represents a combination of social justice (person-in-environment interactions that seek a balance toward social justice or fairness) and the legal environment (which represents the law, the legal process, and institutions that seek individual and community protection). Thus, the SJS perspective allows social workers to pursue optimal social and justice outcomes for their clients across all fields of practice.

Figure 1.3 depicts a HR-SJS map that shows the different pathways individuals and families may travel in across the social service and/or justice systems of care. These service trajectories may span a continuum from the least to most restrictive service environments. The human rights and social justice system is comprised of an individual's proximal social system and the "social and justice sectors of care." Each sector of care represents a service

Figure 1.3 A Conceptual Diagram With Examples of the Different Informal or Formal Systems That Individuals and Families May Use Concurrently and/or Sequentially in the Social and Justice Sectors of Care. It Can Be Used for Prevention, Assessment, and Intervention Mapping

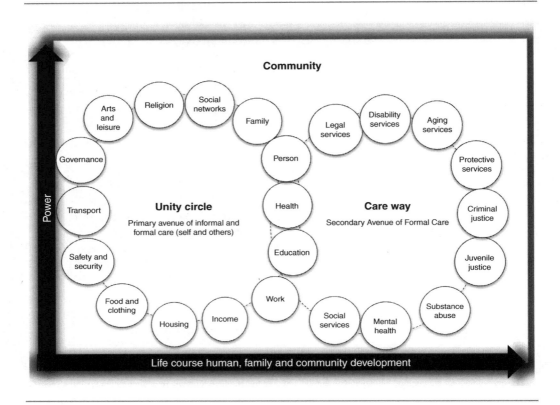

subsystem in which individuals are affected by this sector's laws and policies. Although health and education are universal services, the other subsystems are specifically designed to provide services for individuals and/or families at risk. Individuals and families may have varied patterns of system bias and discrimination, unmet service needs, and/or concurrent and/or sequential service-use patterns that include health, education, social services, child welfare, mental health, substance abuse, and juvenile justice and criminal justice service sectors of care.

The HR-SJS framework builds upon a generalist social systems theory. Social systems theory focuses on "the relationships that exist among members of human systems and between these systems and their impinging environments" (DuBois & Miley, 2012). Within each larger system are smaller nested subsystems. A change in one part of a system affects other parts of the system (L. C. Johnson & Yanca, 2015). For example, social work practitioners commonly assess and intervene in the subsystems of family, health care, education, and social service, as well as political and legal systems.

In an ideal world, these social systems would function at their optimum potential. Families would be able to care for the physical, emotional, and social development of young and elderly family members; health and mental health institutions would assist all individuals in achieving and maintaining optimal physical, mental, emotional, and spiritual health; educational institutions would help all individuals to achieve the knowledge and skills needed to excel in society; social service systems would be able to help all individuals in need; and the political and legal system would provide protection, safety, and human rights to all individuals and families by developing or implementing laws, maintaining order, and fostering their creativity and potential.

However, the reality of our global society, in which oppression of individuals and groups based on difference, does not match this ideal. The interaction between and among systems is often conflicted because of social tension, service barriers, missed opportunities, power struggles, oppression, and other social injustices. L. C. Johnson and Yanca (2015) argue that when applying social systems theory, individuals' needs and rights must be considered in the context of larger systems because of these divergent environmental demands.

When applying a HR-SJS approach, social interactions among individuals and their environment also are viewed as dynamic and multidimensional. The interaction between individuals and the different systems in their environment may significantly affect their level of functioning. For example, a single mother with four children who has no mode of transportation will be unable to travel to obtain much-needed public assistance or food stamps. Because social workers "strive to ensure access to needed information, services, and resources; equality of opportunity; and meaningful participation in decision making for all people" (NASW, 1996), a social worker for this family can apply a two-pronged approach to intervention: He or she may provide resource links to public assistance and employment services and transportation as well as advocating for the development of free or affordable shuttle services for social service recipients.

Social workers also must recognize that individuals and families may be involved in multiple systems concurrently or sequentially (Garland, Hough, Landsverk, & Brown, 2001). For example, a child with emotional and behavioral problems may simultaneously be involved in special education services, community mental health services, and probation. Another child may have initially entered the child welfare system and then later gone through the juvenile justice system. The role of the social worker will include identifying obstacles, making resource linkages, or advocating for needed resources across these social institutions (Finn & Jacobson, 2003).

A HR-SJS approach balances the goal of maximizing outcomes on both individual and societal levels. It also emphasizes the need for the knowledge and skills in forensic or legal issues, interprofessional and intersectoral collaboration, and generalist social work that integrates advanced clinical and/or policy practice. The HR-SJS approach helps to frame social workers' efforts in pursuing social change, especially for vulnerable and oppressed populations affected by systemic issues (e.g., poverty, discrimination). Consistent with the NASW *Code of Ethics* (NASW, 1996), assessing for social and justice outcomes can "ensure access to needed information, services, and resources; equality of opportunity; and meaningful participation in decision making for all people." Thus, the jurisprudent social worker who is savvy with both policy and the law can more competently engage in multilevel intervention strategies that include direct practice, community organizing, supervision, consultation, administration, advocacy, social and political action, policy development and implementation, education, and research and evaluation (NASW, 1996).

Conclusion

This section reviewed the essential definitions and core concepts of social work practice in a sociolegal context. It presented a HR-SJS approach in which the "environment" of the human rights, social justice, and person-in-environment perspective represents social and justice issues. The need for forensic social work to integrate a two-pronged approach to practice, in which practitioners act as facilitators in which individuals, families, and communities empower themselves within sociolegal environments as well as changing those environments directly, was reinforced. Given the complexity of social problems in contemporary communities and societies, adopting a two-pronged approach is one way to uphold U.S. (NASW, 1996) and international (International Federation of Social Work, 2000) mandates for social work practice.

Section Two: Definitions and Central Themes of Forensic Practice

As a professional social worker, inevitably you will encounter diverse individuals, families, or communities affected by social/environmental and legal issues. Poverty, homelessness, parental divorce, exposure to family or community violence, and juvenile or criminal offending are just some of the hardships clients face. Frontline social workers in a variety of settings (e.g., community-based child and family services, health care, education, child welfare, mental health, substance abuse, social services, juvenile justice, and criminal justice systems) interact daily with clients who have multiple problems, including legal ones. For example, a social worker may have a client who is a single father facing allegations of child neglect. He knows little about the child welfare policies and laws affecting his family or how to navigate the court system. Thus, it is imperative that social workers supplement their generalist and specialized practice expertise with knowledge of the laws and policies that influence their client populations. The practice of forensic social work is ideal because social workers are positioned to take action in a sociolegal environment because justice issues are much more explicitly present.

We argue that all social workers across all fields of practice, not just those in juvenile and criminal justice settings, often assist clients affected by laws and policies or problems in accessing resources. Therefore, it is imperative that practitioners integrate their understanding of collaboration, the law, and specialized skills with generalist social work practice. This book helps prepare practitioners with the knowledge, values, and skills to navigate the social and legal issues that affect clients.

Definitions and Themes of Forensic Social Work

- Generalist practice
- Forensic specialization
- Forensic ethics
- Therapeutic jurisprudence
- The use of evidence and evidence-based practices
- Collaboration
- Cultural humility

We also argue that effective forensic social work practice requires a two-pronged approach to helping clients. This dual approach involves intervening with clients on both an individual level to address a client's social well-being (e.g., referral to mental health counseling) and/or at the legal or policy levels (e.g., representing a youth in court as a child advocate or participating in lobbying efforts to advocate for legislation that addresses special population needs). We define forensic social work as an integrated (i.e., generalist, specialized, and collectivistic) approach to social work practice with diverse populations across diverse practice settings in the sociolegal environment. Exhibit 1.1 illustrates this definition. This exhibit depicts a broad definition of forensic social work that integrates the knowledge and skills of generalist and specialized social work, forensic social work, and collaboration.

The integrated role of forensic social workers allows us to assume multiple professional roles, functions, and activities. This strategy is designed to improve clients' social functioning and environmental conditions through collaboration with clients, professionals, and other stakeholders within and across different systems of care. The "forensic" or "legal" aspect of the work situates social workers in a position to honor their professional commitment to social justice through the use of legal knowledge and skills, including advocacy and policy practice.

Exhibit 1.1 A Broad Conceptualization and Definition of Forensic Social Work and Interprofessional Practice

Human Rights, Social Justice, and Legal Framework
Forensic Lens With Nine Core Competencies (Council on Social Work Education, 2015) 1. Demonstrate Ethical and Professional Behavior 2. Engage Diversity and Difference in Practice 3. Advance Human Rights and Social, Economic, and Environmental Justice 4. Engage in Practice Informed Research and Research Informed Practice 5. Engage in Policy Practice 6. Engage With Individuals, Families, Organizations, and Communities 7. Assess Individuals, Families, Organizations, and Communities 8. Intervene With Individuals, Families, Organizations, and Communities 9. Evaluate Practice With Individuals, Families, Organizations, and Communities
Forensic Social Work = Generalist + Forensic + Collaboration
Generalist Social Work • Generalist Knowledge, Values, and Skills • Apply to the Process of Change With Individuals, Families, Groups, Organizations, and Communities • Integrated Strategies Incorporate: Ethics, Direct Practice, Case Management/Care Coordination, Research, and Advocacy
Forensic Specialization • Specialized Social Work at the Intersection of Public Health and Public Safety • Actively Incorporates the Use of Legal Knowledge, Laws • Actively Incorporates Use of Evidence and "Facts" and Evidence-Based Practice/s
Collaboration • Collaboration Knowledge, Values, and Skills With Individuals, Families, Organizations, and Communities • Interprofessional, Interdisciplinary, and Intersectoral Collaboration • Integrative Care and Practice

Definitions

Generalist Social Work

Embedded in our definition of forensic social work are the general principles of social work practice, such as the International Federation of Social Work's (IFSW) definition. According to the IFSW:

> The social work profession promotes social change, problem solving in human relationships, and the empowerment and liberation of people to enhance well-being. Utilizing theories of human behavior and social systems, social work intervenes at the points where people interact with their environments. Principles of human rights and social justice are fundamental to social work. (IFSW, 2000)

Forensic Social Work

There are a number of definitions of forensic social work. They range from general to specific and they may focus on one or more practice settings or populations. For example, Barker and Branson (2000) placed forensic social work in a broad "legal" environment, and they defined it as a "professional specialty that focuses on the interface between society's legal and human service systems." In contrast, Hughes and O'Neal (1983) defined forensic social work as specifically relating to the intersection of mental health and law, in which social workers "function in this space in which mental health concepts and the law form a gestalt." Roberts and Brownell (1999) described forensic social work in terms of the knowledge and skills needed for the specific populations served, particularly victims and offenders. In this case, forensic social work is the "policies, practices, and social work roles with juvenile and adult offenders and victims of crime." In comparison, Green, Thorpe, and Traupmann (2005) defined forensic social work more broadly as "practice, which in any manner may be related to legal issues and litigation, both criminal and civil."

In the scholarly literature, Barker (2003) perhaps provides the broadest definition:

> The practice specialty in social work that focuses on the law, legal issues, and litigation, both criminal and civil, including issues in child welfare, custody of children, divorce, juvenile delinquency, nonsupport, relatives' responsibility, welfare rights, mandated treatment, and legal competency. Forensic social work helps social workers in expert witness preparation. It also seeks to educate law professionals about social welfare issues and social workers about the law.

Forensic Ethics and Evidence-Based Practice

An important part of understanding the landscape of ethical dilemmas in forensic practice involves the recognition that the criminal and juvenile justice systems have vacillated between implementing overly punitive, reactive sentences for offenders (rather than providing opportunities to avoid incarceration) and offering treatment.

Among the most important decisions in juvenile justice, for example, was the U.S. Supreme Court decision to outlaw the death penalty (*Roper v. Simmons*, 2005; a case that involved the murder of elderly women by a 17-year-old during the course of a burglary) on the basis of the finding of developmental neuroscience that the adolescent brain matures into the 20s (Steinberg, 2008). Forensic social workers should consider that in the child welfare and juvenile justice fields, efforts to shape policy are related to helping the public and policy makers apply findings from the empirical literature in comprehensible ways, and understand how specific fields such as neuroscience and structured risk assessment can inform our understanding of adolescent behavior, and what the limitations are in terms of the incomplete understanding of the relationship between an immature brain and immature behavior (S. B. Johnson, Blum, & Giedd, 2009). There are ongoing debates about the ways in which scientific evidence can be used to determine the extent to which adolescents can be held accountable for delinquent or criminal acts (Aronson, 2007). Generally, clarifying the role of the social worker and exactly how evidence-based interventions are conceptualized and applied in forensic settings is an important undertaking.

Ethical questions regarding accountability are intricately tied to the methods of risk determination used in the justice system. Social workers must consider the research evidence concerning the strengths and limitations of specific structured risk assessment tools often used by forensic evaluators to make judgments about the likelihood that a person will commit harm in the future. The interactions of various risk factors used in assessment must be considered, such that a person who is found to be at risk for future violence (e.g., based on an offense history) may also be at risk for health problems and mental health disorders (e.g., depression, suicidality, and substance abuse). In addition to risk factors, protective factors must also be included as part of assessments.

Of relevance to the ethics of risk assessment in forensic practice, there is often a dual relationship between public health and public safety in criminal justice. Integrated health and public safety approaches that combine functions of criminal justice and treatment, such as providing community-based care for drug offenders simultaneously with implementing appropriate monitoring and supervision, can effectively address recidivism and improve social function (NIDA, 2011). Social workers can play a role in advocating for reforms that impact outcomes among specialized populations. For example, regarding registry and community notification policies for sex offender management, we know that policies that are better informed by research evidence result in a better allocation of resources. Such reforms could also address stigma, reduce barriers to offender reintegration, and potentially reduce recidivism (Levenson, Grady, & Leibowitz, 2016).

Therapeutic Jurisprudence

A central concept of the HR-SJS approach is viewing laws and policies as an intervention level. This principle is derived from the therapeutic jurisprudence literature, which examines the therapeutic (i.e., positive) and antitherapeutic (i.e., negative) consequences of legal rules, procedures, and actions (Madden & Wayne, 2003). According to Madden and Wayne (2003), "at the heart of therapeutic jurisprudence is the concept that law, consistent with justice, due process, and other relevant normative values, can and should function as a therapeutic agent" (p. 339). Thus, the impact of the law on a client may have positive or negative effects. For example, an individual with disabilities may win a court case for job discrimination based on legal protections inherent in the Americans With Disabilities Act. This is an example of how a law provides positive protections for this individual. In contrast, a single mother being released from prison on a controlled dangerous substance offense is denied public assistance based on a law that denies benefits to individuals with prior drug charges. This is an example of how a law provides negative or antitherapeutic effects on this mother's ability to receive needed services for herself and her family. Therefore, social workers must evaluate the intervention effects of the legal process and the outcomes on individuals, families, and communities. Based on this evaluation, an intervention strategy that incorporates a two-pronged approach, which enhances social functioning and improves social justice outcomes, can be devised.

Social workers who adopt principles of therapeutic jurisprudence will also be positioned to create conditions that empower clients or influence the development of laws and the ways current laws and policies can be applied most beneficially. Therapeutic jurisprudence is a useful perspective for social workers in interprofessional settings who are working with professionals such as medical providers, psychologists, psychiatrists, police officers, probation officers, or attorneys. This perspective crosses professional boundaries and incorporates another important element, interdisciplinary collaboration, which is particularly concerned with creative problem solving in which the combined knowledge, skills, and techniques of multiple professionals seek to achieve social and justice outcomes (Madden, 2003; Madden & Wayne, 2003; Petrucci, 2007). A professional specialty, forensic social work, which focuses on equipping social workers with additional legal knowledge, is particularly well suited to take a leading role in the rapidly growing practice arena of the sociolegal environment.

Collaboration

As the various definitions suggest, social workers who practice in a sociolegal environment must be well versed in collaboration. This includes working with other professionals (e.g., attorneys, doctors and nurses, and victim advocates), law enforcement personnel, and clients, family members, and other stakeholders.

Historically, social workers have practiced in a variety of "host" agency settings, such as hospitals, schools, industries, psychiatric clinics, police departments, and court and criminal justice settings (Brownell & Roberts, 2002; Jansson & Simmons, 1986; see Section Three in this chapter). With the increasing intricacies of social problems and dwindling resources, social workers' involvement in interdisciplinary collaboration within and across agencies is often unavoidable (Bronstein, 2003; Graham & Barter, 1999; Guin, Noble, & Merrill, 2003; Payne, 2000).

In particular, forensic social workers often work with interdisciplinary teams. When they do, the elements of interdisciplinary team practice often consist of

- a group of professionals from different disciplines;
- a common purpose;
- the integration of various professional perspectives in decision making;
- interdependence;
- coordination and interaction;
- communication;
- role division based on expertise (Abramson & Rosenthal, 1995).

The ability to work interdependently with others is critical to achieving successful client outcomes. As Bronstein (2003) noted, interdisciplinary collaboration is an "effective interpersonal process that facilitates the achievement of goals that cannot be reached when individual professionals act on their own." Social workers who incorporate interdisciplinary collaboration into forensic practice are able to address sociolegal issues with the help of a variety of professionals in a group problem-solving process, which makes it possible to examine the problem from all angles (Abramson & Rosenthal, 1995).

In addition to multidisciplinary practice skills, multicultural competence is critical for forensic social work practice in which diverse populations are served. The following section underscores the important role of diversity in social work practice.

Diversity and Cultural Humility

Diversity or other related terms, such as *cultural humility, multiculturalism, cultural competence,* and *vulnerable populations,* are commonly used in social work practice (Barker, 2003; Beckett & Johnson, 1995; Logan, 2003). The *Social Work Dictionary* defines diversity as "variety, or the opposite of homogeneity" (Barker, 2003). Diversity within social organizations commonly refers to the "range of personnel who more accurately represent minority populations and people from varied backgrounds, cultures, ethnicities, and viewpoints" (Barker, 2003).

Incorporating Cultural Humility in a Human Rights and Social Justice Paradigm

1. to engage in self-reflection and self-critique;
2. to bring into check the power imbalances, by using person-focused interviewing and care;
3. to assess anew the cultural dimensions of the experience of each person/family;
4. to relinquish the role of expert to the client, becoming the student of the client;
5. to see the client's potential to be a capable and full partner in the therapeutic alliance.

Cultural Humility Self Reflection

1. Identify your own cultural and family beliefs and values.
2. Define your own personal culture/identity: ethnicity, age, experience, education, socioeconomic status, gender, sexual orientation, religion . . .
3. Are you aware of your personal biases and assumptions about people with different values than yours?

4. Challenge yourself in identifying your own values as the "norm."
5. Describe a time when you became aware of being different from other people (based on Alsharif, 2012).

The Diversity Dilemma

How can forensic social work develop a "way to be" that is affirming and inclusive of diversity? Many of the professions that collaborate in correctional settings are struggling with this question. In law, attorneys speak of "antioppressive legal practice" and the activation of "privilege and disadvantage" (Kafele, 2005). In psychiatry, a leading text reminds the reader that cultural considerations should be paramount, for example, when offering expert assessment in areas such as competency to stand trial, the presence of mental illness, or the use of psychological testing across cultures (Tseng, Matthews, & Elwyn, 2004). In mental health treatment, the U.S. Department of Health and Human Services Substance Abuse and Mental Health Services Administration (SAMHSA) published extensive guidelines in 2001 mandating that correctional settings create comprehensive plans for addressing cultural practice in their settings.[1] In medicine and health care delivery, practitioners discuss the importance of "providing care within a framework of cultural meaning," expecting all colleagues to do so as standard practice (Hufft & Kite, 2003). And in social work, the core of our ethics mandates cultural competence, even when correctional institutions may not seem responsive to such concepts.[2]

Diversity and the Justice System

A glaring example of the lack of cultural responsiveness, indeed the lack of acknowledgement of the role of privilege and race in the U.S. justice system, can be found in the overrepresentation of persons of color and persons from communities in poverty among the incarcerated population. James (2000) provided a good overview of some of these issues, citing rates of arrest for working-class crime versus typical "white-collar" crime; the use of those in prison as a source of labor; the overrepresentation of African American men in justice system "supervision" (e.g., probation, incarceration, or parole); uneven statistics for lengths of sentences and state executions; and inconsistencies between the U.S. justice system and some provisions of international human rights. James (2000) also noted that when state justice systems deny political rights (including, at times, the right to vote) to those who are or have been incarcerated, this disproportionately affects people of color and the poor. Addressing these issues is squarely within the realm of "diversity practice," and it is social work's responsibility to respond, as a profession that is based on an ethics of human rights.

Diversity in Practice

Diversity and forensic social work practice encompass several overlapping mandates. At the micro end of the spectrum, recruitment and retention of personnel throughout service and justice systems should reflect the diversity of the communities in which those systems operate. Those systems must also accommodate all individuals who are participating, whether accused, aggrieved, or employed, and respond to their diverse characteristics and abilities. Forensic social workers are ethically bound to develop practice skills grounded in an understanding of clients in their contextual identities and lives. In the mezzo section of the spectrum, social service programs and services must be vigilant regarding unintended structural biases that favor or accommodate individuals with certain backgrounds or characteristics over others. This extends to governmental agencies as well, whose policies and procedures may rise to

---

[1] These can be accessed at: http://store.samhsa.gov/shin/content/SMA14-4849/SMA14-4849.pdf

[2] See, for example, Van Wormer (2001) on the conflicting paradigms of the two arenas.

the level of regulation or law and thus have even more impact on individuals' and families' lives. Finally, at the macro end of this continuum, the intersection of forensic social work with considerations of diversity points to the need to work for the improvement of human rights conditions throughout all nations. Wherever a forensic social work practitioner finds herself or himself on this continuum, the remaining segments cannot be ignored.

Conclusion

The broad definition of forensic social work incorporates the knowledge, values, and skills of social work, policy practice, the approaches to the law, collaboration, and diversity. Consistent with the mission of social work, forensic social work involves a two-pronged approach to assessment and intervention with diverse clients in a sociolegal environment. With the increased complexity of social problems, adopting this approach will help increase social and justice outcomes for the diverse populations we serve. Section Three of this chapter describes the history of forensic social work using the United States as the case example to illustrate how a two-pronged approach to practice was integrated throughout this specialized arena of practice.

Section Three: The History and Evolution of Forensic Social Work

Social workers respond to individuals in the criminal justice system, and work to change the system in which such individuals find themselves. Moreover, social workers not only respond to individuals affected by state and federal laws, but also work to change those laws. Forensic social work is as old as social work itself, and it represents the full diversity of our profession, which includes advocating for those accused or convicted of a crime; standing up for victims; responding to youth in juvenile justice systems; testifying in court on behalf of both litigants and defendants; supporting and working alongside law enforcement professionals; and working to improve or change the processes and policies of the U.S. justice system.

How could social work not be present in all these arenas? Our profession revolves around social justice and human rights. Throughout U.S. history, social justice (and in later years, global and universal human rights) has been the core of the theory and practice of social work. Social workers stand for those who cannot; speak for those who have been silenced; and seek to create conditions of empowerment for individuals, families, and communities.

In this light, the history of forensic social work is hard to separate from the history of social work. In fact, one of social work's first professional societies was the National Conference of Charities and Corrections. Formed in 1879, pioneer social worker Jane Addams became the leader of the organization in 1909. This suggests the importance given to corrections, both in early conceptualizations of social services formed over a century ago and in today's understanding of the proper venues for social workers as actors and advocates. To trace the history of forensic social work, we first need to look at the history of forensic policy in the North American colonies and then at the creation of social work and the introduction of social workers to carry out or change those policies. Exhibit 1.2 lists major historical events in the history of forensic social work in the United States.

The History of Forensic Policy

The Colonial Era

No history of social work can be written without reference to the English Poor Laws of 1601. One reason they are significant is that they represent a merging of law and social policy, a codification of society's responses to individuals in distress with an emphasis on government as the entity in charge of those responses. The laws responded to people in poverty, dividing them into three categories: deserving, undeserving, and children (P. J. Day, 2012). The Poor Laws are also significant because they represent the first opportunity for intervention by individuals who would later create the field of social work: advocates for those on the receiving end of the law.

Exhibit 1.2 Major Events in the History of Forensic Social Work in the United States

General U.S. History	Social Work History
Europeans leave European continent, settle in North America. Enslavement of Africans, Native Americans, and later the Irish begins	1700s—Men on patrol looked for "criminals"; punishment was usually corporal
1766—North American colonies become independent from England, create the United States	1790—Concepts of prisons as being rehabilitative grow; the first prison in the United States opens in Philadelphia: the "Walnut Street Jail" Conceptualizations of corrections develop to include proportionate sentencing and programs encouraging reform
1787—An Age of Rationality spreads through Europe and influences the writers of the U.S. constitution	1800s—Theorists note that determinate sentences undermine efforts at individual reformation
1812–1814—United States and Great Britain at war	1875—The Society for Prevention of Cruelty to Children is created
1845—Portions of Mexico are annexed as Texas, setting off the Mexican–American war from 1846 to 1848	1876—The concept of parole is born; the first parolee is released from the Elmira Reformatory in New York
1861–1865—U.S. Civil War	1879—National Conference of Charities and Corrections is formed
Late 1800s—Varieties of internal combustion engines are perfected, setting the stage in the United States for the Industrial Revolution	1899—Illinois opens the first juvenile court
1920—U.S. women gain the right to vote	1907—The National Council on Crime and Delinquency was formed
1929—U.S. stock market crash sets off the Great Depression	1920—Two thirds of U.S. states institute procedures for probation, a concept originated in Massachusetts
1939–1948—Portions of the world fight in World War II and the development of the Universal Declaration of Human Rights (UDHR)	1921—The American Association of Social Workers is formed
	1925—Forty-six states now have juvenile courts
	1940s—Police social workers return to prominence in forensics 1948—Postwar ratification of the UDHR

(continued)

Exhibit 1.2 Major Events in the History of Forensic Social Work in the United States (*continued*)	

General U.S. History	Social Work History
1961—Eleanor Roosevelt is appointed chair of President Kennedy's Commission on the Status of Women; its 1963 report documents discrimination in the workplace	1960s—Federal social policies begin to emphasize social responsibility and deinstitutionalization of prisoners and the mentally ill
	1973—First shelter for female victims of battering opens in Arizona
1960s/1970s—Contemporary rise of mass incarceration; social movements in the United States bring focus on women's rights, civil rights for African Americans, and gay and lesbian rights	1974—The Juvenile Justice and Delinquency Prevention Act passes; The Child Abuse Prevention and Treatment Act passes
2001—On September 11 the United States is hit by three simultaneous crimes of terrorism	U.S. society sours on rehabilitation and begins to "get tough on crime"
	1984—Victims of Crime Act passes
2013—Black Lives Matter (BLM) movement founded with increased social work involvement	2001—On October 26 the U.S. Congress passes the Patriot Act, establishing new executive branch powers for certain crimes 2015–2016—*Journal of Social Work Education* editorial published for the social work profession to embrace its forensic practice roots and leadership in criminal justice reform The science of social work and Grand Challenges in social work gain momentum

Later, early English colonists were influenced by the laws and systems of England. Legally, this meant they also codified responses to the impoverished members of their settlements: individuals were divided up and then either shuffled to almshouses (for those who could not work) or workhouses (for the able bodied). They were reluctant, however, to turn to the government as the appropriate and responsible institution for maintaining law and order (perhaps exhibiting what might now be understood as communal posttraumatic stress disorder from their experiences living under a monarch perceived to be overly rigid and tyrannical). As a result, early police forces were made up of men patrolling neighborhood streets, first at night, and later during the day as well (Blakely & Bumphus, 1999). If a "criminal" were caught, the colonists sought swift punishment, usually of a corporal nature (Popple & Leighninger, 2014). Concepts of right and wrong—and views of human nature at the time—did not suggest that criminals would benefit from rehabilitation or that their victims needed support and advocacy.

The first institutions associated with crime and punishment were jails, which were simple holding cells for individuals, both children and adults, awaiting trial or punishment.[3] The ensuing political break from England and concomitant development of Enlightenment philosophies, however, popularized a valuing of rationality that in many ways survives today.

---

[3] This is well before several professions, such as psychology, helped to develop conceptions of childhood and children as developmentally different from adults.

"Rational man" was thought to be changeable if shown the error of his ways; extrapolated to corrections, this gave rise to "proportional" punishments rather than "punitive" ones and engendered early concepts of rehabilitation. After the Revolutionary War, the first prison in the United States—"Walnut Street Jail"—was constructed in Philadelphia in 1790 (Popple & Leighninger, 2014). Because at that time crime was seen as arising from disorder, prison staff imposed strict discipline, schedules, and order on incarcerated individuals. This philosophy often carried over to almshouses and workhouses, which by definition were not correctional institutions, but whose operation was often indistinguishable from prisons. More opportunities for social work collaborative intervention were thus being created.

The 1800s

The 19th century saw a vigorous application of new legal and correctional policies. By midcentury, however, many were questioning if the philosophy was effective. If prisoners were sentenced to a fixed length of time, and if they were going to be incarcerated until their sentence was completed, regardless of their behavior, what incentive did they have to participate in the rigors of rehabilitative programs? Thus, the concept of early release as a reward for "good behavior" was created: Persons under incarceration began to be released early through parole. The first such individual was set free from the Elmira Reformatory in New York in 1876.

John Augustus, a wealthy shoe manufacturer in Boston, began social reform in the early 1840s when he started the practice of interviewing adults awaiting incarceration, personally posting their bail, and taking responsibility for their reformation, a pattern that was later instituted by Massachusetts as the process of probation. The practice spread to two thirds of the states by 1920 (Popple & Leighninger, 2014). Probation extended the concept of rehabilitation: those committing crimes could change their ways, either through discipline and programs in prison that could lead to early release, or through strict supervision and reform that could prevent incarceration completely. Though we cannot claim Augustus was a social worker, his actions foreshadowed those of the pioneers in forensic social work and helped solidify approaches to human nature that emphasized a person's ability to change and grow. Such views would soon extend to those in other "legal" institutions, such as almshouses and workhouses.

The 20th Century and the Birth of Social Work

National Conference of Charities and Corrections

Having declared independence, fought two wars with Britain, another among its own citizens, and experienced many social upheavals, the United States was grappling with a myriad of social issues. It was in this climate that social work as a profession began to develop. The first social work training school opened in 1898. Earlier, in 1879, the National Conference of Charities and Corrections (formerly the Conference of Boards of Public Charities) was created, becoming the National Conference of Social Work in 1917, and joining a collaborative to become the National Association of Social Workers in 1955 (Zenderland, 1998). Trailblazing social workers were concerned with social reform, and law and justice issues were a primary focus (Barker & Branson, 2000; Roberts & Brownell, 1999). The plight of the poor was a major concern of Mary Richmond, a pioneer in social work and the founding mother of casework (Colcard & Mann, 1930). Jane Addams, a Nobel Prize-winning social work pioneer, targeted the systems and policies that affected the poor of her day. Addams was also the founder of settlement houses (P. J. Day, 2012).

The Creation of Juvenile Courts

A key accomplishment of early social workers was to change the policy regarding young persons charged with criminal offenses (Platt, 1969, 1977). Julia Lathrop, Jane Addams, and Lucy Flower pushed to get children out of penal institutions, where individuals as young as 5 years old were incarcerated with adults. Their efforts led to the birth of the juvenile justice system in 1899 (Center on Juvenile & Criminal Justice, 1999). The new system saw several innovations. The Juvenile Psychopathic Institute, founded as a result of advocacy by several residents of Hull House, including Florence Kelley, Alice Hamilton, Julia Lathrop, Ellen Gates Starr, Sophonisba Breckinridge, and Grace and Edith Abbott, began to conduct psychosocial assessments of children in the justice system (Open Collections Program, Harvard University Library, n.d.). Again, many collaborators came together—this time to create separate juvenile courts, the first seated in Illinois in 1899. By 1925, 46 states and the District of Columbia had created juvenile courts, where hearings considered delinquency as well as the needs of abused and neglected children. The New York Society for Prevention of Cruelty to Children (NYSPCC), founded in New York in 1875 and modeled after the early Societies for Prevention of Cruelty to Animals, presaged these later juvenile justice reforms (NYSPCC, n.d.).

These institutional changes were both fueled by and gave birth to new theories of human nature and childhood. Mary Richmond's efforts, first in Baltimore's Charity Organization Society and later as the director of the Russell Sage Foundation, argued for private social work practice, and for creating a system of social work education for "recognizing human differences and adjusting our systems of . . . law, of reformation and of industry to those differences" (quoted in Colcard & Mann, 1930). Jane Addams's efforts called for structuring policies that saw children not as "mini-adults" but as developmentally different, young individuals needing guidance and care, who could not be expected to see the world or make decisions as adults do. Children were thus afforded closed hearings and, eventually, confidentiality of their court records and limitations of the records' availability once the children attained adulthood (Center on Juvenile & Criminal Justice, 1999).[4]

Collaborative Reforms in Adult Courts

At the same time that juvenile courts were being created, U.S. policies regarding the larger criminal justice system were also in flux. With the advent of parole in the mid to late 1800s and the creation of juvenile courts at the end of the century, reformers gained a renewed commitment to rehabilitation, a concept that had found itself on shaky ground prior to these changes. Prisons were renamed "penitentiaries," and their goals included repentance (hence the name) and reform of the individual (Blakely & Bumphus, 1999). These goals fit well with the dual aims of social work: changing social systems and changing the individuals who have strayed from those systems. For the latter, social casework was the proper response and individuals in penitentiaries were appropriate recipients. With the creation of the American Association of Social Workers in 1921 (forerunner to the National Association of Social Workers), casework became the central focus, and services focused on offenders made "correctional treatment specialists" of social workers (Roberts & Brownell, 1999).

Social Workers Call for Social Change

Social work swung back to an emphasis on social change, however, when the Great Depression began in 1929. Providing services for the "new poor" (i.e., individuals in poverty who were formerly working class or middle class) helped social workers realize that policy change was often the proper arena for their profession. Social workers testified before congressional committees calling for policy revisions, and many New Deal programs were influenced by their expertise. As Secretary of Labor, Frances Perkins, who had been trained by Mary Richmond, was instrumental in creating reforms, including regulations ensuring safe conditions for American workers and the design and establishment of Social Security (P. J. Day, 2012; Frances Perkins Center, 2008). Social worker Harry Hopkins, appointed by President Hoover and again by President Roosevelt, oversaw new initiatives in the Works Projects Administration, which focused on youth; these were the forerunners of today's delinquency prevention programs (Roberts & Brownell, 1999).

---

[4] Although, see Platt's (1977) seminal work critiquing these reforms as ultimately hurting youth, pathologizing them, and institutionalizing their subservient social position.

In the early 1920s, police social workers were common: They were women who provided social work advocacy as members of groups called Women's Bureaus, which functioned as divisions within local police departments. These positions were cut following the Great Depression, but returned to prominence in the 1940s. At that time, youth gangs were growing in number, and hundreds of child guidance clinics opened that employed social workers as court liaisons. Community-based councils and delinquency prevention programs were created; these focused on supporting and intervening with individuals, including children who had dropped out of school, and members of what the courts labeled "problem families" (Roberts & Brownell, 1999).

From World War to Universal Human Rights (1914–1960)

The profession also continued to develop amidst a world struggling with war, peace, and human rights. At that time, World War I (1914–1918) was quickly followed by the rise of Adolf Hitler and the Nazi regime and Japanese imperialism over which World War II was fought (1939–1945). In fact, for three decades of the 20th century the world was emblazoned with two of the most destructive and widescale wars fought by mankind. The inhumane and cruel treatment inflicted by humans on other humans, particularly during WWII, seemed unfathomable. This treatment included the attempted extermination of Jews and other groups, such as homosexuals and persons with disabilities.

The dropping of the atom bomb on the cities of Nagasaki and Hiroshima in Japan transformed a seemingly harmless mushroom cloud into an unprecedented weapon of mass destruction that could wipe out large cities and its inhabitants in a matter of minutes (Gilbert, 2004; Strachan, 2003). Yet, from the ashes of war, most world citizens and their leaders were ready for a new approach to human rights, where dignity and respect for all humans were honored. World leaders sought a new way to address world problems, which included the establishment of the UN in 1945. With Eleanor Roosevelt at the helm and the UN Commission on Human Rights, the UDHR was crafted and then ratified on December 10, 1948. The initial proclamation in the UDHR preamble continues to resound: "We the peoples of the UN [are] determined to reaffirm faith in fundamental human rights, in the dignity and worth of the human person, in the equal rights of men and women and of nations large and small" (UN, 1948).

The UDHR authors crafted the declaration to be a relatively short, inspirational, and energizing document usable by common people. The UDHR consists of 30 articles that are often described by three generations of rights. The first generation of rights (Articles 2–21) are referred to as negative rights, both civil and political. These are generally rights to standards of good behavior by governments or protection of the rule of law including the right to life; to freedom from torture; to own property; and to limiting where government may intrude. The second generation of rights (Articles 22–27) are often referred to as positive rights, which are economic, social, and cultural rights. These rights include the right to social security, the right to work, and the right to freely participate in cultural life. Third generation rights (Articles 28–30) are collective or solidarity rights, such as everyone is entitled to a social and international order (UN, 1948; Wronka, 2008).

The philosophy and actions of human rights are consistent with social work, especially forensic social work aims. Respect for human rights is becoming a universal principle associated with good government practice. According to Wronka (2008), "at the heart of social work, human rights are a set of guiding principles that are interdependent and have implications for macro, mezzo, and micro policy and practice."

Government Policy Includes Forensic Social Work

As great social change unfolded in the United States over the coming decades, changes in policies and approaches to criminal justice also evolved. Within the context of a new emphasis on reform and social responsibility (Center on Juvenile and Criminal Justice, 2017), Presidents Kennedy and Johnson expanded federal policy and funding aimed at preventing or addressing juvenile delinquency. The prototype initiative was the New York City Mobilization for Youth. Created by a federal grant to the Columbia University School of Social Work, it laid the groundwork for a multitude of similar programs to follow (Center on Juvenile and Criminal Justice, 2017). Forensic social workers also increased their role in juvenile and adult probation services. The executive director of the National Council on Crime and Delinquency was social worker Milton Rector, who felt that probation officers should hold master of social work degrees. At the same time, federal dollars were allocated for correctional treatment programs for adults, pretrial diversion programs, and 262 youth service bureaus. During this decade, social workers worked in police departments, psychiatric settings, juvenile justice programs, and at probation offices (Haynes, 1998; Roberts & Brownell, 1999).

In the early 1970s, Massachusetts social worker Jerome Miller created the soon-copied policy of moving youth in juvenile justice systems from institutions to smaller, community-based group homes. In 1974, the passage of the federal Juvenile Justice and Delinquency Prevention Act intensified the focus on deinstitutionalization (Nelson, 1984). At the same time, forensic social workers and child welfare reformers collaborated to highlight the incidence of child maltreatment and to create programmatic responses, first at the state and later at the federal level. This led to the passage of the Child Abuse Prevention and Treatment Act (1974), which appropriated funds for child abuse assessment and treatment teams, which were usually led by medical social workers (P. J. Day, 2012).

In 1973, the first shelter for women battered by their husbands opened in Arizona; later in the decade, shelters for female victims and services for male perpetrators of family violence began to proliferate. Thus, the focus on social responsibility that grew in the 1960s in the United States led to the institutionalization of certain initial reforms in the rights of women and children at the federal level. These initiatives brought a renewed focus on victims' needs and rights to the forensic social work arena.

A Shift From Social Reform to Individual Responsibility

Corrections policies began to focus on "get tough on crime" initiatives in the 1980s. Prison populations grew rapidly, and program dollars were stretched thin. Many correctional administrators spent the majority of their budgets on maintaining order and security in their institutions, leaving little funding for services. Feminists brought the impact of crime on survivors of domestic violence and rape to the national spotlight, highlighted by the landmark Victims of Crime Act (1984). The American public was not convinced that prisons were meeting the goal of reforming individuals and debated what to do in response to violent crime. Some have called what followed a "rage to punish," as harsher sentences and mandatory sentencing laws proliferated (Haney & Zimbardo, 1998). Though treatment services for perpetrators of domestic violence continued to be available, they were in outpatient settings, and the correctional goal of rehabilitation for incarcerated persons began to wane (Haney & Zimbardo, 1998).

The United States was struggling to determine a philosophy for correctional work (Gebelein, 2000). Was it truly "correctional"? Or was the point of prison systems to protect the public from the violent offenders locked inside? Was it to deter those who might otherwise commit violent crime? Was the point of prison simply for members of society to feel better because the "bad guys" were punished?

Faith in the possibility of rehabilitation was dealt a severe blow with the publication—and some would say the misinterpretation—of Robert Martinson's evaluation of reform programs, "What Works?" Martinson was one of three researchers, the last to join the project; he published the results early and without his colleagues, stating that little proof exists to suggest that rehabilitative programs are successful (Martinson, 1974; Wilks, 2004). When the full article was published, the conclusions were not as dramatic, suggesting that some efforts were effective under some conditions with some subsets of incarcerated persons (Lipton, Martinson, & Wilks, 1975). However, it was the first article to make such a claim and its strong questioning of the efficacy of rehabilitation had an impact.

In this climate, forensic social work opportunities shifted from prison-based rehabilitation to community-based victim/witness assistance programs, where it is estimated that approximately one third of the staff are social workers (Barker & Branson, 2000; Roberts & Brownell, 1999). Community-based corrections initiatives, such as halfway programs and community courts, also turned to social workers for expertise. In the mid 1980s, federal monies were appropriated for the RESTTA initiative: Restitution Education, Specialized Training, and Technical Assistance. This program of the federal Office of Juvenile Justice and Delinquency Prevention (OJJDP) offered local probation departments and courts the resources to hold juvenile offenders accountable, either through monetary compensation, community service, or direct victim services (Roberts & Brownell, 1999). Currently such programs can be found in OJJDP Juvenile Accountability Block Grants. Related to these approaches are the youth-focused "boot camp" or "tough love" projects that seek accountability by mandating early intervention for high-risk young offenders. The success of these programs is unclear, and some high-profile failures have affected their support.[5]

Social Work Post 9-11

The horrific crimes that occurred in the United States on September 11, 2001, and the myriad of local, state, and federal law and justice policies that have followed, are creating a new chapter in forensic policy and changing social workers' roles. President George W. Bush's "War on Terror" led to many new laws, perhaps most significant of which was the Patriot Act: Uniting and Strengthening America by Providing Appropriate Tools Required to Intercept and Obstruct Terrorism, passed on October 26, 2001, and revised and reauthorized in March 2006. The Act heightened the role of governmental intervention to anticipate and prevent specific crimes and alters the protections provided for those accused. Although much of the Act focuses on international security concerns, domestic policies have shifted in its wake, affecting immigrants and those seeking refuge or asylum. In this unfolding arena, forensic social workers again face a continuum of tasks and challenges, from individual casework and intervention to policy advocacy and social change.

Forensic Social Work and Human Rights

For 21st-century practice, forensic social workers can choose to play an instrumental leadership role in advancing human rights forward in our country and abroad. So where do we go from here? A good place to start is with the essential document, the UDHR (UN, 1948). Ratified by the UN in 1948, it continues to project a life-affirming message to citizens of the world and is a universally accepted legal mandate by most world governments to fulfill human rights.

Eleanor Roosevelt's hope that the UDHR would become the International Magna Carta for all nations appears to have come to fruition. Following the UDHR, additional international human rights agreements (e.g., covenants and treaties) were adopted by many countries. In 1976, these documents included the International Covenant on Civil and Political Rights. Today the UDHR, along with these covenants, comprise the International Bill of Rights (Wronka, 2012). Despite progress in human rights over the past 50 years, 21st-century practitioners still have remaining gaps to fill. First of all, the United States continues to lag behind in support for human rights. Since the signing of the UDHR, the United States has signed and ratified major parts of the International Covenant on Civil and Political Rights (1966), which recognizes civil and political human rights (e.g., the right to life and liberty and rights to freedom of expression). Additionally, President Carter in 1978 signed the International Covenant on Economic, Social and Cultural Rights (1966) that recognizes economic, social, and cultural rights (e.g., the rights to food, clothing, housing, and health care). However, as of 2010, the United States has made some strides, such as the election of the first African American president and a bill proposing universal health care for all Americans; the U.S. government has not yet ratified this covenant (Wronka, 2008; 2012).

---

[5] For a famous example, consider the case of 14-year-old Martin Anderson, who died in custody in a "boot camp" in Florida in 2006. Retrieved from www.MartinLeeAnderson.com

The United States has ratified only a small number of other human rights international documents and lags far behind many other nations in their legal commitment to human rights. The few documents ratified by the United States include the Convention on the Prevention and Punishment of the Crime of Genocide (1948), International Convention on the Elimination of Racial Discrimination (1965), and the Convention Against Torture and Other Cruel, Inhumane or Degrading Treatment or Punishment (1984). Other important international treaties and documents remain unsigned or unratified by the United States. For example, the United States and Somalia are the only world nations who have not as yet ratified the Convention on the Rights of the Child (1989). The United States also has not ratified the Convention to Eliminate Discrimination against Women (1979), which guarantees the equality of women to men, although U.S. grassroots support for it is growing (Wronka, 2012). Forensic social workers have practice specialty areas where they can concentrate their individual and collective efforts toward advancing human rights. These areas include practice and systems reform in juvenile justice, criminal justice, health care, immigration, mental health, victims' rights, and civil rights for racial–ethnic and homosexual minorities. For example, forensic social workers whose efforts are focused on juvenile and criminal justice human rights reform can advocate for the rights of offenders of all ages detained in penal institutions, the rights of minorities disproportionately involved in the criminal justice system, the rights of criminal offenders to rehabilitation and training, the rights of children born to women prisoners, the rights of juvenile prisoners, the rights of political prisoners, the rights of probationers, and the rights of those sentenced to capital punishment. There also is the potential to greatly improve the dehumanizing aspects of prison, including improving prison conditions themselves, and improving community conditions, such as living in poverty and crime-ridden neighborhoods, that place people at risk of engaging in criminal offenses (UN, 1994; Wronka, 2008).

Some relevant UN documents with direct implications for 21st-century forensic social work for juvenile and criminal justice reform (listed in chronological order) include the UDHR (1948); the Standard Minimum Rules for the Treatment of Prisoners (1955); the International Covenants on Economic, Social, and Cultural Rights (1966); the Convention Against Torture and Other Cruel, Inhumane, or Degrading Treatment or Punishment (1984); the safeguards guaranteeing protection of the rights of those facing the death penalty (1984); the UN Standard Minimum Rules for the Administration of Juvenile Justice (1985); the Basic Principles on the Independence of the Judiciary (1985); and the Convention of the Rights of the Child (1989). Forensic social workers can familiarize themselves with the documents and the UN committees designated to address the issues that are most relevant to their practice issue and/or population (UN, 1994). Forensic social workers as collaborators for human rights also can engage in targeted intervention strategies. The UN (1994) has 10 recommended intervention strategies to help advance human rights that forensic social workers can adapt. These intervention strategies are (a) working with local, regional, and national organizations to promote, develop, and implement needed changes in policy, planning, and programming on human rights issues; (b) recognizing and adapting existing services to maximize effectiveness; (c) developing and involving appropriate and qualified leaders from the community to identify, plan, and implement needed services and advocacy efforts; (d) developing self-capacities of those disadvantaged in their human rights; (e) organizing previously unorganized disadvantaged groups for self-help; (f) forming alliances with like-minded social and political movements; (g) developing mechanisms to enhance local and global awareness, including the use of mass media; (h) fundraising for the cause; (i) assessing the impact of actions undertaken in collaboration with persons and groups affected and associated groups and organizations; (j) documenting and disseminating information on human rights abuses; and (k) promoting legislation that benefits disadvantaged groups. If forensic social workers individually and collectively engage in one or more of these strategies in their local communities, these incremental efforts can make a significant difference as evidenced in the history of forensic social work reviewed.

Black Lives Matter (BLM) Movement

BLM is a global social and protest movement that emerged in 2012 largely as a social media campaign in response to the shooting death of Trayvon Martin in Florida. It campaigns against violence and systematic racism targeting Black people. Issues of concern to the movement include racial profiling, police brutality, and racial inequality, especially disproportionate justice involvement of Black people in the criminal justice (E. Day, 2015). Michelle Alexander's (2011) *The New Jim Crow* has been influential to social work and related causes to address and understand mass incarceration of African Americans. Social work has been advocating for a response to these issues including in the field's major education journals (e.g., Robbins, Vaughan-Eden, & Maschi, 2015). For more information about the Black Lives Matter movement, see http://blacklivesmatter.com.

Conclusion

Over 100 years ago, social workers understood that government, as author and institutor of policy, can and should be an arena for reform. Their efforts in the justice system set a high standard for forensic social workers of today. Our forebearers saw that advocating for their "clients" meant advocating for systemic reform, as they collaborated to apply a two-pronged approach to social welfare: individual and social change. This bifurcation of social action weaves throughout the history of forensic social work. In today's sociolegal environment, the duality becomes a continuum of options for intervention, as social workers offer an integrated approach for clients across diverse settings.

Perhaps Eleanor Roosevelt (1958), in her speech to the UN Commission on Human Rights at the UN in New York on March 27, 1958, suggests where and how we might approach our next steps. She eloquently responded to her own question:

> Where, after all, do universal human rights begin? In small places, close to home—so close and so small that they cannot be seen on any maps of the world. Yet they are the world of the individual person; the neighborhood he lives in; the school or college he attends; the factory, farm, or office where he works. Such are the places where every man, woman, and child seeks equal justice, equal opportunity, equal dignity without discrimination. Unless these rights have meaning there, they have little meaning anywhere. Without concerted citizen action to uphold them close to home, we shall look in vain for progress in the larger world. (Roosevelt, 1958)

Eleanor Roosevelt's words are just as applicable today as they were about a half century ago. We have the opportunity to revel in past achievements and take the lessons learned forward to shape best practices for the 21st century. Forensic social work history suggests that the most effective efforts were when individual and social level action converged. In the 21st century, advancing the mission of forensic social work involves equipping practitioners with a collective vision as well as the knowledge and skills to effectively navigate the legal system. The potential for the next century of forensic social workers is one of high anticipation. Our collective efforts of today will soon become tomorrow's newest history chapter. And together we can make it a most memorable one.

CHAPTER EXERCISES

Human Rights Framework

Protects Civil, Political, Economic, Social, and Cultural Rights

Basic Principles

Universality

Participation

Accountability

Transparency

Nondiscrimination

Human Rights and Social Justice as Ethical Issues in Social Work

International Federation of Social Work

Principles

Human Rights and Human Dignity

Social Justice

http://ifsw.org/policies/statement-of-ethical-principles

National Association of Social Work *Code of Ethics*

www.socialworkers.org/pubs/code/code.asp

Cultural Humility

www.youtube.com/watch? v=SaSHLbS1V4w

Additional Resources

Convention on Elimination of All Forms of Discrimination Against Women: www.ohchr.org/EN/ProfessionalInterest/Pages/CEDAW.aspx

Convention on the Rights of Persons With Disabilities: www.ohchr.org/EN/HRBodies/CRPD/Pages/ConventionRightsPersonsWithDisabilities.aspx

Core International Human Rights Instruments: www.ohchr.org/EN/ProfessionalInterest/Pages/CoreInstruments.aspx

Examples of United Nations Covenants, Conventions, Standards, Other: http://www.ohchr.org/EN/ProfessionalInterest/Pages/UniversalHumanRightsInstruments.aspx

Handbook on Prisoners With Special Needs: www.unodc.org/documents/justice-and-prison-reform/Prisoners-with-special-needs.pdf

Human Rights Instruments Library: www.ohchr.org/EN/ProfessionalInterest/Pages/UniversalHumanRightsInstruments.aspx

Office of the High Commissioner of Human Rights: www.ohchr.org/EN/Pages/WelcomePage.aspx

Optional Protocol to the Convention Against Torture and Other Cruel, Inhuman or Degrading Treatment or Punishment: www.ohchr.org/EN/ProfessionalInterest/Pages/OPCAT.aspx

Standard Minimum Rules for the Treatment of Prisoners: www.ohchr.org/EN/ProfessionalInterest/Pages/TreatmentOfPrisoners.aspx

United Nations Principles for Older Persons: www.ohchr.org/EN/ProfessionalInterest/Pages/OlderPersons.aspx

United Nations Convention Against Torture and Other Cruel, Inhuman or Degrading Treatment or Punishment: www.ohchr.org/EN/ProfessionalInterest/Pages/CAT.aspx

Universal Declaration of Human Rights: www.un.org/en/documents/udhr

References

Abramson, J. S., & Rosenthal, B. S. (1995). Interdisciplinary and interorganizational collaboration. In R. L. Edwards (Ed.), *Encyclopedia of social work* (19th ed., pp. 1479–1489). Washington, DC: National Association of Social Workers Press.

Addams, J. (1910). *Twenty years at Hull house*. New York, NY: Macmillan.

Alexander, M. (2011). *The New Jim Crow: Mass incarceration in the era of color blindness*. New York, NY: New Press.

Alsharif N. Z. (2012). Cultural humility and interprofessional education and practice: A winning combination. *American Journal of Pharmaceutical Education, 76*(7), 1–2.

Aronson, J. D. (2007). Brain imaging, culpability, and the juvenile justice death penalty. *Psychology, Public Policy, and Law, 13*(2), 115–142.

Barker, R. L. (2003). *The social work dictionary* (2nd ed.). Washington, DC: National Association of Social Workers Press.

Barker, R. L., & Branson, D. M. (2000). *Forensic social work: Legal aspects of professional practice* (2nd ed.). New York, NY: Haworth Press.

Bartlett, H. M. (1958). Working definition of social work practice. *Social Work, 3*(2), 5–8.

Bartlett, H. M. (1970). *The common base of social work practice*. Silver Spring, MD: National Association of Social Workers Press.

Beckett, J. O., & Johnson, H. C. (1995). Human development. In R. L. Edwards & J. G. Hopps (Eds.), *Encyclopedia of social work* (pp. 1385–1405). Washington, DC: National Association of Social Workers Press.

Blakely, C. R., & Bumphus, V. W. (1999). American criminal justice philosophy: What's old—What's new? *Federal Probation: A Journal of Correctional Philosophy and Practice, 63*(1), 62–66.

Bronstein, L. R. (2003). A model for interdisciplinary collaboration. *Social Work, 48*, 296–306.

Brownell, P., & Roberts, A. L. (2002). A century of social work in criminal justice and correctional settings. *Journal of Offender Rehabilitation, 35*(2), 1–17.

Center on Juvenile and Criminal Justice. (1999). Second chances: Giving kids a chance to make a better choice. Retrieved from https://www.ncjrs.gov/pdffiles1/ojjdp/181680.pdf

Center on Juvenile and Criminal Justice. (2017). Juvenile justice history. Retrieved from http://www.cjcj.org/education1/juvenile-justice-history.html

Colcard, J. C., & Mann, R. Z. S. (Eds.). (1930). *The long view: Papers and addresses of Mary E. Richmond*. New York, NY: Russell Sage Foundation.

Council on Social Work Education. (2015). *Educational policy and accreditation standards for baccalaureate and master's social work programs*. Alexandria, VA: Author. Retrieved from https://www.cswe.org/Accreditation/Standards-and-Policies/2015-EPAS

Day, E. (2015, November 19). #BlackLivesMatter: The birth of a new civil rights movement. *The Guardian*. Retrieved from https://www.theguardian.com/world/2015/jul/19/blacklivesmatter-birth-civil-rights-movement

Day, P. J. (2012). *A new history of social welfare* (7th ed.). New York, NY: Allyn & Bacon.

DuBois, B., & Miley, K. K. (2012). *Social work: An empowering profession* (5th ed.). Boston, MA: Allyn & Bacon.

Ehrenreich, J. H. (1985). *The altruistic imagination: A history of social work and social policy in the United States*. Ithaca, NY: Cornell University Press.

Finn, H. L., & Jacobson, M. (2003). *Just practice: A social justice approach to social work*. Peosta, IA: Eddie Bowers.

Frances Perkins Center. (2008). Homepage. Retrieved from http://francesperkinscenter.org

Garland, A. F., Hough, R. L., Landsverk, J. A., & Brown, S. A. (2001). Multi-sector complexity of systems of care for youth with mental health needs. *Children's Services: Social Policy, Research, and Practice, 4*, 123–140.

Gebelein, R. S. (2000). The rebirth of rehabilitation: Promise and perils of drug courts. In *Sentencing and corrections: Issues for the 21st century*. Washington, DC: National Institute of Justice.

Gilbert, M. (2004). *The Second World War: A complete history*. New York, NY: Holt.

Graham, J. R., & Barter, K. (1999). Collaboration: A social work practice method. *Families in Society, 80*(1), 6–13.

Green, G., Thorpe, J., & Traupmann, M. (2005). The sprawling thicket: Knowledge and specialisation in forensic social work. *Australian Social Work, 58*, 142–153.

Guin, C. C., Noble, D. N., & Merrill, T. S. (2003). From misery to mission: Forensic social workers on multidisciplinary mitigation teams. *Social Work, 48*, 362–371.

Haney, C., & Zimbardo, P. (1998). The past and future of U.S. prison policy: Twenty-five years after the Stanford Prison Experiment. *American Psychologist, 53*, 709–727.

Harvard University Library. (n.d.). Open Collections Program: Working women: Jane Addams. Retrieved from http://ocp.hul.harvard.edu/ww/addams.html

Haynes, K. S. (1998). The one hundred-year debate: Social reform versus individual treatment. *Social Work, 43*, 501–509.

Hufft, A., & Kite, M. M. (2003). Vulnerable and cultural perspectives for nursing care in correctional systems. *Journal of Multicultural Nursing & Health, 9*(1), 18–26.

Hughes, D. S., & O'Neal, B. C. (1983). A survey of current forensic social work. *Social Work, 32*, 393–394.

International Federation of Social Work. (2000). Definition of social work. Retrieved from http://www .ifsw.org/en/p38000208.html

James, J. (2000). The dysfunctional and the disappearing: Democracy, race and imprisonment. *Social Identities, 6*, 483–492.

Jansson, B. S., & Simmons, J. (1986). The survival of social work units in host organizations. *Social Work, 35*, 339–343.

Johnson, L. C., & Yanca, S. J. (2015). *Social work practice: A generalist approach* (10th ed.). Boston, MA: Pearson.

Johnson, S. B., Blum, R. W., & Giedd, J. N. (2009). Adolescent maturity and the brain: The promise and pitfalls of neuroscience research in adolescent health policy. *Journal of Adolescent Health, 45*, 216–221.

Kafele, K. (2005). *Understanding cultural competence. Fourth colloquium on the legal profession.* Windsor, Ontario, Canada: University of Windsor. Retrieved from http://www.lsuc.on.ca/media/ fourthcolloquiumkafele.pdf

Levenson, J., Grady, M., & Leibowitz, G. S. (2016). Grand Challenges: Social justice and the need for evidence-based sex offender registry reform. *Journal of Sociology and Social Welfare, 43*(2), 3–38.

Lipton, D., Martinson, R., & Wilks, J. (1975). *The effectiveness of correctional treatment: A survey of treatment evaluation studies*. New York, NY: Praeger.

Logan, S. M. L. (2003). Issues of multiculturalism: Multicultural practice, cultural diversity, and competency. In R. A. English (Ed.), *Encyclopedia of social work* (19th ed., pp. 95–105). Washington, DC: National Association of Social Workers Press.

Madden, R. G. (2003). *Essential law for social workers*. New York, NY: Columbia University Press.

Madden, R. G., & Wayne, R. H. (2003). Social work and the law: A therapeutic jurisprudence perspective. *Social Work, 48*, 338–347.

Martinson, R. (1974). What works? Questions and answers about prison reform. *Public Interest, 35*, 22–54.

Maschi, T. (2016). *Applying a human rights approach to social work research and evaluation: A rights research manifesto*. New York, NY: Springer Publishing.

Maschi, T., & Youdin, R. (2012). *Social worker as researcher: Integrating research with advocacy*. Boston, MA: Pearson Publishing.

Miley, K. K., O'Melia, M. O., & DuBois, B. (2012). *Generalist social work practice: An empowering approach* (7th ed.). Boston, MA: Pearson.

National Association of Social Workers. (1996). *Code of ethics of the National Association of Social Workers*. Washington, DC: Author.

National Institute of Drug Abuse. (2011). Treating offenders with drug problems: Integrating public health and public safety. Retrieved from https://www.drugabuse.gov/sites/default/files/drugs_crime.pdf

Nelson, B. J. (1984). *Making an issue of child abuse: Political agenda setting for social problems*. Chicago, IL: University of Chicago Press.

New York Society for the Prevention of Cruelty to Children. (n.d.). Our 129 year commitment to the safety and well-being of children. Retrieved from http://www.nyspcc.org

Payne, M. (2000). *Teamwork in multiprofessional care*. Chicago, IL: Lyceum Books.

Petrucci, C. (2007). Therapeutic jurisprudence in social work and criminal justice. In A. R. Roberts & D. W. Springer (Eds.), *Social work in juvenile and criminal justice settings* (3rd ed., pp. 287–299). Springfield, IL: Charles C. Thomas.

Platt, A. M. (1969). The rise of the child-saving movement: A study in social policy and correctional reform. *Annals of the American Academy of Political & Social Science, 381*, 21–38.

Platt, A. M. (1977). *The child savers: The invention of delinquency* (2nd ed.). Chicago, IL: University of Chicago Press.

Poe-Yamagata, E., & Jones, M. A. (2000). *And justice for some: Differential treatment of minority youth in the justice system*. Washington, DC: Building Blocks for Youth.

Popple, P. R., & Leighninger, L. (2014). *Social work, social welfare, and American society* (6th ed.). Boston, MA: Allyn & Bacon.

Richmond, M. (1917). *Social diagnosis*. Philadelphia, PA: Russell Sage Foundation.

Robbins, S. P., Vaughan-Eden, V., & Maschi, T. M. (2015). Editorial: It's not CSI: The importance of forensics for social work education. *Journal of Social Work Education, 51*(3), 412–424.

Roberts, A. R., & Brownell, P. (1999). A century of forensic social work: Bridging the past to the present. *Social Work, 44*, 359–369.

Roosevelt, E. (1958). Eleanor Roosevelt, the driving force behind the Universal Declaration of Human Rights. Retrieved from http://www.erooseveltudhr.org

Saltzman, A., & Furman, R. (1999). *Law in social work practice* (2nd ed.). Belmont, CA: Wadsworth.

Schroeder, L. O. (1997). *The legal environment of social work* (2nd ed.). Washington, DC: National Association of Social Workers Press.

Steinberg, L. (2008). A social neuroscience perspective on adolescent risk-taking. *Developmental Review, 28*(1), 78–106.

Strachan, H. (2003). The first worldwar: Vol. I. To arms. New York, NY: Oxford University Press.

Tseng, W. S., Matthews, D., & Elwyn, T. S. (2004). *Cultural competence in forensic mental health*. New York, NY: Brunner-Routledge.

Uehara, E., Flynn, M., Fong, R., Brekke, J., Barth, R. P., Coulton, C., . . . Lubben, J. (2013). Grand Challenges for social work. *Journal of the Society for Social Work and Research, 4*(3), 165–170.

United Nations. (1948). *Universal declaration of human rights*. New York, NY: Author. Retrieved from http://www.un.org/en/documents/udhr

United Nations. (1994). *Human rights and social work: A manual for schools of social work and the social work profession*. Geneva, Switzerland: United Nations Centre for Human Rights.

Van Wormer, K. (2001). *Counseling female offenders and victims: A strengths-restorative approach*. New York, NY: Springer Publishing.

Wilks, J. (2004). Revisiting Martinson: Has corrections made progress in the past 30 years? *Corrections Today, 66*, 108–111.

Wronka, J. (2008). Human rights. In T. Mizrahi & L. E. Davis (Eds.), *Encyclopedia of social work* (pp. 425–429). Washington, DC: National Association of Social Workers Press.

Wronka, J. (2012). *Human rights and social justice: Social action and service for the helping and health professions* (2nd ed.). Thousand Oaks, CA: Sage Publications.

Zastrow, C. H., & Kirst-Ashman, K. K. (2012). *Understanding human behavior and the social environment* (9th ed.). Belmont, CA: Brooks/Cole-Thompson.

Zenderland, L. (1998). *Measuring minds*. New York, NY: Cambridge University Press.

CHAPTER 2

Life Course Systems Power Analysis: Understanding Health and Justice Disparities for Forensic Assessment and Intervention

Tina Maschi

George S. Leibowitz

CHAPTER OBJECTIVES

The major objectives of this chapter are to:

- Describe the life course pathways of cumulative health and justice disparities experienced by historical and emerging diverse groups, which are often found among forensic populations.
- Articulate a life course systems power analysis strategy for use with forensic populations and in forensic settings.
- Demonstrate how a data-driven and evidence-based assessment and intervention plan can be used to address clinical and legal issues using case examples of an aging prison population.

CHAPTER COMPETENCIES HIGHLIGHTED

- Competency 2: Engage Diversity and Difference in Practice
- Competency 4: Engage in Practice Informed Research and Research Informed Practice
- Competency 6: Engage With Individuals, Families, Organizations, and Communities
- Competency 7: Assess Individuals, Families, Organizations, and Communities
- Competency 8: Intervene With Individuals, Families, Organizations, and Communities
- Competency 9: Evaluate Practice With Individuals, Families, Organizations, and Communities

The mass incarceration of people of all ages is international in scope but is particularly problematic in the United States, which has the largest incarceration rate per capita. Many incarcerated people, especially older people, have the paradoxical experience of being a victim to interpersonal and social structural violence and cumulative disparities that heighten their risk of being convicted of serious and nonserious offenses during their lifetime. This chapter uses older people in prison, including case vignettes based on actual incarcerated elders, to illustrate the complex life course of health and social structural barriers and needs of incarcerated people who have histories of victimization and criminal convictions. We apply what we refer to as a *life course systems power analysis* for use with assessment and intervention with forensic populations of all ages. We present information about trauma and justice, especially related to the trauma of incarceration, which in itself is often a form of abuse, especially when frail elders are involved and they are at increased risk for victimization, medical neglect, and "resource" exploitation. The chapter concludes with a detailed example of an assessment and intervention plan for programming in a rights-based geriatric specialized unit that offers its program participants safety protections, rehabilitation, and restoration. We assert that the biggest challenges for forensic professionals and forensic settings to best serve an incarcerated population with past and current histories of trauma and criminal justice involvement is to develop competencies to work effectively at the practice intersection of life course development (or again), behavioral health, and the criminal justice system and the incorporation of specialized programming in corrections as warranted.

Case Vignettes

Case 1. Jorge is a 56-year-old male from Puerto Rico and the youngest of nine children. He has a history of trauma and criminal offending that includes the unexpected death of his father at age 5 years, childhood sexual victimization, poverty, prostitution, drug dealing, substance abuse (heroin addiction), and recidivism (incarcerated two times). At age 17 years, he reported committing armed robbery to support his heroin addiction and was sentenced to 20 years in prison. During his prison term, he continued to use drugs. He violated parole within 15 months of release after being charged with sexual offense of a minor and possession of controlled dangerous substances, and as a result is now serving his second and current 45-year sentence. In prison, he has spent 8 of the past 15 years in solitary confinement. He perceives prison as "an overcrowded monster" designed to hold, degrade, and punish people. He views the staff as disinterested and disengaged and is despondent over the limited access to counseling and education rehabilitative services. Jorge was diagnosed with cancer six months ago while in prison and is projected to receive parole in 14 years when he is in his late seventies. He has not had any contact with family in over five years and reports feeling depressed.

Case 2. Mary is a 64-year-old, Caucasian, Catholic woman who is incarcerated in a maximum security facility for women. She identifies herself as a lesbian. As a child, she experienced the divorce of her parents, abandonment by her mother, and sexual, physical, and verbal abuse by her father, whom she described as having serious mental health issues. At age 25 years, Mary married a man 5 years younger, had two children, and divorced. This is her first criminal conviction, and she is serving a 10-year prison sentence (85% minimum) for conspiracy and the attempted murder of her abusive husband, which she describes as in self-defense. Mary describes this sentence as unfair and unjust based on mitigating circumstances. She has a medical history of hypertension, vision impairment, and osteoporosis that makes it difficult for her to walk or use a top bunk bed. At age 64 years, Mary's extensive dental problems have resulted in a premature need for dentures. She describes her current prison experience as "degrading, especially the way correctional officers treat inmates." Although she reports feelings of depression and despair, Mary reports that she copes with her prison experience by "finding meaning" in it through spirituality. Despite her ill health, Mary is resistant to using prison health care services. Her projected parole date is in two years, when she will be 66 years old. Because of the distance, Mary has not had any in-person visits with her family members since her incarceration, but corresponds monthly by mail and every three months by phone with her two adult children and four grandchildren. She says that she misses her family immensely.

(*continued*)

Case 3. Joseph is a 66-year-old Caucasian male of Irish and Polish descent; his family has an intergenerational history of alcoholism. Joseph is a Vietnam war veteran. As a child, he experienced "extreme" corporal punishment from his parents and was fearful of communicating with his parents because of it. Joseph was sexually molested for years by his little league manager. At age 13 years, he made a conscious decision to "get tough" to protect himself. At 18 years he joined the Marine Corp. After his release, Joseph witnessed a man in a bar offering cocaine to several young girls who he believed would be sexually molested. In a blinding rage, he took the man outside the bar with another peer and murdered the man. In prison, Joseph spent time in administration segregation and solitary confinement. During these periods of isolation he describes engaging in self-reflection. His recent visit to the prison infirmary showed that he had signs of cognitive impairment, suggestive of dementia. He is serving a life sentence in prison.

Source: Maschi, Leibowitz, and Mizus (2015).

Background of the Problem

The Case Vignettes of Jorge, Mary, and Joseph represent a tip of the iceberg of the rapidly aging global prison population. The mass incarceration of the individuals that eventually will grow old in prison is an international problem but is particularly problematic in the United States, which has the largest incarceration rate per capita (ACLU, 2012). The cases presented in this chapter are only 3 of the 2.3 million people in custody in the United States, of which 16% ($n = 200,000$) are aged 50 years and older, the age generally designated as elderly in corrections (Guerino, Harrison, & Sabol, 2011). Two major reasons for the rise in the incarcerated elderly population are a general increase in the general aging population as well as the 1980s stricter sentencing and parole release policies and practices. The punitive criminal justice practices have resulted in individuals serving longer, including life prison terms, destining them to grow old and even die in prison (Maschi, Viola, & Sun, 2012). About two out of three of the aging prison population is incarcerated for committing a violent or sexual offense (ACLU, 2012; HRW, 2012).

The Pathways of Cumulative Health and Justice Disparities

The diverse backgrounds and differing pathways to prison among the incarcerated population have implications for culturally responsive assessment and intervention with individuals, families, organizations, and communities. For example, the majority of the U.S. aging prison population are men (96%) and are disproportionately racial ethnic minorities (Black = 40%, Latino = 15%, other = 15%) compared to Whites (40%; Guerino et al., 2011). Maschi, Viola, and colleagues' (2013) typology describes four distinct types of people who reach old age in prison largely based on the length of time served. These four groups are incarcerated persons with long-term sentences (a person with 20 or more years served), the lifer (life sentence), persons with histories of acute and chronic recidivism (two or more incarcerations), and persons who were first convicted as an older adult (first convicted in old age). Health status also varies among all age groups but increases along with the aging process. Some incarcerated individuals maintain their functional capacity while in prison, while others suffer from serious and terminal illnesses such as HIV/AIDs, cancer, and dementia or mental health and substance use problems (36%; James & Glaze, 2006). Those individuals with chronic health and mental health issues may or may not have had these conditions prior to incarceration. In addition to criminal offense histories, many incarcerated individuals have histories of traumatic stress, abuse, and violent victimization that have occurred in the community and/or while in prison. These types of traumatic and stressful life experiences include, but are not limited to, childhood physical and sexual assault, witnessing violence, or a history of family separation or foster care involvement (Maschi, Viola, Morgen, & Koskinen, 2013). Their criminal histories are often the focus of the criminal justice system, and these traumatic and stressful life experiences that have occurred prior to incarceration often go undetected and/or untreated and result in varying levels of adaptive coping responses and access to fair justice, social support, and service networks (Aday, 2005; Maschi, Viola, & Morgen, 2013; Maschi, Viola, et al., 2013).

As illustrated in the Case Vignettes, the pathway that results in prison for incarcerated people may vary in one or more cumulative disparities related to race, education, socioeconomic status, gender, disability, sexual orientation, or legal or immigration status, which can influence their access to health, behavioral health and social services, economic resources, and justice (Figure 2.1). As the international human rights movement is gaining momentum in its efforts to advocate for the rights of incarcerated people of all ages, the forensic practice community is challenged to think creatively and out of the concrete "prison" box on how to respond effectively, especially as it relates to special populations who experience a lifetime of cumulative disadvantages, such as women and children, persons with physical and behavioral health issues, and older people (United Nations [UN], 2012).

The Trauma of Incarceration: Prison as an Abusive System

We argue that the poor social and environmental conditions of confinement, particularly for vulnerable diverse groups, should be classified as abuse and neglect and responded to according to social work's ethical and legal mandates to report abuse (NASW, 1996). The World Health Organization (2012) defines elder abuse as "a single, or repeated act, or lack of appropriate action, occurring within any relationship where there is an expectation of trust which causes harm or distress to an older person." For example, elder abuse may take many forms and consists of physical, sexual, psychological, emotional, financial exploitation, and intentional or unintentional neglect, including medical neglect (WHO, 2012). In the case of elder abuse in prison, situations of physical and sexual victimization, medical neglect, and lack of rehabilitation services and discharge planning exacerbate physical and mental illnesses and are a violation of human rights to safety protections and basic standards of care (ACLU, 2012; HRW, 2012). As suggested in the three Case Vignettes, prison was described as a source of trauma, abuse, and distress, especially for Jorge who spent considerable time in solitary confinement.

As a special population, older adults in prison are often an overlooked group who are at increased risk of many types of elder abuse in prison. Due to their increasing age-related frailty, older adults in prison are at increased risk of victimization and injury, medical and social care neglect, and exploitation of their resources (Maschi, Morrissey, & Leigey, 2013). Yet, despite their vulnerabilities, there is also a growing body of evidence that documents their resilience, such as their use of cognitive, physical, emotional, spiritual, and social coping resources. These multidimensional domains of coping suggest there are avenues for prevention and intervention that promote health and positive human development and rehabilitation (Aday, 2003; Maschi, Viola, et al., 2013).

Assessment and Intervention Using a Life Course Systems Power Analysis Model

When considering the important task of assessment and intervention with incarcerated people in the criminal justice system, conducting a holistic assessment of each person, such as found in the three Case Vignettes, in a social environmental context is essential. Given that this chapter addresses individuals in their social/structural context, a life course forensic interdisciplinary perspective is integrated with ecological systems and critical theories

Figure 2.1 A Life Course System Power Analysis Model for Multilevel Assessment and Intervention

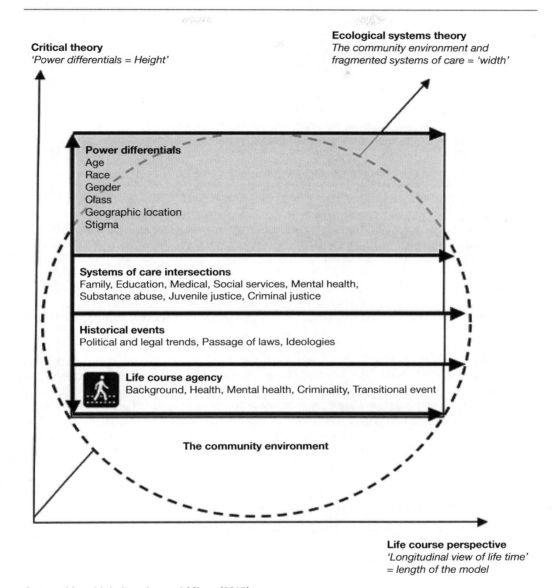

Source: Maschi, Leibowitz, and Mizus (2015).

within the human rights and social justice system (HR-SJS) approach articulated in this text (see Figure 2.1).

As shown in Figure 2.1, a life course systems power analysis assists in identifying the potential areas in the three Case Vignettes of Jorge, Mary, and Joseph that may require an integrated clinical, case management, and/or advocacy response. It allows for an evaluation of the process and current outcomes of older adults in prison and can be used for clinical-, organizational-, community-, and policy-level assessment, prevention, and intervention efforts (Maschi, Viola, & Sun, 2012). The model is discussed next followed by an application of the model to the three Case Vignettes for assessment and intervention.

The Life Course (the Length of the Model)

Consistent with a HR-SJS approach, the life course perspective gives central importance to the whole person, or individual, and his or her dynamically changing inner or subjective experiences; meaning making, of life course events (e.g., objective event—victim of sexual assault and subjective response—adaptive or maladaptive response) and subjective well-being, is the central focus of the model. Human agency is the core component and is commonly used in the life course perspective and social justice capabilities theories (Elder, 2003; Nussbaum, 2004). Human agency is conceptualized as a person's creative life force energy and central driver through which the individual sets his or her intention and pursues his or her life's purpose, passion, and goals in connection to and with others, which in turn ideally fosters an innate and developing sense of well-being and connectedness (Wahl, Iwarsson, & Oswald, 2012). In the case of Jorge, Mary, and Joseph, earlier life traumas and prison experience present a challenge for their pursuit of life course human agency.

Well-being is defined consistent with the World Health Organization (2014) definition of health as a state of multidimensional well-being and not just the absence of disease. Specifically, well-being is defined by seven core domains: root (basic needs), physical, cognitive, emotional, social/cultural, spiritual, and participatory (political/legal) well-being. When cumulative determinants or social and environmental conditions are optimal during the life course, individuals express human agency through concern for self and others and sustain high subjective levels of well-being and meaning making. As older adults in prison describe, domains of well-being include cognitive, physical, emotional, spiritual, and social coping resources. These multidimensional domains of coping suggest there are avenues for prevention and intervention that promote health and positive human development and rehabilitation (Aday, 2003; Maschi, Viola, et al., 2013).

However, when conditions are suboptimal, such as the experience of personal beliefs or attitudes (e.g., negative worldview) or confronted with social environmental barriers (poverty, low educational attainment, adverse neighborhood conditions, long prison sentences), a person's healthy expression of human agency may diminish his or her subjective well-being and negatively manifest as illness (e.g., somatic symptoms) or offending behavior (Maschi & Baer, 2012; Maschi, Kwak, Ko, & Morrissey, 2012; Maschi, Morgen, Zgoba, Courtney, & Ristow, 2011). As the three Case Vignettes show, Jorge, Mary, and Joseph have had adverse life experiences, including prison placement that they describe as challenging their health and well-being.

Systems (the Width of the Model)

During an individual's life course, the systems, such as family, service, and legal systems, often change over time. This type of dynamic interaction between the person in his or her social environment context also consists of practice and stakeholder contexts. Access to services and justice may facilitate or impede an individual's right to human agency and the individual's ability to achieve his or her life goals. When societal conditions are suboptimal, such as in the case of most U.S. state correctional systems' poor health care services, the health and well-being of older adults may be significantly compromised (UN Office on Drugs and Crime, 2009). Other social contexts include society's values and ethics, interdisciplinary perspectives, and the use of evidence-based and evidence-informed practices. Values and ethics can be personal, professional, and societal (UN, 1948)—as Jorge, Mary, and Joseph describe the lack of access to evidence-based services and justice during the course of their criminal justice system experiences. For example, a central value and ethical principle of human rights philosophy is honoring the dignity and worth of all persons and respect for all persons, including people in prison (UN, 1948, 1977, 2012). In many cases, this principle is not honored for older adults in prison, including for the case examples.

Power (the Height of the Model)

The history of access to power and privilege throughout the life course also is important to assess, especially for older adults who have experiences of being victimized and who have committed crimes. Power dynamics across the life course may be balanced (equitable) or imbalanced (oppressive). This social environment factor may facilitate or hinder individuals throughout the life course. Characteristics, such as age, race/ethnicity, gender, social class, income, immigration, and legal status, may serve to open or close doors to advancement in society or result in accumulating disparities across the life course.

According to this model, individuals or groups can be oppressed at the personal (i.e., everyday interactions), structural (e.g., institutional), or cultural levels (e.g., societal attitudes, media). Individuals' internalization of negative self-messages influence behaviors toward others (Mullaly, 2010). For example, societies across the globe often have social structural barriers that enable the dominant group to subjugate oppressed subgroups, as noted earlier (Mullaly, 2010). Life course cumulative disparities often result in criminalization of oppressed persons as evidenced in the disproportionate stricter sentencing and confinement of minority populations and creation of barriers to parole release (Sampson & Laub, 1997).

Interdisciplinary perspectives, which are commonly fragmented when addressing aging people in prison, is another social environmental factor to consider (see Figure 2.1). Given that a social work perspective may vary from a medical perspective that pathologizes, and that philosophies of practice may change over time, an assessment and intervention should address these varying perspectives. In a life course systems power analysis, using a holistic and integrated theoretical base is essential to adequately address the process and outcomes of the crisis (Greenfield, 2012). Lastly, the evaluation of evidence-based and evidence-informed practices is needed to most adequately capture the process and outcomes of interventions for older adults in prison (Glasziou, 2005).

Embedding Restorative Justice and Risk, Need, and Responsivity (RNR)

Embedded in the life course power analysis shown in Figure 2.2 are restorative justice approaches that emphasize strengthening prosocial bonds, community-based management and systems of care for offenders, and enhancing protective factors against sexual and nonsexual criminal reoffense. The promotion of protective factors in restorative justice approaches (such as Circles of Accountability and Support or COSAs; Wilson, Picheca, & Prinzo, 2007) are central in models that focus on offender reintegration that include fostering interrelationships and community engagement and support, as well as mutual accountability in addressing the needs of older adults in prison. Additionally, principles of risk, need, and responsivity (Andrews & Bonta, 2010) coincide with the shift from a punishment/criminalization approach to a rehabilitation model that is more attentive to social and psychological risk and protective factors in designing interventions, which includes substance abuse, trauma, and exposure to violence exemplified in the case vignettes presented earlier. RNR underscores respectful and collaborative working relationships between clients and correctional agencies that promote the use of effective assessments and interventions, resulting in lower recidivism rates (Andrews & Bonta, 2010). RNR is based on three therapeutic principles that focus on matching services to the individual's risk level (risk principle); addressing criminogenic (e.g., sexual drive, the sequelae of traumatic stress, and social rejection) and noncriminogenic needs (need principle); and tailoring interventions based on an individual's motivation, learning style, agency, identity, and systems context (responsivity principle).

Application of Model to Case Vignettes of Jorge, Mary, and Joseph

What perhaps is most challenging for practitioners who work with older adults with histories of victimization prior to and while in prison is that there is no cut-and-dry distinction between being a "victim" and "offender." As these case vignettes of Jorge, Mary,

Figure 2.2 A Practice Model for Assessing and Treating Justice-Involved Individuals, Families, and Communities

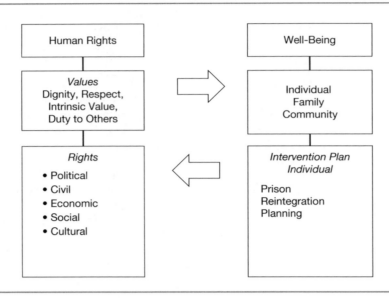

and Joseph suggest, older adults with histories of victimization and criminal conviction histories are diverse. Many people in prison have experienced life challenges related to their marginalized or disadvantaged statuses based on personal or social structural characteristics and personal and trauma histories. As shown in the case examples, their stories reveal an accumulation or aggravation of life course disadvantages, such as being born in poverty; child, adolescent, and adult trauma or exploitation; and juvenile and criminal involvement. Their high-risk life course trajectories present unique challenges for individuals, families, organizations, and communities, including forensic social work and interdisciplinary professionals, to prevent, assess, and intervene as needed. Enhancing social relations compromised by a history of marginalization and victimization; addressing the principles of risks, need, and responsivity (Andrews & Bonta, 2010); and instilling community-based supports attuned to cultural and gender differences in each of these cases can have a stabilizing effect, particularly postrelease, and decrease the likelihood of relapse for sexual and/or violent reoffense. Although social workers may work with individuals in the criminal justice system, it is important they acknowledge that interagency cooperation and mutual support is crucial to good outcomes, and consideration of the context of a criminal justice system is required where the unjust and disproportionate treatment of racial/ethnic minorities, individuals, and families living in poverty, persons with mental health or physical disabilities, and a rapidly growing subgroup of older women are particularly vulnerable (ACLU, 2012). The next section applies the model to assessment and intervention plans, including for the three case vignettes.

Human Rights and Social Justice Assessment and Intervention Plan

In designing an intervention plan for Jorge, Mary, and Joseph, a life course systems analysis was conducted. It consisted of a holistic assessment of biopsychosocial, spiritual, and legal aspects. Exhibit 2.1 highlights the core assessment tools that were used; instruments that assess traumatic stress (e.g., posttraumatic stress disorder [PTSD] checklist [PCL]), as well as instruments that specifically estimate the risk for sexual offense (e.g., Static 99; designed

Exhibit 2.1 Assessment Tools

- **A life course systems power analysis.** As shown in Figure 2.1, a life course systems power analysis allows for an assessment of an individual's life experiences and subjective response to these events, changing systems (access to services and justice over time), and power dynamics that may result in protective advantages and/or cumulative disparities.
- **Human rights and well-being multilevel assessment.** As shown in Figure 2.2, the human rights map is a visual assessment tool, similar to an ecomap, that assesses for biopsychosocial/structural issues in relation to multidimensional well-being (i.e., legal, political, economic, educational, social, physical, mental, spiritual, and cultural well-being) embedded in a human rights framework based on the 30 articles of the Universal Declaration of Human Rights.
- **Traumatic and stressful life experiences.** Trauma and stressful life experiences (cumulative objective occurrences and past year subjective distress) were measured using the 31-item Life Stressors Checklist-Revised (LSC-R). The LSC-R estimates the frequency of the objective occurrences of lifetime and current traumatic events (e.g., being a victim of and/or witness to violence). The LSC-R has good psychometric properties, including use with diverse age groups and criminal justice populations (Wolfe, Kimerling, Brown, Chrestman, & Levin, 1996).
- **Posttraumatic stress symptoms.** Posttraumatic stress symptoms were measured with the PTSD checklist (PCL) for civilian populations (Weathers, Litz, Herman, Huska, & Keane, 1993).
- **Coping resources.** Coping resources were measured using the Coping Resources Inventory (CRI; Marting & Hammer, 2004). The CRI is a valid measure of self-reported coping resources that are available to manage stressors, and has been used with samples of older adults and criminal offenders. This 60-item CRI has five subscales that measure cognitive, emotional, spiritual and philosophical, physical, and social coping resources. The CRI has good convergent and discriminant validity and good internal consistency ($\alpha = .80$) across the subscales.
- **Activities of daily living.** The Katz Index of Independence in Activities of Daily Living, commonly referred to as the Katz ADL, is the most proper scale to assess functional status as a measurement of the person's ability to perform ADLs independently. Although no formal reliability and validity reports could be found in the literature, the tool is used extensively as a flag signaling functional capabilities of older adults in clinical and home environments.
- **Geriatric Depression Scale.** Geriatric Depression Scale (GDS) is a self-reported measure of depression in older adults and had been used with older prison populations (Parmelee, Katz, & Lawton, 1989; Yesavage et al., 1983).
- **Montreal Cognitive Assessment.** The Montreal Cognitive Assessment was used to assess for cognitive impairment (Nasreddine et al., 2005).
- **Substance Abuse.** The Addiction Severity Index (ASI) is a semistructured instrument used in face-to-face interviews conducted by clinicians, researchers, or trained technicians. The ASI covers the following areas: medical, employment/support, drug and alcohol use, legal, family/social, and psychiatric. The ASI obtains lifetime information about problem behaviors, as well as problems within the previous 30 days.
- **Risk and needs assessments/discharge planning:** (a) The Static-99 is a 10-item actuarial assessment instrument for use with adult sexual offenders who are 18 years or older at the time of community release. (b) Correctional Offender Management and Profiling Alternative Sanctions (COMPAS) assesses needs and risk of recidivism (general recidivism, violent recidivism, noncompliance, and failure to appear); (c) LSI-R (Andrews & Bonta, 1995) assesses parole outcome, success in correctional halfway houses, institutional misconducts, and recidivism.

Source: Maschi, Leibowitz, and Mizus (2015).

only for males) and instruments that can assess a broader range of risk factors for both male and female adults (e.g., Level of Service Inventory-Revised [LSI-R]), should be administered in order to help determine appropriate interventions.

Jorge

In the case of Jorge, assessing complex life course issues and risk, need, and responsivity factors that address both sexual and nonsexual issues are salient, including history of victimization, loss, and health issues (recent diagnosis of cancer). It is significant that he recidivated on a sexual offense toward a minor (sexual drive and risk for sexual harm considerations; the Static-99 could be used), signaling significant impairments in interrelationships, after a history of nonsexual crimes and related to substance abuse/addiction. Interventions in Jorge's case should consider dynamic/protective factors including internal and external coping resources and health and mental health factors (e.g., depression) impacting older individuals, as well as criminogenic needs (attuned to his culture) related to risk management and community safety such that he can engage in the community upon reentry. Taking into account the competencies and program components that should be targeted, which includes reengagement with his family and resources that are needed, are crucial in this case (Exhibit 2.2 and Table 2.1).

Mary

In the case of Mary, there are similar considerations in terms of a history of victimization (domestic violence), coping resource issues, health care concerns, and disengagement with family, with the addition of gender-specific considerations and the fact that her only criminal history was related to the attempted murder of her abusive husband. Using risk and needs assessment appropriate for females (e.g., the LSI-R) and gender-specific strategies for establishing therapeutic engagement is crucial in this case.

Joseph

In the case of Joseph, a history of coercive parental discipline, abandonment and subsequent impairment in attachment, and sexual victimization led to substance abuse and traumatic stress symptomatology (hyperarousal as well as dissociative rage), such that he felt compelled to protect potential victims from sexual violence that led to the murder charge. His current constellation of health issues and isolation are salient factors in the consideration of interventions while he serves his life sentence (e.g., possible dementia).

Intervention Plan

All three individuals were referred to a geriatric specialized unit in the prison that included geriatric-specific programming. The geriatric-specific program highlighted in this chapter is based on the Nevada Department of Corrections, Senior Structured Living Program, or True Grit Program (Exhibit 2.2; Harrison, Kopera-Frye, & Harrison, 2017). The program is staffed by an interdisciplinary team of doctors, nurses, social workers, chaplains, lawyers, advocates, and volunteers. The program infuses principles of human rights and social justice, such as dignity and worth of the person, and incorporates comprehensive structured services that foster biopsychosocial well-being among older adults in prison and accountability and has separate programs for men and women. Preliminary analysis of the qualitative data from participants suggests that they view the program as an invaluable part of their lives, helping them cope with daily prison stress while allowing them to offer restitution for their crimes, and planning for community reintegration. Preliminary quantitative analysis suggests that participants who are released from prison have a 0% recidivism rate (Maschi, Leibowitz, Rees, & Pappacena, 2016). As shown in Table 2.1, the intervention plans to which each of the participants was assigned were selected from program components from Exhibit 2.2.

Exhibit 2.2 Program Components

1. **Diversion activities.** Diversion activities are a major segment of the program. Crocheting, knitting, beading, and latch-hook rug-making provide activity that is not only cognitively stimulating, but affords excellent physical therapy for arthritic hands and fingers.

2. **Culturally responsive cognitive interventions.** Cognitive interventions include creative writing, Spanish language study group, ethnodrama, and cultural arts group. The groups produce a newsletter and poetry journal, which are edited by the group members.

3. **Substance abuse/addictions groups.** Weekly meetings of 12-step groups including Alcoholics Anonymous, Narcotics Anonymous, and Sexual Compulsives Anonymous, which are facilitated by volunteer sponsors.

4. **Psychoeducation.** Weekly seminars are held that address aging, health and wellness, sexuality, life skills, cooking, menu planning and healthy life choices, or other relevant activities.

5. **Animal-assisted therapy/end-of-life care.** Volunteers provide animal-assisted therapy (individually and in group). Animal-assisted therapy targets physical, occupational, speech and psychotherapies, special education, pain management issues, and end-of-life support.

6. **Physical exercise.** Program participants are scheduled for daily exercise activities. These activities include wheelchair softball, basketball, or volleyball; aerobics; tennis; measured-distance walking; weight lifting; stationary bicycle; billiards; ping-pong; horseshoes; or dancing.

7. **Peer support groups/vet to vet**. Veteran volunteers assist members with writing and producing artwork about their war experiences.

8. **Spiritual wellness.** Spiritual wellness consists of traditional religious activities by staff, or volunteers, or peer support members. Bereavement services are provided for when the death of a family member or peer in prison occurs.

9. **Correctional mental health activities.** Formal correctional programs facilitated by both staff and community volunteers are available to program participants. These programs include victim awareness, stress management, anger management, conflict resolution, relationship skills, health-related recovery, commitment to change, trauma and recovery, addictions prevention education, sex offender treatment, parenting and grandparenting classes, and special populations programs.

10. **Prison legal services and victims' rights training.** Prison legal services provide program participants access to pro bono lawyers and social workers who are versed in elder and prison rights and law and case management services. Program participants can seek consultation or representation for appeals based on sentencing, parole release, or geriatric, medical, and compassionate release. The prison Ombudsman represents cases of interpersonal victimization and institutional abuse. Community advocates who monitor cases based on the Prison Rape Elimination Act also are available to incarcerated persons at the facility, including program participants.

11. **Family visiting programs.** The family visiting program provides extended time with family members, which includes spouses and partners, children, and grandchildren. Families can request transportation services from faith-based volunteers if there is no access to public transportation to get to the facility. An option for televisiting was available for participants, such as Mary, whose family lived at a distance that did not enable them to visit her in person. For participants without family members who can visit, peer visits and volunteer visitors can be arranged based on request.

12. **Restorative justice/reconciliation and forgiveness groups/long-termers and lifers group.** The program also offers a session for reconciliation and forgiveness. It uses a narrative style writing and group reflection for individuals to process their crime, especially violent or sexual offenses that resulted in harm or death to another person or persons. For participants with life sentences, a weekly lifers group is offered.

(continued)

Exhibit 2.2 Program Components (*continued*)

13. **Education and vocational training.** Program participants may choose from a range of vocational services to obtain general education diploma (GED) or high-school diplomas, college degrees, and vocational training in occupations, such as the culinary arts and select trades.

14. **Discharge planning.** Volunteers provide members with information and referrals concerning their eventual release from prison. This includes collaboration with nonprofit organizations, halfway houses, resources for potential employment, and other assistance, such as veterans or disability benefits.

Source: Maschi, Leibowitz, and Mizus (2015).

TABLE 2.1   Intervention Plan

Intervention	Jorge	Mary	Joseph
Treatment Goals	1. Increase root, cognitive, physical, emotional, social, spiritual, and participatory well-being 2. Reduce disciplinary infractions to zero	1. Increase root, cognitive, physical, emotional, social, spiritual, and participatory well-being 2. Increase preparedness for community reintegration	1. Increase root, cognitive, physical, emotional, social, spiritual, and participatory well-being
Programming assigned			
Arts-based diversion activities	X	X	X
Culturally responsive cognitive interventions	X	X	X
Substance abuse/addictions groups	X	X	X
Psychoeducation	X		X
Animal-assisted therapy	X	X	X
End-of-life care/grief and bereavement			
Physical exercise	X	X	X
Peer support groups/vet to vet			X
Spiritual wellness	X	X	X
Mental health activities	X	X	X
Prisoner legal services and victim rights	X	X	X
Family/peer/volunteer visiting program	X	X	X
Restorative justice/reconciliation/ forgiveness	X	X	X
Education and vocational training	X	X	X
Discharge planning		X	
Lifers and long-termers group	X		X

Source: Maschi, Leibowitz, and Mizus (2015).

Conclusion

As illustrated in the case study examples of Jorge, Mary, and Joseph, the biggest challenges for interdisciplinary professionals and programs to foster health and well-being among incarcerated older adults are in developing competencies in working at the practice intersection of aging, health/mental health, and criminal justice sectors of care. Although the extent to which some skills are used depends upon where a professional is "positioned" in the system (e.g., clinical social worker in prison, reentry program administrator), it involves having competencies in aging (gerontological practice), physical and mental health assessment and intervention, case management, interdisciplinary collaboration, discharge planning, and legal and policy advocacy.

Coupled with society's increased recognition of the elderly as a vulnerable population, as demonstrated by the proposed Convention of the Rights of Older Persons and the growing elder and intergenerational and family justice movements, there is now the potential for older prisoners to achieve access to justice.

Comprehensive promising programs, such as geriatric-specific programming—for example, True Grit prototypes—that bridge prison-to-community services are a leap forward toward addressing human rights-based best practices for older adults in prison, especially with histories of being victims and committing offenses. Promising practices with older adults in prison often honor the dignity and worth of the person, foster human agency and autonomy, and foster holistic well-being. Program components often include geriatric case management services for medical, mental health, substance abuse, family, social services, housing, education or vocational training, restorative justice (e.g., victim or victim–offender mediation services), or spiritual counseling; exercise and creative arts programs; and employment and/or retirement counseling. Program-specific aspects include one or more of the following: age- and cognitive capacity–sensitive environmental modifications (including segregated units), interdisciplinary staff and volunteers trained in geriatric specific correctional care, complementary medicine, specialized case coordination, the use of family and inmate peer supports and volunteers, mentoring, and self-help advocacy group efforts.

If these incarcerated individuals were to be released, a holistic biopsychosocial and structural assessment would be beneficial for transitional care planning. Additionally, a social worker also would need to make the service linkages to all the resources necessary to meet the complex needs of the incarcerated person and his or her families. Recommendations for relevant categories for a holistic assessment and transitional care planning form can be found in Exhibits 2.3 and 2.4.

Exhibit 2.3 Excerpt From Transition Care Assessment Tool

Biopsychosocial Legal Narrative Assessment
1–2 Page Narrative Summary of Case

Completed by: _____

Agency: _____

Date: _____

1. Identifying information (sociodemographic characteristics)
2. Reason for referral/presenting problem
   A. Referral source
   B. Summary of the presenting problem/s
   C. Impact of the presenting problem/s

(continued)

Exhibit 2.3 Excerpt From Transition Care Assessment Tool (*continued*)

2. Client and family description and functioning
3. Relevant history
   A. Family of origin history
   B. Relevant developmental history
   C. Family of creation and current family history
   D. Trauma, oppression, stigma, and discrimination history
   E. Current cognitive, emotional, physical, social, and spiritual health
   F. Educational and employment (past and current) history
   G. Housing (past and current)
   H. Religious (spiritual) participation
   I. Intergenerational social relationships
   J. Dating/marital/sexual relations
   K. Medical service history
   L. Mental health/substance use service use history
   M. Legal issues and criminal justice system involvement
   N. Current and anticipated environmental conditions
   O. Assets, resources, and strengths
   P. Other (if applicable)
4. Worker's assessment

Source: © Tina Maschi, 2016.

Exhibit 2.4 Transitional Care Referral Form

Date:		
Client's name:	Client's DOB: MM/DD/YYYY	
Client's age:		
Contact information:		
Referral types (check all that apply)	Specific comments (*specify type of issue and services needed*)	*INTERNAL USE*
Medical		*Linkage made/date*
• Medical services		
• Medication		
• HIV/AIDS Service Administration (HASA)		
• Health literacy classes		
• Other (please specify)		
Mental health/addiction		
• Mental health		
• Substance abuse/addictions		
• Medication		
• Other (please specify)		
Employment		
• Job referral		
• Training referral		

(*continued*)

Exhibit 2.4 Transitional Care Referral Form (*continued*)

Housing		
• Housing		
• Home energy assistance		
Benefits/social services		
• Aging services		
• SSI/SSD application		
• Food stamps		
• Public assistance		
• Medicaid		
• Medicare		
• Veterans' benefits and services		
• Birth certificate		
• Social Security card		
• Life skills, psychoeducation, socialization		
• Support groups (peer, other)		
• Case management		
• Partner notification		
• Domestic violence, abuse, neglect		
• Escort transportation		
• Family support services		
• Other (please specify)		
Legal		
• Legal services		
• INS (Green Card)		
• Other (please specify)		

INS, Immigration and Naturalization Service; SSI/SSD, Supplemental Security Income/Social Security Disability.
Source: © Tina Maschi, 2016.

CHAPTER EXERCISES

These chapter exercises can be completed by an individual or group as a one-page written exercise, a five-minute class discussion, or a 300-word discussion thread.

Exercise 1. After reviewing these key terms from the chapter, choose at least one term and explain your understanding of how it applies to at least one of the case vignettes.

Exercise 2. Using a life course systems analysis strategy, choose a case from practice to describe the individual, family, organization, or community in terms of life course individual, family, or community development, power dynamic, and social systems. If no case from practice is available, you can use one of the chapter vignettes.

Exercise 3. After reading all three vignettes in this chapter, identify what human rights issues are similar or different across all three cases.

Additional Resources

The Justia Agenda: www.justiaagenda.com

Penal Reform International: www.penalreform.org/about-us

Restorative Practices International: www.rpiassn.org

Substance Abuse and Mental Health Services Administration (SAMHSA) Trauma and Justice Initiative: https://store.samhsa.gov/shin/content/SMA11-4629/04-TraumaAndJustice.pdf

References

Aday, R. H. (2003). *Aging prisoners: Crisis in American corrections.* Westport, CT: Praeger.

Aday, R. H. (2005). Aging prisoners' concerns toward dying in prison. *OMEGA-Journal of Death and Dying, 52*(3), 199–216.

American Civil Liberties Union. (2012). The mass incarceration of the elderly. Retrieved from http://www.aclu.org/files/assets/elderlyprisonreport_20120613_1.pdf

Andrews, D. A., & Bonta, J. (1995). *LSI-R: The level of service inventory-revised.* Toronto, ON, Canada: Multi-Health Systems.

Andrews, D. A., & Bonta, J. (2010). Rehabilitating criminal justice policy and practice. *Psychology, Crime and Law, 16*(1), 39–55.

Elder, G. (2003). The emergence and development of life course theory. In J. T. Mortimer & M. J. Shanahan (Eds.), *Handbook of the life course* (pp. 3–21). New York, NY: Plenum.

Glasziou, P. (2005). Evidence based medicine: Does it make a difference? Make it evidence informed practice with a little wisdom. *British Medical Journal* (Clinical Research Ed.), *330*, 92; discussion 94.

Greenfield, E. A. (2012). Using ecological frameworks to advance a field of research, practice, and policy on aging-in-place initiatives. *Gerontologist, 52*(1), 1–12.

Guerino, P., Harrison, P., & Sabol, W. (2011). Prisoners in 2010 [Bulletin NCJ236096]. Washington, DC: U.S. Department of Justice, Bureau of Justice Statistics. Retrieved from http://bjs.ojp.usdoj.gov/content/pub/pdf/p10.pdf

Harrison, M. T., Kopera-Frye, K., & Harrison, W. O. (2017). A promising practice—True Grit: A structured living program for older adults in prison. In T. Maschi & R. Immagieron (Eds.), *Aging prisoners: A crisis in need of intervention* (White paper; 2nd ed., pp. 57–69). New York, NY: The Justia Agenda. Retrieved from http://justiaagenda.com

Human Rights Watch. (2012). Old behind bars: The aging prison population in the United States. Retrieved from http://www.hrw.org/reports/2012/01/27/old-behind-bars

James, D. J., & Glaze, L. E. (2006). *Mental health problems of prison and jail inmates* (Bureau of Justice Reports NCJ 213600). Washington, DC: U.S. Department of Justice.

Marting, M. S., & Hammer, A. L. (2004). *Coping resources inventory manual-revised.* Menlo, CA: Mind Garden.

Maschi, T., & Baer, J. C. (2012). The heterogeneity of the world assumptions of older adults in prison: Do differing worldviews have a mental health effect? *Traumatology, 19*(1), 65–72. doi:10.1177/1534765612443294

Maschi, T., Kwak, J., Ko, E. J., & Morrissey, M. (2012). Forget me not: Dementia in prisons. *The Gerontologist, 52*(4), 441–451. doi:10.1093/geront/gnr131

Maschi, T., Leibowitz, G. S., & Mizus, L. S. (2015). Best Practices for Assessing and Treating Older Adult Victims and Offenders. In K. Corcoran, A. R. Roberts (Eds.), *Social Workers' Desk Reference*. Oxford University Press.

Maschi, T., Leibowitz, G., Rees, J., & Pappacena, L. (2016). Analysis of US compassionate and geriatric release laws: Applying a human rights approach to global prisoner health. *Journal of Human Rights and Social Work, 1*, 165–174. doi:10.1007/s41134-016-0021-0

Maschi, T., Morgen, K., Zgoba, K., Courtney, D., & Ristow, J. (2011). Age, cumulative trauma and stressful life events, and post-traumatic stress symptoms among older adults in prison: Do subjective impressions matter? *Gerontologist, 51*(5), 675–686. doi:10.1093/geront/gnr074

Maschi, T., Morrissey, M. B., & Leigey, M. (2013). The case for human agency, well-being, and community reintegration for people aging in prison: A statewide case analysis. *Journal of Correctional Healthcare, 19*(3), 194–201. doi:10.1177/1078345813486445

Maschi, T., Viola, D., & Morgen, K. (2013). Unraveling trauma and stress, coping resources, and mental well-being among older adults in prison: Empirical evidence linking theory and practice. *Gerontologist, 54*(5), 857–867. doi:10.1093/geront/gnt069

Maschi, T., Viola, D., Morgen, K., & Koskinen, L. (2013). Trauma, stress, grief, loss, and separation among older adults in prison: The protective role of coping resources on physical and mental well-being. *Journal of Crime and Justice, 38*(1), 113–136. doi:10.1080/0735648X.2013.808853

Maschi, T., Viola, D., & Sun, F. (2012). The high cost of the international aging prisoner crisis: Well-being as the common denominator for action. *The Gerontologist, 53*(4), 543–554. doi:10.1093/geront/gns125

Mullaly, B. (2010). *Challenging oppression and confronting privilege* (2nd ed.). New York, NY: Oxford University Press.

Nasreddine, Z. S., Phillips, N. A., Bédirian, V., Charbonneau, S., Whitehead, V., Collin, I., . . . Chertkow, H. (2005). The Montreal Cognitive Assessment (MoCA): A brief screening tool for mild cognitive impairment. *Journal of the American Geriatrics Society, 53*, 695–699.

National Association of Social Workers. (1996). *Code of ethics of the National Association of Social Workers*. Washington, DC: National Association of Social Workers Press

Nussbaum, M. C. (2004). Beyond the social contract: Capabilities and global justice. *Oxford Development Studies, 32*(1), 1–17.

Parmelee, P. A., Katz, I. R., & Lawton, M. P. (1989). Depression among institutionalized aged: Assessment and prevalence estimation. *Journal of Gerontology, 44*, 22–29.

Sampson, R. J., & Laub, J. H. (1997). A life-course theory of cumulative disadvantage and the stability of delinquency. In T. Thornberry (Vol. Ed.), *Advances in criminological theory: Vol. 7, Developmental theories of crime and delinquency* (pp. 1–29). New Brunswick, NJ: Transaction Publishers.

United Nations. (1948). The universal declaration of human rights. Retrieved from http://www.un.org/en/documents/udhr

United Nations. (1977). Standard minimum rules for the treatment of prisoners. Retrieved from https://www.unodc.org/pdf/criminal_justice/UN_Standard_Minimum_Rules_for_the_Treatment_of_Prisoners.pdf

United Nations. (2012). Report of the United Nations high commissioner for human rights (Substantive session of 2012: Geneva, 23–27 July 2012). Retrieved from http://www.unece.org/fileadmin/DAM/pau/age/wg5/Other-documents/E-2012-51-e.pdf

United Nations Office on Drugs and Crime. (2009). Handbook for prisoners with special needs. Retrieved from http://www.unhcr.org/refworld/docid/4a0969d42.html

Wahl, H.-W, Iwarsson, S., & Oswald, F. (2012). Aging well and the environment: Toward an integrative model and research agenda for the future. *Gerontologist, 52*(3), 306–316.

Weathers, F. W., Litz, B. T., Herman, D. S., Huska, J. A., & Keane, T. M. (1993, October). *The PTSD checklist: Reliability, validity, and diagnostic utility*. Paper presented at the annual meeting of the International Society for Traumatic Stress Studies, San Antonio, TX.

Wilson, R. J., Picheca, J. E., & Prinzo, M. (2007). Evaluating the effectiveness of professionally-facilitated volunteerism in the community-based management of high-risk sexual offenders: Part two–a comparison of recidivism rates. *The Howard Journal*, 46(4), 327–337.

Wolfe, J. W., Kimerling R., Brown, P. J., Chrestman K. R., & Levin, K. (1996). Psychometric review of the Life Stressor Checklist-Revised. In B. H. Stamm (Ed.), *Measurement of stress, trauma, and adaptation* (pp. 31–53). Lutherville, MD: Sidran Press.

World Health Organization. (2012). Elder abuse. Retrieved from http://www.who.int/ageing/projects/elder_abuse/en

World Health Organization. (2014). Mental health and well-being. Retrieved from http://www.who.int/features/factfiles/mental_health/en

Wronka, J. (2010). *Human rights and social justice*. Thousand Oaks, CA: Sage Publications.

Yesavage, J. A., Brink, T. L., Rose, T. L., Lum, O., Huang, V., Adey, M., & Leirer, V. O. (1983). Development and validation of a geriatric depression screening scale: A preliminary report. *Journal of Psychiatric Research, 17*, 37–49.

VOICES FROM THE FIELD

Tammy Leombruno, LCMHC

Susan Robinson, LICSW
Psychotherapists
New England Counseling & Trauma Associates, LLC

Agency Setting

We are a small private practice outpatient office serving children, adolescents, and adults who have been impacted by trauma. The initial iteration of providers was established in November 2001 and was designed to provide comprehensive trauma assessment and treatment services across several counties. Presently, we receive referrals from various child-serving agencies (e.g., Department of Children and Families, schools in the area, designated mental health agencies, or county courts) located in Chittenden County, as well as other counties across the state of Vermont.

Practice Responsibilities

We provide individual psychotherapy, statewide consultation work, and comprehensive trauma and psychosexual evaluations. Additionally, we provide supervision to those seeking licensure with a specific interest in trauma. We are also involved in the field of juvenile justice and, more specifically, work with youth and adults who have engaged in sexually harmful behavior, recognizing that many of these individuals have also experienced trauma.

Expertise Requirements

We have met the Vermont licensure requirements in our respective fields. Both of us have been trained in eye movement and desensitization reprocessing (EMDR), Trauma Focused-Cognitive Behavioral Therapy (TF-CBT), and the Attachment, Self-Regulation, and Competency Treatment Framework (ARC). We receive trauma-specific peer supervision in line with best practice modalities. We have approximately 50 years of combined experience in the field of sexual abuse.

Ethical, Legal, Practice, Diversity, and/or Advocacy Issues Addressed

There is always a delicate balance when working with family systems. With the youth we serve, we need to balance the needs of confidentiality with the need for parents to be informed of concerning or unhealthy behaviors. We need to be mindful about how parents are informed that is respectful to our clients and preserves our treatment alliance. Being a mandated reporter also has its potential negative impact to the therapeutic working relationship. For example, if a 15-year-old is dating and having sex with a 19-year-old, we need to report this to the authorities because it is against the law (the 15-year-old is not yet of the age of legal consent) but this risks losing the relationship with a client or losing a client altogether. Ethical questions often arise: If a minor client is sending naked pictures of himself or herself to others via the Internet, are we obligated to inform parents or authorities given such behavior can be defined as possession or distribution of child pornography? What if a client is engaging in self-harming behavior and says she will never meet with you again if you inform a parent? These are the types of situations we face in private practice.

Moreover, living in a small community presents other challenges. How do therapists navigate situations when they have a son on a football team and a client is on the same team? What if a former client becomes your child's teacher, or coach? We have encountered a situation where one of us was at an adult social gathering and a client's adoptive parent was also present. Another situation that was particularly challenging was when one of us realized that a previous client was on the invitation list to her teenaged son's summer party.

Another practice issue faced is that of the dual role. As licensed therapists, we cannot ethically be involved in a dual role with our clients. We oftentimes are asked to be in a position to advocate for our client. For example, when involved in cases of youth who have engaged in sexually harmful behavior, it is not unusual for parents to request a letter of support on behalf of their child for court. In this situation, we need to explain to parents that we cannot write such letters because it could be construed as advocating for a client. A therapist who is in a dual role can face disciplinary action by the licensure board. Recently, one of us was faced with such a request.

A client was in the process of being substantiated for sexual abuse of another child (exposing his penis). Because the client has a significant trauma history, and emotionally functions at a younger age, his attorney wanted a letter of support to fight the Department of Children and Families (DCF) substantiation. The parent was similarly pushing for this and placing pressure on the therapist. Ultimately, the therapist met with the parent to explain why such advocacy could not occur. A treatment summary was provided to the attorney but the parent was disappointed in the neutral wording.

Interprofessional and Intersectoral Collaboration

As treatment providers, we often work with interdisciplinary or multidisciplinary teams depending on the case. Usually, this involves social workers from the DCF, doctors, psychiatrists, school-based clinicians, home care providers, and probation officers. We provide trainings related to sexual abuse and maltreatment for various agencies and organizations.

CHAPTER 3

Human Rights: Some Implications for Social Work

Rosemary Barbera

CHAPTER OBJECTIVES

The major objectives of this chapter are to:

- Articulate a basic understanding of human rights and how they relate to social work.
- Describe some of the changes that are needed in social work practice in the United States in order to adhere to human rights principles.

CHAPTER COMPETENCIES HIGHLIGHTED

- Competency 2: Engage Diversity and Difference in Practice
- Competency 5: Engage in Policy Practice
- Competency 6: Engage With Individuals, Families, Organizations, and Communities

Social work's commitment to social justice, human rights, and multiculturalism is well known and well documented (Boyle, Nackerud, & Kilpatrick, 1999; Gil, 1998; Ife, 2001; Mama, 2001). "Social work and human rights have a very close relationship" (Eroles, 1997). This relationship calls on social workers to be active in the construction of a new reality so that the human rights of all are respected. Human rights issues permeate all parts of the social realities in which social workers find themselves in the United States, both professionally and personally. Social workers are on the front lines, working with those persons and communities that have been exploited by social conditions that perpetuate massive human rights violations. As a result, social workers should be very familiar with human rights (Sánchez, 1989), integrating human rights into their daily practice. In fact, the International Federation of Social Workers (IFSW) and the International Association of Schools of Social Work (IASSW) consider it imperative that social workers commit themselves fully to the promotion and protection of human rights without reservation (Eroles, 1997). Unfortunately, this is not always the case in the United States, where the population is not educated in the language of human rights.

Social workers also "uphold and defend the dignity of each person's worth" (IFSW, 2004), approaching his or her work with this dignity in mind. However, often the forces of society and structural inequalities mean that "real human beings suffer (because) human rights are not protected" (DeLaet, 2006). This is especially true with regard to the prison system in the United States, where human rights violations run rampant (Golembeski & Fullilove, 2005), as youth are tried as adults and minorities are overrepresented. As a result, the dignity and worth of all humans is severely compromised as there is a clear relationship between human rights and human needs (Wronka, 1995). Wronka stated that the goal of human rights is to fill these human needs: biological (to eat and have shelter), social–psychological (to feel affiliated and loved), productive–creative (to work and create), security (to have privacy and be secure in one's person), and spiritual (to worship and find meaning in one's existence). There are clear implications for social workers who strive to respectfully partner with clients to fulfill the client's needs and gain respect for her or his human rights. In fact, in Latin America, social workers recognized that "with the introduction of human rights into the daily work of social workers, the profession became much more meaningful" (Sánchez, 1989) and more effective in creating real change.

This chapter addresses the implication of human rights for social workers. It offers some background on the concept of human rights, with emphasis on the relationship between human rights and social work and human rights and the law. It includes a discussion of the implication of human rights for social work education and social work practice, with a focus on building community. It also discusses obstacles to social work practice from a human rights perspective, and concludes with a discussion on how social work needs to change to have consistency between discourse and action.

Human Rights

"Today, the language of human rights has become a prominent tool" (DeLaet, 2006) that is used throughout the world by governments, nongovernmental organizations (NGOs), and social movements. However, although the discourse on human rights has increased, the application of that discourse seems to be lacking as evidenced by the growth of poverty and exploitation related to the growth of neoliberal globalization. When human rights are not protected, that is, when the discourse remains discourse and is not applied, "real human beings suffer" (DeLaet, 2006).

The term *human rights* refers to a significant number of rights that each human being deserves; it is what many jurists of international humanitarian law refer to as *basic rights* (Barbera, 2007). These basic rights include the right to housing, health, equitable education, a job at a living wage; in sum, to live a life of dignity and worth. And according to "the keystone instrument of human rights, the Universal Declaration of Human Rights [UDHR], adopted unanimously by the United Nations' General Assembly in 1948" (Bricker-Jenkins, Barbera, & Young, 2008), "all are equal before the law and are entitled without any discrimination to equal protection of the law" and all have certain rights in front of the criminal justice system (see Articles 7–13 of the UDHR). Given the disproportionate number of people of minority status inhabiting the jails and prisons in the United States, and the disproportionate number of economically exploited persons in prison or jail, we can see that there is a link between violations of certain human rights as defined by the UDHR and imprisonment in the United States. Therefore, the original violations to the human rights of housing, education, and jobs that pay a living wage are exacerbated by further violations of the right to be equal in front of the law, to have no cruel or unusual punishment. In this way, there is a clear role for forensic social workers to advocate with and on behalf of people in prison so that their human rights, both within and without the penal system, are respected.

Human Rights and Social Work Practice

The basic human rights just mentioned are central to social work practice.

> No society can call itself truly civilized, or truly committed to human rights, until this minimal protection of first generation rights is effectively achieved. A social worker that is committed to a human rights philosophy must also be committed to working towards such a goal. (Ife, 2001)

To successfully work toward the goal of human rights for all, "social workers need to regard human rights violations or denials as systemic in origin and to address fundamental structural issues through their practice" (Ife, 2001). Therefore, it is clear that social workers should no longer spend most of their time asking people to adjust to a dysfunctional society; rather, we are called to intervene in ways that change the exploitative, unjust structures that perpetuate injustice, oppression, and violations of human rights. It is, therefore, the role of social workers to denounce violations of human rights (Sánchez, 1989).

This becomes especially clear when we think about the fact that human "rights are intimately linked to the idea of 'quality of life'" (Cáceres, 2000), and many people who end up in prisons and jails in the United States do so because of a poor quality of life (Golembeski & Fullilove, 2005). Social workers spend a good deal of their professional time trying to work with people to improve the living conditions that lead to a negative quality of life for the world's vast majority.

Wainwright (2000) noted that "economic and social rights can be protected at a time when poverty and exclusion are recognized as major challenges." The lack of respect for economic, social, and cultural human rights further alienates those members of society who already live on the fringe and are already the most vulnerable. Indeed, it is the role of social workers to work in partnership with the most vulnerable members of society to ensure that such rights are respected and to ensure "continuous improvement in living conditions" (Wainwright, 2000) and quality of life.

Social work that grows from a human rights perspective helps us attain the very basis of our professional principles: the preoccupation with serving and being useful to the weakest members of society, by specifically confronting social problems until we are able to assure that the necessary conditions which guarantee all basic necessities are met (Sánchez, 1989). As a result "social workers have as their task the transformation of societal conditions" (Eroles, 1997), which is an ethical–political commitment. Therefore, to be ethical, it is imperative that social work practice is rooted in human rights.

> Social work practice from [a human rights] framework requires three elements: a theoretical base that gives us a framework for action; action in both the popular/grassroots and professional arenas; and, an organization ideology with three elements: 1) a commitment to basing our work in the knowledge of the people; 2) an ethical commitment to work in partnership with the most affected to ensure human rights; and, 3) interaction with other social actors towards a practice oriented towards social change. (Eroles, 1997)

This framework calls on social workers not to see people as "clients" or "others." Such a viewpoint makes it easier to objectify people and reduce them to their conditions in life. Rather, social workers are called to form partnerships with the people for whom they are working, recognizing that all human beings are actors and can be agents for change.

However, we must be cautious not to fall into the trap of saying one thing while practicing another. "Human rights seems to be a new fad since people from all walks of life and beliefs are discussing this theme. . . . In this way, however, human rights have been distorted" (Johansson, 1989). But for social work and social workers, human rights should be the basis of our action and our work. Human rights are nonnegotiable and we must work to change not only the conditions that lead to the violations of human rights, but also the conditions within our agencies and institutions that do not permit us to practice social work from a human rights framework.

Human Rights and the Law

Human rights law represents a significant paradigm shift as it recognizes that humans are not just subjects, but are also actors (DeLaet, 2006). A major step in this paradigm shift occurred in 1948 when the United Nations' Declaration of Human Rights was signed. "As a resolution passed by the General Assembly, the UDHR is a nonbinding document" (DeLaet, 2006).

Subsequently, two international conventions were developed to codify the aspirations of the UDHR—the International Covenant on Civil and Political Rights and the International Covenant on Economic, Social, and Cultural Rights. "Both documents were signed in 1966 and entered into force in 1976. As treaties that must be signed and ratified in order to enter into force, both covenants are binding under international law" (DeLaet, 2006). Because many international human rights conventions have not been ratified by the United States, their conditions or guidelines are not legal here (Williams, 2001). Regarding these two covenants, the United States has only signed and ratified the first covenant and not the second.

This is also true of other international conventions. For example, the United States and Somalia are the only countries that have not ratified the United Nations (UN) Declaration on the Rights of the Child. And, in 1996, the United States was the only country to reject the right of housing at the Habitat Conference, and the right to food at the World Food Summit (Mittal & Rosset, 1999):

> Melissa Kimble, the head of the United States government delegation to the Food Summit, said that the United States could not support language around the right to food in the Summit's Plan of Action because the new welfare reform law would then be in violation of international law.

This is a clear recognition by a United States government official that social policies in the United States do not measure up to international human rights standards.

In this same vein, it is important to note that the original UDHR includes a call to each signatory country to execute the human rights contained as best as they can given the country's economic situation. With this in mind, the United States, as the richest country on the planet, has a particular responsibility to ensure that the basic human rights of its residents are being met. This includes the right to housing, health, education, food, respect regardless of race, and jobs at living wages. These issues have significant implications in legal contexts as many people who find themselves within the criminal justice system come from exploited and oppressed groups in society in which these human rights are not respected. Therefore, we could say that although the United States is not violating the letter of the law, because the UDHR is not a legally binding document but rather an aspiration, it is violating the spirit of the law, and "public authorities must operate within the law" (Williams, 2001).

By way of comparison, Williams (2001) pointed out that in the United Kingdom, "public authorities are under a legal duty not to act in a way that is incompatible with a Convention right" because of the British Human Rights Act of 1998. However, any country that has ratified an international human rights convention is equally responsible to uphold the rights explicated in such document, so by not ratifying a document, the United States leaves itself open to violate human rights.[1] According to Goodwin-Gill (1989), there is a "distinctive concept" of rights against the state, once of moral but now legal entitlements, of rights inalienable and inherent in humanity, of the rule of law as essential to the resolution of conflicts between rights, that is dominant still in debate about human rights.

As social workers using a collaborative forensic practice framework in the United States, it is important for us to keep abreast of international human rights law as a way of improving the living conditions under which so many human beings are forced to live. It is also important to be up-to-date on human rights so that we can work more effectively in partnerships with people in client status to make change happen.

Implications for Social Work

Social work must revise itself according to the present reality (Colectivo de Trabajo Social, 1989) to bring about the conditions necessary for the respect of human rights. Our ethical

---

[1] However, it must be pointed out that the United States did both sign and ratify the UN Convention on Civil and Political Rights. One of the rights explicated in this document is the right to not be tortured. The United States has continually violated this right, as well as others.

obligation goes "beyond simply providing the best service available within the social worker's agency; it also necessitates looking at all the person's human rights and making sure they are realized and protected" (Ife, 2001). As a result, we need to reconceptualize how we engage in social work practice.

Social Work Practice

Much social work practice in the United States occurs through working one on one with an individual or family unit. This legacy of casework from the early Charity Organization Societies directs the focus of social workers on individuals when oftentimes the problems or challenges these people are facing are structural in nature. At the same time, through this individualized focus, people continue to feel isolated and alone, not recognizing that the challenges they are facing are also being faced by many others. Social workers who work in solidarity with the Poor People's Economic Human Rights Campaign, for example, work together with people living in poverty to understand the structural issues that exist. This is as true for social workers focusing on issues of housing, education, and jobs as it is for clinical social workers (Jennifer Jones, personal communication, April 1, 2003). What these social workers do is to reorganize their practice in a collective way, recognizing that the focus of human rights is group oriented; therefore, individualistic forms of social work do not make sense.

This calls on social workers to live and work in solidarity with people in client status because "social work values the people as historical subjects" (Eroles, 1997) who can be agents for change. For this kind of practice to become more widespread, however, more social workers in agencies and institutions need to demand that their practice be consistent with human rights. It also requires social workers to understand that "as social rights have been chipped away, they have been replaced by 'clientelistic' structures, such as social investment funds created to 'alleviate poverty' with funding from the World Bank and other multilateral sources" (Cáceres, 2000). These clientelistic structures function best when there is a power differential between social worker and "client," because they are partially about perpetuating the status quo. Social workers who are committed to recognizing the dignity and worth of each human being need to be given the tools to analyze clientelistic structures so as to change them. Forensic social workers, particularly, need to address issues of structural (i.e., systemic) violence in society and within the penal system that lead to human rights violations in and out of prison.

Social Work Education

Although it is true that social work practice needs to change, it is equally true that social work education too needs to change. Steen and Mathiesen (2005) pointed out that despite the obvious connections between social work and human rights, and beside the materials made available through the Centre for Human Rights, social work programs in the United States are behind other professional programs in integrating human rights content in their curricula. This is disappointing as "social workers are called to act to change the social condition, not just study it" (Eroles, 1997). Because all social work programs in the United States that are accredited by the Council for Social Work Education (CSWE) must include content about vulnerable populations, students often spend a good deal of time studying poverty and other human rights violations. Often, however, these conditions are not presented as human rights violations; and, more often, students are, at the same time, learning social work practice skills that locate problems at the individual level rather than the structural level. Therefore, there is a disconnection between discourse and practice in this area. Social work education must be based in social action (Sánchez, 1989), making use of pedagogy of human rights in which social work relationships are democratic and based on solidarity; this way social action in social work practice can become more prevalent.

Social work does not have to reinvent the wheel, so to speak. The United Nations' Centre for Human Rights has a document that clearly articulates the fit between social work and human rights. "Human rights are inseparable from social work theory, values and ethics, and practice. . . . Advocacy for such rights must therefore be an integral part of social work" (Centre for Human Rights, 1994). Social work programs can use this document as a guide to help integrate the practice of human rights, and not just its theory and values, into their curricula.

> It is not enough for social workers to profess a commitment to human rights. We have to know how to integrate human rights into our practice. We have to change our educational models so that they integrate theory and practice in human rights. We must generate a style of work that is participative and active. (Sánchez, 1989)

This calls on social work education to bridge the false divide between so-called micro and macro practice.

> The human rights approach to ethical practice suggests that a social worker who insists on maintaining the division between macro and micro practice, and only operates within one of them, is also practicing unethically, and the same criticism could be made of university departments which perpetuate the macro/micro divide in their curricula. (Ife, 2001)

Building Community

Social work committed to human rights must question the "relationships of power that perpetuate exploitation, alienation, discrimination and social exclusion" and act to change those relationships (Eroles, 1997). This calls on social workers to work against the forces of individual consumerism and to work toward building communities of solidarity. This is quite countercultural in a society that worships material goods and the maverick spirit.

"We must criticize the role of 'helper' and clientelism that often characterizes social work; our work should be more about partnerships focused on social change, conscientization, organizing and mass mobilizations" (Sánchez, 1989). Clientelism prohibits us from developing the horizontal relation of partnership; as we perpetuate the idea that social workers "help" others, we also perpetuate the idea that there is a vertical relationship of unequal power distribution between social workers and a person in client status. The very fact that the social worker is in a position to "help" denotes that there is a power differential and that the act of helping maintains that differential. Therefore, "the practice of social work needs to be committed to the values that define how we live together: solidarity, justice, and freedom" (Sánchez, 1989).

Recognizing the Obstacles

Of course, for social workers to be effective human rights advocates and activists, it is necessary to recognize the obstacles that will slow down our work. Issues of state sovereignty present an obstacle because "the principle of sovereignty discourages the use of force for the purpose of influencing the 'internal affairs' of other states" (DeLaet, 2006). DeLaet (2006) later commented that "state sovereignty trumps universal human rights." However, it is important to note that there is a double discourse when discussing state sovereignty. Although each state seems to have the right to enforce international human rights laws and standards as they see fit, at the same time there is universal enforcement of international laws that favor multinational corporations, oftentimes leading to the violation of human rights. Social workers, as advocates, educators, and concerned citizens of the world, can and should be in the forefront of the movement(s) to contest this proliferation of exploitation (Barbera, 2006).

Also relevant is the fact that sovereign states typically are the actors most responsible for perpetuating human rights abuses and are simultaneously the actors responsible for promoting and protecting human rights (DeLaet, 2006); Because many social workers exercise their profession in state-financed institutions, this becomes problematic.

Another obstacle that exists for social workers in the United States particularly, is that the majority of the U.S. population believes that human rights violations occur in other countries, not their own. This is caused in part by the fact that people most often think of human rights in civil and political terms and do not consider that there are also economic, social, and cultural human rights. In this scenario, social workers need to educate (Freire, 1970) the population regarding the full spectrum of human rights.

One final obstacle to be considered here (although there are others that space limitations do not allow us to explore) is that funding agencies might see human rights as too political and this could jeopardize the budgets of social work agencies. Practicing social work from a human rights framework requires recognition that the very structure of society is warped and needs to be transformed, not just reformed. For those who have power in society, this proposition is scary. As Freire (1970) found in his work with Brazilian peasants, the powerful in society do not want those at the bottom to understand their rights because the newly informed will then demand that their rights be respected. The same is the case in the United States today.

Conclusion

> It is not enough for social workers to speak the language of human rights and democracy; before they can even engage in social service work, they have to have in their hearts the conviction that all human beings are worthy. (Eroles, 1997)

Therefore, we must be willing to question our practice and our locations of practice: Do they perpetuate injustice and oppression? Do they question the status quo or accept it? Are they oppressive? How does our practice acquiesce to dominant thinking? Where does financing come from? How does it limit our work? We must not only know methodologies, but we must look at the context in which we practice (Ife, 2001). That is, we must be willing to interrogate all aspects of our social work practice, including our own location in society and how we might benefit from the structures of society as they presently exist. This, of course, can be a scary proposition, but one that is necessary to contribute to building a society in which the human rights of all are respected.

We must be willing to interrogate how our practice of social work might actually perpetuate problems of human rights abuses and inequalities. As Birkenmaier (2003) suggested: "Individualizing problems in direct clinical practice can also serve to maintain unjust social and institutional forces that directly relate to personal problems." Do we knowingly, and against our will, contribute to oppression through our practices? If so, are we willing to make the significant changes necessary to stop this practice? We must ask ourselves these questions and be willing to face the answers.

Social workers in forensic settings must be able to analyze the structures in society that cause many people to turn to crime. We must also be able to reflect critically on inherent injustices and structural violence that exists and that lead to disproportionate numbers of poor and minority persons inhabiting the prisons and jails in the United States. We must work simultaneously to create conditions in which incarcerated persons can empower themselves; change the conditions that lead to human rights violations within the prison system; and change the conditions in society that further exploit, oppress, and violate human rights.

Finally, we must go beyond the idea of individual human rights and think more communally. Human rights are inherently collective. As a result, the idea of social work practice emanating from a perspective of solidarity is essential. Our social work practice must always take into account the "social" in social work; a practice that focuses only on individuals and individual strategies is the antithesis of what it means to be in solidarity, to be "social" workers, working for the advancement of human rights.

CHAPTER EXERCISES

Exercise 1. Choose one of the case studies from *Perfecting Our Union* (Coke & The U.S. Human Rights Fund, 2010) *or Close to Home* (Ford Foundation, 2004). Apply the strategy used by the organization in the case study to an issue that you think is important in the United States today.

- Why is this issue important?
- How is it a human rights issue?
- How could the situation be changed to make sure human rights are not violated?

Exercise 2. Go to the Kairos webpage (https://kairoscenter.org). What can we learn from their work that will advance human rights for incarcerated persons?

Additional Resources

Davis, A. Y. (2003). *Are prisons obsolete?* Toronto: Seven Stories Press.

Fact-Finding Mission to U.S. Looks at Human Rights Condition of African Americans. (2016). Retrieved from http://www.ohchr.org/EN/NewsEvents/Pages/HumanRightsExpertsInUSA.aspx

Farmer, P. (2004). *Pathologies of power: Health, human rights, and the new war on the poor.* Berkeley: University of California Press.

Farmer, P. (2009). I believe in health care as a human right. Retrieved from http://www.youtube.com/watch?v=xJpZnUjtorI

Jones, J., & Bricker-Jenkins, M. (2004). Creating strengths-based alliances to end poverty. In D. Saleeby (Ed.), *The strengths perspective in social work practice* (3rd ed., pp. 186–212). Boston, MA: Pearson.

Kairos: The Center for Religion, Rights, and Social Justice. (n.d.). Retrieved from https://kairoscenter.org/poverty-initiative

Pitts, B. (2008). Dr. Farmer's remedy for world health. Retrieved from http://www.pih.org/blog/60-minutes-to-watch-and-a-lifetime-to-act

United Nations Universal Declaration of Human Rights. (1948). Retrieved from http://www.un.org/Overview/rights.html

References

Barbera, R. A. (2006). Understanding globalization through short-term international field experiences. *Journal of Baccalaureate Social Work, 12*(1), 287–302.

Barbera, R. A. (2007). La vivienda es un derecho humano [Housing is a human right]. *Revista de Trabajo Social, Universidad Autónoma Nacional de México, 16,* 68–73.

Birkenmaier, J. (2003). On becoming a social justice practitioner. *Social Thought, 22*(2/3), 41–54.

Boyle, D. P., Nackerud, L., & Kilpatrick, A. (1999). The road less traveled: Cross-cultural, international experiential learning. *International Social Work, 42,* 201–214.

Bricker-Jenkins, M., Barbera, R., & Young, C. (2008). Poverty through the lens of economic human rights. In D. Saleeby (Ed.), *The strengths perspective in social work practice* (5th ed., pp. 321–331). Boston, MA: Pearson.

Cáceres, E. (2000). Building a culture of rights. *NACLA Report on the Americas, 34*(1), 19–24.

Centre for Human Rights. (1994). *Human rights and social work: A manual for schools of social work and the social work profession.* New York, NY: United Nations.

Coke, T., & The U.S. Human Rights Fund. (2010). *Perfecting our union: Human rights success stories across the United States.* New York, NY: The U.S. Human Rights Fund. Retrieved from http://www.cadre-la.org/core/wp-content/uploads/2013/07/Pefecting-our-Union-0209-314-CST.pdf

Colectivo de Trabajo Social. (1989). *Trabajo social y derechos humanos: Compromiso con la dignidad. La experiencia chilena* [Social work and human rights: A commitment with dignity. The Chilean experience]. Buenos Aires: Editorial Humanitas.

DeLaet, D. (2006). *The global struggle for human rights: Universal principles in world politics.* Belmont, CA: Thompson/Wadsworth.

Eroles, C. (1997). *Los derechos humanos: Compromiso ético del trabajo social* [Human Rights: An ethical imperative for social work]. Buenos Aires: Espacio Editorial.

Ford Foundation. (2004). Close to home: Case studies of human rights work in the United States. Retrieved from www.nesri.org/sites/default/files/close_to_home.pdf

Freire, P. (1970). *Pedagogy of the oppressed.* New York, NY: Continuum International.

Gil, D. (1998). *Confronting injustice and oppression: Concepts and strategies for social work.* New York, NY: Columbia University Press.

Golembeski, C., & Fullilove, R. (2005). Criminal (in)justice in the city and its associated health consequences. *American Journal of Public Health, 95,* 1701–1707.

Goodwin-Gill, G. S. (1989). International law and human rights: Trends concerning international migrants and refugees. *International Migration Review, 23*(3), 526–546.

Ife, J. (2001). *Human rights and social work: Towards rights-based practice.* New York, NY: Cambridge University Press.

International Federation of Social Workers. (2004). Ethics in social work: Statements in principle. Retrieved from http://ifsw.org/policies/statement-of-ethical-principles

Johansson, C. (1989). Los derechos humanos no se transan en el Mercado de valores [Human rights cannot be compromised by the market]. In Colectivo de Trabajo Social (Colectivo), *Trabajo social y derechos humanos: Compromiso con la dignidad. La experiencia chilena* [Social work and human rights: A commitment with dignity. The Chilean experience] (pp. 31–36). Buenos Aires: Editorial Humanitas.

Mama, R. S. (2001). Preparing social work students to work in culturally diverse settings. *Social Work Education, 20,* 373–382.

Mittal, A., & Rosset, P. (1999). *America needs human rights.* Oakland, CA: Food First Books.

Sánchez, M. D. (1989). Trabajo social en derechos humanos: Reencuentro con la profesión [Social work in human rights. A reunion with the profession]. In Colectivo de Trabajo Social (Colectivo), *Trabajo social y derechos humanos: Compromiso con la dignidad. La experiencia chilena* [Social work and human rights: A commitment with dignity. The Chilean experience] (pp. 17–30). Buenos Aires: Editorial Humanitas.

Steen, J. A., & Mathiesen, S. (2005). Human rights education: Is social work behind the curve? *Journal of Teaching in Social Work, 25*(3/4), 143–156.

Wainwright, S. (2000). New rights of responsibilities in anti-poverty work? *British Journal of Social Work, 30,* 249–253.

Williams, J. (2001). 1998 Human rights act: Social work's new benchmark. *British Journal of Social Work, 31,* 831–844.

Wronka, J. (1995). Human rights. *The Encyclopedia of Social Work, 7,* 1405–1418. Washington, DC: National Association of Social Workers Press.

VOICES FROM THE FIELD

Rosemary Barbera, PhD, MSS
Immigrant Rights Organization

Agency Setting

South Philadelphia has a rich tradition of immigration. For years it was known as the Italian section of Philadelphia, although there were also vibrant Jewish and Irish communities, and a growing African American community, as well. However, at the turn of the century the population began to rapidly change with an influx of Mexican immigrants who were fleeing the poverty imposed upon them by the North American Free Trade Agreement (NAFTA). Many of these people—in the majority, young people—could no longer eke out a living growing corn because the United States was now dumping subsidized genetically modified corn as a result of NAFTA. With little prospects for survival for themselves and their families, people began to migrate north. A young university student in Philadelphia noticed the growing population of Mexican immigrants in south Philadelphia and began to offer them free English classes. He then reached out to others in Philadelphia to begin a grassroots organization that would organize immigrants. The organization eventually adopted a human rights framework for community organizing.

Practice Responsibilities

The organization had only one staff person as board members acted like staff. I supervised student interns and worked with the outreach committee. Together we educated people on their rights. Many immigrants were under the impression that they had no rights as they were undocumented. As such, they were being targeted for crime because they were afraid to go to the police as they feared deportation. We did reach out to members of the community to let them know of their rights and we also educated the police about the conditions these immigrants were living in.

Expertise Required

In order to do this work one must be fluent in Spanish, and perhaps even have fluency in one of the over 60 indigenous languages of Mexico as some people who migrate do not speak Spanish. The worker must have knowledge of Mexican culture, with particular emphasis on rural culture and indigenous cultures. They must be fluent in both human rights as well as rights that undocumented immigrants in the United States have. And, they must be willing to use their privilege in the service of a very vulnerable population.

Ethical, Legal, Practice, Diversity, and/or Advocacy Issues Addressed

There are multiple issues that are addressed in this work. Foremost is the human right to live a life of dignity. There are also the human rights to migration, to fair working conditions with livable wages, to recognition before the law, as well as others contained in the United Nations' Universal Declaration of Human Rights. These rights are deeply ethical in principle as they have to deal with the dignity and worth of all human beings.

Interprofessional and Intersectoral Collaboration

This organization worked closely with other organizations such as refugee organizations, social service agencies, legal services, and the local Mexican Consulate. Members from these organizations formed a committee that met on a regular basis to discuss issues related to Mexican immigrants in south Philadelphia. The committee helped with training sessions for various agencies in the city of Philadelphia to educate them on the unique needs of this population, as well as the rich diversity and culture that they added to the city. By definition, the work was intersectional as we were addressing economic, social, cultural, civil, and political human rights.

CHAPTER 4

Social Work and the Law: An Overview of Ethics, Social Work, and Civil and Criminal Law

David Axlyn McLeod

CHAPTER OBJECTIVES

The major objectives of this chapter are to:

- Demonstrate how social work ethics apply to ethical and legal decision making in forensic social work practice.
- Describe and discuss the context of social work practice in legal systems.
- Detail the basic structures of the U.S. civil and criminal legal systems.

CHAPTER COMPETENCIES HIGHLIGHTED

- Competency 1: Demonstrate Ethical and Professional Behavior
- Competency 3: Advance Human Rights and Social, Economic, and Environmental Justice

This chapter begins with an exploration of ethics and ethical decision making in the profession of social work. Ethical decision making models are reviewed. The chapter also lays the foundation for the criminal and civil court processes in the United States and introduces basic terminology and a description of associated activities and progression through these systems.

Forensic social workers function within a unique context that explicitly differentiates them from their fellow social workers in numerous ways. None of these distinctions are more important than the fact that forensic social workers have a responsibility to simultaneously provide competent service to their direct client or client system while also maintaining an explicit commitment to uphold the standards of the law, abiding by the rules and regulations of the court or court system(s) with which they are interacting, and providing a vital service in regards to the safety and well-being of the community. Forensic social workers rarely find themselves in positions where they have the luxury to focus their professional attention and energy on a single individual or entity. Rather, by the nature of this type of practice, they engage in intervention with the recognition that they must balance these multiple roles while providing ethical service to all parties and systems affiliated, along with performing advocacy work to develop equitable laws and reform laws that are unjust or unfair. This is no easy task, but it is one that forensic social workers are prepared to take on. Social work is a profession where practice behaviors are grounded in a system, such as a jail or prison, and governed by a code of ethics; however, forensic social workers must negotiate how to abide by this code of ethics while also navigating service delivery provision in conjunction with criminal and civil legal systems.

The first goal of this chapter is to explore social work ethics and to apply ethical decision-making frameworks to forensic social work practice. Second, this chapter focuses on providing an introductory, and overarching, picture of both civil and criminal law in the United States and introduces the roles social workers play in these systems, many of which are further explored throughout this text. The U.S. justice system is a living and breathing organism that continually evolves and changes over time, and while we are not able to cover all of the complex nuances of the system, it is the aim of this chapter to provide basic frameworks so that the reader may develop a more thorough understanding of the history of social work practice in legal settings, and how social work practitioners continue to play more advanced roles in the future of the U.S. legal system.

Ethics

Ethics are at the core of social work practice and have been since its inception. Mary Richmond is credited with developing the first social work code of ethics almost 100 years ago in 1920. Since that time, the application of evidence-based ethical decision-making practice has been a cornerstone of social work service delivery (Congress, Black, & Strom-Gottfried, 2009). Nowhere is the application of ethical decision making more important than in forensic social work practice. Forensic social workers play significant roles in various parts of the legal system and in numerous stages of the legal process, and, according to the National Association of Social Workers (NASW) *Code of Ethics* (available at www.socialworkers .org/pubs/code/code.asp), have professional responsibility to provide competent service in these often complicated and crucial professional roles (NASW, 2006; 2008). Maintaining competence in forensic social work is no simple task, in that the variety of social work practice interactions with legal systems is as varied and diverse as the profession itself.

Forensic social workers serve as mitigation specialists, mental health clinicians, mandated batterer or sexual offender treatment providers, child custody and divorce specialists, child abuse and neglect workers, and in a wide variety of other capacities across a broad spectrum of service delivery mechanisms. In these roles, it is not uncommon for social workers to be challenged with ethical conflicts and to have to make complicated or nuanced decisions that will have significant implications in the lives of the clients and communities they serve (Forgey & Colarossi, 2003). For example, a forensic psychiatric social worker who works in a competency evaluation and restoration role in a state hospital setting will use his or her clinical expertise to continually evaluate the ability of a psychiatrically unstable client to stand trial and face charges related to crimes of which the client is accused. In this role, the social worker is responsible for ongoing assessment and treatment related to the client's psychological state and the degree to which the client's psychological impairment impacted his or her ability to act within the confines of the law. In these roles, social workers make daily decisions that not only affect their client, but also the families and people who their client may have offended against, and they also make decisions that could have significant implications for community safety as well. It is important to understand the basis of ethics and ethical decision making and how these processes are applied to social work practice, particularly at intersections between social work and legal systems.

Values Versus Ethics

Before moving forward, we need to make a few specific linguistic distinctions. Oftentimes, it is easy to confuse values for ethics, particularly when exploring these concepts in an applied sense. Social work, by its nature, is a value-driven profession. It has long been suggested that perhaps no other profession focuses on the importance of values more than the profession of social work (Brown, 1968). *Values* can be described as ideas or beliefs that are held dear and are often reflective of personal and professional experience, time and context, and external or societal influences. Historically, social work has been a profession that has clung tightly to its values, particularly related to service and social justice, the dignity and worth of all people, the importance of human relationships, and integrity and competence in practice.

Ethics tend to be deducted from values. While values may be concerned with what is good and desirable, ethics focus on what is right or correct in the application of those beliefs or constructs to real-life circumstances. In this sense, values tend to be the more general and broad constructs while ethics, and ethical behavior in particular, can be measured and be prescriptive. For example, a central value of the social work profession is that *all* people are deserving of dignity and respect. To apply this value through ethical behavior, it is important that social workers make themselves aware of any biases they may have as they enter into relationships with clients or client systems. For example, a forensic social worker who works as a juvenile sex offender treatment provider must acknowledge the potential negative feelings he or she may have toward the previous behavior of the client, and find ways to maintain positive and appropriate interaction with the client despite his or her aversion to the client's history. It would be unethical for a social worker to allow any type of bias he or she may have to mitigate the type of services delivered to clients. While on paper the connections between values and ethics may appear straightforward and linear, the application of ethical behavior can be more nuanced and individualized. This can often be because (a) people do not always behave in a manner reflective of the values they espouse to, and (b) people by nature can hold dear a great range of differing personal values. Lowenberg, Dolgoff, and Harrington (2000) make a clear distinction between general ethics and professional ethics. In this they suggest that while closely related, professional ethics, such as those in social work, are derived from the true values of the profession rather than the values of the individual practitioner. Conceptually this is an important distinction, and one that social workers should use to help guide them in their practice and avoid the pitfalls of projecting their own values onto the client or client systems. For forensic social workers, this is remarkably important, as we will often be in situations where our services are being provided to, with, and for people who have engaged in activities that may violate our own personal value structures. To help us, the NASW *Code of Ethics* provides a behaviorally prescriptive exemplar that was set up as a guiding instrument to assist social workers in aligning specific behavioral expectations that we are pledged to uphold as stewards of the profession. Being intentional about ethical decision making can be especially important in forensic social work practice owing not only to the sensitivities and complexities of the services forensic social workers administer, but also to the intricacies of the multiple systems (legal, health, mental health, child welfare, etc.) that forensic social workers navigate.

Difference Between Ethics and Law

Oftentimes people can become confused about noncongruence between law and ethics. In the profession of social work, ethics are related to a specific set of applied behaviors in practice situations. In contrast, the law is related largely to social control and creation of a framework that defines both how citizens will interact with the government and each other, and what type(s) of consequences will be levied if these behavioral expectations are not met (Albert, 1986; Black, 1972; Van Hoose & Kottler, 1985). The contrast between these two can be complicated, particularly because of the tendency for complex critical decision making in social work practice to function in indistinct shades of gray, as opposed to the definitive black-and-white expectations of law. It has been suggested that while behavioral alignment with legal norms is often connected to, and enforced by, an externalized threat of punishment, compliance with ethical principles and moral decision making is highly associated with respect and personal or professional value structures (Lowenberg, Dolgoff, & Harrington, 2000).

Major conflicts can arise at times between ethics and the law. For example, it is unethical for a social worker to treat the client with disrespect even though it is not illegal to do so. For forensic social workers, this can be further complicated as the venue for their practice is often associated with our legal system, and the behaviors they exhibit in the facilitation of their service delivery must abide by the ever-changing code of the law. This has not always been an easy area to navigate. Social workers often have to make decisions at the intersection of law and ethics. For example, social workers are often considered mandated reporters in a variety of areas regarding individual and family safety. Rules around the mandated reporting of social workers (to legal authorities, such as the police or child welfare) may be governed by statutory law in the jurisdiction to which the social worker practices. Social workers often have to navigate the realities of ethical service delivery, as related to confidentiality and self-determination in their practice, as they strive to also abide by the expectations of the legal systems in which they function.

Ethical Decision Making

So, how should forensic social workers go about the process of ethical decision making, and is that a different process than is found in other areas of social work practice? Many social work scholars have attempted the task of creating ethical decision-making frameworks, but often these frameworks rely heavily on philosophical principles and/or theoretical knowledge. In some circumstances, multiple tools should be considered to manage the complexities of the cross-system ethical decisions that forensic social workers encounter. Critiques have surfaced, which suggest that social workers rarely make clinical decisions based on theoretical constructs or in light of philosophical perspectives (Lowenburg, Dolgoff, & Harrington, 2000). For the purpose of this chapter, we focus on the ETHICA model of ethical decision making as a resource and tool that can be used to help forensic social workers process difficult and complex situations across multiple systems.

The *ETHICA model*, as developed and refined by Elaine Congress (2009), seen in Figure 4.1, was created to help social workers make ethical decisions quickly and effectively. This was in response to calls that originated from Reamer (1995) and others who suggested that the focus of ethical decision making had shifted from a concentration on the morality of the client or client system to the ethical behavior of practitioners. In order to help social work practitioners quickly resolve ethical dilemmas and make conscious decisions about their practice and how to behave in an ethical manner, the ETHICA model suggests social workers progress through six distinct steps when assessing complicated situations. This process begins with an examination of one's own personal values and how those values may be aligned with social, cultural, client, and professional values. The social workers then should take into consideration the NASW *Code of Ethics*, as well as the laws, regulations, and policies that may govern their specific service provision area(s). Next, the model suggests hypothesizing different potential scenarios, and moving forward to identify what people or entities may be the most vulnerable and/or could be harmed by each of the potential outcomes of the ethical decisions. The model then suggests that if resolution has not been

Figure 4.1 ETHICA Model

E	Examine values (personal, social, cultural, client, and professional)
T	Think about the *Code of Ethics*, laws, regulations, and agency policies
H	Hypothesize about different scenarios
I	Identify who is most vulnerable and who will be harmed
C	Consult with supervisors and colleagues
A	Advocate for agency, profession, community, and systemic change

Source: Congress (2009).

made, then the practitioners should consult with supervisors and colleagues, and finally that social workers should advocate for improvements in policy and law in order to resolve the issues that contributed to their ethical dilemma.

When using the ETHICA model in forensic social work practice, it may become increasingly important to pay attention to the fourth principle and how your potential decisions could harm others. As mentioned earlier in the chapter, forensic social workers have a responsibility not only to their client, but also to the community at large. Specifically, the decisions that social workers make in clinical settings can have far-reaching implications on individual, family, and community safety, and the responsibility of making these decisions must not be taken lightly. For example, a forensic social worker who is working in a diversion program to help people with criminal charges related to substance abuse issues avoid prison and work toward substance abuse treatment goals must continually assess the program participant's fidelity to the diversion process and the treatment and behavioral expectations associated with it. Many social work scholars have sought to develop frameworks that can help provide guidance in the ethical decision-making process. Perhaps one of the more useful screens developed to help social workers make decisions around vulnerability, safety, and potential for harm would be the ethical principles screen by Lowenberg, Dolgoff, and Harrington (2000).

The ethical principles screen, as detailed in Exhibit 4.1, ranks the ethical principles of social work practice in order of the most important being Ethical Principle 1, the protection of human life (Lowenberg, Dolgoff, & Harrington, 2000). In this framework, the protection

Exhibit 4.1 Ethical Principles Screen

Principle 1	The *protection of human life* applies to all persons, that is, both to the life of a client and to the lives of others. This principle takes precedence over every other obligation.
Principle 2	The *principle of equality and inequality* suggests that equal persons have the right to be treated equally and nonequal persons have the right to be treated differently if the inequality is relevant to the issue in question. Child abuse is one area where this principle applies: Children are not equal to adults.
Principle 3	A social worker should make practice decisions that *foster a person's autonomy, independence, and freedom*. A person does not have the right to decide to harm himself or herself or anyone else on the grounds that the right to make such a decision is her or his autonomous right.
Principle 4	A social worker should always choose the option that will *cause the least harm*, the least permanent harm, and/or the most easily reversible harm.
Principle 5	A social worker should choose the option that *promotes a better quality of life* for all people, for the individual as well as for the community.
Principle 6	A social worker should make practice decisions that strengthen every person's *right to privacy*. Keeping confidential information inviolate is a direct derivative of this obligation.
Principle 7	A social worker should make practice decisions that permit him or her to *speak the truth* and to *fully disclose* all relevant information to the client and to others.

Source: Dolgoff, Harrington, and Loewenberg (2012). © 2012 South-Western, a part of Cengage, Inc. Reproduced by permission. www.cengage.com/permissions

of human life takes precedence over any other ethical obligation of the social worker. This can be of particular importance for forensic social workers. Following closely, and of great importance, are the other ethical principles including explicit focus on equality, autonomy, causing the least harm possible, quality of life, privacy, and truth in full disclosure. Alone, each of these principles is highly important, but collectively they can be used to help social workers make ethical decisions in regards to highly complicated or nuanced practice situations. To apply the screen during an ethical decision-making process, workers should start with Ethical Principle 1 and evaluate their situation moving down through each principle. This tool can be used to help organize the details of the situation so the social worker can focus on the most important issues first, while keeping in mind ancillary details of the situation in context to his or her importance to the overall decision-making abilities. For forensic social workers, tools like this can help them process the implications of making decisions in contexts where multiple systems intersect.

Legal System

When integrating law in practice, social workers commonly intersect with the legal system. So, what are the expectations of the law and how do these expectations relate to social work practice in the legal system? How is it that social workers are involved in the systems? In order to explore these questions more thoroughly, we have to create a basic understanding of what the U.S. legal system looks like. For the sake of brevity, we do not have the opportunity to thoroughly detail all the facets of the system(s); however, the Legal Systems section of this chapter is a summary of information organized by the U.S. State Department with the intent of outlining some of the core constructs to help you understand the basics of civil and criminal law in the United States. (For those readers who want to read beyond this overview, the full report created by the Bureau of International Information Programs can be accessed at http://iipdigital.usembassy.gov/media/pdf/books/legalotln.pdf#popup; for more extended reading and reference see Bureau of International Information Programs [BIIP], 2004.)

Background

The legal system in the United States is a complex and ever-evolving entity. By its very nature, and from its inception, it was created to grow and flex with a purpose of meeting the needs of citizens in the contexts of their own time and community. There are multiple components in the U.S. legal system, and the importance of understanding the distinctions between them cannot be understated. Throughout the next section of this chapter, we explore the origins of law, distinctions among the different types of law, and the differential application of law depending on specific legal systems.

Federal and State Legal System

One of the first things to understand, as we explore the U.S. legal system, is the distinction between federal and state law. The separation of federal and state law is historically derived and connected to the unique development of our country and the reality that the United States was not initially formed as one singular nation, but rather as a collection of independent and sovereign states. In fact, the Declaration of Independence (1776) declares specifically that each state shall remain free and independent with its own rights to self-governance. While this structure allowed for states to independently decide how they would govern and what rules and regulations they would develop for the protection and empowerment of their society, the decentralization of any overarching government structure proved costly and problematic as related to interstate commerce in the ability of states to collectively function. Just a decade after the Declaration of Independence, the U.S. Constitution, adopted in 1788, remedied many of these problems by establishing the Supremacy Clause. This edict dictated how the laws of the federal government would supersede state law to become the supreme law of the land, and that the Constitution of the United States would be used as a benchmark to assess the legal status of state law. This basically means that states are free to develop their own laws, which are contextual to the independent circumstances of the individual states. However, these laws must abide by the rules set forth in the U.S. Constitution and must not violate the rights of sovereign citizens as defined by the Constitution. The U.S. Constitution also established a structure to create separation of powers. In the structure, the executive, legislative, and judicial branches of government were established at a federal level to enable a *system of checks and balances* to ensure that no one part of the government became so powerful that it could control the others. For similar reasoning, most states mirrored this type of separation of powers while establishing their own systems of law. At both federal and state levels forensic social workers serve a variety of purposes and fill a diversity of roles.

Sources of Law

At both federal and state levels, it is important to understand where laws come from. Who writes it? Who approves it? Who applies it? Laws can be derived from several mechanisms in the United States. At the base level, laws are derived from and prescribed in constitutions. This could be referenced both by the development and enactment of the U.S. Constitution and the state constitutions, which set forth the overarching priorities of law in individual states. Additionally, *statutes* are laws that are created by the legislative branches, voted on, and approved by the executive branch representatives such as state governors. *Case law* is a term referencing how law can be created through the judicial process; however, this term can be slightly deceiving. Case law is most typically connected to the interpretation of legal statutes for constitutional rights rather than the construction and development of new laws altogether. *Common law* refers not to any specific law that is explicitly created, but rather to the social norms and rules by which people live, and inherently accept, which are not statutorily defined. Basically, when there is not a law written to define an acceptable behavior in the context of a certain situation, the court systems refer to common law, and examine a collection of social customs or general societal principles that may have been previously accepted as legitimate expectations of behavior, under similar circumstances, in the court system. The courts interpret common law and enforce statutory and other law, based on a system of *judicial precedent*. This basically means that courts adjudicate legal challenges based on what has previously been accepted as the proper outcome for remedy. Forensic social workers often advocate for the improvement, refinement, and adoption of new laws that are data driven, socially just, and focused on improving equity for citizens, particularly in their interactions with legal and court systems.

Goals of Law

What are the goals of law? Why have we developed these extensive sets of rules to govern our interactions with each other? Laws are created, enacted, and enforced for multiple reasons. The first of these is the protection of rights. Since the inception of the United States of America, an explicit focus has been paid to the development of law as it pertains to the protection of individual rights and the freedom and autonomy of individuals from each other and from the government itself. Put simply, from this perspective the goal of law is the protection of personal power and freedom. Another goal of law is to serve as a regulatory mechanism. This is an incredibly important function of our legal system: creating a fair playing field and opportunities so that they are not only available to all citizens now, but also in the future. Another goal of the law is to serve as a mechanism for resolving conflict. Laws basically function as sets of rules, and in many cases these rules are used as tools to guide the resolution of divergence from societal norms in interactions between individuals. Lastly, it is the goal of law to preserve order in the state. Laws are created to prevent, deter, and encourage specific behavioral expectations among citizens related to public and personal safety. To put it most simply, the goals of law are related to defining and enforcing collectively acceptable interactions in our society.

Criminal Law

In the United States, there are two primary court systems in which social workers play significant roles: the civil court system and the criminal court system. Both of these systems are distinctly different and for the purpose of this chapter we explore them separately. We begin our exploration with the criminal court system. The criminal court process is one used to address the realities of crime and criminal activity in our society, and to impose sanctions on those found guilty of involvement in criminal behavior. This is a system that is punitive by nature, with the intention of creating significant consequences for deviation from expected behavioral norms, with the purpose of encouraging people to behave in ways that are beneficial to society as a whole. Forensic social workers serve in a variety of ways in the criminal system. From coordination of victim-centered services to mediation in sentencing for the convicted, they provide crucial advocacy to individuals impacted by crime and involvement in criminal activity.

What Is Crime?

So if something is hurtful to others, does that make it a crime? The short answer is no. An action only constitutes as a crime if it is done in direct violation of criminal statute. Previously we explored how statutory law is created by elected officials at federal, state, and even community levels. In order for someone to be engaged in the criminal court process, and more specifically to be charged with a crime, the specific action for which he or she is accused must be noted in statute as a chargeable offense. Herein lies one of the primary, and distinct, differences between the criminal court processes compared to the civil court processes. To be charged with the crime, the state must acknowledge and bring the case against an individual whose alleged behavior violates the specific statutory code.

Types of Crime

Across the United States, crimes can come in all types, shapes, and sizes. While some of the laws quantifying what constitutes a crime may seem like common sense, others can be unusual, outdated, or unlikely to be prosecuted. There are two basic categories of criminal statutes with a wide range of levels among each which vary from state to state. *Misdemeanors* are typically understood to be violations of a lower severity and in most states carry penalties of lower monetary fines and up to one year in jail. *Felonies,* on the other hand, are crimes classified as more severe and could include penalties including substantial imprisonment and even execution. The U.S. State Department suggests that there are five primary categories of crime. *Conventional crimes* constitute the majority of crimes perpetrated in the United States, and would include such offenses as property crimes, theft, burglary, and the more serious classifications of *violent offenses* such as murder, rape, robbery, manslaughter, and the like. *Economic crimes* could include anything from tax evasion to forgery, misleading advertising, or antitrust violations. All of these offenses are focused on nonviolent mechanisms of illegal activity with the intention of monetary gain. *Organized crimes* are often related to syndicated organizations of individuals who function within a hierarchical structure, and are traditionally linked to *vice crimes,* such as gambling, prostitution, drug trade, and similar activities. *Political crimes* are crimes against the government, such as treason with a bribery or assassination of public officials. The final category is classified as *consensual crimes*, often described as victimless crimes. These could be crimes such as drug use or prostitution, and are often activities engaged in by consenting adults who are active and willing participants.

Elements of Crime

The range of crimes in criminal activities is broad, fluid, and changes from jurisdiction to jurisdiction. However, there are a few specific elements of crime that are shared across the spectrum of activities. It is important that these elements exist in order to pursue a case in the criminal court system. The first of these elements is that there must be an existing law that defines the crime, its statute, and sets forth guidelines for punishment. Next, the *actus reus* (a Latin phrase meaning that a criminal action has been committed, which gives authority to the government to initiate an enforcement action) must be present. This could be in the form of evidence, which suggests an activity, such as an assault, occurred, or evidence that suggests the absence of the required action was present. For example, this could include failure to protect a child from an abusive parent. Next, the court investigates for the *mens rea*. This is basically a measure to assess the malice associated with the crime, and the degree to which the defendant intended to generate an outcome that was hurtful to another. It is then important to quantify how criminal action is related to the level of injury or negative outcome associated with it. This is basically an assessment of how much harm was done. Finally, in order to understand the crime in its totality, causal relationship between the action of the crime and the resultant injury must be assessed. In some cases, the mere intention to commit a crime, such as an attempt to lure the child via the Internet, is enough to continue for the action against a defendant. In other cases, and with other crimes, there is a specific need for harm to have been done in order to facilitate prosecution. Throughout this process, forensic social workers serve in clinical, administrative, and development capacities, and in collaboration with investigative, prosecutorial, and defense teams, as well as directly for the criminal court systems to help provide guidance on the psychosocial history and current conditions impacting both victims and survivors of crime as well as the accused, and work to provide context to inform decision making by the courts.

Legal Intervention

Investigation and Arrest. When criminal activity is detected and brought to the attention of government authorities, entities, or organizations, a chain of events begins to take place. While these events can, and do, vary depending on jurisdiction, many pretrial components are present across a variety of contexts. The first significant intervention on the part of the state is the *arrest*. Arrests are basically the process by which a law-enforcement officer takes into custody someone suspected of being involved in criminal activity. There are two basic types of arrests. The first of these occurs when a law-enforcement officer observes a crime being committed in his or her presence or has significant evidence to suggest the crime has occurred before his or her arrival, or in some circumstances that a crime is about to occur. The second type of arrest is with a *warrant*. A warrant for someone's arrest is issued after an original complaint is filed and the details and evidence surrounding that complaint have been reviewed by a prosecutor, magistrate, grand jury, or other governing body that has agreed that substantial evidence exists to establish probable cause that the defendant has engaged in criminal activity.

So are people arrested for every crime they commit? The simple answer is no. Oftentimes, law enforcement officials use discretion and choose not to arrest or charge people for minor violations. On other occasions, people are issued citations or summons to appear in court in reference to the alleged minor or misdemeanor offense. At other times, the victim of the crime may choose not to press charges, which in cases other than those affiliated with family or domestic violence often lead to the dismissal of a charge or a reluctance to arrest. It could also be possible that a victim in the case engaged in the commission of criminal activity at the time of his or her victimization. In these types of situations, it may also be true that officers could choose not to make an arrest of the offending party. All in all, there are a great many factors that come into play if someone is going to be arrested and charged with the crime and how that process takes place. Oftentimes, forensic social workers provide services to individuals and families who may have experienced or been victims of criminal activity, even if they did not report the crime or become involved in the court system.

After the Arrest. Within a reasonable amount of time after the arrest, a person is to be brought before a local judge, magistrate, or commissioner to be formally informed of the charges and constitutional rights. At this point, it is determined if it is safe for the defendant to be released, and to what level the defendant's bond should be placed as he or she awaits trial. In some minor cases, the accused has the opportunity to plead guilty or not guilty, but in regard to larger level felony cases this is an opportunity for future court dates to be set. In large part, this is the formal beginning of the defendant's adjudication process. Depending on the *venue* (the location and jurisdiction of the official court proceeding), various pretrial events could take place. For example, in federal court all defendants have the right for a grand jury to hear the evidence of the case to determine whether it should proceed to trial. It is also possible for preliminary hearings to be ordered to discuss the validity of evidence, potential possibilities for plea bargains, and the potential for reductions or dismissal of charges.

The Trial and Sentencing. In the United States we employ an adversarial process in our courtrooms. This basically means that there are two sides, one occupied by the state, which brings the prosecution to light of a violation of criminal statute, and the other of the defendant and his or her legal representation. Lawyers represent both sides and are responsible for arguing their side of the case to the best of their abilities and to the full extent of the law. It is the role of the judge to be an impartial arbiter of the law who interprets the facts of the case and applies judgment as required by statute. In cases where a jury is present, it is the responsibility of the jury to hear the sides of the case and conclude if guilt can be determined beyond a reasonable doubt.

Typically, trials begin with opening statements from both the prosecution and defense and an overview of specific expectations, as presented by the judge. The prosecution delivers its case first as the state attempts to present the evidence, which reinforces how the law was broken and how the defendant is connected to the charge. After this, the defense presents its case, where it is not required to produce any additional evidence, but rather focuses on addressing what was presented by the prosecution to show how the defendant cannot be proven to be responsible. Throughout this process, it is important that the judge remains impartial, particularly in the event of a jury trial. In some cases, judges are also social workers. Joint JD/MSW programs are common across the United States, and oftentimes people with a strong interest in both social justice and legal justice pursue these options with an intent to provide person-centered advocacy with attention to the social constructs that impact marginalized people and communities. When the jury is present in a court case, it is their role to hear both sides of the adversarial argument and use critical thinking in their own judgment to come to a conclusion about the guilt or innocence of the accused party. The jury receives explicit instructions from the judge and has the opportunity to deliberate in private so that they can debate and discuss the details presented in the trial in order to make their decision.

After the jury renders its verdict, and if that verdict implicates the defendant as guilty, the next step in the court process is *sentencing*. Sentencing is a formal event where the court renders its final judgment for the defendant, where the details of the punishment associated with the crime are presented. In most circumstances, sentences are administered by the judge who presided over the case. After sentencing occurs, an individual has the opportunity to move on to serving the terms of the sentence, as well as the opportunity to appeal findings of the court. If an appeal is filed, it is typically on the grounds that the defendant suggests he or she did not receive a fair trial or that some part of the process which led to the conviction and sentencing was tainted or illegal.

Civil Law

The civil process shares many traits with the criminal one. There are also, however, several distinct differences worthy of note. The overarching and primary differences between the two are that criminal law is focused on how mechanisms of government can address conduct that is destructive or offensive to societal sensibilities, while civil law pertains more to the responsibilities and obligations that private citizens have to each other. This means that the civil process, rather than having the state bring statutorily based charges against an alleged offender, is a process where one (private) person brings a dispute against another seeking reparation or compensation for an alleged wrong. The state, however, may be involved in civil processes as well, particularly as related to child welfare and/or involuntary commitment, both of which are further explored later in this chapter. Forensic social workers provide an array of services in civil contexts as well. From mediation services during divorce and separation cases, to providing direct services and working in conjunction with child welfare cases, social workers interact with the civil system in a variety of ways.

What Is the Civil Law?

In the application of civil law, the court typically attempts to settle a dispute between two parties by assessing the individual rights of each party within the details of a particular situation. Forensic social workers assist in a variety of capacities throughout this process. Then a determination is made as to the responsibilities each party may have to one another. It is also possible for a person's actions, and one single event, to lead to his or her involvement in both criminal and civil court processes. For example, in recent history, a popular sports figure was arrested and charged for the murder of his former spouse and her friend. Although he was found to be not guilty in a criminal court of law, the family of the victim waged a successful civil suit against the defendant blaming him for wrongful death. In the suit the victim's family was awarded substantial monetary compensation as the court found the defendant guilty for the wrongful death of the victim(s) based on the *preponderance of evidence* in the case. As mentioned earlier, each court has an evidentiary standard. In criminal cases that standard is *beyond a reasonable doubt*, while in civil cases it is typically by a *preponderance of the evidence*. This basically means that in a criminal case, for someone to be convicted as guilty, the prosecution will need to provide evidence to support their argument to the point that the judge and jury are absolutely confident the defendant is responsible for the crime. On the contrary, in a civil case the burden of proof of responsibility is basically that the accused party is more likely than not responsible for the damages. This can sometimes be described numerically as the court needing to be 51% sure someone is responsible for damages (civil) as opposed to 95% sure that someone is guilty of committing a crime (criminal).

Types of Civil Law

In the United States of America, civil cases outnumber criminal ones at both federal and state levels. Basically, any dispute between two parties could lend itself to a civil suit and involvement in the civil court process. There are several different categories of civil law, including *contract law*, which is concerned with voluntary agreements between people; *tort law*, which is focused on civil wrongs primarily associated with personal and corporate negligence resulting in the injury of others; and *property law*, which focuses on quantifying the ownership of personal property. Undoubtedly, however, social workers interact with the civil law process in the two areas of civil commitment and family law far more than any other.

The *civil commitment* process pertains to engaging in a legal procedure to assess if a person can be held against his or her will in an inpatient or correctional capacity. This can be initiated by an individual citizen or petition from local or state government officials, depending on the context. Most typically civil commitments are connected with severe mental illness, but there is a growing emphasis on state-order civil commitments related to individuals assessed as high-risk sexual offenders. This is one of the areas where criminal and civil courts can often overlap. Throughout the process of a criminal court procedure, evaluations can be ordered to assess the mental status and capacity of an individual and if he or she is competent to stand (criminal) trial. The individual can then be ordered into a civil commitment process to assess if he or she meets criteria for what has traditionally been called being *not guilty for a reason of insanity* (NGRI). When a person is determined to be NGRI, a civil commitment process is utilized to maintain his or her mandated inpatient treatment until the point where the individual is deemed competent to stand criminal trial or until the criminal charges are dropped due to his or her inability to attain competence. Social workers serve many roles in the civil commitment process, none more crucial that providing intensive psychosocial assessment in cases associated with competency evaluation and restoration. Forensic social workers are vital team members who play a crucial role in determining if a person meets the criteria for being considered clinically insane and thereby unable to face trial.

By volume, more social workers cross paths with the legal system in the area of *family law* than any other. Family law pertains to issues surrounding marriage, divorce, child custody, and issues of children's rights and child protection. This is also another area where criminal and civil law commonly intersect. For example, a case of a parent who is physically abusive toward his or her minor child will not only result in statutory charges in a criminal court setting but also a civil court process related to child placement and protection. A wonderful resource has been created by the U.S. Department of Health and Human Services that details child welfare work at its intersection with the courts, and can be found here: www .childwelfare.gov/pubPDFs/courts.pdf. Additional information about child welfare work can be found in Chapter 11 of this text.

The Civil Court Experience

Just as the criminal court process has a distinct manner by which people are brought into and progress through it, the civil court experience does as well. An individual, or the state, may begin the civil court process by the filing of a civil suit or petition. From that point forward, the person or entity filing the suit is referred to as the *plaintiff*, and the person or entity being sued is referred to as the *defendant*. Important to note is that the decision around which court should hear certain cases is determined by the concepts of jurisdiction and venue. Not unlike the criminal court experience, *jurisdiction* is related to deciding which court has the authority to exercise judicial power over the particular case that is brought forward. *Venue*, on the other hand, is related to the geographic location in which either a crime or grievance occurred, and/or where the plaintiff, victim, and/or defendants reside. Oftentimes a motion may be filed to request a change in venue if one of the parties believes he or she may not receive a fair trial owing to the geographic location of the court.

Pretrial

Prior to the onset of any civil litigation, several pretrial events may occur. The first, and most important of these, is related to the delivery of notice, or *summons*, to the defendant so that the defendant may know that a claim has been filed against him or her and that the defendant has a responsibility to report to the court and present his or her side of the story. After this has taken place, additional *motions* could be filed with requests for further information from the parties associated with litigation. These motions must be *answered* in compliance with the jurisdictional laws and regulations associated with each case. *Discovery* is another component process of the U.S. legal system in both civil and criminal court proceedings where each side is entitled to the information possessed by the other. Motions of discovery are often filed to ensure both sides have adequate access to evidence which will be used in the trial. It is also possible that a judge may call for a *pretrial conference* in order to clarify the facts of a case and further outline the expectations associated with the civil litigation process.

Civil Trial

In civil court, just as in criminal, there exists a right to a trial by jury. This right may be waived in favor of a *bench trial* where the judge serves as not only the arbiter of the rules and process but also the party responsible for making a decision about the presentation of evidence and facts, and the outcome of the trial. Just as in the criminal court process, the trial begins with opening statements from both sides. Then, in the event that the case was brought forward by an individual, the plaintiff presents his or her case. If the complaint was brought forward by the state, the state serves as the plaintiff or petitioner in the case. In some situations, after the presentation of the plaintiff's case, the defendant may request for a *directed verdict* where they ask the court to dismiss the case due to a lack of sufficient evidence or the inability of the plaintiff to factually pursue the claim. If the directed verdict is not accepted by the court, the defendant then presents the case. After this follows a series of rebuttals from both sides and then closing arguments. Finally, instructions are given to the jury if one was used, deliberations occur, and the *verdict* (final decision) is rendered. If the verdict is in favor of the defendant, the trial is over. If the verdict is in favor of the plaintiff, the judge moves forward with an execution of the verdict where representatives of the state (oftentime sheriff's offices) are used to enforce that the defendant conforms to the terms as issued by the court. Just as in criminal cases, if one party feels that there was an error in the process of law then that party has the right to appeal.

Emerging Alternative Resolutions

So is a trial always necessary? The short answer is no. In many cases, associated with the civil process, decisions are made to avoid a trial and pursue alternative resolution, and forensic social workers play many roles in this process. Alternative resolutions can be sought for a variety of reasons, among which can be that people would often prefer to find a way to avoid going to court. Sometimes the parties agree to *mediation*, which is a confidential process where a private third party can guide both the plaintiff and defendant through a process of discovering the facts and finding mutually agreed-upon resolution. For example, oftentimes people seeking to outline agreements of child custody or visitation rights could use a mediation process to come to an agreement. *Arbitration* is another alternative process that is similar to mediation in that it allows for the parties to avoid going to trial, and involves an outside private party to help guide the process. However, in the arbitration process, rather than having the plaintiff and defendant agree upon the resolution, the arbitrator hears both sides of the case and makes a decision much in the fashion of a verdict. Forensic social workers often provide services to assist people in the processes.

While several other alternative options may exist, perhaps none is growing in popularity more than specialized courts. Varying wildly across jurisdictions, numerous specialized courts have been created in attempts to help manage highly nuanced types of cases and to provide alternative outcomes. This concept began with small claims courts, where the trial process could be fast tracked for cases involving lower monetary damage levels. The specialized court concept has been adapted to child welfare courts, domestic violence courts, substance abuse (drug) courts, and in other contexts in an attempt to provide diversionary programming and specialized intervention. For example, if an individual has the opportunity to enter into a substance-abuse court after receiving a criminal charge, he or she may have the chance to be civilly mandated into a professional treatment program in order to avoid processing through the criminal system. Upon successful completion of treatment, the criminal charges could be dropped completely or suspended for a certain amount of time to ensure the individual's sobriety. These types of hybrid courts have the potential not only to help decarceration efforts across the United States, but also to create space in the court systems for wraparound solutions to address the complicated problems people often face. Forensic social workers serve in a variety of advocacy contexts in diversion courts, often assisting those in need in their transition through the diversion programming and expectations that they must meet to avoid incarceration.

Conclusion

Throughout the next section of this text you will explore multiple systems of care as they intersect with forensic social work practice. All of these have some sort of interaction with the law in their own highly nuanced and individualized ways. Additionally, because of the nature of the law, issues of diversity in the context of individuals and communities are highly influential in the ways that laws are constructed, interpreted, and applied. Throughout this chapter we have explored some of the basic frameworks of our civil and criminal legal system in the United States. We also began with conversations around ethics and applied ethical decision making. As forensic social workers, we are tasked, oftentimes, with filling the gap between the application of the law and respecting the dignity of those involved in the process. For forensic social workers, this often means we never have just one client per case. We work with families and individuals, and must take into account the holistic context in which they engage in the legal process. It is also our distinct responsibility to do this with a commitment to public safety in the boundaries of the law. With this highly complicated process, ethical decision making is of paramount importance. Put quite literally, forensic social workers are making clinical and other complex decisions every day that will impact people, their families, and their communities for lifetimes. Throughout the remainder of this text, social workers can apply the information introduced in this chapter that influences how they intervene; provide treatment, assessment, and recommendation; and advocate in these cases. As a profession, social work focuses on understanding individuals, and their behavior, in the full context of their social environment. Forensic social work goes further to look at this in light of the complexity of the criminal justice system and all the additional systems and services with which it intersects. We have made so many collective advances in our modern U.S. society, but the marginalization and continued oppression of certain sections of our population continues. This is seen over and again in how people traverse the criminal justice and legal systems differentially. Forensic social workers strive to provide context and meaning to advocate for the fair and equal administration of the law as individuals and families process through the legal system, and the work of forensic social workers is nowhere near over. Throughout the remainder of this text, there is the opportunity to delve into specific functions of forensic social workers as they provide services that help people, families, and communities in all kinds of contexts and strive for the fair and equal application of law for all, regardless of age, race, income level, or any other demographic or personal factors. Much progress has been made, but much work is left to do. Forensic social workers are on the front lines of working to effect the kind of change that can ensure both safety in our communities and the equitable administration of justice for all.

CHAPTER EXERCISES

Exercise 1. Apply the ethical decision-making model presented in this chapter with a client in the field. This exercise can be completed as a short paper, or a dyadic or small group discussion. Present your findings to the larger group.

Exercise 2. In a small group discussion, discuss how each participant views the role of law in social work practice. Discuss your findings with the large group.

Exercise 3. Discuss in small and large groups the following short video on racism and the criminal justice system in 10 charts: www.youtube.com/watch?v=InOsF5x1lZw

Additional Resources

Bureau of Justice System: Criminal Justice Flowchart: www.bjs.gov/content/largechart.cfm

Cornell University Law School Databases

- Federal Law Collection: www.law.cornell.edu/federal
- State Law Collection: www.law.cornell.edu/states

National Conference of State Legislatures (State Laws Database): www.ncsl.org/research/telecommunications-and-information-technology/ncsl-50-state-searchable-bill-tracking-databases.aspx

United Nations' International Law Commission: http://legal.un.org/ilc

References

Albert, R. (1986). *Law and social work practice*. New York, NY: Springer Publishing.

Black, D. (1972). The boundaries of legal sociology. *Yale Law Journal, 81*, 1086–1101.

Brown, B. (1968). *Social change: A professional challenge*. Unpublished paper.

Bureau of International Information Programs. (2004). *Outline of the US legal system*. Washington, DC: United States Department of State. Retrieved from http://iipdigital.usembassy.gov/media/pdf/books/legalotln.pdf#popup

Congress, E. (2009). *ETHICA: Expanding the ETHIC model to include advocacy*. Paper presentation at CSWE Baccalaureate Program Directors Meeting, Phoenix, AZ.

Congress, E., Black, N., & Strom-Gottfried, K. (2009). *Teaching social work values and ethics: A curriculum resource* (2nd ed.). Alexandria, VA: Council on Social Work Education Press.

Dolgoff, R., Harrington, D., & Loewenberg, F. M. (2012). *Ethical decisions for social work practice* (Empowerment Series, 9th ed.). Belmont, CA: Brooks/Cole.

Forgey, M. L., & Colarossi, L. (2003). Interdisciplinary social work and the law: A model domestic violence curriculum. *Journal of Social Work Education, 39*, 459–476.

Lowenberg, F., Dolgoff, R., & Harrington, D. (2000). *Ethical decisions for social work practice* (6th ed.). Itasca, IL: Peacock.

National Association of Social Workers. (2006). *NASW code of ethics*. Washington, DC: Author. Retrieved from http://www.socialworkers.org/pubs/code/code.asp

National Association of Social Workers. (2008). *Legal and ethical issues in social worker worker-lawyer collaborations*. Washington, DC: Author. Retrieved from https://www.socialworkers.org/ldf/legal_issue/200801.asp?back=yes&print=1

Reamer, F. (1995). Malpractice claims against social workers: First facts. *Social Work, 40*, 595–601.

United States Constitution. (1788).

United States Declaration of Independence. (1776).

Van Hoose, W., & Kottler, J. (1985). *Ethical and legal issues in counseling and psychotherapy* (2nd ed.). San Francisco, CA: Jossey-Bass.

VOICES FROM THE FIELD

Melissa Elder, MSW
Kids' HOPE Coordinator
Oklahoma City Family Justice Center

Agency Setting

The Kids' HOPE Program is a program of the Oklahoma City Family Justice Center (FJC). The FJC exists to reduce the barriers for victims of domestic violence by bringing all of the services that a victim might need under one roof. The Oklahoma City FJC houses law enforcement, legal services, prosecution, domestic violence advocacy, on-site child care, counseling, and medical services. The FJC opened its doors in the Fall of 2016. The Oklahoma City FJC is based on a national model recognized by the Department of Justice in 2007 as a best practice model in the field of domestic violence intervention and prevention. As 78% of domestic violence victims are women with children, addressing the trauma that children experience or witness as a result of family violence is also a function of the FJC.

Practice Responsibilities

The Kids' HOPE Program is the arm of the FJC that addresses children and trauma. The main role of the Kids' HOPE Program is to organize and host a fully funded summer camp experience for children who have witnessed or experienced domestic violence called Camp HOPE America. In Oklahoma City, the FJC took 29 kids, ages 7 to 11 years; 13 camp counselors, ages 17 to 27 years; and 6 adult administrative staff to camp in July 2016, for our first ever Camp HOPE America in Oklahoma City. Camp HOPE America relies on young adult volunteer camp counselors who build relationships with the campers and continue the relationships through bimonthly reunions. As the Kids' HOPE Coordinator, my job is to plan and organize camp each summer; build and sustain a working relationship with a partner camp; find community partners to fund camp; recruit and train volunteers for camp; recruit campers; build and sustain relationships with community partners, volunteers, campers, and their families; organize and plan a work group of experts who specialize in helping kids with trauma; and work with the Camp HOPE America team in California to ensure proper implementation of the Camp HOPE America model.

Expertise Required

Camp HOPE America is the only camping and mentoring model specifically designed for children exposed to domestic violence. As an affiliate of Camp HOPE America, Camp HOPE America in Oklahoma City received extensive hands-on support from experts in trauma-informed camping and mentoring from the months leading up to camp and during the week of camp. Two Camp HOPE America staff attended our Oklahoma City camp as resources. I am the first Kids' HOPE Coordinator for the FJC in Oklahoma City and the position requires at least a bachelor's degree in social work and some experience working with children. As a Masters in Social Work (MSW), mother of two, with 15 summers worth of camp counselor experience, I was able to bring that unique perspective with me into the position of Kids' HOPE Coordinator.

Ethical, Legal, Practice, Diversity, and/or Advocacy Issues Addressed

One of the issues I encountered in recruiting volunteers was helping the FJC governing entities and partner agencies understand the importance of having counselors who were ethnically diverse and had similar life experiences of the campers. For kids who have been exposed to trauma by a trusted adult in their lives, building trust and developing meaningful relationships can sometimes be a challenge. I felt that eliminating these barriers would play an important role in helping campers build trust with our counselors. My goal was to get volunteers who looked like our campers—racially, ethnically, and socioeconomically—and who had similar life experiences to my campers: foster care, incarcerated parents, and other adverse childhood experiences. As we talked about Camp HOPE to our board of directors, the other partner agencies, and other FJC governing boards, it was difficult for them to understand why we would want counselors who had a "past." Advocating for our campers' needs was tedious, and required me to be very selective in our volunteer recruitment. In fact, we were only able to find five male counselors; to keep our minimum child-to-counselor ratio of 3:1, we were only able to take 15 male campers. Originally we wanted a 2:1 ratio for 16 campers. Luckily, I was able to find top-notch counselors who were excelling in their educational and career paths who also had similar life experiences and were of a similar ethnic makeup as our campers.

Interprofessional and Intersectoral Collaboration

One of our most involved partners for Camp HOPE and the lead agency for the FJC in Oklahoma City has been the Oklahoma City Police Department (OCPD). OCPD sent two female officers and one male cadet to camp as counselors. As most of our campers have had interactions with police, I was unsure of how a police presence would be interpreted by the campers. I made sure to talk about it with all our campers during the precamp interview. The officers were so engaging with the campers. They brought their squad car to camp, which ended up being a big hit with the campers. Both campers' and officers' influence on each other was amazing. The campers were so proud to have officers as "their" counselors and having them there seemed to add an element of safety for the campers. The officers, who work together on a night shift and see many incidents of domestic violence on their patrol, said that the experience of camp would change how they policed the community. It helped them see a different perspective of the effects of domestic violence and the effects of their actions in police work. And the campers were so excited to know that they knew a police officer who was "fun."

PART II

SYSTEMS OF CARE AND FORENSIC PRACTICE

CHAPTER 5

Education, Social Work, and the Law

Carolyn Bradley
Karen J. Dunn

CHAPTER OBJECTIVES

The major objectives of this chapter are to:

- Demonstrate the complexity of the role of the school social worker.
- Describe how to respond collaboratively and effectively to the variety of issues presented within public schools.

CHAPTER COMPETENCIES HIGHLIGHTED

- Competency 2: Engage Diversity and Difference in Practice
- Competency 8: Intervene With Individuals, Families, Organizations, and Communities

Social workers working in educational settings strive to ensure that children develop intellectually, socially, and emotionally. Struggling families often, either willingly or unwittingly, bring their problems with their children to social workers in the schools.

A school social worker must have knowledge, skills, and expertise to be able to successfully negotiate multiple systems on behalf of the client. The school, which so often serves not only as an educational setting but also as a community resource center, deals with health care agencies, law enforcement, the courts, probation, corrections, and child protective services (CPS). The effective school social worker must be knowledgeable about community resources as well as be up-to-date regarding the numerous federal and state laws concerning services within the public school.

This chapter provides a brief history of social work services in schools. It addresses recent demographics and trends and the scope of the problems in this specialty area. Relevant theoretical frameworks are examined from the perspective of the varied roles of the school social worker. Common issues requiring social work services in a school setting, as well as common practice settings and collaborative practice with other professionals, are also addressed. Specific legal and ethical issues of concern in the practice of school social work are reviewed, and issues of assessment, prevention, and intervention are discussed. Finally, cases are reviewed that exemplify the issues, skills, and collaborative aspects of social work practice in schools.

Overview of Field of Practice

History

Early 1900s

Social work services in U.S. schools began in 1906, primarily out of concern for the needs of urban students. Services began with "visiting teachers," employed by private agencies and civic organizations, whose primary role was to improve attendance and foster understanding and communication between the school and the community. Coinciding with the development of "visiting teachers," attention to attendance was an enactment of compulsory education laws (National Conference of State Legislatures [NCSL], n.d.). These laws, developed on a state-by-state basis between 1852 and 1918, mandated that children attend school between certain ages and for a minimum number of days per year. These initial school social work services began in New York City, Boston, and Hartford. In 1913, the first school social workers were employed by the Board of Education in the city of Rochester, New York (Constable, Massat, McDonald, & Flynn, 2008).

In 1916, at the National Conference of Charities and Corrections, a presentation given by Jane Culbert defined the role of the school social worker (Constable et al., 2008). Culbert's description of the work of the "visiting teacher" detailed the need for respect for differences, inclusion, focus on the child in his or her environment at home and in school, and recognition of education as a relational process. Almost 100 years later, this description still applies.

The early years of social work services in schools focused on family and neighborhood conditions that interfered with attendance and helping the teacher understand the home conditions of the child. By the 1920s, concerns with delinquency and the influence of the mental hygiene movement moved the focus of school social workers away from community issues and more on individual psychological concerns. Social workers were called on to assist in understanding the emotional needs of children and how these needs, left unmet, could lead to social maladjustment (Huxtable, 1998).

1940s to 1960s

The 1940s through the 1960s saw the role of the school social worker become even more focused on working with socially and/or emotionally maladjusted children. Services during this period primarily involved casework with individual students and their families, consultation with teachers, and referrals to community agencies (Huxtable, 1998).

However, by the late 1960s, recognition of increasing problems within the schools and the communities in which they were located caused another shift in focus in school social work. The struggle for social and economic equality created an awareness of the disparity in the quality of education provided to children based on their race, economic status, and geographic location. Remedies were sought through the development of programs such as Head Start, a federally funded program created in 1965 to promote school readiness through services to low-income children and their families (Administration of Children and Families [ACF], n.d.). In response to issues such as these, social workers began to move away from the traditional focus on individual casework and began to engage in more advocacy (Huxtable, 1998).

1970s and 1980s

Since the 1970s, the role of the school social worker has changed in response to the mandates of specific legislation. In 1975, schools were affected by the enactment of the Education for All Handicapped Children Act of 1975 (PL 94-142). This federal law created a new role for social workers: They were part of a *child study team* (CST), an interdisciplinary team responsible for specific services and focused primarily on the identification of children with learning disabilities within the school setting.

1990s to the Present Day

In March 1994, the Goals 2000: Educate America Act (1994) was enacted. This federal legislation recognized the personal and social factors that affect a child's ability to learn. Issues such as substance abuse; behavioral difficulties; and the complex interaction of emotional, family, and social factors were acknowledged as impeding academic achievement. The law recognized the need for specialized help with problems of this type. Such specialized help could be provided through social work services. Amendments in 1997 to the Individuals With Disabilities Education Act (IDEA) of Amendments of 1997 (PL 105-17) provided additional social work services in the schools, including more traditional casework and counseling services, especially for children with behavioral and attention deficit problems. This legislation also strengthened the rights and the involvement of parents, which, as always, strengthened the social work liaison and advocacy function (Constable et al., 2008).

Focus of School Social Work

The primary focus of school social work is the resolution of issues that children bring from their families and their communities into the schools. Through the resolution of such sociolegal issues, social workers hope to assist the students they serve in improving attendance, raising academic achievement, and reducing violence in schools and neighborhoods. How this work is done is shaped in part by federal and state legislation and regulations, by local resources, and by the definition of the role of the social worker within each individual school district.

Recent Demographics

In the United States, it is difficult to estimate the number of social workers working in schools. Services provided by social workers are often done under different titles, for example "crisis intervention counselor," "behavioral counselor," or "student assistance counselor" (SAC). In 2011 to 2012 the number of full-time equivalent social workers was 31,030 (National Center for Education Statistics [NCES], 2016).

In the Fall of 2016, it was estimated that there are 50.4 million students in public elementary and secondary schools in the United States (NCES, 2016). The types of services provided through social work in schools, ranging from traditional CST work to reentry services for students returning from correctional and/or treatment facilities, varies based on funding, the number of staff members, and the ages of the students.

Current Trends

The practice of school social work as a specialty area has gained legitimacy. This is evidenced in several ways: professional journals devoted to the topic, professional organizations dealing solely with the area, legislation mandating such services, states requiring licensing or credentialing, and the National Association of Social Workers (NASW) creating a national specialty credential. Despite these gains and the specialized sociolegal expertise offered by school social workers, school social work in its many manifestations is often one of the first services to be reduced when school budget constraints are encountered.

The primary tasks of the school social worker are casework with students and their parents and collaboration with staff. Issues addressed are broad and multifaceted, ranging from completion of required documentation for special education services to child abuse, attendance, and family issues, for example, death, separation or divorce, health issues, pregnancy, substance abuse, suicide, and homelessness (Constable et al., 2008).

Background and Scope of the Problem

The need for school social work is easily documented when one reviews national trends concerning truancy, dropout rates, violence, and other social problems (NCES, 2016). The development of prevention and intervention programs to address such issues is uniquely suited to the skills and training of the professional social worker. Counseling and advocacy services for students with learning problems and/or family problems are also areas in which social work services have been demonstrated to make noticeable and sustainable change (Usaj, Shine, & Mandlawits, n.d.). Therefore, social work services should be available to students, families, and staff from preschool through high school. Such services should be provided at a reasonable student-to-worker ratio.

Relevant Theories or Frameworks

The social worker providing services in a school needs to be aware of a variety of theories, depending on the function she or he performs. Social workers providing traditional CST services must be familiar with learning theories as well as counseling approaches.

In general, school social workers do not provide therapy. Short-term, problem-focused counseling as well as crisis intervention may be provided. Approaches such as *reality therapy* (Glasser, 1965) or *motivational interviewing* (Miller & Rollnick, 2013) are often used. *Family systems theory* (Nichols, 2013) is a useful approach in the school setting because the concepts can be applied when working with students or in understanding the organizational context. Additionally, social learning theories assist with changing behaviors, problem solving, and altering dysfunctional thoughts that influence behaviors (Bandura, 1969).

An understanding of *organizational theory* (Bolman & Deal, 2013) is also useful within the school setting when negotiating the school system's hierarchy as well with interagency collaboration, such as law enforcement and/or corrections.

Common Issues

Myriad issues are referred to the services of the school social worker. The exact role and responsibility of the worker is often dictated by the title under which the worker functions, relevant federal and state laws and regulations that mandate functions, and the local school governing body that employs the social worker.

Functions of the school social worker—for example, CST assessments, attendance and truancy interventions, collaboration with child welfare services, bullying and violence prevention services, crisis counseling, and other mental health services—are mandated or suggested by specific legislation (Constable et al., 2008). Other functions are determined by the specific district. The best summary of the scope and function of the school social worker is to improve attendance; reduce violence; assist students with transition from school to adult life; address emotional, social, and/or family problems; and assist with raising academic achievement. In addition, the social worker may also be responsible for providing consultation services to school personnel. The manner in which these tasks are envisioned and carried out varies widely.

Common Practice Settings

Settings/Jobs

The most common setting for a social worker in a school is as a member of a CST. As a member of a CST, the social worker assists in the identification, evaluation, and remediation of students with learning disabilities. This process requires determining eligibility for services, testing, and, if classified, the development of an individualized education program (IEP), which requires periodic review and updating. This function is the same whether the service is provided at the elementary or high school level. CST members are required to be knowledgeable of federal legislation such as the Individuals With Disabilities Act (IDEA) (PL 105-117) and federal and state codes regarding the provision of special education services (Constable et al., 2008).

Social workers may also work in schools under a variety of titles providing crisis intervention services, specialized counseling services (e.g., substance abuse prevention and intervention, truancy intervention, conflict resolution), and supervising specific programs. When providing these types of services, the worker also must be knowledgeable of the specific laws and regulations that govern the provision of these services.

Each of these positions may require specific educational licenses or certifications issued by the department of education of the state in which the school is located. Information regarding licensure and/or certification may be obtained through the department of education website in the state in which a person intends to practice.

School social work services are provided in public and private schools. Some private schools do not require the social worker to have a state license and/or an educational credential.

Professionals Involved

School social workers interact with a variety of professionals within and outside of the school. As previously noted, within the school, social workers often function as part of an interdisciplinary CST. The other members of the CST may include a school psychologist, a learning consultant, a speech therapist, and a school nurse, as well as other consultants and specialists as needed. The social worker also interacts with guidance counselors, teachers, and administrators within the school.

The social worker as a CST member, or under another title providing services within the school, may also be involved with juvenile officers, probation officers, hospital personnel, and mental health and addiction professionals. Social workers are often the contact person in the school for CPS workers with whom students and their families are involved. Because of the likelihood of the need for collaboration with outside systems, it is necessary for the worker to be aware of the regulations regarding how the school may interact with them. Although professional social workers must always function within the guidelines for practice specified within the NASW *Code of Ethics* (NASW, 2008), school social workers must also consider the confidentiality guidelines of the School Social Work Association of America (2001) and comply with laws such as the Family Educational Rights and Privacy Act of 1974 (FERPA) (PL 93-380), which governs the dissemination of school records, and the federal confidentiality regulations regarding the release of substance abuse information (42 CFR-2 [Section 42 of the Code of Federal Regulations, Part 2] and the Health Insurance Portability and Accountability Act of 1996 [HIPPA]; Constable et al., 2008).

The Role and Function of Social Workers in Schools

School social workers have varying and multifaceted roles and functions, which is the result of federal and state legislation, legal decisions, the characteristic focus of social work, and how the school district understands and values social work services. The social worker's role is often formed by the interaction of the professional and personal focus of the individual worker with the structure and expectations of the particular school (Constable et al., 2008). The school social worker is responsible to multiple constituencies: students and their families, faculty, school administrators, local school governing bodies (e.g., boards of education), and the community. Therefore, the school social worker performs all the functions associated with professional social work, for example, counselor, advocate, developer of linkages, policy analyst, and researcher.

One of the most common roles for a school social worker is as part of a CST often comprised of a school psychologist and a learning consultant. This team is responsible for identifying, assessing, and providing remediation plans for students with learning disabilities. In this capacity, the school social worker is responsible for the social assessment of the student. This assessment is conducted by observing the child in school, meeting with the parent(s) to obtain a social and developmental history, talking with the teacher, and reviewing any available, pertinent school records.

If a child is found to have a learning disability a remediation plan is developed, such as an IEP, as required by the IDEA (Constable et al., 2008), with the consultation and written consent of the parents. One of the CST members is then assigned to the student as a case manager. The case manager is responsible for monitoring the student's progress and determines any changes that might be needed to the student's remediation plan. The case manager must meet annually with the student, parents, and teacher to review and update this plan as long as the student receives special education remediation services. In addition to assessment and case manager responsibilities, school social workers may also provide counseling to special education students, either individually or in groups. Counseling may include social skills and behavioral management issues. Consultation services may also be provided to teachers working with special education students.

Within schools there is often a team responsible for interventions with students with academic and/or behavioral problems but who are not eligible for special education services. These teams are often made up of a building administrator, a guidance counselor, a social worker, a teacher, and other appropriate school personnel. The social worker involved with such a team has the opportunity to provide prevention and/or early-intervention services. Students referred to this type of service are often involved in truancy or have other problems in the community that affect school performance. The social worker is often the most knowledgeable and appropriately trained among school personnel to intervene with students and their families in these types of situations.

Many schools have developed specific programs (often entitled *student assistance programs*) to identify and intervene with students with substance abuse problems or who come from families with substance abuse problems. These teams are often led by social workers with specialized training in addictions. When students are identified as using substances, the social worker is responsible for the initial assessment and determination of the need for referral for treatment services. This role requires interaction with parents, treatment providers, and often law enforcement and/or correctional personnel.

As federal mandates have been enacted to ensure that public schools are safe and drug free, violence prevention programming has been added to the duties of the SAC.

Social workers working in student assistance programs use advanced direct practice, policy, and community-organizing skills. In the role of the school substance abuse and violence prevention specialist, the social worker is responsible for the development and implementation of prevention programs (Slovak, 2006), often delivered in the form of assembly programs and classroom presentations, faculty and parent education programs, and psychoeducational groups for students.

Crisis intervention teams are another service found within schools that require social workers. These teams are set up to manage crises such as the death of a student or a faculty member or any other type of traumatic event (Constable et al., 2008). A member of this team is most likely to be called on to perform a threat assessment of a student presenting with either suicidal or violent thoughts or behavior. These teams, developed as a result of federal mandates for safe and disciplined schools, operate under specific local education governing body policies and procedures.

Relevant Ethical, Legal, and Policy Issues

All assessment and remediation services provided by CSTs require signed consent by a student's parent if that student is under 18 years of age. The provision of special education remediation services involves the completion of numerous legal and educational documents requiring the signatures of school personnel and parents. Failure to complete the required paperwork within specified timelines can result in legal action by the student's family. Cases of this nature are usually resolved in an administrative law or civil rights hearing.

Counseling services provided to a student under 18 years of age other than crisis intervention requires parental notification and consent. The exception to this rule is services to a substance abusing student provided through a SAC. The provision of such services is covered under 42 CFR-2. Parental notification of the provision of such services to students may be done only with the written consent of the student. Although adherence to this level of confidentiality is mandated by federal regulation, it often creates ethical dilemmas for the social worker regarding parental involvement, which may be necessary to obtain a higher level of care for a substance abusing student.

Relevant Assessment, Prevention, and Intervention Strategies

Assessment, prevention, and intervention services provided in a school setting by a social worker vary, depending on the title and function of the social worker. Usually such services entail assessment, remediation planning, and monitoring done by a social worker as part of a CST. In some school districts, the social worker may also be responsible for providing counseling services to students receiving special education services.

Social workers providing services through student assistance programs are responsible for prevention, education, identification, assessment, intervention, and referral services concerning substance abuse. Social workers may plan and provide programs for students, their families, and the community on prevention of substance abuse. In schools, social workers functioning as SACs may teach lessons on substance abuse prevention in classrooms. SACs are also responsible for identification, assessment, intervention, and referral of students who are abusing substances or who come from homes where substance abuse is a problem. SACs are able to assess for substance abuse, refer for outside treatment services, and provide individual counseling and in-school support groups. Students who require inpatient services for substance use will, on return to school, have reentry plans developed with the SAC, the student, and rehabilitation center staff.

Schools are increasingly confronted with students who have a myriad of emotional and social issues that affect their academic performance. Social workers in the school are often seen as the experts called in to deal with students with such problems. Emotional and social issues presented in the school run the gamut from severe psychiatric problems (e.g., depression with suicidal ideation and/or gestures) to relationship problems, harassment, sexual identity issues, attention deficit/hyperactivity disorder (ADHD), eating disorders, parental divorce, physical and sexual abuse, aggression, and violence (National Center for Educational Statistics, 2016).

Given the wide range of possible issues presented by students, social workers need to have excellent assessment skills and knowledge of crisis intervention strategies (Richmond, 1917). Assessments, regardless of the role of the social worker within the school, need to be multidimensional and address cultural considerations. The assessment process within the school can be complex, because of the various specialized tasks performed by the social worker. In general, a social work assessment covers problem identification, identification of the client system (i.e., who is asking for services), and the target system (i.e., what is expected to change). The assessment covers multiple domains within the client's life and focuses on her or his strengths. Components to be addressed may include demographics and data source, referral source, presenting problem, family information, health/physical/intellectual/emotional functioning, interpersonal/social relationships, religion/spirituality, strengths/problem-solving capacity, economics/housing, impressions/assessment, and goals/interventions (Miley, O'Melia, & DuBois, 2017). The product of the assessment process—a social assessment report—is a written document that becomes part of the student's record. The format for the final report is usually determined by the school district.

Some districts provide standardized assessment instruments for use by the social workers based on the service they provide. School social workers working on CSTs at an elementary level often use the Behavior Assessment System for Children Structured Developmental History (BASC-SDH; Reynolds & Kamphaus, 1992). SACs have a variety of assessment instruments available based on the age of the student, for example, Adolescent Substance Abuse Subtle Screening Inventory (SASSI). Crisis intervention or behavioral specialists may use standardized instruments specific to their services (e.g., Beck Depression Inventory [Beck, Steer, & Brown, 1996]). A variety of assessment formats and instruments may be reviewed in the text *Clinical Assessment for Social Workers* (Jordan & Franklin, 2015).

Resources for social workers in schools are most frequently available through the professional associations specific to the title under which the social worker operates. Three national organizations providing resources are the NASW's School Social Work Section, the School Social Work Association of America, and the National Association of Student Assistance Programs. All three organizations provide resources and information about national/regional conferences.

Forensic Practice Skill Set

Social workers providing services in schools must possess a variety of skills. Excellent verbal and written language skills are necessary. The ability to communicate clearly and effectively with people from different socioeconomic and educational levels is a requisite for this work.

School social workers must have knowledge of and the ability to interact with people from different racial, ethnic, and cultural backgrounds. Social workers in schools provide case management and advocacy services for the students and their families. They often assist students' families in identifying and applying for eligible services within the school and in the outside community.

As the liaison to the community, the school social worker needs to be able to interact with law enforcement, treatment providers, and, often, correctional personnel. In these interactions, the social worker must be cognizant of ethical and legal considerations in the disclosure of an exchange of information regarding students.

Case Examples and Application

Given the breadth of services provided by social workers in schools, it would be difficult, if not impossible, to present one case that typifies what issues may be presented by students. Therefore, three cases follow: one student with developmental/learning problems, another student with behavior problems, and a final case regarding sexual orientation issues.

Case 1

James is a 3-year-old African American male who resides with his maternal grandmother, 14-year-old maternal aunt, and a 7-year-old cousin. The other two children are reported to do well in school and participate in general education classes. There are no other adults in the home.

James is referred for CST evaluation by his pediatrician because of delays in language development and difficulties with attention and behavior. James uses only single words and short phrases and has a vocabulary of approximately 50 words. He has problems following direction and staying on task. When frustrated or upset, James screams, kicks, bangs his head, and/or throws objects. Grandmother uses "time-outs" for discipline.

James requires constant supervision, and he is described as impulsive and showing poor judgment. He is reported to dart into the street. When the family is outdoors, James requires his hand to be held by other family members at all times for safety reasons.

James is reported to be affectionate with his family but shy with strangers. The 14-year-old aunt, the grandmother's main support in caring for James, and the 7-year-old cousin are reported to be gentle and supportive with James.

The family is active in the Baptist church, where James participates in a child care program during services. In that setting, James is reported to enjoy playing with cars and trucks, pushing vehicles back and forth with another boy. In this program, James's interest in activities is described as short lived.

James was born at 31 weeks gestation, weighing 2 lbs 4 oz.; he was 17 in. in length. Head circumference appeared smaller than normal. At birth, James experienced difficulty breathing and eating. He was placed in a neonatal care unit for 11 weeks. It is reported that James's mother used crack cocaine and marijuana throughout the pregnancy.

His grandmother brought James home upon his discharge. His mother lived in the home for a short period after James came home. The grandmother reports that currently the mother visits occasionally but is mostly absent from James's life. The mother is reported to continue using drugs and to be "living on the streets." James's father is incarcerated for selling drugs. He has not developed a relationship with James. The grandmother has sole custody of the child.

James experienced a delay in attaining developmental milestones. He spoke his first word at 2½ years and continues to have speech difficulties. He walked without assistance at 17 months. James is mostly toilet trained with occasional episodes of nocturnal enuresis. He is able to dress himself.

(continued)

James is reported to be generally healthy. There is no history of head injuries, convulsions, or hospitalizations. He is reported to have a healthy appetite. He is a restless sleeper and snores. He has a history of ear infections.

James was evaluated by the CST and found to be eligible for services as a student with learning disabilities. He was enrolled in a preschool handicapped program in which he received speech services and occupational therapy services. A behavioral plan was developed to address time-on-task concerns and to help James develop more appropriate ways to deal with frustration.

Case 2

Brian is a seventh-grade student who fails several subjects, does little homework, comes to school late, and presents behavioral difficulties. Although appearing academically uninterested, he presents as sociable and enjoys the social aspects of school.

Brian began to experience academic problems during middle school. His standardized test scores are all in the average range. Although usually friendly and sociable, he becomes sullen and uncommunicative when discussion focuses on academic problems. Brian does not receive special education services.

The school has attempted to address Brian's declining academic performance through conferences with his parent. Brian resides with his biological mother, her boyfriend, and a younger female sibling. His mother often does not attend scheduled conferences.

Brian came to the attention of the SAC after an incident with a teacher in which he was verbally disrespectful and insubordinate. After being referred to the assistant principal for this behavior, Brian was noted to be unusually tired, irritable, and red eyed. Brian was then asked to submit to a drug test, which he refused. As required, Brian's mother was contacted regarding the behavior and the request for a drug test.

On notification of the request for the drug test, Brian's mother did come to school. Brian and his mother conferred regarding the drug test. The mother seemed unusually concerned about the outcome of such a test.

The SAC, Brian, and his mother met. From this discussion, it became known that the family was using marijuana together and that the parental figures and Brian were selling marijuana as well. Brian and his mother agreed to the drug test, which came back positive for high levels of tetrahydrocannabinol (THC), the chemical in marijuana. The level was indicative of someone who smoked marijuana daily.

The family was referred to CPS and the police. The mother denied dealing as did Brian. Police involvement ended as dealing could not be proven. CPS continued to support the mother's recovery.

Brian's behavior continued to deteriorate in school and resulted in a CST referral. He was determined to be eligible for special education services as a student with severe behavioral difficulties.

Brian became known to the juvenile court as a result of incidents in the community. The SAC advocated with the court to order Brian into rehabilitation rather than a correctional facility. The court accepted the recommendation of the SAC and Brian was sent to an inpatient rehabilitation facility.

Brian successfully completed inpatient treatment for substance abuse. He returned to the school with a recommendation for outpatient treatment and in-school support services provided by the SAC.

Brian's mother relapsed and did not follow through with Brian's aftercare program. Brian began using again and was involved in a series of burglaries in the community. Brian was caught, convicted, and sent to a juvenile correctional facility.

(*continued*)

Case Example and Application (*continued*)

Case 3

Irina is a 14-year-old ninth-grade student. She immigrated to the United States from Russia with her family when she was 12 years old. She does well academically and maintains a "B" average. There are no attendance problems. Although she speaks perfect English, Irina remains isolated socially. She presents some discipline problems for teachers.

Irina is rejected socially by the other girls. They report that she tells "outrageous stories" regarding going to bars in a large city within access to the school district through public transportation. Although a fairly good soccer player, Irina refuses to be involved with organized sports. Teachers report problems with verbal exchanges between Irina and other students. When requested to cease the exchange, Irina disregards the teacher's directives, resulting in a referral for insubordination to the main office.

Irina's parents have participated in conferences at school regarding discipline problems. They report that they are experiencing similar problems at home. They express concern that Irina often stays out late on the weekends and that they do not always know her whereabouts. They report that she is sullen and withdrawn at home. Attempts by school personnel to engage Irina in discussions about problems with other girls have been unsuccessful.

Over the course of Irina's ninth-grade school year, her appearance changed. She began wearing more dark-colored clothing and appeared to take less interest in her hair. She stopped using any make-up and wore no jewelry other than a watch. Her jackets and backpack were covered with buttons with slogans and rainbow flags.

After wearing a t-shirt to school with a slogan about dating women, Irina was referred to the SAC for an interview. Although affirming Irina's right to wear the t-shirt, the SAC tried to open a conversation with her on why that t-shirt and what she was trying to tell everyone. With much support and gentle probing, Irina was able to disclose the questions that she was beginning to have regarding her sexual orientation. Irina was able to disclose her anger and frustration at feeling that she did not fit in with girls her own age, her increasing depression, and a somewhat detailed plan for suicide. The t-shirt provided a vehicle for someone to ask Irina a direct question regarding her sexual orientation.

Irina met with her parents and the SAC. A referral was made to a local therapist comfortable with dealing with adolescent sexual orientation issues.

Discussion

James's case highlights the skills required of a social worker on a CST. In this capacity, the worker must be able to establish rapport so as to obtain a detailed history and to provide a biopsychosocial assessment of the student and his family. The ability to engage the student and family at this level may allow for the provision of services at an early age to remediate the learning problem. Often, early remediation can prevent school dissatisfaction, which can lead to social and behavioral problems.

Brian's case demonstrates the function of the SAC in the school setting. The knowledge base of the SAC, the ability to handle crises, and the strategies that need to be employed to obtain treatment for the student are highlighted in this case.

Irina's case highlights an emerging issue regarding sexual orientation in adolescents and the need for the school social worker to be knowledgeable and aware of such issues. The case highlights the clinical skills that are often needed in the school setting to be able to deal effectively with adolescents.

In all of the cases presented, the social worker had to be aware of and adhere to all federal and state laws and regulations and local governing board policies and procedures as well as to follow the appropriate confidentiality regulations.

Conclusion

This chapter presented an overview of social work services in the school. It examined the origin and development of such services in the United States. Contemporary functions of the school social worker and the various legal, academic, and social emotional issues addressed were presented.

CHAPTER EXERCISES

Exercise 1. Using the case examples, role-play how a social worker may interact with one of these clients.

Exercise 2. Read the following article on education in juvenile justice: www.edjj.org/focus/ education. Form two debate teams to argue why we should or why we should not provide quality education to juveniles in prison.

Exercise 3. Watch the following short video: School to Prison Pipeline: www.youtube.com/ watch?v=4FCGUaOKRks. Discuss in a small, then large, group how social work can play a role in preventing and intervening in breaking the school-to-prison pipeline for youth.

Additional Resources

Council of State Governments: https://csgjusticecenter.org/youth/posts/critical-elements-of-juvenile -reentry-in-research-and-practice

National Center on Education, Disability and Juvenile Justice: www.edjj.org

Office of Juvenile Justice and Delinquency Prevention: www.ojjdp.gov and www.ojjdp.gov/programs/ system_involved_youth.html#relpubs

PBS Film: Education Under Arrest: www.pbs.org/wnet/tavissmiley/tsr/education-under-arrest

References

Administration of Children and Families. (n.d.). Office of Head Start. Retrieved from http://eclkc.ohs .acf.hhs.gov/hslc/About%20Head%20Start

Bandura, A. (1969). *Principles of behavior modification*. New York, NY: Holt, Rinehart & Winston.

Beck, A. T., Steer, R. A., & Brown, G. K. (1996). *Manual for Beck Depression Inventory II (BDI-II)*. San Antonio, TX: Psychology Corporation.

Bolman, L. G., & Deal, T. E. (2013). *Reframing organizations* (5th ed.). San Francisco, CA: Jossey-Bass.

Constable, R., Massat, C. R., McDonald, S., & Flynn, J. P. (2008). *School social work* (7th ed.). Chicago, IL: Lyceum Books.

Education for All Handicapped Children Act, Pub. L. No. 94-142. (1975). Retrieved from https://www .gpo.gov/fdsys/pkg/STATUTE-89/pdf/STATUTE-89-pg773.pdf

Family Educational Rights and Privacy Act, 20 U.S.C.S. § 1232. (1974). Retrieved from http://www .ed.gov/policy/gen/guid/fpco/ferpa/leg-history.html

Glasser, W. (1965). *Reality therapy*. New York, NY: Harper & Row.

Health Insurance Portability and Accountability Act, Pub. L. No. 104-191. (1996). Retrieved from https://www.hhs.gov/hipaa; updates of the Act are retrieved from http://www.hhs.gov/about/ news/2013/01/17/new-rule-protects-patient-privacy-secures-health-information.html

Huxtable, M. (1998). School social work: An international profession. *Social Work in Education, 20*(2), 95–109.

Individuals With Disabilities Education Act Amendments, Pub. L. No. 105-17, 20 U.S.C. (1997). Retrieved from http://www2.ed.gov/offices/OSERS/Policy/IDEA/index.html

Jordan, C., & Franklin, C. (2015). *Clinical assessment for social workers* (4th ed.). Chicago, IL: Lyceum Books.

Miley, K. K., O'Melia, M., & DuBois, B. (2017). *Generalist social work practice* (8th ed.). Boston, MA: Pearson.

Miller, W. R., & Rollnick, S. (2013). *Motivational interviewing* (3rd ed.). New York, NY: Guilford Press.

National Association of Social Workers. (2008). *Code of ethics.* Washington, DC: Author. Retrieved from https://www.hhs.gov/hipaa

National Association of Social Workers. (2012). *NASW standards for school social work services.* Washington, DC: Author. Retrieved from https://www.socialworkers.org/practice/standards/NASWSchoolSocialWorkStandards

National Center for Educational Statistics. (2016). Overview of public elementary secondary schools and districts. Retrieved from http://nces.ed.gov/index.asp

National Conference of State Legislatures. (n.d.). Compulsory education. Retrieved from http://education.findlaw.com/education-options/compulsory-education

Nichols, M. P. (2013). *The essentials of family therapy* (6th ed.). Boston, MA: Allyn & Bacon.

Reynolds, C. R., & Kamphaus, R. W. (1992). *BASC—Behavioral assessment system for children: Manual.* Circle Pines, MN: American Guidance Service.

Richmond, M. (1917). *Social diagnosis.* New York, NY: Russell Sage Foundation.

School Social Work Association of America. (2001, March 15). School social workers and confidentiality. Retrieved from http://education.findlaw.com/education-options/compulsory-education

Slovak, K. (2006). School social workers' perceptions of student violence and prevention programming. *School Social Work Journal, 31*(1), 30–42.

Usaj, K., Shine, J., & Mandlawitz, M. (n.d.). Response to intervention: New roles for school social workers. Retrieved from http://www.wisconsinpbisnetwork.org/assets/files/2012%20Conference/Session%20Material/Roles_School_Social_Workers_RTI.pdf

VOICES FROM THE FIELD

Karen J. Dunn, MSW, LSW
School Social Worker

Agency Setting

My agency is a public school district in Monmouth County, New Jersey. My primary work location is in the high school where I serve on the child study team as a school social worker. Our school district serves five towns; therefore, it is considered a large district with three elementary schools, one intermediate school, and one high school.

Practice Responsibilities

My primary function is to assist each child to attain his or her maximum school potential through the development of a cooperative home–school relationship to promote a better mutual understanding of the child and his or her needs. My primary responsibility is to assist students in the resolution of such personal, emotional, and/or social problems that interfere with their adjustment in school and their capacity to utilize the benefits of the education offered.

Expertise Required

In New Jersey, the qualifications for being a school social worker are set by the state Department of Education and include a valid New Jersey Educational Services Certificate and a School Social Worker Endorsement. A knowledge of and thorough understanding of the New Jersey State Code for Special Education and Related Services is mandatory. Experience working with families, community health, and social service agencies is desirable. A background in mental health and substance abuse is also valuable. School social workers must be effective problem solvers and must have excellent communication and organizational skills.

Ethical, Legal, Practice, Diversity, and/or Advocacy Issues Addressed

Ethical issues arise around maintaining state-mandated timelines, which at times hinder parents' involvement with their child's meetings during school hours due to parent employment. In addition, there are times where minorities may be discouraged to take advantage of the benefits of Special Education and Related Services. One of the goals of the Department of Education is to not overclassify minorities. Frequently, minorities are immigrants who may need the support of special education and related services.

Interprofessional and Intersectoral Collaboration

Our school district has involvement with mental health agencies, social service agencies, and child protection agencies so as to meet the needs for care of children who have emotional and behavioral needs. Additionally, there are professional relationships with private special education schools, which provide placements for students who require more support and/ or services than can be provided within the public school setting.

CHAPTER 6

Thinking Outside the Box: Tackling Health Inequities Through Forensic Social Work Practice

Karen Bullock

Jodi Hall

David Fitzpatrick

CHAPTER OBJECTIVES

The main objectives of this chapter are to:

- Emphasize the importance of improving health literacy.
- Incorporate Cultural Competence Standards in forensic social work practice perspectives.
- Promote engagement of informal support networks in promoting health and well-being among diverse groups.

CHAPTER COMPETENCIES HIGHLIGHTED

- Competency 2: Engage Diversity and Difference in Practice
- Competency 8: Intervene With Individuals, Families, Organizations, and Communities

The number of people incarcerated in the United States quadrupled from approximately 500,000 to 2.3 million between 1980 and 2008, with three decades of growth in the prison populations disproportionately impacting Black men and women. According to reports by the Pew Public Safety Performance Project, the hues of prison communities are becoming more Black, brown, and gray as incarceration tends to be more heavily concentrated among ethnic minorities, and they are more likely to have longer sentences "behind bars" than nonminority groups (Pew Charitable Trusts, 2008). Moreover, one in three African American men and one in six Hispanic men born in 2001 are projected to be incarcerated during their lifetime (Ahalt, Bolano, Wang, & Williams, 2015). According to the National Institute for Justice, health disparities abound among prison populations (U.S. Department of Justice, 2004).

Extending justice and human rights to incarcerated persons is a means to address the "differences in the incidence, prevalence, mortality, and burden of diseases and other adverse health conditions that exist among specific groups in the United States" (Hofrichter & Bhatia, 2010), especially among those persons who may have often spent a lifetime of exposure to violence, discrimination, and low educational attainment prior to their encounters with the justice system. Besides, the increase in chronically ill, terminally ill, and elderly inmates (U.S. Department of Justice, 2004) demands a shift in research focus, service delivery, health policy, and practice approaches. The capacity of forensic social workers to provide health care in accordance with the values, ethics, and standards of the profession requires knowledge and skills in the area of cultural competence. This chapter highlights two theoretical frameworks that help to inform the perspective on health disparities in prisons and provides a case example for application of the practice skill set.

Background and Scope of the Problem

The United States comprises 5% of the world's population and has 25% of the prisoners of the world locked behind bars, on its home soil (Center on Juvenile and Criminal Justice, 2008). Combining the number of people in prisons, jail, probation supervision, and parole, 1 in every 31 adults, or 3.2% of the population, is under correctional control or criminal justice oversight. Because people of African descent, or African Americans, who self-report their race as Black are disproportionately among this population, the National Association for the Advancement of Colored People (NAACP) issued its own report on the state of criminal justice for/or against African Americans (2013), emphasizing the fact that African Americans make up "nearly 1 million of the 2.3 million" Americans who are incarcerated in U.S. prisons today. Moreover, 58% of all prisoners in the United States in 2008 were African Americans and Hispanics, in spite of the fact that these groups represent only 25% of the total U.S. population.

If these demographic trends continue, with one in six Black men continuing to be incarcerated over time, and 1 in 100 Black women imprisoned (NAACP, 2013), continually, the disparity among those persons spending their lifetime "behind bars" will lead to another social justice concern for forensic social workers, which is the access to health care for individuals who are elderly, chronically, and/or terminally ill (U.S. Department of Justice, 2004). Scholars (Maschi, Viola, Morgen, & Koskinen, 2015) have documented that about two out of three inmates experience trauma and stress in prison. This can include physical and sexual abuse, bullying, neglect, exploitation by staff and younger inmates, food and water depravation, and solitary confinement.

The National Association of Social Workers *Code of Ethics* (NASW, 2008) speaks of the value of social justice, as well as social and political action for marginalized groups. To advocate for health care reform, and especially for the most effective intervention approaches, so that people will access the health care that is available to them, is in keeping with social work values and standards for practice. In the 1960s, we saw some of the most significant strides of history in the passage of legislation aimed specifically at protecting the rights of those who had been discriminated against based on race, color, religion, or national origin (Pollard, 2008). Since this era, the United States has successfully ushered in an abundance of legislation and policies intended to improve the quality of life for the poor and disabled persons (Pollard, 2008). Yet, programs and services to meet the needs of the most infirmed and elderly incarcerated persons have fallen short of meeting equal access and parity thresholds (Maruschak, 2008), and some would argue this to be true for women inmates across age, race, and ethnic groups as well (Williams & Rickard, 2004).

Persons who are incarcerated as convicted criminals are often treated as if they are less valued in society (Hochstetler, Murphy, & Simmons, 2004) and thus receive less attention when policies and services are being considered on a national level to address health care for the chronically ill, terminally ill, and the elderly. National Institute of Corrections (NIC) reports provide documentation that "some of the most dangerous and persistent criminals who were sentenced to life in prison without parole 30 years ago are now old, debilitated, frail, chronically ill, depressed, and no longer considered a threat to society or the institution," yet they will remain behind bars for as long as they live.

System and Population Overview

In the past decade, the number of elderly and infirm prisoners has increased dramatically. Less than a decade ago, the number of state and federal prisoners age 50 years and older increased from 41,586 to 113,358, a staggering increase of 172.6% (Camp & Camp, 2001). This population (age 50 years and older) represented only 5.7% of the correctional population, but continued to increase incrementally (Sabol & Couture, 2008). Aging in prison could soon reach epidemic proportions due, in part, to the same trends and concerns that gerontologists have for the general population, stemming from the increase in baby boomers, with little prospect for generating the necessary financial resources to fund their health and human service's needs (Reimer, 2008). In the penal system, however, the criminal charges and sentencing trends that disproportionately impact racial and ethnic minorities are generating an alarm as health care providers strive to understand the challenges of promoting health care among a population with burgeoning complex needs.

Sociocultural factors exacerbate the scope of the problem. Several studies have reported that Hispanic and African Americans are more likely to rely on informal supports and services across the life course (Delgado, 2014; Miles & Smith, 2013). Moreover, persons of these race/ethnic groups tend to have higher rates of morbidity and mortality than nonminority individuals (Mehta, Sudharsanan, & Elo, 2013). They are also less likely to utilize and complete mental health treatment programs (Saloner & Le Cook, 2013). When they have a history of incarceration, the continuum of care, in the community, for older adults is almost nonexistent of formal providers. In a study of formerly incarcerated older adults—a qualitative research, with primarily (80%) Latino and African Americans—participants reported that the bulk of their health care needs were met by family members and peers (Maschi & Koskinen, 2015). Furthermore, data show that persons of racial and ethnic minority groups have unequal access to health care as compared to Whites (Agency for Healthcare Research and Quality, 2009). These disparities persist through the end of life. Furthermore, at the end of life, racial/ethnic minorities fail to adequately use hospice care and palliative-care services, which could vastly improve pain management and overall quality of life in the final days of life (National Hospice and Palliative Care Organization, 2016). Literacy may be a contributing factor to the underutilization (Rickard, Hall, & Bullock, 2015; Stansbury, Peterson, & Bleecher, 2013), but the lack of cultural appropriateness and collective decision making could also serve as sociocultural determinants of disparities in behavioral health (Hall & Bullock, 2015); medical utilization (Bullock & Allison, 2015) and end-of-life care (Bullock & Volkel, 2014) also influence poor health outcomes.

The impact of implementation of cultural competence-based assessments and interventions may serve to mitigate sociocultural barriers that contribute to disparities in correctional confinement, and ultimately to reduce disparities in access to health and human services in forensic social work. This chapter emphasizes the importance of improving health literacy and incorporating cultural competence standards into the discussions about practice perspectives and theoretical frameworks to promote the engagement of informal support networks in achieving health and well-being among diverse groups of incarcerated persons.

Current Practice, Policy, and Social Movement Trends and Debates

Disadvantaged racial and ethnic minorities in the United States have long been overrepresented in the criminal justice systems (Iguchi, Bell, Ramchand, & Fain, 2005). Particular attention should be given to subgroups that experience higher prevalence of chronic diseases such as hypertension, coronary heart disease, and diabetes. Although racial and ethnic minority groups are considered a hard-to-reach population to engage in health care research (Benoit, Jansson, Miller, & Phillips, 2005), identifying and incorporating culturally appropriate practice approaches are challenging, yet necessary undertakings for forensic social workers.

With the Bureau of Justice Statistics (2015) reporting disproportionate increases in incarceration across groups (age, sex, race, and Hispanic origin) for the past three decades, it behooves social workers to be prepared to engage diversity and differences in practice, and to engage diverse individuals, families, groups, and communities in their efforts to achieve cultural competence in standards of practice. Taking into account these attributes, Black males have the highest rate of incarceration overall. Black or African American females are more likely to be incarcerated than females of other race/ethnic groups. Next to African Americans, Hispanics have the highest rate of incarceration nationwide, and persons of these race/ethnic groups receive the longest incarceration sentences (Bureau of Justice Statistics, 2015). In regards to the health profile among the general population, African Americans are twice as likely to die from certain noncurable diseases (i.e., cancer) as their White counterparts (U.S. Department of Health and Human Services, 2015) and have an even greater likelihood of requesting life-sustaining treatment at the end of life (Fried, Bullock, Iannone, & O'Leary, 2009). Scholars (Carriòn & Bullock, 2012; Smith, Sudore, & Perez-Stable, 2009) have argued that care for this population is inadequate and ineffective in terms of the provision of palliation and hospice referrals (National Hospice and Palliative Care Organization, 2016) in addition to being devoid of advance directives (Carriòn & Bullock, 2012; McKinley, Garrett, Evans, & Danis, 1996).

The elimination of health care disparities and ensuring the health care delivery system is responsive to minority groups is a national priority (Agency for Healthcare Research and Quality, 2015). Forensic social work models allow practitioners to move beyond a medical model's conceptualization, taking into account linkages between and among culture, psychosocial dynamics, and the person in environment (Dewees & Lax, 2009). The strength of an intervention can correlate directly with the effectiveness of treatment plans that drive it, as well as the case management to monitor and promote success among persons at risk of poor health care outcomes. In regards to higher morbidity rates among incarcerated persons, there was a call for action almost two decades ago to improve treatment for chronic conditions and preventive services for females and elderly inmates (Lindquist & Lindquist, 1999). However, social work services are designed to promote and maintain health and wellness. Ideally, the goals for care would focus on preventing illness and treating the "whole" person, with attention given to the psychosocial–spiritual and emotional needs of the consumer of services. Incarceration should not be a barrier to culturally appropriate, quality care. The forensic social worker should advocate for high-quality care that engages the recipient of care as an autonomous decision maker with the right to self-determine, to the degree that inmates are permitted to self-determine, during such life transitions and difficult periods of stress associated with chronic illness, terminal illness, and a life sentence in prison. Concomitantly, it is important to allow dignity and self-worth to prevail when there is a shift toward less autonomous treatment planning to focus services more on those disabling health conditions that may make it difficult for the individual to achieve personal self-fulfillment, intensified by criminal justice-managed care and other institutional policies and regulations. Mental health decline, for example, may be one of those disability health conditions.

Core Roles and Functions of Forensic Social Work in This System

Cantor (1991) proposed a social care model over two decades ago that is still very useful in understanding the psychosocial components of a serious illness that becomes terminal. For many persons who are spending their lifetime in prison, or any years of their lives in which they are chronically incarcerated, at the center of a series of concentric events of illness there is an ever-widening and more formal domain of care that they need. For an older person who is incarcerated, the problems are magnified and surrounded by a myriad of needs. Each phase of care, potentially, leads to more formal care needs when, perhaps, the older person has spent a lifetime relying on informal supports for his or her care needs, including family members, friends, and even church and/or other community members. For many persons of racial and ethnic minority populations, the care providers and care recipients engage in an interdependent, reciprocal model of care (Bullock, Crawford, & Tennstedt, 2003; Mehta, Sudharsanan, & Elo, 2013). This level of engagement with informal support members is not possible for incarcerated persons in criminal justice systems. These persons of racial/ethnic minority groups may be accustomed to family members and informal community supports typically being the foundation of a caregiving network and receiving supplemental care from fictive kin, friends, and neighbors (Bullock, Crawford, & Tennstedt, 2003), while formal providers were not visible nor welcomed into some cultural networks as a care option, especially among people who did not have health insurance or access to health care prior to incarceration.

The roles and function of forensic social workers who provide services to persons with these cultural norms can be expanded using a broader ecological framework and the applied social care model to develop intervention strategies and care plans. Psychosocial barriers to health care utilization may begin on the individual level with emotions, such as fear and denial about the health condition, in a confined environment that limits decision-making capacity and options. Furthermore, mistrust of formal providers can make the engagement and rapport phase of the contact with inmates challenging for practitioners (Carrión & Bullock, 2012). When barriers are not appropriately identified as such nor addressed or dismantled, the individual in need may forgo or refuse the available treatment options offered by the social workers. The Standards and Indicators for Cultural Competence in Social Work Practice (National Association for Social Workers, 2015) "reinforce the concept of culture as being inclusive beyond race and ethnicity; inclusive of, but not limited to, sexual orientation, gender identity and expression, and religious identity or spirituality." Similarly, these standards reinforce practice norms and expectations for social work practice at the micro, mezzo, and macro levels. Furthermore, there is intersectionality between micro, mezzo, and macro components of the social environment and living conditions that influence the health and well-being of individuals, families, groups, and communities.

Relevant Theories or Frameworks

The World Health Organization (2010) maintains that health is the condition of "complete physical, mental, and social well-being and not merely the absence of disease or infirmity." Access to care within correctional facilities, especially jails and prisons, has been deemed to be less than adequate in terms of meeting the health care needs of incarcerated persons. One explanation may be related to the findings that minority groups tend to have poorer outcomes in health intervention programs (Saloner & Le Cook, 2013; Snowden, 2001). However, we argue that mental health intervention with incarcerated, racial, and ethnic minority persons is a neglected area of research and practice. The lack of educational promotion of mental health interventions with and among family members and informal support networks warrants attention. Increasing literacy among any group of people includes outreach and education campaigns to bring about awareness (Rickard, Hall, & Bullock, 2015). Furthermore, the literature that addresses health care in jails confirms the lack of attention given to holistic care theories and models (Kulkarni, Baldwin, Lightstone, Gelberg, & Diamant, 2010; Lindquist & Lindquist, 1999; Pew Charitable Trusts, 2008).

Theories that frame the discourse on behavioral change actions tend to be psychodynamic in nature and function. Cognitive theories are among this classification of theories and are well known as cognitive behavioral theories. They developed in response to behavioral psychology's exclusive focus on actions and behavior. Cognitive theorists view breakdown in mental health as the result of faulty or irrational thinking and underlying beliefs. Research (Ellis & Ellis, 2011) has identified irrational beliefs central to mental health function, while perhaps there is actually a cognitive triad associated with poor mental health outcomes and behaviors (WHO, 2004). This negative cognitive triad consists of negative thoughts related to self (e.g., "I'm defective"), the world (e.g., "all I do results in failure"), and the future (e.g., "it's hopeless"). Both of these research studies suggest that people with poor mental health tend to ignore positive information, dwell on the negative, and overgeneralize. Ellis and Ellis (2011) developed rational emotive behavior therapy as a means to address such conditions. Incarcerated persons may benefit from such intervention.

Cognitive behavioral therapy tends to be a short-term, present-focused framework. This therapeutic approach incorporates action-oriented components, as well as didactic instruction on the presumed connection between cognition and affect (i.e., between thoughts and feelings). Understanding how culturally competent assessments can inform this framework and lead to successful negotiations in a treatment plan blends theory and practice frameworks for effectiveness. Furthermore, members of informal support networks can participate in family group conferencing to augment the social worker's impact and legitimize the importance of the intervention with the incarcerated person. A well-designed study to examine the two approaches is warranted. It is important to incorporate the cultural competence standards and indicators (NASW, 2015) to guide the implementation and evaluation of evidence-based practices.

Relevant Ethical, Legal, and Policy Issues

Since the United States has an incarceration rate four times that of the world average and we imprison more women than any other country worldwide (Hartney, 2006), forensic social work should be at the forefront of creating knowledge for best practices among forensic social workers. In 2001, at a meeting on minority health disparities sponsored by the National Institute on Drug Abuse, researchers outlined and explicated how the disproportionate entry of racial and ethnic minorities impacts their communities at large, especially upon their release from prison (Iguchi, Bell, Ramchand, & Fain, 2005). In a more recent study, Kulkarni et al. (2010) examined whether or not a lifetime history of incarceration was associated with access to medical and dental care. They found that incarceration history was independently associated with disparities in access to care. The progress of implementing health care reform in prisons has been slow.

Prison communities and/or facilities, both public (federal, state, county) and private institutions, are grappling with the issue of how best to meet the demands for health care for the chronically ill, terminally ill, and the elderly, although prisoners are constitutionally guaranteed rights to community-standard care, as legislated in the 1976 Supreme Court case *Estelle v. Gamble* (Bonczar, 2003). The knowledge gap about best practices that inform relevant ethical, legal, and policy issues is widening as correctional institutions continue to be tasked with the responsibility of responding to policy makers with recommendations for addressing health disparities in prisons (Ahalt et al., 2015; U.S. Department of Justice, 2004).

Relevant Assessment, Prevention, and Intervention Strategies

Having outlined the health care challenges that practitioners face with providing care for diverse populations in correctional institutions, the evidence for culturally competent approaches to assessment, prevention, and intervention becomes apparent. Understanding theoretical perspectives and frameworks for engaging chronically ill, terminally ill, and elderly prisoners can improve practitioners' awareness and skill level for working effectively across groups and for developing culturally appropriate treatment plans. Many people are denied access to services, including access to nursing homes, because of their incarceration histories (Maschi & Koskinen, 2015). Moreover, older adults who have been formerly incarcerated continue to be exposed to social injustices that often began with limited access to health care, jobs, and career advancement opportunities.

Culture represents race, class, ethnicity and a whole host of other differences that can facilitate or impede intervention strategies. For practitioners, the capacity to design and implement culturally relevant assessment tools requires that they ask questions about the values, attitudes, norms, and traditions of the inmate's worldview and unique needs for psychosocial care. Avoid stereotypes and bias, which can undermine the provider–recipient relationship. Instead, ask guiding questions that enable individuals to "tell their story" and create narrative data, which can be incorporated into prevention strategies. Incorporating informal supports in family group conferencing has proven to be effective with health care research (Carriòn & Bullock, 2012) as well as didactic educational interventions that increase health literacy (Kulkarni et al., 2010). Knowing what has worked in the past, at the micro, mezzo, and macro levels, and what has not, can be constructive data for developing and delivering care that is responsive to a wide range of needs and to diverse populations. Because lived experiences, customs, traditions, and values affect how individuals and groups make decisions, identifying these cultural components is a tool for successful engagement. If the goal of care is to ensure that all persons receive optimal care, knowledge and skills must be honed to address disparities among disenfranchised populations.

Forensic Practice Skill Set

The key to address the challenges of a more inclusive practice model is to identify and incorporate culturally appropriate and effective assessment tools and strategies. Flexible screening tools that are used to identify the complexity of health needs, either physical, mental, or emotional, that may cause inmates functional difficulty in their daily lives, including getting along with others, are essential. It is important to develop and administer screening questions that identify circumstances associated with diverse experiences and provide critical information that leads to person-centered decisions about treatment and/or desired outcomes. Practice skills that align with cultural competence standards (NASW, 2015) can inform policy and programming to ensure effective, efficient, and humane programming for inmates in all correctional institutes. Public health homes grew out of policies with a social justice focus and were intended to create access to primary care providers for persons with low income to take advantage of the services. Vulnerable populations receive care, including comprehensive medical, nutrition services, outreach, health education, and case management, from the "safety net" providers. However, state spending on prison health care peaked before 2011 and federal programs, such as Medicaid, have historically played a very limited role in covering inmate health care costs (Gates, Artiga, & Rudowitz, 2014).

Forensic social workers were challenged in figuring out how to provide the plethora of much-needed services, including emergency services, diagnosis, treatment, referral, and community education and coordination. Promoting health literacy, and the engagement of informal support networks in health intervention, may help to bridge gaps in the development and delivery of care that is intended to eliminate disparities.

Case Example and Application

Jose is a 70-year-old Hispanic man. He has a life sentence in a maximum security prison after repeated criminal offenses, with one resulting in the death of another person. He was brought to see the social worker–doctor's office because of his continuous complaints regarding pain in his legs and hands over the past months. He was diagnosed with arthritis about five years ago, but felt strongly that a doctor "can help" him. Additionally, Jose was diagnosed with type 2 diabetes, hypertension, and kidney problems that resulted from 30 years of alcohol use and abuse. Although he is still able to do many things for himself, Jose is becoming more disoriented and confused cognitively.

According to his family informants, Jose has always been a stoic man. He found comfort in his faith community and the close friends he played cards with at the local bar. He and his wife have five grown children and 12 grandchildren. All lived in the city, and the correctional institution where he now resides is a three-hour bus ride "upstate." They kept in touch mostly by phone and as often as they could.

Recently, Jose has developed vision problems and painful rheumatoid arthritis. As a result, he spends long hours in his bed, with very little physical activity incorporated into his daily life. Jose does not like relying on people for help and is reluctant to burden his friends (inmates) with helping him. He now also refuses formal intervention and does not take his medications as prescribed. Most recently, he has started to feel tired all the time and has trouble concentrating and sleeping at night. Overall, Jose feels useless and devalued as a human being. The recurring thought in his head is: "It just was not supposed to be this way."

Conclusion

Disadvantaged racial and ethnic minorities in the United States have long been overrepresented in the criminal justice systems. The elimination of health care disparities and ensuring the health care delivery system is responsive to minority groups is a social justice issue. The roles and function of forensic social workers that provide services to persons with these cultural norms can be expanded using a broader ecological framework and the applied social care model to develop intervention strategies and care plans with incarceration persons. Identifying and incorporating culturally appropriate practice approaches are challenging, yet necessary undertakings for forensic social workers.

CHAPTER EXERCISES

Exercise 1. How would you proceed to assess Jose's psychosocial needs? What information in the case example is most significant? Why?

Exercise 2. What are some areas to target for assessment to ensure cultural competence in the intervention plan?

Additional Resources

Books

Britto, S., & Beck, E. (2009). *In the shadow of death: Restorative justice and death row families.* New York, NY: Oxford University Press.

Delgado, M., & Humm-Delgado, D. (2008). *Health and health care in the nation's prisons: Issues, challenges, and policies.* Lanham, MD: Rowan & Littlefield.

Johnston, D., & Sullivan, M. (2016). *Parental incarceration: Personal accounts and developmental impact.* New York, NY: Routledge.

Reports

Health in Prisons: A WHO Guide to the Essentials in Prison Health: www.euro.who.int/__data/assets/pdf_file/0009/99018/E90174.pdf

This guide outlines some of the steps prison systems should take to reduce the public health risks from compulsory detention in often unhealthy situations, to care for prisoners in need, and to promote the health of prisoners and staff. This especially requires that everyone working in prisons understand well how imprisonment affects health and the health needs of prisoners and that evidence-based prison health services can be provided for everyone needing treatment, care, and prevention.

Online Resources

Forensic Healthcare Online: www.forensichealth.com

Forensic Healthcare Online offers information for the purpose of enhancing clinical excellence by promoting scientific literature, peer-reviewed technical guidance, and free and low-cost continuing education. It serves as a gateway to a variety of professional services, from curriculum development to training to expert witness testimony, offered by forensic clinicians. The site does not provide legal advice on any matters.

The Justia Agenda

American Civil Liberties Union—Healthcare Not Handcuffs: www.drugpolicy.org/sites/default/files/Healthcare_Not_Handcuffs_12.17.pdf

The Center for Prisoner Health and Human Rights: www.prisonerhealth.org

Federal Interagency Reentry Council: https://csgjusticecenter.org/reentry/issue-areas/health/health-policy

The Justia Agenda: http://justiaagenda.com

The mission of the Justia Agenda is to build awareness of and take action on human rights and social justice issues through research, practice, advocacy, writing, and education. Justia Agenda activities foster reflection, dialogue, and action on how human rights and social justice can be realized in everyday and professional practice.

References

Agency for Healthcare Research and Quality. (2009). AHRQ activities to reduce racial and ethnic disparities in health care. Rockville, MD: Author. Retrieved from http://www.ahrq.gov/research/findings/factsheets/minority/disparities/index.html

Agency for Healthcare Research and Quality. (2015). *2015 national healthcare quality and disparities report and 5th anniversary update on national quality strategy*. Retrieved from https://www.ahrq.gov/sites/default/files/wysiwyg/research/findings/nhqrdr/nhqdr15/2015nhqdr.pdf

Ahalt, C., Bolano, M., Wang, E. A., & Williams, B. (2015). The state of research funding from the National Institutes of Health for criminal justice health research. *Annual of Internal Medicine, 162*(2), 345–352.

Benoit, C., Jansson, M., Miller, A., & Phillips, R. (2005). Community-academic research on hard-to-reach populations. Benefits and challenges. *Qualitative Health Research, 15*(2), 263–282.

Bonczar, T. P. (2003). *Prevalence of imprisonment in the U.S. population, 1974–2001*. National Center for Justice 19796. Washington, DC: U.S. Department of Justice, Office of Justice Programs, Bureau of Justice Statistics.

Bullock, K., & Allison, H. (2015). Access to medical treatment for African American populations: The current evidence base. In G. Christ, C. Messner, & L. Behar (Eds.), *Handbook of oncology social work* (pp. 293–298). New York, NY: Oxford University Press.

Bullock, K., Crawford, S. L., & Tennstedt, S. L. (2003). Employment and caregiving: An exploration of African American caregivers. *Social Work, 48*(2), 150–162.

Bullock, K., Hall, J. K., & Leach, M. T. (2013). End-of-life care. In K. E. Whitfield & T. A. Baker (Eds.), *Handbook of minority aging* (pp. 265–276). New York, NY: Springer Publishing.

Bullock, K., & Volkel, J. (2014). Culturally competent care in an increasingly diverse society. In C. Staudt & J. H. Ellens (Eds.), *Our changing journey to the end: Reshaping death, dying, and grief in America* (Vol. 2, pp. 145–158). Santa Barbara, CA: Praeger.

Bureau of Justice Statistics. (2015). Correction Statistical Analysis Tool (CSAT)–Prisoners. Retrieved from http://www.bjs.gov/index.cfm?ty=nps

Camp, G., & Camp, C. (2001). *The corrections yearbook, 2001*. Middletown, CT: Criminal Justice Institute.

Cantor, M. H. (1991). Family and community: Changing roles in an aging society. *The Gerontologist, 31*(3), 337–346.

Carriòn, I. V., & Bullock, K. (2012). A case of Hispanics and hospice care. *International Journal of Humanities and Social Sciences, 2*(4), 9–16.

Center on Juvenile and Criminal Justice. (2008). Proof of facts, 3D series (Vol. 103). Retrieved from http://www.cjcj.org/uploads/cjcj/documents/proof_of_facts-expert_testimony_at_sentencing.pdf

Delgado, M. (2014). *Baby boomers of color: Implications for social work policy and practice*. New York, NY: Columbia University Press.

Dewees, M., & Lax, L. K. (2009). A critical approach to pedagogy in mental health. *Social Work in Mental Health, 7*(1–3), 82–201.

Ellis, A., & Ellis, D. J. (2011). *Rational emotive behavior therapy.* Washington, DC: American Psychological Association.

Fried, T. R., Bullock, K., Iannone, L., & O'Leary, J. R. (2009). Understanding advance care planning as a process of health behavior change. *Journal of the American Geriatrics Society, 57*(9), 1547–1555.

Gates, A., Artiga, S., & Rudowitz, R. (2014). Health coverage and care for the adult criminal justice-involved population. The Henry J. Kaiser Family Foundation. Retrieved from http://kff .org/uninsured/issue-brief/health-coverage-and-care-for-the-adult-criminal-justice-involved -population

Hall, J. K., & Bullock, K. (2015). A practicum partnership approach to addressing barriers to mental health among racially diverse older adults. *International Journal of Humanities & Social Sciences, 5*(8), 10–19.

Hartney, C. (2006). Research from the National Council on Crime and Delinquency: U.S. rates of incarcerations. Retrieved from http://www.nccdglobal.org/sites/default/files/publication_pdf/ factsheet-us-incarceration.pdf

Hochstetler, A., Murphy, D. S., & Simons, R. L. (2004). Damaged goods: Exploring predictors of distress in prison inmates. *Crime and Delinquency, 50*, 436–457.

Hofrichter, R., & Bhatia, R. (Eds.). (2010). *Tackling health inequities through public health practices.* New York, NY: Oxford University Press.

Iguchi, M. Y., Bell, J., Ramchand, R. N., & Fain, T. (2005). How criminal system racial disparities may translate into health disparities. *Journal of Health Care for the Poor and Underserved, 16*, 48–56.

Kulkarni, S. P., Baldwin, S., Lightstone, A. S., Gelberg, L., & Diamant, A. L. (2010). Is incarceration a contributor to health disparities? Access to care for formerly incarcerated adults. *Journal of Community Health, 35*(3), 268–274.

Lindquist, C. H., & Lindquist, C. A. (1999). Health behind bars: Utilization and evaluation of medical care among jail inmates. *Journal of Community Health, 24*(4), 285–303.

Maruschak, L. M. (2008). *Medical problems of prisoners* (NCJ Publication No. 221740). Rockville, MD: U.S. Department of Justice.

Maschi, T., & Koskinen, L. (2015). Co-constructing community: A conceptual map of reuniting aging people in prison with the families and communities. *Traumatology, 21*(3), 208–218.

Maschi, T., Viola, D., Morgen, K., & Koskinen, L. (2015). Trauma, stress, grief, loss, and separation among older adults in prison: The protective role of coping resources on physical and mental well-being. *Journal of Crime and Justice, 38*(1), 113–136.

McKinley, E., Garrett, J., Evans, A., & Danis, M. (1996). Differences in end-of-life decision making among Black and White ambulatory cancer patients. *Journal of General Medicine, 11*, 651–656.

Mehta, N. K., Sudharsanan, N., & Elo, I. T. (2013). Race/ethnicity and disability among older Americans. In K. E. Whitfield & T. A. Baker (Eds.), *Handbook of minority aging* (pp. 111–130). New York, NY: Springer Publishing.

Miles, T. P., & Smith, M. L. (2013). Does health care quality contribute to disparities? An examination of aging and minority status issues in America. In K. E. Whitfield & T. A. Baker (Eds.), *Handbook of minority aging* (pp. 237–256). New York, NY: Springer Publishing.

National Association for the Advancement of Colored People. (2013). Criminal justice fact sheet. Retrieved from http://www.naacp.org/pages/criminal-justice-fact-sheet

National Association of Social Workers. (2008). *Code of ethics.* Retrieved from http://www.socialworkers .org/pubs/code/code.asp

National Association of Social Workers. (2015). *NASW standards and indicators for cultural competence in social work practice*. Retrieved from https://www.socialworkers.org/practice/standards/index.asp

National Hospice and Palliative Care Organization. (2016). Facts and figures: Hospice care in America. Retrieved from http://www.nhpco.org/sites/default/files/public/Statistics_Research/2015_Facts_Figures.pdf

Pew Charitable Trusts. (2008). The Pew Center on the States: One in 100—behind bars in America 2002. Retrieved from http://www.pewtrusts.org

Pollard, W. L. (2008). Civil rights. In T. Mizrahl & L. E. Davis (Eds.), *Encyclopedia of social work* (20th ed., pp. 301–309). New York, NY: National Association of Social Workers Press and Oxford University Press.

Reimer, G. (2008). The graying of the U.S. prisoner population. *Journal of Correctional Health Care, 14,* 202–208.

Rickard, R. V., Hall, J. K., & Bullock, K. (2015). Health literary as a barrier to trauma-informed care across diverse groups. *Traumatology, 21*(3), 227–236.

Sabol, W. J., & Couture, H. (2008). *Prison inmates at midyear 2007* (NCJ Publication No. 221944). Rockville, MD: U.S. Department of Justice.

Saloner, B., & Le Cook, B. (2013). Blacks and Hispanics are less likely than Whites to complete addiction treatment, largely due to socioeconomic factors. *Health Affairs, 32*(1), 135–145.

Smith, A. K., Sudore, R. L., & Perez-Stable, E. J. (2009). Palliative care for Latino patients and their families: Whenever we prayed, she wept. *Journal of the American Medical Association, 301*(10), 1047–1057.

Snowden, L. R. (2001). Barriers to effective mental health services for African Americans. *Mental Health Services, 3*(4), 181–187.

Stansbury, K. L., Peterson, S. L., & Bleecher, B. (2013). An exploration of mental health literacy among older African Americans. *Aging & Mental Health, 17*(2), 226–232.

U.S. Department of Health and Human Services. (2015, December 2). HHS action plan to reduce racial and ethnic health disparities: Implementation progress report 2011–2014. Retrieved from https://minorityhealth.hhs.gov/assets/pdf/FINAL_HHS_Action_Plan_Progress_Report_11_2_2015.pdf

U.S. Department of Justice. (2004). *Health care: Addressing the needs of elderly, chronically ill, and terminally ill inmates*. Washington, DC: National Institutes of Corrections.

Williams, M. E., & Rickard, R. V. (2004). Marginality or neglect: An exploratory study of policies and programs for aging female inmates. *Women & Criminal Justice, 15*(3/4), 121–141.

World Health Organization. (2004). Prevention of mental disorders: Effective interventions and policy options [Summary report] (pp. 1–65). Geneva, Switzerland: Author. Retrieved from http://www.who.int/mental_health/evidence/en/prevention_of_mental_disorders_sr.pdf

World Health Organization. (2010). WHO definitions of health. Retrieved from http://www.who.int/maternal_child_adolescent/topics/quality-of-care/definition/en

VOICES FROM THE FIELD

Gia N. Marshall, LCSW
Clinical Social Worker
North Carolina Correctional Institution for Women

Agency Setting

The North Carolina Correctional Institution for Women (NCCIW) is the primary correctional facility for women in the state. It consists of all custody levels and control statuses including death row, maximum, close, medium, minimum, and safe keepers. The facility houses over 1,600 offenders and is the central processing center for all women entering the prison system. NCCIW provides the primary medical, mental, and alcohol and chemical dependency treatment for female offenders.

Practice Responsibilities

As a Licensed Clinical Social Worker at the NCCIW, my responsibilities are vast. I manage a mental health caseload of 60 to 70 patients seen every 30 to 45 days or sooner if needed. Review and recommendation of older Americans With Disabilities Act (ADA) accommodation requests are completed as assigned. I provide crisis coverage one day a week on the outpatient mental health unit, as well as facilitating mental health restrictive housing checks on offenders in segregation. Medical aftercare for all referred offenders is provided. This could include one or all of the following: scheduling follow-up medical equipment and securing medically appropriate housing, assisting in applying for Medicaid and/or Social Security benefits on an as-needed basis, along with coordinating all approved medical releases for end-stage terminally ill or medically fragile cases. NCCIW does not currently house hospice patients in the inpatient infirmary; therefore, those patients are generally approved for medical release and I will identify and coordinate medically appropriate housing: hospice, skilled nursing facility, or private residence with additional in-home hospice/medical care. I facilitate the patient/offender's signing of a release form allowing specific departments within the Department of Public Safety (DPS) to access patient medical information. The patient signs an authorization for release forms prior to releasing any medical information on the individual. Health care benefits are obtained if benefits were not approved prior to incarceration. If benefits were being received prior to incarceration, efforts are made to ensure reinstatement upon placement into DPS-approved setting. An attending physician in the community must be identified for the patient/offender and a signed memorandum from the physician agreeing to provide care must be obtained. If the patient/offender is on a mental health caseload, a brief statement from the psychologist/psychiatrist indicating the course of treatment and follow-up recommended after release must be secured. The name and contact information for the mental health provider must also be obtained. Contact is made and maintained with the patient/offender's next of kin to keep them abreast of the medical release/aftercare plan. Once all aspects of the release are in place, an official medical release/aftercare plan is drawn up and forwarded to the DPS risk manager.

Expertise Required

A formal master's degree in clinical social work in the area of mental health along with a Licensed Clinical Social Work (LCSW) qualification are the initial requirements to include continuous educational training in the area of practice, along with exploration of other clinical areas. Specific areas and expertise that would prove valuable to the social worker providing medical aftercare and end-stage life care would be policies and procedures governing medical treatment of offenders, patient rights, ethics and diversity, geriatric care, hospice, and grief therapy. Possessing competent skill sets in the areas of empathy, compassion, commitment, advocacy, and case management, while maintaining professional boundaries with the patient/offender and his or her family, when necessary, is crucial to the delivery of quality and human services.

Ethical, Legal, Practice, Diversity, and/or Advocacy Issues Addressed

Maintaining the privacy and confidentiality of all patients is paramount and is done by ensuring that Authorization for Release of Information forms are signed by patients before disclosing any medical information to referring agencies. Due to the varying cultures within the prison system, efforts are made to respect the ethical imperatives of each patient, as long as they do not pose a conflict with the policies of the N.C. Department of Public Safety. Tireless efforts are spent in advocacy for incarcerated patients. I have found many skilled nursing facilities across North Carolina to be biased in accepting incarcerated patients even with nonviolent crimes. For some, the hardship of untimely financial reimbursement is communicated as the reason for denial and for some no specific reason is provided; others simply reserve the right to deny active offenders. However, the two experiences I have had with actual hospice placements have been wonderful.

Interprofessional and Intersectoral Collaboration

When coordinating services for medical release it is often a necessity to consult with the following: nursing bed manager, the attending physician, the attending psychologist/psychiatrist, referring mental health providers, the physical therapist, the director of nursing, the medical director, the hospital administrator, the Department of Public Safety risk manager, parole officers, the community attending physician, Medicaid case worker and/or supervisors, Social Security administration, and hospice or skilled nursing facility administrators.

CHAPTER 7

Housing

Tam Perry
Vanessa Rorai
Claudia Sanford

CHAPTER OBJECTIVES

The major objectives of this chapter are to:

- Enhance understanding of the multifaceted challenges that individuals, especially older adults, seeking housing with a criminal background face (Section One).
- Review the ways in which individuals, especially older adults, can be vulnerable in terms of safety and security in their housing settings (Section Two).
- Discuss ways in which forensic practitioners can support vulnerable populations, including older adults.

CHAPTER COMPETENCIES HIGHLIGHTED

- Competency 3: Advance Human Rights and Social, Economic, and Environmental Justice
- Competency 5: Engage in Policy Practice
- Competency 9: Evaluate Practice With Individuals, Families, Organizations, and Communities

Section One: Older Adults Seeking Housing With a Criminal Background

Affordable and safe housing is a concern for many individuals in the United States. Options depend on one's financial situation, family network, and the make-up of one's community supports. Identifying and applying for rental housing can be a time of uncertainty as applications are subject to scrutiny by professionals who may not know the individual's character, as well as his or her ability to get along with other tenants and to follow the rules of the housing complex. For those seeking government-subsidized housing, this uncertainty can be compounded if they have a criminal background that is identified on the application. These issues of access and accompanying discrimination are complex across all age groups; however, they become complicated for older adults who may be concerned with navigability of housing available (e.g., working elevator) and experiencing physical and mental health concerns and related expenses (e.g., prescription costs). With the expertise of the authors, we offer a perspective on how these processes affect older adults. However, we emphasize that housing stability is a challenge for many vulnerable populations including low-income and other marginalized populations (Perry, Archambault, & Sanford, in press), and hope that the insights brought forth here through the lens of older adults can be applied by the readers for the populations they work with and as they advocate for equitable, safe, and affordable housing. Therefore, the remainder of the chapter discusses the complexities of affordable and safe housing using case examples and descriptions focusing on the older adult population.

Background and Scope of the Problem

As of 2014, there are 46.2 million older adults living in the United States, which makes up 14.5% of the country's population (U.S. Department of Health and Human Services, Administration for Community Living, Administration on Aging, 2015). This population is expected to more than double to 98 million by 2060 (U.S. Department of Health and Human Services, Administration for Community Living, Administration on Aging, 2015). Within the older adult population, 22% self-identify as a minority with the majority being African American (9%), followed by Hispanic (8%) (U.S. Department of Health and Human Services, Administration for Community Living, Administration on Aging, 2015). Looking at the income level of older adults within the United States reveals that, in 2014, over 10% of older adults were below the poverty line. Falling below the poverty line does not affect all older Americans equally; more African American (19.2%) than White (7.8%) and Hispanic (18.1%) older adults fall below the poverty line. However, it is important to note the relatively new Supplemental Poverty Measure (SPM) released by the Census Bureau to provide a more accurate measure of poverty among the elderly. The SPM includes collecting information on impacting costs to older adults such as housing costs, food stamps, low-income tax credits, and out-of-pocket medical expenses. Although the SPM does not replace the official measure of poverty, when taking these impacting costs into account, it reports a higher level of poverty for older adults at 14.4% compared to the official poverty measure of 10% (U.S. Department of Health and Human Services, Administration for Community Living, Administration on Aging, 2015).

A deeper look at the older adults living in subsidized housing provides a clearer understanding of this population. Based on the 2010 Census, there are just over 5 million subsidized units available across the country with a 92% occupancy rate (U.S. Department of HUD, Office of Policy Development and Research, 2015). Of those living in subsidized housing, 33% are aged 62 years or older and 65% self-identified as a minority (U.S. Department of HUD, Office of Policy Development and Research, 2015). Thus, the difficulty of securing housing can be compounded for those with a criminal record.

System and Population Overview

The population in focus concerns older adults who are aged 65 years and older and live in public housing. Although these individuals function within several systems, scarcity of available housing is the system in focus. However, a search for housing is layered in other systems, including the number of previously mentioned housing units available and occupancy rates. Acknowledging the interconnectedness of employment and financial well-being, one's ability to secure housing also depends on one's income levels, either through expected government payments like Social Security, Disability, or a pension. Depending on the length of incarceration, he or she may not have paid into Social Security for a sufficient number of years, and having a low income may result in choosing only among subsidized housing options (Center for Justice at Columbia University, 2015).

Current Practice, Policy, and Social Movement Trends and Debates

In April 2016, the Department of Housing and Urban Development (HUD) Office of General Council released "new" guidance for looking at one's criminal past when reviewing the Tenant Selection Plan (TSP) for Section 8 Housing, which includes project-based housing. Each property must submit a TSP that is nondiscriminatory and related to program eligibility. Property managers review applicants for eligibility including U.S. residency, age, income, credit history, rental history, and criminal background. HUD states that "because of widespread racial and ethnic disparities in the U.S. criminal justice system, criminal history-based restriction on access to housing are likely disproportionately to burden African-Americans and Hispanics" (HUD Fair Housing Act Standards, 2016).

A housing provider's use of a blanket policy to deny housing based on criminal history without considering other factors would likely be a violation of the Fair Housing Act even if it is not the intention of the provider to discriminate. This screening policy would have a disparate impact on racial minorities and includes policies that deny housing based on a prior arrest that may not have resulted in a conviction. This does not mean that housing providers cannot consider criminal history; they have the option to look at the nature and severity of the crime and whether the individual, in their opinion, would still pose a threat to the community.

> Policies that exclude persons based on criminal history must be tailored to serve the housing provider's substantial, legitimate, nondiscriminatory interest and take into consideration such factors as the type of the crime and the length of the time since conviction. (HUD Fair Housing Act Standards, 2016)

Persons who have been *convicted* of manufacturing or distributing drugs are not covered under the Fair Housing Act.

HUD requires that the housing provider chooses a less discriminatory way of screening applicants—one that does not look at criminal record alone but one that looks at the individual and the offense. The Office of General Counsel Guidance outlines a three-step process for analyzing the discriminatory effect of denying housing based on criminal background alone:

- Evaluating whether the criminal history policy or practice has a discriminatory effect
- Evaluating whether the challenged policy or practice is necessary to achieve a substantial, legitimate, nondiscriminatory interest
- Evaluating whether there is a less discriminatory alternative

Core Roles and Functions of Forensic Social Work in This System

Forensic practitioners need to be aware and intervene in the following ways. Most often a person applying to Section 8 Housing would be applying directly to a property of his or her choice based on income and physical needs. More often than not, if that person is denied, he or she just walks away and seeks housing elsewhere; this housing could be a weekly rental at a single rent occupancy (SRO), a shelter, or living on the street. Some applicants who are already connected to a service provider might seek assistance if they are denied housing. When housing providers assist someone who has a criminal conviction, they can look at the circumstances around that conviction, nature of the crime, and when it was committed, and advise the tenant on his or her rights based on the current HUD policies. In addition, a forensic practitioner can assist the applicant if denied housing with requesting an appeal and can even accompany the applicant to the appeal. Not all housing providers understand the new HUD guidance and would not understand the Fair Housing issues around the decision. A forensic practitioner would be able to verbalize the guidelines better than many tenants.

HUD's new guidance in the screening of applicants for housing prevents exclusion for arrest without conviction and places the burden of proving that any policy regarding criminal convictions is not contrary to the Fair Housing Act on the housing provider.

Relevant Theories or Frameworks

Intersectionality

To understand the challenges of a low-income older-adult population residing in public housing and their experiences with (a) the justice system and its impact on their ability to find housing, or as addressed in Section Two, and/or (b) the potential for older adults to be victims of crimes in their residences, a theoretical framework that addresses multiple identities may serve as a useful perspective (Crenshaw, 1991). Intersectionality theory provides a lens to understand how multiple types of identity contribute to one's health and well-being (Crenshaw, 1991); conversely, it is understanding how the intersection of multiple experiences of marginalization due to race, class, gender, sexual orientation, and, relevant for this book, criminal history and/or potential to be victimized connect with the aging experience. Importantly, scholars have explored how these intersectional inequalities are reproduced in differing social spaces (from social roles in the family to social roles in the workplace), and how these reactions also contribute to maintenance of these stratified opportunities (Tilly, 1998; Verloo, 2013).

From a criminal justice perspective, recent work has examined how multiple facets of identity shape one's experience with the criminal justice system counteracting a dominant paradigm of analyzing identity categories as separate and distinct when analyzing this population. Given the great inequities of racial representation in the U.S. justice system, some scholars are promoting a qualitative look at experiences of identity with this population, emphasizing the importance of self-perception and the perception of others in terms of how threatening or how deviant a person is assessed to be (Trahan, 2011).

Scholars have particularly examined the combination of important identities such as race and gender and its impact on health from both a quantitative and qualitative perspective. Warner and Brown (2011) explored race and gender in terms of how persons experience disability, finding that the levels of disability from order of least affected were White men, White women, and racial/ethnically non-White men, and at the top were Black and Hispanic women. They also noted the difference between the latter two groups, finding aging with disability accelerated for Black women. Other studies have underscored the usefulness of the intersectionality framework for understanding social ties and its impact on depression for older adults (Mair, 2010).

Relevant Ethical, Legal, and Policy Issues

HUD cites that people with criminal convictions have less recidivism when they have access to housing and that the further in the past the conviction, the less likely an individual's prospect of committing another offense; eventually, the likelihood becomes the same as an individual without a criminal conviction (HUD Fair Housing Act Standards, 2016).

Perspectives From the Ground: Criminal Activity

How criminal offenses are dealt with depends on the onsite manager and policies of the management company. Some managers are sympathetic to the senior population; especially in the absence of a building service coordinator, they try to give the tenant a chance to change the behavior before moving forward with eviction proceedings. Some managers are punitive and issue eviction notices for any infraction without seeking outside assistance for the tenant.

Recently, one of the coauthors' agencies, United Community Housing Coalition, legally assisted two elderly tenants for drug dealing. One tenant who used an electric wheelchair for mobility had been working with a young man he stated was his "grandson"; according to the building manager he was not related to the senior. The grandson was using the tenant's apartment as a base for selling drugs. There did not appear to be any intimidation, and the tenant apparently was reaping a benefit from this activity. The second elderly tenant living in the same building also had mobility issues. He was essentially selling drugs out of his apartment and allowing the activity to take place in his unit. It also appeared that he was an addict. In the first case the onsite manager attempted to help the senior by restricting the grandson from entering the building but could not get cooperation from the tenant. Termination of tenancy cases were brought against both seniors.

The housing practitioner was able to make a deal through management and the attorney, before their court date, to give both men 30 days to move and a neutral reference. The judgment would be entered as consent and, along with a neutral reference, would give them the opportunity to find housing. The first senior was a veteran, whose mental status seemed to be deteriorating, so he would have support networks to assist him. The agency worked to understand the needs of these older adults throughout their cases.

Relevant Assessment, Prevention, and Intervention Strategies

Further work needs to be done in this area of intervention strategies as potential tenants prepare applications for housing. One way is to assist tenants in completing housing applications by answering questions honestly and succinctly. Often, tenants feel that they have to overexplain their past, possibly raising more questions than being helpful. For example, one of the coauthors assisted a tenant who had been convicted of manslaughter 10 years in the past and she wrote it in every blank space she could find on the page. By simply answering the question, she was accepted into a senior Section 8 building. Some applicants for low-income housing have poor written, verbal, and cognitive skills; without assistance, they would not be able to complete the application process, let alone understand how to cope with the issues around a criminal conviction. A forensic practitioner can help the applicant with completing the application and obtaining needed documents, and assist in understanding how to discuss his or her criminal background with a housing provider.

Forensic Practice Skill Set

Comprehensive case management skills are vital to working with postincarceration clients to successfully address housing and related needs. Helping clients fill out applications for housing in appropriate and supportive ways is important, as highlighted earlier. A significant related need is providing help with finding employment as some older adults also try to seek employment to supplement income. In 2015, about 3.8% of older adults 65 years and older were unemployed (U.S. Department of Health and Human Services, Administration for Community Living, Administration on Aging, 2015); however, that percentage may be misleading, since people may not be actively seeking employment or only seeking employment in part-time and informal positions. If older adults are seeking work, having a criminal record may inhibit their ability to obtain employment. Although obtaining employment has a strong connection to supporting oneself to pay for housing, in both cases—applications for housing and for employment—criminal records may be disclosed. Forensic practitioners should be informed on recent guidelines and movements for both employment and housing (e.g., the international campaign called "Ban the Box," which seeks to remove the criminal history check box on employment applications).

Case Example and Application

A 30-year-old male tenant, Mr. Jones, lived with his wife and child at a property housing seniors and persons with disabilities. Mr. Jones had been convicted of criminal sexual conduct in another state prior to his tenancy at the building. However, he had lived in this project-based Section 8 community for 12 years in good standing and now he had to relive this past offense over again. The family was denied a voucher based on his criminal conviction. Ultimately Mr. Jones opted to leave the family and move into a unit of his own so his wife and child would have the benefit of the Section 8 voucher.

In another case, a female tenant, Alexa, from a senior project-based Section 8 property contacted a tenant organizer for assistance. Her sister, Hannah, had been recently released from prison and wanted to move in with her. Her sister was not only denied tenancy at that property, she was banned from entering the building.

Section Two: Older Adult Safety and Security Concerns in Housing

Security and safety in one's residence are concerns across the life span. Various issues of safety can be experienced across all ethnicities, socioeconomic statuses, genders, and age groups. The authors have extensive experience working with older adults, which illustrates the unique impact these issues have on this vulnerable population; therefore, this section continues to focus on this age group. Older adults may be particularly concerned about security and safety at home because their homes have been shown to be places where they can be victimized, either by telephone scams, door-to-door solicitation, bullying in age-congregate settings, and witnessing other crimes occurring in their residences. The section also presents case studies of older adults in low-income senior housing, based on data collected in an urban setting following relocation of many seniors. When seniors are relocated, there is concern that their former social networks change. These social supports might have been helpful against victimization in multiple ways.

Background and Scope of the Problem

The issue of safety and security within public housing focuses on the same population as described earlier in the chapter: older adults aged 65 years and older who live in public housing. In 2014, the U.S. Department of Justice released a special report on crimes against older adults (Bureau of Justice Statistics, 2014). Results from this report revealed that during 2003 to 2013, older adults living in a variety of household settings experienced 2% of violence and 2% of serious violence each year across all ages within the United States. Among these experiences, 59% reported being victimized at or near their home. The report revealed that older adults experience crime at or near their home more than any other age group. Consequently, the most common type of crime older adults encountered was property crime (93%), which includes burglary and theft.

Older adult victims of property crime mostly lived in urban areas, followed by suburban and then rural areas. The only difference in rates of reporting crime based on age was older adults had higher rates of reporting crime than persons aged 12 to 24 years. It is worth noting that this special report limited data collection only to older adults living in household settings; thus, those living in facilities such as long-term care, hospitals, hospice, and the homeless were not included.

Bullying is one form of victimization older adults can experience in their housing settings. There has been little research conducted on elder-to-elder bullying as most research has focused on older adults being bullied by family members, caregivers, or professional staff. Consequently, few studies have investigated bullying within public housing (Parker-Cardinal, 2015). Forensic social workers need to understand the context their clients live within. It is imperative for forensic social workers to utilize this knowledge to gain accurate assessments of older adult clients that include sense of safety and security outside and within their home. While a review of bullying interventions is beyond the scope of this chapter, the authors encourage forensic practitioners to better understand the complex dynamics of bullying and to be attuned to the possibility of bullying and difficult peer relationships in congregate housing settings. In other words, having housing creates other challenges of vulnerability and victimization that may need to be addressed by forensic practitioners.

Perspectives From the Ground: Bullying

Bullying can also come from bad onsite managers, sometimes encouraged by uncaring owners. Onsite managers are important to the health of any senior building or project-based building. Some managers seem to lack the proper training in HUD regulations or how to assist tenants in crisis. Better standards for management companies and onsite managers would seem to be necessary and a requirement that all buildings have service coordinators not aligned with management. Service coordinators should be well trained in how to access services in the community, legal, drug treatment, mental health, and housing areas, when necessary.

For instance, one of the worst examples of bullying comes from drug dealers who take over vulnerable tenants' units. Management is sometimes so interested in keeping the appearance of being a model building that they suppress tenant complaints about drug dealing in the building and other illegal activities. They have even gone so far as to not allow local police in the building to deal with tenant complaints. From a macro perspective, well-organized and trained tenant groups are another way to assist tenants.

The next two sections provide further recommendations on other areas of assessment and intervention that forensic social workers can conduct.

Core Roles and Functions of Forensic Social Work in This System

Forensic practitioners need to be aware and intervene in the following ways. Assessment of older adults' housing concerns should also include an understanding of their social network and how their community may offer support or protection from victimization. Likewise, any relocation may alter one's social network, so investigating the proximity and density of social supports in a new residence and/or community is important to understand the older person's vulnerabilities. If an older adult is new to a community, it is important to broker community support to help with the transition and prevent/minimize victimization. Forensic social workers can work to develop and support tenant groups to address these issues as a building and to develop peer-led systems of support for residents.

Forensic Practice Skill Set

In addition to understanding vulnerabilities and potential for victimization, for work with older adults, knowledge of aging processes is useful for a skill set. Understanding the symptoms and signs of cognitive and physical decline, as well as the ability to assess one's social network, are important skills. In addition, understanding the meaning(s) of one's home and community, which is unique to every older adult, is vital to then assess what moving means to a senior. The skilled forensic practitioner understands how an older adult's physical, social, and emotional needs/well-being may be enhanced by a perception of safety where one lives. Lastly, social workers assigned to working with those in this process can help address these safety concerns and develop strategies. For example, if an older adult does not feel safe walking in the community at a certain time of day, the social worker may facilitate an assessment of reorganizing a daily schedule or participating in group "buddy" systems that both meets the older adult's needs and enhances safety and security.

Case Example and Application

Mrs. Yola is a new client. She is 74 years old and lives alone in an apartment building. She is able bodied and in good physical and mental health. She was recently forced to relocate from her previous apartment that she lived in for 15 years, to a new apartment building in a different neighborhood. You are responsible for assessing her needs and connecting her to any needed resources. While conducting your initial assessments, Mrs. Yola tells you she does not feel safe in her new apartment building owing to lack of security present. Mrs. Yola describes two recent robberies occurring within the building office and common areas, and suspects drug activity is happening within and outside the building. Mrs. Yola tells you she only feels safe to walk to the store during certain hours of the day owing to feeling unsafe walking alone in the neighborhood.

Conclusion

Addressing the severe housing needs of vulnerable populations, including older adults, requires understanding the difficulties in obtaining housing and the ways populations can be vulnerable in their residential communities. Interventions should support vulnerable populations in the application process and in assessing safety concerns in their housing environments. Forensic practice skill sets for social workers include supporting clients through housing applications and advocating for fair housing standards, as well as assessing cognitive and physical decline of the individuals and their social support networks to address safety concerns.

CHAPTER EXERCISES

Exercise 1. Given Mr. Jones' case, what would you address first? How would you proceed? How would you work with him? How would you work with members of his family?

Exercise 2. Given Alexa and her sister's challenges, whose interests would you prioritize? Alexa's or Hannah's? How can you support/advocate for both of them?

Exercise 3. In both cases, what are their logistical and psychosocial needs?

Exercise 4. What strategies would you devise with Mrs. Yola to help her feel safe?

Exercise 5. What strategies would you devise within your organization? Within the community?

Exercise 6. What areas of Mrs. Yola's life do you think are impacted by her low sense of safety in her home?

Exercise 7. What short-term plan of action would you develop for Mrs. Yola? What long-term plan of action would you develop?

Additional Resources

HUD guidelines on use of criminal records: www.enterprisecommunity.org/2016/04/guidelines-criminal-families

National Center on Elder Abuse: https://ncea.acl.gov

National Employment Law Project: www.nelp.org/campaign/ensuring-fair-chance-to-work

National Housing Law Project: https://nhlp.org/node/1253

National Low Income Housing Coalition: http://nlihc.org/article/hud-issues-bold-fair-housing-guidance-use-criminal-records

References

Bureau of Justice Statistics. (2014). Crimes against the elderly, 2003–2013 (Special Report NCJ 248339). Retrieved from http://www.bjs.gov/content/pub/pdf/cae0313.pdf

Center for Justice at Columbia University. (2015). Aging in prison: Reducing elder incarceration and promoting public safety. Retrieved from http://centerforjustice.columbia.edu/files/2015/10/AgingInPrison_FINAL_web.pdf

Crenshaw, K. (1991). Mapping the margins: Intersectionality, identity politics, and violence against women of color. *Stanford Law Review*, *43*, 1241–1299.

Mair, C. (2010). Social ties and depression: An intersectional examination of Black and White community-dwelling older adults. *Journal of Applied Gerontology, 29*(6), 667–696. doi:10.1177/0733464809350167

Parker-Cardinal, K. (2015). From social bullying in schools to bullying in senior housing (Master's capstone project). Retrieved from University of Massachusetts Boston database.

Perry, T., Archambault, D., & Sanford, C. (in press). Preserving senior housing in a changing city: Innovative efforts of an interprofessional coalition. *Public Policy & Aging Report*.

Perry, T., Wintermute, T., Carney, B., Leach, D. E., Sanford, C., & Quist, L. (2015). Senior housing at a crossroads: A case study of a university/community partnership in Detroit, Michigan. *Traumatology*, *21*(3), 244–250. doi:10.1037/trm0000043

Tilly, C. (1998). *Durable inequality*. Berkeley: University of California Press.

Trahan, A. (2011). Qualitative research and intersectionality. *Critical Criminology*, *19*(1), 114.

U.S. Department of Health and Human Services, Administration for Community Living, Administration on Aging. (2015). Profile of older Americans. Retrieved from http://www.aoa.acl.gov/Aging_Statistics/Profile/index.aspx

U. S. Department of Housing and Urban Development. (2016). Office of general counsel guidance on application of Fair Housing Act Standards to the use of criminal records by providers of housing and real estate-related transaction. Retrieved from https://portal.hud.gov/hudportal/documents/huddoc?id=HUD_OGCGuidAppFHAStandCR.pdf

U.S. Department of Housing and Urban Development, Office of Policy Development and Research. (2015). Picture of subsidized households. Retrieved from https://www.huduser.gov/portal/datasets/picture/yearlydata.html

Verloo, M. (2013). Intersectional and cross-movement politics and policies: Reflections on current practices and debates. *Signs: Journal of Women in Culture and Society*, *38*(4), 893–915. doi:10.1086/669572

Warner, D., & Brown, T. (2011). Understanding how race/ethnicity and gender define age trajectories of disability: An intersectionality approach. *Social Science & Medicine*, *72*(8), 1236–1248. doi:10.1016/j.socscimed.2011.02.034

VOICES FROM THE FIELD

Claudia Sanford, BFA
United Community Housing Coalition

Agency Setting

United Community Housing Coalition (UCHC) is a 501(c)3 nonprofit organization, which provides comprehensive housing assistance to Detroit's low-income residents. Since 1973, the organization has worked with tenants, homesteaders, homeowners, the homeless, and community organizations, rebuilding neighborhoods and providing affordable housing, as well as religious, civil rights, labor, and housing advocacy, to improve, preserve, and expand affordable housing opportunities for low-income Detroiters.

Today, the organization is primarily focused on the following areas of work: landlord–tenant legal counseling, housing placement, tenant organizing, and tax and mortgage foreclosure prevention. Services are provided to income-eligible families and individuals free of charge.

UCHC has several programs that assist families and individuals at risk of homelessness using legal and housing placement assistance. UCHC does not own or operate housing so there is no organizational policy regarding people with criminal backgrounds. The issue most often arises with attempting to place a senior and/or families in project-based Section 8 housing.

Practice Responsibilities

I have been with UCHC for over 10 years. My first position was as a housing placement counselor assisting low-income families at risk of homelessness find housing, jobs, and financial resources to move. Overlapping this role along with Ted Phillips, UCHC executive director, we assisted tenants living in a low-income property who were being forced to relocate because the property was purchased by a local casino; the building was scheduled for demolition. HUD issued Section 8 vouchers but tenants did not have the financial resources to relocate and casino executives were unwilling to cover the cost of the move. UCHC organized tenants and we were able to negotiate a comprehensive relocation package with the casino owners. My next role at UCHC was to oversee a new two-year program with two funding sources—city and state—that provided a combined total of over $1,600,000.00 to assist at-risk low-income Detroiters to find and maintain housing.

Expertise Required

I was born, raised, and educated in Detroit. I left to attend college in Boston and moved to New York City to pursue a career as a graphic designer. This transitioned into my owning and operating a business in New York. I have lived and worked in different cities including two years in England. I have traveled extensively through Europe, South America, the south Pacific, and as far as Australia.

I returned to Detroit in 2000 and chose to make my home in the city. What prepared me for my current job was the displacement of 250 neighbors in my apartment building. I was one of the tenant leaders and we were assisted by Executive Director Ted Phillips, UCHC.

This experience profoundly affected my view of how this type of displacement impacted tenants in Detroit and made me want to continue to help tenants. I overheard one of the long-time senior residents say that she had only expected to leave that building feet first.

Ethical, Legal, Practice, Diversity, and/or Advocacy Issues Addressed

In 2013, the Department of Housing and Urban Development (HUD) approved funds to support a program Tenant Resource Network (TRN). The National Alliance of HUD Tenants (NAHT) lobbied for these funds to place tenant organizers in project-based Section 8 properties with expiring HUD contracts. UCHC applied for a grant to employ two organizers and contract with Michigan Legal Services. One of the properties covered under the TRN grant was sold and opted out of the Section 8 program. Tenants were told that they would get Section 8 vouchers to move but they would have to submit applications and go through a normal screening process. This process required that tenants complete applications with an approved state authority housing agent and meet all the supporting document requirements and deadlines.

In this work, I have also become interested in advocacy around preserving low-income housing for older adults, in addition to direct work helping tenants find new housing options. I am part of a coalition in Detroit aiming to work on these issues. Many service providers in Detroit, including UCHC, recognized several of their older adult clients were being forced to relocate from their low-income apartment buildings. Once these agencies came together, it was clear that many seniors in the Detroit area were being displaced as their Section 8 apartment contracts expired and the buildings were then renovated to market-rate apartments. These various senior service providers that recognized this growing issue in Detroit took action to form the Senior Housing Preservation of Detroit (SHP-D). I have been active in this coalition by helping to create a relocation assessment tool (see Perry et al., 2015) to understand the needs of older adults if they need to relocate, and have produced a documentary for the coalition to be shown to local policy makers.

Interprofessional and Intersectoral Collaboration

At UCHC I work closely with Executive Director Ted Phillips, an attorney and staunch advocate for protecting housing for all low-income residents of Detroit. I also work with other attorneys and trained social workers. Often I have collaborated on grants with other agencies such as The Heat and Warm Fund, Homeless Action Network of Detroit, Neighborhood Service Organization, Coalition on Temporary Shelters, and Wayne County Neighborhood Legal Service. Other partners in Detroit have been the Luella Hannan Memorial Foundation and St. Aloysius Church organizations that provide valuable resources for seniors in Detroit.

One important interprofessional and intersectoral collaboration I have recently participated in is a John A. Hartford-funded study titled, "Relocation Amidst Revitalization: Recreating Social Worlds for Older Adults" where I worked alongside Dr. Perry, a gerontological social work researcher from a local university, and Kathleen Carsten, a parish nurse, to track older adults who have recently experienced involuntary relocation out of downtown Detroit, furthering our understanding of how these adults respond to the ongoing challenges of resettlement.

CHAPTER 8

Employment at the Intersection of the Juvenile Justice System

Rebecca Linn-Walton

CHAPTER OBJECTIVES

The major objectives of this chapter are to:

- Enhance understanding of the role employment services play in forensic social work with youth.
- Present relevant findings from recent research on employment services for justice-involved youth and their effects on recidivism.
- Describe and discuss the targeted programs and services for justice-involved youth, providing case examples and discussion of how social workers assist this population, and the skills required for effective intervention.

CHAPTER COMPETENCIES HIGHLIGHTED

- Competency 2: Engage Diversity and Difference in Practice
- Competency 3: Advance Human Rights and Social, Economic, and Environmental Justice
- Competency 8: Intervene With Individuals, Families, Organizations, and Communities

This chapter covers the history, context, and evidence for the importance of employment services for justice-involved youth. Topics covered include relevant context and history, policies, and theories behind why employment is such a large component of programming for juvenile justice agencies. You have learned a lot about forensic social work, and the various roles you can play to advocate for and treat those who come in contact with the justice system. This chapter builds upon these themes and provides a basic understanding for how employment services fit within the system. You learn about the scope of the problem, theoretical background including several frameworks, policies previously and currently employed, and some examples of services designed for this population, and a case example to help you imagine work in this capacity. Employment services provide a much-needed and empowering pathway to reduce recidivism for justice-involved youth. This chapter aims to connect research with real-life examples. Although the topics of juvenile justice and employment services do not at first appear obviously connected, by the end of this chapter you will have an understanding of how and why they came to be connected.

Background and Scope of Problem

The latest national report from the National Center on Juvenile Justice (2014) reported 1.7 million juveniles (under 18 years) were involved in the U.S. criminal justice system; 37.5% were arrested for property offenses (damage or theft), 27% were arrested for public-order offenses (e.g., running away, missing school), 24.3% for violence toward other persons, and 11.2% for drug or alcohol use or sales. The report also found that juvenile arrests have decreased by 17% in the past decade (Sickmund & Puzzanchera, 2014). However, on any given day, 70,000 juveniles are living in jails, prisons, and other detention settings in the United States. This report found that over 20,000 of these individuals have not been convicted (found guilty of a crime) and are awaiting trial. Detention disrupts a young person's development by removing him or her from school, family, community, and everything he or she knows, as well as supports (Hoge, 2016). Sickmund and Puzzanchera (2014) found that 20% of arrested juveniles are detained. Two thirds of these charges are nonviolent, with the most prevalent cases being property theft (e.g., stealing another student's property), drug or alcohol offense, skipping school, and running away or breaking curfew. Many of these offenses would not be considered a crime if the individual were not a minor.

Further, many U.S. detention facilities are at or over capacity (Davidson & Rowe, 2008; Sickmund & Puzzanchera, 2014), which limits detainees' access to counseling, medical attention, and other necessary services, and delays court processing, thereby lengthening time detained. Research has found that even one day in detention negatively impacts educational attainment, mental health, and family integrity (Cantwell, 2013). In the United States, juveniles are detained in overcrowded facilities designed to punish adults, rather than support adolescent development (Decker, Spohn, Ortiz, & Hedberg, 2014; Hoge, 2016). For youth, these same studies found that detention during adolescence led to an increased risk of dropping out of high school, negatively impacting employment for decades. In contrast, employment training during adolescence leads to better employment outcomes over the entire life span (Burt, 2014). For these reasons, one of the most effective methods for changing the trajectory of justice-involved youth is to provide effective employment services.

Although alternatives to incarceration services have been available in the United States and Europe since the 19th century, youth alternatives are relatively recent (Harris, 1995). In response to issues in juvenile detention of overcrowding, child development, poor outcomes, and the disruptive nature of detention, in the 1960s, U.S. agencies started opening up to provide supervision of justice-involved youth in the community (Bond, 2013). One example is the Court Employment Project at the Center for Alternative Sentencing and Employment Services in New York City (www.cases.org). This agency was created to provide in-community services to youth offenders in order to reduce recidivism while enabling them to remain in the community, with family. Services include oversight of court involvement and reporting, mental health counseling, family counseling, and legal services (Bullis & Yovanoff, 2006). These services can include attending court hearings with the client, providing counseling for the individual and family, and making phone calls to or visiting schools to document school attendance. Employment-related tasks include psychoeducation and training clients in employment skills; assisting in the job application process; providing ongoing updates to and receiving feedback from employers; and providing employment-related supportive counseling. Many of these services are provided by social workers. This support helps families and individuals avoid future crime (recidivism), function as a cohesive unit, and help the justice-involved individual return to or remain in the community where he or she can progress in productive community engagement (Bond, 2013). Employment services provide a key role in reducing recidivism for justice-involved individuals, both youth and adult (Bond, 2013). This chapter focuses on how these services help reduce recidivism for justice-involved youth, and accelerates their success.

Core Roles and Functions of Forensic Social Work in This System

Social workers provide a myriad of roles in the juvenile justice system. This section provides some illustrative examples for the reader, taken from Cantwell (2013). Clinical and macro setting examples are presented. For justice-involved youth, services can begin at the point of arrest. Examples of roles include coresponse units where social workers are paired with police or emergency response workers. Social workers can serve as court representatives, advocating that instead of being remanded to detention, youth can remain in the community, under supervision, while participating in programs aimed at reducing recidivism through mental health, employment, and education services. In agency settings, social workers can provide these services. A social worker can be an employment counselor, a case manager, a psychotherapist working with justice-involved individuals and overseeing employment, a group leader, or in the team-leader capacity. Social workers can also fulfill administrative capacities, supervising the direct care providers, or serve as senior managers in such agencies. Social work researchers can study these services while working in academic settings, research institutions, or government agencies.

Whether a social worker chooses to work in direct employment services or not, all social workers working in juvenile justice need to understand the impact effective employment services can play in their role within the system. For instance, a court representative will need to know the structure of the youth's employment program so that he or she can report on progress made to the judge and court. A clinical social worker can use employment accomplishments, impediments, and conflicts as material during psychotherapy when using motivational interviewing, cognitive behavioral therapy (CBT), or family therapy, for example, as discussed subsequently. Likewise, a social worker serving as an employment counselor will need to understand and counsel regarding how mental health, medical concerns, family illness, or lack of economic resources impact one's ability to sustain employment.

Relevant Theories or Frameworks

CBT and Juvenile Justice

The simplest way of understanding CBT is that our thoughts lead to our actions (Minjoo, Mpofu, Brock, Millington, & Athanasou, 2014). Therefore, researchers, policy makers, and intervention creators have hypothesized that justice-involved youth have cognitions that lead to offending behaviors (Viljoen, McLachlan, & Vincent, 2010). Such thoughts include beliefs that stealing or other illegal activity is "no big deal" or is socially acceptable, or a belief that impressing or pleasing one's peers by engaging in illegal activity is a way to get ahead. Treatment then becomes helping the individual see the negative consequences of his or her thinking. There is a wide variety of interventions developed for juvenile justice populations that implement CBT (Davidson & Rowe, 2008). Some of them are described at length elsewhere in this text. In the context of juvenile justice and employment, interventions become focused on replacing criminal behavior with healthy and productive activities, such as developing employment skills and securing lasting employment (Calloway, 2006). There is a common saying, "move a muscle, change a thought," and employment services provide that framework.

Risk, Need, and Responsivity

Out of CBT and case management frameworks came the risk–need–responsivity (RNR) model shown in Table 8.1 (Vaswani & Merone, 2013). This model proposes that the likelihood of an individual recidivating (being arrested or convicted again) is based on patterns of thinking associated with offending, inadequate resources in specific areas, and service needs. These factors are labeled "criminogenic needs" (Andrews & Bonta, 2007). Criminogenic need factors include antisocial patterns of thinking; historic and present thoughts, attitudes, and

TABLE 8.1   RNR Model

Criminogenic Need Factor	Risk
History of antisocial behavior	Early and continuing involvement in a number and variety of antisocial acts and a variety of settings
Antisocial personality pattern	Adventurous pleasure seeking, weak self-control, restlessly aggressive
Antisocial cognition	Attitudes, values, beliefs, and rationalizations supportive of crime; cognitive–emotional states of anger, resentment, and defiance
Antisocial associates	Close association with criminal others and relative isolation from anticriminal others; immediate social support for crime
Family and/or marital	Two key elements are nurturance and/or caring and monitoring and/or supervision
School and/or work	Low levels of performance and satisfaction in school and/or work
Leisure and/or recreation	Low levels of involvement and satisfaction in anticriminal leisure pursuits
Substance abuse	Abuse of alcohol and/or other drugs

RNR, risk–need–responsibility.
Source: Adapted from Andrews and Bonta (2007).

beliefs that committing crime is acceptable; friends or associates with similar beliefs; lack of strong family connections; insufficient school and employment; substance misuse; and a lack of noncrime-related hobbies or prosocial activities (Andrews & Bonta, 2007). What does that mean? The RNR model paints a picture of an individual who thinks stealing is not a big deal ("All my friends are doing it so I can too"), with low parental and family involvement, not attending school or working, drinking alcohol or doing drugs, and who lacks hobbies. The more of these characteristics that are present, the more likely an individual will be to offend or reoffend. Therefore, researchers have found that interventions aimed at these factors reduce recidivism (Wasserman et al., 2003). As employment is a key factor in reducing recidivism, agencies have developed programs to provide connection to employment for justice-involved youth.

Criticism of this model has grown in recent years (Vaswani & Merone, 2013). You may have noticed that the premise of criminogenic need is built upon antisocial thoughts and beliefs. The human brain does not develop fully until adulthood, however, which is why children and adolescents cannot be diagnosed with antisocial personality disorder (Vaswani & Merone, 2013). Although the RNR model is used for and provides assessment tools for use with minors, these authors argued that the assessment labels normal adolescent impulsivity and lack of development as antisocial. The RNR model fails to take strengths into account, and ignores systemic inequality and impact (Vaswani & Merone, 2013).

Youth Empowerment (a Framework)

In response to these and other criticisms came the youth empowerment model (Jennings, Parra-Medina, Hilfinger-Messias, & McLoughlin, 2006). This model posits that youth commit crime when they are not provided with adequate resources, opportunity, and care. When youth are provided with safety, respect between themselves and from adults, opportunities to engage with and effect change in their environment, and tools to critically appraise society, they become productive members of the community (Jennings et al., 2006). When they do not receive some or all of these opportunities, negative behaviors and criminal involvement can ensue. Therefore, interventions that were developed out of this framework seek to empower youth to have a voice in their community and family, and provide the tools to create change through activism, employment, and education (Cargo, Grams, Ottoson, Ward, & Green, 2003). These authors cite the importance of making youth aware of how systems affect them, so that they may change the system from within. Providing employment services is reflective of this model, as it provides the opportunity for justice-involved youth to become participative and productive members of their communities.

Relevant Ethical, Legal, and Policy Issues

A topic that is inherently relevant to juvenile justice and employment but has not yet been covered is systemic oppression and inequality. This section outlines two of the ways inequality and oppression impact juvenile justice and employment. This review is not exhaustive, but other chapters in this book outline other resources on the topic. This section focuses on inequality and oppression related to employment for justice-involved youth.

As mentioned earlier, criminogenic need factors in the RNR model label youth as potentially having personality disorders or symptoms associated with psychopathy that are not developmentally appropriate for youth (Takahashi, Mori, & Kroner, 2013). Personality disorders are a maladaptive fixed set of beliefs, and as the juvenile mind is still developing, the previously noted authors questioned the assessment's validity for this population. We could be mislabeling a developing brain as maladaptive. These labels can be stigmatizing for youth, and increase the likelihood that schools will suspend or expel them, employers will fire/dismiss them, and family members will be less supportive of them (Bullis & Yovanoff, 2006; Burt, 2014). These same researchers found that minority and poor youth are more likely to be misdiagnosed, and receive harsher penalties of expulsion, longer sentences from courts, and have poorer employment outcomes. In this way what starts as misdiagnosis becomes an issue of inequality and oppression.

Another way in which inequality and oppression can impact employment services for justice-involved youth is with regards to funding. In the United States, minorities are more likely to live in poorer neighborhoods with less funding for their schools (Wald & Losen, 2003). These authors found that lower-funded schools attracted less competent teachers, reported higher numbers of suspensions and expulsions, and maintained a higher police presence, leading to more arrests from student fights than in other schools. We already know from earlier in the chapter that even one arrest can impact employment for decades, owing to lost school time, disrupted development, resulting anger from family members, and higher likelihood of expulsion. In this way, economic and racial inequality make it more likely for minority youth to be arrested and be disadvantaged in employment prospects and every other aspect of the youth's life.

That being said, a forensic social worker can have a strong, positive influence in the lives of justice-involved youth. Social work is based on an understanding of how one's environment and the systems with which one comes into contact have an impact on one's present circumstances (Cantwell, 2013). Understanding how upstream inequality impacts youth who go on to commit crime allows the social worker to treat the individual with empathy and compassion. Social work's strengths-based mission and focus on working with the oppressed, giving voice to the voiceless, and working in a collaborative environment allow forensic social workers not only to advocate for their clients, but to impart these skills directly to justice-involved youth. Some forensic social workers have personal histories of justice involvement (Ericson, 1975). What better outcome for juvenile justice and employment than a justice-involved young person going on to obtain a graduate degree in social work?

Relevant Assessment, Prevention, and Intervention Strategies

RNR Assessment

The first question social work students often ask when they arrive in the classroom is, "But what do I do with my client?" The answer to the question is to ask a different question, however: "How do I know what to do with my client?" The answer is simple: assessment. Knowing "what to do" should come from the clients themselves, rather than a prescriptive plan. A good assessment offers a comprehensive picture of the client, the systems with which he or she interacts, previous history that led to the current "presenting problem," and the relevant obstacles and supports the client has in place or could put in place to create positive change in his or her own life. Assessments are surveys or questionnaires with a series of questions designed to help social workers understand the scope and depth of the problem in its current state, as well as the short- and long-term needs of the client. Through conducting comprehensive assessments of our clients, social workers determine which specific tasks he or she must carry out, which goals are relevant to the client's needs and desires, and with which systems the social worker will need to interact, such as the courts, schools, and employers.

In juvenile justice, these assessments include measuring the risk of recidivism through criminogenic needs that drive one's risk for recidivism, as this is the primary role of programming for justice-involved individuals. This model of assessment is called "risk-need responsivity" (Hoge, 2016). Alternative to incarceration (ATI) programs seek to provide monitoring for the individual until his or her case or probation is closed, and to provide services to reduce future offense through promoting behaviors associated with productivity and community membership.

In order to keep the individual in the community, it is necessary to assess which needs he or she has that would make him or her more or less likely to be involved in future criminal activity. An example of a widely used assessment tool for justice-involved youth is the level of service/case management inventory, which has both youth (12–15 years) and adult (over 16 years) versions (Takahashi et al., 2013). This tool allows social workers to assess the following areas of need, and the degree to which services are needed: antisocial cognitions, companions, personality, as well as family and marital relationships, substance misuse, employment, education, and leisure/recreation (Hoge, 2016; Takahashi et al., 2013). After the social worker and individual complete the survey, they can score the answers using a predetermined rubric to objectively assess whether the individual is at low, medium, high, or very high risk of recidivating using a standardized method. Additionally, through the conversations had to complete a survey, the social worker gains a comprehensive understanding of service needs and goals of treatment. For example, the assessment could determine that the individual has low skills and limited work experience. The social worker would then be able to create a treatment plan that would build the skill set and experience base. These services have been found to reduce recidivism and increase community engagement for justice-involved youth (Vaswani & Merone, 2013). Providing youth with opportunities for growth and economic independence is the goal, and recidivism is minimized along the way.

Intervention Strategies

This section discusses two evidence-based employment intervention strategies that are available to justice-involved youth in New York. The first program, "Ready, Set, Work!" (RSW), is a skills-based training program designed for justice-involved individuals (Chautauqua County Jail graduates 'Ready, Set, Work' participants, 2013). The second intervention, "Jobs for America's Graduates," is a combination of education and employment services for out-of-school individuals who have dropped out without completing high school (Calloway, 2006). This intervention was not created specifically for justice-involved individuals, but has a track record of efficacy, and is in the process of being adapted for and tested on justice-involved youth up to age 24 years (Calloway, 2006, and see www.jag.org).

Manualized training programs such as these provide social workers with a variety of tools to aid their work (Bond, 2013). A structured curriculum of workshops with youth ensure that all necessary skill-development topics are delivered to the client (Burt, 2014). Flexible session order, content within the session, and setting for the training provide the social worker with flexibility to adapt the training to meet the needs of the particular client. For instance, if a client already has solid communication skills, the worker can move on to time management, if this is an area of inexperience for the client.

Ready, Set, Work!

RSW is a 20-hour skill-based training to equip probationers with the necessary tools to get and retain quality employment. The model includes an emphasis on career planning and advancement to encourage longevity in legitimate employment (rather than internships). While limited evaluation of RSW has been performed, the model has produced promising employment outcomes and recidivism reductions among justice-involved participants in jurisdictions across New York state consistent with a 2011 study by the National Institute for Corrections finding that offenders receiving this type of Offender Workforce Development services have a 33% lower risk of recidivism. This model provides social workers with a concrete framework to deliver skills training to their clients (Chautauqua County Jail graduates 'Ready, Set, Work' participants, 2013).

Jobs for America's Graduates Out-of-School (JAG OOS) Model

JAG OOS involves six months of regular engagement in classes and activities built around a 20-module job readiness curriculum. The program emphasizes youth empowerment through cohort-based community and/or entrepreneurial projects. JAG OOS also involves up to 12 months of aftercare services to continue to support a young person to secure employment and/or retain and progress in that job. The model was developed as a dropout-recovery approach and typically services youth with significant barriers to success including inadequate or no work experience, lack of marketable occupational skills, low academic performance, and lack of motivation or maturity to pursue education or career goals. According to a 2006 evaluation, despite their significant challenges, 50% of JAG OOS graduates secured full- or part-time unsubsidized employment, 6% went on to full-time college or university studies, and 1% enlisted in the armed services (Calloway, 2006), reflecting significant progress from their out-of-school and out-of-work status only 12 to 18 months prior. One strength of this model is that it provides educational assistance in tandem with employment services. This combination has been found to be more effective in reducing recidivism and improving client pathways to recovery than either service alone (Calloway, 2006).

As discussed earlier, previous iterations of employment services for justice-involved youth included solely employment linkages to entry-level positions. Without providing pathways to careers, as distinct from jobs, agencies failed to effectively reduce recidivism (Minjoo et al., 2014). The JAG OOS program provides entry-level skills with attainment of a high-school equivalency, as well as comprehensive career and employment counseling, so that successful graduates can go on to earn higher degrees or advance their positions in the workforce. These outcomes both reduce recidivism and create stronger community and family members.

Though these are just two evidence-based interventions to promote employment for justice-involved youth, the reader should now have a sense of the policies and areas of concern driving the intervention. As mentioned earlier, law makers and researchers have identified that, in many cases, juvenile populations have better outcomes through services than through detention. Funding for programming reflects this, with many states funding programs aimed at reducing criminogenic need and promoting employment, education, and family interaction.

But what if these are not the most effective strategies? This chapter pointed out multiple ways in which systemic oppression affects education, opportunity, and even how thoughts are labeled. An adolescent who gets in a fight at school can have multiple outcomes. A school counselor can meet with that student, assess him or her, and might diagnose an anxiety disorder as the root cause of the impulsivity leading to the fight. The adolescent can then engage in counseling and learn to manage his or her symptoms with no further violence. In another scenario, there might be a police officer on site at the adolescent's school. He or she might then be arrested, detained in a juvenile facility (where we have already learned that resources for recovering from mental illness are limited), and have that experience impact his or her employment for decades, not to mention the effects of untreated anxiety. Here we have an example of one individual whose life can have widely varying outcomes based on one instance of justice system involvement. It is for this reason social workers are encouraged to take a variety of career paths when working as forensic social workers. If we use our systems and strengths-based approach, we can change the system from the inside out, and even teach our clients to do so in the process.

Case Example and Application

Samuel is a 17-year-old male in New York City. When he was 16 years, he was arrested for a felony gun charge, meaning that the police arrested him for having a gun, which turned out was not registered, and for which he did not have a license. This was his first offense, so instead of being incarcerated, he was sentenced to an ATI program. The program provided a variety of services, including employment and education counseling to help Samuel set goals, mental health counseling, family support, and court advocacy (all of these roles can be staffed by social workers). When he attended services, Samuel was very clear from day one that he wanted to get a job. He lived in a neighborhood with a strong gang presence, but not many businesses. The employment counselor worked with him to explore career goals he had for himself and expose Samuel to multiple different careers to help him identify his interests. Samuel already had his high school diploma, and was very bright, but said he had attended some continuing education and did not like it. He wanted "a job." The social worker supported him in securing a job at an automobile repair shop. He was a reliable worker, but his boss took advantage of inexperienced employees, underpaying them for hours worked. So the social worker helped him find a second job, this time in a law firm, school admissions office, or dentist's office, for example. The social worker's sessions were focused on helping Samuel develop the soft skills necessary to succeed at work, including planning so as to arrive on time, time management to complete assignments, professional conflict resolution when misunderstandings or disagreements arose at work, and communication skills so that he could demonstrate to his supervisor what he was working on, strengths he brought to the job, and what he accomplished during the workday. Over time, Samuel went from the job being a subsidized placement (the ATI provides a portion of the salary, and oversees a trial period of work) to full time, permanent employment. By supporting the client's goals, rather than setting the agenda himself, the social worker was able to help Samuel master not one but two positions, and, when he was working in an unsuitable environment, to secure employment elsewhere. By remaining available to Samuel even after his probation ended, the social worker provided a positive role model for Samuel. In recent months, Samuel has referred friends to the agency's voluntary education and employment services. In this way the social worker has helped Samuel help himself, connect to his community, and make positive change in the lives of those around him. Samuel's employment counselor still holds out hope that Samuel will go back to school and become a counselor himself someday. "I just keep planting the seed and being a role model."

Conclusion

Working with justice-involved youth and employment-related services requires a wide range of social work and systems knowledge, skills, and expertise. Social workers must be adept in collaborating with multiple parties in education, employment, and justice service agencies; the courts; and the youth participant himself or herself. Justice-involved youth can have histories of trauma and symptoms of depression, anxiety, or other behavioral health needs. In some cases, justice-involved youth have families who present with these same needs. Forensic social workers must employ skills in assessment, linkages to additional services, case management, and facilitate relationships with employers. This type of work requires flexible and adaptive skills, and provides a broad range of intervention opportunities to change the lives of justice-involved youth for the better.

CHAPTER EXERCISES

Exercise 1. Theory-informed practice choices: Form small groups of students. Choose one theory/framework from this chapter. Choose one policy mentioned in this chapter. Discuss the following: How does theory inform this policy? Does it? Where are theory and policy at odds? Is there a different policy that could be described as theory driven? Explain.

Exercise 2. Case-in-action: Form groups of three students. Take five minutes to create or look up a case example. The case should include a justice-involved youth with employment needs and at least three family members. Specify one to two systems with which the individual interacts. One student will be the social worker. One will be the youth client. Another will be the observer. The social worker will conduct an informal assessment of the youth client's mental health, employment, and other needs (biopsychosocial assessment). What are the needs of the individual? What are the needs of the family (housing, employment, mental health, other)? How do these impact the individual needing employment services? Do the family's needs create obstacles for the justice-involved individual? How would family/community support help him or her succeed? How does current policy impact these needs or support these strengths? How can social workers work within this environment? What are some strategies that can empower the client? The family? Those observing should take notes and share feedback with the group.

Additional Resources

American Society of Criminology: www.asc41.com

Bureau of Justice Assistance: www.bja.gov

Coalition for Juvenile Justice: www.juvjustice.org

National Association of Social Worker's Juvenile Justice: www.socialworkers.org/ldf/lawnotes/juvenile.asp

References

Andrews, D. A., & Bonta, J. (2007). *Risk-need-responsivity model for offender assessment and rehabilitation.* Ottawa, ON, Canada: Public Safety Canada.

Bond, G. R. (2013). Supported employment for justice-involved people with mental illness. Rockville, MD: GAINS Center for Behavioral Health and Justice Transformation. Retrieved from https://www.prainc.com/wp-content/uploads/2015/10/article-supported-employment-justice-involved-people-mental-illness.pdf

Bullis, M., & Yovanoff, P. (2006). Idle hands: Community employment experiences of formerly incarcerated youth. *Journal of Emotional and Behavioral Disorders, 2*(14), 236–250.

Burt, R. M. (2014). More than a second chance: An alternative employment approach to reduce recidivism among criminal ex-offenders. *Tennessee Journal of Law & Policy, 6*(1), 1–37.

Calloway, J. P. (2006). Jobs for America's graduates: A school-to-career program. *Applied Technology Training and Development, 3,* 1–92.

Cantwell, N. (2013). The role of social work in juvenile justice. *The United Nations Children's Fund.* Retrieved from http://www.unicef.org/ceecis/UNICEF_report_on_the_role_of_social_work_in_juvenile_justice.pdf

Cargo, M., Grams, G. D., Ottoson, J. M., Ward, P., & Green, L. W. (2003). Empowerment as fostering positive youth development and citizenship. *American Journal of Health Behavior, 27*(1), 66–79.

Chautauqua County Jail graduates 'Ready, Set, Work' participants. (2013, May 13). *Westfield Republican*. Retrieved from http://www.westfieldrepublican.com/page/content.detail/id/520677/Chautauqua -County-Jail-graduates--Ready--Set--Work-participants.html?nav=5070

Davidson, L., & Rowe, M. (2008). *Peer support within criminal justice settings: The role of forensic peer specialists*. Delmar, NY: The Center for Mental Health Services National GAINS Center. Retrieved from https://www.prainc.com/wp-content/uploads/2015/10/peer-support-criminal-justice -settings-role-forensic-peer-specialists.pdf

Decker, S. H., Spohn, C., Ortiz, N. R., & Hedberg, E. (2014). *Criminal stigma, race, gender and employment: An expanded assessment of the consequences of imprisonment for employment*. Washington, DC: National Institute of Justice.

Ericson, R. V. (1975). *Young offenders and their social work*. Lexington, MA: Saxon House.

Harris, R. (1995). *Probation and related measures*. New York, NY: United Nations Publications.

Hoge, R. D. (2016). Risk need, and responsivity in juveniles. In K. Heilbrun, D. DeMatteo, N. S. Goldstein, K. Heilbrun, D. DeMatteo, & N. S. Goldstein (Eds.), *APA handbook of psychology and juvenile justice* (pp. 179–196). Washington, DC: U.S. American Psychological Association. doi:10.1037/14643-009

Jennings, L. B., Parra-Medina, D. M., Hilfinger-Messias, D. K., & McLoughlin, K. (2006). Toward a critical social theory of youth empowerment. *Journal of Community Practice, 14*(1), 31–55.

Minjoo, K., Mpofu, E., Brock, K., Millington, M., & Athanasou, J. (2014). Cognitive-behavioral therapy effects on employment-related outcomes for individuals with mental illness: A systematic review. *SA Journal of Industrial Psychology/SA Tydskrif vir Bedryfsielkunde, 40*(2), Art. #1188. doi:10.4102/sajip .v40i2.1188

Sickmund, M., & Puzzanchera, C. (Eds.). (2014). Juvenile offenders and victims: 2014 national report. Pittsburgh, PA: National Center for Juvenile Justice. Retrieved from http://www.ojjdp.gov/ ojstatbb/nr2014/downloads/NR2014.pdf

Takahashi, M., Mori, T., & Kroner, D. G. (2013). A cross-validation of the Youth Level of Service/Case Management Inventory (LS/CMI) among Japanese juvenile offenders. *Law and Human Behavior, 37*(6), 389–400.

Vaswani, N., & Merone, L. (2013). Are there risks with risk assessment? A study of the predictive accuracy of the Youth Level of Service–Case Management Inventory with young offenders in Scotland. *British Journal of Social Work, 44*, 2163–2181.

Viljoen, J. L., McLachlan, K., & Vincent, G. M. (2010). Assessing violence risk and psychopathy in juvenile and adult offenders: A survey of clinical practices. *Assessment, 17*(3), 377. doi:10.1177/1073191109359587

Wald, J., & Losen, D. J. (2003). Defining and redirecting a school-to-prison pipeline. *New Directions for Youth Development, 99*, 9–15.

Wasserman, G., Jensen, P., Ko, S., Cocozza, J., Trupin, E., Angold, A., & Grisso, T. (2003). *Mental health assessments in juvenile justice: Report on the consensus conference*. New York, NY: Center for the Promotion of Mental Health in Juvenile Justice.

VOICES FROM THE FIELD

April Harvin, LCSW

Clinical Director of Youth Programs
The Center for Alternative Sentencing and
Employment Services (CASES)

Agency Setting

CASES was formed in 1989 through the merger of two long-running programs created by the Vera Institute of Justice, located in New York City. One of these programs, the Court Employment Project (CEP), was established in 1967 to provide a meaningful alternative to incarceration (ATI) for judges in New York City Supreme Courts when sentencing young people facing jail or prison as the result of felony charges. The core goals of CEP are to divert youth who can be safely supervised in the community, engage them in a case management model that includes education and employment services, and help them address challenges while building skills and accessing meaningful opportunities to improve their short- and long-term prospects. These services provide much needed assistance for young people, aged 16 to 24 years. In addition to CEP, CASES currently operates nine other youth programs at sites across New York City serving young people including those returning to the community following incarceration and those at high risk for arrest due to factors including gang involvement. Our youth programs collectively serve nearly 700 young people age 12 to 24 every year. Within CASES, there are also five additional ATI/detention programs, serving thousands of youth annually. Rather than go to jail or prison, young people are provided supportive and supervised wraparound services including employment and education, youth empowerment, mental health counseling, family counseling, substance abuse counseling, and cultural and skill-developing enrichment opportunities. Counselors help participants identify and address issues that arise from acclimating to employment, attending court appointments, and reintegrating with family and community.

Practice Responsibilities

Ms. Harvin is the clinical director for both voluntary and mandated services for youth at CASES. Agency clients have either been arrested and in many cases sentenced, or are at risk of justice involvement based on factors such as gang involvement, family involvement in the justice system, or living in high-crime neighborhoods. Ms. Harvin oversees the licensed staff in these programs, from mental health counselors to licensed psychotherapists. She provides clinical supervision, participates in program planning to ensure quality clinical practice, and advocates for ethically responsive programming to meet the needs of clients and their families. Examples of collaboration include working with the agency's educational and employment program, as well as the agency's mental health clinic and newly opened primary care treatment.

Expertise Required

Ms. Harvin has over 20 years of experience in multiple capacities and types of social work. She began her career as a direct practice social worker, working with family and children's services. Since then she has worked in emergency mental health centers, mental illness and substance misuse treatment centers, and a variety of other agencies. She has worked as a clinical social worker, a case manager, a supervisor, and now as a clinical director. Ms. Harvin says,

> Everywhere you go, there is justice involvement. In children's services, sometimes it's not the parents but the child who is justice involved. Kids with substance abuse diagnoses get arrested for using drugs. Parents working 50 to 60 hours a week at minimum wage don't make enough to survive on, so sometimes supplement their wages with illegal activities such as selling drugs, and then ACS [Administration for Children's Services] becomes involved. Justice involvement touches so many lives, so you need to know what to do in every setting, and know all the systems, from Children's Services to the court system to shelters and employment.

She describes the work as addressing three main concerns: communication, affect regulation, and accessing resources. Social workers work with clients to increase communication skills at home, at work, and when appearing in court. When a judge lengthens probation, or a boss is difficult, justice-involved youth need to know how to process resulting emotions and respond in a productive manner. Finally, clients will need to be given the tools to access support in the future, from finding and applying for jobs to looking for mentorship in employers.

Ethical, Legal, Practice, Diversity, and/or Advocacy Issues Addressed

When asked about what the ethical concerns or issues are, Ms. Harvin replied, "Do you have several days?" She discussed the fact that many employment programs for juvenile justice participants provide opportunities for minimum wage jobs. Ms. Harvin detailed long work hours in order to earn a paycheck that does not match the cost of living. She mentioned the stress this puts on social workers, specifically in cases where the client decides to supplement his or her income through illegal activity. She highlighted the need for collaboration with other providers within and outside the agency. "If I can get my client an education program, I can help them work toward sustainable employment. That means working with the education staff person, but also talking about it in my mental health sessions." Ms. Harvin works in an agency with multiple programs for youth, covering mental and physical health needs, employment, and education. Referrals are often made within the agency, necessitating close collaboration with staff and programs. Social workers are charged not simply with supervising youth before or after sentencing, but enabling them to engage in additional services, such as employment, in order to reduce long-term recidivism.

Another concern raised was regarding diagnosis and stigmatization.

> What if we diagnose someone as having "criminogenic need" or "antisocial beliefs" when what they really have is depression or trauma or poverty and generations of systemic oppression? The World Health Organization classifies racism and poverty as a public health crisis. Terms and punishments used by the criminal justice system don't reflect and treat that.

So what can a social worker do? Ms. Harvin has had great success in this area.

> You provide the services mandated, but as a social worker, you come from a strengths-based approach, understanding systems. Maybe I can't change our justice system today, but I can empower my clients to join me in this work. I can empower youth to participate in the system in a positive way, through working, through education, through helping their families.

Interprofessional and Intersectoral Collaboration

Ms. Harvin described the varied roles of forensic social workers, and the common thread of practice that runs through all positions. "You teach them communication, affect regulation, and accessing resources. You can be a clinical social worker, a case manager, or an employment specialist. The words and the goals change, but the content doesn't." Ms. Harvin illustrates a key point for forensic social workers specializing in employment services for justice-involved youth. Whether learning how to explain to a judge the progress he or she has made, or explaining to a boss how one has completed an assignment, communication skills are needed. When a young person hears from the judge that his or her probation is not being ended early, or when a boss denies a vacation request, being able to manage one's anger or immediate reaction effectively is the skill at hand. Even more important, forensic social workers in all settings must help their clients learn to access resources independently.

> Being able to identify when you need help, being able to ask, and knowing whom to ask are the most important skills we all learn as adults. Yes, I spend some of my time filling out housing work for my clients, but teaching them to apply for an apartment is more lasting.

Ms. Harvin also chronicles the need to collaborate with other staff, agencies, and systems. "You can't have services solo, even though they tend to be," she said.

> The employment counselor can't just provide employment services while the clinical social worker delivers CBT [cognitive behavioral therapy]. That won't change anything. It all has to work in tandem. The therapist works with the client to develop techniques to tolerate frustration or boredom. Then the employment counselor helps the client find a job. They might get a lot of practice at that entry-level position and become bored, but have to learn not to quit or get fired. And both the therapist and employment counselor need to know if the client has a health problem. Maybe you couldn't get to work because you are caring for a sick parent. We need to work with you to address that and find help caring for that family member during work hours, and a means of communicating effectively to the employer.

This is a perfect example of how skills, roles, and even agencies intersect, all in a day's work.

CHAPTER 9

Families as a System in Forensic Practice

Nancy J. Mezey

Tina Maschi

George S. Leibowitz

CHAPTER OBJECTIVES

The main objectives of this chapter are to:

- Illustrate how factors outside of families affect the lives of people within families.
- Examine the potential impact that two major issues—work–family conflict and mass incarceration—can have on the lives of family members.

CHAPTER COMPETENCIES HIGHLIGHTED

- Competency 7: Assess Individuals, Families, Organizations, and Communities
- Competency 8: Intervene With Individuals, Families, Organizations, and Communities

Background and Scope of the Problem

Social workers often find it necessary to interact with, assess, and develop and implement intervention plans for families and their individual members involved in some way with the justice system. Although many of us talk about "the family," families in the United States exist in a variety of structures and have very different needs. Single-parent families; divorced families; lesbian, gay, bisexual, and transgender families; blended families; grandparents raising grandchildren; dual-income-earning families; families in which a member or members are incarcerated or affected by the criminal justice system; families living in poverty; and a host of other "postmodern" families make up approximately 90% of U.S. families today (Ameristat, 2003). While changes to family structures and interpersonal dynamics have occurred in part because of changing social norms and values, most families are changing because of critical structural changes that exist outside of families. Changes in the economy, changing gender and sexual relations, ongoing wars, and the enormous growth of mass incarceration due in large part to the "war on drugs" and "colorblind racism" are a few examples of external factors that greatly impact families.

Family scholars have noted that laws and policies regarding families rarely keep pace with family changes. Part of the dilemma for policy makers is trying to figure out how best to support families, which families to support, and how to make such support economically and socially feasible (Bogenschneider, 2014). In addition, most existing laws are not expressly written to shape families. In fact, other than laws governing marriage and divorce, and the Family Medical Leave Act (FMLA) of 1993, very few laws and policies are explicitly "family" laws. Despite the lack of explicit family laws, many laws and policies directly affect families. For example, laws regarding poverty, suicide, unemployment, long-term health care, transportation, physical and mental health, crime and punishment, sexuality, drug and alcohol use/abuse, education, drunk driving, economics, racial/class/gender/age discrimination, immigration, work, community development, and wars all greatly affect families.

This chapter describes the ways in which laws governing systems external to families, particularly work and criminal justice, can disrupt families in ways that may lead those families to use the services of social workers. The chapter also aims at providing the necessary understanding of how social workers can help support such families, keeping in mind that family needs often develop from the social and economic context in which each family is situated.

Although most problems that families encounter manifest themselves within the family (e.g., drug or alcohol abuse, intimate partner violence, child abuse, abandonment), many of those problems arise out of a context that exists external to the family, including laws and policies. Because many issues that affect the health of families are shaped by a variety of laws (both directly and indirectly aimed at families), social workers must be aware of those laws and the impact they have. In addition, for families to successfully navigate and access resources, there must be laws and policies in place to make doing so possible. Families need safe housing, adequate medical care, reliable and high-quality child care, reproductive health services, sufficient nutritional food, education, safe neighborhoods, and support services. Understanding laws that affect families, and working to improve or change those laws, are key ways that social workers can help families in need.

System and Population Overview

Social science research suggests that there is a general misconception of what families are, what goals they can accomplish, and how they can accomplish those goals (Dill, Baca Zinn, & Patton, 1998). Many Americans use a very narrow definition of what constitutes a healthy family. In addition, they tend to believe that healthy families are the key to creating a healthy society. Although we cannot have a fully healthy society without having healthy families, in order to be healthy, the social environment, including laws, must support all our families in a variety of ways. This chapter helps social workers conceptualize how to help create healthy families.

In order to be "healthy," families must meet three criteria. First, they must have quality relationships between and among family members. Second, they must be able to access important material resources such as schooling, jobs, health care, housing, safe environments, drug and alcohol treatment, family planning, marriage, divorce, child care, legal counseling, and psychological counseling. Third, families must be able to negotiate the different systems through which those resources are obtained. Families must have the ability to speak and cooperate with educators, workers, and medical, financial, and legal officials in order to fully access and benefit from the resources people provide within their specific institutions.

Part of the social worker's job is to help families become healthy by addressing family members' internal concerns, connecting those concerns to external resources, and helping family members negotiate external systems. Because of the bureaucratic nature of many of the systems offering assistance to families, families must have a fair level of sophistication to navigate, access, and maintain such assistance. Centralization of services and a holistic, team-oriented approach that views the entire family's needs together and in relation to influences external to the family are vital to ensure continued access to family-sustaining services (Dewees, 2006). The social work profession can be an instrumental force in developing and maintaining such a system.

More specifically, social workers who work with families may find themselves in a variety of settings completing many different tasks. For example, they may be involved in public and/or private human service agencies in the planning and implementation of services to single women who become pregnant (i.e., single-parent services). These services typically include counseling about the choices surrounding continuing the pregnancy, childbirth preparation, legal counseling regarding parental rights, family planning, education and employment counseling, money-management counseling, and child care and child-development counseling (Zastrow, 2009).

Social workers involved in family issues may also have a place in the courtroom, testifying about the best custody situation for a child whose parents are separating, divorcing, or in a custody dispute. Such testimony would be based on the prescribed involvement with family members in interview settings, home visits, and review of materials. In supervised custody arrangements, social workers may find themselves supervising visitation between parents and children. In cases of family violence, social workers may provide crisis intervention and long-term counseling to the adult, child, or elderly survivors. They may also serve as legal advocates who accompany survivors of violence to court-related appointments. In addition, social workers may provide safety planning to children and families who are attempting reunification into a previously violent home.

Should a parent relinquish parental rights and a child be placed in foster care, pending-adoption social workers may be involved in recruitment, selection, and training of foster parents as well as in counseling parents who are considering placing their children for adoption. In certain adoptions, social workers may make home visits and file reports regarding the home environment into which a potential adopted child would be placed. They also may work with a variety of parents, including single- and same-sex parents.

Current Practice, Policy, and Social Movement Trends and Debates

There are myriad issues that families currently face. This section focuses on two of the most pressing issues—work–family conflict and the system of mass incarceration that affects over 2.3 million people and their families, particularly Black families—to show how laws and policies shape families in a variety of ways in which social workers should be aware.

Work–Family Conflict

Balancing the responsibilities of work and family is one of the major challenges facing families in the United States today. Such balancing can cause conflict for families "when roles and responsibilities at home and at work are incompatible, forcing workers to make hard choices about how to divide their fixed pool of resources, especially time and energy, between the two spheres" (Berheide & Linden, 2015). Although politicians use the rhetoric of "family values" and "valuing families," only one meager law—FMLA of 1993—supports work–family conflict. According to the U.S. Department of Labor,

> FMLA requires covered employers to provide up to 12 weeks of unpaid, job-protected leave to eligible employees for 1) incapacity due to pregnancy, prenatal medical care, or childbirth, 2) caring for one's birth, adopted, or foster child, or 3) caring for one's spouse, child, or parent who has a serious health condition. (Department of Labor, n.d.)

In addition to the FMLA, many organizations, particularly private organizations, have developed and incorporated additional work–family conflict policies. For example, some companies allow part-time work, flexible hours, flexible workplace (e.g., working from home), and subsidized child care or child care on premises (Sallee, 2014; Solomon, 2015). While such opportunities are usually available to all employees, women are much more likely than men to make use of work–family balance policies (Berheide & Linden, 2015).

Studies show that having policies is not enough. Rather, work–family conflict policies are only beneficial if there is a culture within the company that encourages use of the policies (Anderson, 2015). Furthermore, such policies tend to be available mostly to those working in professional positions. Therefore, those in blue-collar or unskilled jobs find themselves with few ways to support their need to resolve work–family conflict. The lack of work–family conflict policies at certain job levels is exacerbated by a lack of affordable quality child care.

The result is that parents, and particularly women, are torn between earning a living for their family and providing proper care for their children. Indeed, women who are trying to move off of welfare and into the workforce often return home full-time because of the inability to balance the two (Hays, 2003).

When poor women "fail" to move into the workforce, social workers need to be able to assess why this "failure" occurs. Most states have subsidized child care so that poor women can look for and maintain work. Ironically, the cost of subsidized child care is far more expensive for the state than simply paying poor parents to stay home with their children. However, the most recent welfare reform—the Personal Responsibility and Work Opportunity Reconciliation Act of 1996—mandates that after two years of receiving aid, single mothers cannot receive welfare for another two years, and can only repeat this cycle for up to five years in total, thus forcing poor mothers to find child care for their children. Despite the fact that states have child care subsidies, fewer than one third of eligible mothers receive such subsidies (Hays, 2003). Furthermore, the choices of affordable child care are often substandard. Therefore, poor single mothers are often forced to put their children into questionable child care situations; and they often end up leaving their jobs in order to save their children from suffering in such conditions (Hays, 2003).

Social workers need to be aware of the laws and policies that exacerbate work–family conflict, even when those very laws claim to help poor women create a balance. Social workers should also be careful not to misinterpret the lack of support that facilitates women and men in maintaining productive work lives while still having their children cared for as being a lack of interest on the part of parents in becoming gainfully employed. Indeed, social workers should help their clients determine how to best mitigate work–family conflict in order to help their clients successfully move into the paid labor force while still being able to care for, and find adequate daycare for, their children.

Mass Incarceration

Since the 1970s and due to the "war on drugs" and "color blind racism," over the past 30 years the prison population has grown from approximately 300,000 in the 1970s to over 2 million in the 1990s, with the vast majority of those incarcerated being economically compromised people of color (Alexander, 2012). The negative effects the growth of mass incarceration has had on families, particularly families of color, are extraordinary. In particular, incarceration takes a huge economic toll on poor families of color. These families often experience a loss of income and housing, loss of child care, and the increased cost of supporting and maintaining contact with incarcerated family members. In addition, the high cost of phone calls from prison creates such an economic burden through collect calls that many families disconnect their phones within two months of the incarceration because of the cost. Other families stop accepting collect calls. Furthermore, prisons are often located in remote areas, thus increasing costs to visit the family member in prison, including car rental, gas, motel costs, food, and possible days away from work. In addition, families spend money to send packages and letters to the incarcerated family member (Braman, 2007).

There are also emotional costs of incarceration caused by many unknowns for family members. Will the incarcerated family member be injured in prison? Will he or she get necessary medical treatment? Will advocacy for the family member's rights cause retaliation against the family member? Who will be able to visit the inmate, how many times, and will the prison allow them in to see their loved one? Often rifts occur within families about who is visiting (or not), who is willing to accept phone calls (or not), and who is helping out (or not) in general. Many family members are embarrassed by the incarceration and experience social isolation, which leads to greater hardship at the loss of the valuable social network of friends and family (Travis & Waul, 2003).

Incarceration also affects family organization and structure because incarceration often means the removal of fathers from families and the increase in single female-headed households. At the time of reentry, previously incarcerated people have difficulty finding jobs, thus creating a financial burden on their families. The large number of Black men who are incarcerated means fewer "marriageable" men. This leads to an uneven gender ratio, which encourages men to dominate women because men have more women to choose from than women have to choose from men (Braman, 2007). Incarceration greatly affects children as well. Studies suggest that 2.7 million (or 1 in 28) children in the United States have an incarcerated parent. In addition, approximately 10 million children have experienced parental incarceration at some point in their lives. One in nine African American children (11.4%), 1 in 28 Hispanic children (3.5%), and 1 in 57 White children (1.8%) in the United States have an incarcerated parent. Approximately one half of children with incarcerated parents are under 10 years of age (Christian, 2009).

Children experience the loss of a parent as a traumatic event. That trauma diverts children's energy away from developmental tasks, and causes anxiety in coping in an uncertain situation and having to face the stigma of having a parent in prison (Travis & Waul, 2003).

Regarding laws, social workers working in prison settings will need to be familiar with the 1997 Adoption and Safe Families Act (ASFA). ASFA mandates that a state initiate termination of parental rights if that person's child or children have "been in foster care for 15 out of the past 22 months—6 months if the child is younger than [3]-years-old" (Bernstein, 2000). Often the parents whose rights are being terminated are incarcerated. Because most parents who are in prison have mandatory minimum sentences longer than ASFA time limits, they often lose parental rights (Saltzman, Furman, & Ohman, 2016).

Additional issues complicate reunification between an incarcerated parent and child. Nearly every parole and child reunification plan requires that the ex-offender or parolee have gainful employment within days or weeks of release. In the United States, women earn on average 38% less than men, even for the same work. Moreover, having served time in prison restricts the type of work an ex-offender may find and dramatically reduces the number of companies willing to hire her or him. Many of the "pink-collar" employment opportunities requiring limited training or education that would be a mainstay for low-income or working-on-advancement women, such as child care positions, teacher's aide, nursing assistant, and recreation aides in nursing homes, are unavailable. In addition, because an ex-offender usually cannot be bonded except by a state program, other entry-level jobs such as bank teller or even cleaning personnel at companies that bond their employees are unattainable.

An additional complication is that even if ex-offenders find gainful employment, they may find their wages garnished under child-support enforcement laws (Bernstein, 2000). To complicate matters, if addiction was part of the problem that initially led to involvement with the criminal justice system, getting clean and staying sober may require in-patient treatment, making parental responsibilities more difficult to maintain.

Given that "an estimated 1,706,600 minor children, accounting for 2.3% of the U.S. resident population under age 18," have a parent in prison (Glaze & Maruschak, 2008), ASFA has the potential to affect many of our nation's children. Although many of the children whose parents are incarcerated faced family instability prior to their parent's incarceration (Johnston, 2001), research suggests that children are greatly affected by parental incarceration. The uncertainty in their lives raises children's stress levels. Because schools and communities have few, if any, programs to help children of incarcerated parents, such children face a number of barriers to successfully completing the tasks that school and home demand (Travis & Waul, 2003).

Given these numbers, social workers need to meet the needs of children whose parents are incarcerated, as well as nonincarcerated parents whose partners are incarcerated. Social workers also have to address the family needs of parents in prison. This is true for social workers "who work in child welfare, mental health, infant and child development, schools, criminal justice, juvenile justice, and health care" (Social Work Policy Institute, 2008).

Core Roles and Functions of Forensic Social Work in This System

Families are involved in the justice system for civil issues, such as divorce or adoption, or criminal issues related to child abuse and neglect. To this end, social workers working with intergenerational families affected by the justice system have several core roles or functions in the system. These roles may involve assessment, such as evaluating families for child custody arrangements or allegations of child abuse and neglect. Another core function or role is that of mediator. For example, with intergenerational families affected by divorce or child abuse and neglect, serving the role of mediator is as in the case of restorative justice. This may have involved mediation or family-group conferencing (Maschi, Leibowitz, & Mizus, 2014). Another central role or function is as an advocate for a family member or family. For example, some social workers may be a child or elder advocate in the courts in cases of child or elder abuse (Maschi, Bradley, & Ward, 2009).

Relevant Theories or Frameworks

Family policy specialist Karen Bogenschneider (2014) states that "theoretical frameworks explaining the causes of social problems help lawmakers develop viable solutions to social problems, thereby indicating which decisions or interventions may offer the best chance for success." The same is true for social workers. Theory in its simplest form answers the question, "Why?" Why are some families healthier than others? Why do some family members engage in risky or harmful behavior? Why do laws support some families and constrain others? Different theories prompt us to ask different questions and help us answer questions in different ways. Because the questions we ask and the answers we get are critical to assessment and intervention, social workers must understand a variety of theoretical frameworks to help guide their work. Although there are many theories pertaining to families that are relevant to social workers, this section highlights two of them.

Multiracial Feminism

Multiracial feminism is important because it provides a useful framework from which to consider how power, privilege, and oppression shape families and their interpersonal relations. Multiracial feminism is a social structural and constructionist approach that places difference at the center of its analysis to examine how women are dissimilar from one another based on race, class, and sexuality (Baca Zinn & Dill, 1996). The theory focuses on power structures that exist both within and external to families and that help families survive, pull them apart, and/or change them in general.

Multiracial feminism addresses three main issues that can help social workers think about the families and family members they counsel. First, the theory recognizes that there is no "normal" family; rather, it is critical to understand the social context in which each family exists. Second, multiracial feminism understands power as being central to human relations, and race, class, gender, and sexuality as fundamental organizing principles that distribute rewards and resources in unequal ways to different groups of people. Third, multiracial feminism recognizes that people within families negotiate, challenge, and/or capitalize on social inequality. Social workers can greatly benefit from understanding how multiracial feminism examines the relationship between social forces and people's negotiations of these forces in shaping family experiences.

Life-Course Perspective

The life-course perspective (also known as the family life cycle framework) examines how "most families, regardless of structure or composition, progress through certain predictable marker events or phases (such as marriage, the birth of a first child, children leaving home, the death of grandparents)" (Goldenberg, Stanton, & Goldenberg, 2016). The family is a developmental system, one that changes with the events that occur over the course of the family's lifetime. The life-course theory maps out eight common transition points through the life cycle: married couple, childbearing family, preschool children, school children, teenagers, and launching children into adulthood, middle-aged parents, and aging family members. Social workers should be cautioned, however, that because of changing factors outside of families, these transitional points are often complicated by external factors (Goldenberg et al., 2016).

A main issue that life-course theorists examine is the conditions under which families cope with life changes, and the conditions under which life changes cause families to become unstable. The social worker's concern is to help families remain stable, or regain stability. Another issue is how families might lack the flexibility or ability to effectively make the transition through an event. To address such issues, social workers must look at a variety of factors, including those outside families (e.g., social, cultural, political, economic, and community-related factors), as well as those within families (e.g., family structure and interpersonal family dynamics; Goldenberg et al., 2016).

Relevant Ethical, Legal, and Policy Issues

Following the two issues discussed earlier in the chapter, this section discusses the more relevant ethical, legal, and policy issues facing work–family conflict and mass incarceration. The ethical issues regarding work–family conflict lie largely in gender and class inequalities. The expectation that child care is mostly women's responsibility remains a reality in the United States (Rehel, 2014). Therefore, women often bear the largest challenge when trying to balance work and family. While many companies offer some form of work–family conflict policies such as flex-time or flex-place, such positions are available mostly to professional-class women. Women in working-class positions rarely reap the benefits of such policies.

The lack of laws that could help alleviate the pressure of work–family conflict adds to the burden on the family. Compared to other industrialized countries such as Sweden and France, the United States lags seriously behind in offering real ways for families to balance work and family. Sweden follows a gender egalitarian model that allows both women and men to work and mind children. Child care is subsidized such that parents pay only 13% of the total child care costs, as opposed to nearly 98% in the United States. In addition, there is a focus on quality care in the Swedish model in order to nurture child development. The program was initially tailored to poor, working, single mothers but now extends to all parents, including fathers. In addition to initial parental leave, parents are entitled to 18 months of leave that includes a "wage replacement of 80% for the first year, with a flat rate for the following months" (Henderson & Jeydel, 2007).

Similar to Sweden, France has proactive child care policies aimed at helping parents balance work and family, as well as encouraging parents to have more children. France's main goal is to establish a freedom of choice for both parents. By doing this, they provide parents the option to stay at home for a long or short period of time after the birth of a child, or to take paid work, while also giving parents the option between different types of nonparental care. Parent fees are income related and are capped at 25% of the total child care costs. Preschool programs are publicly funded and are free for an eight-hour day. In addition, France offers families many different allowances to help offset the costs of child rearing. To ensure quality child care providers, France has specific training regulations for those working in the different child care settings (Henderson & Jeydel, 2007).

While work—family conflict is a pressing issue for most U.S. families, the ethical, legal, and policy issues of mass incarceration and their effects on families, particularly Black families, are deep seated and disturbing. In her 2012 book, *The New Jim Crow*, Michelle Alexander reveals the apparatus that politicians, law makers, and the police have instituted to nearly guarantee that the vast majority of Black men in the United States will be entangled in the criminal justice system either through jail, prison, parole, or probation. Through the "war on drugs," the United States has created a legal system of corruption in which local law enforcement agencies are incentivized to make drug arrests. Such incentives include the promise of military style weapons and the sharing of proceeds of property seized through drug busts.

In addition, laws that allow police officers to make arrests on a "hunch" or a pretext of some other offense, such as minor traffic violations, encourage large numbers of arrests.

Similarly, policies that encourage large sweeps for drugs that interrogate many people in hopes of catching a few drug users or dealers leads to a reign of terror over people of color that is often devastating to those involved. And despite the fact that a vast majority of drug users and sellers are White, "African Americans constitute 80% to 90% of all drug offenders sent to prison" (Alexander, 2012).

Once released from prison, laws are designed to prevent the successful reentry into legitimate society. Legally blocked from public housing and many types of work, broad and strict probation and parole regulations, and the lack of educational programs available to many people both in and out of prison, are examples of how our laws are designed specifically to send people back to prison and deepen what Alexander (2012) calls the American undercaste. What is most astounding and deeply disturbing about the mass incarceration of African Americans is that politicians—both conservative republican and liberal democratic—have created a mythical fear of drugs and Black people that is now embedded in our belief system, and therefore supports a carefully crafted set of laws and policies that serve to continually oppress Black people. The system thus privileges White people by masking the reality that while White people are drug offenders at far greater rates than Black people, they are rarely policed or convicted of drug-related crimes. Thus, because Black people are targeted as the problem, White people eschew suspicion, blame, and the humiliation and devastation of the criminal justice system.

Relevant Assessment, Prevention, and Intervention Strategies

Following the two issues discussed earlier, this section discusses the relevant assessment, prevention, and intervention strategies regarding work–family conflict and mass incarceration. When working with clients who face challenges within their families, some social workers may jump to the conclusion that those challenges exist within the character of the client, rather than caused by factors external to the clients themselves. Assuming that psychological distress is the cause of behavior indicative of a mental illness (e.g., anxiety, depression) may lead to a treatment plan based on curing psychological ills rather than understanding the social and economic factors that shape the mental well-being of a client. Therefore, this chapter encourages social workers to look beyond the individual—indeed, outside the individual—to the systems in which individuals are situated and often constrained, to better understand the behaviors, decisions, and mental health of individual clients. By helping clients and their families successfully negotiate social systems that constrain them, social workers will undoubtedly find that their clients' personal mental health will greatly improve.

Studies show that when family and work responsibilities conflict, family members—particularly the primary parental caregiver—suffer from psychological distress and marital dissatisfaction (Eby, Casper, Lockwood, Bordeaux, & Brinley, 2005; St. Vil, 2014). For example, in a study of 190 journal articles on work–family conflict between 1980 and 2002, Eby et al. (2005) found that work–family conflict creates stress for family members both at work and at home. This is true for those in professional careers who work long hours (Eby et al., 2005), as well as those living in poverty who are concerned about their children's welfare while the parents are at work (Hays, 2003). Similarly, St. Vil (2014) found that across racial boundaries, the greater the ability to balance work and family, the lower the marital stress. St. Vil (2014) also found that wives were most satisfied when they perceived the work–family balance to be fair between them and their husbands. Husbands, on the other hand, were most satisfied when there was little conflict at home regarding work–family issues.

Because the United States is reluctant to use tax dollars to implement and subsidize high-quality, low-cost child care for families, as discussed earlier, the solution for helping families mitigate and reduce work–family conflict is largely the responsibility of the workplace. Despite the evidence that the male breadwinner/female homemaker model is nearly nonexistent in the United States today, most organizations still "continue to operate as if families still adhere to such a traditional division of labor" (Sallee, 2014). In addition, many employers expect their workers to be "ideal workers," that is, workers who are willing to work long hours unimpeded by other responsibilities (Sallee, 2014). The combination of assumptions about family structure and the cultural norm of the ideal worker leads to a high stress level, particularly for single parents, parents with young children, workers with ailing parents, and people who want to advance in their careers but also want to be involved in their families.

Evidence suggests that a major way to reduce work–family conflict involves the implementation of family friendly policies, as well as the development of a workplace culture that allows employees to comfortably and confidently make use of those policies (Berheide & Linden, 2015; Sallee, 2014). Types of work–family conflict reduction efforts may include a combination of a compressed work week, telework, remote work, part-time work, job sharing, paid leave to care for sick family members, emergency time off, shift swapping, occasional flexibility, and subsidized child care (Eby et al., 2005; Santa Rosa Chamber of Commerce, n.d.) Research suggests, however, that the more white collar the job, the more work–family benefits workers may receive (Eby et al., 2005; Sallee, 2014). Therefore, while policies and workplace culture promise to help alleviate work–family conflict, those in the working class and those working minimum wage jobs often find themselves with little institutional help for alleviating such stress.

The implications of the research presented is that social workers should regularly assess the level of their client's work–family conflict to determine what effect such conflict has on their clients' mental health and interpersonal relationships (St. Vil, 2014). To be effective, social workers need to obtain the knowledge and skills to help their clients successfully negotiate and reduce work–family conflict. Efforts to aid clients might include making adjustments to family dynamics and work patterns. In addition, social workers "should actively engage in and advocate for policies that will increase work–family balance and decrease work–family conflict. Social workers can advocate for flexible hours, decreased work hours, and child care" (St. Vil, 2014).

In addition to finding interventions to help alleviate work–family conflict, social workers can find interventions to successfully help alleviate some of the stress that comes with having an incarcerated family member. In thinking about how to best help those who are incarcerated, who have partners in prison, or children who have parents in prison, consider that over the past 30 years, "parents of minor children held in the nation's prisons increased by 79%." In addition, most inmates have a minor child, and 25% are under the age of five. Moreover, approximately 50% of inmates were the primary breadwinner for their children (Glaze & Maruschak, 2008). Given the grave circumstances that face millions of families with a family member who is incarcerated, how can social workers help alleviate some of the challenges such families face?

Studies indicate that for children with incarcerated parents, social workers should approach the children with the assumption that these children have faced much trauma. Such trauma may be due to seeing their parent arrested and "the sudden separation from a parent upon arrest and imprisonment" (The Federal Interagency Working Group for Children of Incarcerated Parents, 2013). Studies also show that children of incarcerated parents may have experienced other trauma connected to the environment in which they lived prior to their parent's arrest (The Federal Interagency Working Group for Children of Incarcerated Parents, 2013).

Social workers working in social welfare agencies can intervene during the entire process from arrest to reentry. For example, by helping law enforcement agencies at the time of arrest, social workers can "potentially prevent placements and eliminate harm to children" (Lincroft, 2011). Furthermore, social workers can try to mitigate the trauma through working on changing systems and practices in ways that help children. For example, social workers can help by ensuring jail and prison visiting conditions are sensitive to the needs of children; offering opportunities for incarcerated parents to increase their parenting capacities to nurture and support their children; promoting opportunities for positive communication between incarcerated parents and their children, where appropriate; and working to facilitate a parent's involvement in his/her child's schooling where appropriate, despite the obstacles inherent in incarceration (The Federal Interagency Working Group for Children of Incarcerated Parents, 2013).

Social workers can also help children communicate with their incarcerated parents, and vice versa. They can also help maintain child–parent contacts during the time in which the parent is in prison. And social workers can help inmates create a reentry plan so that their reentry is as successful as possible (Lincroft, 2011).

Forensic Practice Skill Set

Forensic social workers are often proficient in generalist and specialized micro, mezzo, and macro skills that are drawn from working with intergenerational families involved in the justice system. Family counseling and mediation skills are important skills for social workers providing clinical or supportive services for justice-involved families. Mediation, or family-group counseling skills, are also skills useful for working with families in conflict, or in which abuse and neglect or other types of trauma have occurred in families. Case- and legislative-level advocacy are also important. Social workers may be involved in advocating for need resources or family rights when agency or organizational policies negatively impact a family. For example, a forensic social worker may advocate for the right of a father in prison to see his child when the mother has not been honoring this right. At a legislative level, a social worker may advocate for family visiting rights for people in prison (Maschi et al., 2009).

Case Example and Application

To help build healthy families, social workers in family services must guard against potential biases toward what constitutes a "good" or "normal" family based on their own experiences. For example, there is some evidence that social workers prefer and therefore recommend to the court a continued placement with a middle-class foster family as opposed to reunification with a child's working-class family, even once any reasons for foster placement have been resolved, simply because the social worker feels that the child would have better opportunities in the middle-class family (Saltzman et al., 2016). Advocacy for the child's best interest is paramount, but social workers must carefully consider their own prejudices when they consider what constitutes a "best" placement.

Case Study

Theresa B., a White 26-year-old mother of a biracial 7-year-old daughter, presents some ways social workers may become involved with a family in need of services in which they would need to show both a cultural understanding, as well as an understanding of structural forces and constraints. Theresa was convicted of attempted murder when she was 24 years old. Under the influence of drugs and alcohol, and possibly based on unaddressed psychiatric problems, Theresa stabbed her father repeatedly at their home, thinking he was attacking her. Her father, though he required prolonged medical care, survived the attack and eventually resumed his normal life. A social worker was involved with the family while the father was hospitalized because the family had no health care coverage and required access to in-home nursing care for which they could not provide funds. The social worker helped the family access the required health care and the other agencies that provided medical assistance to the father. The social worker also assisted with child care for their granddaughter during the convalescence and recovery time.

(continued)

Once arrested, Theresa felt consumed with remorse and became suicidal; she was consequently placed on suicide watch while awaiting her trial. Social workers visited her at the county jail where she was held without bond until her trial. The testimony and assessments of the social workers and psychiatrists who interviewed her were part of the legal process that determined Theresa should serve a 10-year term for her actions. Once incarcerated at the prison, social workers there assessed her again, and developed a treatment plan for Theresa's addiction and anger issues. Her long-time boyfriend, an IV-drug user, died of an overdose shortly after she was incarcerated and, because he was not immediate family, there was no provision for her to be able to attend a private viewing of his remains or to attend the funeral. Social workers ran the grief management support group and saw Theresa individually as she coped with this loss. She became suicidal again at this time, and remained under the care of counselors and a psychiatrist for psychotropic medication.

Because Theresa's sentence was long, and because social workers for the child welfare services organization in her state determined Theresa's parents' home to not be the best placement for her daughter's long-term best interests, they started the process to terminate Theresa's parental rights, which ultimately were terminated. Social workers were part of the process on her daughter's behalf, assessing the girl's performance in school and at home, as well as her current and projected relationship with her mother and extended family, and making recommendations to the court as to what placement would suit her needs most effectively in the long term. Rather than the same social worker completing all the phases of intervention in this case, many social workers were involved in the various needs this family presented. Theresa's case illustrates the need for social workers to carefully assess each person's life circumstances, needs, and limitations. Because many factors shape people's lives in a variety of ways, social workers must be careful to assess many issues that may force them to reconsider their own definitions and assumptions about what makes for a healthy family.

Conclusion

Understanding how factors external to families greatly affect the interpersonal relationships and problems within families is critical for social workers. Laws and practices shaping employment, policing, and incarceration, for example, as well as laws beyond those discussed in this chapter, can disrupt families in serious and personal ways. To best support and serve families, social workers will need to draw on their micro, mezzo, and macro skills. For example, family social workers should have strong skills in family counseling, family group counseling, and mediation. They should also be able to engage in case and legislative level advocacy, particularly advocating for resources or rights when policies negatively impact families.

CHAPTER EXERCISES

Exercise 1. Drawing on the case study, write a treatment plan based on two of the issues raised in the case study.

Exercise 2. Research two policies affecting families and incarceration, or families balancing work and home responsibilities. Present those policies, focusing on how social workers can help families negotiate the relevant social institutions that create barriers to being healthy families.

Exercise 3. Research work–family policies at two different types of work sites. After comparing the two, explain how these policies affect family dynamics and what role social workers can play in helping family members negotiate their work–family balance issues.

Exercise 4. Research the impact of incarceration on the children and adults who are on the outside. Describe how social workers can help children and adults whose family members have been incarcerated.

Additional Resources

The Annie E. Casey Foundation, When a Parent Is Incarcerated: A Primer for Social Workers: www.aecf .org/resources/when-a-parent-is-incarcerated

Careers in Psychology.org, Start a Family Social Work Career: http://careersinpsychology.org/become -a-family-social-worker

United Nations Department of Economic and Social Affairs, Work-family balance benefits families and society: www.un.org/en/development/desa/news/social/work-family-balance-benefits -families-and-society.html

References

Alexander, M. (2012). *The new Jim Crow: Mass incarceration in the age of colorblindness* (Rev. ed.). New York, NY: The New Press.

Ameristat. (2003, March). Traditional families account for only 7 percent of United States households. Retrieved from http://www.prb.org/Publications/Articles/2003/TraditionalFamiliesAccountfor Only7PercentofUSHouseholds.aspx

Anderson, E. K. (2015). "Could I be THAT guy?": The influence of policy and climate on men's paternity leave use. In E. K. Anderson & C. R. Solomon (Eds.), *Family-friendly policies and practices in academe* (pp. 51–68). New York, NY: Lexington Books.

Baca Zinn, M., & Dill, B. T. (1996). Theorizing difference from multiracial feminism. *Feminist Studies*, 22(2), 321–331.

Berheide, C. W., & Linden, R. (2015). [Do work/life policies matter? The importance of work/life policies for reducing faculty intention to quit]. In E. K. Anderson & C. R. Solomon (Eds.), *Family-friendly policies and practices in academe* (pp. 27–50). New York, NY: Lexington Books.

Bernstein, N. (2000). Motherless children: The drug war has stamped an entire class of parents as permanently unfit. Retrieved from http://www.salon.com/2000/10/25/drug_families

Bogenschneider, K. (2014). *Family policy matters: How policymaking affects families and what professionals can do* (3rd ed.). New York, NY: Routledge.

Braman, D. (2007). *Doing time on the outside: Incarceration and family life in urban America*. Ann Arbor: University of Michigan Press.

Christian, S. (2009). Children of incarcerated parents. Retrieved from http://www.ncsl.org/ documents/cyf/childrenofincarceratedparents.pdf

Department of Labor. (n.d.). FMLA (family & medical leave). Retrieved from http://www.dol.gov/ general/topic/benefits-leave/fmla

Dewees, M. (2006). *Contemporary social work practice*. Boston, MA: McGraw-Hill.

Dill, B. T., Baca Zinn, M., & Patton, S. (1998). Valuing families differently: Race, poverty and welfare reform. *Sage Race Relations Abstracts*, 23(3), 4–30.

Eby, L. T., Casper, W. J., Lockwood, A., Bordeaux, C., & Brinley, A. (2005). Work and family research in IO/OB: Content analysis and review of the literature (1980–2002). *Journal of Vocational Behavior, 66*, 124–197. doi:10.1016/j.jvb.2003.11.003

The Federal Interagency Working Group for Children of Incarcerated Parents. (2013). Promoting social and emotional well-being for children of incarcerated parents. Retrieved from https:// csgjusticecenter.org/wp-content/uploads/2013/06/Promoting-Social-and-Emotional-Well -Being-for-Children-of-Incarcerated-Parents.pdf

Glaze, L. E., & Maruschak, L. M. (2008). Parents in prison and their minor children. Retrieved from http://www.bjs.gov/content/pub/pdf/pptmc.pdf

Goldenberg, I., Stanton, M., & Goldenberg, H. (2016). *Family therapy: An overview* (5th ed.). Boston, MA: Cengage.

Hays, S. (2003). *Flat broke with children: Women in the age of welfare reform*. New York, NY: Oxford University Press.

Henderson, S., & Jeydel, A. S. (2007). *Participation and protest: Women and politics in a global world*. New York, NY: Oxford University Press.

Johnston, D. (2001). *Incarceration of women and effects on parenting*. Paper presented at the Institute for Policy Studies conference on "The Effects of Incarceration on Children and Families," Northwestern University, Evanston, IL.

Lincroft, Y. (2011). Children of incarcerated parents. Retrieved from https://firstfocus.org/resources/ fact-sheet/children-incarcerated-parents

Maschi, T., Bradley, C., & Ward, K. (Eds.). (2009). *Forensic social work: Psychosocial and legal issues in diverse practice settings*. New York, NY: Springer Publishing.

Rehel, E. M. (2014). When dad stays home too: Paternity leave, gender, and parenting. *Gender & Society, 28*, 110–132. doi:10.1177/0891243213503900

Sallee, M. W. (2014). *Faculty fathers: Toward a new ideal in the research university*. Albany, NY: SUNY Press.

Saltzman, A., Furman, D. M., & Ohman, K. (2016). *Law in social work practice* (3rd ed.). Boston, MA: Cengage.

Santa Rosa Chamber of Commerce. (n.d.). Family-friendly workplace policies that you can adopt. Retrieved from http://www.santarosachamber.com/wheel/family-friendly-workplace-policies -that-you-can-adopt

Social Work Policy Institute. (2008). Children with incarcerated parents. Retrieved from http://www .socialworkpolicy.org/research/children-with-incarcerated-parents.html

Solomon, C. R. (2015). University family-friendly policies: Professors' experiences and perceptions. In E. K. Anderson & C. R. Solomon (Eds.), *Family-friendly policies and practices in academe* (pp. 9–26). New York, NY: Lexington Books.

St. Vil, N. M. (2014). African American marital satisfaction as a function of work-family balance and work-family conflict and implications for social workers. *Journal of Human Behavior in the Social Environment, 24*, 208–216. doi:10.1080/10911359.2014.848694

Travis, J., & Waul, M. (Eds.). (2003). Prisoners once removed: The children and families of prisoners. In J. Travis & M. Waul (Eds.), *Prisoners once removed: The impact of incarceration and reentry on children, families, and communities* (pp. 1–28). Washington, DC: Urban Institute Press.

Zastrow, C. (2009). *Introduction to social work and social welfare: Empowering people* (10th ed.). Belmont, CA: Brooks/Cole.

VOICES FROM THE FIELD

Victoria Marini, PhD
Claire Gilligan, PsyD
Forensic Psychologists
Vermont Forensic Assessment, PLLC

Agency Setting

Vermont Forensic Assessment, PLLC is an established group practice comprised of four independent licensed doctoral psychologists based in Shelburne, Vermont. Dr. Gilligan is a partner of the practice and Dr. Marini is an associate on the partnership track. The practice conducts a range of forensic psychological evaluations, including general psychological, psychosexual, violence risk, fitness-for-duty, criminal responsibility, and parenting capacity evaluations. We meet with and observe evaluees in a variety of settings across the state to include at our offices, jails, attorney and agency offices, homes, and schools. We also provide consulting services to Vermont's incarcerated and community sex offender treatment program, probation and parole offices that manage sex offenders in the community, and schools that have identified students with violent and/or sexual behavior challenges, among other agencies. We often testify as experts in our fields, both in state criminal and juvenile court, and federal court.

Practice Responsibilities

As noted earlier, our main responsibilities are to conduct evaluations from numerous referral sources. Less frequently, we are called to testify in court with regard to our findings. There is no "typical day," but rather in a given day we might be interviewing an evaluee; conducting collateral interviews; administering, scoring, or interpreting psychological testing; preparing reports; and/or consulting with referral sources. Some weeks are spent largely on the road, interviewing evaluees around the state. Others are spent quietly in our private office writing reports and billing. To promote quality work and ethical practice, we also meet formally as a group once weekly to consult on cases and engage with guest speakers from our community (e.g., state agencies and evaluators).

Expertise Required

In order to be a practicing forensic psychologist, you must obtain a graduate degree, typically doctoral, and psychology licensure within your state. Many forensic psychologists obtain a degree in clinical psychology and specialize in forensic psychology by obtaining additional training and experience typically through supervision, consultation, and education. In addition, forensic psychologists must also have a working knowledge of the legal system. This includes the ability to apply legal statutes and standards in cases, communicate findings and opinions with relevant parties (e.g., lawyers, judges, and other authoritative bodies), and serve as an expert witness.

Ethical, Legal, Practice, Diversity, and/or Advocacy Issues Addressed

The evaluations we complete often have important ramifications for the individual being assessed. In a fitness-for-duty evaluation, for example, the results could dictate whether or not a particular individual remains in his or her job. In a risk assessment, the results could make the difference between community supervision or incarceration. Because of the high stakes of our work, we must operate at high levels of ethical and professional standards. We must stay up-to-date on current research and invest in additional training by routinely attending conferences and workshops. We belong to a listserv for our profession so we are constantly exposed to current debates on how to approach difficult topics, cases, and scenarios.

We also have to acknowledge that because of the high stakes associated with our work and referral questions, we, like other forensic psychologists, are exposed to an evaluee taking legal action against us at a higher rate than psychologists providing outpatient treatment, for example. As a means of ensuring integrity, we routinely ask our colleagues in the practice to consult and review our work. We value the opinion of our colleagues at Vermont Forensic Assessment, and could not imagine doing this work in isolation. Working in a group practice also helps prevent against burnout, which is a reality of ours due to the nature of the cases, many of which involve perpetrators of sexual and violent crimes and other forms of trauma. Our colleagues become a sounding board to retain perspective or simply blow off steam.

Although we can speak of many practice issues, one that comes to mind is recognizing your bias—especially allegiance to the retaining party (e.g., defense versus state). Psychologists are typically helpers and want to please others. These tendencies must be acknowledged and left at the door as we communicate with referral sources who may try to sway us toward a particular opinion. We must remain true to our role as a neutral party by relying on our data and methodology, developing and testing hypotheses, and considering alternative explanations. We must also learn not to take our work personally when a referral source disagrees with our findings or an opposing attorney calls our expertise or findings into question during testimony. It is all part of the highly rewarding job.

Interprofessional and Intersectoral Collaboration

As forensic psychologists, we are, by definition, working at the nexus of psychology and the law. Particularly when we testify, but also when approaching a case, formulating recommendations, and preparing a report, we must operate through the lens of our referral source, using their language and being guided by their practices. On a given day, we communicate with attorneys or social workers as our referral sources, interview community mental health providers and educators as collateral sources, and/or provide consultation to treatment providers and other agencies throughout the state. As a result, we must learn the language of many disciplines, including correctional, community mental health, and legal.

CHAPTER 10

Family and Social Services: Meeting Basic Human Needs of Income, Food, and Shelter

Anne Sparks

CHAPTER OBJECTIVES

The major objectives of this chapter are to:

- Examine the significance for vulnerable groups of social welfare policies and advocacy to meet basic human needs.
- Identify key policies and programs established to meet needs of income, food, and shelter.
- Encourage students to begin using research and statistical data to assess needs and adequacy of programs.
- Identify social work's role and skills in addressing needs of vulnerable groups.

CHAPTER COMPETENCIES HIGHLIGHTED

- Competency 3: Advance Human Rights and Social, Economic, and Environmental Justice
- Competency 5: Engage in Policy Practice
- Competencies 7 and 8: Assess and Intervene With Individuals, Families, Organizations, and Communities
- Competency 9: Evaluate Practice With Individuals, Families, Organizations, and Communities

Through the passage of the Social Security Act of 1935, the United States made a commitment to provide a national safety net for poor and vulnerable populations. The act established a social justice framework that includes governmental and societal responsibility for assisting individuals and families who have difficulty meeting their basic human needs. This chapter focuses on the key role of social work professionals in establishing, maintaining, and improving programs needed to ensure a basic level of income for families with children (i.e., income security), access to adequate nutrition (i.e., food security), and access to adequate shelter (i.e., housing security). The activities of social workers in legal arenas regarding basic human needs include influencing the passage and implementation of laws that establish the necessary programs and advocating for clients' rights to access the programs, along with directly serving clients involved with the criminal justice system.

The general category of people whose basic needs have not been, or may not be, adequately met includes those considered poor (i.e., living at or below the poverty level), those living in economically distressed communities that lack adequate resources, and those who are vulnerable owing to factors such as age and discrimination based on gender or race/ethnicity. Women have been considered vulnerable because of barriers to employment, lower earnings in comparison to similarly employed men, and (for mothers) the responsibilities of caring for children. Women subjected to violence and abuse are considered particularly vulnerable, and social work has provided leadership in advocating and developing specialized services for battered women and their children. Children are vulnerable because of their dependence on others and their environment for healthy development. In 2014, 21% of children in the United States lived in families officially considered poor, and the percentage of African American and Latino children in low-income families was twice as high as the percentage of White children in low-income families (National Center for Children in Poverty, 2016).

As part of our ethical duty to promote the general welfare of society, social workers contribute to the ongoing debate about how to create and maintain "living conditions conducive to the fulfillment of basic human needs" (National Association of Social Workers [NASW], 1999); as practitioners we use our professional knowledge and skill to connect individual clients with basic resources. Social workers collaborate with other professions and interest groups to establish programs and services at local, state, and national levels and to monitor programs' responsiveness and adequacy. The fact that people who grow up in poverty face a greater likelihood of experiencing incarceration makes it especially important to lower poverty rates and increase resources for offenders who reenter poor communities after completing their sentences. Some victims of crime, particularly women with children attempting to leave abusive partners, are also at high risk for poverty.

Social work has historically been involved with public welfare agencies and provision of financial assistance. The profession's advocacy role is evident in the strong opposition it mobilized to the initiative known as "welfare reform" that ended Aid to Families with Dependent Children (AFDC) in 1996 and replaced it with Temporary Assistance to Needy Families (TANF). The profession has supported expansion of national programs to prevent hunger, such as the Supplemental Nutrition Assistance Program (SNAP/food stamps) and the National School Lunch Program. Social workers help establish and maintain community programs that provide food to those without adequate incomes or in emergency situations. The profession's involvement in the housing arena includes advocating for subsidized housing for people with low and moderate incomes and creating residential programs for groups needing transitional housing, such as offenders reentering the community and people recovering from substance abuse.

This chapter provides a brief overview of three arenas of basic human needs (income, food, and housing) and discusses the challenges faced by social workers who serve populations with these needs, including offenders and victims of crime. The chapter draws particular attention to the increased hardships caused by the Great Recession from 2007 to 2009 (Pilkauskas, Currie, & Garfinkel, 2012) and the slow economic recovery. A greater focus on the financial environment and policy making will enable social workers to assist in establishing a stronger "safety net" for vulnerable populations.

Public Assistance or "Welfare"

The Social Security Act of 1935 established Aid to Dependent Children (later known as AFDC). The program provided assistance to children in poor families without a male breadwinner, based on the rationale that mothers were needed by the children and should not be forced to work outside the home. During the 1970s, as role expectations based on gender changed and more mothers entered the labor market, public debate began to focus on the increasing number of female-headed households receiving public assistance. During the 1980s, criticisms of AFDC were bolstered by concerns that childbearing among unmarried adolescents had increased, and many unmarried fathers took no financial responsibility for their children. The push for welfare reform gained momentum from the argument that welfare dependency was becoming a way of life for some families and from recognition that the bureaucratic culture of welfare agencies did not provide the means or incentives for recipients to become self-sufficient. Qualitative researchers found that although AFDC recipients often sought employment, low-wage jobs did not provide the income or stability they needed in order to care for their children adequately (Edin & Lein, 1997). Despite lack of support from research, the idea that poverty was caused by childbearing outside marriage continued to influence the public. A more restrictive program, TANF, replaced AFDC through passage of the Personal Responsibility and Work Opportunity Act (PRWOA) of 1996.

Fundamental changes in public assistance as a result of PRWOA included limiting receipt of cash assistance to a maximum of five years in a person's lifetime, the requirement that recipients must participate in work or work-related activities, and new latitude for each state in deciding how to spend TANF funds (now received as a Block Grant). During the first five years of welfare reform, a strong economy and the increased earned-income tax credit (EITC) made it possible for many TANF recipients (primarily single mothers) to transition successfully from welfare to work. Some in this group received training that enabled them to obtain jobs with benefits and the possibility of advancement; others, however, obtained low-wage positions without benefits or job security. A study of the impact of welfare reform that focused on the income of former recipients found that one group had increased their income since leaving TANF, whereas another group had dropped into deeper poverty (Acs & Loprest, 2007). Some recipients who had not benefited from work-preparation programs had been permitted to continue as TANF recipients as a result of documented hardships (e.g., severe health problems or caring for family members with disabilities). Allard (2002) found that 42 states were enforcing a lifetime ban preventing felony drug offenders from ever receiving welfare.

Regulations in the reauthorization of TANF placed more requirements on the states, including new restrictions on what states could count as work or work-related activities for current recipients. The National Association of Social Workers (NASW) unsuccessfully campaigned against the new rules (NASW, 2006a). In testimony to the House Committee on Ways and Means, NASW (2006b) pointed out that meeting the new rules would increase recipients' needs for child care, although no additional funding for child care was being provided. The Center for Law & Social Policy (2007) recommended to the House Ways and Means Committee that Congress remove arbitrary limits on education and training for TANF recipients, allow modifications of participation requirements for individuals with disabilities, and restore cuts in funding for child-support enforcement.

The limitations of the assumptions underlying TANF and the inability of the program to respond to sharp increases in costs of food and fuel (while homelessness and unemployment increased) raise profound concerns (Dillon, 2008). Social workers as individual professionals and as members of organizations and coalitions are encouraged to use advocacy skills to strengthen the safety net function of TANF and improve its ability to lead to stable, decently paying employment (Pavetti & Schott, 2016).

Because of variations among the states in regulations and the amount of cash assistance a family may receive per month, there is no manual that can be used in every state to inform TANF applicants and recipients of all the relevant procedures, available benefits, and eligibility requirements. The eligibility of ex-offenders for TANF also varies from state to state. However, in all states, applicants and recipients do have the right to request a fair hearing when they believe that an adverse decision affecting their status was incorrect. Such decisions include denying benefits, sanctioning a client, and terminating benefits. Besides setting the individual maximum lifetime limit of five years on receiving TANF (although permitting states to grant some exemptions), federal regulations require that states sanction recipients by decreasing their cash assistance when recipients fail to comply with work requirements. Social workers serving low-income families need to be aware of the hardships that sanctioning causes (Reichman, Teitler, & Curtis, 2005) and the rights of recipients to appeal the decision to impose sanctions (as well as decisions to deny and terminate benefits) through the fair hearing procedure (U.S. Department of Public Health & Human Services, 2007). Lens (2006) analyzed administrative data from fair hearing decisions in Texas and found that 49% of the hearings resulted in reversing the action that had been taken by the welfare office. The fair hearing records showed that the most frequent reasons for reversing decisions were that welfare workers had failed to provide or obtain necessary information, had applied the rules too rigidly without considering the goals of the program, or had entered case information incorrectly (Lens, 2006). Social workers should obtain information about the policies and procedures of the welfare offices serving their clients. If a client receives a notice of denial, sanction, or termination from TANF, the social worker should explore with the client whether grounds may exist for appealing this decision (e.g., the possibility of administrative error or documented conditions that interfere with the clients' ability to understand and comply with requirements). If such grounds exist, the client may decide to request a fair hearing. Social workers also need to be aware of TANF's Family Violence Option (FVO), which gives states the flexibility to exempt victims of domestic violence from certain program requirements and to extend the time limits on benefits so that they can obtain safety for themselves and their children (Postmus & Ah Hahn, 2007).

Food Insecurity

To indicate the degree to which people lack adequate means of obtaining food and risk malnourishment, the U.S. Department of Agriculture (USDA) replaced the term *hunger* with two categories of "food insecurity": *Low* food security means that people have a reduced quality or quantity of food because of budget limitations; *very low* food security means that people have to cut back on eating or skip meals on a frequent basis. Food hardship is defined as not having enough money to purchase food needed for oneself and one's family. According to the Food Research & Action Center (FRAC), over 19% of people in the United States experienced food hardship due to the Great Recession, and that rate had only fallen to 16% in 2015 (FRAC, 2016). The main safety net provided by the federal government for people experiencing food insecurity is the Supplemental Nutrition Assistance Program (SNAP), still commonly known as the Food Stamp Program. It now subsidizes the purchase of food by low-income individuals and families through an electronic benefit transfer system. An increase in the number of families receiving SNAP, as well as the improved employment rate, helped reduce food hardship in 2015 (FRAC, 2016). Eligibility requirements for SNAP vary somewhat from state to state, but, in general, households with a net income equal to or less than 100% of the poverty guidelines are eligible (U.S. Department of Agriculture, 2017). Poverty-level income for a household of four in 2015 was $24,250 (U.S. Department of Health & Human Services, 2015). Food stamps, combined with unemployment insurance, have helped prevent hunger in communities facing the loss of jobs. However, many of the working-poor families that are eligible for food stamps do not receive them.

A survey of 23 U.S. cities found that the needs for emergency food assistance were not adequately met in 2007, at the beginning of the Great Recession (U.S. Conference of Mayors, 2007). The survey found that the recent jump in foreclosures on home mortgages and increases in the cost of living, including food costs, had exacerbated the current "hunger crisis." Cities reported that the Food Stamp Program benefit levels had not kept up with the increasing price of food, causing some families to seek emergency food assistance when their food stamps were used up before the end of the month (U.S. Conference of Mayors, 2007).

Hunger in itself is cause for concern, but being able to avoid hunger does not mean that the person is receiving adequate nutrition. Among the people who utilized Feeding America's food pantries in 2014, almost four fifths reported that to provide for their household they purchased the cheapest food available, even if they knew it was not the healthiest for them (Feeding America, 2016).

Social workers are involved in local campaigns to collect food in response to downturns in the economy and emergencies, as well as ongoing need. They also educate the public about the availability of assistance programs such as SNAP and emphasize the rights and dignity of recipients in order to decrease the perceived stigma of receiving such help. However, the consequences of poor nutrition for infants and children and the importance of adequate diet for managing serious health conditions indicate a need for continued efforts on all levels to reduce food hardship and insecurity. Feeding America's website (www.feedingamerica .org) has a feature enabling people to locate the closest food bank and other free sources of food and meals in their area. Both Feeding America and the Food Research and Action Center (http://frac.org) provide guidelines for effective advocacy to strengthen food assistance programs and decrease hunger.

Homelessness

National policy began to address the needs of homeless people in 1987 through the Stewart B. McKinney Homeless Assistance Act. During the 1990s, shelter services expanded throughout the United States, and increased numbers of people sought these services. Social workers provide a variety of services to individuals and families who are homeless (or in danger of becoming homeless) and also work at local, state, and national levels to improve these services and address the causes of homelessness. The groups at greatest risk of homelessness are those with unstable or low incomes, including those working full-time jobs paying the minimum wage (Doran, 2015). Physical disabilities and health and mental health problems (including substance abuse) are risk factors, as are limited education or skills training; community risk factors include the gap between wages for unskilled work and the cost of housing (Burt, 2001). For youth, experiences of physical and sexual abuse, foster home placement, and incarceration (for males) are predictors of homelessness. Children who experience homelessness have more cognitive and emotional difficulties than other children and are also at greater risk for homelessness in adulthood (Burt, 2001). The experience of even a brief period of homelessness, for children or adults, is stressful and disruptive.

In a 2007 survey of 23 major cities, the U.S. Conference of Mayors (2007) found that 23% of those using emergency shelters and transitional housing programs were members of homeless families, whereas 76% were single adults and 1% were unaccompanied youth. Six cities reported an increase in the overall number, and 10 cities reported an increase in the number of households with children who used shelters and transitional housing services in 2007. Twelve cities reported that they were not able to serve everyone who requested shelter. Cities in 2007 identified the lack of affordable housing, poverty, and domestic violence as common causes of homelessness for households with children; for single individuals, the most common causes were mental illness and substance abuse. Fifteen of the surveyed cities foresaw the increase in requests for emergency shelter among households with children in 2008 as a result of the foreclosure crisis and increased poverty. The officials' most common response to the question of what their city needed to do to reduce homelessness was to provide more permanent housing (U.S. Conference of Mayors, 2007).

Although generally critical of federal housing policy, social work analysts support programs such as Section 8 housing vouchers, which expand opportunities for the poor to obtain decent housing in economically stable communities (Gilbert & Terrell, 2005). Social work strongly supports the Violence Against Women Act, which includes funding for emergency shelters, transitional housing, and permanent housing for victims of domestic violence (National Low Income Housing Coalition, 2007). Social work supports transitional services, including housing, for prisoners reentering the community, and social workers actively participated in President Obama's Homeless Veterans Outreach Initiative, which has significantly decreased the percentage of veterans who are homeless (Malai, 2013).

Housing Crisis and Predatory Lending

Beginning early in 2007, the percentage of home mortgages going into default began to rise as homeowners faced steep increases in the monthly payments due. This was the beginning of the Great Recession. In 2008, more than 3 million Americans lost their homes due to inability to pay their monthly mortgage bills (Ross & Squires, 2011). Increases in monthly mortgage payments stemmed from variable interest rates and other features of subprime lending, in which lenders are not held to the same regulations as traditional banks (Wharton School of the University of Pennsylvania, 2007). In subprime lending, borrowers whose income levels and credit histories would not normally qualify them for loans were offered loans at higher interest rates and with higher fees than those offered by traditional lenders. The term *predatory lending* is used when borrowers are not knowledgeable about the actual terms of the agreement, or clearly lack the means to meet the terms of repayment, and deceptive promotional offers may be involved (Hirsh, 2008).

Social workers became more aware of consumer rights and protections in order to advocate for clients who had been exploited, including those in danger of losing their homes, due to predatory lending. For example, Metropolitan Family Services, a comprehensive social service agency in Chicago, campaigned for regulation of predatory lending. Social workers are beginning to analyze and address the impact of financial practices on low-income communities (Caplan, 2014). Social service agencies should expand resources available to assist clients who want to improve their financial literacy, avoid inappropriate loans, and effectively manage debt (Karger, 2015).

Chapter Vignette—Applying Theories and Skills

Systems theory is helpful when working with client populations who struggle to meet basic human needs, and especially those with legal and criminal justice involvement, because it enables social workers to understand clients' interactions with a range of institutions and complex systems. The social worker links clients to necessary services, using "resource consultation or case management" skills (Greene, 1999, p. 240), and often provides input to develop or strengthen those resources as well. Social workers use systems theory to understand structural aspects of organizations and programs that control resources; they use systems theory together with ecological theory to assess the needs in a given community and develop and implement strategies to address those needs. In the criminal justice arena, social workers must translate their knowledge of the system's requirements and available resources into information that clients can comprehend and use. Following is a description of situations in which the social worker in a shelter for the homeless uses the skills of case management, collaboration, advocacy, and education to provide ways for people to access resources and establish stable living situations.

The agency is a faith-based organization with a range of programs including a shelter serving several counties in rural Appalachia. The social worker initially meets with each homeless individual and family staying in the shelter to conduct an assessment and develop a service plan. The homeless clients come from many backgrounds: some experienced personal difficulties that made them particularly vulnerable, whereas others have lived for long periods in extreme poverty without heat and running water. Some people have lived in rental storage units; others have "coasted from couch to couch." Youths with experience in foster care often become homeless. Clearly, it is vital for the social worker to coordinate services and communicate regularly with other organizations that assist shelter residents and/or have authority in their lives, such as probation officers and Child Protective Services.

(continued)

Clients have the opportunity to receive a positive reference from the shelter staff, based on following their case plan and demonstrating their willingness and ability to keep their living area clean and interact appropriately with staff and other residents. This reference has a positive impact because the shelter is a respected agency with a history of collaborating effectively with other institutions within the community. The reference may help the client obtain an apartment or open a bank account without providing a credit check; it may persuade a judge to sentence the client to community service instead of a term in jail. The social worker advocates on behalf of clients with other agencies, for example, clients may have been unaware of requirements they were expected to meet, perhaps in order to continue to receive food stamps, because they had no residence where they could receive mail. The shelter allows clients to use the agency's address and makes it possible for them to accomplish basic tasks that are taken for granted by people with housing, for example, making phone calls, obtaining identification, and traveling to health care services and agencies where they can apply for permanent housing or disability benefits. The social worker educates clients about the systems that affect their current and future ability to reach their goals. The social worker also educates people in the community about the causes and prevalence of homelessness and involves them in the program as volunteers. The social worker is currently facing an ethical dilemma because of federal funding requirements. To maintain its funding, the shelter is required to collect extensive personal information from every shelter resident and enter it into an online database. Respecting clients' rights to privacy and informed consent, the social worker tells new residents about the information system and asks if they are willing to give the information and have it entered into the database. Clients' wishes have been respected, and usually a minimal amount of information is entered; however, pressure to obtain complete data from every resident has recently increased.

Conclusion

Social workers across the range of professional settings must be prepared to assist vulnerable individuals and families in need of income, food, and shelter. Forensic social work requires application of case management, collaboration, advocacy, and education skills in directly assisting vulnerable clients; application of systems knowledge is necessary to build and maintain supportive community resource networks.

The profession works in legal arenas related to meeting basic human needs by influencing passage and implementation of laws that establish effective programs and by advocating for clients' rights to access benefits and services. The recent Great Recession and subsequent slow economic recovery in the United States have made the inadequacies of current income, food, and housing assistance programs apparent. Social workers mobilized to address the housing crisis brought on by massive foreclosures in 2007 and 2008 and continue working to meet ongoing needs of struggling communities. In response to the damaging effects of predatory lending and other types of financial exploitation, the profession has successfully joined other advocacy groups to improve consumer protection and require accountability in the lending and banking industries. New directions include developing programs to strengthen clients' financial capability and acquiring expertise in order to influence economic as well as social welfare policy.

CHAPTER EXERCISES

Exercise 1. Using the chapter vignette, role-play how a social worker may interact with a client requesting shelter services.

Exercise 2. Watch the following YouTube video, "My Path Out of Poverty": www.youtube .com/watch?v=CpaFX6Ei0nU

Discuss in small or large groups the skills social workers can use to assist individuals in getting out of poverty.

Exercise 3. In small groups, choose an article to read from those posted on the following web page: www.mothersmovement.org/resources/welfare.htm. Discuss in large group the information you found and/or debate the pros and cons of the major argument of that paper.

Exercise 4. Review the following webpage: http://nlihc.org/issues/criminal-justice. Discuss in class how social work can play a role in helping individuals overcome housing barriers.

Exercise 5. Listen to the following NPR podcast: www.npr.org/sections/thetwo -way/2016/04/04/472878724/denying-housing-over-criminal-record-may-be -discrimination-feds-say. Debate in class whether or not denying housing to people with criminal justice histories is discrimination or not.

Additional Resources

Council on State Governments Justice Center-HUD and Housing: https://csgjusticecenter.org/reentry/ posts/hud-continues-push-to-increase-access-to-housing-for-people-with-criminal-records

The Mother's Movement: www.mothersmovement.org/resources/welfare.htm

National Low Income Housing Coalition: http://nlihc.org/issues/criminal-justice

References

Acs, G., & Loprest, P. (2007). *TANF caseload composition and leavers synthesis report*. Washington, DC: The Urban Institute. Retrieved from http://www.urban.org/UploadedPDF/411553_tanf_caseload .pdf

Allard, P. (2002). *Life sentences: Denying welfare benefits to women convicted of drug offenses*. Washington, DC: The Sentencing Project: Research and Advocacy for Reform. Retrieved from https://www .opensocietyfoundations.org/reports/life-sentences-denying-welfare-benefits-women-convicted -drug-offenses

Burt, M. (2001). *What will it take to end homelessness*? Washington, DC: The Urban Institute. Retrieved from http://www.urban.org/url.cfm?ID=310305

Caplan, M. A. (2014). Communities respond to predatory lending. *Social Work, 59*(2), 149–156.

Center for Law & Social Policy. (2007). Congress should take action to restore flexibility and funding lost in 2006 welfare reauthorization and HHS regulations. Retrieved from http://www.clasp.org/ publications/flexibility_2006_tanf_testimony.pdf

Dillon, S. (2008). Hard times hitting students and schools. *The New York Times*. Retrieved from http:// www.nytimes.com/2008/09/01/education/01school.html?hp

Doran, L. (2015). As rental costs rise, incomes fall, and low-income renters are left behind. National Alliance to End Homelessness. Retrieved from http://www.endhomelessness.org/blog/entry/ rental-costs-rise-incomes-fall-and-low-income-renters-are-left-behind#.V9NgK0fW59M

Edin, K., & Lein, L. (1997). *Making ends meet: How single mothers survive welfare and low-wage work*. New York, NY: Russell Sage Foundation.

Feeding America. (2016). Key findings from hunger in America 2014. Retrieved from http://www .feedingamerica.org/hunger-in-america/our-research/hunger-in-america/key-findings.html

Food Research & Action Center. (2016, June). FRAC's national, state, and local index of food hardship. Retrieved from http://frac.org/wp-content/uploads/food-hardship-2016-1.pdf

Gilbert, N., & Terrell, P. (2005). *Dimensions of social welfare policy*. Boston, MA: Allyn & Bacon.

Greene, R. (1999). *Human behavior theory and social work practice* (2nd ed.). Hawthorne, NY: Aldine de Gruyter.

Hirsh, M. (2008, May 24). How questionable loans created a Cleveland slum. Retrieved from http://www.newsweek.com/how-questionable-loans-created-cleveland-slum-89885

Karger, H. (2015). Curbing the financial exploitation of the poor: Financial literacy and social work education. *Journal of Social Work Education, 51*, 425–438.

Lens, V. (2006). Examining the administration of work sanctions on the frontlines of the welfare system. *Social Science Quarterly, 87*, 573–590.

Malai, R. (2013). Programs work to end veteran homelessness. *NASW News*. Retrieved from http://www.socialworkers.org/pubs/news/2013/11/veteran-homelessness.asp

National Association of Social Workers. (1999). *Code of ethics of the National Association of Social Workers*. Washington, DC: Author.

National Association of Social Workers. (2006a). Oppose the Temporary Assistance for Needy Families (TANF) interim final rule. Retrieved from http://www.socialworkers.org/advocacy/alerts/2006/082106.asp

National Association of Social Workers. (2006b). Written testimony of Elizabeth J. Clark, Hearing to "Review outcomes of 1996 Welfare reform." Retrieved from http://www.socialworkers.org/advocacy/letters/2006/072406.asp

National Center for Children in Poverty. (2016). Basic facts about low-income children. Retrieved from http://www.nccp.org/publications/pub_1145.html

National Low Income Housing Coalition. (2007). Violence against women act. Retrieved from http://www.nlihc.org/detail/article.cfm?article_id=2809&id=46

Pavetti, L., & Schott, L. (2016). TANF at 20: Time to create a program that supports work and helps families meet their basic needs. *Center on Budget and Policy Priorities*. Retrieved from http://www.cbpp.org/research/family-income-support/tanf-at-20-time-to-create-a-program-that-supports-work-and-helps

Pilkauskas, N., Currie, J., & Garfinkel, I. (2012). The great recession, public transfers, and material hardship. *Social Service Review, 86*, 401–427.

Postmus, J., & Ah Hahn, S. (2007). The collaboration between welfare and advocacy organizations: Learning from the experiences of domestic violence survivors. *Families in Society: The Journal for Contemporary Services, 88*, 475–484.

Reichman, N., Teitler, J., & Curtis, M. (2005). TANF sanctioning and hardship. *Social Service Review, 79*, 215–236.

Ross, L. M., & Squires, G. D. (2011). The personal costs of subprime lending and the foreclosure crisis: A matter of trust, insecurity, and institutional deception. *Social Science Quarterly, 92*, 140–163. doi:10.1111/j.1540-6237.2011.00761.x/epdf

U.S. Conference of Mayors. (2007). Hunger and homelessness survey: A status report on hunger and homelessness in America's cities. Retrieved from http://www.ncdsv.org/images/USCM_Hunger-homelessness-Survey-in-America's-Cities_12%202007.pdf

U.S. Department of Agriculture. (2017). Supplemental Nutrition Assistance Program (SNAP) eligibility. Retrieved from https://www.fns.usda.gov/snap/eligibility

U.S. Department of Health & Human Services. (2015). The 2015 HHS poverty guidelines. Retrieved from https://aspe.hhs.gov/2015-poverty-guidelines

U.S. Department of Public Health & Human Services. (2007). TANF program policy manual, section 1500, case management, subsections 1506–1, 1506–2 and 1506-3. Retrieved from http://www.dphhs.mt.gov/hcsd/tanfmanual

Wharton School of the University of Pennsylvania. (2007). *How we got into the subprime lending mess*. Knowledge @ Wharton. Retrieved from http://knowledge.Wharton.upenn.edu/article.cfm?articleid=1812#

VOICES FROM THE FIELD

Diane Pfaff, MSW, LISW-S

Community Services Manager
The Alcohol, Drug Addiction and Mental Health
Services Board Serving Athens, Hocking, and Vinton Counties

Agency Setting

The Alcohol, Drug Addiction and Mental Health Services Board provides mental health and addiction services to the residents of Athens, Hocking, and Vinton Counties—three Appalachian counties in southeast Ohio. The Board's funding comes from the Ohio Department of Mental Health and Addiction Services and two local levies. The agency assesses service needs, contracts with local service providers, and evaluates performance via outcomes achieved. It pays for services not reimbursable by Medicaid or health insurance and for services received by persons without health insurance coverage.

Practice Responsibilities

As a social worker at the Board (which has a small staff of eight), I have many responsibilities and roles including community and program planning, contract administration, and program evaluation. As a social worker in macrolevel practice, I apply engagement, assessment, planning, and intervention skills at the community and agency level. The Board works collaboratively across many systems to address needs of vulnerable populations including housing, employment, social security, and legal services. I write grants and work with partner organizations to address unmet needs and to increase organizational capacity to deliver high-quality services and supports.

Expertise Required

My position requires administration and public management skills. I have both undergraduate and graduate degrees in social work and a dozen years of direct service experience. This work requires all of the core direct services skills of listening, empathy, engagement, and empowerment. In addition, skills in working with data, report and grant writing, and policy analysis are required.

Ethical, Legal, Practice, Diversity, and/or Advocacy Issues Addressed

Advocacy is a primary role of the Board. We are charged with listening to the needs of the community and working to advocate at legislative and local levels to address those needs. The Board takes a leadership role in providing community education to reduce the stigma associated with mental health and substance use disorder diagnoses. We prioritize issues involving clients' rights and follow formal procedures to address client concerns or grievances with any of the agencies funded by the Board.

Interprofessional and Intersectoral Collaboration

The Board collaborates with all community partners to promote wellness and access to resources for persons with behavioral health issues. Partners include providers in the fields of housing and homelessness, employment, child welfare, developmental disabilities, domestic violence, and health care, as well as courts, law enforcement, and corrections. As an example, the Board has provided leadership to help develop the Athens County Housing Coalition. This group serves as a local "continuum of care" to address homelessness in the community. The Housing Coalition meets every quarter and includes representatives from housing, social services, criminal justice, and government. The Board assisted members in identifying state and federal funding opportunities that were available but not currently accessed in the community. Through networking and collaboration, the Board helped providers to apply for and receive significant new funding for capital projects and ongoing rental assistance. The new funding offers Permanent Supportive Housing to Veterans and persons with long-term disabilities—most often mental illness and substance use disorders. The Permanent Supportive Housing addresses the ex-offender population by providing low-barrier access and supportive services to help them maintain housing and increase income. Funding has also been obtained to address the needs of homeless, transition-aged young adults—ages 18 to 24 years. The Housing Coalition has developed a Ten-Year Plan to End Homelessness and conducts an annual "Point-in-Time" count to help increase understanding of the local sheltered and unsheltered homeless population.

VOICES FROM THE FIELD

Jeff Yungman, MSW, LISW-CP, MPH, JD
Clinical Director of Crisis Ministries and
Director of Crisis Ministries Homeless Justice Project

Agency Setting

Crisis Ministries, located in Charleston, South Carolina, provides social services, primary care, and mental health care and counseling in addition to the basic needs of food and shelter to over 150 homeless men, women, and children every night. In January 2006 the Crisis Ministries Homeless Justice Project was created as a partnership among Crisis Ministries, the Charleston School of Law, Nelson Mullins Law Firm, and Pro Bono Legal Services. It is designed to help homeless individuals and families by removing obstacles, both legal and social, which prevent homeless men and women from regaining self-sufficiency. The Crisis Ministries Homeless Justice Project is one of therapeutic jurisprudence designed to be client centered in that services are provided to the client on site; and it is holistic in that it assesses all the needs of the individual to provide not only legal services, but social services as well.

Practice Responsibilities

As the clinical director, I am responsible for supervision of the eight case managers in addition to carrying a caseload composed of individuals with mental health issues and/or legal issues. As director of the Crisis Ministries Homeless Justice Project, I take the initial referrals for any individual with a legal issue (primarily civil issues). Each referral is then forwarded to the Nelson Mullins Law Firm and Pro Bono Legal Services for assignment. At the monthly legal clinic, the client meets with his or her attorney and a law student to discuss his or her case. I then provide follow-up on identified legal and social issues with the assistance of the law student assigned to the case, an MSW intern, and the Crisis Ministries case management staff. In addition, I assume responsibility for some cases, primarily disability cases.

Expertise Required

The position requires an MSW with extensive knowledge of the legal system and legal issues. I started in the position prior to receiving my law degree and except for representing individuals in court, a legal degree is not absolutely necessary.

Practice Challenges

The greatest practice challenges for working with the homeless in general are lack of affordable housing, lack of universal health care, and lack of a living minimum wage. The greatest practice challenges as director of the Homeless Justice Project are the increasing criminalization of homelessness, the snail-paced disability process, and the difficulty recruiting volunteer attorneys.

Ethical, Legal, Practice, Diversity, and/or Advocacy Issues Addressed

The common legal issues handled by the Crisis Ministries Homeless Justice Project include disability claims; family law, including divorce, child custody, and child support; landlord/ tenant issues; wills and power of attorney; expungements and pardons; employment claims; and some municipal criminal charges. Although not an ethical issue per se, I have found it difficult at times to reconcile my veteran social work approach to a problem with my new legal approach to that same problem.

Collaborative Activities With Professionals and/or Other Stakeholders

I am a member of the Crisis Ministries Homeless Justice Project advisory board that is tasked with developing the project to its maximum potential and with recruitment of both attorney and law students. In that regard, I have presented at information sessions and continuing legal education (CLEs) at the Charleston School of Law. In addition, I am a member of the South Carolina Re-entry Initiative program, a group of community members and professionals who help individuals released from prison reintegrate themselves into society.

CHAPTER 11

Child Welfare

George S. Leibowitz

R. Anna Hayward-Everson

Carl Mazza

CHAPTER OBJECTIVES

The major objectives of this chapter are to:

- Detail the scope of the problem of child maltreatment, and current evidence-based assessment and interventions in the child welfare system.
- Describe the foster care crisis in the United States, including the foster care to prison pipeline, the impact of parental incarceration, and current policies such as reforms in the juvenile jurisdiction system.
- Review the relevant theoretical and practical approaches, including the application of neuroscience research, trauma-informed care, father engagement, and addressing secondary trauma among child welfare professionals.

CHAPTER COMPETENCIES HIGHLIGHTED

- Competency 3: Advance Human Rights and Social, Economic, and Environmental Justice
- Competency 7: Assess Individuals, Families, Organizations, and Communities
- Competency 8: Intervene With Individuals, Families, Organizations, and Communities

This chapter covers the history of child protection legislation and addresses the impact of child maltreatment in the child welfare system, including the foster care crisis, the prison pipeline, and the effects of parental incarceration. Additionally, trauma-informed care and the juvenile jurisdiction system are examined in light of recent trends to more closely align systems of care with neuroscience research and best practices for serving children and adolescents. A case study is presented and Voices From the Field section illustrates the challenges of working with incarcerated fathers who may have children in the child welfare system.

Background and Scope of the Problem: Child Maltreatment

In 2014, there were 3.6 million referrals involving the alleged maltreatment of 6.6 million children; 702,000 were identified as "victims" of abuse or neglect (Child Welfare Information Gateway, 2016). During 2013, among children who experienced maltreatment or abuse, nearly 80% suffered neglect (the most common form of reported abuse); 18% suffered physical abuse; and 9% suffered sexual abuse. Just under 80% of reported child fatalities as a result of abuse and neglect were caused by one or more of the child-victim's parents, and children in the first year of their life had the highest rate of victimization of 23.1 per 1,000 children in the national population of the same age (Children's Alliance, 2013). Compared with caregivers of older children, caregivers of infants are more likely to abuse drugs or alcohol, have trauma and domestic violence histories, have a serious mental health problem, and may be involved in the criminal justice system (Wulczyn, Hislop, & Jones Harden, 2002).

These official statistics represent the number of cases that come to the attention of Child Protective Services (CPS) or other authorities. Estimating the true rates of abuse, however, is challenging. A smaller number of cases referred for abuse are substantiated by CPS, for example, in 2010 only 500,000 were substantiated (Administration on Children, Youth and Families, Children's Bureau, 2012). Additionally, as confirmed by the Adverse Childhood Experiences (ACEs) research discussed subsequently, individuals reported experiencing measurable emotional and physical neglect as well as physical, sexual, and emotional abuse.

Research on polyvictimization has confirmed that cumulative and multiple victimizations are common, and that individuals who are exposed to multiple types of abuse are more likely to experience distress. In a study assessing polyvictimization among 2,030 children ages 10 to 17 years using the Juvenile Victimization Questionnaire (JVQ), Finkelhor, Ormrod, Turner, and Hamby (2005) found that 22% of the children in the sample had experienced four or more different kinds of victimization in separate incidents within the previous year, and that polyvictimization predicted posttraumatic symptomatology.

In addition to maltreatment, complex trauma is associated with other forms of violence or loss (e.g., chronic exposure to community violence; loss of caregiver in early childhood; Cook et al., 2005). Outcomes of maltreatment include the costs associated with chronic health and mental health problems, as well as child welfare and judicial system involvement. Other outcomes include juvenile delinquency and criminal justice system involvement (see Chapter 14 for more on the link between trauma and delinquency).

Adverse Childhood Experience Survey

The ACEs research described various types of abuse, neglect, and traumatic experiences occurring in individuals during their childhood and examined relationships between ACEs and reduced health and well-being later in life. Over 17,000 people receiving physical exams completed confidential surveys containing information about their childhood experiences and current health status and behaviors (Felitti et al., 1998).

Childhood experiences have a lifelong impact on health and the quality of our lives. In the initial ACEs study, 9% of the study participants also reported three or more adverse family experiences (AFEs), and one in four to one in five grew up in a household with someone who had alcohol or drug problems, with caregivers who were divorced or separated, or with someone who was mentally ill or depressed. The ACEs study showed not only the relationship between adverse childhood experiences and behavioral, mental, and physical outcomes, but also revealed the potential magnitude of the effect between these experiences and risky behavior, psychological issues, serious illness, and reduced life expectancy. Some of the more prevalent outcomes and risk behaviors include depression, suicide attempts, alcoholism, and drug use (e.g., Campbell, Walker, & Egede, 2016).

System and Population Overview

Child maltreatment impacts all families regardless of race, ethnicity, or income. However, children from poor families are more likely to end up in the child welfare system. Numerous studies have documented racial and ethnic disproportionality in all levels of the child welfare system, from report to substantiation, to removal, out-of-home placement, and ultimately reunification with biological parents. African American and Native American children in particular are overrepresented in the child welfare system, especially in foster care and residential facilities (Child Welfare Gateway, 2016). Although evidence suggests that (after controlling for poverty) there are no differences in actual perpetration of child maltreatment in these families, they continue to be represented in the child welfare system at alarming rates. Various strategies to address racial disparities include community-based initiatives, culturally informed home-based and preventative strategies, and blinded determination reviews. Some of these strategies are discussed subsequently.

History of Child Welfare

In the late 1800s, social worker Eta Wheeler discovered that Mary Ellen Wilson was severely neglected and physically and emotionally abused by her stepmother. Given the absence of child protective services during that period, the case was brought to the Society for the Prevention of Cruelty to Animals (SPCA). The public outcry after the stepmother was found guilty of assault led to the creation of the Society for the Prevention of Cruelty to Children (SPCC) in 1874. By the beginning of the 20th century, over 250 such agencies had developed across the country (Costin, 1985; Pecora, Whittaker, Maluccio, & Barth, 2000). In the 1960s, *battered child syndrome* (Kempe et al., 1967) was described by C. Henry Kempe and colleagues as medical and physical conditions resulting from physical abuse, and the medical community began working collaboratively with child protection professionals.

An important development in the protection of Native American children who were removed from their homes at high rates was the establishment of the Indian Child Welfare Act (ICWA). In the mid-1970s, advocacy efforts to address the alarming high rate of out-of-home placement (and placement into non-Indian homes and institutions) led to the development of ICWA, which became a federal law in 1978. The purpose of ICWA is to "promote the stability and security of Indian tribes and families" and allows for the child and families of the tribe and local community to have input in any cases of child maltreatment—of particular importance is the provision that child maltreatment cases can be heard in the tribal court.

Protective Legislation for Children

This history of U.S. child welfare policy development includes the Social Security Act of 1935, the Child Abuse Prevention and Treatment Act of 1974 (CAPTA), the Adoption Assistance and Child Welfare Act of 1980 (AACWA), and the Adoption and Safe Families Act (ASFA) of 1997. The Social Security Act established that each state must have a plan for child protection; CAPTA set standards for prevention and treatment services and formally recognized each of the multiple forms of abuse inflicted on children. The AACWA worked to set standards for family preservation, reunification, foster care, and adoption; ASFA was enacted to further define and specify these standards, replacing the previous policy under the AACWA. AFSA's goals are to ensure that child welfare services across the United States protect children from harm, preserve families, and promote child well-being. However, many of AFSA's provisions for permanency, which prevent children from spending undue time languishing in out-of-home care, may be difficult to navigate if parents are incarcerated or contending with multiple interrelated issues such as substance abuse, mental health, poverty, and other family issues that can prevent children from returning to their family of origin. In addition, ICWA's provisions provide culturally relevant interventions and priority placement in homes in the child's tribe and community for Native American children.

Current Trends and Debates in Child Welfare

Foster Care to Prison Pipeline

Children may enter the child welfare system because of ongoing family problems including maltreatment, substance abuse, and parental incarceration. Often these issues are long-standing, deep rooted, and intergenerational. Rarely does a child enter the system because of an isolated crisis; rather, the child enters the system because of a long-term systemic problem such as substance abuse or mental health issues.

Children who then grow up in the child welfare system may lack the same level of family support that other children have, whether owing to separation from their family of origin or myriad problems in that family from early childhood. After experiencing multiple moves through foster homes, children "in the system" may grow up feeling disconnected and alone. Although interventions provided by the child welfare system are designed to be temporary, it is often not the case (as underscored by the case example in this chapter). Under the federal AFSA, as well as individual states' policies, the day the child enters the system, plans must be developed projecting his or her discharge from the system (McWey, Henderson, & Tice, 2006; Whitt-Woosley & Sprang, 2014). Children's initial discharge goal is most often to return to his or her parent. This means that those working with the family and child must focus on the family's initial problem that caused the child welfare placement and work to overcome the problem so that the child can return home. However, this approach ignores the context of family problems and the interrelated nature of difficulties related to poverty, substance addiction, history of trauma, and neighborhood stress. Overcoming the family's issues often takes more time than allowed by government regulations. Even after initial out-of-home placement, birth families are only required to be minimally adequate in order to have the children return to them. This means that the children either return to fragile families with limited resources, limited supports, and great challenges or they remain in the child welfare system with a goal change from return to parent to either adoption or independent living.

In the United States, the majority of birth families involved in the child welfare system are low income and reside in low-income communities. When a child is discharged from child welfare back to his or her birth family, more than likely the child returns to a low-income community. This is particularly true in urban areas. In 1982, two economists, James Q. Wilson and George L. Kelling, developed the broken windows theory (Kelling, 2015). This economic theory posed that if a business dealt with a small problem at its initiation, then it would prevent a larger problem down the road. This economic policy was then adopted by New York City Mayor Rudolph Giuliani. Giuliani adapted this theory to policing and crime. He and his advisors posed that if police presence focused on concentrated low-income neighborhoods and the police "cracked down" on small crimes and violations, then the larger more serious crimes would never occur (Chappell, Monk-Turner, & Payne, 2011). They equated someone loitering or writing graffiti as leading to murder and arms dealing. As unproven as the broken windows theory is, it had been replicated in many U.S. cities. In New York City and other large cities with these types of aggressive police tactics, a young person discharged from child welfare back to his or her parents may be more apt to have contact with police than youth from wealthier communities. Being stopped for jaywalking can easily lead to involvement in the criminal justice system. Added to this is the advent of "stop and frisk" policies where police have the authority to stop and frisk anyone (Ferrandino, 2015). Most "stop and frisk" searches occur in low-income neighborhoods and the victims are African American and Latino youth. This population directly overlaps with child welfare populations and those incarcerated in both juvenile and adult correctional facilities (Warde, 2016).

For young people going before a judge for the first time, the court process can be an intimidating experience. Children in the child welfare system may be even more vulnerable due to a lack of family support. In addition, their familiarity with the court from family court may actually make them appear dismissive or unaffected by the gravity of a criminal court visit.

An additional concern for children in the child welfare system is that the label of foster child or resident of a group home or treatment center can be stigmatizing and may impact the judge's impression of youth from these vulnerable groups. In addition, youth in the child welfare system may have few significant support systems. Birth families may still struggle with limited resources to address both emotional and physical challenges. The child welfare system often terminates all supports soon after discharge. All of this may lead to an appearance in criminal court with no evidence of support or strong positive ties to the community. Anyone who has worked with the criminal court systems can attest to the fact that if an individual is charged with a crime, it is highly advantageous to have family members—mothers, fathers, grandparents, children, aunts, and uncles—in the courtroom. Their presence can mean an enhanced sense of community support, and connectedness, as social isolation and lack of support among youth can result in worse outcomes and increased risk for future problematic behavior.

Core Roles and Functions of Forensic Social Work in This System

Applying strategies from trauma-informed care, safety planning, caregiver engagement, and risk assessment processes, social workers can engage directly with children, family members, and caregivers in the community and institutional settings. Social workers may also provide public and professional education, collaborate with others on social and legal reforms, conduct research, and disseminate findings to reach diverse groups. A social worker who has applied some of these strategies to working with parents in the criminal justice system is depicted in the Voices From the Field section.

Relevant Theories and Applications From Neuroscience

Systems Theory

Systems theory is widely used in the practice and social planning of child welfare. Systems of care, and what are known as *wraparound services*, work to address the biopsychosocial and cultural needs of children and families. Wraparound services link statewide services from medical assistance and mental health directly to child service divisions and their specific populations. Moreover, wraparound services use collaborative treatment teams of professionals, caregivers, and community resources for each child and his or her family, working to meet their specific needs (Anderson, McIntyre, & Somers, 2004; Ferguson, 2007).

Attachment Theory

Attachment theory is another relevant theory for child welfare practice. The use of attachment theory is critical in the assessment of the child's current functioning, her or his development, and coping. Attachment theory also provides insight into the bond and relationship between the child and his or her parent. Attachment and relational experiences, or the manner in which a child reciprocally interacts with and develops trust, reliance, and dependency on others, have long been purported as key to positive youth development (Ainsworth & Bowlby, 1991).

Attachment theorists have conjectured that accessibility and responsiveness, to and from others, advances a secure bond, whereas indifferent, abusive, or unpredictable response patterns are associated with avoidant, ambivalent, or disorganized attachment styles (Bowlby, 1988). Attachment classifications are derived from the supposition that relationships are joint connections with the self and others, such that internal self-worth match feelings of external support and trust (Bartholomew & Horowitz, 1991). Among youth involved in child welfare and juvenile justice systems, recent research showed that lower levels of mother and peer trust and communication were associated with more severe sexual offenses; low levels of mother trust were associated with more victims; and low levels of mother trust and high father alienation were associated with more nonsexual behavioral problems (delinquency) (Yoder, Leibowitz, & Peterson, 2016). Practice implications of this research suggest the need to incorporate families more consistently into treatment and apply findings from attachment research.

Neurodevelopmental Impact of Abuse

The child welfare system, and indeed the social work profession in general, has increasingly incorporated neuroscience research in order to understand and treat traumatic stress among children and families. Traumatic experiences can impair the integration of the cortical and subcortical regions of the brain, and EEG abnormalities were found in studies of sexually abused and maltreated children in community-based and juvenile justice settings (Ito et al., 1993; Kaiser & Meckley, 2013). Moreover, impairments in numerous structural parts of the brain are associated with posttraumatic stress, including the parietal lobes, the amygdala (decreasing empathy and guilt), the hippocampus, and corpus callosum (Teicher et al., 2003; van der Kolk, 2001). Adolescents with posttraumatic stress disorder (PTSD) may have decreased hippocampal volume, which can cause behavioral disinhibition—such youth may have problems with taking in and processing information and learning from new experiences.

In a study comparing participants diagnosed with PTSD and traumatized individuals without PTSD, both groups showed behavioral activation on the stop-signal task, but individuals with PTSD exhibited significant disinhibition (Casada & Roache, 2005). Findings of that study suggest that disinhibition along with behavioral activation may explain PTSD-related impulsivity and aggression. Social workers in the child welfare system will find such behavioral challenges and socioemotional disturbances among victimized children very common, complicating case planning and decisions regarding reunification between children and caregivers.

It should be noted that correlates between research findings on the brain and PTSD vary, and brain activation studies using functional MRI (fMRI) techniques are inconclusive regarding whether individuals with PTSD can also have diminished activation in other areas of the brain (e.g., cingulate cortices) besides the emotional centers (amygdala and insula), areas commonly known to be associated with anxiety disorders (Uttal, 2011). Forensic social workers and practitioners should be aware that cognitive neuroscience in many ways has progressed substantially, but additional research on the neural substrates of behavior is required. In cases of childhood sexual abuse, the limbic system, associated with attachment, social connectedness, and attentional processes, is also impacted.

While neuroscience has been used to support an investment in early intervention and this is indeed one of the goals of forensic social work, one caveat for practitioners and researchers concerns the *dual-use dilemma* in which neuroscience could also be utilized to "prove" poor parenting or attempt to predict future criminality among children and families (Walsh, 2011). Huntington (2012) argues that neuroscience is relevant to these types of policy-related questions. She upholds that the child welfare system should consider prevention as essential, with a focus on the well-being of children, using research about the sensitive periods of neurodevelopment, and promoting attachment/bonds between children and primary caregivers that is implicated in the development of the architecture of the brain.

Relevant Ethical, Legal, and Policy Issues

In Vermont, recent legislation known as H.95 impacts both the child welfare and juvenile justice systems. H.95 is a bill that reforms the juvenile jurisdiction system to more closely align with brain development research (as discussed previously) and best practices for serving youth. Vermont is one of the few states where 16- and 17-year-olds are charged in criminal court as adults for any offense, including misdemeanors. These charges potentially have major collateral consequences for youth charged in adult court, including a public record, exclusion from the military, and ineligibility for college loans. This is contraindicated with unintended consequences to best practices for youth and the findings from neuroscience, attachment, and child development research. Studies have shown that youth are much more amenable to treatment and rehabilitation, and as such should be treated differently from adults. The Vermont Department for Children and Families (DCF) has collaborated with the Vermont Defender General's Office, State's Attorney's Office, Department of Corrections, victims' rights organizations, the Vermont Judiciary, Vermont American Civil Liberties Union (ACLU), and members of the Vermont House and Senate in drafting this bill (Lindy

Boudreau, Vermont DCF, personal communication; http://legislature.vermont.gov/bill/status/2016/H.95).

Relevant Assessment, Prevention, and Intervention Strategies

Effective programs to prevent and respond to child maltreatment include holistic family services that seek to reduce risk factors and increase protective factors in families. Family Connections, an evidence-based intervention that began in Baltimore, Maryland, serves families in their homes with weekly social work services. Addressing basic needs, including food, clothing, and housing, can help prevent child neglect; trauma-informed in-home counseling services address intergenerational trauma and child neglect and maltreatment.

Interventions that provide intensive in-home services for new parents have also been found to reduce child maltreatment and prevent later involvement in the juvenile justice system. For example, the Nurse–Family Partnership (NFP) provides home-based services delivered through nurses in the homes of new parents who may be at risk for involvement in the child welfare system (Olds et al., 2013).

While most child welfare programs focus on families or on mothers as the primary caregiver, recent investments in father-focused programming hold promise for prevention of family violence including child maltreatment. Programs that promote father involvement can prevent both child welfare and later criminal justice involvement of children and adolescents. Further, addressing the economic needs of fathers can have a positive impact on children and families and potentially prevent poverty-associated child neglect. The Suffolk County, New York Fatherhood Initiative (SCFI—highlighted in the Voices From the Field section) provides economic stability, father involvement, and positive relationship skills to low-income fathers in one large New York county. This initiative works with fathers in the community and those transitioning from incarceration to encourage increased involvement with children and positive relationship skills. Program goals are focused on preventing family violence and strengthening families. By working with men who are currently incarcerated or transitioning from the criminal justice system or residential drug treatment facilities, father-focused programs can potentially prevent children's involvement in child welfare systems or facilitate reconnection and reunification with children and families.

Trauma-Informed Evidence-Based Practice

In light of the fact that a history of trauma and polyvictimization is common among child welfare-involved youth, trauma-informed approaches are consistent with a mental health model that provides comprehensive assessment and individualized treatment (Griffin, Germaine, & Wilkerson, 2012). Trauma-focused cognitive behavioral therapy (TF-CBT) has been found to be more effective in randomized controlled trials in treating PTSD in sexually abused children and adolescents than other interventions, such as supportive therapy, stress management, narrative therapy, or psychoeducational work (Cohen, Berliner, & Mannarino, 2010; Deblinger, Steer, & Lippmann, 1999). Components of TF-CBT include psychoeducation and parenting skills, affect modulation skills, cognitive coping skills, conjoint parent–youth sessions, and trauma narrative and processing.

Another model designed for children with complex trauma is the attachment, self-regulation, and competency (ARC; Arvidson et al., 2011) framework, which is delivered in the context of caregiver systems and addresses various targets (from attunement and affect identification to executive functioning) in the three core domains leading to trauma experience integration and competency.

The National Child Traumatic Stress Network (NCTSN) has developed online resources that summarize the clinical and research evidence regarding trauma-informed interventions, especially as these interventions relate to diverse cultural groups (with attention to race, ethnicity, sexual orientation, socioeconomic status, spirituality, disability, and geography).

Forensic Practice Skill Set

Addressing Secondary Trauma

The literature has documented occupational risks for practitioners who work with children and adults who have experienced loss (Cunningham, 2004; Figley, 1995; Hooyman & Kramer, 2006; Ryan & Cunningham, 2007). Practitioners who work with bereaved children, especially if it involves trauma, are at risk for work-related adverse effects, including chronic bereavement, psychological distress, countertransference, burnout, secondary trauma/ compassion fatigue, and vicarious trauma (Maschi, 2016; Maschi & Brown, 2010).

Secondary Trauma Stress (STS) and Compassion Fatigue (CF)

STS, or CF, is another occupational risk directly related to a practitioner's work with the bereaved and children with traumatic stress. This is especially true when the child's loss was due to sudden traumatic circumstances, such as the loss of a parent in a terrorist attack or an unexpected natural disaster. In contrast to burnout, which is not necessarily linked to work with clients, STS is related. STS (or CF) is the "natural consequent behaviors and emotions resulting from knowing about a traumatizing event experienced by a significant other—the stress resulting from helping or wanting to help a traumatized or suffering person" (Figley, 1995). Similar to a person directly exposed to a traumatic event, through the context of the work relationships, practitioners are exposed secondarily. Whereas STS disorder is based on clinical symptoms and diagnostic criteria, its related "cousin," vicarious trauma, is based on theoretical constructs and is important for practitioners to understand (Pearlman, 1999; Saakvitne et al., 1996, 1999). Pearlman and Saakvitne (1995a, 1995b) defined vicarious trauma as:

> The transformation that occurs within the trauma counselor as a result of empathic engagement with clients' trauma experiences and their sequelae. Such engagement includes listening to graphic descriptions of horrific events, bearing witness to people's cruelty to one another, and witnessing and participating in traumatic reenactments. It is an occupational hazard and reflects neither pathology in the therapist nor intentionality on the part of the traumatized client. (p. 31)

Addressing secondary stress and vicarious trauma through self-care strategies, which include obtaining effective supervision, is particularly important for social workers and professionals working in the child welfare system, given the complexity and intensity of cases as illustrated in the following example.

Case Example and Application

Fred is a 16-year-old Latino male referred for an evaluation and treatment recommendations by the DCF. He has been in DCF custody since he was 12 years old due to parental incarceration, exposure to domestic violence, neglect, and caregiver substance use. He is currently residing in his third foster home. Fred is ill with cystic fibrosis, requiring regular medical care.

Fred's biological parents divorced, and he has a 15-year-old brother, John, and an 11-year-old sister, Virginia. Virginia was adopted out of state. Fred indicates he talks to his father on the phone approximately once a week but has not seen him in the last few months. He further indicates he has contact with his brother but has not seen him since last year. Fred reports he has several half-siblings as well. On his father's side, he has a 3-year-old brother, Matt. On his mother's side, he has a 20-year-old sister, Haley, and three other siblings who were adopted out (Victoria, age 9; Jasmine, age 7; and Jaden, age 6).

(continued)

Fred reports he has been placed in DCF custody on three separate occasions. Prior to his age of 7 years, he lived with his mother, who resided with her parents. From his age of 7 years until he was 13 years old, he reports he lived with his maternal grandparents: He says he could not live with his mother at that time, because she had a prescription drug problem. Fred indicates that when he was 13 years old his grandmother became ill with cancer and could not care for him so he went to live with his mother's brother until he was 13 years old. From his uncle's home, he entered DCF custody and was placed in a foster home. He went to a group home for boys in Texas, and he says his behaviors were unproblematic while there. He was then placed in a group home for mentally challenged people with specialized medical needs in order to be closer to his grandmother. Fred believes he was going to be adopted by a group home there, but was also discussing living with his father.

Fred describes his father as someone who has had a "hard life." He explains that his father was released from prison about five years ago. He believes his father was incarcerated for drug possession or burglary. He says his father went to prison when he was a 1-year-old and was incarcerated for a few years. Once released, he returned home and stayed with them; however, he returned to prison for selling drugs after he "got caught with lots of drug money."

Fred says he has had a "pretty hard life." He indicates that when his mother raised him, there was no positive male role model for him. He reports his grandfather was a strong figure for him but he is currently in prison. He believes if he had had his father in his life when he was younger, "things would have been a lot different." He says growing up without his father was difficult and he would "always cry" about not having him in his life. He says his father was incarcerated on and off for several years during his childhood, but he used to call "every once in a while." Fred states it is also difficult for him not being able to see his other siblings and it has been about five years since he saw his half-siblings. He reports missing them and recalls positive memories of them. He also maintains he wishes his parents were back together.

Fred has experienced some victimization in his childhood. He recalls he was the victim of frequent bullying when he was in elementary school. Reportedly, students would make fun of him because of how he walked. He denies any history of emotional or sexual abuse, but indicates he was physically abused and neglected. He states his stepfather, Al, got in trouble for spanking him with a belt when he was approximately 6 years old. He also recalls witnessing domestic violence: Al was physically abusive of his mother and went to jail for domestic violence. Fred says on one occasion he witnessed Al hit his mother when he was visiting her. He asserts he pulled a knife on Al and kicked him out of the house, never to see him again.

Academically, Fred indicates he struggles, and he was retained in the first grade, primarily due to attentional issues. He indicates school is "too hard" for him. (On the Youth Self Report [YSR; Achenbach, 2001], he stated he "hates" school.) Fred reports, "No matter how hard I try I fail." Fred also reports he is on an individualized education program (IEP), but is uncertain about why.

Case Formulation and Recommendations

Fred is a young Latino man who has been through a significant amount of hardship in his life. He has experienced inconsistent caregiving, numerous moves, involvement in the DCF and foster care system in various states, caregiver substance abuse problems, caregiver incarceration, and a father who was largely absent from his life until the last few years. His siblings have been adopted out of the family. In short, Fred has experienced significant loss

(*continued*)

and disruption. Furthermore, he has been the victim of bullying, physical and verbal abuse by his mother's partner, and he was exposed to domestic violence. Fred is a young man feeling wronged by the system, and he has a severe illness impacting his lungs and digestive system, requiring significant medical and social supports.

Recommendations include scheduling a family group conference as soon as possible with all the key players involved (Fred, his mother, father, foster parents, DCF workers) to determine the next steps for this severely ill young man. It is important that, given his disrupted attachments, a predictable and consistent permanency and reunification plan be developed, with trauma-informed interventions in place to help his caregivers develop attunement to his needs and understand how to work to support him and manage his potentially terminal medical condition.

Conclusion

Working with children and families in the child welfare system requires skills and knowledge about complex family dynamics and the impacts of poverty, substance abuse, mental illness, trauma, and racial disparities in both the child welfare and criminal justice systems. Interventions that assist families in the child welfare system, or prevent such involvement, focus on the entire family system, are trauma informed, and provide concrete support services to children and the entire family system. Forensic practice skill sets for social workers include safety planning and assessment, understanding risk and protective factors for child maltreatment, engaging with all family members including fathers and extended families, and working with complex systems across disciplines.

CHAPTER EXERCISES

Exercise 1. In the case application, which aspects of Fred's developmental and family history are important to consider when conducting an assessment and making recommendations for treatment? What kinds of interventions would be appropriate in this case?

Exercise 2. Considering the Voices From the Field section, how would a social worker in a forensic setting work with a father who wishes to reengage with his family?

Additional Resources

Administration for Children & Families' Children's Bureau: www.acf.hhs.gov/cb

Child Welfare Information Gateway: www.childwelfare.gov

For Secondary Trauma: Rothschild, B., & Rand, M. L. (2006). *Help for the helper: The psychophysiology of compassion fatigue and vicarious trauma.* New York, NY: Norton.

How Childhood Trauma Affects Health, Nadine Burke Harris: www.ted.com/talks/nadine_burke_harris_how_childhood_trauma_affects_health_across_a_lifetime

Kempe Center: www.kempe.org

The National Child Traumatic Stress Network: www.nctsn.org

References

Achenbach, T. M. (2001). *Child behavior checklist for ages 6 to 18*. Burlington: University of Vermont, Research Center for Children, Youth, and Families.

Administration on Children, Youth and Families, Children's Bureau. (2012). Child maltreatment 2011. Retrieved from https://www.acf.hhs.gov/cb/resource/child-maltreatment-2011

Ainsworth, M. D. S., & Bowlby, J. (1991). An ethological approach to personality development. *American Psychologist, 46*, 333–341.

Anderson, J. A., McIntyre, J. S., & Somers, J. W. (2004). Exploring the experiences of successful completers of a system of care for children and their families through case narratives. *Journal of Family Social Work, 8*(1), 1–25.

Arvidson, J., Kinniburgh, K., Howard, K., Spinazzola, J., Strothers, H., Evans, M., . . . Blaustein, M. A. (2011). Treatment of complex trauma in young children: Developmental and cultural considerations in the application of the ARC intervention model. *Journal of Child & Adolescent Trauma, 4*, 34–51. doi:10.1080/19361521.2011.545046

Bartholomew, K., & Horowitz, L. M. (1991). Attachment styles among young adults: A test of a four-category model. *Journal of Personality and Social Psychology, 61*, 226–244. doi:10.1037/0022-3514.61.2.226

Bowlby, J. (1988). *A secure base: Parent-child attachment and healthy human development*. New York, NY: Basic Books.

Campbell, J. A., Walker, R. J., & Egede, L. E. (2016). Associations between adverse childhood experiences, high-risk behaviors, and morbidity in adulthood. *American Journal of Preventive Medicine, 50*(3), 344–352. doi:10.1016/j.amepre.2015.07.022

Casada, J. H., & Roache, J. D. (2005). Behavioral inhibition and activation in posttraumatic stress disorder. *Journal of Nervous and Mental Disease, 193*(2), 102–109.

Chappell, A. T., Monk-Turner, E., & Payne, B. K. (2011). Broken windows or window breakers: The influence of physical and social disorder on quality of life. *Justice Quarterly, 28*(3), 522–540.

Child Welfare Information Gateway. (2016). Child maltreatment 2014. Retrieved from https://www.acf.hhs.gov/cb/resource/child-maltreatment-2014

Cohen, J. A., Berliner, L., & Mannarino, A. (2010). Trauma focused CBT for children with co-occurring trauma and behavior problems. *Child Abuse & Neglect, 34*, 215–224.

Cook, A., Spinazzola, P., Ford, J., Lanktree, C., Blaustein, M., Cloitre, M., . . . van der Kolk, B. (2005). Complex trauma in children and adolescents. *Psychiatric Annals, 35*, 390–398.

Costin, L. B. (1985). The historical context of child welfare. In J. Laird & A. Hartman (Eds.), *A handbook of child welfare: Context, knowledge, and practice* (pp. 53–76). New York, NY: Free Press.

Cunningham, M. (2004). Avoiding vicarious trauma: Support, spirituality, and self-care. In N. B. Webb (Ed.), *Mass trauma and violence: Helping families and children cope* (pp. 327–343). New York, NY: Guilford Press.

Deblinger, E., Steer, R. A., & Lippmann, J. (1999). Two-year follow-up study of cognitive behavioral therapy for sexually abused children suffering from post-traumatic stress symptoms. *Child Abuse & Neglect, 23*(12), 1371–1378.

Felitti, V. J., Anda, R. F., Nordenberg, D., Williamson, D. F., Spitz, A. M., Edwards V., . . . Marks, J. S. (1998). Relationship of childhood abuse and household dysfunction to many of the leading causes of death in adults: The adverse childhood experiences study. *American Journal of Preventive Medicine, 14*, 245–258.

Ferguson, C. (2007). Wraparound: Definition, context for development, and emergence in child welfare. *Journal of Public Child Welfare, 1*(2), 91–113.

Ferrandino, J. (2015). Minority threat hypothesis and NYPD Stop & Frisk policy. *Criminal Justice Review, 40*(2), 209–229.

Figley, C. R. (1995). Compassion fatigues as secondary traumatic stress disorder. In C. R. Figley (Ed.), *Compassion fatigue: Coping with secondary traumatic stress disorder in those who treat the traumatized* (pp. 1–20). New York, NY: Routledge.

Finkelhor, D., Ormrod, R. K., Turner, H. A., & Hamby, S. L. (2005). Measuring poly-victimization using the Juvenile Victimization Questionnaire. *Child Abuse & Neglect, 29*(11), 1297–1312.

Griffin, G., Germaine, E. J., & Wilkerson, R. G. (2012). Using a trauma-informed approach in juvenile justice institutions. *Journal of Child and Adolescent Trauma, 5*, 271–283.

Hooyman, N. R., & Kramer, B. J. (2006). *Living through loss: Interventions across the lifespan.* New York, NY: Columbia University Press.

Huntington, C. (2012). Neuroscience and the child welfare system. *Brooklyn Journal of Law and Policy, 21*, 37–57.

Ito, Y., Teicher, M. H., Glod, C. A., Harper, D., Magnus, E., & Gelbard, H. A. (1993). Increased prevalence for aberrant cortical development in abused children: A quantitative EEG study. *Journal of Neuropsychiatry and Clinical Neuroscience, 10*, 298–307.

Kaiser, D. A., & Meckley, A. (2013). Brain function assessment and neurotherapy for sexual abuse. In R. E. Longo, D. S. Prescott, J. Bergman, & K. Creeden (Eds.), *Current perspectives & applications in neurobiology: Working with young persons who are victims and perpetrators of sexual abuse* (pp. 113–130). Holyoke, MA: NEARI Press.

Kelling, G. (2015). An author's brief history of an idea. *Journal of Research in Crime & Delinquency, 52*(4), 626–629.

Kempe, C. H., Silverman, F. N., Steele, B. F., Droegemueller, W., & Silver, H. K. (1967). The battered-child syndrome. *Journal of the American Medical Association, 181*(1), 17–24.

Maschi, T. (2016). Professional self-care and prevention of secondary trauma. In N. B. Webb (Ed.), *Play therapy with children in crisis* (4th ed., pp. 102–122). New York, NY: Guilford Press.

Maschi, T., & Brown, D. (2010). Professional self-care and prevention of secondary trauma. In N. B. Webb (Ed.), *Helping bereaved children: A handbook for practitioners* (4th ed., pp. 335–355). New York, NY: Guilford Press.

McWey, L. M., Henderson, T. L., & Tice, S. N. (2006). Mental health issues and the foster care system: An examination of the impact of the Adoption and Safe Family Act. *Journal of Marital & Family Therapy, 32*(2), 195–214.

National Children's Alliance. (2013). National statistics on child abuse. Retrieved from http://www .nationalchildrensalliance.org/media-room/media-kit/national-statistics-child-abuse

Olds D., Donelan-McCall, N., O'Brien, R., MacMillan, H., Jack, S., Jenkins, T., . . . Beeber, L. (2013). Improving the nurse-family partnership in community practice. *Pediatrics, 132*(Suppl. 2), 110–117.

Pearlman, L. A. (1999). Self care for trauma therapists: Ameliorating vicarious traumatization. In B. Hudnall Stamm (Ed.), *Secondary traumatic stress: Self-care issues for clinicians, researchers, and educators* (pp. 51–64). Baltimore, MD: Sidran Press.

Pearlman, L. A., & Saakvitne, K. W. (1995a). *Trauma and the therapist.* New York, NY: W. W. Norton.

Pearlman, L. A., & Saakvitne, K. W. (1995b). Treating therapists with vicarious traumatization and secondary traumatic stress disorders. In C. R. Figley (Ed.), *Compassion fatigue: Coping with secondary traumatic stress disorder in those who treat the traumatized* (pp. 150–177). New York, NY: Routledge.

Pecora, P. J., Whittaker, J. K., Maluccio, A. N., & Barth, R. P. (2000). *The child welfare challenge: Policy, practice and research.* New York: Aldine de Gruyter.

Ryan, K., & Cunningham, M. (2007). Helping the helpers: Guidelines to prevent vicarious traumatization of play therapist working with traumatized children. In N. B. Webb (Ed.), *Play therapy with children in crisis: Individual, group and family treatment* (pp. 443–460). New York, NY: Guilford Press.

Saakvitne, K. W., Gamble, S., Pearlman, L. A., & Tabor Lev, B. (1999). *Risking connection: A training curriculum for working with survivors of childhood abuse.* Baltimore, MD: Sidran Press.

Saakvitne, K. W., & Pearlman, L. A. (1996). *Transforming the pain: A workbook on vicarious traumatization.* New York, NY: W. W. Norton.

Teicher, M., Andersen, S., Polcari, A., Anderson, C., Navalta, C., & Kim, D. (2003). The neurobiological consequences of early stress and childhood maltreatment. *Neuroscience and Biobehavioral Reviews, 27*, 33–44.

Uttal, W. R. (2011). *Mind and brain: A critical appraisal of cognitive neuroscience.* Cambridge, MA: MIT Press.

van der Kolk, B. A. (2001). The psychobiology and psychopharmacology of PTSD. *Human Psychopharmacology, 16*, 49–64.

Walsh, C. (2011). Youth justice and neuroscience: A dual-use dilemma. *British Journal of Criminology, 51*, 21–39.

Warde, B. (2016). *Inequality in U.S. social policy: An historical analysis.* New York, NY: Routledge.

Whitt-Woosley, A., & Sprang, G. (2014). When rights collide: A critique of the adoption and Safe Family Act from a justice perspective. *Child Welfare, 93*(3), 111–134.

Wulczyn, F., Hislop, K., & Jones Harden, B. (2002). The placement of infants in foster care. *Infant Mental Health Journal, 23*(5), 454–475.

Yoder, J. R., Leibowitz, G., & Peterson, L. (2016). Parental and peer attachment characteristics: Differentiating between youth sexual and non-sexual offenders and associations with sexual offense profiles. *Journal of Interpersonal Violence* [First published online February 12, 2016]. doi:10.1177/0886260516628805

VOICES FROM THE FIELD

Romarie McCue, BA
Program Director, Suffolk County Fatherhood Initiative
Retreat, Inc.

Agency Setting

The Retreat is a nonprofit, community-based agency that has been providing direct domestic violence services in Long Island, New York, for 29 years. The Retreat's mission is to provide safety, shelter, and support for victims of domestic abuse and to break the cycle of family violence. In addition to providing high-quality shelter, counseling, and legal advocacy services, we have also implemented programs designed to prevent domestic violence, including education of at-risk fathers, youth and their parents/caregivers, community members, and children/adolescents through school-based education programs.

Suffolk County Fatherhood Initiative (SCFI), a program of the Retreat, is a community-level collaboration that addresses the needs of low-income, at-risk fathers who often have a history of incarceration; it succeeds by engaging such men in catalytic skill-building activities designed to leverage and activate their strengths. Anticipated outcomes of SCFI include reduction of criminal activity and family violence. The program is funded by the Healthy Marriage/Responsible Fatherhood (HMRF) initiative discretionary grant through the Office of Family Assistance (OFA). The program provides responsible fatherhood and healthy relationship education, case management, economic stability, and mentoring to fathers living in Suffolk County who are struggling economically. Since 2011, we have served over 900 low-income fathers, about 15% who are incarcerated or transitioning from incarceration and more than 75% with prior criminal justice involvement. Within the context of Retreat's domestic violence prevention mission, we weave prevention throughout our interventions and meet fathers where they are—in one of our two community-based sites, in halfway houses, or in the local county jail.

Practice Responsibilities

As program director, I oversee all programs' day-to-day operations. I am responsible for coordinating and overseeing project activities (outreach to fathers, client assessments, case management, skill-building education in fathering/parenting, healthy marriage/relationship education, peer mentoring and workforce development, and economic stability activities). In addition, I am responsible for recruiting project staff, training, and coordinating efforts among project partners, tracking and analyzing program statistics and goals, adhering to contract compliance, implementing and enhancing the sustainability plan, and all the other programmatic reporting and functions. I supervise the case management coordinator and education coordinator and oversee the supervision of all related program staff.

Expertise Required

This position requires organizational and management skills, as well as an ongoing and evolving knowledge of service providers and county staff in our local jails. More important than level of education in this job is the ability to work with staff at all levels and throughout different delivery systems. For example, I have to be able to communicate with and maintain working relationships with case managers, program directors, correctional officers, and other jail staff, as well as the sheriff's office and the department of probation.

Ethical, Legal, Practice, Diversity, and/or Advocacy Issues Addressed

There are several challenges to this work including challenges executing the mission of the program to help fathers connect with and build relationships with their children. Working with fathers who may have limited access to their children both before and after incarceration presents one unique challenge; often the focus of our work is helping fathers negotiate the child welfare system and repair relationships with their children's mother. Navigating family relationships within the context of the real constraints of both the criminal justice and child welfare systems is an everyday challenge. Although the fathers we serve have criminal histories, we center them in their work and provide services regardless of past criminal history.

Interprofessional and Intersectoral Collaboration

The primary interprofessional collaboration is with the local jail system; staff on all levels (case managers, educators, program management) must develop positive and collaborative working relationships with staff in the local jail. In addition, this work requires ongoing collaboration with other providers, especially around the time of release, to allow them to finish participating in the program and integrate into the community.

CHAPTER 12

Domestic Violence

Joan Pennell

CHAPTER OBJECTIVES

The major objectives of this chapter are to:

- Present ways in which forensic social workers respond flexibly, collaboratively, and effectively to situations of domestic violence.
- Describe ways to engage men who abuse in becoming better fathers and partners.

CHAPTER COMPETENCIES HIGHLIGHTED

- Competency 2: Engage Diversity and Difference in Practice
- Competency 8: Intervene With Individuals, Families, Organizations, and Communities

Increasingly the United States is resorting to legal strategies to stop domestic violence (Goodmark, 2012). This national trend has both benefits and costs. Treating domestic violence as a crime validates the suffering of those who are victimized and offers valuable legal remedies. Who benefits from the law, however, too often reflects biases based on gender, sexuality, race, nationality, and income. These biases are especially problematic because the targets of domestic violence are disproportionately women and lesbian, gay, bisexual, and transgender (LGBT) individuals and because low-income communities that are predominantly African American, Latino, or indigenous receive fewer supports and protections (U.S. Department of Justice, 2015b).

The lopsided reliance on the legal system limits funding of other necessary services that not only deter domestic violence but also help families to heal and flourish (Huntington, 2014). Forensic social work, encompassing a broad range of programs and policies in the sociolegal context, has much to offer in righting this imbalance. This chapter examines how social workers can foster culturally respectful partnerships with and around families that safeguard all family members. These systems of care have the potential to respond in a manner that helps men who abuse become better partners and fathers. An example is provided of a fathering program for men with a history of committing domestic violence, and the lead coordinator of this program is highlighted in the Voices From the Field section.

Background and Scope of the Problem

The U.S. Department of Justice (U.S. Department of Justice, 2015a) defines domestic violence as

> . . . a pattern of abusive behavior in any relationship that is used by one partner to gain or maintain power and control over another intimate partner. Domestic violence can be physical, sexual, emotional, economic, or psychological actions or threats of actions that influence another person.

Other common terms for domestic violence are *women abuse* and *intimate partner violence*.

Globally, women abuse is widespread and can be attributed to both gender and economic inequality (World Health Organization [WHO]/London School of Hygiene and Tropical Medicine, 2010). Levels vary widely by country and are lowest where community sanctions prohibit women abuse and where women have access to sanctuary from the violence (WHO/London School of Hygiene and Tropical Medicine, 2010). As codified by the United Nations, the freedom of women is a fundamental human right, and gendered violence is not excusable on the grounds of customary practices (United Nations, General Assembly, 1993).

Within the United States, the cultural norms of the various populations, native and settler, differed in regards to gendered relationships and domestic violence. Precontact with Europeans, many American Indians traced their lineage through their mothers, men and women had equitable gender relations, and women exerted considerable leadership socially, economically, and politically (Smith & Wilson, 1999). War, disease, and forced removal from their traditional lands pushed American Indians into farming and into patrilineal and patriarchal systems.

Black couples had relative sexual equality and drew upon support from their extended kinship network, a legacy from their African cultures (Gilmore, 1996). Many of the slaves came from western Africa with a philosophy of human connectedness and an ethic of communal labor. The relatively egalitarian systems of American Indians and African Americans were marginalized by the practices of the early British colonists, who had an abiding influence over the development of mores and laws in the country.

The British settling in the colonies had quite disparate family ways, and these reflected their entwined beliefs about class, race, gender, and generation (Fischer, 1989). The Puritans in Massachusetts banned wife beating as well as cruelty against children and servants in order to ensure harmony under the rule of the father and to forestall divine retribution. In contrast, the Royalist elites in Virginia upheld the moral authority of the patriarch to punish his wife, children, servants, and slaves but used public shaming to temper the severity of beatings by White men against their wives. The pacifist Quakers in the Delaware valley espoused tender and attentive care of children to improve moral character and viewed men and women as "helpmeets for each other" (Fischer, 1989). Taking a different tack, settlers in the Appalachian backcountry used permissive practices, interspersed with violent outbursts, which fostered self-assertion by boys and self-denial by girls and a warrior culture.

The views of the settlers affected domestic violence law and interventions. In 1641, the Puritans passed the Body of Liberties, the first Western legislation outlawing family violence, and they used collective monitoring to ensure safety within the home. Their communities had lower rates of domestic homicide than reported in other British colonies (Fischer, 1989; Pleck, 1987), and state crime statistics show that those differences persisted into the 21st century (Violence Policy Center, 2015).

In the early 19th century, U.S. courts upheld the husband's right to govern his family, including wife beating in moderation, and women were rarely granted a divorce on grounds of spousal abuse (Pleck, 1987). The proposal of first-wave feminists that women should have the right to divorce abusive husbands lost traction at the onset of the American Civil War in 1861. After the devastating war, wife-beating interventions were primarily limited to calls to flog abusers. In the southern states, the Ku Klux Klan, a vigilante group formed by White

Confederate veterans, whipped wife beaters, both White and Black. Nevertheless, over the next 100 years, White women and later women of color made gains in legal rights, voting, education, employment, and social welfare. These gains laid the foundation for second-wave feminism in the latter half of the 20th century.

In the 1970s, feminists advocating for women's rights propelled women abuse into the forefront of national discussions. Challenging male domination, battered-women activists across the country established shelters offering refuge to abused women and their children (Schechter, 1982). Although wary of the police and courts perceived as revictimizing women, advocates over the 1980s and 1990s increasingly urged mandatory arrest laws, no-drop policies by prosecutors, and enforcement of no-contact orders. The results of these interventions were mixed in large measure because they lacked the flexibility to be responsive to individual situations (Goodman & Epstein, 2011).

On the one hand, legal interventions helped women leave abusers and upheld domestic violence as a crime, which was of immense importance to the emotional healing of abused women. On the other hand, mandatory policies led to arrests not only of men who abused but also women who fought back against the abuse or refused to testify in court. Women had good reason not to give testimony: doing so could lead to the incarceration of a loved partner or father or of the family breadwinner, retaliation by the abuser or condemnation from their faith or cultural communities, and deportation of undocumented family members.

All these adverse impacts were keenly experienced in communities of color for whom the lack of service options outside the legal system only exacerbated the disproportional imprisonment of their men. Moreover, the dominant paradigm of male violence against women reinforced heterosexist assumptions with the courts unable to identify who was perpetrating abuse in lesbian, gay, bisexual, transgender, and queer (LGBTQ) couples.

Outcomes of restraining orders from civil courts were more promising because they not only prohibited contact between the former partners but could also address financial support, housing, and child visitation arrangements, all essential to the well-being of families. Women of color and from low-income neighborhoods reported that court orders restraining men from contacting their victims prevented or reduced further violence. The effectiveness of these orders, however, depended on whether they were enforced and what other measures were taken at the time. In particular, mothers who did not stay apart from their abusers could be subject to child protection services removing their children, and abusive men often continued the harassment through child custody challenges in court (Hannah & Goldstein, 2010).

Other legal strategies were taken to control abusers. In 1996, a nearly unanimous Congress amended the federal Gun Control Act to prohibit individuals with a domestic violence protective order from owning a firearm. During this period, judges also began ordering men into batterer intervention programs in the hope that with treatment or reeducation, they would change for the better. These groups challenged power and control tactics used to coerce partners and had high attrition rates averaging 50%, but if the men completed the group, they were less likely to commit further partner violence (Gondolf, 2002). Recommendations to improve the batterer intervention programs included being culturally congruent, attentive to fathering, working with other services to address economic and behavioral health issues, and engaging previously abusive men in violence prevention (Bent-Goodley, Rice, Williams, & Pope, 2011). These recommendations reflected the need for a coordinated response that supported safe relationships for all family members from different backgrounds. Given all these efforts to stop domestic violence, we examine its extent today and whether rates are decreasing.

System and Population Overview

Intimate partner violence cuts across social groups in the United States and has very serious consequences. A national survey (Black et al., 2011) found that 35.6% of women and 28.5% of men identify themselves as a victim of intimate partner abuse in their lifetime, most commonly at the hands of men. As compared to heterosexual populations, prevalence is greater for individuals who identify as LBGT, with the exception of gay men (Walters, Chen, & Breiding, 2013). Abusing partners may entrap their victims by threatening to reveal the victims' sexual orientation or gender identity.

Levels of victimization are higher for American Indian, multiracial, and Black populations than for White and Hispanic populations (Black et al., 2011). Among those victimized, over one third of the women report more than one form of violence (i.e., rape, stalking, and/ or physical violence); in contrast, less than one tenth of the men report anything other than physical violence. Experiencing multiple forms of partner violence results in more negative consequences such as posttraumatic stress disorder, injuries, work absenteeism, and unwanted pregnancies (Black et al., 2011).

The impact of abuse undermines women's autonomy as individuals to direct their lives and their capacity as mothers to care for and protect their children. Even though fathers usually spend far less time than mothers with children, fathers are involved in approximately half the child maltreatment and fatalities found by public child welfare (U.S. Department of Health and Human Services, Administration for Children and Families, Administration on Children, Youth and Families, Children's Bureau, 2015).

Current Practice, Policy, and Social Movement Trends and Debates

Given the widespread prevalence of domestic violence and its severe impact, a major question is whether the rate of domestic violence is falling in the United States. To answer this question, data collected directly from victims is used rather than police records because people, especially victims of domestic violence, frequently do not file reports with law enforcement. Rate, rather than prevalence, is analyzed because prevalence refers to the proportion of a population having experienced prior or new occurrences of domestic violence within a time period while rate refers to the proportion of a population experiencing new occurrences of domestic violence within a time period. Comparing new occurrences for different time periods makes it possible to determine if rates are waning, rising, or staying the same.

A national self-report survey of nonfatal intimate partner violence perpetrated in the previous six months found that rates declined by 64% from 1994 to 2010 (U.S. Department of Justice, 2012/2015). This survey observed that from 1994 to 2000, the decrease in intimate partner violence paralleled the decrease in overall violent crime; however, from 2001 to 2010 the level of intimate partner violence stabilized, unlike that for overall violent crime which continued to decrease. These U.S. trends may be a function of how the data were analyzed.

An analysis of British data from 1994 to 2014 shows domestic abuse against both women and men falling until 2008 when their and the U.S. economies were adversely affected by the Great Recession (Walby, Towers, & Francis, 2015). After 2008, the British survey observed a rise in the rate of domestic violence against women and a stabilizing of the rate of domestic violence against men. Falling incomes coupled with cuts to social services in all likelihood made it more difficult for women to leave abusive relationships. A difference between the British and the U.S. (U.S. Department of Justice, 2012/2015) studies is that the British researchers took into account the number of incidents up to 60 committed against individual victims while the U.S. researchers capped the series of incidents at 10. This U.S. approach may have underestimated the violence because many victims are abused on a frequent basis, often weekly.

Core Roles and Functions of Forensic Social Work in This System

The history of the second-wave feminist movement to end violence against women is also a history of social work. A prime example is social worker Susan Schechter, who challenged her profession to engage in these struggles (Danis, 2006). Activists included and continue to include battered women, women's advocates, professionally educated men and women, and combinations of all these. Today, social workers are involved in preventing, stopping, and promoting healing from domestic violence. Social workers engage directly with family members, develop and manage programs, provide public and professional education, collaborate with others on social and legal reforms, conduct research, and disseminate findings to reach diverse groups. A social worker who has applied all these strategies to ending domestic violence is profiled in the Voices From the Field section.

Relevant Theories or Frameworks

Fathers make a difference to their children's lives and future prospects. Involved, caring fathers support their children's growth emotionally, cognitively, socially, and morally (Lamb, 2010). In the context of domestic violence and child maltreatment, however, fathers pose a risk to their children's development. Simply dismissing all men who abuse as incapable of change is a missed opportunity for creating safe, loving homes for some families. An alternative is helping the men become better parents and partners.

Few services are available for men who abuse to learn how to become responsible parents, and evaluations of these programs are even more limited. Thus, knowledge in this field is scarce. Two exceptions are a Canadian program called Caring Dads and a North Carolina program called Strong Fathers. These responsible fatherhood programs seek to raise the men's awareness of the deleterious impact of children's exposure to domestic violence and to enhance the men's skills in communicating and parenting. Increased awareness of the harm motivates men to change and improvement in skills makes it possible for the men to act on these aspirations.

The Caring Dads compared the participants' self-reports before and after they completed the 17-week fathering program (Scott & Lishak, 2012). The data showed a significant decrease in the men's overreacting to their children's behaviors and significant progress in how they communicated with and respected the children's mothers.

The Strong Fathers program used multiple data sources, including the participants, their current or former partners, the group facilitators, and child protection reports. Notably, the findings from all these data sources point to benefits for the men's children and former or current partners. Over the course of the 20-week group, the men progressed in their parenting skills and set positive goals for themselves and for relating to their children and the mothers of their children (Pennell, Sanders, Rikard, Shepherd, & Starsoneck, 2013). Pre/post data show reductions in child protection findings and family risk level (Pennell, Rikard, & Sanders, 2014).

Relevant Ethical, Legal, and Policy Issues

Responsible fatherhood programs such as Strong Fathers deviate from batterer intervention programs, which usually emphasize men's accountability through fees, acknowledging harm, and mandatory participation. These programs highlight the general negative effects of domestic violence on children and do not use fatherhood as a motivation to reduce violence. The resulting inattention to parenting skills is problematic because the majority of men in batterer intervention programs are in some kind of fathering relationship (Salisbury, Henning, & Holdford, 2009). Strong Fathers also represents a departure from the majority of available parenting programs in that fathers, rather than mothers, are the intended participants. Moreover, fathering educational programs and batterer intervention programs alike have had a poor track record of including men of color and low-income men (Jewell & Wormith, 2010; Julion, Breitenstein, & Waddell, 2012).

Relevant Assessment, Prevention, and Intervention Strategies

At the beginning of each Strong Fathers session, the men reflect back over the last week and complete a weekly parenting log. On the log, they record their key successes and struggles as a father and rate their parenting decisions on a scale of 1 ("I did not feel good at all") to 5 ("I felt great"). This means that the men assess their performance, and their self-evaluation becomes the basis for group dialogue about ways to manage the risk that the men pose to their families.

Self-assessment is a way to enhance risk assessment that is usually based on professional judgment or risk assessment tools. The ability of workers to assess risk is limited by the fact they are often unaware of the extent of domestic violence on their caseloads (Kohl, Barth, Hazen, & Landsverk, 2005). Risk assessment tools help workers refrain from bias against certain populations and instead focus on likely predictors of domestic violence, but these instruments only modestly increase the accuracy of the assessments (Kropp & Gibas, 2010).

Forensic Practice Skill Set

In order to foster a positive learning environment, the Strong Fathers facilitators need to simultaneously foster a safe context for expressing views and to challenge the men's norms and practices. Maintaining this balance is especially delicate when the parenting skills taught in the group run counter to the participants' cultural upbringing. In particular, the participants express deep-felt unease with using praise to reinforce children's good behavior. After one session on praise, a facilitator noted,

> This was a great discussion they [the men] felt like praise could be a sign of weakness. After giving examples they began to understand the importance of praising your child. One of the fathers expressed not having any praise as a child from his parents, only abuse.

Once the men practice these skills at home, they are rewarded by their improved relationships within the family.

Overwhelmingly, the men's feedback on the group was that it helped them become better fathers (Pennell & Brandt, 2017). An area of some disagreement was whether the facilitators spoke in a way that the men could understand. Interestingly, the men who had difficulty comprehending the facilitators were also the ones who identified that the group helped them see their world in a new way.

Case Example and Application

A very committed Strong Fathers participant was a young father of three little girls.* From the outset of joining the group, he recognized that he and the children's mother "get along better when we're not together." While living together, they had been investigated by the police and then Child Protective Services for family violence incidents that involved their children. No protective orders were put in place. Initially the children moved between their parents' households, but by the end of the Strong Fathers group, they resided with their mother and their father visited them regularly.

His strong attendance record stood out: He was absent from only one session. Even more noteworthy were the strides that he made in his understanding of how to relate to his daughters and former partner. The pretest and posttests backed up his progress. At three points during the group, he completed a questionnaire testing his knowledge of child development. He progressed from a low of 62% correct answers to 69% and finally to a high of 85%. For example, on the first test, he agreed that "you should be careful not to praise your children too much because they'll get used to it and take it for granted." By the final session, he disagreed with this statement. More poignant, though, than the test scores were his self-commentary on the various worksheets completed during the group sessions.

(continued)

When asked early in the group to identify his goals, he wrote, "Love myself and love my kids." He further recognized that there were aspects of his own childhood that he did not want to pass on to his own children, in particular, "my attitude." By the seventh session on the impact of violence, it was obvious that he put much thought into his goals, and these related to changing his attitude toward his children. He wrote about "less yelling" and paying "more attention" to his children. During the eighth session, he identified the impact of domestic violence on his daughters and highlighted "mental abused" and "physical abused." By the 15th session on abusive relationships, he connected his masculinity with being a good father. When asked about how he served as a role model to his children during the past week, he wrote, "Praised them, help(ed) them when they need something, and be a real man around" them.

This progression in his fathering is evident in his self-assessments. At each session, he rated how he felt about his parenting during the past week on the 5-point scale of 1 ("Did not feel good at all about the parenting decisions that I made") to 5 ("Felt great about those decisions"). He started with a 3 and wrote that his greatest struggle as a father in the past week was having his children stay at his home because they "messed with everything." When he gave himself a 5, it was because of areas in which he was rightly proud of his growth, for example: "talking to my kids," "waking up early" to make sure his children were ready for school, and praising his children for "reading good." And he lowered his self-ratings when he had not visited with his children to a 1 or 3. Even then, he made a point of checking in by phone. For example, he wrote: "I didn't go to the movies with my [children] yesterday, but I talk(ed) to them and they said they had a good time."

In regards to his former partner, he recognized from the outset of the group that she was "a good mother." By the seventh session, which focused on the impact of violence, he set as goals for his relationship with her—"treat with respect" and "helping her" by taking care of the children while she was recovering from an illness. During the 16th session, he had advanced his understanding of his own emotional abusiveness and how this "messed" up his life and served to "break up" his family. How did he make these changes?

The Strong Fathers curriculum and supportive group context gave him the opportunity to learn new information, set his goals, assess his performance, and change how he related to his children and their mother. For his part, he affirmed the importance of receiving support from "God, grandmother, and mother." He went on to write, "I pray to God that I be a better man and a better father, and my grandmother and mother tells me all the time that they are proud of me."

Note: The collection of the Strong Fathers data used in this chapter was funded by the North Carolina Department of Health and Human Services, Division of Social Services from 2009 to 2014, prime Family Violence Prevention and Services Act, U.S. Department of Health & Human Services.
*The identity of the family has been masked to protect confidentiality.

Conclusion

Domestic violence is a pattern of abuse committed most commonly by men against an intimate partner. The abuse has far-reaching adverse impacts on everyone in a family and on their community ties. Increasingly, the United States has turned to the police and courts to stop domestic violence. Legal measures rightly validate that domestic violence is a crime but fail to develop the potential of those who abuse to become better partners and parents. Preventing domestic violence requires putting in place the safeguards, supports, and services necessary for advancing the autonomy of those who are victimized and the healing of families.

CHAPTER EXERCISES

Exercise 1. Father's self-assessment. In completing his weekly parenting logs, a father reflected on his parenting in the past week. He also rated his parenting decisions on a 5-point scale. The following table displays his comments and self-ratings for 4 of the 20 sessions. From his comments, why do you think he gave himself these self-ratings? Over these sessions, what challenges do you see him facing as a father? What progress do you see him making as a father?

Session 2	Session 4	Session 8	Session 19
"I'm learning new thing but finding it hard to use what I'm learning because I can't see or talk to my kid's mother and don't get to see my little girl for two hours once a week."	"Tried to listen more and talk less. Working on controlling my temper. Looking at how my actions affect my kids."	"[Domestic violence is harmful] Because it lets [my daughter] see a side of me that she should never have to see! Could make her find herself with a man like I was!"	"Working with my little girl with her homework on my visit. Played store with her she really enjoyed that. I tried to tell her she was doing a great job as much as possible."
Self-Rating 3	Self-Rating 2	Self-Rating 1	Self-Rating 3

Note: A self-rating of 1 means "I did not feel good at all about my parenting decisions;" a self-rating of 5 means "I felt great about my parenting decisions."

Exercise 2. Mother's perspective. In an interview, the wife of one Strong Fathers participant shared, "During the program there were some things brought out that affected him in a good way. . . . Evaluating himself and seeing where he could be better." What is she saying about the group's impact on her husband's capacity to assess his own behaviors and to identify areas where he needed to change?

Additional Resources

National Coalition Against Domestic Violence: www.ncadv.org

United States Department of Health and Human Services, Administration for Children and Families, Administration on Children, Youth and Families, Children's Bureau: www.acf.hhs.gov

United States Department of Justice, Office on Violence Against Women: www.justice.gov/ovw

References

Bent-Goodley, T., Rice II, J., Williams, O., & Pope, M. (2011). Treatment for perpetrators of domestic violence. In M. Koss, J. White, & A. Kazdin (Eds.), *Violence against women and children: Navigating solutions* (Vol. 2, pp. 199–213). Washington, DC: American Psychological Association.

Black, M. C., Basile, K. C., Breiding, M. J., Smith, S. G., Walters, M. L., Merrick, M. T., . . . Stevens, M. R. (2011). *The national intimate partner and sexual violence survey: 2010 summary report.* Atlanta, GA: National Center for Injury Prevention and Control, Centers for Disease Control and Prevention. Retrieved from http://www.cdc.gov/ViolencePrevention/pdf/NISVS_Report2010-a.pdf

Danis, F. S. (2006). A tribute to Susan Schechter: The visions and struggles of the battered women's movement. *Affilia, 21*(3), 336–341. doi:10.1177/0886109906288899

Fischer, D. H. (1989). *Albion's seed: Four British folkways in America.* New York, NY: Oxford University Press.

Gilmore, G. E. (1996). *Gender and Jim Crow: Women and the politics of White supremacy in North Carolina, 1896–1920.* Chapel Hill: University of North Carolina Press.

Gondolf, E. W. (2002). *Batterer intervention systems: Issues, outcomes, and recommendations.* Thousand Oaks, CA: Sage.

Goodman, L. A., & Epstein, D. (2011). The justice system response to domestic violence. In M. P. Koss, J. W. White, & A. E. Kazdin (Eds.), *Violence against women and children: Navigating solutions* (Vol. 2, pp. 215–235). Washington, DC: American Psychological Association.

Goodmark, L. (2012). *A troubled marriage: Domestic violence and the legal system.* New York, NY: University Press.

Hannah, M. T., & Goldstein, B. (Eds.). (2010). *Domestic violence, abuse, and child custody: Legal strategies and policy issues.* Kingston, NJ: Civic Research Institute.

Huntington, C. (2014). *Failure to flourish: How law undermines family relationships.* New York, NY: Oxford University Press.

Jewell, L. M., & Wormith, J. S. (2010). Variables associated with attrition from domestic violence treatment programs targeting male batterers: A meta-analysis. *Criminal Justice and Behavior, 37*(10), 1086–1113. doi:10.1177/0093854810376815

Julion, W. A., Breitenstein, S. M., & Waddell, D. (2012). Fatherhood intervention development in collaboration with African American non-resident fathers. *Research in Nursing & Health, 35,* 490–506. doi:10.1002/nur.21492

Kohl, P. L., Barth, R. P., Hazen, A. L., & Landsverk, J. A. (2005). Child welfare as a gateway to domestic violence services. *Children and Youth Services Review, 27,* 1203–1221. doi:10.1016/j.childyouth.2005.04.005

Kropp, P. R., & Gibas, A. (2010). The Spousal Assault Risk Assessment Guide (SARA). In R. K. Otto & K. S. Douglas (Eds.), *Handbook of violence risk assessment* (pp. 227–250). New York, NY: Taylor & Francis.

Lamb, M. E. (Ed.). (2010). *The role of the father in child development* (5th ed.). Hoboken, NJ: Wiley.

Pennell, J., & Brandt, E. (2017). Men who abuse their intimate partners: Their evaluation of a responsible fathering program. In T. August-Scott, K. Scott, & L. M. Tutty (Eds.), *Innovations in interventions to address intimate partner violence: Research and practice* (pp. 227–243). New York, NY: Routledge.

Pennell, J., Rikard, R. V., & Sanders, T. (2014). Family violence: Fathers assessing and managing their risk to children and women. *Children and Youth Services Review, 47,* 36–45.

Pennell, J., Sanders, T., Rikard, R. V., Shepherd, J., & Starsoneck, L. (2013). Family violence, fathers, and restoring personhood. *Restorative Justice, 1*(2), 268–289.

Pleck, E. (1987). *Domestic tyranny: The making of social policy against family violence from colonial times to the present.* New York, NY: Oxford University Press.

Salisbury, E. J., Henning, K., & Holdford, R. (2009). Fathering by partner-abusive men: Attitudes on children's exposure to interparental conflict and risk factors for child abuse. *Child Maltreatment, 14*(3), 232–242. doi:10.1177/1077559509338407

Schechter, S. (1982). *Women and male violence: The visions and struggles of the battered women's movement.* Boston, MA: South End Press.

Scott, K. L., & Lishak, V. (2012). Intervention for maltreating fathers: Statistically and clinically significant change. *Child Abuse & Neglect, 36,* 680–684. doi:10.1016/j.chiabu.2012.06.003

Smith, M. S., & Wilson, E. H. (1999). *North Carolina women making history.* Chapel Hill: University of North Carolina Press.

United Nations, General Assembly. (1993). *Declaration on the elimination of violence against women.* Geneva, Switzerland: 85th Plenary Meeting. Retrieved from http://www.un.org/documents/ga/res/48/a48r104.htm

U.S. Department of Health and Human Services, Administration for Children and Families, Administration on Children, Youth and Families, Children's Bureau. (2015). Child maltreatment 2013. Retrieved from http://www.acf.hhs.gov/sites/default/files/cb/cm2013.pdf

U.S. Department of Justice. (2012/2015). *Intimate partner violence, 1993–2010* [NCJ 239203]. Washington, DC: Bureau of Justice Statistics. Retrieved from http://www.bjs.gov/content/pub/pdf/ipv9310.pdf

U.S. Department of Justice. (2015a). Domestic violence. Retrieved from http://www.justice.gov/ovw/domestic-violence#dv

U.S. Department of Justice. (2015b). Identifying and preventing gender bias in law enforcement response to sexual assault and domestic violence. Retrieved from http://www.justice.gov/opa/file/799476/download

Violence Policy Center. (2015). *When men murder women: An analysis of 2013 homicide data*. Washington, DC: Author. Retrieved from http://www.vpc.org/studies/wmmw2015.pdf

Walby, S., Towers, J., & Francis, B. (2015). Is violent crime increasing or decreasing? A new methodology to measure repeat attacks making visible the significance of gender and domestic relations. *British Journal of Criminology, 56*(6), 1203–1234. doi:10.1093/bjc/azv131

Walters, M. L., Chen, J., & Breiding, M. J. (2013). *The National Intimate Partner and Sexual Violence Survey (NISVS): 2010 findings on victimization by sexual orientation*. Atlanta, GA: National Center for Injury Prevention and Control, Centers for Disease Control and Prevention. Retrieved from http://www.cdc.gov/violenceprevention/pdf/nisvs_sofindings.pdf

World Health Organization/London School of Hygiene and Tropical Medicine. (2010). *Preventing intimate partner and sexual violence against women: Taking action and generating evidence*. Geneva, Switzerland: World Health Organization. Retrieved from http://www.who.int/violence_injury_prevention/publications/violence/9789241564007_eng.pdf

VOICES FROM THE FIELD

Joetta Shepherd, MSW, LCSW

Director, Safe Relationships Division
Family Services, Inc.

Agency Setting

Family Services is a nonprofit organization serving Forsyth County, North Carolina, by providing professional services and participating in partnerships that foster the development of children; advance the safety, security, and success of families and individuals; and help build a sustainable community. These services are delivered through three major divisions: Child Development, Family Solutions, and Safe Relationships.

Practice Responsibilities

- Program development and management
- Supervision
- Budgetary control
- Grant writing and reporting
- Community education and prevention
- Direct services
- Collaborative initiatives

Expertise Required

- Master's degree in human services
- Knowledge of management practice and principles
- Ability to provide clinical services
- Knowledge of the area of victimization

Ethical, Legal, Practice, Diversity, and/or Advocacy Issues Addressed

Domestic violence is a crime that not only affects survivors and their families, but society as a whole. It is rooted in a social structure that perpetuates the inequality in relationships. All people have the right not to be abused, and interventions must hold abusers accountable through a coordinated community response. Principles that help to shape the intervention strategies of the Safe Relationships division are victim safety and abuser culpability. When providing services to victims of domestic violence, the Empowerment Model is practiced. This model serves as a framework for noncontrolled living and allows victims to experience personal power and self-determination. It establishes safety as the highest priority and acknowledges the patriarchal cultures, institutions, and laws that have permitted gender violence. Furthermore, this model believes that everyone is susceptible to battering. When providing legal services to victims of domestic violence, it is important that social workers not practice law. Sometimes, it can be a thin line, particularly when assisting victims with a restraining order.

Services to batterers are based on the Duluth Model, which believes that "violence is used to control people's behavior." In addition, this model theorizes that abusive behavior is intentional, and tactics used on the Power and Control Wheel are typical behaviors of those who want to dominate others. The structured psychoeducational program delivered through the agency is designed to encourage accountability by the participant and explore noncontrolling and nonviolent ways of relating to partners.

The importance of providing comprehensive services to the family unit is considered in this division's mission/goals. Children, 3 years of age and older, accompanying their parent to the shelter are provided services. The agency was accepted for the Child Advocacy and Services Enhancement (CASE) project through the North Carolina Coalition Against Domestic Violence. CASE is designed to "promote dialogue and raise awareness of the needs of children exposed to domestic violence and co-occurring child maltreatment." Children are screened by victim advocates to determine what additional services may be needed. A designated licensed therapist is located at the shelter to assist with the clinical needs of families at our residential program.

Individual and family values are recognized as an important part of therapeutic intervention. The agency uses a variety of therapeutic methodologies and modalities that are specifically selected to meet the client's needs based on the diagnostic assessment and treatment plan. In addition to accommodating variations in lifestyles and situational change, the treatment plan emphasizes personal growth and gives special consideration to the client's cultural, ethnic, and religious perspective.

Interprofessional and Intersectoral Collaboration

Collaborations include various sectors of the community. The Safe Relationships division facilitates several community teams: the Domestic Violence Community Council, the Sexual Assault Response Team, and the Child Abuse Multidisciplinary Team. Membership includes representatives from law enforcement, educational systems, volunteer advocates, health and medical professionals, and human service representatives. As appropriate, subcommittees have been established to address issues related to the medical and health care profession, clergy, educational institutions, criminal justice, and others. These teams allow us to examine best practice models in our mission to eradicate violence and create a safer community. The results of these collaborations have included the following:

- Creation of "Safe on Seven" which is a multiagency center for victims to pursue no-contact orders
- Revisions of this community's protocol for child abuse and neglect
- Training of clergy and lay leaders
- Implementation of screening tools for health care facilities
- Development of training and printed materials for victims

CHAPTER 13

Substance Use and Co-Occurring Psychiatric Disorders Treatment: Systems and Issues for Those in Jail, Prison, and on Parole

Keith Morgen

Kelsey Denison-Vesel

Abigail Voelkner

Carolyn Brouard

Jaclyn Smith

Alissa Nowak

CHAPTER OBJECTIVES

The major objectives of this chapter are to:

- Show how mental health and substance use interact with criminal justice involvement.
- Examine the common assessment and intervention strategies for comorbid mental health and substance abuse in the forensic population and settings.

CHAPTER COMPETENCIES HIGHLIGHTED

- Competency 7: Assess Individuals, Families, Organizations, and Communities
- Competency 8: Intervene With Individuals, Families, Organizations, and Communities

Substance use disorders (SUDs) and co-occurring psychiatric disorders are an epidemic problem in U.S. prisons (Center for Substance Abuse Treatment [CSAT], 2005). For instance, the National Center on Addiction and Substance Abuse (CASA, 2010) found that 67.6% of inmates used illegal drugs regularly, 64.5% met the diagnostic criteria for SUD, and 24.4% struggled with co-occurring SUD and psychiatric disorders. Furthermore, CASA (2010) noted how only between one third to one half of all the prisons and jails report that they include co-occurring disorders within their addiction treatment services.

Other national data support this relationship. The Treatment Episode Dataset (Substance Abuse and Mental Health Services Administration [SAMHSA], 2013) surveys all SUD treatment admissions each year. In the most recent available data, findings show that of all admissions referred from the criminal justice system (CJS), substantial proportions of co-occurring SUDs and psychiatric disorders exist within the referral sources of prison (35.2%) and probation/parole (26.3%). In addition, the most recent findings from the National

Survey of Substance Abuse Treatment Services (N-SSATS; SAMHSA, 2014) found that only 33.6% of all SUD treatment programs nationwide offer specialized services for CJS clients.

These numbers are disturbing. Morgen (2017) underscores the need for SUDs treatment provided by clinicians and other professionals who are trained and experienced in the myriad nuances of SUD and co-occurring psychiatric care. CASA (2010) goes further, stating that all CJS personnel require training in an effort to bridge the chasm between the CJS and adequate SUD/co-occurring psychiatric disorder care.

Consequently, this chapter attempts to discuss some of the concepts relevant in bridging this gap. Publications from CASA (2010) and CSAT (2005) have already done a thorough job of providing a comprehensive scope of the SUD/psychiatric disorder epidemic within the CJS. This chapter does not try to restate these findings. We start with a brief review of how SUDs co-occur with psychiatric disorders. Next, we delve into key issues relevant to treatment and aftercare services. Recognizing the heterogeneous nature of co-occurring SUD/psychiatric disorders as well as jail and prison services and policies, we do not presume to offer any type of universal solution. Rather, this chapter simply points out these issues as in need of further dialogue between the addiction treatment, mental health treatment, and CJS.

Prevalence of Co-Occurring Disorders in General

To understand the impact of co-occurring SUDs/psychiatric disorders, the reader needs to review the prevalence and complexity of this issue within the general SUD population (and not just the CJS). Many in the CJS population come to jail/prison with diagnosed SUD/co-occurring psychiatric disorders, whereas many others enter jail/prison without the benefit of a diagnosed condition. The key psychiatric disorder areas are briefly reviewed here.

Anxiety/Depression

Myriad findings (e.g., Brooner, King, Kidorf, Schmidt, & Bigelow, 1997; Stewart, Zvolensky, & Eifert, 2002) support the conclusion that anxiety and depressive symptoms occur frequently within the SUD treatment population. For instance, in an SUD population, the lifetime rates of affective and anxiety disorders run between 49% and 79% (Langås, Malt, & Opjordsmoen, 2012). Other studies have documented the temporal sequencing of SUD and anxiety. First, a preexisting anxiety disorder leading to self-medication increases as predicting (Odds-Ratio = 2.50–4.99) the risk of SUD onset (Robinson, Sareen, Cox, & Bolton, 2011). Second, Menary, Kushner, Maurer, and Thuras (2011) documented that approximately 20% of the anxiety disorder population self-medicates with alcohol owing to the anxiolytic effect of alcohol. Third, anxiety disorder onset seems to come prior to opioid use disorder onset (Fatséas, Denis, Lavie, & Auriacombe, 2010) or alcohol use disorder (AUD) onset (Birrell, Newton, Teesson, Tonks, & Slade, 2015). Fourth, it is reported that at least 25% of individuals with depressive disorders use substances to relieve symptoms (Bolton, Robinson, & Sareen, 2009). Mood disorders also commonly co-occur with SUDs and trigger a significant risk for suicidal behavior (CSAT, 2009). For example, a review of psychological autopsy studies showed that mood disorders (particularly major depression) and SUDs were the most common disorders for those who died by suicide.

Bipolar Disorders

Bipolar disorders and SUDs are a common (e.g., Hawton, Sutton, Haw, Sinclair, & Harriss, 2005) and complex combination. Evidence from treatment populations indicates that one third of bipolar clients met the old *DSM-IV* abuse or dependence criteria (Baethge et al., 2005). The co-occurring relationship between these disorders complicates the course and duration of the bipolar depressive and manic episodes. These clients are also dangerous to self as they demonstrate medication nonadherence (Teter et al., 2011) as well as a higher risk for suicide (CSAT, 2009). Specifically, the mixed episode (most recent depressed and manic) bipolar client with rapid cycling seems to most commonly report a co-occurring SUD (Agrawal, Nurnberger, & Lynskey, 2011).

Psychotic Disorders

Psychotic symptoms are also common in SUDs, whether due to withdrawal, substance-induced, or non–substance-related co-occurring disorder (SAMHSA, 2005). Recently, 23 psychotic heroin-dependent patients, at their first agonist opioid treatment, were compared with 209 nonpsychotic individuals. Findings showed that psychotic heroin-dependent clients presenting for agonist opioid treatment demonstrated more severe psychopathology but a shorter, less severe addiction history than the nonpsychotic comparison group. Maremmani et al. (2012) reasoned that as the psychotic clients requested agonist opioid treatment earlier, and with a less severe addiction history, these clients primarily benefited from an opioid medication alleviating their psychiatric symptoms and not necessarily their heroin addiction. However, Maremmani et al. (2012) noted that psychotic symptoms may also develop after substance use (i.e., heroin) onset, thus confusing the non–substance-related versus substance-induced diagnostic deliberation. This finding supports earlier research regarding how methadone maintenance helps prevent psychotic relapses in clients with a history of psychotic episodes. The cessation of methadone with these clients led to a reemergence of psychotic symptoms (Levinson, Galynker, & Rosenthal, 1995). Similarly, research involving heroin addicts admitted for inpatient treatment of manic and/or acute psychotic episodes found that regardless of the reasons for hospitalization, those receiving increasing dosages of methadone were found to be less in need of antimanic and antipsychotic drugs at discharge (Pacini & Maremmani, 2005).

Personality Disorders

Antisocial personality disorder (ASPD) clients present as complex cases (R. B. Goldstein, Dawson, & Grant, 2010) and are associated with a more severe course of SUD (Morgen, 2017). Among clients with co-occurring disorders, ASPD is associated with more severe addiction and worse overall functioning (Crocker et al., 2005). Borderline personality disorder (BPD) is also prevalent within the SUD treatment population. A large survey found that 50.7% of individuals with a lifetime BPD diagnosis also qualified for a diagnosis of an SUD over the previous 12 months. This same survey found that for individuals with a lifetime diagnosis of an SUD, 9.5% also had a lifetime diagnosis of BPD (Grant et al., 2008). Co-occurring SUD and BPD present a few challenges. Both BPD and SUD are associated with emotional dysregulation (Beatson & Rao, 2012) and linked with impulsivity, suicidality, and self-harm risks, and all these risk factors are likely exacerbated by substance use. Thus, it is plausible to conclude that BPD may contribute to the severity of SUD symptoms and that SUD treatment may be more complicated for clients who also have BPD (SAMHSA, 2014).

Posttraumatic Stress Disorder (PTSD)

PTSD is common in the SUD population (Coker, Stefanovics, & Rosenheck, 2016; Morgen, Maschi, Viola, & Zgoba, 2013). Those with a PTSD diagnosis have nearly a twofold risk of a lifetime SUD diagnosis (Pietrzak, Goldstein, Southwick, & Grant, 2011). Furthermore, many SUD clients have a heightened risk of developing PTSD and/or other co-occurring psychiatric disorders (Green, Calhoun, Dennis, & Beckham, 2010). Like many other substances mirroring psychiatric symptoms, careful diagnostic deliberation is required with PTSD as many of the symptoms of this trauma disorder (such as arousal or reactivity) strongly resemble some symptoms of use and/or withdrawal (Saxon & Simpson, 2015). In addition, Maschi and colleagues (Maschi, Gibson, Zgoba, & Morgen, 2011; Maschi, Morgen, & Viola, 2014; Maschi, Morgen, Zgoba, Courtney, & Ristow, 2011; Maschi, Viola, Morgen, & Koskinen, 2015) have noted the potential for consistent reexposure and retraumatization as a contributing factor in deteriorating psychiatric well-being.

Prevalence of Psychiatric Disorders in the Prison/Jail Systems

Incarcerated individuals struggling with co-occurring SUD and psychiatric disorders are a population in need of study and improved treatment services (van Wormer & Persson, 2010).

TABLE 13.1   Selection of Studies on Psychiatric Disorders/Symptoms Within an Incarcerated Population

Disorder	Citation
Bipolar disorders	Baillargeon, Binswanger, Penn, Williams, and Murray (2009) Fovet et al. (2015) Kamath et al. (2010) Kamath et al. (2013)
Depressive disorders	Baier, Fritsch, Ignatyev, Priebe, and Mundt (2016) Baillargeon, Black, Contreras, Grady, and Pulvino (2001) Zlotnick et al. (2008)
Anxiety disorders	Osasona and Koleoso (2015) Værøy (2011)
Psychotic disorders	Denzel, van Esch, Harte, and Scherder (2016) Tamburello, Bajgier, and Reeves (2015) Young (2003)
Borderline personality disorder	Adams, Stuewig, and Tangney (2016) Hochhausen, Lorenz, and Newman (2002) Nee and Farman (2005)
Antisocial personality disorder	Warren and Burnette (2013) Yang, Chen, Xu, and Qian (2014)
Posttraumatic stress disorder	Maschi, Morgen et al. (2011) Maschi et al. (2014) Maschi et al. (2015)

CASA (2010) and CSAT (2005) are just two of the recent reports highlighting the prevalence of SUDs in the prison/jail systems. Numerous other studies underscore the prevalence of psychiatric disorders and symptoms within the prison/jail systems. Considering the highly evident relationship shown between psychiatric disorders and SUDs, many inmates reporting psychiatric disorders also likely present with an SUD(s). Table 13.1 highlights just some of these reported psychiatric disorders within the incarcerated population. These disorders, in conjunction with SUDs, shape the complex challenges discussed—in part—in the following sections.

Challenge 1

Use of Medication-Assisted Therapies (MATs)

MATs are pharmacological treatments primarily for opioid use disorders. Past pharmacotherapy for opioid withdrawal utilized methadone, a synthetic opiate. Methadone is administered in decreasing doses over a period not exceeding 30 days (for short-term detoxification) or 180 days (for long-term detoxification). A recent review of the research (Amato, Davoli, Minozzi, Ali, & Ferri, 2005) found that slow tapering with temporary substitution of long-acting opioids can reduce withdrawal severity. One issue with methadone treatment was that federal restrictions limited the distribution to a small number of methadone clinics. Thus, there was an inconvenience factor that inhibited the detoxification process. Furthermore, there were limited provisions for home or medical office administration of methadone due to concerns regarding the diversion of the methadone to illicit use (i.e., use of methadone to get high or unlawful sale of methadone).

These concerns were first addressed in 2000 with the passage of the Drug Addiction Treatment Act (DATA), which legalized the office-based management of opioid addiction.

This was not legal prior to DATA owing to the existing federal laws that had prohibited physicians from prescribing a narcotic for the sole purpose of maintaining the individual in a narcotic-addicted state. Next, in 2002, buprenorphine was approved for opioid withdrawal treatment. The first of two formulations approved, Subutex, contains only buprenorphine and is intended for use at the beginning of treatment. The other, Suboxone, contains both buprenorphine and the opiate antagonist naloxone, and is intended to be used in maintenance treatment of opiate addiction. The use of buprenorphine for medically supervised opioid withdrawal provides a transition from physical dependence to an opioid-free state with minimal withdrawal symptoms (CSAT, 2004).

Despite the myriad SUDs in the CJS population, MATs are underutilized (Oser, Knudsen, Staton-Tindall, Taxman, & Leukefeld, 2009). The CJS typically aligns with sanctions instead of treatment approaches such as MAT (Couture & Sabol, 2008). For example, Matusow et al. (2013) note how a survey of drug courts found that 98% of their clients report opioid problems and many of these individuals struggle with prescription opioids as opposed to heroin. But, despite these statistics, most drug court rules do not permit MATs with strong opposition to MATs from judges and other court/county officials, typically on ethical/moral grounds (Ludwig & Peters, 2014).

As limited resources are devoted to CJS SUD treatment, many inmates with addiction histories leave prison untreated (Taxman, Perdoni, & Harrison, 2007). This is unfortunate and not necessary as studies demonstrate that offenders leaving incarceration show high rates of fatal and nonfatal overdose (Binswanger, Blatchford, Mueller, & Stern, 2013; Kinner et al., 2012) and that MATs can reduce opioid-related deaths during incarceration (Larney et al., 2014). Further discouraging statistics come from a survey of CJS respondents that found how those reentering the community from jail/prison were actually the least likely to receive any MAT services (Friedmann et al., 2012). Thus, those with opioid addiction histories or an active opioid addiction are paroled with no treatment support.

Some estimates are as high as 80% of inmates with an opioid use disorder history not receiving appropriate SUD treatment (Aronowitz & Laurent, 2016). Many of these individuals may have been receiving opioid use disorder treatment prior to incarceration because many such struggling individuals already receiving MAT from community-based providers (e.g., methadone programs, in-office Suboxone treatment) are entering jails and prisons (Morgen, 2017). As a result, prisons and jails increasingly must interrupt community-based MAT when offenders enter a CJS facility. Aronowitz and Laurent (2016) emphasized that inmates who lost MAT access upon incarceration reported excessive struggles. Consequently, the rigid rules prohibiting MAT in jails/prisons may contribute to the addiction and mental health struggles of the inmates. For example, imagine an individual with an undiagnosed psychotic disorder who had been self-medicating using illegal opioids. If on MAT at the time of incarceration, the cessation of the MAT within one month of incarceration may likely produce the onset of the co-occurring psychotic symptoms that had been (though dysfunctionally) managed via opioid use and subsequent MAT for withdrawal purposes. Now, the jail or prison is facing a serious mental illness issue in a new inmate.

However, the one exception to this rule tends to be pregnant women entering incarceration with an opioid use disorder. Pregnant women struggling with addiction are a growing treatment subpopulation and one in need of increased attention. For this reason, many correctional facilities that house women offenders provide them with MAT (e.g., methadone) during pregnancy. The MAT is often ceased very soon after delivery. However, these women are also at high risk for relapse after delivery and urgently need follow-up SUD care (Denison-Vesel, Brouard, & Morgen, 2016).

Inmates entering prison with SUDs may be coming directly from an MAT program, or will soon require one due to withdrawal symptoms experienced once incarcerated. In addition, the high number of co-occurring SUD/psychiatric disorders seen in the CJS make the treatment of opioid (or other substance) withdrawal quite critical. Thus, we make three recommendations (earlier versions of these recommendations were discussed in Morgen & Voelkner, 2014).

One, all inmates with an opioid (or any substance) use disorder should be screened both at onset of incarceration and consistently throughout the first 90 days of their sentence. This will enable any co-occurring, substance-induced, or withdrawal-based symptoms (Morgen, 2017, for a review of withdrawal and substance-induced symptoms) to be caught early enough for a safe and successful intervention with minimal psychological/physiological discomfort experienced by the inmate. Two, increased collaboration must occur between the mental health and addiction treatment service sectors within the CJS. Recall from the CASA (2010) findings how most addiction treatment service systems within a prison/jail do *not* take into account psychiatric disorders. It is important for the CJS to truly and fully adopt the philosophy of *co-occurring disorders as the norm in the SUD population* (Morgen, 2017), *including those within the CJS*. Finally, the third recommendation is that all prison/jail systems (federal or state) implement an evidence-based and well-monitored MAT service for those struggling with withdrawal due to cessation of use.

Challenge 2

Treatment and Aftercare Services

Aftercare services are critical. For instance, Burdon, Dang, Prendergast, Messina, and Farabee (2007) studied 4,165 male and female parolees who received prison-based therapeutic community substance abuse treatment and who subsequently participated in only outpatient or only residential treatment following release from prison. Findings indicated that the participants benefited equally from outpatient and residential aftercare, regardless of the severity of their drug/alcohol problem. It is important to note that as states and the federal prison system further expand prison-based treatment services, the demand for aftercare treatment services will also increase. As this occurs, systems and policies governing the transitioning of individuals from prison- to community-based treatment should include a systematic and validated assessment of postprison treatment needs and a valid and reliable means to assess the quality of community-based treatment services. Finally, all parolees must experience a truly uninterrupted continuum of care.

Accomplishing this uninterrupted and well-designed continuum of care and support is challenging. CSAT (2005) reviews a long list of aftercare services necessary for successful reentry into the community without relapse and/or exacerbation of SUD and/or psychiatric disorder. These include the following:

- Case management to assist the parolee at the start of reentry
- Ease of communication with parole officer(s)
- Medical care
- Residential or outpatient SUD treatment as warranted
- Relapse prevention services
- Drug testing and monitoring
- Self-help education and support
- HIV/AIDS education, testing, and counseling
- Mental health services including medications when indicated
- Social and other support services for the offender and family members
- Vocational and educational training
- Family services
- Assistance in managing social support services (e.g., food stamps, veterans benefits)
- Housing assistance

All of these services take time, money, and staffing. In addition, there is complicated coordination required between numerous agencies (some private, some public) with different policies and caseloads. Typically, aftercare SUD services for parolees are seen as a unique component and distinctive from the prison/jail system. However, you could argue that effective SUD/co-occurring psychiatric aftercare services following prison/jail *must* commence with effective SUD/co-occurring psychiatric treatment services in prison/jail.

One good example of a strong in-prison treatment experience serving as a foundation for effective aftercare services is the Residential Drug Abuse Program (RDAP). RDAP is a voluntary, 500-hour, 9- to 12-month treatment program for federal prisoners with substance abuse problems. It is authorized by 18 U.S.C. § 3621, which directs the Bureau of Prisons (BOP) to provide "residential substance abuse treatment (and make arrangements for appropriate aftercare) . . . for all eligible prisoners." As an incentive for participation, federal law allows the BOP to reduce the sentences of RDAP graduates convicted of "nonviolent" offenses by up to one year (see www.bop.gov/inmates/custody_and_care/substance_abuse_treatment.jsp).

RDAP is divided into three phases. Phase I is the *unit-based* component providing 6 to 12 months of SUD treatment (500 hours) where inmates live in a special section of the prison and divide their time between treatment and prison work/educational programs. Upon completion of this phase, participants receive a certificate of completion. Phase II is the *follow-up services* component. Here, inmates will either go to a halfway house for follow-up care (if scheduled to do so) or return to the prison population and utilize prison services for follow-up care. This phase reflects one half of the aftercare requirement. Phase III is the *transitional drug abuse treatment* (TDAT) phase component that occurs in a halfway house. This phase lasts up to six months and is the other half of the aftercare requirement.

Eligibility for the program includes a willingness to participate in the program, have at least 24 months of their sentence remaining, and are able to complete all three phases of the RDAP, which includes the community-based program in a halfway house. The RDAP is limited to those who have real, verifiable substance use problems and desire treatment. "Verifiable"—as per this program—refers to a diagnosis that is documented, preferably in a document called the presentence report (PSR). However, letters/reports from a medical doctor mental health/addictions professional, a parole or probation officer, or a judge's recommendation help to document that the prisoner has a "verifiable" substance use disorder. Furthermore, two or more convictions for driving under influence (DUI) or driving while intoxicated/impaired (DWI) in the five-year period before the prisoner's most recent arrest may also verify that the prisoner has a substance use disorder. Not all federal prisons have an RDAP (see Table 13.2 for the most recent roster of prisons that offer RDAPs).

The BOP may deny someone access to the RDAP by claiming that the person is in "sustained remission." According to the *DSM-5* (American Psychiatric Association, 2013), a person is in "sustained remission" if she or he has not used substances for 12 consecutive months prior to his arrest. One exception to this rule is when the person is in a "controlled environment" during that 12-month period (i.e., closely supervised and substance-free jails, therapeutic communities, or locked hospital units). If a person is in a "controlled environment" during the 12-month period before his arrest, and does not use drugs during that 12-month period, the *DSM-5* says the person is not in "sustained remission." Consequently, the addiction history prior to incarceration is the determining factor.

Other programs also provide SUD/co-occurring psychiatric disorder care in-prison/jail treatment. Two of the most common types of treatments for those in the CJS are cognitive behavioral therapy (CBT) and 12-Step groups. Each will briefly be addressed in the following text, specifically through the perspective of the CJS population.

Cognitive Behavioral Therapy

Cognitive theory states that thought patterns and cognitive themes (schemas) play a large role in both causing and maintaining psychological distress (Beck, 1976). Often in cases of SUDs and psychiatric disorders, these schemas tend to be negative, thus setting up the individual for a pattern of unhealthy coping mechanisms and symptoms. For instance, Beck, Wright, Newman, and Liese (1993) noted that addressing these schemas and other dysfunctional thought processes is the fundamental component of cognitive-related work with SUDs. Once schemas in SUD individuals become activated, automatic thoughts, cognitive distortions, and other errors tend to fixate on the use of substance as a source of relief. According to the cognitive theory of substance abuse, the dysfunctional beliefs about substances and their effects perpetuate the disorder (Beck et al., 1993). Beck et al. (1993)

TABLE 13.2 RDAP Locations as of 2015

NORTHEAST REGION
FCI Allenwood - L (PA)
FCI Allenwood - M (PA)
FCI Berlin (NH)
USP Canaan (PA)
FCI Danbury (CT)
FCI Elkton (OH)
FCI Fairton (NJ)
FCI Fort Dix I (NJ)
FCI Fort Dix 2 (NJ)
FPC Lewisburg (PA)
FPC McKean (PA)
FCI Schuylkill (PA)

MID-ATLANTIC REGION
FPC Alderson 1 (WV)✹
FPC Alderson 2 (WV)✹
FPC Beckley (WV)
FCI Beckley (WV)
USP Big Sandy (KY)
FCI Butner M1 (NC)
FCI Butner M2 (NC)
FCI Cumberland (MD) FPC
Cumberland (MD)
SFF Hazelton (WV)✹
FMC Lexington 1 (KY)
FMC Lexington 2 (KY)★
FCI Memphis (TN)
FCI Morgantown 1 (WV)
FCI Morgantown 2 (WV)
FCI Petersburg - M (VA)
FCI Petersburg - L (VA)

SOUTHEAST REGION
FCI Coleman - L (FL)
USP Coleman II (FL)
FPC Edgefield (SC)
FSL Jesup (GA)
FCI Marianna (FL)
FCI Miami (FL) Ś
FPC Miami (FL)
FPC Montgomery 1 (AL)
FPC Montgomery 2 (AL)
FPC Pensacola (FL)
FPC Talladega (AL)
FCI Tallahassee (FL)✹
FCI Yazoo City (MS)

NORTH CENTRAL REGION
FPC Duluth (MN)
FCI Englewood (CO)
FPC Florence (CO)
FCI Florence (CO)
FPC Greenville (IL)✹
FCI Leavenworth (KS)
FPC Leavenworth (KS)
USP Marion (IL)
FCI Milan (MI)
FCI Oxford (WI)
FPC Pekin (IL)
FCI Sandstone (MN)
MCFP Springfield (MO)★
FCI Terre Haute (IN)
FCI Waseca (MN)✹
FPC Yankton 1 (SD)
FPC Yankton 2 (SD)

SOUTH CENTRAL REGION
FCI Bastrop (TX)
FPC Beaumont (TX)
FCI Beaumont - L (TX)
FCI Beaumont - M (TX)
USP Beaumont (TX)
FPC Bryan (TX)✹
FMC Carswell 1 (TX)✹★
FMC Carswell 2 (TX)✹Ś
FCI El Reno (OK)
FCI Forrest City - L (AR)
FCI Forrest City - M (AR)
FCI Fort Worth 1 (TX)
FCI Fort Worth 2 (TX)
FCI La Tuna (TX)
FCI Seagoville 1 (TX)
FCI Seagoville 2 (TX)
FPC Texarkana (TX)

WESTERN REGION
FCI Dublin 1 (CA)✹
FCI Dublin 2 (CA)✹
FCI Herlong (CA)
FCI Lompoc (CA)
FCI Phoenix (AZ)
FPC Phoenix (AZ)✹
FCI Safford (AZ)
FCI Sheridan (OR)
FPC Sheridan 1 (OR)
FPC Sheridan 2 (OR)
FCI Terminal Island 1 (CA)
FCI Terminal Island 2 (CA)★

CONTRACT FACILITY
RCI Rivers, (NC)

KEY
FCC = Federal Correctional Complex
FCI = Federal Correctional Institution
FMC = Federal Medical Center
FPC = Federal Prison Camp
FSL = Federal Satellite (Low Security)
MCFP = Medical Center for Federal
Prisoners
RCI = Rivers Correctional Institution
SFF = Secure Female Facility
USP = United States Penitentiary
✹Female Facility
★Co-occurring Disorder Program
Ś Spanish program

Updated: 09/09/15

**89 RDAPs at 77 RDAP
Locations.**

**RDAPs in grey were activated in FY
2013. RDAPs in underline are at the
same location.**

RDAP, Residential Drug Abuse Program.
Source: www.bop.gov/inmates/custody_and_care/substance_abuse_treatment.jsp

argued that dysfunctional beliefs contribute to the formation of urges. The theory stipulates a linear process that starts with a belief, which leads to an expectation, which then produces an urge to use. Each time this linear process plays out with a satisfactory result, the model is reinforced. This is because CBT holds that the dysfunctional beliefs about the substance use include one or more of the following:

- The substance use will help the client maintain an overall sense of stability.
- The substance will make the client better, smarter, more capable, and so forth.
- The substance effects will be pleasurable in some manner.
- The substance will relieve negative mood or affect.
- The substance will help manage any cravings.

Within the CJS, CBT for offenders strive to accomplish four tasks: (a) define problems producing a conflict with authorities; (b) select goals; (c) generate new alternative prosocial solutions; and (d) implement these prosocial solutions (Cullen & Gendreau, 2000). Milkman and Wanberg (2007) reviewed several CBT programs specifically designed for offenders. Two will briefly be reviewed.

Aggression Replacement Training (ART)

The ART is a multimodal intervention designed for adolescents involved with juvenile justice systems (A. P. Goldstein, Glick, & Gibbs, 1998), but the model has been adapted for use in adult correctional settings. ART consists of a few CBT components. One, social skills training (the behavioral component) teaches interpersonal skills for anger-provoking situations. Skills covered include some of the following: understanding the feelings of others, managing difficult conversations, coping with another person's anger, and responding to personal failure. Two, the anger control training (the affective component) trains participants to reduce their affective impulses. Topics covered include: managing triggers that facilitate emotions that may lead to anger responses, reacting to physical responses indicating anger, and coping skills to reduce anger. Three, the moral reasoning training (the cognitive component) raises the sense of social fairness, justice, and concern with the needs and rights of others.

Strategies for Self-Improvement and Change (SSC)

The SSC (Milkman & Wanberg, 2007) is a long-term (9 months to 1 year), intensive, cognitive behavioral-oriented treatment program for adult substance abusing offenders across three phases. In Phase I, a series of lessons build a working relationship with the client to help the client develop motivation to change. Sessions are also directed at providing basic information on how people change, the role of thought and behavior in change, and basic information about substance abuse and criminal conduct. A big part of this process is confronting their past and then challenging them to bring that past into a present change focus. The individual identifies areas of change and develops a comprehensive relapse and recidivism prevention plan. Phase II focuses on basic skills for change and learning CBT methods for changing thoughts and behaviors contributing to substance use and criminal behaviors. Phase III is the stabilization and maintenance phase, and involves treatment experiences that reinforce the commitment to established behavior and thought changes. This phase includes discussions of the thoughts and behaviors associated with relapse and recidivism.

12-Step Programming

Many prisons/jails do operate an Alcoholics Anonymous (AA)/Narcotics Anonymous (NA) meeting owing to their effectiveness while requiring little to no prison/jail costs. However, the use of 12-Step meetings are a common but understudied component of CJS SUD care (Magaletta & Leukefeld, 2011). For instance, Johnson, Schonbrun, and Stein (2014) pilot tested an enhanced referral approach introducing a 12-Step volunteer to a woman in jail who would attend a meeting with her after release, with 57% of participants who met with AA volunteers in jail contacting those volunteers after release from jail. Participants had significantly fewer drinking days, heavy drinking days, alcohol problems, and drug-using days during the postrelease follow-up than they did before jail detention. Consequently, 12-Step groups seem beneficial to both the incarceration and aftercare periods.

However, the 12-Step meeting in a prison or jail faces unique challenges. CSAT (2005) reviewed some of these challenges. In jails, the principal obstacle involves time constraints. Inmates housed in jails are there for shorter sentences. Due to these shorter sentences and the schedule run by the jail, inmates may not have the time to participate in all services and may choose another program (i.e., educational or vocational) over 12-Step. Furthermore, some inmates (those in the pretrial stage) are housed for an uncertain amount of time and could be released or transferred to a longer term facility with little notice. Thus, the stability and community of a 12-Step group would be challenging to develop and maintain. In prisons, the principal obstacle may be the larger percentage of inmates struggling with mental illness, trauma, and hopelessness (CSAT, 2005). In this setting, many inmates may first require more intensive SUD/co-occurring psychiatric treatment before joining a 12-Step group.

Conclusion

SUDs and co-occurring psychiatric disorders are epidemic within the U.S. jail and prison systems. Furthermore, these individuals are leaving jail/prison and returning to the community. Unfortunately, many in need of in-jail/prison SUD/co-occurring psychiatric care are either being grossly undertreated or receiving no treatment. This is due to numerous issues, such as overcrowding and costs for staffing and treatment services that require major systemic changes and priority adjustments at the federal and state levels.

Offenders, whether in jails or prisons, will best be served by treatment and CJS systems working together to foster effective treatment and aftercare programs. Coordinating these efforts will be difficult and time consuming. However, without strong treatment programs, these offenders will enter aftercare shaky (at best) in their recovery, which in turn increases the risk of relapse and criminal recidivism. The issues of MAT, best treatment practices, and aftercare services discussed in this chapter are only a brief sampling of the myriad concepts inherent in slowing the revolving door of addiction and criminal recidivism.

CHAPTER EXERCISES

Exercise 1. Watch the following webinar prior to class and come prepared to discuss: Screening and Assessment of Co-Occurring Disorders and Criminal Justice: www.youtube.com/watch?v=ZsHrXuNk2zs

Exercise 2. Watch the following webinar prior to class and come prepared to discuss: Sharing Information Between Behavioral Health and Criminal Justice Systems: www.youtube.com/watch?v=cH2fFC6lDC4

Exercise 3. Watch the following webinar prior to class and come prepared to discuss: Improving Outcomes for Court-Involved Youth With Co-Occurring Disorders: www.youtube.com/watch?v=yDA99Win4fY

Additional Resources

Gains Center SAMHSA: www.samhsa.gov/gains-center

National Institute of Drug Abuse (NIDA): www.drugabuse.gov/related-topics/criminal-justice/drug-addiction-treatment-in-criminal-justice-system

Substance Abuse and Mental Health Service Administration (SAMHSA): www.samhsa.gov/criminal-juvenile-justice/behavioral-health-criminal-justice

References

Adams, L. M., Stuewig, J. B., & Tangney, J. P. (2016). Relation of borderline personality features to preincarceration HIV risk behaviors of jail inmates: Evidence for gender differences? *Personality Disorders: Theory, Research, and Treatment, 7*(1), 40–49. doi:10.1037/per0000124

Agrawal, A., Nurnberger, J. I., & Lynskey, M. T. (2011). The bipolar genome study: Cannabis involvement in individuals with bipolar disorder. *Psychiatry Researcher, 185*, 459–461.

Amato, L., Davoli, M., Minozzi, S., Ali, R., & Ferri, M. (2005). Methadone at tapered doses for the management of opioid withdrawal. *Cochrane Database of Systematic Reviews, 20*(3), CD003409.

American Psychiatric Association. (2013). *Diagnostic and statistical manual of mental disorders* (5th ed.). Arlington, VA: American Psychiatric Publishing.

Aronowitz, S. V., & Laurent, J. (2016). Screaming behind a door: The experiences of individuals incarcerated without medication-assisted treatment. *Journal of Correctional Health Care, 22*(2), 98–108. doi:10.1177/1078345816634079

Baethge, C., Baldessarini, R. J., Khalsa, H. K., Hennen, J., Salvatore, P., & Tohen, M. (2005). Substance abuse in first-episode bipolar I disorder: Indications for early intervention. *American Journal of Psychiatry, 162*(5), 1008–1010. doi:10.1176/appi.ajp.162.5.1008

Baier, A., Fritsch, R., Ignatyev, Y., Priebe, S., & Mundt, A. P. (2016). The course of major depression during imprisonment—A one year cohort study. *Journal of Affective Disorders, 189*, 207–213. doi:10.1016/j .jad.2015.09.003

Baillargeon, J., Binswanger, I. A., Penn, J. V., Williams, B. A., & Murray, O. J. (2009). Psychiatric disorders and repeat incarcerations: The revolving prison door. *The American Journal of Psychiatry, 166*(1), 103–109. doi:10.1176/appi.ajp.2008.08030416

Baillargeon, J., Black, S. A., Contreras, S., Grady, J., & Pulvino, J. (2001). Anti-depressant prescribing patterns for prison inmates with depressive disorders. *Journal of Affective Disorders, 63*(1–3), 225–231. doi:10.1016/S0165-0327(00)00188-9

Beatson, J. A., & Rao, S. (2012). Depression and borderline personality disorder. *The Medical Journal of Australia, 1*(4), 24–27. doi:10.5694/mjao12.10474

Beck, A. T. (1976). *Cognitive therapy and the emotional disorders.* New York, NY: Meridian.

Beck, A. T., Wright, F. D., Newman, C. F., & Liese, B. S. (1993). *Cognitive therapy of substance abuse.* New York, NY: Guilford Press.

Binswanger, I. A., Blatchford, P. J., Mueller, S. R., & Stern, M. F. (2013). Mortality after prison release: Opioid overdose and other causes of death, risk factors, and time trends from 1999 to 2009. *Annals of Internal Medicine, 159*(9), 592–600.

Birrell, L., Newton, N. C., Teesson, M., Tonks, Z., & Slade, T. (2015). Anxiety disorders and first alcohol use in the general population. Findings from a nationally representative sample. *Journal of Anxiety Disorders, 31*, 108–113. doi:10.1016/j.janxdis.2015.02.008

Bolton, J. M., Robinson, J., & Sareen, J. (2009). Self-medication of mood disorders with alcohol and drugs in the National Epidemiologic Survey on Alcohol and Related Conditions. *Journal of Affective Disorders, 115*(3), 367–375. doi:10.1016/j.jad.2008.10.003

Brooner, R. K., King, V. L., Kidorf, M., Schmidt, C. W., & Bigelow, G. E. (1997). Psychiatric and substance use comorbidity among treatment-seeking opioid users. *Archives of General Psychiatry, 54*, 71–80.

Burdon, W. M., Dang, J., Prendergast, M. L., Messina, N. P., & Farabee, D. (2007). Differential effectiveness of residential versus outpatient aftercare for parolees from prison-based therapeutic community treatment programs. *Substance Abuse Treatment, Prevention, and Policy, 2*, 16. doi:10.1186/1747 -597X-2-16

Center for Substance Abuse Treatment. (2004). *Clinical guidelines for the use of buprenorphine in the treatment of opioid addiction (Treatment Improvement Protocol [TIP]) Series 40.* DHHS Publication No. [SMA] 04–3939. Rockville, MD: Substance Abuse and Mental Health Services Administration.

Center for Substance Abuse Treatment. (2005). *Substance abuse treatment for adults in the criminal justice system (Treatment Improvement Protocol [TIP]) Series 44.* HHS Publication No. [SMA] 13-4056. Rockville, MD: Substance Abuse and Mental Health Services Administration.

Center for Substance Abuse Treatment. (2009). *Addressing suicidal thoughts and behaviors in substance abuse treatment (Treatment Improvement Protocol [TIP]) Series, No. 50.* HHS Publication No. [SMA] 15-4381. Rockville, MD: Substance Abuse and Mental Health Services Administration.

Center on Addiction and Substance Abuse. (2010). *Behind bars II: Substance abuse and America's prison population.* New York, NY: Author.

Coker, K. L., Stefanovics, E., & Rosenheck, R. (2016). Correlates of improvement in substance abuse among dually diagnosed veterans with post-traumatic stress disorder in specialized intensive VA treatment. *Psychological Trauma: Theory, Research, Practice, and Policy, 8*(1), 41–48. doi:10.1037/tra0000061

Couture, H., & Sabol, W. J. (2008). *Prison inmates at midyear 2007 (NCJ 221944).* Washington, DC: Bureau of Justice Statistics, U.S. Department of Justice.

Crocker, A. G., Mueser, K. T., Clark, R. E., McHugo, G. J., Ackerson, T., & Alterman, A. I. (2005). Antisocial personality, psychopathy and violence in persons with dual disorders: A longitudinal analysis. *Criminal Justice and Behavior, 32,* 452–476.

Cullen, F., & Gendreau, P. (2000). Assessing correctional rehabilitation: Policy, practice, and prospects. In J. Horney (Ed.), *Criminal justice 2000* (Vol. 3, pp. 109–175). Washington, DC: U.S. Department of Justice, Office of Justice Programs, National Institute of Justice.

Denison-Vesel, K., Brouard, C., & Morgen, K. (2016). *Pregnant women and substance use disorder treatment: TEDS findings 2013.* Poster presented at the 87th Annual Meeting of the Eastern Psychological Association, New York, NY.

Denzel, A. D., van Esch, A. M., Harte, J. M., & Scherder, E. A. (2016). Ethnic variations in psychotic disorders in the criminal justice system: A systematic review. *Aggression and Violent Behavior, 29,* 20–29. doi:10.1016/j.avb.2016.05.006

Fatséas, M., Denis, C., Lavie, E., & Auriacombe, M. (2010). Relationship between anxiety disorders and opiate dependence—A systematic review of the literature: Implications for diagnosis and treatment. *Journal of Substance Abuse Treatment, 38*(3), 220–230. doi:10.1016/j.jsat.2009.12.003

Fovet, T., Geoffroy, P. A., Vaiva, G., Adins, C., Thomas, P., & Amad, A. (2015). Individuals with bipolar disorder and their relationship with the criminal justice system: A critical review. *Psychiatric Services, 66*(4), 348–353. doi:10.1176/appi.ps.201400104

Friedmann, P. D., Hoskinson, R. J., Gordon, M., Schwartz, R., Kinlock, T., Knight, K., & Frisman, L. K. (2012). Medication-assisted treatment in criminal justice agencies affiliated with the criminal justice-drug abuse treatment studies (CJ-DATS): Availability, barriers, and intentions. *Substance Abuse, 33*(1), 9–18. doi:10.1080/08897077.2011.611460

Goldstein, A. P., Glick, B., & Gibbs, J. C. (1998). *Aggression replacement training* (Rev. ed.). Champaign, IL: Research Press.

Goldstein, R. B., Dawson, D. A., & Grant, B. F. (2010). Antisocial behavioral syndromes in adulthood and alcohol use disorder treatment over three-year follow-up: Results from wave 2 of the National Epidemiologic Survey on Alcohol and Related Conditions. *Journal of the American Psychiatric Nurses Association, 16*(4), 212–226. doi:10.1177/1078390310375846

Grant, B. F., Chou, S. P., Goldstein, R. B., Huang, B., Stinson, F. S., Saha, T. D., . . . Ruan, W. J. (2008). Prevalence, correlates, disability, and comorbidity of *DSM-IV* Borderline Personality Disorder: Results from the Wave 2 National Epidemiologic Survey on Alcohol and Related Conditions. *Journal of Clinical Psychiatry, 69*(4), 533–545.

Green, K. T., Calhoun, P. S., Dennis, M. F., & Beckham, J. C. (2010). Exploration of the resilience construct in posttraumatic stress disorder sensitivity and functional correlates in military combat veterans who have served since September 11, 2001. *Journal of Clinical Psychiatry, 71*(7), 823–830. doi:10.4088/JCP.09m05780blu

Hawton, K., Sutton, L., Haw, C., Sinclair, J., & Harriss, L. (2005). Suicide and attempted suicide in bipolar disorder: A systematic review of risk factors. *Journal of Clinical Psychiatry, 66*(6), 693–704.

Hochhausen, N. M., Lorenz, A. R., & Newman, J. P. (2002). Specifying the impulsivity of female inmates with borderline personality disorder. *Journal of Abnormal Psychology, 111*(3), 495–501. doi:10.1037/0021-843X.111.3.495

Johnson, J. E., Schonbrun, Y. C., & Stein, M. D. (2014). Pilot test of 12-Step linkage for alcohol-abusing women in leaving jail. *Substance Abuse, 35*(1), 7–11. doi:10.1080/08897077.2013.794760

Kamath, J., Temporini, H., Quarti, S., Zhang, W., Kesten, K., Wakai, S., . . . Trestman, R. (2010). Best practices: Disseminating best practices for bipolar disorder treatment in a correctional population. *Psychiatric Services, 61*(9), 865–867. doi:10.1176/appi.ps.61.9.865

Kamath, J., Zhang, W., Kesten, K., Wakai, S., Shelton, D., & Trestman, R. (2013). Algorithm-driven pharmacological management of bipolar disorder in Connecticut prisons. *International Journal of Offender Therapy and Comparative Criminology, 57*(2), 251–264. doi:10.1177/0306624X11427537

Kinner, S. A., Milloy, M., Wood, E., Qi, J., Zhang, R., & Kerr, T. (2012). Incidence and risk factors for nonfatal overdose among a cohort of recently incarcerated illicit drug users. *Addictive Behaviors, 37*(6), 691–696. doi:10.1016/j.addbeh.2012.01.019

Langås, A., Malt, U. F., & Opjordsmoen, S. (2012). In-depth study of personality disorders in first admission patients with substance use disorders. *BioMed Central Psychiatry, 12*(1), 180. Retrieved from http://www.biomedcentral.com/1471-244X/12/180

Larney, S., Gisev, N., Farrell, M., Dobbins, T., Burns, L., Gibson, A., Kimber, J., & Degenhardt, L. (2014). Opioid substitution therapy as a strategy to reduce deaths in prison: Retrospective cohort study. *British Medical Association Open, 4*(4), e004666. doi:10.1136/bmjopen-2013-004666

Levinson, I., Galynker, I. I., & Rosenthal, R. N. (1995). Methadone withdrawal psychosis. *Journal of Clinical Psychiatry, 56*(2), 73–76.

Ludwig, A. S., & Peters, R. H. (2014). Medication-assisted treatment for opioid use disorders in correctional settings: An ethics review. *International Journal of Drug Policy, 25*(6), 1041–1046. doi:10.1016/j.drugpo.2014.08.015

Magaletta, P. R., & Leukefeld, C. (2011). Self-help. In C. Leukefeld, T. P. Gullotta, J. Gregrich, C. Leukefeld, T. P. Gullotta, & J. Gregrich (Eds.), *Handbook of evidence-based substance abuse treatment in criminal justice settings* (pp. 245–257). New York, NY: Springer Publishing. doi:10.1007/978-1-4419-9470-7_14

Maremmani, A. G. I., Bacciardi, S., Rovai, L., Rugani, F., Dell'Osso, L., & Maremmani, I. (2012). Natural history of addiction in psychotic heroin-addicted patients at their first agonist opioid treatment. *Addictive Disorders and Their Treatment, 12*(1), 31–39.

Maschi, T., Gibson, S., Zgoba, K., & Morgen, K. (2011). Trauma and life event stressors among young and older adult prisoners. *Journal of Correctional Healthcare, 17*, 160–172.

Maschi, T., Morgen, K., & Viola, D. (2014). Unraveling trauma and stress, coping resources, and mental well-being among older adults in prison: Empirical evidence linking theory and practice. *The Gerontologist, 54*, 857–867.

Maschi, T., Morgen, K., Zgoba, K., Courtney, D., & Ristow, J. (2011). Age, cumulative trauma and stressful life events, and post traumatic stress symptoms among older adults in prison: Do subjective impressions matter? *The Gerontologist, 51*(5), 675–686. doi:10.1093/geront/gnr074

Maschi, T., Viola, D., Morgen, K., & Koskinen, L. (2015). Trauma, stress, grief, loss, and separation among older adults in prison: The protective role of coping resources on physical and mental well-being. *Journal of Crime and Justice, 38*, 113–136. doi:10.1080/0735648X.2013.808853

Matusow, H., Dickman, S. L., Rich, J. D., Fong, C., Dumont, D. M., Hardin, C., . . . Rosenblum, A. (2013). Medication assisted treatment in US drug courts: Results from a nationwide survey of availability, barriers and attitudes. *Journal of Substance Abuse Treatment, 44*(5), 473–480. doi:10.1016/j .jsat.2012.10.004

Menary, K. R., Kushner, M. G., Maurer, E., & Thuras, P. (2011). The prevalence and clinical implications of self-medication among individuals with anxiety disorders. *Journal of Anxiety Disorders, 25*(3), 335–339. doi:10.1016/j.janxdis.2010.10.006

Milkman, H., & Wanberg, K. (2007). *Cognitive behavioral treatment: A review and discussion for corrections professionals.* Washington, DC: National Institute of Corrections.

Morgen, K. (2017). *Substance use disorders and addictions.* Thousand Oaks, CA: Sage.

Morgen, K., Maschi, T., Viola, D., & Zgoba, K. (2013). Substance use disorder and the older offender [VISTAS Online, Article 97]. Retrieved from http://www.counseling.org/knowledge-center/ vistas/vistas-2013

Morgen, K., & Voelkner, A. (2014). *Clinical and data management issues for the older offender on parole.* Paper presented at the Conference on 21st Century Forensic Practice: Moving Beyond Cultural Competence, New York, NY.

Nee, C., & Farman, S. (2005). Female prisoners with borderline personality disorder: Some promising treatment developments. *Criminal Behavior and Mental Health, 15*(1), 2–16. doi:10.1002/cbm.33

Osasona, S. O., & Koleoso, O. N. (2015). Prevalence and correlates of depression and anxiety disorder in a sample of inmates in a Nigerian prison. *International Journal of Psychiatry in Medicine, 50*(2), 203–218. doi:10.1177/0091217415605038

Oser, C., Knudsen, H. K., Staton-Tindall, M., Taxman, F., & Leukefeld, C. (2009). Organizational-level correlates of the provision of detoxification services and medication-based treatments for substance abuse in correctional institutions. *Drug and Alcohol Dependence, 103S,* S73–S81.

Pacini, M., & Maremmani, A. G. I. (2005). Methadone reduces the need for antipsychotic and antimanic agents in heroin addicts hospitalized for manic and/or acute psychotic episodes. *Heroin Addiction & Related Clinical Problems, 7*(4), 43–48.

Pietrzak, R. H., Goldstein, R. B., Southwick, S. M., & Grant, B. F. (2011). Prevalence and Axis I comorbidity of full and partial posttraumatic stress disorder in the United States: Results from Wave 2 of the National Epidemiologic Survey on Alcohol and Related Conditions. *Journal of Anxiety Disorders, 25*(3), 456–465. doi:10.1016/j.janxdis.2010.11.010

Robinson, J., Sareen, J., Cox, B. J., & Bolton, J. M. (2011). Role of self-medication in the development of comorbid anxiety and substance use disorders: A longitudinal investigation. *Archives of General Psychiatry, 68*(8), 800–807. doi:10.1001/archgenpsychiatry.2011.75

Saxon, A. J., & Simpson, T. L. (2015). *Co-occurring substance use disorders and PTSD.* In N. C. Bernardy & M. J. Friedman (Eds.), *A practical guide to PTSD treatment: Pharmacological and psychotherapeutic approaches* (pp. 135–150). Washington, DC: American Psychological Association. doi:10.1037/14522 -010

Stewart, S. H., Zvolensky, M. J., & Eifert, G. H. (2002). The relations of anxiety sensitivity, experiential avoidance, and alexithymic coping to young adults' motivations for drinking. *Behavior Modification, 26*(2), 274–296.

Substance Abuse and Mental Health Services Administration. (2005). *Substance abuse treatment for persons with co-occurring disorders (Treatment Improvement Protocol [TIP]) Series, No. 42.* HHS Publication No. [SMA] 1339920. Rockville, MD: Author.

Substance Abuse and Mental Health Services Administration. (2013). *National Survey of Substance Abuse Treatment Services (N-SSATS): 2012.* Data on Substance Abuse Treatment Facilities (BHSIS Series S-66, HHS Publication No. [SMA] 14-4809). Rockville, MD: Author.

Substance Abuse and Mental Health Services Administration. (2014). An introduction to co-occurring borderline personality disorder and substance use disorders. *In Brief, 8*(3), 1–8.

Tamburello, A. C., Bajgier, J., & Reeves, R. (2015). The prevalence of delusional disorder in prison. *Journal of the American Academy of Psychiatry and the Law, 43*(1), 82–86.

Taxman, F. S., Perdoni, M. L., & Harrison, L. D. (2007). Drug treatment services for adult offenders: The state of the state. *Journal of Substance Abuse Treatment, 32*(3), 239–254. doi:10.1016/j.jsat.2006.12.019

Teter, C. J., Falone, A. E., Bakaian, A. M., Tu, C., Öngür, D., & Weiss, R. D. (2011). Medication adherence and attitudes in patients with bipolar disorder and current versus past substance use disorder. *Psychiatry Research, 190*(2–3), 253–258. doi:10.1016/j.psychres.2011.05.042

Værøy, H. (2011). Depression, anxiety, and history of substance abuse among Norwegian inmates in preventive detention: Reasons to worry? *BioMed Central Psychiatry, 11.* doi:10.1186/1471-244X-11-40

van Wormer, K., & Persson, L. (2010). Drug treatment within the U.S. Federal Prison System: Are treatment needs being met? *Journal of Offender Rehabilitation, 49*, 363–375.

Warren, J. I., & Burnette, M. (2013). The multifaceted construct of psychopathy: Association with APD, clinical, and criminal characteristics among male and female inmates. *The International Journal of Forensic Mental Health, 12*(4), 265–273. doi:10.1080/14999013.2013.857739

Yang, Y., Chen, F., Xu, K., & Qian, M. (2014). Self-control strength in prison inmates with antisocial personality disorder. *Journal of Forensic Psychiatry & Psychology, 25*(5), 613–622. doi:10.1080/14789949.2014.933859

Young, D. S. (2003). Co-occurring disorders among jail inmates: Bridging the treatment gap. *Journal of Social Work Practice in the Addictions, 3*(3), 63–85. doi:10.1300/J160v03n03_05

Zlotnick, C., Clarke, J. G., Friedmann, P. D., Roberts, M. B., Sacks, S., & Melnick, G. (2008). Gender differences in comorbid disorders among offenders in prison substance abuse treatment programs. *Behavioral Sciences & the Law, 26*(4), 403–412. doi:10.1002/bsl.831

VOICES FROM THE FIELD

Keith Morgen, PhD, LPC, ACS

Clinician

Discovery Psychotherapy & Wellness Centers

Agency Setting

I see patients in—using the American Society of Addiction Medicine criteria—an outpatient (Level 1) facility for substance use disorders and co-occurring psychiatric disorders. It is an outpatient psychotherapy group practice. Some of my patients fall within the "forensic" population.

Practice Responsibilities

The patients I see in the "forensic" category have some involvement with the criminal justice system. At the outpatient level, that sometimes means seeing patients as a component of a pretrial intervention program where they engage in psychotherapy with me to address their substance use and psychiatric disorders that facilitated the current legal difficulties. This entails creating a treatment plan relevant to their psychological and legal problems. This also entails balancing the needs and wants of various parties. For example, the patient's lawyer is sometimes not satisfied with a report or other documentation I provide on the patient (e.g., documentation on diagnosis, progress, or engagement with treatment). In these instances, I need to explain my reasoning for the letter written while also holding to my professional judgment and ethics regarding why I chose to write the letter in that manner.

Expertise Required

A *comprehensive* understanding of the interface between substance use disorders and co-occurring psychiatric disorders is needed. This requires knowing the symptom presentations (behavioral, cognitive, and emotional) for substance intoxication, substance withdrawal, substance-induced disorders (such as substance-induced depressive, anxiety, psychotic, or bipolar disorders), and co-occurring psychiatric disorders.

I also need to know the basic processes of the legal system in my state. This knowledge allows me to understand (a) where my patient currently stands in the legal system, (b) what are typically the next step(s), and (c) what the typical best/worst case scenarios may be based on their current charge(s) and past legal history. Though I am not a lawyer, knowing the basics of the process assists my thinking process about the case.

Ethical, Legal, Practice, Diversity, and/or Advocacy Issues Addressed

You try to advocate for the patient as much as possible, but within the bounds of recognizing it is their responsibility to follow through to help themselves. For example, I have written a last second letter to a lawyer or a judge on a number of occasions. In these instances I drop everything so that my letter can advocate on behalf of the client. However, I have also had to help patients face consequences of their own actions such as when they failed to follow-up with appointments. In these cases I have to report their inaction to the court, which typically results in increased legal difficulties for the patient. This is the biggest challenge—how to advocate for the patient while simultaneously mandating the patient own responsibility for all action/inaction on his or her own behalf.

Ethically, the forensic cases I see are no different than any other patients. As a Licensed Professional Counselor in New Jersey, I must adhere to the legal regulations as set forth by the state as well as the ethics of the profession as stipulated in the current ethics code of the American Counseling Association. In addition, there are legal/ethical requirements regarding the handling of substance use disorder patient records (i.e., CFR-42, part 2). These regulations are—in many ways—more stringent than Health Insurance Portability and Accountability Act (HIPAA) regulations, so I have to always be mindful of how any substance use disorder patient record is being handled.

Interprofessional and Intersectoral Collaboration

When working with a forensic patient, my interprofessional collaborations are with lawyers, probation officers, and court officials as well as—if warranted—a psychiatrist regarding medication prescriptions and monitoring.

CHAPTER 14

Critical Issues, Trends, and Interventions in Juvenile Justice

Wesley T. Church II
George S. Leibowitz
Tina Maschi

CHAPTER OBJECTIVES

The major objectives of this chapter are to:

- Assist the reader to develop a basic orientation to the critical issues, history, trends, policies, programs, and intervention strategies of the juvenile justice system.
- Review the types, functions, and legal responsibilities of the various juvenile justice agencies and institutions.
- Describe the case flow within the juvenile justice system.
- Discuss systems of care in juvenile justice, and specialized assessment and treatment issues with adolescents, including sexually abusive youth.

CHAPTER COMPETENCIES HIGHLIGHTED

- Competency 3: Advance Human Rights and Social, Economic, and Environmental Justice
- Competency 6: Engage With Individuals, Families, Organizations, and Communities
- Competency 7: Assess Individuals, Families, Organizations, and Communities
- Competency 8: Intervene With Individuals, Families, Organizations, and Communities

History

As illustrated in Chapter 1, social work's history is closely interwoven with the history of juvenile justice. The origins of the juvenile justice system can be traced back to the child-saving movement of the late 1800s (Platt, 1969). The child savers, particularly the "feminist" reformers, such as Jane Addams, were viewed as making an "enlightened effort to alleviate the miseries of urban life and juvenile delinquency caused by an unregulated capitalist society" (Platt, 1977). Successful lobbying efforts for a rehabilitative approach made by Jane Addams and fellow reformers resulted in the creation of the Cook County (Illinois) Juvenile Court on July 3, 1899.

The establishment of the Illinois juvenile court system created a justice system for children with the underlying premise of the protection and rehabilitation of youth. This premise was different from the punishment approach taken by the criminal justice system. The juvenile court was also designed to see to the needs of abused and neglected children and delinquent children. By 1925, the juvenile court system model had been adopted across the United States and Canada, as well as by countries in Europe and South America (Justice Policy Institute, 2000), which underscores how the collaborative efforts of social workers and other advocates led to wide-scale legal reform.

The contemporary mission of the juvenile justice system has been described as having three parts: (a) to protect public safety, (b) to hold juvenile offenders accountable for their behavior, and (c) to provide treatment and rehabilitation services for juveniles and their families (Bartollas & Miller, 2005). However, more recent trends for addressing juvenile crime combine rehabilitative and punitive approaches. For example, rehabilitative approaches include alternatives to detention or community programs that attempt to keep youth in the community and divert them from the formal juvenile justice system (Bruns et al., 2004; Burns & Hoagwood, 2002; Cocozza & Skowyra, 2000; National Mental Health Association [NMHA], 2004). For example, since the 1960s, teen courts have been steadily growing as an alternative to juvenile courts, especially for youth aged 10 to 15 years who have been charged with minor offenses (Butts & Buck, 2000). What is unique about teen courts is that sentencing is done by other teens, rather than an "official" judge (Herman, 2002). In contrast, recent punitive approaches feature tougher policies and laws, such as the juvenile waiver to adult court and the death penalty for juveniles (Justice Policy Institute, 2000). Social workers working within this system should be aware of the tension between the rehabilitative approach (which is more consistent with the philosophy of social work) and the opposing punitive approach and how this tension might influence their ability to achieve practice objectives that are consistent with social work's mission to enhance social functioning and increase social justice outcomes.

Background and Juvenile Justice Overview

Each year, in the United States, delinquent acts are committed by several million youth. As a society, we are saturated with graphic depictions of individual youths and gangs committing violence in our schools, in our streets, in our parks, and even in our homes. The reality is that although almost 1.5 million juvenile arrests were reported by the National Center for Juvenile Justice (NCJJ) and the Office of Juvenile Justice and Delinquency Prevention (OJJDP) in 2014 (last year for complete data), the approximate number of juvenile delinquent acts could be between 13 and 15 million annually because many crimes committed by juveniles go unreported or undetected, or no arrest is made. Nevertheless, almost all types of juvenile violent and property crimes have been declining since the mid-1990s. Most legislators, agency administrators, practitioners, and students are unaware of the latest model juvenile offender treatment and prevention programs and of the growing research evidence of their success in sharply reducing recidivism.

This chapter provides an orientation to the history, critical issues, trends, policies, programs, and intervention strategies of the juvenile justice system. We discuss the types, functions, and legal responsibilities of the various juvenile justice agencies and institutions. Within the chapter, we lay the foundation and groundwork for the study of juvenile delinquency and the juvenile justice system while delineating the legal definitions of *juvenile status offenses* and *juvenile delinquency*, examining the nine steps in the juvenile justice case-flow process. Later in the chapter, attention is given to systems of care and the link between trauma and delinquency, as well as the assessment and treatment considerations for forensic social workers when addressing the specialized needs of juveniles in the justice system.

In general, youths can be charged with two types of juvenile offenses within the juvenile justice system: juvenile delinquency offenses, which are criminal acts (e.g., auto theft, forcible rape, breaking and entering), for which they would be held accountable if they were adults, and status offenses (e.g., truancy, incorrigibility, and running away from home), which are illegal activities committed by juveniles. In fact, the criminologist and political scientist John Dilulio (1995) wrongly predicted what he termed *super predators*—a group of youth who have no regard or respect for human life. Thus, violent juvenile crimes receive the most media attention and serve to intensify the fear and outrage of concerned citizens. This fear and outrage, in turn, frequently influence prosecutors, juvenile court judges, and correctional administrators to subject more juvenile offenders to harsher penalties even though the ideology has been deemed inaccurate by academics of all fields. Juveniles who commit status offenses or nonviolent property crimes are far more prevalent in the juvenile justice system than those that commit violent crime; unfortunately, society has been "scared" into the notion that any crime committed by a youth needs to be punished harshly, with no regard to past history, living environment, and family dynamics.

Professionals and mental health practitioners working in juvenile justice agencies often encounter the discretionary, deficient, flawed, and often overcrowded system with which we are placing the youth of our society. At other times, they encounter caring and compassionate juvenile justice volunteers and practitioners. Although the primary goal of justice-oriented agencies is to protect society and to humanely care for and rehabilitate our deviant children and youth, in actuality the juvenile justice system sometimes labels, stigmatizes, mistakenly punishes, and reinforces delinquent patterns of behavior. In a number of jurisdictions, the controlling, biased, and punitive orientation of some juvenile justice officials has led to a revolving-door system in which we find an overrepresentation of children and youth from Black, low-income, neglectful, and/or abusive homes. For example, in 2014 a disproportionate number of juvenile arrests involved minorities.

Although juvenile arrest rates have been declining overall, the proportion of delinquency cases that involved Black youth increased from 25% in 1985 to 34% in 2009 (Puzzanchera, Adams, & Hockenberry, 2012). After converting the total reported arrest numbers into arrest rates per 1,000 juveniles in each racial group, the number of delinquent arrests for Black youth (103.2) was more than double the rate for White (40.3) and American Indian (50.9) juveniles. With regard to crimes against persons, the arrest rate for Black juveniles (30.2) was approximately 3 times the arrest rate for American Indian juveniles (11.6) and White juveniles (8.8) and 11 times the arrest rate for Asian American juveniles (2.8). OJJDP conducted an analysis of studies that spanned over 12 years and found approximately two thirds of the studies to have a "negative race effect" (meaning that race explained why minorities remained in the system) during various stages of the juvenile justice process (Armour & Hammond, 2009). This has led to many academics examining disproportionate minority contact with the juvenile justice system.

Defining Juvenile Justice

How is the juvenile justice system defined within the United States of America? It is the agencies and institutions whose primary responsibility is handling juvenile offenders who commit either juvenile delinquency offenses or status offenses. In addition, these agencies concern themselves with delinquent youths and with those children and youths labeled incorrigible, truant, or runaway. Juvenile justice attempts to focus on all the needs of youth who are taken into custody, diverted into special programs or processed through the juvenile court and adjudicated, placed on probation, referred to a community-based day treatment program, or placed in a group home or a secure facility.

The history of juvenile justice has involved the development of policies, programs, and agencies for dealing with youth involved in legal violations. As we examine the juvenile justice system, we focus on the interrelated, yet different, functions of several agencies and programs: the police, the school system, the juvenile court, detention facilities, juvenile correctional facilities, the mental health system, community-based programs, and gang prevention programs.

Defining Juvenile Delinquency

Juvenile delinquency is a broad, generic term that includes many diverse forms of antisocial behavior committed by a minor. In general, most state criminal codes define juvenile delinquency as behavior that is in violation of the criminal code and committed by a youth who has not reached adult age. The specific acts by the juvenile that constitute delinquent behavior vary from state to state; however, a broad definition that is commonly used was developed by the U.S. Children's Bureau (1967):

> Juvenile delinquency cases are those referred to courts for acts defined in the statutes of the State as the violation of a state law or municipal ordinance by children or youth of juvenile court age, or for conduct so seriously antisocial as to interfere with the rights of others or to menace the welfare of the delinquent himself or of the community.

Other agencies define as delinquent those juveniles who have been arrested or contacted by the police, even though many of these individuals are merely reprimanded or sent home to their parents with a warning. In fact, less than half of the juveniles who come in contact with the police are referred to the juvenile court. These are the children and youths the Children's Bureau would classify as delinquents.

The legal definitions of what constitutes juvenile delinquency appear in state juvenile codes and statutes and vary somewhat from state to state. Generally, a criminal law definition of juvenile delinquency holds that any person, usually under 18 years of age, who commits an illegal act is considered a delinquent when he or she is officially processed through juvenile or family court. A juvenile does not become a delinquent until he or she is officially labeled as such by the specialized judicial agency (e.g., the juvenile court). For example, the Louisiana Children's code defines specifically for those who are in the care of the Louisiana Office of Juvenile Justice:

1. **Title VI** deals with Child in Need of Care Proceedings, the provisions under which the Office of Community Services (OCS) may be given custody of a child by the court.
2. **Title VII** is Families in Need of Services (FINS). Both OCS and Office of Juvenile Justice (OJJ) can receive custody of juveniles under this title.
3. **Title VIII** is the delinquency title, containing a section on the constitutional rights afforded to juveniles (see Ch. C. Art. 808–811). The only constitutional right denied to juveniles is the right to a jury trial. Because the focus in juvenile court is rehabilitation rather than punishment, the judge is in the best position to decide the juvenile's case.

It is important to carefully note the difference between a "delinquent" and a delinquent act. The specific act is the behavior that has violated the state criminal code, and the term *delinquent* is the official label frequently assigned to a youth who deviates from the accepted community norms. A juvenile who commits an illegal act is not immediately or automatically defined as a delinquent. Assaulting another youth or breaking a school window does not automatically make one a delinquent. Isolated single incidents usually are tolerated by the community or neighborhood. For the most part, society at large reserves judgment until after a number or series of legally defined delinquent acts are committed. Police officers and prosecutors handle juveniles differently depending on age and the nature, severity, and frequency of the juvenile's acts. Prosecutorial and judicial discretion with juvenile offenders and their beliefs about punishment versus rehabilitation explain why two different youths are usually handled differently by the juvenile court, even if they commit the same offense.

There are two primary types of juvenile delinquency. As discussed earlier, the first are the *criminal offenses*: those acts considered illegal whether committed by an adult or a juvenile. Such illegal acts include aggravated assault, arson, homicide, rape, burglary, larceny, auto theft, and drug-related crimes. These types of serious offenses are the primary concern of juvenile corrections officials. According to the national and local statutes on juvenile criminality, burglary and larceny are the most frequently committed offenses. The brutal crimes of homicide and forcible rape are only a small percentage of the total number of crimes committed by juveniles.

The second major type of juvenile delinquency is known as *status offenses*: misbehavior that would not be considered a crime if engaged in by an adult. Examples of status offenses are truancy, incorrigibility, curfew violations, and running away from home. Approximately half of the states include status offenses in their definition of juvenile delinquency offenses. Other states have passed separate legislation that distinguishes juveniles who have committed criminal acts from those who have committed status offenses. In those states, status offenders are viewed as individuals "in need of supervision" and are designated as CHINS, CINS, MINS, PINS, or JINS. The first letter of the acronym varies, based on whether the initial word is *children*, *minors*, *persons*, or *juveniles*, but the rest of the phrase is always the same: in need of supervision.

Juvenile Justice Processing and Case Flow

The processing of youth within the juvenile justice system often involves the formal agencies and procedures developed to handle those children and youth suspected or accused of violating their state's juvenile code. The agencies that often constitute the juvenile justice system are law enforcement (if the jurisdiction has a juvenile division they will be involved), juvenile and family courts, and community-based and institutional juvenile correctional facilities. There are nine stages in delinquency case processing through the juvenile justice system:

1. Initial contact with law enforcement
2. Law enforcement's initial handling of the case—diversion, arrest, and/or referral to the juvenile court
3. Juvenile court intake
4. Preadjudication juvenile detention
5. Prosecutors file a delinquency petition in juvenile court or waive to adult criminal court
6. Investigation or predisposition report
7. Juvenile court judge's adjudicatory decision and sanctions
8. Participation and completion of mandated juvenile offender treatment program
9. Juvenile aftercare plan

Owing to differences between jurisdictions, there is some variation from one city or county to the next in the processing of juvenile cases. Therefore, while there is a sequential series of critical decision points in case processing, there is also some variation in how, when, and which types of decisions are made. In general, the steps outlined are consistent, with first contact being with law enforcement; thus, this contact is often important in the "life cycle" of the case.

Initial Contact With Law Enforcement

When possible, law enforcement officers use their discretion and attempt to divert juveniles they come into contact with out of the juvenile justice system. However, if an officer has sufficient evidence to arrest a juvenile and immediately bring the suspect to the police precinct, he or she will do so. An *arrest* is defined as taking an individual into custody for purposes of interviewing or charging an individual with an offense—delinquent or status. Upon arresting the youth, a decision is made based on whether there is sufficient evidence to either send the case to juvenile court or to attempt to divert the case out of the system into an alternative program. In most cases, the officer makes this decision after discussions with the victim, the juvenile, and the parent or guardian and after carefully determining the nature and extent of the youth's previous contacts with the police and juvenile courts.

Federal regulations clearly discourage detaining juveniles in adult county or city jails and lockups. If it becomes necessary to detain a youth in secure custody for a short period, the youth should be placed in a local juvenile detention facility, then federal regulations require that the youth be detained for a maximum of six hours and in a restricted area from where no adult detainees can be observed or heard.

Juvenile Court Intake and Pre-Adjudication

The majority of juvenile court referrals come from police sending the juvenile to the probation intake unit. In general, juvenile court intake units are staffed by the juvenile probation department or the prosecutor's office. At this decision point, the probation intake officer must decide whether to dismiss the case, handle the juvenile informally, or request formal adjudication by the juvenile court. Before making this decision, the intake officer is required to examine the type and seriousness of the alleged offense and to make a determination of whether there is clear and convincing evidence to prove the allegation. If there are no clear legal merits, such as eyewitnesses, then the case is dismissed. If there is sufficient evidence, then the intake probation officer makes a determination as to whether official juvenile court processing is appropriate.

Approximately half of all juvenile cases referred by intake officers are handled informally. The overwhelming majority of these cases are dismissed. In the other informally handled cases, the youth voluntarily signs a written agreement outlining specific conditions for an informal disposition for a specified time period.

Filing of a Case in Juvenile or Criminal Court

Several states have mandated that prosecutors waive certain (generally serious or violent) juvenile cases to the adult criminal court. These are cases in which the state law has been codified that a youth should be waived to criminal court and be handled as a criminal offender due to the seriousness of the crime. In a growing number of states, the legislature has allowed the prosecutor the sole discretion of filing a defined list of serious cases in either juvenile court or adult criminal court. In these states, the prosecutor selects the court that will hear the case. If the case is handled by a juvenile court judge, then two types of formal petitions may be filed: delinquency or waiver to adult court.

A delinquency petition formally describes the allegations and requests the juvenile court to *adjudicate* (or judge) the juvenile a delinquent, making the juvenile offender a ward of the court. This legal language is different from that applied in the criminal court system, where an offender is *convicted and sentenced*. With regard to delinquency petitions, an adjudicatory judicial hearing is scheduled. At the adjudicatory hearing (trial), the juvenile is represented by counsel, and witnesses are called to present the facts of the case. In most adjudicatory hearings, the judge (rather than a jury) determines whether the juvenile committed the offense(s).

Investigation or Predisposition Report Prepared by a Probation Officer

There are three main types of juvenile dispositions: *nominal, conditional*, and *custodial* options. Nominal dispositions are frequently utilized with nonviolent first offenders and include reprimands or warnings that the juvenile will be incarcerated for a long time if he or she returns to the court for a new offense. Conditional dispositions often require juvenile offenders to comply with certain conditions of probation, such as participating in two months of addictions treatment including six days a week of intensive group therapy, psychosocial assessment and individual clinical treatment twice a week, completion of a vocational evaluation and placement program, or full restitution to victims and the juvenile court, which are monitored by the probation officer. Custodial dispositions limit juveniles' freedom of movement by placing them in nonsecure custody foster homes, community-based temporary confinement, secure custody, or secure confinement, including home detention with electronic monitoring devices, group homes, forestry camps, structured wilderness programs, schools, and secure juvenile institutions.

The Juvenile Court Judge's Decision and Sanctions

Juvenile court judges have the responsibility of ordering sanctions on adjudicated delinquents, which can result in a turning point for juvenile offenders. Participation in short-term residential or community treatment programs can break the cycle of habitual delinquency and criminality. Regular probation, intensive probation supervision, and probation-monitored restitution are the preferred sanctions of many juvenile court judges. However, about one third of these delinquents are committed to residential treatment programs.

Upon release from a state juvenile correctional institution, the juvenile may be ordered to a period of intensive aftercare or parole. During this period, the juvenile may be monitored or under the supervision of the juvenile court or the corrections department. Aftercare programs should include a continuum of services and scheduled activities, such as after-school recreational and creative arts programs, alternative dispute resolution programs, mentoring and tutoring programs, career development and vocational training programs, religious group meetings, family counseling, volunteer work with the homeless and disabled, and neighborhood crime prevention projects. The juvenile who does not adhere to the conditions of aftercare may be remanded to the same juvenile correctional facility or to another facility.

The Processing of Status Offense Cases Differs From That of Delinquency Cases

As discussed earlier in this chapter, a delinquency offense is an act committed by a minor, the kind for which an adult could be prosecuted in criminal court. Nevertheless, status offenses are behaviors that are violations of the state juvenile code only for children and youths of minor status, for example, running away from home, chronic truancy, ungovernability, staying out all night without permission, and underage drinking. In a number of ways, the law enforcement and court processing of status offense cases parallels that of delinquency cases.

However, not all states consider all of these behaviors to be law violations. Most states view these behaviors as indications that the youth is in need of closer supervision and respond to the behavior through the provision of social and family services. This different perspective of status offenses often results in their being handled more like dependency than delinquency cases. Status offenders are just as likely to enter the juvenile justice system through a child welfare agency as through law enforcement.

The landmark Juvenile Justice and Delinquency Prevention Act of 1974 strongly discouraged holding status offenders in secure juvenile correctional facilities, either for detention or placement. This important legislation and policy mandate is called *deinstitutionalization of status offenders*. An exception to this deinstitutionalization policy takes place when the juvenile status offender violates a valid court order, such as a probation order that requires the adjudicated status offender to reside in a group home for 30 days or one that requires attendance at school five days a week and an 8 p.m. curfew. The status offender who violates the court order or group home placement may then be confined in a secure detention or correctional facility.

Juvenile Court Referrals and Case Dispositions

It is the juvenile court judge's responsibility at the disposition hearing to determine the most reasonable and appropriate sanction, as a result of carefully reviewing a predisposition psychosocial and delinquency history report prepared by the county or city probation department. The full range of adjudication options available to a typical juvenile court includes commitment to a juvenile institution or a residential drug treatment facility; placement in a group home or foster care; traditional or intensive probation supervision; court-monitored home-based electronic monitoring; referral to an outside community agency, prevocational program, psychosocial day treatment, or a community mental health program; a fine; community service in a local hospital, nursing home, or public works program; or restitution.

With regard to juvenile court dispositional hearings, judges usually do their best to determine appropriate and effective sanctions for delinquent youth in order to break the cycle of juvenile delinquency recidivism. In a growing number of delinquency dispositions, the juvenile court imposes a combination of sanctions, such as probation for one year with the first three months spent in a residential drug treatment facility or commitment to a group home for six months, with the stipulation that the adjudicated youth attend an alternative school five days a week and two hours of group therapy every night. Other sanctions include commitment to a juvenile correctional institution's maximum security unit for mentally ill and chemically dependent (MICA) juvenile offenders, probation, and/or electronically monitored home detention.

According to the U.S. Department of Justice data, probation is the most common form of sanction given by the juvenile court. Between 1997 and 2009, the number of juvenile offenders formally placed on probation has decreased across all four types of offenses. Specifically, the percentage of youth adjudicated to formal probation has decreased the most for property offenses (40%), followed by drug offenses (17%), offenses against persons (12%), and public order offenses (5%).

With the decreases in the number of overall juvenile court cases from 1997 to 2009, decreases in the number of sanctions given out by the court should be expected. This trend has also been reflected in other fields as well. Specifically, similar decreases have been reflected in youth substance use (Johnston, O'Malley, Bachman, & Schulenberg, 2013), school violence (Pitner, Astor, & Benbenishty, in press), and school dropout (Aud et al., 2012). Some have hypothesized that the emphasis on delivering evidence-based intervention to at-risk youth may be reducing and diverting youth from these problematic trajectories (Greenwood & Edwards, 2011).

Assessment and Management of Juvenile Status Offenders

The debate over the appropriate way to handle status offenders has been going on for many years. The major issue is whether the juvenile court should retain authority over them or if these cases should be handled by Child Services. Those in favor of the court's continuing authority believe that a youth's habitual misbehavior will eventually lead to more serious delinquent acts; therefore, the court should retain jurisdiction over them. An opposing view (often advanced by deviance theorists with a societal reaction or labeling-theory perspective) holds that status offenders who are defined as delinquents may actually become delinquents as the result of a self-fulfilling prophecy, leading to secondary deviance (Becker, 1963; Lemert, 1971; Schur, 1973).

An alternate belief is that the needs of status offenders can be better met within the community social service and child welfare service systems (Boisvert & Wells, 1980; Roberts, 1987; Springer, 2001). For example, Roberts (1987) states that there is a need for a full range of social services, including 24-hour telephone hotlines, short-term runaway shelters, family treatment programs, education and treatment services for abusive parents, and vocational training and placement services.

At issue is the type of treatment status offenders should receive. Should they be sentenced to a secure juvenile facility or referred to a community social service agency for counseling? For many years, it was common for juvenile status offenders to be sentenced to juvenile correctional facilities, where they were confined in the same institution with youths convicted of serious crimes. The practice of sending status offenders to juvenile correctional institutions has become much less common in recent years because of the deinstitutionalization of status offenders.

Probation officers often believe that although most status offenders do not pose a danger to others, they do frequently exhibit destructive behavior patterns such as drug abuse, alcohol abuse, or suicide ideation. They often come from dysfunctional, conflict-ridden families where physical, sexual, or emotional abuse is prevalent. Thus, the social work perspective urges that a continuum of services be provided for status offenders and their families through a social service agency, a family service agency, or a juvenile court-based program. Available services should include family counseling, individual and group counseling, addiction treatment, alternative education programs, and vocational evaluation, education, and training.

When working with juveniles with status or delinquency offenses, forensic social workers should use developmentally appropriate risk assessment tools that include an assessment of traumatic stress, and other factors known to be associated with recidivism, when making a recommendation about the level of treatment and continuum of services for juvenile justice-involved youth (particularly important when working with specialized populations as discussed subsequently).

Systems of Care: Addressing Mental Health in Juvenile Justice

Mental health problems among adolescents are often addressed in the juvenile justice system as a last resort. In fact, 50% to 75% of all youth in juvenile justice facilities may have a mental disorder (OJJDP, 2012) including attention deficit hyperactivity disorder (ADHD), disruptive disorders, suicidality, and co-occurring substance use. Youth with serious socioemotional and behavioral challenges, who often also present with histories of victimization and traumatic stress, are shuffled from the child welfare system or from a mental health agency into the correctional system (Koppleman, 2005). The following sections address interdisciplinary collaboration, specialized assessment, and primary, secondary, and tertiary prevention. The subsequent sections cover risk assessment and complex trauma among sexually abusive adolescents.

Collaboration in the Juvenile Justice System

Knowledge and skills in interdisciplinary collaboration are essential to serve juvenile justice-involved clients. As noted previously, collaboration in the juvenile justice system involves different individuals, groups, and organizations across a variety of practice settings. It is useful to conceptualize these individuals (professionals, nonprofessional individuals, or groups) as stakeholders because they all have a vested interest in youth and/or community safety outcomes. The different systems and their stakeholders include:

- the family (e.g., juvenile, parents, legal guardians, siblings, and extended family);
- the community (e.g., neighborhoods and community volunteers);
- the schools (e.g., teachers and other educational staff);
- law enforcement (e.g., police officers, juvenile police officers);
- the juvenile courts (e.g., juvenile court judges, intake officers, probation officers, court-appointed advocates, prosecuting attorney for the state, defense attorney for the youth, and social workers);
- teen courts (e.g., other teens);
- juvenile detention centers (e.g., social workers, mental health and medical professionals, juvenile correctional facilities); and
- social welfare agencies (e.g., social workers), such as inpatient mental health or substance abuse services (e.g., alcohol and drug counselors) and court-mandated foster care services (e.g., child welfare workers).

The presence of multiple "actors" across juvenile justice systems underscores the need for combining multiple perspectives in assessment and intervention planning that involves youth, their families, and their communities. However, practitioners should be aware that this combination of diverse perspectives may not always result in harmonious interactions. Conflict may occur among interdisciplinary professionals who have been trained with a particular set of personal and professional values and ethics, as well as professional areas of expertise.

Therapeutic jurisprudence outcomes (e.g., positive outcomes) that address juvenile public policy issues must transcend the expertise of one profession and must include open interactions across the disciplines (Madden & Wayne, 2003). Effective strategies that social workers can use include open communication, cooperation, coordination, and the resolution of disciplinary conflicts through debate (Abramson & Rosenthal, 1995; Garland, Hough, Landsverk, & Brown, 2001; Payne, 2000; Petrucci, 2007). These cooperative efforts, particularly among interdisciplinary professionals, extend to assessment, prevention, and intervention strategies across the juvenile justice system. A review of assessment, prevention, and intervention with the juvenile justice populations follows.

Relevant Assessment, Prevention, and Intervention Strategies

Assessment, prevention, and intervention efforts occur at each step of the juvenile justice process, from entry in the system (e.g., the courts) to aftercare services (e.g., when a youth is paroled from prison). It is common for assessments of juveniles to be completed by social workers, psychologists, and/or psychiatrists. Ellis and Sowers (2001) defined social work assessment as the "examination of the client and his social systems to identify the problems that may contribute to his deviant behavior and the strategies that might be used to curb it."

Biopsychosocial Assessment

Biopsychosocial assessment is a tool that serves the critical function of guiding decision-making processes for youth involved in the juvenile justice system. A biopsychosocial assessment commonly includes information on the presenting problem, the demographic background of the client, and relevant history, including family history; developmental history; educational, vocational training, and employment history; family and peer relations; medical, mental health, substance abuse history, and treatment; and legal history (Vogelsand, 2001).

A social worker conducting a biopsychosocial assessment engages in a broad and comprehensive process that often includes interviews with the youth, collateral contacts, case record reviews, and a review of the relevant theoretical and empirical literature. An expert consultation is frequently used to help explain information gathered. Obtaining multiple sources of information helps to ensure reliability and validity (Vogelsand, 2001).

The biopsychosocial assessment can have different functions in different settings. For instance, in private agency settings, the information can be used to inform treatment or intervention planning, or to develop community resources. In public settings, such as the court, the assessment may be used to provide information that would assist the judge or jury in decision making related to the juvenile defendant (Ellis & Sowers, 2001).

For social workers, particularly clinical social workers, a biopsychosocial assessment plays an important role in expert testimony. Vogelsand (2001) had several recommendations on how social workers can best prepare for court testimony, including knowing how to define psychosocial assessment and being able to explain one's area of expertise and training in conducting biopsychosocial assessments.

Specialized Assessment

In addition to general assessments, there are also specialized risk assessments at every stage of the judicial decision-making process for youth (Roberts, 2004). These assessments provide recommendations that may serve to influence placement decisions and the type of treatment received. Some of the more specialized assessments include an assessment for danger to self (i.e., suicidal assessment) or others (e.g., violence and sexual offending behavior), mental health issues (e.g., competency and need for treatment), and substance abuse (Borum & Verhaagen, 2006; Hoge & Andrews, 1996; Perry & Orchard, 1992).

Suicide Risk Assessment

Suicide risk assessment often occurs in the juvenile justice system. Youth, especially in the first 72 hours of detention, may be at an elevated risk for suicidal behavior. A suicidal risk assessment attempts to determine the level at which a youth is a danger to himself or herself. This assessment includes determining the presence of recent stressors, the degree of suicidal ideations, suicidal intent, suicidal plans, and past suicidal history. Risk assessment for an offender's potential for being a danger to others (e.g., violence) attempts to determine the propensity of risk for repeat offending (Borum & Verhaagen, 2006; Perry & Orchard, 1992). Often conducted by a psychologist or psychiatrist, recommendations from these reports may significantly influence the placement of youth.

Substance Abuse and Mental Health Assessments

Substance abuse and mental assessments may also be conducted with youth involved in the juvenile justice system (Roberts, 2004). Substance abuse evaluations attempt to determine the level to which a youth has a substance abuse problem. This type of assessment may include the degree to which juveniles use alcohol or drugs and whether this constitutes dependence or abuse and/or the need for treatment (American Psychiatric Association, 2000).

Mental health evaluations are designed to determine a youth's level of mental health competence or his or her need for treatment. Youth may be assessed for competency at various points in the juvenile justice process. For example, before making an arrest, police may need to assess a youth's ability to comprehend his or her Miranda rights. Court officials may need to determine a youth's ability to stand trial or whether a waiver to criminal court is warranted (Grisso, 1998; Hoge & Andrews, 1996). Examples of mental health screening instruments used in the juvenile justice system are the *Massachusetts Youth Screening Instrument* (*MAYSI-2*; Grisso & Barnum, 2006) and the *Brief Symptom Inventory* (*BSI*; Derogatis, 1993).

Massachusetts Youth Screening Instrument. The *MAYSI-2* is one of the most widely used mental health screening tools; it may be used at entry or transitional points during the juvenile justice process (e.g., intake, probation, or pretrial) (Grisso & Barnum, 2006). Designed for youth aged 12 to 17 years, the *MAYSI-2* takes approximately 15 minutes to administer and identifies youth with special needs (e.g., alcohol/drug use, suicidal ideation, anger and irritability, depression, and trauma histories).

Brief Symptom Inventory. The *BSI* is the short version of the Symptom Checklist-90-Revised (SCL-R-90; Derogatis, 1993). It is a 53-item self-report instrument and takes 8 to 12 minutes to administer. It identifies psychological symptoms in adolescents and adults using a 5-point Likert scale (0 = not at all to 4 = extremely) to measure one's level of distress (e.g., somatic complaints, anxiety, depression, hostility, paranoia, and psychoses) over the course of seven days (Derogatis, 1993).

Primary, Secondary, and Tertiary Prevention Strategies

In addition to assessment, there are prevention and intervention strategies social workers use to address youth concerns.

Primary Prevention

Prevention and intervention strategies geared toward enhancing youths' positive developmental assets may occur at the primary, secondary, and/or tertiary levels (Rapp-Paglicci, Dulmus, & Wodarski, 2004). The first level, *primary prevention,* involves a universal approach. Primary prevention programs target all youths in community and school settings. An example of a violence prevention approach for all children is the Second Step: A Violence Prevention Curriculum (D. C. Grossman et al., 1997). It is an emotional literacy program that was developed to increase the social and emotional skills of youth. This program includes modules on empathy, anger management, and emotional learning. Research on the Second Step Program has shown that youth who have participated in this program increased their social and emotional skills and decreased their use of physical and verbal aggression and disruptive behavior (D. C. Grossman et al., 1997; McMahon, Washburn, Felix, Yakin, & Childrey, 2000).

Secondary Prevention

Secondary prevention strategies specifically target at-risk youth populations. The focus of secondary prevention activities is on preventing repeated occurrences of problem behavior through targeted interventions (Howell, 2001). For example, a social worker can provide a student, who has more than one disciplinary referral for fighting in a given month, special instruction in conflict resolution or social skills. Another example of a secondary prevention strategy is establishing mentoring programs in neighborhoods with high levels of youth gang affiliation. These programs provide at-risk youths the opportunity to bond with prosocial adults or peers. Mentoring programs, such as the Juvenile Mentoring Program (JUMP) and Big Brothers/Big Sisters are examples of evidence-based mentoring programs that can improve prevention or treatment outcomes for at-risk youth (J. B. Grossman & Garry, 1997; Keating, Tomishima, Foster, & Alessandri, 2002). Evidence suggests that at-risk youth who participate in mentoring programs are less likely to engage in antisocial activities, such as substance use and violence, than youth who do not; mentoring programs also improve the participants' academic performance (Blechman, 1992; OJJDP, 1998).

Tertiary Prevention

The most intensive level of support is *tertiary prevention.* Tertiary prevention strategies specifically target delinquent youth, especially serious and chronic offenders. Interventions are geared toward reducing the impact of a condition or problem on the individual's ability to function in the least restrictive setting (Catalano, Arthur, Hawkins, Berglund, & Olson, 1998; Howell, 2001). Wraparound services and multisystemic therapy (MST) are examples of tertiary level interventions.

Wraparound Services. Wraparound services are designed to enable children with severe, multiple needs and risks (including delinquency) to remain at home rather than be placed in institutionalized care. They generally refer to a set of individualized services for youth and their families being helped by multiple agencies. These services may include treatment as well as personal support services. These services emphasize a partnership among the families, educators, and service providers responsible for the child (Burns & Hoagwood, 2002). The NMHA and Substance Abuse and Mental Health Services Administration's (SAMHSA) Center for Mental Health Services (CMHS) have endorsed this approach and since the 1990s have promoted it as part of its systems of care initiatives (NMHA, 2004). Wraparound services generally include a collaborative, community-based interagency team, a formal interagency agreement, care coordinators, child and family teams, a unified plan of care, and systematic, outcome-based services. Social workers may work in wraparound services as a program administrator or as a practitioner providing services.

Multisystemic Therapy. MST is an intervention strategy designed to help identified youth reduce antisocial behavior (e.g., disobedience, running away, drug use, arson, vandalism, theft, and violence against persons). MST provides multilevel intervention strategies in individual, family, and community domains (Henggeler et al., 1991; Swenson, Henggeler, Taylor, & Addison, 2005). There is a debate over the effectiveness of MST (Henggeler, Schoenwald, Borduin, & Swenson, 2006; Littell, 2006). Proponents of MST cite methodologically sound outcome studies for treating violent and chronic juvenile offenders and their families from diverse backgrounds, including offending behavior and substance use problems (Brown, Borduin, & Henggeler, 2001; Henggeler et al., 1991; Swenson et al., 2005). MST also has been shown to provide cost savings, especially among substance abusing juvenile offenders (Schoenwald, Ward, Henggeler, Pickrel, & Patel, 1996). In contrast, Littell and colleagues' systematic review of published and unpublished studies on MST (conducted for the Campbell and Cochrane Collaborations) found that MST is not as effective as previously thought (Littell, 2005; Littell, Popa, & Forsythe, 2005).

Complex Trauma and Polyvictimization

Alongside racial disparities and negative peer influences (e.g., Dodge, Dishion, & Lansford, 2007), and community and neighborhood factors related to delinquency, significant percentages of youth entering into the justice system have salient traumatic experiences that require intervention. Complex trauma experiences among juvenile justice-involved youth is linked with sexual and nonsexual behavior problems and delinquency (Ford, Chapman, Connor, & Cruise, 2012; Marini, Leibowitz, Burton, & Stickle, 2013). More than 90% of youth in the juvenile justice system reported having experienced at least one traumatic event (Arroyo, 2001), and youthful offenders in the prison system in the United States have experienced cumulative life course trauma, a potential pathway to delinquency. Researchers have found that cumulative trauma, or multiple (re)victimizations, and polyvictimization are also common among general population-based adolescents, with 38.7% having experienced two or more victimizations in the previous year, and 10.9% having experienced five or more direct victimizations in the past year (Finkelhor et al., 2005).

Evidence for the trauma–delinquency link was also found among youth adjudicated for sexual offenses (Burton, Leibowitz, Eldredge, Ryan, & Compton, 2011), a specialized population many forensic social workers come in contact with in the juvenile justice system. Complex trauma includes sexual and physical abuse and neglect, and is associated with sequelae that include a range of emotional and behavioral impairments in core competencies related to attachment, self-regulation, executive functioning, conduct, and psychiatric concerns (Cook et al., 2005).

Working With Specialized Populations: Sexually Abusive Youth

The effective management and treatment of juvenile justice-involved adolescents can be especially challenging for forensic social workers. The research on delinquency, and particularly on adolescent sexual abusers, is needed to assist in the development of more effective policies, risk assessment protocols, and interventions.

Advancements include the research on the link between trauma and delinquency and understanding complex trauma and maltreatment (Ford et al., 2012; Maschi & Bradley, 2008) as previously discussed, including neurodevelopmental approaches to working with sexually abusive adolescents, which underscore that early adversity and trauma impact the brain and behavior (e.g., Longo, Prescott, Bergman, & Creeden, 2013). Additionally, the recidivism research and empirical findings regarding the validity of risk assessment tools in predicting future offenses (Prescott, 2006; Reitzel & Carbonell, 2006; Viljoen et al., 2009; Worling, Littlejohn, & Bookalam, 2010) must be considered, as well as practice frameworks delineating the family and social–ecological context in which sexual abuse occurs.

The number of adolescents involved in the legal system for sexually abusive behavior increases at age 12 years and plateaus after age 14 years. Early adolescence is the peak age for offenses against younger children (Finkelhor, Ormrod, & Chaffin, 2009). Sexually abusive behavior among juveniles encompasses hands-on, nonassaultive, and hands-off offenses that include child-on-child sexual harassment, rape, incest, exhibitionism, and voyeurism (Rich, 2003). In terms of juvenile justice policy and forensic practice, the fact that juveniles constitute more than one third of those who commit sexual offenses against minors underscores the need for sexual abuse prevention and treatment efforts to target the risks and needs of these youthful offenders.

Sexual victimization has been found to have the greatest impact on subsequent sexual offending and sexual fantasy in developmentally sensitive periods (ages 3–7 years) when children rapidly acquire inhibition skills and cognitive flexibility (Grabell & Knight, 2009). These findings illustrate the importance of early intervention as well as the need to account for the differences in the developmental trajectories between youth who offend against children and their counterparts (i.e., delinquent youth and sexually abusive youth who offend against peers; Leibowitz, Burton, & Howard, 2012; Netland & Miner, 2012; Seto & Lalumiere, 2010). The causes and etiology of adolescent sexual offending can be understood as multifactorial, with diverse pathways to sexual aggression; therefore, multimodal interventions that include family-based approaches show promising outcomes. MST has been found effective in addressing the needs of delinquent youth at the individual and family levels, and has also been found to reduce sexual behavior problems among juvenile sex offenders (Letourneau et al., 2009).

Social workers should evaluate the context in which sexualized behaviors occur, including the family system, and caution should be exercised to avoid pathologizing normative behaviors. Moreover, it is important to consider that sexual offenses committed by youth do not fit the profile of the adult "pedophile" or that of a predatory sex offender (Finkelhor et al., 2009), in that their arousal patterns are not fixed. Moreover, sexually harmful behavior is not explained by general delinquency theories; however, nonsexual crimes are important to address in treatment (Leibowitz, Burton, & Howard, 2012; Seto & Lalumiere, 2010). Clinical case studies highlight a range of characteristics and behaviors among sexually abusive youth, including sexual arousal patterns and fondling over or under clothes, performing oral or vaginal sex on younger children, and boundary violations with peers (see Exhibit 14.1 for a summary of characteristics of sexually abusive youth and considerations for treatment).

As discussed earlier, the caveat about negative labeling of youth that can result in stigma and social rejection applies to adolescents with sexually abusive behavior. Contemporary adult sex offender registration and community notification policies, which began with the Jacob Wetterling Act (named after a heinous case in which an 11-year-old boy was abducted in Minnesota in 1989; his remains were found in 2016), can be iatrogenic and result in negative unintended consequences, including suicidality and harassment and violence toward

---

Exhibit 14.1 Summary of Considerations for Working With Youth With Sexually Harmful Behaviors

1. Sexually abusive youth are a heterogeneous group with a variety of developmental, attachment, personality, and mental health considerations.
2. The etiology of sexually abusive behavior is multifactorial and there are a number of pathways leading to sexual aggression.
3. Assessment and treatment should be an ongoing process, should be sensitive to developmental changes in the youth, and should be based on a developmental perspective, incorporating static, stable, and dynamic risk factors (Ryan, Leversee, & Lane, 2010).
4. Developmental/contextual approaches include a consideration of multiple developmental antecedents, including a history of sexual, physical, and emotional abuse and social learning or "modeling" in which an adolescent learns sexually abusive behavior (from peers, caretakers, and/or pornography; Burton & Meezan, 2004).
5. Youthful sexual abusers are not the same as adult sex offenders and they do fit the profile of "pedophiles." There are differences in terms of amenability to treatment, mental health issues, and the conceptualization of "deviant sexual interests" (i.e., youth are not as "habituated").
6. Sexually harmful behavior is not explained by general delinquency theories, but nonsexual crimes are important to address in treatment. Differences between youth with sexual offenses and delinquent youth include atypical sexual interests and greater sexual victimization and social isolation (Seto & Lalumiere, 2010).
7. Treatment should address risk and protective factors, be family-based where possible, and draw from treatment areas derived from using appropriate sex offense-specific risk assessment instruments. Sexual recidivism among sexually abusive youth is relatively low and "offense-specific" treatment can be effective and reduce recidivism (Carpentier & Proulx, 2011).
8. Treatment approaches for complex trauma (Ford et al., 2012) are integral to working with youth with sexual and nonsexual offenses, as are family-based approaches such as MST.

Source: From LeCroy and Anthony (2014). Republished with permission of John Wiley and Sons Inc.

youth (Levenson, Grady, & Leibowitz, 2016). Indeed, a recent Human Rights Watch report documented the irreparable harm of juvenile registration on youth and their families (Pittman & Parker, 2013). Forty-one states have some form of registration for juveniles adjudicated delinquent for a sex crime, 30 states permit or require website publication of the registration information, and most states require registration for juveniles convicted in adult court (Office of Sex Offender Sentencing, Monitoring, Apprehending, Registering, and Tracking, 2015).

Psychosexual Evaluations

Conducting assessments with sexually abusive youth is one of the most challenging responsibilities for forensic social workers, psychologists, and professionals in related fields.

Psychosexual evaluators are called upon to be attentive to the multiple domains associated with a youth's functioning and developmental/contextual factors. A comprehensive psychosexual mental health evaluation includes a clinical interview with youth and current caretakers and consultation with professionals/past treatment providers, review of collateral information, psychological testing, and the use of risk assessment instruments appropriate for use with sexually abusive males. Assessment of risk, protective factors (including traumatic sequelae), strengths, and amenability to intervention are part of the assessment, as are recommendations for treatment, supervision, and risk management. The evaluator should use assessment tools for general delinquency and mental health described in the previous section, as well as tools designed to assess sexual behavior problems among youth.

It is important to note that there are no empirically validated risk assessment tools for juveniles who have sexually harmed, but there are sex offense instruments that assess the likelihood of attenuated or elevated risk based upon both *static* (fixed, historical) and *dynamic* (changeable) factors (Prescott, 2006). These include the Juvenile Sex Offender Assessment Protocol-II (J-SOAP II; Prentky & Righthand, 2003), designed to be used with males ages 12 to 18 years (they are not designed to assess risk among females), who have been adjudicated for sexual offenses, as well as nonadjudicated youths with a history of sexually coercive behavior. The instrument has four subscales, two major historical (static) domains that are of importance for risk assessment—Scale 1: Sexual drive/sexual preoccupation, and Scale 2: Impulsive and antisocial behavior—as well as the two major dynamic areas that could potentially reflect behavior change—Scale 3: Clinical/treatment, and Scale 4: Community adjustment. Another commonly used instrument with sexually abusive youth, the Estimate of Risk of Adolescent Sexual Offense Recidivism (ERASOR; Worling & Curwen, 2001), is an empirically guided tool for youth between 12 to 18 years consisting of 25 risk factors falling into five categories: (a) sexual interests, attitudes, and behaviors; (b) historical sexual

Case Example and Application

Arturo is a 14-year-old Latino male placed in residential treatment, and he is on probation for delinquency (theft, fire-setting, and property destruction). Arturo's biological mother was a victim of domestic violence and childhood physical and sexual abuse, and she has a history of substance abuse. Because of sexual and nonsexual (delinquency) behavioral issues that emerged as early as 7 years old and persisted as he became older, Arturo was recently placed in a more structured treatment setting with plans for reunification with his adoptive family. A year prior to his placement, three younger female cousins made an outcry that Arturo sexually abused them. He reportedly used games to gain their trust before he abused them, eventually escalating to threats to gain compliance, the same modus operandi or tactics used during Arturo's own victimization as a child.

Previous psychological evaluations highlighted that Arturo's early life experiences were characterized by exposure to violence in the home, parental substance abuse, and

(continued)

medical complications that were life threatening. His biological mother's various boyfriends reportedly sexually abused both Arturo and his older sister, Cheryl, on several occasions. Subsequently, Arturo experienced challenges in interpersonal relationships, oppositional behaviors in both home and in school, and achieving fulfilling connections to his peers that increased as he entered adolescence. Sexual behavioral problems and paraphilias (inappropriate recurrent sexual interests) also appeared to be emerging. Arturo's early life was marked with traumatic stress and it played an important role in his neurological development and capacity for self-regulation.

Although trauma can manifest in multiple ways, unresolved trauma can be integral to the development of life-course persistent conduct disorder, affect dysregulation, and adolescent antisocial behavior. Arturo's strengths include that he can be articulate; is friendly; enjoys working with his hands, such as in woodworking; has a sense of humor; and appreciates music. He also can form substantive relationships with school officials and counselors. Trauma, however, can obviate empathy, reduce inhibitions concerning delinquent acts, and increase aggressiveness. Arturo was previously diagnosed with ADHD (with mixed response to medications). His discharge plan reflected the additional diagnosis of major depressive disorder, without psychotic features, and concerns about fire-setting. Clinicians also noted that he appeared dissociative when discussing details of his trauma history as well as his current actions and aggression toward his adoptive family (threatening them, etc.). His clinical picture matches a young person with complex trauma symptomatology, which includes emotional dysregulation co-occurring with sexual behavior issues. Nonsexual behavioral concerns have been identified by other professionals, including fire-setting, stealing, and running away. Given that research on juvenile sexual abusers has established a relationship between trauma and nonsexual crimes (e.g., Burton et al., 2011), these factors should be carefully assessed and addressed in the course of treatment.

Early on during Arturo's treatment, there were indications of callous-unemotional traits; for example, lack of empathy and impulsivity, and evidence of executive functioning issues. During the course of treatment, Arturo's threatening behavior and aggression toward his adoptive parents eroded his parents' trust and feelings of safety concerning their son (but they remained hopeful and very active in seeking strategies to help Arturo). While Arturo endorsed some feelings of shame and anxiety regarding his sexual and nonsexual behavior at times, his frustration tolerance and level of remorse remained low, and mood management and self-regulation skills were clearly the focus of intervention, in the context of individual and family-based work.

Treatment Plan for Arturo

Drawing from information derived from risk assessment tools described earlier, a treatment plan was created for Arturo addressing hypersexuality, sexual interests and attitudes, and history of victimization, as well as his family environment. Given his combined type of emotional functioning, impulsivity, and aggressive behavior, Arturo is more likely to develop life-course persistent antisocial behavior, *but* he is still young—trauma-informed work in a structured setting (i.e., residential milieu) and wraparound that includes family interventions can increase protective factors (e.g., MST) and improve self-control, particularly as he works toward reunification with his adoptive family. Engaging in reparative work and demonstrating empathy and accountability with the victims' families is also indicated in this case, as is working on understanding the ways his behavior impacts others in general. Interventions should also focus on his risk for nonsexual offenses, boundaries, improving emotional awareness, signaling behavior (methods for expressing his needs), peer relationships, safety planning, and self-care, which would also help achieve increased stability. Targeting both cognitive and affective vulnerabilities may enhance clinical interventions.

assaults; (c) psychosocial functioning; (d) family/environmental functioning (high stress levels); and (e) treatment (i.e., practicing realistic safety/treatment plans).

Conclusion

Forensic social work in juvenile justice settings is a complex undertaking, requiring an understanding of the history of practices and legislation impacting juveniles processed in the court system and how delinquency cases are handled in court, and the appropriate use of juvenile risk assessment tools to help inform treatment planning when working with specialized populations, as well the implementation of evidence-based interventions. Social justice issues must also be considered, which include the iatrogenic application and unintended effects of specific policies (reflected in the history of juvenile justice systems), such as community notification and registration in the case of sex offenses committed by adolescents.

CHAPTER EXERCISES

Exercise 1. Drawing from the case of Arturo, in small groups, develop a treatment plan with an adolescent in your field placement or work setting. Consider risk assessment tools and other ways of collecting relevant case information as well as complex trauma in developing your plan. Offer recommendations for treatment.

Exercise 2. In the same small group, role-play engaging with Arturo and his family concerning ways they might work together with you as a practitioner who is part of an interdisciplinary team. Then, role-play conducting a risk assessment and engaging with a justice-involved youth in your field placement. Who would be part of the multidisciplinary team and how might you collaborate with other professionals to best serve the client and her/his family?

Exercise 3. As a class, research and discuss juvenile justice processing and case flow in your state. What systems of care are available to juvenile justice-involved youth in your state?

Additional Resources

Blueprint for Health Youth Development: Center for the Study of Prevention of Violence: www .colorado.edu/cspv/blueprints

Human Rights Watch: www.hrw.org/report/2013/05/01/raised-registry/irreparable-harm-placing -children-sex-offender-registries-us

Multisystemic therapy (MST): http://mstservices.com/what-is-mst/what-is-mst

Office of Juvenile Justice and Delinquency Prevention: www.ojjdp.gov

References

Abramson, J. S., & Rosenthal, B. S. (1995). Interdisciplinary and interorganizational collaboration. In R. L. Edwards (Ed.), *Encyclopedia of social work* (19th ed., pp. 1479–1489). Washington, DC: National Association of Social Workers Press.

American Psychiatric Association. (2000). *Diagnostic and statistical manual of mental disorders* (4th ed., text rev.). Washington, DC: Author.

Armour, J., & Hammond, S. (2009). *Minority youth in the juvenile justice system: Disproportionate minority contact.* Washington, DC: National Conference of State Legislatures.

Arroyo, W. (2001). PTSD in children and adolescents in the juvenile justice system. In S. Eth (Ed.), *PTSD in children and adolescents* (Vol. 20, pp. 59–86). Arlington, VA: American Psychiatric Publishing.

Aud, S., Hussar, W., Johnson, F., Kena, G., Roth, E., Manning, E., . . . Zhang, J. (2012). *The condition of education 2012* (NCES 2012-045). Washington, DC: U.S. Department of Education, National Center for Education Statistics.

Bartollas, C., & Miller, S. J. (2005). *Juvenile justice in America* (4th ed.). Upper Saddle River, NJ: Pearson Prentice Hall.

Becker, H. S. (1963). *Outsiders: Studies in the sociology of deviance.* New York, NY: Free Press.

Blechman, E. A. (1992). Mentors for high-risk minority youth: From effective communication to bicultural competence. *Journal of Clinical Child Psychology, 21,* 160–169.

Boisvert, M. J., & Wells, R. (1980). Toward a rational policy on status offenders. *Social Work, 25,* 230–234.

Borum, R., & Verhaagen, D. (2006). *Assessing and managing violence risk in juveniles.* New York, NY: Guilford Press.

Brown, T. L., Borduin, C. M., & Henggeler, S. W. (2001). Treating juvenile offenders with mental health disorders in community settings. In J. B. Ashford, B. D. Sales, & W. H. Reid (Eds.), *Treating adult and juvenile offenders with special needs* (pp. 445–464). Washington, DC: American Psychological Association.

Bruns, E. J., Walker, J. S., Adams, J., Miles, P., Osher, T., Rash, J., . . . National Wraparound Initiative Advisory Group. (2004). *Ten principles of the wraparound process.* Portland, OR: National Wraparound Initiative, Research & Training Center on Family Support & Children's Mental Health, Portland State University.

Burns, B. B., & Hoagwood, K. (2002). *Community treatment for youth: Evidence-based interventions for severe emotional and behavioral disorders.* New York, NY: Oxford University Press.

Burton, D. L., Leibowitz, G. S., Eldredge, M. A., Ryan, G., & Compton, D. (2011). The relationship of trauma to non-sexual crimes committed by adolescent sexual abusers: A new area of research. *Journal of Aggression, Maltreatment, & Trauma, 20*(5), 579–593.

Burton, D. L., & Meezan, W. (2004). Revisiting recent research on social learning theory as an etiological proposition for sexually abusive male adolescents. *The Journal of Evidence-Based Social Work, 1*(1), 41–81.

Butts, J. A., & Buck, J. (2000). *Teen courts: A focus on research* [Bulletin]. Washington, DC: Office of Juvenile Justice Delinquency Prevention.

Carpentier, J., & Proulx, J. (2011). Correlates of recidivism among adolescents who have sexually offended. *Sexual Abuse: A Journal of Research and Treatment, 23,* 434–455.

Catalano, R. F., Arthur, M. W., Hawkins, J. D., Berglund, L., & Olson, J. J. (1998). Comprehensive community and school based interventions to prevent antisocial behavior. In R. Loeber & D. P. Farrington (Eds.), *Serious and violent juvenile offenders: Risk factors and successful interventions* (pp. 248–283). Thousand Oaks, CA: Sage.

Cocozza, J., & Skowyra, K. (2000). Youth with mental health disorders: Issues and emerging responses. *Office of Juvenile Justice and Delinquency Prevention Journal, 7*(1), 3–13.

Cook, A., Spinazzolla, J., Ford, J., Langtree, C., Blaustein, M., Cloitre, M., . . . van der Kolk, B. (2005). Complex trauma in children and adolescents. *Psychiatric Annals, 35*(5), 390–398.

Derogatis, L. R. (1993). *BSI Brief Symptom Inventory. Administration, scoring, and procedures manual* (4th ed.). Minneapolis, MN: National Computer Systems.

Dilulio, J., Jr. (1995, November 27). The coming of the super-predators. *The Weekly Standard.* Retrieved from http://www.weeklystandard.com/the-coming-of-the-super-predators/article/8160

Dodge, K. A., Dishion, T. J., & Lansford, J. E. (Eds.). (2007). *Deviant peer influences in programs for youth: Problems and solutions.* New York, NY: Guilford Press.

Ellis, R. A., & Sowers, K. M. (2001). *Juvenile justice practice: A cross-disciplinary approach to treatment.* Belmont, CA: Wadsworth.

Finkelhor, D., Ormrod, R., & Chaffin, M. (2009). *Juveniles who commit sexual offenses against minors.* Washington, DC: Office of Juvenile and Delinquency Prevention.

Ford, J. D., Chapman, J., Connor, D. F., & Cruise, K. R. (2012). Complex trauma and aggression in secure juvenile justice settings. *Criminal Justice and Behavior, 39*, 694–724. doi:10.1177/0093854812436957

Garland, A. F., Hough, R. L., Landsverk, J. A., & Brown, S. A. (2001). Multi-sector complexity of systems of care for youth with mental health needs. *Children's Services: Social Policy, Research, & Practice, 4*(3), 123–140.

Grabell, A. S., & Knight, R. A. (2009). Examining childhood abuse patterns and sensitive periods in juvenile sexual offenders. *Sexual Abuse: A Journal of Research and Treatment, 1*(2), 208–222.

Greenwood, P. W., & Edwards, D. L. (2011). Evidence-based programs for at-risk youth and juvenile offenders: A review of proven prevention and intervention models. In D. W. Springer & A. R. Roberts (Eds.), *Juvenile justice and delinquency* (pp. 369–390). Sudbury, MA: Jones & Bartlett.

Grisso, T. (1998). *Forensic evaluation of juveniles.* Sarasota, FL: Professional Resource Press.

Grisso, T., & Barnum, R. (2006). *Massachusetts Youth Screening Instrument-Version 2: User's manual and technical report.* Sarasota, FL: Professional Resource Press.

Grossman, D. C., Neckerman, H. J., Koepsell, T. D., Liu, P. Y., Asher, K. N., Beland, K., . . . Rivara, F. P. (1997). The effectiveness of a violence prevention curriculum among children in elementary school. *Journal of the American Medical Association, 277*, 1605–1611.

Grossman, J. B., & Garry, E. M. (1997). *Mentoring—A proven delinquency prevention strategy.* Washington, DC: Office of Juvenile Justice and Delinquency Prevention.

Henggeler, S. W., Borduin, C. M., Melton, G. B., Mann, B. J., Smith, L., Hall, J. A., . . . Fucci, B. R. (1991). Effects of multisystemic therapy on drug use and abuse in serious juvenile offenders: A progress report from two outcome studies. *Family Dynamics of Addiction Quarterly, 1*(3), 40–51.

Henggeler, S. W., Schoenwald, S. K., Borduin, C. M., & Swenson, C. C. (2006). Methodological critique and meta-analysis as Trojan horse. *Children & Youth Services Review, 28*, 447–457.

Herman, M. M. (2002). *Teen courts: A juvenile justice diversion program. Report on trends in the state courts.* Williamsburg, VA: National Center for State Courts.

Hoge, R. D., & Andrews, D. A. (1996). *Assessing the youthful offender: Issues and techniques.* New York, NY: Plenum Press.

Howell, J. C. (2001). Juvenile justice programs and strategies. In R. Loeber & D. P. Farrington (Eds.), *Child delinquents: Development, intervention, and service needs* (pp. 305–322). Thousand Oaks, CA: Sage.

Johnston, L. D., O'Malley, P. M., Bachman, J. G., & Schulenberg, J. E. (2013). *Monitoring the future national results on drug use: 2012 Overview, key findings on adolescent drug use.* Ann Arbor: Institute of Social Research, University of Michigan.

Justice Policy Institute. (2000). *Second chances: 100 years of the children's court: Giving kids a chance to make a better choice.* Washington, DC: Author.

Keating, L. M., Tomishima, M. A., Foster, S., & Alessandri, M. (2002). The effects of a mentoring program on at-risk youth. *Adolescence, 37*, 717–734.

Koppelman, J. (2005). Mental health and juvenile justice: moving toward more effective systems of care. *National Health Policy Forum Issue Brief, 805*, 1–24.

LeCroy, C. W., & Anthony, E. K. (2014). *Case studies in child, adolescent, and family treatment* (2nd ed.). Hoboken, NJ: John Wiley and Sons Inc.

Leibowitz, G. S., Burton, D. L., & Howard, A. (2012). Part II: Differences between sexually victimized and nonsexually victimized adolescent sexual abusers and delinquent youth: Further group comparisons of developmental antecedents and behavioral challenges. *Journal of Child Sexual Abuse, 21*, 315–326.

Lemert, E. M. (1971). *Instead of court: Division in juvenile justice.* Chevy Chase, MD: National Institute of Mental Health, Center for the Studies of Crime and Delinquency.

Letourneau, E., Henggeler, S., Borduin, C., Schewe, P., McCart, M., Chapman, J., & Saldana, L. (2009). Multisystemic therapy for juvenile sexual offenders: 1-year results from a randomized effectiveness trial. *Journal of Family Psychology, 23*(1), 89–102.

Levenson, J., Grady, M., & Leibowitz, G. S. (2016). Grand challenges: Social justice and the need for evidence-based sex offender registry reform. *Journal of Sociology and Social Welfare, 43*(2), 3–38.

Littell, J. H. (2005). Lessons from a systematic review of effects of multisystemic therapy. *Children & Youth Services Review, 27*, 445–463.

Littell, J. H. (2006). The case for multisystemic therapy: Evidence or orthodoxy? *Children & Youth Services Review, 28*, 458–472.

Littell, J. H., Popa, M., & Forsythe, B. (2005). Multisystemic therapy for social, emotional, and behavioral problems in youth aged 10–17. *Cochrane Database of Systematic Reviews, 3*, CD004797. doi:10.1002/14651858.CD004797.pub4

Longo, R. E., Prescott, D. S., Bergman, J., & Creeden, K. (Eds.). (2013). *Current perspectives & applications in neurobiology: Working with young persons who are victims and perpetrators of sexual abuse.* Holyoke, MA: New England Adolescent Research Institute Press.

Madden, R., & Wayne, R. H. (2003). Social work and the law: A therapeutic jurisprudence perspective. *Social Work, 48*, 338–347.

Marini, V., Leibowitz, G. S., Burton, D. L., & Stickle, T. R. (2013). Victimization, substance use, and sexual aggression in male adolescent sexual offenders. *Criminal Justice & Behavior, 20*(10), 1–15.

Maschi, T., & Bradley, C. (2008). Exploring the moderating influence of delinquent peers on the link between trauma, anger, and violence among male youth: Implication for social work practice. *Child and Adolescent Social Work Journal, 25*(1), 125–138.

McMahon, S. D., Washburn, J., Felix, E. D., Yakin, J., & Childrey, G. (2000). Violence prevention: Program effects on urban preschool and kindergarten children. *Applied & Preventive Psychology, 9*, 271–281.

National Mental Health Association. (2004). *Mental health treatment for youth in the juvenile justice system: A compendium of promising practices.* Alexandria, VA: Author.

Netland, J. D., & Miner, M. H. (2012). Psychopathy traits and parental dysfunction in sexual offending and general delinquent males. *Journal of Sexual Aggression, 18*(1), 4–22.

Office of Juvenile Justice and Delinquency Prevention. (1998). *1998 report to Congress: Juvenile mentoring program (JUMP).* Washington, DC: U.S. Department of Justice, Office of Juvenile Justice and Delinquency Prevention.

Office of Juvenile Justice and Delinquency Prevention. (2012). Upper age of jurisdiction. Retrieved from http://www.ojjdp.gov/ojstatbb/structure_process/qa04101.asp

Office of Sex Offender Sentencing, Monitoring, Apprehending, Registering, and Tracking. (2015). Sex offender management, assessment, and planning initiative. Office of Justice Programs. Retrieved from http://smart.gov/SOMAPI/sec2/ch6_registration.html

Payne, M. (2000). *Teamwork in multiprofessional care.* Chicago, IL: Lyceum Books.

Perry, G. P., & Orchard, J. (1992). *Assessment and treatment of adolescent sex offenders.* Sarasota, FL: Professional Resource Press.

Petrucci, C. (2007). Therapeutic jurisprudence in social work and criminal justice. In A. R. Roberts & D. W. Springer (Eds.), *Social work in juvenile and criminal justice settings* (3rd ed., pp. 287–299). Springfield, IL: Charles C. Thomas.

Pitner, R. O., Astor, R. A., & Benbenishty, R. (in press). Violence in schools. In P. Allen-Meares (Ed.), *Social work in schools* (7th ed.). Boston, MA: Allyn & Bacon.

Pittman, N., & Parker, A. (2013). Raised on the registry: The irreparable harm of placing children on sex offender registries in the U.S. (1623130085). *Human Rights Watch*. Retrieved from https://www .hrw.org/report/2013/05/01/raised-registry/irreparable-harm-placing-children-sex-offender -registries-us

Platt, A. M. (1969). The rise of the child-saving movement: A study in social policy and correctional reform. *Annals of the American Academy of Political & Social Science, 381*, 21–38.

Platt, A. M. (1977). *The child savers: The invention of delinquency* (2nd ed.). Chicago, IL: University of Chicago Press.

Prenky, R., & Righthand, S. (2003). Juvenile Sex Offender Assessment Protocol-II (JSOAP-II) manual (NCJ 202316). Office of Juvenile Justice and Delinquency Prevention. Retrieved from http://www .csom.org/pubs/JSOAP.pdf

Prescott, D. S. (Ed.). (2006). *Risk assessment of youth who have sexually abused*. Oklahoma City, OK: Wood & Barnes.

Puzzanchera, C., Adams, B., & Hockenberry, S. (2012). *Juvenile court statistics 2009*. Pittsburgh, PA: National Center for Juvenile Justice.

Rapp-Paglicci, L. A., Dulmus, C. N., & Wodarski, J. S. (2004). *Handbook of preventive interventions for children and adolescents*. Hoboken, NJ: Wiley.

Reitzel, L. R., & Carbonell, J. L. (2006). The effectiveness of sexual offender treatment for juveniles as measured by recidivism: A meta-analysis. *Sexual Abuse: A Journal of Research and Treatment, 18*, 401–422.

Rich, P. (2003). *Understanding, assessing and rehabilitating juvenile sexual offenders*. Hoboken, NJ: Wiley.

Roberts, A. R. (1987). *Runaways and nonrunaways*. Chicago, IL: Dorsey.

Roberts, A. R. (Ed.). (2004). *Juvenile justice sourcebook: Past, present, and future*. New York, NY: Oxford University Press.

Ryan, G., Leversee, T., & Lane, S. (2010). *Juvenile sexual offending: Causes, consequences, and correction* (3rd ed.). San Francisco, CA: Jossey-Bass.

Schoenwald, S. K., Ward, D. M., Henggeler, S. W., Pickrel, S. G., & Patel, H. (1996). Multisystemic therapy treatment of substance abusing or dependent adolescent offenders: Costs of reducing incarceration, inpatient, and residential placement. *Journal of Child & Family Studies, 5*, 431–444.

Schur, E. (1973). *Radical nonintervention: Rethinking the delinquency problem*. Englewood Cliffs, NJ: Prentice Hall.

Seto, M. C., & Lalumière, M. L. (2010). What is special about male adolescent sexual offending? A review and test of explanation through meta-analysis. *Psychological Bulletin, 136*(4), 526–575.

Springer, D. W. (2001). Runaway adolescents: Today's Huckleberry Finn crisis. *Brief Treatment and Crisis Intervention, 1*(2), 131–152.

Swenson, C. C., Henggeler, S. W., Taylor, I. S., & Addison, O. W. (2005). *Multisystemic therapy and neighborhood partnerships: Reducing violence and substance abuse*. New York, NY: Guilford Press.

U.S. Children's Bureau. (1967). *Juvenile court statistics, 1966* (Statistical Series 90). Washington, DC: U.S. Government Printing Office.

Viljoen, J. L., Elkovitch, N., Scalora, M. J., & Ullman, D. (2009). Assessment of reoffense risk in adolescents who have committed sexual offenses: Predictive validity of the ERASOR, PCL: YV, YLS/CMI, and Static-99. *Criminal Justice and Behavior, 36*, 981–1000.

Vogelsand, J. (2001). *The witness stand: A guide for clinical social workers in the courtroom.* Binghamton, NY: Haworth Press.

Worling, J. R., & Curwen, T. (2001). Estimate of risk of adolescent sexual offense recidivism (Version 2.0: The "ERASOR"). In M. C. Calder (Ed.), *Juveniles and children who sexually abuse: Frameworks for assessment* (pp. 372–397). Lyme Regis, Dorset, UK: Russell House Publishing.

Worling, J. R., Littlejohn, A., & Bookalam, D. (2010). 20-year prospective follow-up study of specialized treatment for adolescents who offended sexually. *Behavioral Sciences and the Law, 28*, 46–57.

VOICES FROM THE FIELD

Judith L. F. Rhodes, PhD, LMSW

Program Manager
YEP Village—Youth Empowerment Program

Agency Setting

Youth Empowerment Program (YEP) Village is a grant-funded (U.S. Department of Health and Human Services [DHHS], Office of Minority Health) violence prevention program. The purpose of YEP Village is to promote positive and prosocial behavior and to prevent the development of violent behavior and progression into the juvenile justice system among a cohort of African American boys attending inner city schools in Baton Rouge, Louisiana. The cohort, originally in the fourth and fifth grades, will be served for three years; therefore, the boys will progress into middle school (grades 6 and 7) by the third year of the intervention. YEP Village provides an after-school and summer program, whereby it (a) promotes healthy decision making with the evidence-based Positive Action intervention, (b) strengthens academic learning with Academic All Stars/Summer Scholars, and (c) develops prosocial relationships while being engaged in an array of fun and interactive activities with an Enrichment Component. The YEP Village family engagement component consists of monthly workshops or Family Fun Nights, which use curriculum aligned with the students' Positive Action intervention to strengthen and teach families the skills needed to raise healthy and successful children. YEP Village operates as a vehicle to expose the children to new ideas, experiences, and adult influences that are not readily prevalent to children living in distressed communities and attending struggling schools.

Practice Responsibilities

YEP Village uses a team approach to deliver the various program components. The team leaders are mental health professionals (licensed clinical social worker [LCSW] and licensed professional counselor [LPC]). Staff with clinical skills are beneficial in that the approximately 50 young children served reside in distressed communities prone to violence who may require counseling referrals. The staff serve as positive role models as they interact with the children. Practical logistical tasks include scheduling transportation and meal services as well as interfacing with the children's schools. YEP Village staff work with social work interns and university students who provide additional assistance with the program.

Expertise Required

YEP Village staff leadership (director and coordinator) must be licensed mental health professionals with at least five years of experience working with at-risk youth or youth in the juvenile justice system. Knowledge of working in school-based programs is preferred. Training to administer the evidence-based intervention is provided. A credentialed LCSW allows for social work interns to be placed in the program.

Ethical, Legal, Practice, Diversity, and/or Advocacy Issues Addressed

While YEP Village works with a school-age population who are at higher risk of school suspension and expulsion, the YEP team works with a "no ejection" approach. YEP Village operates as a place for children to develop an internal locus of control; therefore, removing a child for infractions is not an option. Clear expectations are set for behavior and interactions among the peers, and staff work closely with the child, his school, and his parents to promote positive interactions. Children are treated as individuals with accountability for one another. YEP Village strives to create an environment where the children can be problem solvers and succeed.

Interprofessional and Intersectoral Collaboration

YEP Village intersects with a variety of educational partners. It is located on the Louisiana State University campus, where the program is highly visible and the staff have ample opportunities to inform school administration, university students, and the community about prevention and intervention efforts of the program. The children attend public and charter schools within the district system and staff are openly invited to participate in other school initiatives and programs. The City of Baton Rouge is a My Brother's Keeper Community, and YEP Village works with the city and other community partners to address the opportunity gaps faced by boys and young men of color.

CHAPTER 15

The Criminal Justice System: A History of Mass Incarceration With Implications for Forensic Social Work

Kirk James

CHAPTER OBJECTIVES

The major objectives of this chapter are to:

- Promote social workers' understanding of mass incarceration from a historical and contemporary framework.
- Demonstrate how to create more holistic practice for impacted people.
- Explore how to advance socially just policies rooted in empirical data.

CHAPTER COMPETENCIES HIGHLIGHTED

- Competency 3: Advance Human Rights and Social, Economic, and Environmental Justice
- Competency 4: Engage in Practice Informed Research and Research Informed Practice

The United States, often considered "the land of the free," currently holds the dubious distinction of being the world's largest prison warden (Walmsley, 2016). While comprising a mere 5% of the world's population, the United States nonetheless has managed to account for 25% of the world's prisoners. No country, much less one that purports a democracy, has managed to incarcerate so many of its inhabitants. To put this in perspective, the incarceration rate for the rest of the world per 100,000 people currently stands at 155; while for the same rate, the United States stands at 716.

Further, 1 in every 100 Americans is currently behind bars. The number of people incarcerated has risen by over 500% in the last 40 years (The Sentencing Project, 2017). Women are the fastest growing prison population. Millions of children report having a parent incarcerated, and in spite of copious amounts of neuroscience data on brain development, we continue to arrest, charge, and sentence young children as adults (Rios, 2006).

Despite the significant rates of incarceration, most people will eventually be released. However, the challenges postrelease are often insurmountable; longitudinal research indicates that most people will return to prison within three years (Langan & Levin, 2002).

The enmeshed consequences of incarceration and prisons are omnipresent throughout the social work profession (K. James & Smyth, 2014). Social justice is often described as the "organizing value," or catalyst, that drives the profession of social work. The National

Association of Social Workers' (NASW; 2008) *Code of Ethics*, as well as the curriculum policy statement of the Council on Social Work Education (CSWE), mandate that social workers and schools of social work education pay explicit attention to social and economic justice for *all* people. Yet, it is startling that critical discourse in schools of social work pertaining to mass incarceration is marginal, or in some cases completely absent (Cnaan, Draine, Frazier, & Sinha, 2008; K. A. James, 2013).

This chapter aims to provide social workers with a historical and contemporary understanding of mass incarceration in the United States. Its goal is to facilitate informed forensic social work practice and advocacy with individuals, families, and communities impacted by this destructive phenomenon.

Background and Scope of the Problem

Prison abolitionist and human rights advocate Angela Davis has long urged the United States to *radically* examine its mass incarceration problem. By radical, she asserts we must simply get to the root—it is here we will find the understanding necessary for an informed intervention. So while many scholars advance the conversation of mass incarceration by pointing to the "get tough on crime" policies and practices indicative of the 1960s and 1970s, the author believes it is important that we dig even deeper into our history.

The 13th Amendment is often hailed as the legislation that ended legalized chattel slavery in the United States. However, few people are aware that the amendment permits legalized slavery for someone convicted of a crime. The amendment declares that "Neither slavery nor involuntary servitude, except as a punishment for crime whereof the party shall have been duly convicted, shall exist within the United States, or any place subject to their jurisdiction" (U.S. Const. amend. XIV).

The southern states, desperate to replace the free labor thought lost with chattel slavery, established "Black Codes" immediately preceding the amendment. These codes essentially criminalized every facet of the Black experience post slavery. Former slaves, many homeless, penniless, and at a significant disadvantage in every sense of the word, had to again deal with a *legalized* system, specifically designed to control and exploit their labor.

Historian, sociologist, and civil rights activist W. B. Du Bois (1910) declared the Black Codes as nothing more than "neo-slavery." The codes criminalized unemployment, and barred Blacks from occupations outside of farming and servitude to Whites. They also prohibited Blacks from looking Whites in the eye, walking on the same side of the street, and even allowed Whites to incarcerate and beat Blacks for breaking what were often exploitive and oppressive contracts. The codes further prohibited Blacks from testifying against Whites in any court proceeding (Muhammad, 2011).

With little to no means of defending oneself, an arrest under the Black Codes almost certainly led to a lengthy conviction for the former slaves (Alexander, 2010). While little research exists to quantify the impact of the codes, it is safe to say that they created a boom in the prison population; at this point in U.S. history, we truly witness the genesis of mass incarceration, or "hyper incarceration" as some scholars have countered, owing to the racialized disparity of arrest and convictions.

Once convicted, former slaves were leased out for a fee through a mechanism titled the "convict leasing system." Railroads, coal mines, and of course plantations all lined up to take advantage of the relatively cheap and abundant labor. The convict leasing system became a very profitable business for prisons and the numerous industries that had historically relied on cheap slave labor. The financial incentive, coupled with the general anxiety surrounding the newly freed slaves, allowed the convict leasing system to usher in a perverse, but legalized form of neoslavery, as Dubois noted (Alexander, 2010).

Mancini's (1996) *One Dies, Get Another* exemplifies in title and content the cruel disregard the system showed toward the former slaves. There existed no oversight within the system;

individuals were often *literally* worked to death. Graveyards were often adjacent to work sites. Friedman (1993) declares the former slaves were treated worse than animals due to their abundance and ease of replacement.

Frederick Douglass (1950), in observance of the codes and convict leasing system, noted the United States' inclination to "impute crime to color." This practice would be further ideologically substantiated by the work of "social scientists"—many of whom heavily contributed to quasi-theories fostering Black inferiority at the height of chattel slavery. These practices were now enrolled to ideologically substantiate Black criminality.

A highly visible publication of the time, Hoffman's (1896) *Race Traits and Tendencies of the American Negro*, asserted that "crime, pauperism, and sexual immorality" (p. 217) were inherent tendencies of Blacks. This ideological premise, coupled with the sheer numbers of Blacks in prison, would now serve to create the imprint of Black criminality in the U.S. psyche (K. James & Smyth, 2014; Muhammad, 2011).

Alexander (2010) asserts in *The New Jim Crow* that mass incarceration is nothing more than a tool for labor exploitation and social control—specifically utilized in periods of U.S. history representing significant racial and social unrest. If that assertion is true, then the first wave of mass incarceration, or more specifically the hyper incarceration, of Blacks began with the Black Codes established during the uncertainty that preceded the 13th Amendment and Reconstruction.

The second and current wave of mass incarceration is often traced to about 1972—a mere four years from the close of the Civil Rights Movement—which was *again* a period similar to Reconstruction, representing significant racial and social unrest in America (Pratt, 2009). While the assertion may be debatable to many, what took place at the conclusion of both periods in history is well documented.

In 1972, the prison population stood at about 300,000. Today it stands at more than 2 million. One would naturally attribute this to higher crime rates, yet from 1960 to 1990, "official crime rates in Finland, Germany and the United States were close to identical. Yet the U.S. incarceration rate quadrupled, the Finnish rate fell by 60%, and the German rate was stable in that period" (Alexander, 2010).

Neo–conservative ideology of the era, very similar to ideas used to justify Black Codes and the convict leasing system, rejected any socioeconomic rationale to crime. Reagan proclaimed that "here in the richest nation in the world where more crime is committed than any other nation, we are told that the answer is to reduce poverty. This isn't the answer" (Beckett & Sasson, 2004). He went on to say that Americans had "lost patience with liberal leniency and pseudo-intellectual apologies for crime." The Bush presidency would echo a similar stance, stating, "we must raise our voices to correct an insidious tendency—the tendency to blame crime on society rather than the criminal."

The "get tough on crime" mandate became the dominant rallying cry by politicians— and any who dared to go contrary to this neo–conservative paradigm were attacked and dismissed as "being soft on crime," a label equivalent to political purgatory (Blomberg & Lucken, 2010). President Reagan officially launched the war on drugs in 1982, but many point to the passage of the New York Rockefeller Drug Laws of 1973 as its true genesis (Alexander, 2010; Pratt, 2009; Rotman, 1990).

The Rockefeller Drug Laws of 1973 legitimized the most draconian sentencing guidelines this country had witnessed. They called for a 15-year (to life) mandatory prison term for anyone convicted of selling more than two ounces of a controlled substance, or anyone possessing more than four ounces of a controlled substance (Hartnett, 2010).

By 1984, most states had mandatory prison terms for offenses ranging from drug to firearm possession (McShane & Williams, 1997). Mandatory minimums limited court and prosecutorial discretion. U.S. District Court Judge Spencer Letts was so perplexed by this loss of discretion that he verbally attacked Congress for the creation of laws which negated the court's ability to adequately weigh all the factors necessary to determine guilt or innocence (Blomberg & Lucken, 2010). Mandatory laws were then further supported through "Truth in Sentencing."

Truth in Sentencing, enacted by the federal government in 1987, ensured that individuals convicted of a criminal offense would serve at least 85% of their sentence prior to being eligible for parole/release from prison. Truth in Sentencing did away with early release from prison as a result of good behavior (Alexander, 2010). As indeterminate sentencing with the opportunity for early release was once used as the carrot on the stick to entice unwilling prisoners to participate in the rehabilitative process, federal funding would now be utilized to entice states to implement Truth in Sentencing–like laws.

The 1994 crime bill allocated more than 10 billion dollars to states who were willing to implement some form of Truth in Sentencing legislation. Federal aid to construct new state prisons was also used as an enticement; thus, by 1995 almost 30 states passed some facet of Truth in Sentencing (Dyer, 2000). "Three-strikes legislation" emerged around the same time as Truth in Sentencing. It allowed prosecutors to give a life sentence to someone convicted of a felony with two prior "serious or violent" convictions. The federal government and at least 24 states would implement some form of three-strike legislation by 1997. There would, however, be varying consensus regarding implementation. Some states regarded drug offenses as serious while others did not, and in eight states only two strikes were necessary to bring about a life sentence (Walker, 1998).

However, even with punitive approaches such as Truth in Sentencing and "mandatory minimums," most people incarcerated will eventually be released from prison. The process of incarcerated individuals returning to society has been termed *reentry*. It is estimated that almost 700,000 people are released annually; however, their transition is often short lived (K. James & Smyth, 2014).

Recidivism is often defined as rearrest and conviction for a new crime, or in some cases a parole violation, which implies that the terms set out by the Department of Parole or Probation were not adhered to. Statistics show that recidivism numbers are extremely high. In a 1994 longitudinal study, it was determined that 68% of people released from prison were arrested for a new offense within three years, with 47% being reconvicted of a new crime while on parole (Langan & Levin, 2002). Further research also concluded that individuals who were sentenced to prison versus probation tended to have higher levels of recidivism, leading the researchers to question the efficacy of prisons as a deterrent (Spohn & Holleran, 2002).

This section highlighted the historical and contemporary mechanisms that have fostered mass incarceration in the United States. The following section examines the prevalence of jails and prisons, as well as an overview of the people who inhabit them.

System and Population Overview

The Prison Policy Initiative (2016) report titled, "Mass Incarceration: The Whole Pie 2016," states that over 11 million people cycle in and out of jails each year. They further report that "The American criminal justice system holds more than 2.3 million people in 1,719 state prisons, 102 federal prisons, 942 juvenile correctional facilities, and 3,283 local jails."

Many of these facilities are often located in remote regions, lacking significant oversight, and prone to gross human rights violations. In a report following the 1971 Attica riots, arguably the most famous prison riot in U.S. history, the National Advisory Commission on Criminal Justice Standards and Goals recommended in a report that no new prison facilities be built. The Commission also strongly recommended closing all juvenile facilities. The report concluded that prisons, jails, and reformatories have all failed; and "there is overwhelming evidence that these institutions create crime rather than prevent it. Their very nature insures failure" (Miller, 2009).

Many people incarcerated in these facilities are nonviolent offenders, poor, of color, and come from communities permeated by trauma, despair, and hopelessness (K. James & Smyth, 2014). Less than half of all prisoners have completed a high-school diploma (Williford, 1994). Western and Wildeman (2009) further indicate that "By the early 2000s, more than a third of young Black non-college men were incarcerated." They also go on to state "that incredibly, 34% of all young Black male high school dropouts were in prison or jail on an average day in 2004, an incarceration rate forty times higher than the national average." Many individuals incarcerated come from poor urban communities with notoriously poor schools, where funding has continued to decrease in favor of prisons and policing (Hawkins, 2010).

Weedon (2005) reports that there are almost five times as many mentally ill people in jails than hospitals. D. J. James and Glaze (2006) estimate that as many as 64% of prisoners have a mental illness. Many of these individuals also have comorbid substance abuse challenges—often utilized as a coping mechanism in lieu of treatment. Researchers also note that there exists a bidirectional relationship between homelessness and incarceration—each increasing the risk factor of the other.

"Justice is [not] blind." More Black men are currently incarcerated than were enslaved in 1850 (Alexander, 2010). At the current pace of incarceration, it is expected that one in three Black men and one in six Hispanic men are expected to spend some time in jail or prison during their lives (Gottschalk, 2006). Federal statistics also show that the average federal sentence for Black drug offenders was 11 times higher than that of White drug offenders through 1986, but those numbers rose exponentially by 1990. The rate of Blacks convicted of drug offenses is 49% higher than their White counterparts; yet, research has shown that the usage and sale of drugs is consistent among Whites and Blacks (Alexander, 2010).

Women, specifically Black women, are at significant risk of incarceration; those incarcerated report severe histories of abuse and trauma. Zlotnick (1997) reported in one study of women in prison that 87% report being assaulted at least once, 55% report being abused as children, 53% reported being raped as adults, and almost 50% met the criteria for posttraumatic stress disorder. The rise in female incarceration also puts significant stress on already compromised families; it is reported that more than 70% of incarcerated women lived with their children as primary caretakers prior to their arrest.

There is also mounting evidence that transgender communities have been disproportionately impacted by the criminal justice system. Research indicates that transgender people have a greater likelihood of incarceration; face higher risk of "police discrimination and abuse"; and while incarcerated, they are at greater risk for sexual abuse. Reports further indicate that transgender people face significant employment discrimination, thus leading many to criminalized activities and the constant risk of incarceration (The Editorial Board, 2015)

Current Practice, Policy, and Social Movement Trends and Debates

In 2015 and 2016, President Obama released via clemency, pardons, and other legal mechanisms thousands of nonviolent drug offenders. The administration pointed to punitive sentencing policies as a rationale for their decision. Obama himself stated that this is "another step forward in upholding our ideals of justice and fairness" (Horwitz, 2015). And while the historical release of prisoners earned praise from criminal justice reformers, many urged the president to give greater examination to the root causes of mass incarceration, as well as the collateral consequences.

An example advocates point to is the release of 6,000 drug offenders in 2015—of which approximately 2,000 were targeted for deportation. So while there is a recognition from the administration that justice policies and practices with historical racial bias are in many ways responsible for their arrest, conviction, and sentence, there exists a dissonance in recognizing that those same factors are also now responsible for their deportation.

The "Nix 96" coalition is made up of immigration and criminal justice reform advocates who argue that criminal justice and immigration policies are intrinsically linked—with the former feeding the latter. And thus for any reform to be truly effective, it must also examine and correct the collateral consequences (i.e., detention and deportation, education, employment and housing discrimination) faced by people postrelease.

Core Roles and Functions of Forensic Social Work in This System

In one of the darkest periods in U.S. prison history, a period marked by unparalleled prison riots, culminating in the San Quentin Massacre and the Attica riots, the brotherhood of Attica demanded to have "social workers" in their struggle for justice (J. James, 2005). Of all helping professionals, they identified social workers.

Social workers have a long history working directly and indirectly with justice-involved populations. Social workers provide clinical services for people in prisons, jails, and varied treatment services. Social workers also work with children and families impacted by mass incarceration. Further, social workers are very involved in policy and advocacy to change racial and oppressive laws.

The NASW has even released a policy statement illustrating the impact of mass incarceration while calling for the "increased use of forensic social workers to provide culturally competent treatment and intervention for the growing population of incarcerated individuals."

Relevant Theories or Framework

Cognitive behavioral theory (CBT) is often hailed as the paragon of evidence-based practices. CBT has its roots in behavioral and cognitive theory. It is a series of "interventions based on a common theory about the connection between our thoughts, attitudes and beliefs—cognitions—and our behavior" (Feucht & Holt, 2016). It posits that maladaptive thoughts, beliefs, and behaviors can be altered by fostering self-awareness through the utilization of individual and/or group therapy, and by further providing the strategies and tools to make healthier decisions.

The National Institute of Justice (NIJ) created crimesolutions.gov as a clearinghouse for best practices with justice populations. A recent meta-analysis examining 50 CBT-rated programs by crimesolutions.gov found that "CBT programs that have been rigorously evaluated are effective at deterring crime, assisting victims and preventing recidivism" (Feucht & Holt, 2016).

The programs included in the meta-analysis provided services to adults, juveniles, or both. The research indicated that CBT appeared to be more effective with juvenile offenders. The researchers attribute the discrepancy to the belief that adults are hardwired with "deeply rooted maladaptive cognitive processes that may be more difficult to change."

Relevant Ethical, Legal, and Policy Issues

On August 18, 2016, Deputy Attorney General Sally Yates issued a memorandum instructing the federal government to reduce, and ultimately end, the utilization of private prisons. She cited an "800" percent hike in federal prison populations from 1980 to 2013 as a rationale for their initial utilization, but noted that criminal justice reform from arrest, sentencing policy, clemency initiatives, as well as the "smart on crime" initiative, have resulted in a drastic drop in federal prison populations. The deputy attorney general also noted that private prisons "simply do not provide the same level of correctional services, programs, and resources . . ."—factors she noted were "essential to reducing recidivism and improving public safety."

Many criminal justice reformers hailed the move as significant, but pointed out that the memorandum only applies to less than 23,000 people (the number of federal prisoners in private prisons). The executive director of the Sentencing Project, Marc Mauer, thought that the move, while lacking the practicality many reformers crave, should be seen as "symbolic" toward an "evolving climate on criminal justice reform."

Relevant Assessment, Prevention, and Intervention Strategies

Restorative justice (RJ) is often hailed as a prevention, and/or intervention, in justice settings. RJ practitioners work with harmed communities, law enforcement, and the court system to identify and institutionalize practices that benefit all parties. RJ has specifically been utilized with great results in public school settings, which have seen significant rates of suspensions and expulsions due to zero-tolerance policies.

High levels of suspensions have seen schools become feeders not for college, but for the juvenile and adult criminal justice systems. This phenomenon has been titled *the school to prison pipeline*; its impact can be felt predominantly among poor students of color. Research has demonstrated the effectiveness of restorative justice in both juvenile justice and school settings.

RJ is grounded in cultivating relationships that allow voice to be given to the harmed, as well as the person who caused the harm. RJ also works to stigmatize "the act, rather than the offender" (Braithwaite, 1989). It is through these processes that mutual understanding is cultivated—leading to personal reflection and accountability necessary for restoration/reparation. It is through this process that RJ practitioners argue that we can take a dignified stance toward harm that truly allows for justice, and not just punishment.

RJ is further supported by empirical data. One school in Oakland, California, found that by implementing a RJ approach, suspensions dropped by 87%, and expulsions to zero. A West Philadelphia High School reported an over 50% reduction in suspensions, combined with a 52% decrease in acts of violence committed within the school (Schiff, 2013).

Research on the utilization of RJ programming for juvenile offenders also found it to be effective in reducing recidivism, and in general far more effective than the traditional juvenile court process (Bergseth & Bouffard, 2012).

Forensic Practice Skill Set

Karl Menninger (1968) famously criticized what he deemed the "cold war between lawyers and psychiatrists" in lamenting the criminalization of people plagued by mental health challenges. Social workers in forensic settings are often faced with a similar burden. They are often working under a system whose main priority is punishment and control, often reducing mitigating factors such as mental health, poverty, economics, and various other social determinants of behavior in favor of a paradigm that trumps individual behavior.

Social workers are trained to meet "people where they are at"—meaning a holistic examination of the individual, inclusive of *all* relevant mitigating factors, in weighing an intervention. This social work value is often in contradiction to the American ideal of meritocracy, which assumes that opportunity is indeed equal, and success, or the lack thereof, can be simply reduced to a choice.

Case Example and Application

A 21-year-old client, Eric (not real name), is assigned a social worker by his public defender. Eric was charged and convicted of an assault when he was 18 years old and spent two-and-a-half years in an upstate correctional facility where he did not engage with any reentry supports. He is currently charged with a quadruple attempted murder. He is alleged to have entered a home with a gun and shot two women while two toddlers were present. One woman was paralyzed from the gunshot and the other made a full physical recovery. The children were not physically harmed but witnessed the entire incident.

The social worker was tasked with uncovering Eric's family and social history to try and elicit a more favorable plea offer from the prosecutor. Through the investigation, it was revealed that Eric's mother had a problematic pregnancy and birth. Eric was her 13th child. His mother was diagnosed with preeclampsia and she had pneumonia during her third trimester. She went into early labor and suffered several complications during delivery, one of which restricted Eric's oxygen supply. Eric's mother could tell from an early age that her son was not developing in the same way as her other children; he was slow in attaining developmental milestones. It was revealed when Eric was a toddler that he suffered high levels of lead in his blood, likely due to lead poisoning in utero or during his youngest years.

(continued)

Case Example and Application (*continued*)

As he grew older, he continued to have a very low IQ according to his special education records; he also dropped out of school in middle school. Eric cannot read or write.

The task of the social worker in this case is to present the information not as an excuse for Eric's actions, or negate the harm inflicted, but rather to give context to Eric and his actions to thus determine an appropriate outcome.

Conclusion

From Michelle Alexander's *The New Jim Crow* to Ava DuVernay's powerful documentary "13," it is clear that the United States has intentionally facilitated a perverse form of neoslavery under the facade of criminal justice. It is thus imperative that the social work profession, with its organizing value of social justice, become a preeminent voice of opposition to mass incarceration; however, for that to occur, the social work profession must be willing to engage in critical dialogue with impacted people. We must also radically assess the impact of capitalism, racism, sexism, and countless other traumas within the academy, within organizations, within society, and within ourselves. It is through this dialogue, this reflection, that we can reach the roots of injustice, and it is by reaching the roots that we can truly begin to utilize that knowledge to inform our education, our practice, and our advocacy to end systems that perpetuate mass incarceration. But maybe even more fundamentally, we must use this knowledge to hold the United States accountable for her promise: the promise of justice and democracy for all people irrespective to race, religion, class, or creed.

CHAPTER EXERCISES

Exercise 1. With the rates of incarceration in the United States being so high, your likelihood as a future social worker to work with justice-involved individuals or impacted populations is extremely high. How prepared are you? Discuss three ways in which this chapter has helped, and three ways in which you can further prepare yourself. What (if any) socially learned biases about this population do you have? What are some ways in which you can address them? On a clinical level, how can you best balance treatment modalities focused on behavioral change, while still acknowledging, and factoring for, racial, social, economic, and the various other discrimination this population often faces?

Exercise 2. On a policy level, many activists are debating the merits of prison reform versus prison abolition. Examine current trends in these areas, and list three pros and cons for each. What do you feel is necessary for reform to be successful? What is necessary for prisons to be abolished? What are alternate ways of addressing crime/harm that can be instituted? Are there international models you can highlight?

Additional Resources

Crime Solutions: www.crimesolutions.gov

Bureau of Justice Statistics: www.bjs.gov

The Marshall Project: www.themarshallproject.org/#.SkBztcYJn

References

Alexander, M. (2010). *The new Jim Crow: Mass incarceration in the age of colorblindness.* New York, NY: New Press.

Beckett, K., & Sasson, T. (2004). *The politics of injustice: Crime and punishment in America* (2nd ed.). Thousand Oaks, CA: Sage.

Bergseth, K. J., & Bouffard, J. A. (2012). Examining the effectiveness of a restorative justice program for various types of juvenile offenders. *International Journal of Offender Therapy and Comparative Criminology, 57*(9), 1054–1075. doi:10.1177/0306624x12453551

Blomberg, T. G., & Lucken, K. (2010). *American penology.* New Brunswick, NJ: Aldine Transaction, Transaction.

Braithwaite, J. (1989). *Crime, shame and reintegration.* Cambridge, UK: Cambridge University Press.

Cnaan, R. A., Draine, J., Frazier, B., & Sinha, J. W. (2008). Ex-prisoners' re-entry: An emerging frontier and a social work challenge. *Journal of Policy Practice, 7*(23), 178–198.

Douglass, F. (1950). *The life and writings of Frederick Douglass.* P. S. Foner (Ed.). New York, NY: International Publishers.

Du Bois, W. B. (1910). Reconstruction and its benefits. *The American Historical Review,* 781–799.

Dyer, J. (2000). *The perpetual prisoner machine: How America profits from crime.* Boulder, CO: Westview Press.

The Editorial Board. (2015, November 5). Prisons and jails put transgender inmates at risk. *The New York Times.* Retrieved from https://www.nytimes.com/2015/11/09/opinion/prisons-and-jails -put-transgender-inmates-at-risk.html?_r=0

Feucht, T., & Holt, T. (2016). Does cognitive behavioral therapy work in criminal justice? A new analysis from crimesolutions.gov. Retrieved from http://nij.gov/journals/277/Pages/crimesolutions-cbt .aspx

Friedman, L. M. (1993). *Crime and punishment in American history.* New York, NY: Basic Books.

Gottschalk, M. (2006). *The prison and the gallows: The politics of mass incarceration in America.* Cambridge, UK: Cambridge University Press.

Hartnett, S. J. (Ed.). (2010). *Challenging the prison-industrial complex: Activism, arts, and educational alternatives.* Urbana: University of Illinois Press.

Hawkins, S. (2010). Education vs. incarceration. Retrieved from http://prospect.org/article/education -vs-incarceration

Hoffman, F. L. (1896). *Race traits and tendencies of the American Negro.* New York, NY: Macmillan.

Horwitz, S. (2015, December 18). President Obama commutes sentences of 95 federal drug offenders. *The Washington Post.* Retrieved from https://www.washingtonpost.com/world/national-security/ president-obama-commutes-sentences-of-about-100-drug-offenders/2015/12/18/9b62c91c-a5a3 -11e5-9c4e-be37f66848bb_story.html?utm_term=.de4b5d8e5af1

James, D. J., & Glaze, L. E. (2006). Mental health problems of prison and jail inmates. Retrieved from http://www.bjs.gov/content/pub/pdf/mhppji.pdf

James, J. (2005). *The new abolitionists: (Neo) slave narratives and contemporary prison writings.* Albany: State University of New York Press.

James, K., & Smyth, J. (2014). Deconstructing mass incarceration in the United States through a human rights lens: Implications of social work education and practice. In M. Bethold, L. Healey, K. Libal, & R. Thomas (Eds.), *Advancing human rights in social work education.* Alexandria, VA: CSWE Press.

James, K. A. (2013). *The invisible epidemic: Educating social work students towards holistic practice in a period of mass incarceration* (Doctoral Dissertation). Retrieved from http://repository .upenn.edu/cgi/viewcontent.cgi?article=1039&context=edissertations_sp2&sei-redir =1&referer=http%3A%2F%2Fwww.bing.com%2Fsearch%3Fq%3Dkirk%2Bjames%2Bthe%2Binvis ible%2Bepidemic%26src%3DIE-TopResult%26FORM%3DIETR02%26conversationid%3D#search= %22kirk%20james%20invisible%20epidemic%22

Langan, P. A., & Levin, D. J. (2002). Recidivism of prisoners released in 1994. *Federal Sentencing Reporter*, *15*(1), 58–65.

Mancini, M. (1996). *One dies, get another: Convict leasing in the American South, 1866–1928*. Columbia: University of South Carolina Press.

McShane, M., & Williams, F. P. (1997). *Drug use and drug policy*. New York, NY: Garland.

Menninger, K. (1968). *The crime of punishment*. New York, NY: Viking.

Miller, J. M. (Ed.). (2009). *21st century criminology: A reference handbook* (1st ed.). Thousand Oaks, CA: Sage.

Muhammad, K. G. (2011). *The condemnation of blackness: Race, crime, and the making of modern urban America*. Cambridge, MA: Harvard University Press.

National Association of Social Workers. (2008). *Code of ethics of the National Association of Social Workers*. Washington, DC: Author.

Pratt, T. C. (2009). *Addicted to incarceration: Corrections policy and the politics of misinformation in the United States*. Los Angeles, CA: Sage.

Prison Policy Initiative. (2016). Mass incarceration: The whole pie 2016. Retrieved from http://www .prisonpolicy.org/reports/pie2016.html

Rios, V. M. (2006). The hyper-criminalization of Black and Latino male youth in the era of mass incarceration. *Souls, 8*(2), 40–54.

Rotman, E. (1990). *Beyond punishment: A new view on the rehabilitation of criminal offenders*. New York, NY: Greenwood.

Schiff, M. (2013). *Dignity, disparity and desistance: Effective restorative justice strategies to plug the "school-to-prison pipeline."* Paper presented at the Center for Civil Rights Remedies National Conference. Closing the School to Research Gap: Research to Remedies Conference, Washington, DC.

Spohn, C., & Holleran, D. (2002). The effect of imprisonment on recidivism rates of felony offenders: A focus on drug offenders. *Criminology, 40*(2), 329–358.

The Sentencing Project. (2017). Issues. Incarceration. Retrieved from http://www.sentencingproject .org/issues/incarceration

Walker, S. (1998). *Sense and nonsense about crime and drugs: A policy guide* (4th ed.). Belmont, CA: West/ Wadsworth.

Weedon, J. R. (2005). The incarceration of the mentally ill. *Corrections Today, 67*(1), 16–20.

Western, B., & Wildeman, C. (2009). The Black family and mass incarceration. *The Annals of the American Academy of Political and Social Science, 621*(1), 221–242.

Williford, M. (1994). Higher education in prison: A contradiction in terms? *American Council on Education Series on Higher Education*. Phoenix, AZ: Oryx Press.

Zlotnick, C. (1997). Posttraumatic stress disorder (PTSD), PTSD comorbidity, and childhood abuse among incarcerated women. *The Journal of Nervous and Mental Disease, 185*(12), 761–763.

VOICES FROM THE FIELD

Julie Smyth, LMSW
Adolescent Defense Project Social Worker
The Bronx Defenders

Agency Setting

The Bronx Defenders is a community-based, multiservice organization dedicated to addressing the underlying problems of poverty in the Bronx. Our staff of 265 provides approximately 35,000 low-income residents of the Bronx with comprehensive legal services, social services, and community programs each year. Our holistic model of representation brings criminal defense attorneys, family defense attorneys, civil attorneys, social workers, civil legal advocates, parent advocates, investigators, community organizers, and support staff together under one roof to efficiently and quickly address the intersecting issues and challenges faced by individual clients. Housed within our criminal defense practice, our Adolescent Defense Project (ADP) provides specialized representation to our youngest clients: 14-, 15-, and 16-year-olds who are being prosecuted as adults. Clients in this age group face unique challenges, including homelessness, family instability, mental health issues, drug addiction, and lack of appropriate educational services. The ADP consists of three criminal defense attorneys and an experienced social worker who works with our adolescent clients to navigate those challenges and resolve their cases without a criminal record and by finding community-based alternatives to incarceration.

Practice Responsibilities

As the social worker in The Bronx Defenders' ADP, I work collaboratively on an interdisciplinary team of advocates working to provide high-quality, holistic representation to youth accused of crimes in Bronx County. Strategizing with attorneys and other advocates, I work with clients to address both the circumstances driving them into the criminal justice system as well as the devastating consequences of that involvement. In my role, I build rapport with both clients and family members through consistent meetings in a variety of settings, including the courthouse, our community-based office, and visits to homes, jails, and juvenile detention facilities. I work with attorneys to ensure my clients understand court procedures and the legal issues they face. I advocate on the record in court and write comprehensive "prepleading investigations" for adolescent clients, which require comprehensive interviews with collateral contacts and examination of medical and treatment records. These reports are submitted to judges and prosecutors with the goal of humanizing my client's story and making a compelling argument for why a reduced or nonincarceratory sentence is appropriate and serves the purpose of justice.

Expertise Required

This job requires a Masters in Social Work (MSW) degree from an accredited graduate school of social work and a license to practice social work. A social worker in this role must use a strengths-based approach and have experience with adolescent clients who have histories of trauma, mental health issues, and habitual absence from school. Most importantly, this role requires that you are a true advocate, meaning that no matter the charges or allegations against your client you fight for the best case outcome.

Ethical, Legal, Practice, Diversity, and/or Advocacy Issues Addressed

One of the ethical challenges involved in my work is the issue of client confidentiality from parent(s). My responsibility is to the adolescent, not the parent(s), so even if my client is under 18 years old, I only share details of the case with a parent or guardian if my client gives me explicit permission to do so. The criminal justice system is the only place where the parent does not have overt access to information regarding his or her child. While this practice of attorney–client privilege may frustrate a parent, it is a critical component of our practice to protect the rights of our clients and advocate on their behalf.

Interprofessional and Intersectoral Collaboration

At The Bronx Defenders, social workers collaborate daily with public defenders and other advocates and liaise with staff at local jails and various community-based organizations, including alternative-to-incarceration programs. Adolescents in the criminal justice system are often at the intersection of various other systems, such as child protective services, foster care agencies, and schools. One of my priorities is to connect adolescent clients to any services that will help them achieve their goals in life and also assist in resolving their legal matters in a favorable way. To that end, I introduce them to after-school programs, mental health providers, and youth programming that can provide them with empowering experiences. A social worker entrusted with advocating for an adolescent involved in the criminal justice system cannot afford to work in a silo. It is essential that the person in this role be committed to engaging the various systems in a youth's ecological framework in order to truly understand the client's perspective and represent her or his best interests.

CHAPTER 16

Adult Protective Services at the Intersection of Aging and Disability

Joy Swanson Ernst
Patricia Brownell
Tina Maschi

CHAPTER OBJECTIVES

The major objectives of this chapter are to:

- Describe how Adult Protective Services responds to and intervenes in the abuse, neglect, and exploitation of vulnerable older adults and disabled adults.
- Articulate policy issues connected to elder justice.
- Explore human rights issues related to elder abuse, aging, and disabilities, particularly how to balance rights to self-determination and safety when working with abused, neglected, and exploited older adults.

CHAPTER COMPETENCIES HIGHLIGHTED

- Competency 3: Advance Human Rights and Social, Economic, and Environmental Justice
- Competency 5: Engage in Policy Practice

This chapter focuses on the role that Adult Protective Services (APS) and related service systems play in protecting vulnerable older adults and adults with disabilities from abuse, neglect, and exploitation. While the nature and scope of services provided by APS vary by state and locality, APS is the first responder to vulnerable adult abuse in most states. With a growing population of older adults, the need for APS is expected to increase in the 21st century. This chapter provides information to increase understanding of this vital practice area.

Social workers who work with older and disabled adults who are vulnerable due to their frailty, physical disabilities, cognitive impairment, mental disorders, and developmental disabilities must develop knowledge and skills needed to effectively work with APS and other entities that respond to and intervene in cases of abuse, neglect, and exploitation. They must be aware of the continuum of services available, the limitations of those services, and ways to build a more effective response to abuse and exploitation. Working with this vulnerable population requires an awareness of the risk for abuse and ways to respond that balance the need for safety and protection with the adult's freedom to choose how and with whom to live.

Background and Scope of the Problem

APS is the social service system that serves older adults and adults with disabilities who need services and support because they are at risk of being abused, neglected, or exploited. In all states, APS responds to and investigates reports of abuse, neglect, and exploitation. Using a philosophy that maximizes client self-determination, APS works with adults who need care, protection, supervision, and assistance with accessing community services and supports.

Elder justice involves efforts to prevent, identify, and respond to elder abuse (U.S. Government Accountability Office, 2013). *Elder abuse* refers to physical, psychological, and sexual abuse, neglect, and financial exploitation. What distinguishes elder abuse from other sorts of crime committed against elders is the presence of a trust relationship, such as that with a family member, paid caregiver, or family lawyer. Evidence from epidemiological studies conducted within the past 10 years suggests that 1 in 10 older adults experiences elder abuse each year (Lachs & Pillemer, 2015).

Self-neglect occurs when older persons, due to their physical or mental incapacity, engage in behavior that puts them at risk for substantial physical, psychological, or emotional harm. Although many researchers and policy makers do not consider self-neglect to be a form of elder abuse, it is subject to mandatory reporting in most states and accounts for a substantial proportion of the cases handled by APS (Teaster et al., 2006).

Most recently, APS agencies have noted the increase in financial exploitation of older adults, which harms them through misappropriation of their money or property and leaves them vulnerable to poor care and diminished resources in their later years. It is very difficult to recover assets lost due to financial exploitation even if the case is pursued by APS or law enforcement. Many states now have laws that mandate that employees of financial institutions report suspected financial exploitation of older or vulnerable adults.

The United States has the most developed APS system for vulnerable disabled and older adults in the world. As a result, prevalence data on abuse of disabled adults internationally is limited and available data come from the United States. While existing studies suggest that the rate of abuse of women with disabilities is similar or higher compared to the general population, there continues to be a lack of attention to this issue. Women with disabilities are at particularly high risk of abuse both through typical forms of violence (physical, sexual, and emotional) and those that target the disability (Plummer & Findley, 2012). In one study using a multiethnic sample of 511 women ages 18 to 64 years, a 9.8% prevalence of abuse was found during the past 12 months (McFarlane et al., 2001). Men with disabilities have been found to experience higher rates of intimate partner violence (IPV) than either women with disabilities or men without disabilities. Results of a retrospective descriptive study found an IPV prevalence rate of 66.2%, with 77.7% describing physical abuse as the most serious type of abuse perpetrated (Ballan, Freyer, & Powledge, 2015).

The salient human rights issues raised in the system include the right to live free of abuse, neglect, and exploitation; the right to self-determination; and the ability to fully participate in one's community and to live in the least restrictive environment. Elder abuse, like any other type of abuse, is a violation of human rights and a "significant cause of illness, injury, loss of productivity, isolation, and despair" (World Health Organization, 2008). Article 16 of the Convention on the Rights of Persons With Disabilities addresses rights to live in freedom from exploitation, violence, and abuse and requires the promotion of recovery, rehabilitation, and social integration of persons with disabilities in a number of ways including "through provision of protection services." The United Nations Principles for Older Persons include principles for care that call for "access to social and legal services that enhance autonomy, protection, and care" and the ability to enjoy human rights and fundamental freedoms when residing in care and treatment facilities. These principles were recognized in the establishment of APS in the United States.

A recommendation to establish protective services for adults came out of the 1961 White House Conference on Aging (WHCoA) and the Administration on Aging funded several demonstration projects in the early 1960s. From the beginning, principles of self-determination and the inherent tensions in providing protective services, including the tension between considering a person's physical and mental health status along with the right of competent people to live as they choose, were noted (Lehmann & Mathiasen, 1963).

The widespread development of APS took place after Title XX of the Social Security Amendment, passed in 1974, gave states permission to use the funds for protective services for adults as well as children (Otto, 2000). With no national direction to follow, states developed their own systems with different laws and definitions of mistreatment. Most states fund APS agencies through federal Social Services Block Grants and state discretionary funds. Distribution and application of these funds varies widely by state and individual programs, creating marked discrepancies in services (Teaster, Wangmo &, Anetzberger, 2010).

Elder abuse as a social problem garnered public attention on the national level in the late 1970s when members of Congress sponsored hearings and issued reports (Wolf, 2003). Senator Claude Pepper of Florida sponsored legislation that eventually established the National Center on Elder Abuse through an amendment to the Older Americans Act. The concern on the part of Congress sparked new interest in APS as a response to elder abuse, but no dedicated federal funds were forthcoming (Otto, 2000). Bipartisan support for the elder justice cause led to the introduction of the Elder Justice Act (EJA) in 2002, which passed in 2009 as part of the Affordable Care Act. The EJA authorized the first dedicated federal funds for APS, but to date, the provisions of the act have never been fully funded. However, several of the programs and provisions of the EJA have been advanced through other means, as discussed further subsequently.

System and Population Overview

APS is an important component in a comprehensive and multidisciplinary service system for older adults and adults with disabilities that ideally will allow people to live as they choose in the least restrictive environment free from the threat of abuse, neglect, or financial exploitation. State statutes, which vary in their definition of who is eligible for APS programs, sanction and guide the delivery of adult protective services. Each state statute allows for investigation of physical abuse and financial exploitation and most include sexual abuse and neglect. Over half of the states also mandate the investigation of reports of self-neglect (Brandl et al., 2006). Currently, most state APS systems are challenged by lack of sufficient funds and challenges related to the complexity of cases and the absence of adequate support systems.

All states except New York have mandatory reporting laws for abuse of older adults living in the community that are based on the premise that vulnerable older and disabled adults need protection by the state if they are being harmed by others, are unable to care for themselves, are unwilling to accept services, and meet some predetermined criteria for diminished capacity to make informed decisions on their own behalf. Most APS programs use intervention models such as case management, crisis intervention, and guardianships and other involuntary services, including removal to a hospital or skilled nursing facility. APS workers are guided by core values that include these beliefs: (a) Adults have a right to safety; (b) adults retain their civil and constitutional rights unless those rights have been restricted by court action; (c) adults have the right to make decisions that fall outside social norms unless those decisions harm others; (d) adults have presumed to have the capacity to make decisions unless a court has deemed otherwise; and (e) adults can refuse services (Brandl et al., 2006).

The APS system serves people whose social identity, past history, and/or current situation make working within the system especially challenging. APS clients are often in poor health, and APS workers must become familiar with the ways in which poor health status adds to risk. As they age, many people experience various "geriatric syndromes," which are common health conditions such as frailty, pressure ulcers, falls, incontinence, delirium, and declining functional status that have multiple causes and involve multiple organ systems and affect quality of life and disability status (Inouye, Studenski, Tinetti, & Kuchel, 2007). Many APS clients have Alzheimer's disease or other dementias, which creates vulnerability for all forms of elder abuse. Individuals who are receiving home-based hospice or palliative care are also vulnerable because hospice professionals do not always recognize or report abuse and neglect that they observe (Jayawardena & Liao, 2006).

Studies have revealed how experiencing financial exploitation may differ by racial group or immigration status. Older African American elders are more likely to be victims of financial abuse than other older adults (Beach, Schulz, Castle, & Rosen, 2010). A study compared how elderly Korean immigrants and American-born older adults of Korean origin characterized a vignette depicting financial exploitation. While most identified the situation as abusive, American-born Korean Americans were more likely to express willingness to seek help while Asian-born immigrants were more likely to tolerate or characterize the problem and its resolution as a family matter (Lee & Eaton, 2009).

The majority of cases of elder abuse are not reported (Lifespan of Greater Rochester Inc., Weill Cornell Medical School of Cornell University, & New York City Department for the Aging, 2011). Many older adults fear the involvement of APS or legal authorities. An example of underreported mistreatment in one ethnic group comes from a study of the prevalence of abuse and neglect among non–cognitively impaired Spanish-speaking Latinos in Los Angeles. The data were collected by *promotores*, or Latino health workers, who are not mandated reporters in California. Findings revealed that 40.4% of the sample of 198 were abused, neglected, or financially exploited, with 22.7% experiencing severe abuse. Two percent reported the abuse to APS (DeLiema, Gassoumis, Homeier, & Wilber, 2012).

In a number of UN documents, older women are identified as especially vulnerable to human rights abuses related to neglect, abuse, and violence. These include the Madrid 2002 International Plan of Action on Ageing (United Nations, 2003); the Convention for the Elimination of All Forms of Discrimination Against Women General Recommendation (CEDAW) No. 27 (Committee on the Elimination of All Forms of Discrimination Against Women, 2010); United Nations Principles of Older Persons (United Nations, 1991); and Discussion Paper and Follow-Up to the Expert Group Meeting (EGM) on the Department of Economic and Social Affairs (DESA) on Neglect, Abuse, and Violence Against Older Women (Department of Economic and Social Affairs, 2013). The human rights perspective includes the concept of older people, including older women, as rights holders and requires that enabling environments must be created for rights holders (Martin, Rodríguez-Pinzón, & Brown, 2015).

Older people, whether actively contributing to families, communities, and society, or limited by cognitive and physical impairments, have the right to live in homes, communities, and societies in which their inherent individual worth is recognized and their needs respected. In the human rights framework, governments are duty bearers, and have the responsibility for ensuring that older people's rights are observed. In this frame, older people are not simply victims and recipients of charity; rather, they are fully entitled to the rights and privileges we all expect (United Nations, 1991).

The overarching theme of the Second World Assembly on Ageing, held in Madrid, Spain, in 2002, was active aging. Recommendations for action are organized around three priority directions: older people and development; advancing health and well-being into old age; and ensuring enabling and supportive environments. Priority area three (enabling environments) addresses elder neglect, abuse, and violence. It states "older women face greater risk of physical and psychological abuse due to discriminatory social attitudes and nonrealization of the human rights of women" (p. 43) and addresses cumulative disadvantages for women in society and harmful stereotypes. "Women's poverty is directly related to absence of economic opportunity and autonomy" (p. 43) and "older women are particularly affected by misleading and negative stereotypes" (p. 44). Remedies include "minimizing the risks to older women of all forms of neglect, abuse, and violence through public awareness and protections; promote positive image of older women" (p. 45), and ending discriminatory laws and practices against older women that continue to fuel violence and abuse. These include witchcraft accusations and harmful practices involving widows, including financial abuse of denying rights to inheritance and property (United Nations, 2003).

On December 16, 2010, the United Nations General Assembly ratified the CEDAW No. 27 on older women and protection of their human rights. While nonbinding, this recommendation states the following:

> States parties have an obligation to draft legislation recognizing and prohibiting violence, including domestic, sexual violence and violence in institutional settings, against older women including those with disabilities. States parties have an obligation to investigate, prosecute and punish all acts of violence against older women, including those committed as a result of traditional practices and witchcraft. (Committee on the Elimination of All Forms of Discrimination Against Women, 2010)

The EGM on DESA, held at the United Nations in 2013 to address a normative gap in human rights protection of violence against older women, further recommended ending the exclusion of women age 60 years and older from studies on women and violence based on ageist assumptions that older women do not experience domestic violence or sexual abuse, do not remember abuse due to age-specific cognitive limitations, and refuse to disclose or dwell on unpleasant memories. A key recommendation was that disaggregated data by gender and age must be captured and reported for indicators on violence by all nations. It noted that older women experience aging differently than men, and that the full development and advancement of women cannot be achieved without taking a life cycle approach (DESA, 2013).

Also at the national and international level is another often overlooked group of elder abuse victims, which are older people in prison. However, there are not many empirical studies documenting this abuse among elders in prison. However, there is at least one study by Maschi, Viola, and Koskinen (2015) of 677 adults aged 50 years and older. This study found that over half of the older participants reported some type of abuse, such as sexual or physical assault and medical neglect. Older participants reported that these forms of abuse were complicated by other forms of stressors, such as separation from family and witnessing daily violence, bullying, and harassment in prison. Despite these forms of abuse, the elder justice community has yet to fully embrace this vulnerable population as deserving of protection. Therefore, more advocacy for older people in prison is warranted, including the development or improvement of prison ombudsman programs.

Current Practice, Policy, and Social Movement Trends and Debates

Efforts have been made to increase the coordination of elder justice activities, including APS, from the federal government in conjunction with national practice, research, and advocacy organizations and individual advocates and scholars from multiple professional and scholarly disciplines. For example the U.S. Department of Justice (DOJ) has funded and overseen research activities related to the criminalization and victimization sides of elder abuse. The Administration for Community Living (ACL) in the Department of Health and Human Services (DHHS) funds a number of elder abuse prevention and intervention activities, including efforts related to APS. The DOJ and DHHS funded development of the Elder Justice Roadmap (Connolly, Brandl, & Breckman, 2014). The roadmap is the distillation of the priorities of 750 practitioners, policy makers, researchers, and advocates on solutions and areas for action in elder justice (Connolly et al., 2014).

The 2015 WHCoA included elder justice as a focus and helped bring national attention to elder justice issues, particularly the frightening rise of financial exploitation among older adults. The WHCoA final report detailed several efforts by federal agencies to prevent elder abuse and support victims. For example, these efforts include new advice from the Consumer Financial Protection Bureau to help financial institutions develop procedures to recognize, prevent, and report elder abuse and development of guidelines for state APS agencies (White House Conference on Aging, 2015).

The EJA, which represents Congress's first attempt at comprehensive legislation to address abuse, neglect, and exploitation of the elderly at the federal level, focuses on providing a coordinated federal response through various public health and social service approaches to the prevention, detection, and treatment of elder abuse. The major provisions of the EJA include national coordination of elder justice research and activities; programs to promote elder justice, which includes APS; and enhanced efforts to protect residents of long-term care facilities (Colello, 2014). The EJA established the Elder Justice Coordinating Council (EJCC), which includes representatives from all the federal agencies and offices that address abuse, neglect, and exploitation. The EJCC submits a report to Congress every two years in which federal departments and agencies describe processes on elder justice-related activities. For example, the Social Security Administration, which administers Social Security benefits, has increased efforts—through increased training and the representative payee program, which provides financial management of benefits for older adults who cannot manage for themselves—to ensure that older Americans are not defrauded out of their benefits.

While the lack of funds for the EJA and the difficulty of passing new legislation have been frustrating for advocates, efforts and leadership at the federal level have brought increased attention to the needs of abused and neglected elders. Kathy Greenlee, the Assistant Secretary for Aging under President Obama, used the influence of her position to increase attention to elder justice-related issues. She oversaw the development of demonstration grants to test new approaches to identify, intervene, and prevent elder abuse in the hopes that successful programs will be replicated and expanded (Administration for Community Living, 2016).

Currently, there is no national database of APS clients and there are no national standards for APS programs. The National Adult Maltreatment Reporting System that is under development will collect data from states to help build a national picture of APS clients, services, and problems addressed. Starting in 2015, the ACL directed an effort that calls upon the expertise of state and local APS agencies, elder justice advocates, and researchers to develop voluntary guidelines for state APS agencies that will guide them in delivering the most effective services possible.

World Elder Abuse Awareness Day (WEAAD) became a UN Day in December 2010, when the UN General Assembly voted to add WEAAD to the UN Calendar of special days. June 15 is the designated day to reflect on the neglect, abuse, and violence experienced by older people as a human rights violation.

Core Roles and Functions of Forensic Social Work in This System

Social workers have a number of roles in the APS system. While educational requirements for the APS workers may vary from state to state, many APS agencies require workers to have a social work degree (either Bachelors in Social Work [BSW] or Masters in Social Work [MSW]) and social work skills; knowledge and values contribute or are a good fit for the work of APS investigation, assessment, and service provision. Both APS and the NASW *Code of Ethics* share the value of honoring client self-determination, which focuses on putting a client in the least restrictive environment. The skills needed by APS workers include the ability to develop and use the worker–client relationship as a means of achieving intervention goals. The person-in-environment orientation of the social worker allows the social worker to appreciate multiple competing factors that have an impact on the older person. In addition, the social work knowledge base includes knowledge related to aging and disabilities, the impact of multiple dimensions of diversity, relevant laws and social policies, and the range of formal and informal supports and services available in the community. Given the complexities of problems addressed, work in APS requires knowledge of aging, disabilities, assessment of client capacity, family dynamics, and community resources that can address a range of needs ranging from mental health to victims' services to housing conditions and other environmental adjustments.

The core activities of APS are intake, investigation, needs/risk assessment, findings, service planning and monitoring, case closure, and documentation. The intake involves screening all reports for safety and risk factors in order to determine the initial response (screening out, emergency response, reporting to law enforcement, investigation, or referral). APS workers often make unannounced home visits. They examine all components of the situation including talking with the victim, the alleged abuser, and all collateral contacts; they also review relevant documentation such as bank records (for allegations of financial exploitation) or medical records. Often during the investigation phase, the APS worker determines that law enforcement or regulatory agencies (an option that is there in any phase of the process) must be contacted. APS workers determine if a specialized capacity assessment to determine how much the older adult understands about what is going on is warranted. The APS worker also assesses the vulnerable adult. This assessment looks at personal health and functional ability, the person's mental health status and capacity to understand his or her situation, the extent of formal and informal supports and caregiver's needs, and health and safety issues in the environment. The worker also examines the financial situation (National Adult Protective Services Association, 2013).

After the investigation is complete, the APS worker, upon consulting with supervisors and colleagues, determines whether or not abuse (physical or sexual), neglect, self-neglect, and/or financial exploitation have occurred. Then the worker develops a plan to address the identified risks and needs of the client and offers these services, keeping in mind guiding principles of APS that prioritize client self-determination and the client's right to refuse services. However, APS workers may also deal with situations where they determine that the older adult does not have sufficient understanding or awareness of the risks present. In some cases, APS agencies must initiate involuntary services. They need to obtain permission of the court in order to do this. For example, an APS worker may determine that the older person did not have the capacity to understand that she was risking her financial well-being by allowing her grandson access to her ATM card, and may determine that the court must appoint someone to manage the older person's finances in a way that will serve the older adult's best interests.

APS workers play a key role in helping to determine whether guardianship, which takes away a person's rights to make decisions related to finances, health care, and living arrangements, is necessary. The decision to seek guardianship raises legitimate concerns and highlights the ethical dilemma of self-determination versus protection of older adults. General concerns about guardianship include challenges in determining legal standards for incompetence and incapacity, concerns that those protected are family members rather than the person needing guardianship, and insufficient oversight of the system by the courts. In general, advocates for older adults see guardianship as a last resort process and that other, less restrictive options should be exhausted beforehand (Wood, 2012).

If investigation reveals that a crime, such as severe physical abuse, stealing of assets, or sexual assault, has been committed, then appropriate involvement of the legal system must take place. An example of a challenge is that, owing to ageism or weak or ineffective response, sexual assault cases involving older victims in nursing facilities are not followed up in a timely manner and evidence is not collected (Burgess, Ramsey-Klawsnik, & Gregorian, 2008).

Relevant Theories or Frameworks

While evidence-based research on APS interventions is lacking, much work is being done to improve the evidence base of interventions designed to address elder abuse, including work on developing and generating empirical evidence on outcomes in APS. One of the issues faced in delivering APS is balancing the need to preserve client self-determination while simultaneously helping reduce the risk for continuing abuse and achieve safety. In addition, there is little evidence available about which intervention models work the best. The ability to persuade cognitively capable older adults to accept services that will reduce risk is very important. Burnes (2016) has developed a community elder mistreatment practice model that is theory based and empirically testable to use with older adults who are cognitively capable.

Burnes' model puts forth three fundamental tenets that, if applied to programs that aim to increase victim safety, have the potential to improve practice and increase service acceptance. The tenets are voluntariness (victims must accept services voluntarily), self-determination, and least restrictive intervention path, which means that social workers and others must be open to proposing service plans that maximize the adult's choice and control even if risk is not reduced to the lowest possible level. This model recognizes that many elderly victimized clients want to reduce risk but also protect a perpetrator who is a family member from involvement in the justice system. This practice model focuses on harm reduction, client centeredness, and the need for a multidisciplinary approach. The skills needed for this approach center on the ability to engage and develop a therapeutic alliance (Burnes, 2016).

Restorative justice is another framework that has been applied to the prevention and amelioration of elder abuse situations. Restorative justice approaches provide opportunities, through structured meetings, for victims, perpetrators, and supportive parties to come together to develop plans to ameliorate the harm resulting from abuse and neglect. The Family Care Conference model, piloted in several Native American communities, involves a structured family meeting attended by the older person, family members, and involved agencies. The goal of the meeting is to develop a plan that will provide for the protection of the older adult while meeting the needs and desires of the family unit (Holkup, Salois, Tripp-Reimer, & Weinert, 2007).

Relevant Ethical, Legal, and Policy Issues

Many ethical challenges exist when working within the APS system, including determination of client capacity, decisions to override client self-determination, and limited resources for APS and agencies providing supportive services. Capacity assessment, which requires special training and expertise and knowledge of the person being assessed, helps APS personnel determine whether older adults can live independently. It helps determine whether to compel older adults to accept services or whether an intrusive intervention such as guardianship is warranted. Capacity is task specific and exists on a continuum; persons can have the capacity to decide what to eat or wear, but not to make decisions about finances. On the other hand, competence is a legal concept. A person either is, or is not, competent as declared by a court of law (Dong & Gorbien, 2005).

While legal remedies such as guardianship are available to protect people if needed, the APS worker must understand the potential negative outcomes of taking away a person's rights to make decisions. The guardianship system is flawed; guardianship is a drastic move that should be used as a last resort because it requires that persons be determined incompetent to make their own decisions and handle their own affairs. Unfortunately, legal guardians do not always act in the best interests of their wards. The public guardianship system does not have sufficient resources, and high caseloads mean that monitoring of vulnerable adults in this system may be insufficient and leave them vulnerable to further mistreatment (Wood, 2012).

In addition to stretched resources for guardianship systems, the entire APS system is overwhelmed. APS services are stretched thin. Some challenges include reduced staffing due to state cutbacks and inadequate training for APS workers (National Adult Protective Services Association and National Association of States United for Aging and Disabilities, 2012).

Relevant Assessment, Prevention, and Intervention Strategies

APS workers must recognize that victims of abuse and neglect experience a loss of control and that they may have been isolated, intimidated, and coerced by their perpetrators. The principle of self-determination reminds APS workers that the ultimate decision-making power lies with the victim. The principle of empowerment helps APS workers to focus on restoring power to victims to make decisions about services and interventions to pursue

(Brandl et al., 2006). In addition to APS, a number of service systems may become involved in the resolution of an elder abuse case including the criminal and civil justice systems, the health care system, the long-term care ombudsman, and domestic violence and sexual assault services. The number of services and potential interventions may leave victims overwhelmed with options instead of adequately served and protected, making collaboration among service providers imperative (Brandl et al., 2006).

Because of the complexity of the cases and the difficulty of sorting out various legal, medical, psychological, and social issues connected to many of the situations that APS handles, many APS agencies rely upon multidisciplinary teams, both internal and external to the agency, to assist in complex cases. Social workers may also serve as members of interdisciplinary or multidisciplinary teams that complete capacity assessments or forensic investigations. Other communities have established multidisciplinary teams to address more challenging APS cases, for example, financial abuse specialist teams that focus on identifying and prosecuting financial abuse. Most teams include representatives from APS, law enforcement, and health care; other team members depend upon the team's focus and purpose (Brandl et al., 2006).

The EJA promotes the establishment of Elder Abuse Forensic Centers (EAFC), which are multidisciplinary teams of experts in health care, social services, and criminal justice that can address complex cases by combining their forensic expertise to establish facts and evidence in complex cases of elder abuse (Schneider, Mosqueda, Falk, & Huba, 2010). Research has demonstrated that financial exploitation cases reported to APS and then referred to the EAFC are significantly more likely to be referred to the district attorney for prosecution (Navarro, Gassoumis, & Wilber, 2013).

Forensic Practice Skill Set

The APS investigator needs superb skills in building rapport and interviewing. Working with older and disabled adults in the protective services system requires patience, persistence, and the ability to work with individuals who have experienced multiple health problems, severe trauma, and victimization at multiple points during their lives. Social workers need to know how to ask questions that will elicit information needed to establish whether abuse has occurred and to also lay the groundwork for the individual to accept services that will reduce his or her risk of further victimization. Social workers must accept that their clients may be suspicious, uncomfortable with questions, and protective of caregivers or other family members who have harmed them. They must learn effective interviewing techniques for persons with disabilities, such as using pictures to communicate with individuals with speech impairments (Brandl et al., 2006). Social workers must also understand the need for patience and that while victims of elder abuse may initially refuse help, many of them will accept services after subsequent investigations.

Social workers must develop the skills and expertise to work as members of multidisciplinary teams, which includes being aware of their own role and professional identity and understanding how professional roles may differ and that team members may have conflicting goals for clients. For example, the goal of the social worker to preserve and prioritize client autonomy may conflict with a doctor or nurse's goal to uphold the safety and best interests of client (Brandl et al., 2006).

Case Example and Application

Jane Smith, who has dementia and is medically frail, is a 95-year-old woman who resides in the suburban home that she and her husband purchased 50 years ago. She is unable to care for herself. Jane and her husband never had children of their own. Her nephew Bill, age

(continued)

Case Example and Application (*continued*)

50 years, has lived with her for the past 10 years after she invited him to live with her because she could no longer take care of the house and she wanted to do something for Bill who was, as she said, "down on his luck." In truth, Bill has an explosive temper, abuses alcohol and cocaine, and depends on Jane for a place to live and financial support. Some years ago, Jane made him the sole heir of her house and her medical power of attorney.

One evening he brings Jane to the emergency room (ER). Jane is emaciated, disoriented, and has a number of decubitus ulcers (bedsores), which occur when a person lies in bed in the same position for long periods of time. Physical examination and lab tests reveal dehydration and poor nutrition. Even though the ER wants to place Jane in a skilled nursing facility, Bill insists that Jane be discharged back home. Bill states that he is legally and morally obligated to carry out her wish to remain in her own home until she dies.

The ER physician consults the medical record and sees that Bill has brought Jane to the ER three times within the past year, with Jane always discharged home in spite of concerns noted in the record. He consults with the hospital social worker and she meets with Bill and Jane separately. Jane is unable to communicate with her. The social worker talks to Bill to determine what he knows about her condition and care needs. Bill reveals that he thinks that nursing homes are a "rip-off" that will use up all of Jane's assets (because of its location, the house is worth $1 million) and that the nursing home will neglect Jane.

Upon discharge from the ER, the hospital social worker contacts APS and describes her concerns. The APS social worker makes a home visit to investigate the allegations. They find Jane alone in a small bedroom at the back of the house. The room has a powerful odor of urine and feces, and dirty clothes and linens are piled on the floor. Jane is in bed on a mattress pad with no sheets. When asked why he has not sought help in caring for Jane, Bill stated that he cares for her and "knows" what she needs and that home health agencies are only after his money. He demonstrates little concern for Jane's health and well-being.

Concerned that Bill's desire to preserve his inheritance supersedes his ability to meet Jane's needs for care, the APS worker involves the elder abuse forensic team. The doctor on the team reviews Jane's health records and law enforcement conducts an investigation to determine whether criminal neglect has taken place. The APS worker recommends that a guardian be appointed to oversee Jane's care. While the petition for guardianship is granted, no criminal neglect charges are filed due to lack of sufficient evidence to build a case.

This case illustrates how important it is for health care and other agencies that come into contact with older adults to document their concerns about caregivers and to report suspicions of abuse and neglect to APS so the evidence needed to support prosecution will be available if needed.

Conclusion

Forensic social work in the APS system requires the ability to address the varied needs of vulnerable older and disabled adults who have been abused, neglected, and exploited. APS operate within a continuum of services that challenge social workers in their efforts to respond effectively to elder abuse. In addition to knowledge of aging, disabilities, the dynamics of family violence and caregiving, community resources and skills in capacity assessment, working in multidisciplinary teams, advocacy, and systems navigation, social workers need commitment to values of self-determination and empowerment to guide their work in this system.

CHAPTER EXERCISES

Exercise 1. Review the adult protection statute in your state to determine (a) who is mandated to report and how to make the reports; (b) how abuse and neglect are defined; and (c) who is eligible for services.

Exercise 2. Have a class discussion on this question: Should eligibility for APS be determined by age alone or should the adults meet some definition of vulnerability?

Additional Resources

International Network for the Prevention of Elder Abuse: http://inpea.net

National Adult Protective Services Association: www.napsa-now.org

National Clearinghouse for Abuse in Later Life: www.ncall.us

National Center on Elder Abuse—United States Administration on Aging: https://ncea.acl.gov

National Committee for the Protection of Elder Abuse: www.preventelderabuse.org

United States Department of Justice Elder Justice Initiative: www.justice.gov/elderjustice

References

Administration for Community Living. (2016). *The elder abuse prevention interventions program.* Retrieved from https://www.acl.gov/programs/elder-justice/elder-abuse-prevention-intervention-demonstrations

Ballan, M. B., Freyer, M. B., & Powledge, L. (2015). Intimate partner violence among men with disabilities: The role of health care providers. *American Journal of Men's Health,* 1–8. doi:10.1177/1557988315606966

Beach, S. R., Schulz, R., Castle, N. G., & Rosen, J. (2010). Financial exploitation and psychological mistreatment among older adults: Differences between African Americans and non-African Americans in a population-based survey. *The Gerontologist, 50*(6), 744–757. doi:10.1093/geront/gnq053

Brandl, B., Dyer, C. B., Heisler, C. J., Otto, J. M., Stiegel, L. A., & Thomas, R. W. (2006). *Elder abuse detection and intervention: A collaborative approach.* New York, NY: Springer Publishing.

Burgess, A. W., Ramsey-Klawsnik, H., & Gregorian, S. B. (2008). Comparing routes of reporting in elder sexual abuse cases. *Journal of Elder Abuse & Neglect, 20*(4), 336–352. doi:10.1080/08946500802359250

Burnes, D. (2016). Community elder mistreatment intervention with capable older adults: Toward a conceptual practice model. *The Gerontologist.* doi:10.1093/geront/gnv692

Colello, K. J. (2014). *The elder justice act: Background and issues for Congress.* Washington, DC: Congressional Research Service. Retrieved from https://www.fas.org/sgp/crs/misc/R43707.pdf

Committee on the Elimination of All Forms of Discrimination Against Women. (2010). *General recommendation No. 27 on older women and protection of their human rights.* Retrieved from http://www.refworld.org/docid/4ed3528b2.html

Connolly, M. T., Brandl, B., & Breckman, R. (2014). The elder justice roadmap: A stakeholder initiative to respond to an emerging health, justice, financial, and social crisis. Retrieved from https://www.justice.gov/elderjustice/file/829266/download

DeLiema, M., Gassoumis, Z. D., Homeier, D. C., & Wilber, K. H. (2012). Determining prevalence and correlates of elder abuse using promotores: Low income immigrant Latinos report high rates of abuse and neglect. *Journal of the American Geriatrics Society, 60*(7), 1333–1339. doi:10.1111/j.1532-5415.2012.04025.x

Department of Economic and Social Affairs. (2013). Neglect, abuse and violence against older women. Retrieved from http://www.un.org/esa/socdev/documents/ageing/neglect-abuse-violence-older-women.pdf

Dong, X., & Gorbien, M. (2005). Decision-making vapacity: The core of self-neglect. *Journal of Elder Abuse & Neglect, 17*(3), 19–36.

Holkup, P. A., Salois, E. M., Tripp-Reimer, T., & Weinert, C. (2007). Drawing on wisdom from the past: An elder abuse intervention with tribal communities. *The Gerontologist, 47*, 248–254.

Inouye, S. K., Studenski, S., Tinetti, M. E., & Kuchel, G. A. (2007). Geriatric syndromes: Clinical, research, and policy implications of a core geriatric concept. *Journal of the American Geriatrics Society, 55*(5), 780–791.

Jayawardena, K. M., & Liao, S. (2006). Elder abuse at end of life. *Journal of Palliative Medicine, 9*(1), 127–136. doi:10.1089/jpm.2006.9.127

Lachs, M. S., & Pillemer, K. A. (2015). Elder abuse. *New England Journal of Medicine, 373*(20), 1947–1956. doi:10.1056/NEJMra1404688

Lee, H. Y., & Eaton, C. K. (2009). Financial abuse in elderly Korean immigrants: Mixed analysis of the role of culture on perception and help-seeking intention. *Journal of Gerontological Social Work, 52*(5), 463–488. doi:10.1080/01634370902983138

Lehmann, V., & Mathiasen, G. (1963). *Guardianship and protective services for older people: The report of a National Council on the Aging Project.* New York, NY: NCOA Press.

Lifespan of Greater Rochester Inc., Weill Cornell Medical School of Cornell University, & New York City Department for the Aging. (2011). Under the radar: New York state elder abuse prevalence study. Retrieved from http://ocfs.ny.gov/main/reports/Under%20the%20Radar%2005%2012%2011%20final%20report.pdf

Martin, C., Rodríguez-Pinzón, D., & Brown, B. (2015). *Human rights of older people: Universal and regional legal perspectives.* Dordrecht, Netherlands: Springer Science + Business Media.

Maschi, T., Viola, D., & Koskinen, L. (2015). Trauma, stress, and coping among older adults in prison: Towards a human rights and intergenerational family justice agenda. *Traumatology, 3*, 15–30. doi:10.1037/trm0000021

McFarlane, J., Hughes, R. B., Nosek, M. A., Groff, J. Y., Swedlend, N., & Mullen, P. D. (2001). Abuse assessment screen-disability (AAS-D): Measuring frequency, type, and perpetrator of abuse toward women with physical disabilities. *Journal of Women's Health & Gender-Based Medicine, 10*(9), 861–866.

National Adult Protective Services Association. (2013). Adult protective services recommended minimum program standards. Retrieved from http://www.napsa-now.org/wp-content/uploads/2014/04/Recommended-Program-Standards.pdf

National Adult Protective Services Association and National Association of States United for Aging and Disabilities. (2012). *Adult protective services in 2012: Increasingly vulnerable.* Washington, DC: National Association of States United for Aging and Disabilities.

Navarro, A. E., Gassoumis, Z. D., & Wilber, K. H. (2013). Holding abusers accountable: An elder abuse forensic center increases criminal prosecution of financial exploitation. *The Gerontologist, 53*(2), 303–312. doi:10.1093/geront/gns075

Otto, J. M. (2000). The role of adult protective services in addressing abuse. *Generations, 24*(2), 33–38.

Plummer, S., & Findley, P. A. (2012). Women with disabilities' experience with physical and sexual abuse. A review of the literature and implications for the field. *Trauma, Violence & Abuse, 13*(1), 15–29.

Schneider, D. C., Mosqueda, L., Falk, E., & Huba, G. J. (2010). Elder abuse forensic centers. *Journal of Elder Abuse & Neglect, 22*(3–4), 255–274. doi:925746408 [pii] 10.1080/08946566.2010.490137

Teaster, P. B., Dugar, T. A., Mendiondo, M. S., Abner, E. L., Cecil, K. A., & Otto, J. M. (2006). The 2004 survey of state adult protective services: Abuse of adults 60 years of age and older. Retrieved from http://www.napsa-now.org/wp-content/uploads/2012/09/2-14-06-FINAL-60+REPORT.pdf

Teaster, P. B., Wangmo, T., & Anetzberger, G. J. (2010). A glass half full: The dubious history of elder abuse policy. *Journal of Elder Abuse & Neglect*, 22(1/2), 6–15. doi:10.1080/08946560903436130

United Nations. (1991). UN principles of older persons. Retrieved from http://www.un.org/documents/ga/res/46/a46r091.htm

United Nations. (2003). *Political declaration and Madrid international plan of action on ageing: Second world assembly on ageing 2002*. New York, NY: Author.

U.S. Government Accountability Office. (2013). *ELDER JUSTICE: More federal coordination and public awareness needed*. Washington, DC: Government Printing Office.

White House Conference on Aging. (2015). *White House Conference on Aging: Final report*. Washington, DC: Author. Retrieved from https://archive.whitehouseconferenceonaging.gov/2015-WHCOA -Final-Report.pdf

Wolf, R. S. (2003). Elder abuse and neglect: History and concepts. In R. J. Bonnie & R. B. Wallace (Eds.), *Elder mistreatment: Abuse, neglect, and exploitation in an aging America*. Washington, DC: National Academies Press.

Wood, E. F. (2012). The paradox of adult guardianship: A solution to—and a source for—elder abuse. *Generations*, 36(3), 79–82.

World Health Organization. (2008). *A global response to elder abuse and neglect: Building primary health care capacity to deal with the problem worldwide: Main report*. Geneva, Switzerland: Author. Retrieved from http://apps.who.int/iris/bitstream/10665/43869/1/9789241563581_eng.pdf

VOICES FROM THE FIELD

Paula Price, LCSW-C

Adult Protective Services Investigator

Agency Setting

The Washington County Department of Social Services is one of 24 local departments of social services in the state of Maryland. Adult Protective Services (APS) is responsible for the investigation of allegations of abuse (physical, sexual), neglect, and exploitation of elder and vulnerable adults. The largest city in Washington County, Hagerstown, has a population of about 41,000; we serve many individuals who live in small towns and rural areas.

Practice Responsibilities

My primary practice responsibilities are to investigate reports of the mistreatment and self-neglect of vulnerable older adults and disabled adults (over 18 years old) and to provide advocacy and information to link the vulnerable adult with the appropriate services and agencies. The philosophy of APS is to promote self-sufficiency, independence, and safety. I have to be prepared to work with a wide variety of complex situations involving abuse, neglect, and exploitation of disabled, mostly older, adults, including assessment for possible guardianship. APS has to have a good screening process, and ongoing assessment of functional abilities and decision-making capacity is very important.

I deal with people from all social, cultural, and economic backgrounds. One of the biggest things I learned when I first started working for APS is that if people want to live in an awful situation, they can. Adults who are competent can refuse our services as long as they possess the capacity to understand the consequences of refusal. I have learned law enforcement cannot make someone open his or her door for us to investigate without a court order. I have also learned that in APS there is the possibility to make somebody angry because you are intervening in situations that people are reluctant to change, even if they are being harmed by a family member or living in an unsafe situation.

While financial exploitation has always occurred, Maryland passed a new banking law in 2012 that requires bank tellers and other bank personnel to report their suspicions of elder financial abuse to APS. The banks and other financial institutions doing business in Maryland can work collaboratively with APS without liability. As a result, I have spent more time dealing with cases of financial exploitation and working with the court system to bring these cases to justice. The new law allows us to examine bank records to begin to build a case. However, APS deals with "gray area crime" and it is not always easy to prove a criminal case from the cases of financial exploitation that are reported to us. Being persistent about pursuing cases is one of the most difficult parts of the job.

Expertise Required

An APS worker should have a background in social work and good skills in assessment. Knowledge about the dynamics of elder abuse and neglect, family systems, and the aging process is very important.

You have to be able to establish relationships with the older adults you are investigating. You have to deal with what is in front of you, so in some ways you develop expertise as you go along. Being able to ask personal, sometimes socially unacceptable questions and engage the client and others in unpleasant discussions is an acquired skill needed by an APS worker. Recognizing and overcoming the need not to know is important to fully investigate abuse and neglect allegations. APS workers develop skill in detecting when people are not telling the truth or are hiding information.

Ethical, Legal, Practice, Diversity, and/or Advocacy Issues Addressed

I can deal with competent adults who are still very vulnerable. It can be very hard to get people to accept our services. I grew up in this county and sometimes I have to recuse myself from certain cases because I know the individuals involved.

Some people think that the solution to the vulnerable elder's problem is to establish a guardian for him or her. Guardianship is an intervention of the very last resort because guardianship takes away a person's rights to make his or her own decisions. Guardianship does not give the guardian arrest powers or total control over the disabled person's actions.

Interprofessional and Intersectoral Collaboration

The new banking law in Maryland has made it much easier for me to work with bank personnel. In many cases of financial exploitation, the bank has the evidence in the form of cancelled checks. The banks are required to train their staff in reporting financial abuse of older persons and to work collaboratively with APS and law enforcement. Bank personnel can identify changes in customer behaviors and "new people" in their life as well as changes in their monthly banking habits. Bank personnel are valuable reporters of the first signs of financial exploitation.

I have worked closely with the police and a state attorney to get perpetrators of financial exploitation convicted of crimes. If prosecution is successful, our goal is to get coverage in the newspaper to raise awareness and we hope to prevent more exploitation. Sadly, some of the perpetrators of financial exploitation are considered to be upstanding members of the community. One of my successful cases involved a minister who was financially exploiting his mother; another involved a retired school teacher who was exploited by a caregiver of 20 years.

APS works collaboratively with the Commission on Aging as well as Meritus Hospital and physicians' offices. As APS investigates adults age 18 years and older, APS works with high schools at times as well as hospice. These agencies are primary referral sources to APS as they have initial contact with possible victims of abuse, neglect, or exploitation. The information reported is screened and, if an investigation is warranted, it is assigned for investigation. APS recognizes the importance to these agencies of maintaining good working relationships with victims and even perpetrators. At times APS plays "the heavy" in these partnerships to motivate the vulnerable adults to accept help, to discourage the perpetrators, and to make the changes needed to prevent further maltreatment.

CHAPTER 17

Justice-Involved Veterans: Programs and Services

Kelli Canada

Clark Peters

Danielle Easter

CHAPTER OBJECTIVES

The major objectives of this chapter are to:

- Enhance understanding of the justice-involved veteran population including the extent of involvement, risk, and protective factors associated with offending, and the impact of criminal justice involvement on the veteran and the veteran's family system
- Describe and discuss the targeted programs and services for justice-involved veterans, how social workers assist this population, and the specific skill set required for effective intervention

CHAPTER COMPETENCIES HIGHLIGHTED

- Competency 3: Advance Human Rights and Social, Economic, and Environmental Justice
- Competency 8: Intervene With Individuals, Families, Organizations, and Communities

Social workers intervene with justice-involved veterans at multiple points within the criminal justice system including arrest, court, community supervision (i.e., probation or parole), jail, prison, and reentry into the community. Programs and services targeting justice-involved veterans are situated at different points within the criminal justice system. Although many services are provided by the U.S. Department of Veterans Affairs (VA), not all veterans are eligible for treatment and services through the VA. Many community-based providers also offer assistance to justice-involved veterans. Social workers engage in case management, skill building, and therapy through preventive services with veterans who are at risk of criminal justice involvement. After arrest, social workers intervene by providing direct services to veterans and their families, assisting with benefit eligibility, facilitating access to treatments, coordinating care and advocacy, and providing therapy. Social workers also engage in macrolevel activities, including assessing community need, advocating for and establishing new programs for veterans, and conducting trainings on veteran-related issues. Regardless of the level of practice, social workers interested in working with justice-involved veterans should have knowledge regarding the military, military culture, VA benefits, mental health problems, and substance use, in addition to the issues that arise as a consequence of criminal justice system involvement.

Background and Scope of the Problem

Census data collected between 2003 and 2013 indicate approximately 21.3 million military veterans in the United States, which is about 9% of the population (Kromer & Holder, 2015). The vast majority of military veterans do not enter the criminal justice system. However, those who do face disproportionate risk of suicide, exacerbation of psychiatric and physical health symptoms during incarceration, and increased risk of homelessness upon release from prison. Felony charges on veterans' records can interfere with benefits, securing employment, and obtaining safe housing. Incarceration can also disrupt the family system, compromise caregiver responsibilities, deplete financial assets, and limit employment opportunities.

Accurate estimates of the number of veterans who have been arrested, are on probation or parole, and are incarcerated are difficult to obtain. A key challenge involves inconsistent practices of documenting veteran status and varying approaches to data collection (e.g., self-reported veteran status). One study indicated that approximately 10% of people in federal and state prisons in 2004 identified as military veterans, with women comprising only 1% of this population (Noonan & Mumola, 2007). Across studies and time, this rate has varied considerably. In 1978, nearly 25% of inmates identified as military veterans (Berzofsky, Bronson, Carson, & Noonan, 2015). Recent trends suggest that there is a decline in the proportion of veterans in confinement; in 2012, approximately 8% of the incarcerated population were identified as veterans, with 1.1% of veterans in prison and 3.2% of veterans in jail being female (Berzofsky et al., 2015). These estimates, however, capture only incarcerated veterans and do not account for veterans involved in the criminal justice system outside of confinement, including those on probation or in jail-diversion programs (Berzofsky et al., 2015).

Health and Mental Health of Incarcerated Veterans

Participation in the military places individuals at a high risk of experiencing trauma (Berzofsky et al., 2015). Incarcerated veterans indicate high rates of trauma exposure, particularly during childhood (Hartwell et al., 2014), and they are twice as likely to be diagnosed with posttraumatic stress disorder (PTSD) compared with the general population of prisoners (Berzofsky et al., 2015). PTSD is a type of anxiety disorder that occurs after exposure to a life-threatening event, injury, or a highly stressful event. PTSD is characterized by intrusion (e.g., reoccurring thoughts or dreams; flashbacks), avoidance, numbing (e.g., avoidance of thoughts or feelings of the traumatic event), negative cognition (e.g., lapse in memory; distorted cognitions), and arousal symptoms (e.g., anger outbursts and hypervigilance; American Psychiatric Association, 2013). In comparison with the general population of prisoners, incarcerated veterans are more likely to have a diagnosable mental illness, traumatic brain injury (TBI), and co-occurring disorders. TBI is associated with substance use, difficulty controlling anger, and general aggression, all of which increase the risk of criminal misconduct (Tanielian & Jaycox, 2008).

Research has well established that substance misuse is strongly associated with criminal justice system involvement among those in the general population (see Fazel, Bains, & Doll, 2006). Similarly for veterans, an estimated 60% of justice-involved veterans have a substance use disorder, one quarter of whom were using drugs and alcohol at the time of arrest (Noonan & Mumola, 2007). The Institute of Medicine (2012) characterizes military substance misuse as a "public health crisis." More than 25% of those aged 18 to 25 years old in the military have problematic alcohol use, compared with 16% of civilians in the same age group, and heavy drinking among military personnel rose more than 25% from 1998 to 2008. An estimated 12% of service members report illicit substance use, including misuse of prescription drugs. Illicit and problematic substance use increases the risk of encountering the criminal justice system. Veterans with co-occurring mental illnesses and substance use disorders face the highest risk of incarceration (Pandiani, Rosenheck, & Banks, 2003).

Causes and Consequences of Arrest Among Veterans

In order to reduce arrests among military veterans, it is important to understand the conditions and contexts that may increase the risk of arrest. However, research seeking to better understand the unique causes of arrest among veterans is largely mixed and inconclusive (Taylor, Parkes, Haw, & Jepson, 2012). Some stakeholders argue that veterans, particularly combat veterans, may be encountering the criminal justice system due to unmet mental health needs (Greenberg & Rosenheck, 2009). Incarcerated veterans report more psychiatric and substance use problems, as well as higher unemployment rates prior to arrest, in comparison with homeless veterans in the community (McGuire, Rosenheck, & Kasprow, 2003), but the link to involvement with the criminal justice system has not yet been firmly established.

Others argue that an inability to adjust to civilian life following military service increases the risk of criminal justice involvement. For some veterans, the military training and adaptive behaviors required for being successful in the military may conflict with civilian culture and create barriers for successful adjustment (Huskey, 2015). Difficulty adjusting to civilian life often impairs occupational and social functioning and may lead to anger for some people (Worthen & Ahern, 2014), increasing the risk of involvement in the criminal justice system. Studies indicate that veterans with mental illnesses, histories of family violence, conduct problems in childhood or adolescence, or antisocial traits are at an increased risk of contact with the criminal justice system; most of these traits are also associated with arrest among the general population in the United States. The best documented correlate for criminal justice involvement among veterans is alcohol and drug use problems (Weaver, Trafton, Kimerling, Timko, & Moos, 2013).

Once a veteran has been arrested, they face myriad psychological, social, and physical health risks. The environment of jails and prisons poses numerous risks to physical and mental health. For the general population, life expectancy declines two years for every year served in prison (Patterson, 2013). Individual differences in the ability to adapt to confinement, limited health care, social isolation, segregation, and stress resulting from risk of violence and prison conditions can lead to adverse health and mental health outcomes. Prisoners are at high risk of communicable diseases like sexually transmitted diseases, poor treatment of chronic health conditions, and higher mortality. Incarcerated veterans are also thought to be at an elevated risk of suicide and suicidal ideation (Wortzel, Binswanger, Anderson, & Adler, 2009). For veterans with mental illness, adjusting to incarceration can be especially difficult, which can worsen symptoms. Symptom exacerbation may result from the stress of prison environments; interrupted, poor, or absence of treatment; stigma; or a combination of factors. In addition to health and mental health consequences, veterans who are arrested may face financial burdens, suspension of benefits, and disruption in family and work life. Felony convictions can interfere with finding and securing employment and housing (Addlestone & Chaset, 2008).

As noted, most veterans will never come into contact with the criminal justice system. Indeed, for some, military service itself may be a kind of diversion program and duty can be a turning point for many service men and women through the broad range of experiences and opportunities not available to civilians. However, service may also have negative consequences, such as instilling aggressive problem-solving strategies, interpersonal stress due to separation from family, and risk of trauma from combat or other military-related situations (Bouffard, 2005). Preventive programming is needed to reduce the risk of arrest that some veterans face, but few evidence-based preventive programs exist. However, there are numerous programs that help assist veterans once they enter the criminal justice system. Social workers play key roles in connecting veterans to these programs and providing both short- and long-term care.

Relevant Frameworks: Trauma-Informed Care

The use of trauma-informed care models and other interventions designed to address trauma are critical for addressing the complex needs of justice-involved veterans. In a sample of male veterans who participated in a jail diversion program, 93% reported trauma exposure during their lifetimes, with most experiencing trauma before the age of 18 years (Hartwell et al., 2014). Moreover, many veterans have experienced complex trauma—that is to say, extended exposure to trauma or multiple trauma experiences. Trauma-informed care suggests that programming must address the multifaceted impact of trauma, identify the symptoms of trauma in individuals and their respective systems, and respond to symptoms with practice and policy that does not retraumatize the client (SAMHSA, 2015).

Exposure to trauma can impact the way clients respond to treatment, including verbal and nonverbal engagement, alliance building, and trust. It is important for social workers to keep in mind power dynamics, be sensitive to taking personal histories and asking specific questions about trauma, and be mindful of physical positioning during meetings, as well as possible barriers to working together, such as dissimilarity in gender. It may take time before clients with histories of trauma are able to disclose personal information. Facilitating empowerment, a core value in social work, is essential to promoting recovery. Examples of how social workers can facilitate empowerment include: (a) developing a collaborative and respectful relationship; (b) providing clients with options, such as the ability to not answer questions that make them feel uncomfortable; (c) using empathy, warmth, and support; (d) utilizing strengths-based assessments; and (e) recognizing and acknowledging successes and gains in treatment and life (SAMHSA, 2015).

Core Roles and Functions of Forensic Social Work in This System

One major role for forensic social workers is through the work of a Veteran Justice Outreach worker (VJO). VJOs work in VA medical centers across the country and act as liaisons between the VA and criminal justice systems (Department of Veterans Affairs, 2016a). VJOs conduct outreach to identify veterans who are involved in the local court system and jail, assess need, and offer short- and long-term case management. For example, VJOs assist in benefit eligibility and referral to mental health services, substance abuse treatment, vocational services, and homeless programs. VJOs conduct trainings for law enforcement on a range of veteran-related issues including veteran needs, TBI, and the impact of PTSD. As court-based interventions, such as veteran treatment courts, continue to grow, more VJOs are serving as members of alternative sentencing court teams and collaborating with community partners.

In addition to the role of a VJO, forensic social workers may encounter justice-involved veterans through their work in jail or prison settings, community-based treatment facilities, inpatient mental health and substance abuse treatment hospitals, probation or parole, and court-based programming (e.g., alternative sentencing courts). Forensic social workers assist justice-involved veterans through case management services like coordinating housing, applying for benefits, and assisting in the enrollment of vocational training (Canada & Albright, 2014). Forensic social workers also provide clinical services to veterans through evidence-based treatments for mental illness and substance abuse. Common evidence-based practices used with veterans include motivational interviewing, moral reconation therapy (MRT), cognitive processing therapy, prolonged exposure, acceptance commitment therapy, and programs for dual diagnosis (i.e., veterans with mental illness and substance abuse problems; Blodgett, Fuh, Maisel, & Midboe, 2013; Department of Veterans Affairs, 2015). When working with justice-involved veterans, it is important to determine if they are eligible for VA benefits and services, if they are not already connected. Veteran eligibility for services will increase the number of resources and treatment options available to clients (Department of Veterans Affairs, 2016a).

Preventive Programs and Services

Programs and services for justice-involved veterans are provided across the criminal justice continuum. Although there are no evidence-based interventions designed to prevent criminal justice involvement among veterans, there are ways for forensic social workers to intervene with veterans who may be at risk for arrest. The VJO program aims to prevent homelessness among veterans. One key service in preventing homelessness is the Department of Housing and Urban Development–Veterans Administration Supportive Housing (HUD-VASH) program. HUD-VASH offers housing vouchers, case management, and clinical services to qualified veterans who are homeless (Veterans Affairs National Center on Homelessness Among Veterans, n.d.). The program is especially important given the strong correlation between homelessness and arrest (Tsai, Rosenheck, Kasprow, & McGuire, 2014). Support services such as those offered through HUD-VASH may ultimately prevent arrest for some veterans. Given veterans who abuse drugs and alcohol are at considerable risk of arrest, preventive services including substance abuse treatment and dual diagnosis programming are important. Dual diagnosis programming is intended to treat substance abuse issues alongside mental health issues (VA National Center on Homelessness Among Veterans, n.d.). Social workers can work directly with the military to help people transition to civilian life through counseling and case management. Screening tools to identify veterans who are abusing substances or who experienced trauma will help facilitate referral to needed services. The VA offers both inpatient and outpatient substance abuse treatment for qualified veterans. A variety of inpatient and outpatient substance abuse treatments are also offered in the community for veterans who lack VA benefits (Department of Veterans Affairs, 2015).

Jail-Diversion Programs

Despite prevention efforts, some veterans will nevertheless encounter the police. For those who have police contact or have been arrested, jail-diversion programs such as Crisis Intervention Teams (CIT) and alternative sentencing courts are increasingly available. Many jail-diversion programs have been created or modified to specifically target military veterans and their unique needs. CIT contains two main components: specialized training and community partnerships with providers and police (Watson, Morabito, Draine, & Ottati, 2008). The specialized training involves a 40-hour curriculum providing police officers with knowledge and response strategies through education about mental illness, substance use, medications, symptoms identification, tools for effective intervention for a person exhibiting psychiatric symptoms, and de-escalation skills to use in crisis. The CIT curriculum involves skill building, role-play scenarios, site visits to providers, and exercises to simulate symptoms' impact on daily living. CIT also establishes community partnerships available for crisis transport and/or service referral. Community partnerships allow for police officers to have additional resources to assist them when responding to a person in crisis, which expands their dispositional options beyond arrest (Watson et al., 2008). Many communities are developing partnerships with veteran service providers and including information about the unique needs of veterans within their initial CIT 40-hour training and in advanced CIT trainings. VJOs often assist with CIT training or conduct specialized trainings with police officers on core issues that justice-involved veterans may face (PTSD, TBI; Shia, Miller, Swensen, & Matthieu, 2013).

Many communities are developing court-based diversion programs for veterans. Court-based programs include veteran treatment courts, a docket or track within an existing alternative sentencing court (e.g., drug treatment or mental health court) for veterans, a docket dedicated to veterans within a criminal court, as well as other hybrid programs that involve court and treatment professionals. In 2014, there were 351 of these programs in operation in the United States according to an inventory conducted by the VA (Department of Veterans Affairs, 2016b).

The most common program being implemented to assist justice-involved veterans are veteran treatment courts, which accounts for approximately three quarters of the programs (Department of Veterans Affairs, 2016b). Veteran treatment courts vary based on the unique needs of their communities, but share some common characteristics. All veteran treatment courts are voluntary programs in which eligible military veterans are diverted from serving time for their crime in jail or prison and provided intensive community-based treatment instead. Eligibility for veteran treatment courts vary on admission criteria including conditions (e.g., mental illness, substance abuse), adjudication status (i.e., preplea or postplea), crime (e.g., felony, misdemeanor, nonviolent), and VA benefit eligibility. Most veteran treatment courts require veterans to participate in regular status hearings before the judge, random drug testing, individual and group treatments, vocational training, and peer mentoring. The veteran treatment court team (i.e., judge, administrators, probation, VJOs, police, mentor coordinator) provides intensive oversight throughout program participation. Court personnel use rewards and sanctions to incentivize treatment adherence and compliance with supervision requirements. Veterans who successfully complete the program, often termed "graduation," are rewarded with dismissal or reduction of the charges they face. Veteran treatment court participation lasts, on average, 12 months, but duration varies by program.

To date, the impact of veteran treatment courts is scant but growing. Knudsen and Wingenfeld (2015) provide one of the few evaluations of veteran treatment courts. They found that after a year of participation, veterans indicated a decrease in PTSD symptoms, sleep disturbances, self-harming behaviors, and substance abuse. Family relationships, emotional well-being, and overall functioning improved. Approximately 31% of participants moved from unstable to stable housing while only 10% of participants were rearrested during the program. It is hypothesized that the peer mentoring program, trauma-informed treatment, and psychiatric medications led to positive outcomes.

Another court-based program for veterans is called Mission Direct Vet (MDV). MDV is a federally funded, postadjudication program involving treatment in the community in lieu of incarceration. Team members, which may include forensic social workers, conduct clinical assessments with potential MDV participants and present the assessment to defense counsel. If approved, veterans participate in MDV for 12 months. Services are trauma informed and include case management, peer support, dual recovery therapy, and care coordination. Positive outcomes of MDV participation include increased community functioning and reduced PTSD symptoms in the 12 months following participation (Hartwell et al., 2014). MDV differs from veteran treatment courts in that participants are not required to attend regular court hearings and are supervised only by the treatment team.

Jail and Prison-Based Programs and Services

Therapy, case management, and benefits coordination occur while veterans are incarcerated and as they prepare for community reentry (Blue-Howells, Clark, van den Berk-Clark, & McGuire, 2013). Forensic social workers assist with these services. Treatment in jails and prisons can be limited to medication, although some facilities do offer more extensive rehabilitative services such as individual and group therapy, vocational training, education, and skill-building groups. Most jails and prisons conduct an assessment of the individual upon entry to the facility. Clinical social workers and psychologists are often part of the clinical teams that conduct the assessments. Although not a common practice, some jails and prisons are creating units or pods exclusively for veterans (Blue-Howells et al., 2013). Thus, veterans have the opportunity for camaraderie and veteran-specific services offered within their unit.

When a veteran is identified in jails, VJOs come to the jail and conduct a thorough assessment to identify the treatment and benefit needs of the veteran. VJOs seek to build rapport while the veteran is incarcerated to ease the transition from jail to the community (Blue-Howells et al., 2013). Lengths of stay are considerably shorter in jails compared to prisons, but many veterans in jail have considerable needs upon release, and often require help in securing housing, maintaining sobriety, and obtaining vocational training. VJO plays a critical role in intervening prior to release to ensure needs are addressed. VJO support for veterans being released from jail varies from picking them up or providing transportation from detention, to setting up appointments for treatment at the VA, to referring homeless veterans to the HUD-VASH program.

In addition to VJO, forensic social workers and other health care professionals work within the VA's Health Care for Re-Entry Veterans Program (HCRV). The HCRV is intended to address the needs of veterans in prison as they plan for community reentry (Blue-Howells et al., 2013). Services include comprehensive assessments of need while the veteran is still in prison and referral to social services, medical and psychiatric providers, and employment services to be used upon release. HCRV workers also provide case management including transportation and follow-up with linkages to additional services. These activities are essential, and forensic social workers here often play a critical role, as reentry is a perilous time for many exiting jail and prison. People are at an increased risk of death including suicide, overdose, homelessness, and victimization. Having services and resources in place as soon as a veteran is released provides support essential for a successful and safe transition (Blue-Howells et al., 2013).

Relevant Ethical, Legal, and Policy Issues

The military experience of veterans, access to special benefits, and particular position in U.S. society makes them eligible for special considerations and services, but also invites special challenges to policy makers and practitioners involving legal and ethical considerations. Forensic social workers with familiarity in legal contexts can be especially helpful in negotiating this difficult terrain. The first issue arises from the benefits for which veterans have access through the VA and community-based programs. Coordination between court-based and veteran services will present challenges, but of particular concern is the risk of loss of the benefits; eligibility for some programs will be compromised with criminal conviction, adding to the potential severity of court-based sanctions (Institute for Veteran Policy, 2011). Moreover, public defenders and other legal advocates are unlikely to have a deep understanding of the nuances of federal military benefits and the consequences of conviction. It is important for any plea bargain, which is the most common means to disposition for most prosecutions, to be informed by its effect on veterans' eligibility for benefits (Hunter & Else, 2014). VJO and community social workers serving veterans in the criminal justice system may bring to bear information to help veteran defendants and their legal representatives as they consider options for plea deals and the risks of conviction. A full awareness of options and consequences and close collaboration with legal counsel are essential, especially in cases where the veteran may be suffering from PTSD or TBI, which evidence shows can affect decision making.

A second policy concern arises from the small evidence base that has so far developed to support court-based programs seeking to serve veterans. While these well-intentioned programs tend to emerge from well-established clinical needs of veterans, the scarcity (discussed earlier) of evidence-based programs to address those needs raises the concern that these programs may fall short of their aspirations and ultimately do little to help veterans in the criminal justice system. Indeed, without rigorous evaluation we have little assurance, beyond anecdote, that these programs improve (or possibly compromise) the outcomes of veterans. Diverting limited resources to serve a subpopulation of offenders should be done only with careful outcomes monitoring to inform a good return on investment.

These programs also involve a higher degree of supervision that may end up identifying (and acting on) misbehavior that would otherwise be overlooked. Rigorous monitoring (and prompt sanctions) ultimately may serve the interests of the veteran, but such supervision ensures that these individuals will face a different experience than their nonveteran peers. Indeed, the individuated service plans that make for good forensic social work practice also can be seen to run afoul of a cornerstone legal principle of equality under the law.

The final concerns in this area are common to other court diversion efforts. Program participation is generally contingent on pleading guilty and waiving the right to contest charges, which may compromise important due process protections (Gambill, 2010). These programs also may engage in "creaming"; that is, devising programs that select for individuals who are predisposed to succeed (and generally present less vexing clinical profiles) with or without intervention. From a policy perspective, the problem here is twofold. First, by excluding the most difficult offenders from eligibility (such as violent offenders), the program excludes those who may have the greatest need. Secondly, creaming may also occur in practice, as uncooperative participants are dropped from the program and—having failed to complete the program—are not counted in measuring the success of the program itself. The consequences for these dropped participants can be serious; having pled guilty, they generally face criminal sentencing without the ability to challenge the evidence or present a defense of any kind (Holbrook, 2010). They are also generally prevented from presenting any due process challenges from their time in the diversion program itself. To address these issues of creaming, the remedy is, again, careful evaluative strategies that examine program efficacy using an intent-to-treat model.

Forensic Practice Skill Set

Forensic social workers who work with veterans must employ the same basic social work skills that they use with all clients. These skills include using empathy, reflective listening, and collaboration. Some forensic social workers may not have extensive knowledge of the military culture. Using open-ended questions for exploration and clarification are essential for ensuring cultural competency. For veterans who have PTSD or a history of trauma, it is especially important to take time to create a safe environment, demonstrate trustworthiness and support, and promote empowerment. Some veterans may have to face probation or parole requirements that require them to change their behavior, or find themselves having to attend mandatory treatment sessions owing to court sanctions. When working with involuntary clients, motivational interviewing can be an important tool for exploring the problem area, identifying where clients are in the change process, and elevating client awareness of how behaviors impact their life. As is the case with any involuntary client, social workers need to address court orders and, in addition, explore what personal goals clients want to pursue while in treatment (NASW, 2012).

Case Example and Application

Brad is a 35-year-old male, originally from Idaho Falls. Brad always knew he wanted to follow in his father's and uncle's footsteps and enlist in the U.S. Armed Forces. Following the events of September 11, 2001, Brad felt it was his duty to enlist. At the age of 23 years, he joined the army and worked as a combat medic. Prior to enlisting, Brad described himself as easygoing and social. He had a lot of friends and hobbies like snowboarding and skiing. Although his relationship with his father was tenuous, he was very close to his mother and relied on her for emotional support. He drank socially with friends but denied alcohol or other drug abuse. Brad described his childhood as "normal" and denied any traumatic experiences prior to his time in the military.

As a combat medic, Brad was responsible for helping wounded soldiers. He received his training in the United States and soon after deployed to Iraq. Not only did Brad see the horrific wounds of hundreds of soldiers, he also experienced the deaths of many of them. Brad spent 18 months in Iraq. Shortly after he returned home, his mother died. He also had two friends who were in the military commit suicide when they returned home. While deployed, Brad was involved in an accident that resulted in him sustaining a TBI. Due to his injuries, Brad was discharged from the military under honorable conditions.

(continued)

Case Example and Application (*continued*)

After discharge, Brad moved back to Idaho Falls and rented a house where he lived alone. He noticed changes in himself including racing thoughts, panic symptoms (e.g., tightness in his chest, sweaty palms, heart palpitations), thoughts of death and suicidal ideation, and isolation. Brad did not want to talk to friends or family. He spent most of his time in his home watching television and playing video games. Brad was unable to work and struggled to leave the house to shop for groceries. Brad's symptoms became worse with time. He started having nightmares about his time as a medic. He had increasing thoughts of death and panic symptoms. Although Brad was eligible for VA services, he did not seek help because he thought he could handle the symptoms on his own.

One of Brad's old friends suggested he try smoking marijuana to deal with his symptoms. Brad tried marijuana and felt temporary relief from his symptoms, which led to more use. After months of marijuana use, Brad decided to start growing it himself. Almost a year after being discharged from the army, Brad found himself in jail following an arrest for growing marijuana. Brad had never been charged with a crime before but did stay overnight in jail on two occasions for drunk driving while he was in the military. Shortly after his arrest, a VJO visited Brad in jail and conducted an assessment of Brad's needs. The VJO determined that Brad would benefit from VA assistance for both physical and mental health needs. The VJO assisted by scheduling appointments for Brad and providing him transportation and support when needed. Brad began individual therapy and psychiatric medications through VA providers to address his PTSD, major depressive disorder, and agoraphobia symptoms. He also began seeing a neurologist to monitor the impact of his TBI.

Brad's VJO referred him to the local veteran treatment court. Brad received a felony conviction but his sentence was suspended pending successful completion of the veteran treatment court. Brad was required to continue with his treatment at the VA and regularly check in with his VJO as a condition of court participation. Brad was also assigned a veteran mentor who offered support, friendship, and guidance to Brad throughout his time in the veteran treatment court. After one year, Brad successfully graduated. His symptoms were under control and he learned new skills to help him manage his anxiety. He was able to drive again and grocery shop without panic. He was also able to slowly build a network of friends again. Brad, like many justice-involved veterans, required comprehensive physical and mental health treatment from an interdisciplinary team of doctors, psychologists, and forensic social workers.

Conclusion

Social workers working with justice-involved veterans utilize a multitude of skills and theories when intervening along the criminal justice continuum. Interventions for veterans involved in the criminal justice system often involve an interdisciplinary team of health and mental health professionals who work directly with veterans and their families. The forensic social worker skill set includes using empathy, reflective listening, cultural competency, and collaboration along with evidence-based interventions for mental health, physical health, and substance use problems.

CHAPTER EXERCISES

Exercise 1. Form small groups of three people. One student is the social worker, one is the client, and the other is the observer. Practice conducting a biopsychosocial assessment with a military veteran who you are seeing in jail. Pay particular attention to the reentry needs of this veteran (e.g., Where will he or she go upon release? Does he or she have transportation?). After the role-play, discuss as a group: What questions were asked that are unique for veterans? What direct skills were especially helpful for creating rapport?

Exercise 2. Select a policy issue discussed earlier and examine how this particular policy impacts your community.

Additional Resources

Justice for Vets: www.justiceforvets.org/what-is-a-veterans-treatment-court

National Center on Domestic and Sexual Violence: www.ncdsv.org/images/va_structured-evidence -review-to-identify-treatment-needs-of-justice-involved-veterans_2013.pdf

National Institute of Corrections: nicic.gov/veterans

U.S. Department of Veterans Affairs: www.va.gov/homeless/vjo.asp

References

Addlestone, D. F., & Chaset, A. (2008). Veterans in the criminal justice system. In Veterans for America (Eds), *The American veterans and service members survival guide: How to cut through the bureaucracy and get what you need and are entitled to* (pp. 311–322). Los Angeles, CA: National Veterans Legal Services Program. Retrieved from http://www.nvlsp.org/images/products/survivalguide.pdf

American Psychiatric Association. (2013). *Diagnostic and statistical manual of mental disorders* (5th ed.). Arlington, VA: American Psychiatric Publishing.

Berzofsky, M., Bronson, J., Carson, E. A., & Noonan, M. (2015). *Veterans in prison and jail*. Bureau of Justice Statistics Special Report. Washington, DC: U.S. Department of Justice.

Blodgett, J. C., Fuh, I. L., Maisel, N. C., & Midboe, A. M. (2013). A structured evidence review to identify treatment needs of justice-involved veterans and associated psychological interventions. Retrieved from http://www.ci2i.research.va.gov/docs/structured_evidence_review.pdf

Blue-Howells, J. H., Clark, S. C., van den Berk-Clark, C., & McGuire, J. F. (2013). The U.S. Department of Veterans Affairs veterans justice programs and the sequential intercept model: Case examples in national dissemination of intervention for justice-involved veterans. *Psychological Services, 10*(1), 48–53.

Bouffard, L. A. (2005). The military as a bridging environment in criminal careers: Differential outcomes of the military experience. *Armed Forces & Society, 31*, 273–295.

Canada, K. E., & Albright, D. L. (2014). Veterans in the criminal justice system and the role of social work. *Journal of Forensic Social Work, 4*, 48–62.

Department of Veterans Affairs. (2015). Guide to VA mental health services for veterans and families. Retrieved from http://www.mentalhealth.va.gov/docs/MHG_English.pdf

Department of Veterans Affairs. (2016a). Veteran justice outreach program. Retrieved from http://www .va.gov/homeless/vjo.asp

Department of Veterans Affairs. (2016b). Veterans court inventory 2014 update. Retrieved from http:// www1.va.gov/HOMELESS/docs/VTC-Inventory-FactSheet-0216.pdf

Fazel, S., Bains, P., & Doll, H. (2006). Substance abuse and dependence in prisoners: A systematic review. *Addiction, 101*(2), 181–191.

Gambill, G. (2010, May 5). Justice-involved veterans: A mounting social crisis. *Los Angeles Daily Journal*, pp. 6–7.

Greenberg, G. A., & Rosenheck, R. A. (2009). Mental health and other risk factors for jail incarceration among male veterans. *Psychiatric Quarterly, 80*, 41–53.

Hartwell, S. W., James, A., Chen, J., Pinals, D. A., Marin, M. C., & Smelson, D. (2014). Trauma among justice-involved veterans. *Professional Psychology: Research & Practice, 45*(6), 425–432.

Holbrook, J. G. (2010, November 10). Veterans' courts and criminal responsibility: A problem solving history & approach to the liminality of combat trauma. Retrieved from http://ssrn.com/abstract=1706829

Hunter, B. D., & Else, R. C. (2014). *The attorney's guide to defending veterans in criminal court.* Minneapolis, MN: Veterans Defense Project.

Huskey, K. A. (2015). Reconceptualizing "the crime" in veterans treatment courts. *Federal Sentencing Reporter, 27*(3), 178–186.

Institute for Veteran Policy. (2011). *Veterans and criminal justice: A review of the literature.* San Francisco, CA: Swords to Plowshares.

Institute of Medicine. (2012). *Substance use disorders in the U.S. armed forces.* Washington, DC: National Academies Press.

Knudsen, K. J., & Wingenfeld, S. (2015). A specialized treatment court for veterans with trauma exposure: Implications for the field. *Community Mental Health Journal, 52*(2), 127–135.

Kromer, B., & Holder, K. (2015). Taking a look at veterans across America [Blog post]. Retrieved from https://www.census.gov/newsroom/blogs/random-samplings/2015/11/taking-a-look-at-veterans-across-america.html

McGuire, J., Rosenheck, R. A., & Kasprow, W. J. (2003). Health status, service use and costs among veterans receiving outreach services in jail or community settings. *Psychiatric Services, 54*(2), 201–207.

National Association of Social Workers. (2012). NASW standards for social work practice with service members, veterans, and their families. Retrieved from https://www.socialworkers.org/practice/military/documents/MilitaryStandards2012.pdf

Noonan, M. E., & Mumola, C. J. (2007). Veterans in state and federal prison, 2004. *Bureau of Justice Statistics Special Report.* Washington, DC: U.S. Department of Justice.

Pandiani, J. A., Rosenheck, R., & Banks, S. M. (2003). Elevated risk of arrest for Veteran's Administration behavioral health service recipients in four Florida counties. *Law & Human Behavior, 27*, 289–298.

Patterson, E. J. (2013). The dose-response of time served in prison on mortality: New York State, 1989–2003. *American Journal of Public Health, 103*(3), 523–528.

Substance Abuse and Mental Health Services Administration. (2015). Trauma-informed approach and trauma-specific interventions. Retrieved from http://www.samhsa.gov/nctic/trauma-interventions

Shia, S. S., Miller, M. J., Swensen, A. B., & Matthieu, M. M. (2013). Veterans justice outreach and crisis intervention teams: A collaborative strategy for early intervention and continuity of care for justice-involved veterans. *Military Behavioral Health, 1*(2), 136–145.

Tanielian, T., & Jaycox, L. (2008). *Invisible wounds of war: Psychological and cognitive injuries, their consequences, and services to assist recovery.* Santa Monica, CA: RAND.

Taylor, J., Parkes, T., Haw, S., & Jepson, R. (2012). Military veterans with mental health problems: A protocol for systematic review to identify whether they have an additional risk of contact with the criminal justice systems compared with other veteran groups. *Systematic Reviews, 1*, 53–61.

Tsai, J., Rosenheck, R. A., Kasprow, W. J., & McGuire, J. F. (2014). Homelessness in a national sample of incarcerated veterans in state and federal prisons. *Administration & Policy in Mental Health & Mental Health Services Research, 41*(3), 360–367.

Veterans Affairs National Center on Homelessness Among Veterans. (n.d.). HUD-VASH resource guide for permanent housing and clinical care. Retrieved from http://www.va.gov/HOMELESS/docs/Center/144_HUD-VASH_Book_WEB_High_Res_final.pdf

Watson, A. C., Morabito, M. S., Draine, J., & Ottati, V. (2008). Improving police response to persons with mental illness: A multi-level conceptualization of CIT. *International Journal of Law and Psychiatry, 31,* 359–368.

Weaver, C. M., Trafton, J. A., Kimerling, R., Timko, C., & Moos, R. (2013). Prevalence and nature of criminal offending in a national sample of veterans in VA substance use treatment prior to the OEF/OIF conflicts. *Psychological Services, 10*(1), 54–65.

Worthen, M., & Ahern, J. (2014). The causes, course, and consequences of anger problems in veterans returning to civilian life. *Journal of Loss & Trauma, 19,* 355–363.

Wortzel, H. S., Binswanger, I. A., Anderson, C. A., & Adler, L. E. (2009). Suicide among incarcerated veterans. *Journal of the American Academy of Psychiatry & the Law Online, 37*(1), 82–91.

VOICES FROM THE FIELD

Danielle Easter, MSW, LCSW
Veteran Justice Outreach Coordinator,
Harry S. Truman Memorial Veterans' Hospital

Agency Setting

The Veteran Justice Outreach (VJO) program is part of Truman Veterans Affairs (VA's) psychosocial rehabilitation team. The program was established in May 2009 when each VA medical facility was given the directive to name a VJO specialist who would be charged with serving as the medical center's liaison with the local justice system, specifically to law enforcement, the courts, and jails. The VJO program is part of the VA's initiative to ensure access to services for the justice-involved veteran population at risk for homelessness, substance abuse, mental illness, and physical health problems. Truman VA has a coverage area that includes 43 Missouri counties and one county in the state of Illinois. I am one of two VJO specialists out of the Truman VA who provides services to veterans within this coverage area. There are currently three veteran treatment courts in my coverage area. We serve on the veteran treatment court team and coordinate, monitor, and report on participants' treatment activities.

Practice Responsibilities

As a full-time social worker in the VJO program, I am responsible for conducting outreach to veterans involved in the justice system. I work with the justice system to determine the best way to identify veterans within their systems. Once identified, I conduct interviews with the veterans to assess their eligibility for VA services and treatment needs. Once their eligibility is determined, I assist them with establishing care. For veteran treatment court participants, I am responsible for the coordination of participants' treatment and monitoring of their progress during their participation in the court program.

Expertise Required

A VJO specialist is required to be either a licensed clinical social worker or a psychologist. It is preferred that the VJO specialist has at least one year experience working with individuals in the criminal justice system. It helps if the VJO specialist is knowledgeable about VA eligibility and services. VJO specialists also participate in extensive training related to the operations of treatment courts utilizing best practices.

Ethical, Legal, Practice, Diversity, and/or Advocacy Issues Addressed

One of the challenging issues that I face in this position is balancing a client's right to privacy and reporting treatment progress within the treatment court process. It is important to establish appropriate releases and to communicate with my clients about my role in veteran treatment court. It is also important to ensure that both VA and legal partners learn and understand each other's professional roles. In doing this, your community partners have a better understanding about the type of information that can be released and the extent to which you will communicate with them regarding clients. It is just as important to educate my coworkers, supervisors, and administrative staff about my role in the court and the process that I am taking to ensure that we are protecting the privacy of our clients. Another very challenging dilemma in my position is advocating for the client who you know needs treatment but who is making poor decisions that violate the rules of the treatment court program. This can be difficult as you want the best chance for the client while also considering the need to maintain the integrity of the program.

Interprofessional and Intersectoral Collaboration

I am part of the psychosocial rehabilitation team at the VA. I also attend several other program meetings to ensure a good working relationship with VA treatment services. This also helps me to stay abreast of any concerns regarding client participation in services as well as any changes related to that specific treatment. I serve on several committees at the VA, which is key to keeping peers up to date about the VJO program. I participate in regional and national VJO and VA homeless program calls. I serve on the veteran treatment court teams and have good working relationships with each of the disciplines including probation and parole. I maintain communication with local attorney agencies such as the Office of the Public Defenders, Missouri Bar Association, Mid-Missouri Legal Aid, and County Prosecutor's office.

CHAPTER 18

The Immigrant Justice System

Carol L. Cleaveland

CHAPTER OBJECTIVES

The major objectives of this chapter are to:

- Explain the paths and obstacles that immigrants face when they navigate the justice system in an attempt to stay in the United States.
- Provide an insight into why 11.9 million immigrants have entered the United States without authorization rather than attempt legal means to immigrate.
- Explore how social workers can support immigrants who are involved in the immigration justice system.

CHAPTER COMPETENCIES HIGHLIGHTED

- Competency 3: Advance Human Rights and Social, Economic, and Environmental Justice
- Competency 5: Engage in Policy Practice
- Competency 8: Intervene With Individuals, Families, Organizations, and Communities

Campaign speeches targeting immigrants for deportation arguably helped businessman Donald Trump win the presidency. He lured followers by his contention that illegal immigration take jobs from Americans and fill communities with dangerous criminals; two proposed solutions were a wall across the Mexico–U.S. border, and escalated deportation enforcement. These proposals resonated with a number of angry Americans, many who likely think of immigrants as "illegals," "illegal immigrants," or "illegal aliens." Other Americans, however, may argue that newer arrivals are the same as immigrants throughout U.S. history—people who have come to this country seeking opportunities and who should be given the chance to be here legally and become citizens. Thus, not only is the question of immigration controversial, but it is complicated legally and has implications for both human and civil rights.

This chapter provides an overview of the system of laws traversed by immigrants who arrive legally, as well as the challenges for immigrants who enter the United States without authorization—a system fraught with obstacles. Undocumented immigrants can be deported unless they can make a convincing claim for asylum. If convicted of a misdemeanor, a legal permanent resident—an immigrant who has a "green card" and who may hope to one day become a citizen—may also be deported. To give readers an understanding of why so many enter the United States without permission, this chapter discusses paths to authorized immigration, including application for resident visas using the family or merit-based immigration systems.

This chapter encompasses the following: (a) the question of why 11.9 million people living in the United States—about 5% of the workforce—entered the country without authorization (Passell, 2015), and thus became eligible for deportation by Immigration and Customs Enforcement (ICE); (b) obstacles to authorized entry including a potential 20-year wait to receive a visa under the family-based immigration program; (c) the potential arrest, detaining, and deporting of undocumented immigrants; and (d) recommendations for social work practice. Though undocumented immigrants are the minority in a population of 43.5 million U.S. immigrants (Zong & Batalova, 2015), this chapter primarily focuses on those who either crossed the border without authorization or who remained here despite the expiration of their visas. Given that this population is subject to arrest, legal proceedings, and possible deportation, social workers are likely to encounter them while working not only in courts and detention centers but in a variety of advocacy and faith-based organizations serving immigrants.

Background and Scope of the Problem

The prospect of jobs and opportunity, the hope of escape from persistent violence in countries such as El Salvador and Honduras, and, in many cases, the wish to join family here may compel an immigrant to cross the U.S. border without authorization (Massey, 2005; Valenzuela, 2003; Vogt, 2013; Zong & Batalova, 2015). Immigrants have been encouraged by the promise of jobs in construction, home repairs, landscaping, house cleaning, informal childcare, and restaurants (Hondagneu-Sotelo, 2007), work that might not be sought by Americans. As noted by Hanson (2010), half of U.S.-born adult workers had not completed a high school diploma in 1960, compared to 8% today. As the proportion of low-skilled native-born workers has fallen, employers continue to require less-educated workers in U.S. agriculture, food processing, construction, building cleaning and maintenance, and other low-end jobs (Hanson, 2010).

Since 2000, approximately 500,000 people have crossed the border each year without authorization (Passell & Cohn, 2009). As many as two-thirds cross the Mexico/U.S. border surreptitiously; the other 30% to 40% arrive on temporary visas but stay here after their visas expire (United States Department Homeland Security, 2013). Approximately 75% of the nation's undocumented immigrants are Latino, with 59% having come from Mexico and another 18% from Central and South America (Passel & Cohn, 2009). Demographers note that the others are from Asia (11%) and the Caribbean (4%), and a small minority (less than 2%) are from the Middle East (Passel & Cohn, 2009).

System and Population Overview

Americans often argue that prospective immigrants should just "get in line" and enter the country legally—a process that, as explained in the following, is easier to discuss than to do. In order to support social workers' knowledge of this process for potential advocacy, this section focuses on the restricted avenues for legal immigration. It begins by addressing a common misconception in the nation's immigration debate: the idea that immigrants have avenues to come here legally if they simply wait their turn. For all but a handful of immigrants, however, options for legal entry and residency simply do not exist. As explained in the following, someone who hopes to become an immigrant has few opportunities to do so legally. "There is no line available for them and the 'regular channels' do not include them" (American Immigration Council, 2013). Immigrants can qualify for visas and "green cards" (legal permanent residency status) through three channels: (a) meeting the need for highly skilled labor such as neurosurgery, aerospace engineering, or professional sports; (b) via sponsorship by a "legal" family member; or (c) by being admitted as a refugee from political, religious, or ethnic persecution.

Only 124,000 work visas were granted in 2013 (U.S. Department of State, Bureau of Consular Affairs, n.d.). Work visas may be granted to employers who prove that they face dire staff shortages. As noted by the U.S. Department of State's Immigration Center, these visas are typically for workers with advanced degrees in such fields as science and engineering. Low-skilled workers—those most likely to immigrate here for jobs in construction and the service industry—would not typically be able to immigrate with a work visa. Instead, they are likely to try to receive permission to live and work here within the family-based system immigration, the U.S. family reunification program. Of 4.4 million people seeking permission to permanently live and work here, 4.3 million have applied through the family-based system (U.S. Department of State, Bureau of Consular Affairs, n.d.). Unfortunately, this route is fraught with obstacles including per country quota systems as well as priorities for certain categories of family members, such as adult children of immigrants. Immigrants from countries that have a large number of people applying for visas, such as Mexico or the Philippines, are disadvantaged simply by virtue of numerical odds. A prospective Mexican immigrant has many more competitors in the per country quota system than a rival from a western European state with a relatively low rate of emigration. State Department statistics show that though a spouse or child of a country with relatively few applicants may wait only three years for a visa, a sibling from Mexico will wait 20 years with no promise of ever receiving a visa. Not wanting to be thwarted by this backlog, some emigrants resort to entering the United States without authorization, thus becoming "illegal."

During these separations as they await permission to enter legally, immigrants and their family members are uncertain as to how long it might be before they are given a visa that would allow family reunification—or if they will even receive a visa as one is never guaranteed. "Children who were infants at the time the permanent resident emigrated may become teenagers before visas become available" (Hatch, 2010). Critical in this discussion is the understanding that only immigrants with legal residency may try to bring family here through the legal system; immigrants who came here without authorization are left hoping that their families can also enter without permission, a process that often includes the use of coyotes (human smugglers) to ensure passage across the border (Cvajner & Sciortino, 2010; Márquez, 2012). Cecelia Menjívar, a sociologist who studies immigration, detailed the experiences of immigrants from Guatemala and El Salvador. She described the experience of one woman whose son finally came here without authorization, via human smuggling from El Salvador. When they finally meet again, the parents and children often find little semblance of a family in each other and sometimes cannot even recognize each other physically. "A Salvadoran woman I interviewed in San Francisco laughed endlessly when she told me about her encounter with her son, whom she had left as a child in El Salvador and had not seen in 10 years. When she went to meet him at a coyote's house in Los Angeles, she kissed and hugged the wrong man because she could no longer recognize her own son" (Menjívar, 2006).

The difficulty of obtaining asylum—granted to refugees from war and/or political, religious/ethnic persecution—may also contribute to immigration without authorization. The numbers of undocumented immigrants from El Salvador, Honduras, and Guatemala have increased steadily since 2010, while the rate of entry from Mexico has declined slightly in the same time period (Migration Policy Institute, 2015). Fueling these demographic shifts are both an improved Mexican economy and an escalation of gang crime in Central America. Gang violence has rendered Central America's northern triangle of Honduras, El Salvador, and Guatemala the most dangerous region of the world; high homicide rates stem from civil wars and political destabilization during the 1990s, as well as extreme income inequality and being located between two of the world's largest producers (Colombia) and consumers (United States) of illegal drugs (Ribando, 2007). A study of unaccompanied migrant children ($n = 322$) in El Salvador who were deported after crossing the U.S. border found that violent crime and gang threats were the strongest determinants informing decisions to emigrate (Kennedy, 2014). Though asylum claims may be granted in U.S. immigration courts for those who can prove they would be subject to persecution for their religion, ethnicity, or religious beliefs, statistics indicate that petitions based on criminal rather than political violence are less likely to succeed. A review of petitions for asylum in the United States showed that while almost 46% of Chinese applicants were granted refuge here in 2013, less than 2% from El Salvador were awarded asylum (Executive Office for Immigration Review, 2014). As is the case for immigrants who hope to enter the United States legally through the family-based immigration system, the possibility of admission based on petitions to escape Central America's pervasive criminal violence is limited.

The Trafficking Victims Protection and Battered Women Protection acts of 2000 may help an immigrant obtain a visa if he or she is a victim of certain violent crimes, if it is determined that the individual will assist law enforcement in criminal prosecution (U.S. Citizenship and Immigration Services [USCIS], n.d.). Only 10,000 people are allowed legal entry to the United States through this program annually, though an immigrant who is admitted with this visa may obtain visas for family and would later be eligible for legal permanent residency if certain conditions are met (USCIS). The crime must have occurred in the United States.

Legal and Policy Frameworks

The U.S. Supreme Court ruled in 1896 that the 14th Amendment's equal protection clause extends to foreign nationals. "The Fourteenth Amendment of the United States Constitution is not confined to U.S. citizens. . . . These provisions are universal in their application to all persons within the territorial jurisdiction" (*Wong Wing v. United States*). This ruling has been upheld in subsequent Supreme Court decisions, most recently in 2001, when it ruled that an immigrant cannot be incarcerated after a deportation order has expired (*Zadvydas v. Davis*). But legal scholars note that while the Supreme Court has upheld the right of undocumented immigrant children to attend public school (*Pyler v. Doe*, 1982), debate persists over questions about whether it is constitutional for law enforcement to question a suspected "illegal" immigrant solely on the basis of race or ethnicity.

It is worth noting that the Department of Homeland Security—which has authority for patrolling the borders, making arrests, and detaining immigrants—refers to this population as "aliens" throughout its policies and procedural documents. The term is used to describe "Any person not a citizen or national of the United States" (U.S. Department of Homeland Security, n.d.). The term *aliens* has been used in American immigration law since President John Adams signed the "Alien and Sedition Act" into law in 1798. The 1798 law gave the federal government the power to deport noncitizens from the United States. Despite its appearance in countless legal documents, the term *alien*, with its connotations of otherness and exclusion, is not without controversy today. Prominent immigration historian Mae N. Ngai (2014) argues that the word *alien* has become pejorative and racist, as it is associated almost exclusively with Mexicans and/or Latinos. California Governor Jerry Brown agreed: He used his executive powers to ban the term from the state's labor laws in August 2015.

In what follows, the question of civil rights for undocumented immigrants is examined, together with an overview of what can happen to an immigrant when he or she is processed through the justice system. It begins with an overview of legal considerations before describing what happens when someone is arrested, detained, and deported.

Despite 14th Amendment protections for immigrants against illegal search of homes or arrest without probable cause, all non-U.S. citizens can legally be deported (American Immigration Council, 2011). Of 485,000 immigrants deported in 2013, approximately 49,000 were legal permanent residents, those known colloquially as "green card holders" (American Immigration Council, 2011; Pew Research Center, 2014). Though a green cardholder can work legally and apply to become a U.S. citizen, he or she also may be deported for both serious and minor infractions. A legal permanent resident may be deported for failing to notify immigration officials of a change of address; by law, he or she has 10 days to do so. The 1996 Illegal Immigrant Reform and Immigrant Responsibility Act (IIRIRA) expanded the list of crimes for which permanent residents can be deported by classifying such offenses as nonviolent theft, receipt of stolen property, and nonviolent drug charges. Under the 1996 law, an immigration judge may adjudicate a misdemeanor as an aggravated felony.

> You can't judge a crime by its name—people who have been convicted of misdemeanors, or of other crimes that were not charged as felonies in their state, have been found to have committed an aggravated felony and been deported. (Bray, n.d.)

U.S. courts have upheld forced deportations for such crimes as possession of stolen transit passes, petit larceny, shoplifting, and turnstile jumping, as these offenses were said to constitute moral turpitude (Harvard Law Review, 2015).

An immigrant may face challenges in the criminal justice system that a citizen would not. For example, a criminal lawyer may advise an immigrant to take a guilty plea to avoid prison time though an immigration lawyer would encourage the immigrant to fight the charges to avoid deportation (Bray, n.d.). And although a low-income immigrant charged would be provided a public defender in the criminal justice system, a consultation with an immigration attorney for a deportation hearing is not provided by the justice system. The immigrant must cover those costs. This is because immigration hearings, conducted before judges appointed by the U.S. Department of Justice, are considered civil rather than criminal proceedings (Global Detention Project, 2010).

Current Practice, Policy, and Social Movement Trends and Debates

Arrests and Deportation

The number of deportations per year reached its peak in 2013, when the United States deported about 438,421, more than double the total in 2001 (Pew Research Center, 2014). That total includes immigrants who had green cards, overstayed a visa, or entered the country illegally. Less than half of the deported had a criminal conviction (Pew Research Center, 2014). An immigrant's risk of deportation depends to a large extent on the policy priorities of the president. A review of statistics in this century shows that the number of deportations reached its peak in 2012 as President Obama escalated forced removals of immigrants to its highest point in U.S. history, prompting disgruntled activists to call him the "deporter in chief" (Gambino, 2014). The Obama Administration dramatically reduced the number of deportations later in his term, after ordering the departments of Justice and Homeland Security to focus efforts on terror risks, convicted criminals, and recent undocumented arrivals (Markon, 2015).

Two recent policies shape what may happen to an immigrant at the Mexico/U.S. border, as he or she attempts to swim across the Rio Grande or navigate a stretch of the Sonoran Desert in Arizona so deadly that the U.S. Border Patrol avoids it; death by exposure, snake bites, hunger, and thirst is possible (Urrea, 2008). The first, Operation Gatekeeper, was designed to dramatically escalate arrests with more police and high technology military equipment including drones. The second, Operation Streamline, seeks to increase criminal penalties for unlawful border crossing. An immigrant apprehended near the border will likely experience a different journey through the legal system than someone who is arrested by local police in New Jersey for a crime such as drunk driving, or during a raid by ICE at a North Carolina meat processing plant.

Operation Gatekeeper began in 1994; since then, the United States has more than doubled the number of Border Patrol officers policing the border in California, Arizona, New Mexico, and Texas (Nevins, 2010). Federal appropriations for immigration enforcement have spiraled from $232 million in 1989 to $3.8 billion in 2010 (U.S. Congressional Research Service, 2014). At the border, that money is used for motion detectors, drones, cameras, towers, reinforced steel fences, remote video surveillance, stadium lighting, and thermal imaging sensors, as well as U.S. Border Patrol officers and dogs (Pew Charitable Trusts, 2015). In addition to preventing unauthorized immigration, the Border Patrol is charged with protecting the United States from drug smuggling and illegal entry by terrorists.

Immigrants who cross the border without authorization do so via clandestine routes, and these have become increasingly more treacherous with the border's militarization, as immigrants seek more remote routes in the Sonoran Desert. When Gatekeeper began, 14 immigrant deaths were reported near the Mexico/U.S. border, but by 1998, when more people began crossing through the desert to avoid arrest, 147 died (Michalowski, 2007). By 2005, as border militarization stretched from San Diego to El Paso, approximately 500 people began dying annually (Michalowski, 2007). The intensified policing is designed to deter people from attempting to immigrate, though some scholars question whether this strategy is effective given the widespread use of human smugglers (Nevins, 2010; Vogt, 2013), or whether statistics showing reduced arrests near the border reflect a declining interest in unauthorized crossing because of a weakened U.S. economy (U.S. Congressional Research Service, 2014).

> Gatekeeper has pushed migrants from urban areas into more unforgiving and risky terrain and forced them to rely on high-priced smugglers. . . . Perhaps the greatest accomplishment of Gatekeeper has been to make undocumented immigrants less visible and thus give the appearance of a border under control. Meanwhile, growing numbers of migrants perish beyond the media spotlight in the mountains and deserts of California's border region. (Nevins, 2004)

The use of smugglers (known as coyotes or guias) to lead people through treacherous passages has become commonplace; despite the high cost of this journey (having risen from approximately $1,000 at Gatekeeper's inception to $4,000 today), indications are that immigrants still attempt unauthorized entry (U.S. Congressional Research Service, 2014).

A second border enforcement initiative, the Department of Homeland Security's Operation Streamline (No More Deaths, 2012), now determines what happens to an immigrant if he or she is arrested within certain enforcement zones near the border. Prior to Streamline, immigrants who had never been arrested trying to cross without permission were given the option by Border Patrol agents to be voluntarily returned to their home countries or given the opportunity to plead their case through the civil immigration system (Lydgate, 2010). Criminal prosecution was reserved for people with criminal records, or for those who made repeated attempts at an unlawful crossing. After Operation Streamline was initiated in 2005, prosecutorial discretion was eliminated and all undocumented immigrants were required to be prosecuted in criminal courts rather than the civil immigration system. The initiative's goal is simple: to deter undocumented immigrants by treating them as criminals.

Border Patrol officers typically bring detainees to holding cells near the border; there, they may be subject to expedited processing (U.S. Congressional Research Service, 2014). An immigrant may be moved from a holding cell to a criminal court and sent home in a single day, with a public defender who might represent as many as 80 clients in a single day (Lydgate, 2010). They are tried en masse.

Once convicted, a sentence of up to six months can be imposed for a single entry with the possibility for up to 20 years for people who have entered without authorization more than once. People incarcerated under these circumstances spend on average between 4 and 72 days in one of the 833 prison facilities under the custodial jurisdiction of the U.S. Marshals until being transferred to the custody of ICE for deportation or an asylum hearing (Global Detention Project, 2010).

Detention

Thirty-thousand immigrants are detained daily in U.S. jails and detention centers—six times the number incarcerated 20 years ago (International Human Rights Clinic (IHRC), Seattle University School of Law, 2008). Last year, the House of Representatives committed to funding immigration incarceration at a rate of more than $5 million daily—double the total than in 2005 (NIF, 2013). To understand how the detention system may affect even an immigrant with legal permanent residence (a green card), this section begins with the discussion of a case study recently analyzed in the Harvard Law Review (2015). Robert Cuellar-Gomez, who was admitted to the United States as a legal permanent resident in 1992, twice pled guilty to misdemeanor marijuana charges. Following the second conviction in 2008, the Department of Homeland Security initiated removal proceedings. He spent four years incarcerated in a detention center as he challenged the initial ruling through appeals in the immigration court system. He was finally deported in 2012. The 1996 IIRIRA permits releasing immigrants to await adjudication only in very rare circumstances; otherwise, they are to be incarcerated as they await immigration court hearings (Harvard Law Review, 2015). Cases such as Cuellar-Gomez's are now fairly common, and explain why the United States is spending more money than ever before to incarcerate immigrants.

Once incarcerated, an immigrant may be housed in one of 13 "Criminal Alien Requirement" detention facilities (American Civil Liberties Union [ACLU], 2014). Human and legal rights advocacy organizations have become increasingly alarmed by the length of incarceration for immigrant defendants, as well as the conditions and treatment they receive in detention centers (ACLU, 2014; Human Rights First, 2014; National Immigration Justice Center, 2015). An immigrant may also be encouraged to sign a voluntary consent to return, which leads to deportation without seeing a judge. Advocates are concerned that immigrants have been pressured to sign these documents without understanding them.

As noted earlier, a substantial proportion of those detained have no criminal record; they are being held while advocating to be allowed to remain in the United States as refugees from violence or persecution. An analysis using an ICE database obtained through the Freedom of Information Act found 32,000 inmates being housed in ICE detention facilities on January 25, 2009 (Kerwin & Lin, 2009). The Associated Press investigation showed that 18,690 had no criminal conviction, not even for minor crimes such as trespass or illegal reentry to the United States. Four hundred of the noncriminal detainees had been incarcerated for more than one year. Noncriminal detainees had been held for a mean of 65 days. Immigration statutes and regulations do not establish any limits to the period of time a noncitizen may be held in immigration detention (Global Detention Project, 2010). In other words, an immigrant faces the risk of being held for a lengthy stay despite a clean record. Human rights organizations blame policies designed to discourage asylum seeking and migration for the large numbers of people being held in detention (ACLU, 2014; Amnesty International, 2007; IHRC, Seattle University School of Law, 2008).

Fifty-nine percent (18,900 of the 32,000) of the detained immigrants were held in cells leased by ICE at local jails and state prisons. The others were in ICE detention facilities, which are leased for-profit private prisons. Though some with criminal convictions included very serious crimes such as homicide ($n = 156$) and sexual offenses ($n = 430$), more were being held for driving offenses ($n = 1,738$) and immigration offenses ($n = 812$) such as fraud or reentry. In June 2015, Human Rights First reported that among those being held in leased detention were 5,000 children with family members. More than half the children were very young, from newborns to age 6 (Human Rights First, 2014). Families are petitioning for asylum as they flee Central America; Honduras and El Salvador have the world's highest homicide rates, as well as cities controlled by gangs (United Nations News Centre, October 29, 2015). As reported by the United Nations, Guatemala and certain areas of Mexico have also become so dangerous as to threaten families.

Advocacy organizations have filed lawsuits seeking to end the incarceration of families in detention centers as they await asylum hearings. Conditions in detention centers have led to outrage by detainees, advocacy organizations, and some members of Congress. In July 2015, 29 members of the House of Representatives wrote to the Department of Homeland Security demanding an investigation of the for-profit prison provider, GEO Group Inc., for allegations of medical maltreatment and neglect at detention centers. One man who had been detained for five years died of intestinal cancer, a condition that had not been diagnosed until three days prior to his death (U.S. Congress, 2015). The Representatives also noted that a partially paralyzed inmate developed an infection after he was instructed by medical staff to reuse his catheters—an unsanitary practice. Hunger strikes and one riot have erupted as inmates complained of being forced to eat spoiled food, some of it infested with insects, as well as verbal and physical abuse by guards (U.S. Commission on Civil Rights, 2015). In short, an immigrant who seeks asylum in the country as he or she escapes violence in Honduras or El Salvador may endure months of harsh conditions in a U.S. detention center or jail.

Local Law and Lawsuits

This section gives a brief overview of how state and local ordinances, lawsuits, and court decisions may affect life for an undocumented immigrant in a variety of realms: from working to housing to an arrest following a traffic ticket. It is important to understand that these ordinances, laws, and policies are fluid because the courts may intervene in halting their implementation. Legal challenges from both anti-immigrant and pro-immigration rights advocacy organizations are common.

An immigrant living in the United States—especially someone who is here without authorization—may face more barriers to enjoying a good quality of life in some states and cities. Since the start of this century, local and state governments have engaged in lawmaking to address what they see as problems or concerns with the presence of immigrants in their communities. Most notably, Arizona passed SB 1070 in 2010 to escalate arrests of suspected undocumented immigrants. Police officers in that state are required to check immigration status for people who appear as if they might be in the country without authorization. The Supreme Court upheld the law despite lawsuits alleging that it would lead to racial profiling and the possible incarceration of American citizens (ACLU, 2014). As noted by the ACLU, the courts have struck down provisions giving the police the right to arrest suspected undocumented immigrants without a warrant and making it a crime not to carry immigration papers. "Copycat" laws were passed in Alabama, Georgia, Indiana, South Carolina, and Utah (ACLU, 2014).

Some cities and states have adopted policies and/or laws to restrict police from handing over immigrants who have been arrested to ICE, preferring instead to treat these individuals as they would an American who has been arrested. These are often known as "sanctuary cities." There are currently 200 localities with these policies, which have become more controversial since the murder of a San Francisco woman by an undocumented man who had been released from jail following his arrest on a drug charge (Pearson, 2015). ICE had asked that the man be handed over for deportation proceedings but San Francisco, according to its policy, did not cooperate.

Core Roles and Functions of Forensic Social Work in This System

By understanding immigration law, a social worker knows how to advise an immigrant who has been arrested to consult an immigration attorney before deciding whether to accept a guilty plea. Social workers are also advised to take detailed information on families to find out if a relative is being held in detention (National Association of Social Workers [NASW], 2011). In these cases, a social worker could assist the family in finding affordable or pro bono legal counsel since an attorney is not provided for immigration court proceedings. Clients may need to be informed that relatives can assist an inmate by putting money in an account to make purchases from the detention center or jail canteen. Families may not know that an inmate can make collect calls. Relatives may also be in duress because they do not know where a loved one is being incarcerated. In that case, social workers may assist by searching ICE's online prisoner locator website. However, if an immigrant is being incarcerated in a jail, he or she will not appear in the locator. It is then up to the social worker to help the family to call local jails and prisons for that information.

In addition, immigrant families may be coping with severe disruption if a parent has been detained. When parents are held in detention, the subsequent family separation poses great risks for their children. Whether as a result of witnessing their parents' arrest or simply not understanding why their parents cannot come home, children are likely to face multiple consequences when separated from their primary caregivers. Children experience emotional trauma, safety concerns, economic instability, and diminished overall well-being. This can lead to interruptions in these children's schooling, depression, aggression, and rebellion (NASW, 2011). Child welfare workers may need to advise family court judges why a parent may not be able to appear for a custody hearing (NASW, 2011).

In its position paper on immigration law and detention, NASW (2011) encouraged social workers to discuss the issues of immigration and detention with other practitioners as well as the community to raise awareness, and to form or join grassroots coalitions to advocate for improved conditions in detention centers and jails. Finally, NASW noted that the *Code of Ethics* (2008) applies to social workers with the following imperatives: (a) Social workers are ethically obligated to engage in social and political action to ensure that all people have access to resources, employment, and opportunity to develop fully; and (b) social workers are ethically obligated to ensure that no group is subject to discrimination based on race, ethnicity, origin, or immigration status. Thus, the ethical imperatives are clear for social workers as immigrants remain a vulnerable population.

Relevant Theories or Frameworks

Undocumented immigrants are not eligible for most services provided by social workers and/or social service programs including the Supplemental Nutrition Assistance Program (SNAP), Temporary Assistance for Needy Families (TANF), and Medicaid, and social work researchers are still in the exploratory phase of identifying service needs. Some undocumented immigrants may encounter social workers in public schools, child protective services, and in detention. The prohibition against social service receipt, coupled with the omnipresent threat of deportation, constitutes clear burdens on this population, exacerbating their marginalization and vulnerability. Therefore, it is argued here that social workers should engage in policy practice, defined here as efforts to influence the development, enactment, and implementation of policies at the local, state, and national levels (Jansson, 2007). Brueggemann (2013) defined policy practice as a core social work competency, specifying that professionals identify social policy at federal, state, and local levels to assess impact on well-being, service delivery, and access to services. CSWE has also mandated that students show competence in assessing how social welfare and economic policies affect social services, and in advocating for policies that advance human rights, as well as social and economic justice. In addition, social work scholars have called on all social workers to engage in policy practice as well as their work with individual clients (Rocha, Poe, & Thomas, 2010).

Conclusion

Social workers need to understand the complexity of the immigration legal system to support individuals, families, and communities. A single family could have "mixed status"

Case Example and Application

A social worker in a suburban community learned that local police had been harassing Mexican immigrants, many of whom had recently rented houses in the township as they sought jobs in construction and childcare. Specifically, police and municipal housing inspectors had begun making late-night visits to residents to write citations for minor infractions that required court appearances. In addition, a vocal neighborhood coalition had organized calling for the removal of "illegals" from the town, and advocating a new ordinance requiring landlords to obtain proof of legal residency in the United States from prospective tenants. Upon hearing about these developments, activists called a meeting with community members who had contact with the immigrants including faith leaders and others who were known to be potentially sympathetic to the immigrants (e.g., a retired teacher who had volunteered his time to help with minor medical concerns). The meeting led to the decision to contact legal organizations with histories of service to Latinos, such as the Puerto Rican Legal Defense Fund. A social worker realized that she could help by providing pro bono time to meet with immigrants and volunteer translators to take statements from immigrants describing the late-night "inspections." By doing the pro bono work, she would be meeting the NASW ethical imperative for service: "Social workers are encouraged to volunteer some portion of their professional skills with no expectation of significant financial return (pro bono service)" (National Association of Social Workers, 2008, Core Value: Service).

The social worker and other volunteers collected several dozen testimonials from immigrants, who described their fear upon being visited by police and municipal officials late at night. They believed that they had to comply with the surprise inspections, and thus let police and inspectors into their homes, sometimes on multiple occasions. In one incident, the social worker joined a legal assistant as he interviewed a 28-year-old Mexican man. The man handed over copies of tickets he had been issued during a late-night housing inspection. The man had been living in a small apartment in a house that had been converted to multiple rental units. One night after 11 p.m., he and his two roommates were startled by a knock on the door. Standing at the entrance were two men: a uniformed police officer and a housing inspector. They did not understand why the police officer was there. "We were just all there watching television. The other two and me," he said. The men were given tickets for overcrowding. The social worker's role in these interviews was to be supportive, and to assist in any way possible. Given their undocumented status, many were apprehensive about the process and a social worker's skills in engaging clients were useful.

The efforts to document municipal harassment proved fruitful, though the legal process was lengthy. Three years after filing suit, a federal judge ordered the municipal government to cease late-night housing inspections. In addition, the judge ordered that police cease giving tickets for "officer's discretion," citations that had typically been issued to day laborers for waiting on corners to find work.

members, including legal permanent residents, citizens, and undocumented relatives. The outcomes of interactions in the immigrant legal system potentially have grave outcomes, including separation of family members through deportation. Practitioners may need to help families find a relative who has been incarcerated and to obtain a credible attorney who would take a pro bono client or adjust legal fees. In addition, social workers are obligated by the NASW *Code of Ethics* to advocate for reforms on behalf of vulnerable immigrants. Such a strategy could begin by addressing a common misconception in the nation's immigration debate: the idea that immigrants have avenues to come here legally if they simply wait their turn. For all but a handful of immigrants, however, options for legal entry and residency simply do not exist.

CHAPTER EXERCISES

Exercise 1. In small groups, discuss how social work services might be implemented for undocumented immigrants in the following settings: immigration court, detention centers, day labor sites, and homeless shelters. What services might immigrants need in this setting? What are the current service barriers? How would funding be developed to pay social workers for services in these settings?

Exercise 2. Select a local, state, or national policy pertaining to immigration and analyze it from a social work perspective. How can social workers engage in policy reform to support immigrant populations?

Additional Resources

American Immigration Council: https://www.americanimmigrationcouncil.org/topics/immigration -101

Global Detention Project: www.globaldetentionproject.org

Mexican American Legal Defense Fund: http://maldef.org

National Immigration Forum: https://immigrationforum.org

References

American Civil Liberties Union. (2014). Warehoused and forgotten: Immigrants trapped in our shadow private prison system. Retrieved from https://www.aclu.org/warehoused-and-forgotten -immigrants-trapped-our-shadow-private-prison-system

American Immigration Council. (2011). Secure communities: A fact sheet. Retrieved from http://www .immigrationpolicy.org/just-facts/secure-communities-fact-sheet

American Immigration Council. (2013). The math of immigration detention. Retrieved from https:// immigrationforum.org/blog/themathofimmigrationdetention

Amnesty International. (2007). Jailed without justice: Immigration detention in the USA. Retrieved from https://www.amnestyusa.org/pdfs/JailedWithoutJustice.pdf

Bray, I. (n.d.). An aggravated felony can get a non-citizen removed (deported). Retrieved from http:// www.alllaw.com/articles/nolo/us-immigration/aggravated-felony-get-non-citizen-removed- deported.html

Brueggemann, W. G. (2013). *The practice of macro social work.* Belmont, CA: Brooks/Cole.

Chavez, L. (2007). Commentary: The condition of illegality. *International Migration, 45,* 192–196.

Cvajner, M., & Sciortino, G. (2010). Theorizing irregular migration: The control of spatial mobility in differentiated societies. *European Journal of Social Theory, 13*(3), 389–404.

DeGenova, N. (2002). Migrant "illegality" and "deportability" in everyday life. *Annual Review of Anthropology, 31,* 419–437.

Executive Office for Immigration Review. (2014). FY 2013 statistics yearbook. Retrieved from http:// www.justice.gov/sites/default/files/eoir/legacy/2014/04/16/fy13syb.pdf

Gambino, L. (2014, October 15). Orphaned by deportation: The crisis of the children left behind. *The Guardian.* Retrieved from https://www.theguardian.com/us-news/2014/oct/15/immigration -boy-reform-obama-deportations-families-separated

Global Detention Project. (2010). Immigration detention and the law: U.S. policy and legal framework. Retrieved from http://www.globaldetentionproject.org/fileadmin/docs/US_Legal_Profile.pdf

Hanson, G. H. (2010). *The economics and policy of illegal immigration in the United States*. Washington, DC: Migration Policy Institute.

Harvard Law Review. (2015). A prison is a prison is a prison: Mandatory immigration detention and the Sixth Amendment right to counsel. Retrieved from http://harvardlawreview.org/2015/12/a-prison-is-a-prison-is-a-prison

Hatch, P. (2010). *US immigration policy: Family reunification*. Seattle, WA: League of Women Voters.

Hondagneu-Sotelo, P. (2007). *Domestica: Immigrant workers cleaning and caring in the shadows of affluence*. Berkeley: University of California Press.

Human Rights First. (2014). How to protect refugees and prevent abuse at the border. Retrieved from http://www.humanrightsfirst.org/sites/default/files/HRF-Asylum-on-the-Border-noApps.pdf

International Human Rights Clinic, Seattle University School of Law. (2008). Voices from detention: A report on human rights violations at the Northwest Detention Center in Tacoma, Washington. Retrieved from http://law.seattleu.edu/documents/news/archive/2008/DRFinal.pdf

Jansson, B. (2007). *Becoming an effective policy advocate: From policy practice to social justice*. Boston, MA: Cengage.

Kennedy, E. (2014). No childhood here: Why Central American children are fleeing their homes. American Immigration Council. Retrieved from http://www.immigrationpolicy.org/perspectives/no-childhood-here-why-central-american-children-are-fleeing-their-homes

Kerwin, D., & Lin, S. Y. Y. (2009). *Immigrant detention: Can ICE meet its legal imperatives and case management responsibilities?* Migration Police Institute. Retrieved from http://www.migrationpolicy.org/pubs/detentionreportSept1009.pdf

Lydgate, J. J. (2010). Assembly-line justice: A review of operation streamline. *California Law Review, 98*, 481–544.

Markon, J. (2015, July 2). Obama Administration scales back deportations in policy shift. *The Washington Post*. Retrieved from https://www.washingtonpost.com/politics/dhs-scales-back-deportations-aims-to-integrate-illegal-immigrants-into-society/2015/07/02/890960d2-1b56-11e5-93b7-5eddc056ad8a_story.html?utm_term=.d6873fa79dbe

Márquez, J. D. (2012). Latinos as the living dead: Raciality, expendability, and border militarization. *Latino Studies, 10*(4), 473–498.

Massey, D. S. (2005). Five myths about immigration: Common misconceptions underlying US border-enforcement policy. *Immigration Daily*. Retrieved from https://www.ilw.com/articles/2005,1207-massey.shtm

Menjívar, C. (2006). Liminal legality: Salvadoran and Guatemalan immigrants' lives in the United States. *American Journal of Sociology, 111*(4), 999–1037.

Michalowski, R. (2007). Border militarization and migrant suffering: A case of transnational social injury. *Social Justice, 34*, 62–76.

National Association of Social Workers. (2008). *Code of ethics of the National Association of Social Workers*. Washington, DC: Author.

National Association of Social Workers. (2011). The impact of immigration detention on children and families. Retrieved from https://www.socialworkers.org/practice/intl/2011/HRIA-FS-84811.Immigration.pdf

National Immigration Forum. (2013). The math of immigration detention. Retrieved from https://immigrationforum.org/blog/themathofimmigrationdetention

National Immigration Justice Center. (2015). The immigration detention transparency and human rights project. Retrieved from http://immigrantjustice.org/immigration-detention-transparency-and-human-rights-project-august-2015-report

Nevins, J. (2004). The United States is to blame for illegal immigrant fatalities. In W. Dudley (Ed.), *Illegal immigration: Opposing viewpoints*. San Diego, CA: Greenhaven Press.

Nevins, J. (2010). *Operation gatekeeper and beyond: The war on "illegals" and the remaking of the US–Mexico boundary*. New York, NY: Routledge.

Ngai, M. M. (2014). *Impossible subjects: Illegal aliens and the making of modern America*. Princeton, NJ: Princeton University Press.

No More Deaths. (2012). Operation Streamline fact sheet. Retrieved from http://forms.nomoredeaths .org/wp-content/uploads/2014/10/nmd_fact_sheet_operation_streamline.pdf

Passell, J. S. (2015). Testimony of Jeffrey S. Passel–unauthorized immigrant population: National and state trends, industries and occupations. Retrieved from http://www.pewhispanic.org/2015/03/26/ testimony-of-jeffrey-s-passel-unauthorized-immigrant-population

Passel, J. S., & Cohn, D. (2009). *Mexican immigrants: How many come? How many leave?* Washington, DC: Pew Research Center. Retrieved from http://www.pewhispanic.org/2009/07/22/mexican -immigrants-how-many-come-how-many-leave

Pearson, M. (2015). What's a sanctuary city and why should you care? Retrieved from http://www.cnn .com/2015/07/06/us/san-francisco-killing-sanctuary-cities

Pew Charitable Trusts. (2015). Immigration enforcement along U.S. borders and ports of entry. Retrieved from http://www.pewtrusts.org/en/research-and-analysis/issue-briefs/2015/02/immigration -enforcement-along-us-borders-and-at-ports-of-entry

Pew Research Center. (2014). U.S. deportation of immigrants reaches record high in 2013. Retrieved from http://www.pewresearch.org/fact-tank/2014/10/02/u-s-deportations-of-immigrants-reach -record-high-in-2013

Ribando, C. M. (2007). *Gangs in Central America*. Washington, DC: U.S. Congressional Research Service.

Rocha, C., Poe, B., & Thomas, V. (2010). Political activities of social workers: Addressing perceived barriers to political participation. *Social Work, 55*(4), 317–325.

United Nations News Centre. (2015). UN agency warns of "looming" refugee crisis as women flee Central America and Mexico. Retrieved from http://www.un.org/apps/news/story.asp?NewsID =52410#.Vo0zUfGA0ZQ

U.S. Citizenship and Immigration Services. (n.d.). Victims of criminal activity: Nonimmigrant status. Retrieved from http://www.uscis.gov/humanitarian/victims-human-trafficking-other-crimes/ victims-criminal-activity-u-nonimmigrant-status/victims-criminal-activity-u-nonimmigrant -status#U%20Visa%20Cap

U.S. Commission on Civil Rights. (2015). With liberty and justice for all: The state of civil rights at immigration detention facilities. Retrieved from http://www.usccr.gov/OIG/Statutory_ Enforcement_Report2015.pdf

U.S. Congress. (2015). Correspondence to the Department of Homeland Security. Retrieved from https://www.documentcloud.org/documents/2165708-adelanto-letter.html

U.S. Congressional Research Service. (2014). Border security: Immigration enforcement between ports of entry. Retrieved from http://fas.org/sgp/crs/homesec/R42138.pdf

U.S. Department of Homeland Security. (n.d.). Definition of terms. Retrieved from http://www.dhs .gov/definition-terms

U.S. Department of Homeland Security. (2013). Yearbook of immigration statistics: 2013. Retrieved from http://www.dhs.gov/publication/yearbook-immigration-statistics-2013-enforcement-actions#

U.S. Department of State, Bureau of Consular Affairs. (n.d.). Overview: Family-based immigrant visas. Retrieved from http://travel.state.gov/content/visas/en/immigrate/family/family-preference .html#1

Urrea, L. A. (2008). *The devil's highway*. Boston, MA: Back Bay Books.

Valenzuela, Jr., A. (2003). Day labor work. *Annual Review of Sociology, 29*(1), 307–333.

Vogt, W. A. (2013). Crossing Mexico: Structural violence and the commodification of undocumented Central American migrants. *American Ethnologist, 40*(4), 764–780.

Wong Wing v. United States, 163 U.S. 228 (1896).

Zadvydas v. Davis, 533 U.S. 678 (2001).

Zong, J., & Batalova, J. (2015). Frequently requested statistics on immigrants and immigration in the United States. Migration Policy Institute. Retrieved from http://www.migrationpolicy.org/article/frequently-requested-statistics-immigrants-and-immigration-united-states

CHAPTER 19

Intersectoral Collaboration: Mental Health, Substance Abuse, and Homelessness Among Vulnerable Populations

David Fitzpatrick
Jodi Hall
Karen Bullock

CHAPTER OBJECTIVES

The major objectives of this chapter are to:

- Explore the use of Addiction Recovery Management (ARM) principles in the recovery process of vulnerable populations.
- Examine factors that may impede or foster successful completion of the long-term recovery process for those experiencing home insecurity.

CHAPTER COMPETENCIES HIGHLIGHTED

- Competency 2: Engage Diversity and Difference in Practice
- Competency 3: Advance Human Rights and Social, Economic, and Environmental Justice

Substance abuse is a significant problem among persons who are homeless (Substance Abuse and Mental Health Services Administration [SAMHSA], 2006; Tucker, Wenzel, Golinelli, Zhou, & Green, 2011). Conventional mental health and substance abuse recovery programs may not be the best suited for this population. Research has suggested that social, peer-led recovery programs may be more effective in addressing the specific needs of persons faced with the intersectionality of mental health, addictions, and home insecurity. The objective of this chapter is to explore the application of ARM principles for developing practice skills in the recovery process among vulnerable populations. This chapter examines demographic and social action factors that may impede or foster successful completion of this long-term recovery for persons who are experiencing home insecurity.

Background and Scope of the Problem

A recent report by the Institute of Medicine (IOM, 2015) documents that mental health and substance disorders affect approximately 20% of the U.S. population. Drug and alcohol misuse can lead to substance disorders, which are classified as mental health conditions.

When untreated, these disorders can have harmful effects on individuals and society (Hahm, Le Cook, Ault-Brutus, & Alegria, 2015). In some cases, these mental health disorders lead to episodic and/or chronic homelessness (North & Smith, 1994), and for some people, the need to support drug misuse leads them to resort to petty theft or other crimes that initiate contact with the criminal justice system (Le Cook & Alegria, 2015). Treatment providers should take into consideration core roles and functions within the system of care that may impede successful practice outcomes.

Forensic social work has expanded its reach in most recent years to include court-mandated mental health, substance abuse treatment, and welfare rights (Robbins, Vaughan-Eden, & Maschi, 2014). In a study that assessed whether criminal history and socioeconomic status reduce or contribute to disparities in substance abuse treatment, the research (Le Cook & Alegria, 2015) documented a higher percentage of referrals to substance abuse treatment from the criminal justice system and a strong correlation between involvement in the criminal justice system and receipt of substance abuse treatment. Furthermore, there were racial–ethnic differences in the receipt of substance abuse treatment, which resulted from the fact that participants with lower income were more likely to use substance abuse treatment, and Blacks and Latinos were more likely to be impoverished.

Health care coverage for the treatment of mental health and substance disorders is a major issue of concern in the United States that continues to be debated in the social, political, and religious arenas. There is much agreement that one approach does not fit all (Clemmens, 2016), and the need to focus on underserved, vulnerable persons is important. One of these underserved populations is persons who experience episodic or chronic homelessness. The existing research on best practices is inconclusive; therefore, the development and refinement of skills, knowledge, and approaches that best address substance use disorders and home/housing insecurity are essential for the practice of forensic social work.

Broader, more integrative approaches that emphasize social justice and human rights as critical components for applying the intersectionality framework must take into consideration race; gender; social class; lesbian, gay, bisexual, and transgender (LGBT); mental health (Maschi & Killian, 2011; Robbins et al., 2014); and substance abuse status (active/inactive). It behooves social work educators to lead the charge in preparing practitioners for this interdisciplinary field of practice because it is often the responsibility of the social worker to (a) document evidence that will be used in the defense of individuals, (b) attend court preceding and proceeding in order to develop effective treatment plans, (c) provide expert testimony to substantiate individuals' narratives, and (d) evaluate competency for participating in civil and criminal trials, and more. Yet, research scholars have argued that "although social workers are trained in various aspects of social work practice, they are rarely trained in the forensic or legal arena" (Robbins et al., 2014). Understanding addictions, recovery, and home/housing insecurity can foster professional growth and development around two specific competencies.

System and Population Overview

Recovery Factors in a Long-Term, Social Recovery Program for Homeless Populations

Mental health and substance abuse disorders among underserved populations have been explored extensively. While 235,823 homeless individuals were admitted to treatment programs in the United States in 2009, research findings suggested services were still lacking for mental health and substance abuse treatment overall and particularly among homeless populations (SAMHSA, 2006; Tucker et al., 2011). According to a more recent report (2015) from the IOM, no standard system is in place to ensure that people will receive the necessary psychosocial intervention as a part of routine clinical care plans. Fortunately, there is existing research that offers hope for persons who are homeless and who are experiencing problems with substance use. Many of these citizens can be rehabilitated and improve their quality of life (Stahler & Stimmel, 1995; Zerger, 2002). The literature on food insecurity (Townsend, Peerson, Love, Achterberg, & Murphy, 2001) helped to provide a strengths-based framework for conceptualizing the problem as home/housing insecurity among the populations that participated in this program evaluation report.

Conventional, professionally led programs that are facilitated by persons trained and educated—typically with degrees, such as social workers—may be able to increase its effectiveness with persons who are homeless by incorporating peer-led, social rehabilitation models of intervention. Previous research (Zerger, 2002) that has examined practice and policy effectiveness suggests "starting where the client is" and pairing him or her with someone who has experienced home/housing insecurity or who has been homeless to create a level of identification that is highly regarded in conventional addiction and recovery intervention models. Additionally, research (Zerger, 2002) indicates social rehabilitation programs can be offered more cost-effectively than conventional programs and result in a net fiscal gain to society while simultaneously increasing the quality of life for the person who has substance abuse problems, his or her family, or social support network. The ARM is one such framework that can be successfully implemented with this population and it can be a useful tool in sustaining long-term recovery efforts in a variety of programs, including social recovery programs (White, 2008).

ARM principles have received support (Fitzpatrick, 2014; Kelly & White, 2011) across disciplines, including social work, psychology, and other mental health professions. Moreover, the social recovery program for homeless individuals implementing ARM principles evaluated in our research documented a 70% success rate for the persons completing the program, remaining sober, and living productive lives at the one-year follow-up. Despite challenges inherent to the treatment of mental health and substance abuse disorders, an ARM framework can be successfully integrated into social recovery programs for homeless individuals. In fact, principles of ARM integrated into comprehensive psychosocial intervention plans seek to initiate "networks of indigenous and professional supports designed to initiate, sustain and enhance the quality of long-term addiction recovery for individuals and families and to create value and policies in the larger cultural and policy environment that are supportive of these recovery processes" (Kelly & White, 2011). This chapter offers insight for forensic social workers about how to engage diversity and differences in practice, as well as advance human rights and social, economic, and environmental justice.

Current Practice, Policies, and Social Movement Trends and Debates

The research on the cause and effect of substance misuse and abuse is inconclusive. One might argue that it is less important to know and document the causes than it is to meet the individuals where they are and to develop an effective plan for moving forward with a successful treatment plan. Regardless of whether or not substance abuse contributes to homelessness, the development of effective interventions for this population is especially important. Evidence-based approaches are essential. Documenting the incidence and prevalence helps to understand the magnitude of the program and who are most affected by it. Research shows a positive correlation between alcohol abuse (2%–86%), drug abuse (2%–70%), and those suffering from home/housing insecurity in various subpopulations (Zerger, 2002). These rates are considerably higher than those for the general population. Some of the most notable research findings in this area suggest (a) substance abuse treatment can be effective and lead to sustained recovery in homeless individuals (Dietz, 2007; Zerger, 2002); (b) substance abusing homeless populations are underserved and often overlooked by treatment programs and outreach efforts (Maguire, Sheahan, & White, 2012); (c) substance abuse treatment programs must use culturally sensitive intervention strategies to engage and retain persons who have experienced homelessness, as opposed to those who have not been homeless; and (d) effective engagement and retention of these individuals in treatment include providing housing and case management (Stahler & Stimmel, 1995; Zerger, 2002).

For social workers, understanding that every person, regardless of position in society, has a fundamental right to freedom, safety, privacy, an adequate standard of living, health care, and education is a core competency in practice. Moreover, the advancement of human rights and social, economic, and environmental justice can be achieved through outcomes-oriented approaches (Council on Social Work Education [CSWE], 2015).

Core Roles and Functions of Forensic Social Work in This System

The ability to integrate and apply social work knowledge, values, and skills rests upon purposeful, intentional (CSWE, 2015), and ethical behaviors. The roles and functions that practitioners take on in order to promote human and community well-being need to be explicated. To this end, the recovery model, which is a social movement that mental health providers have found to be effective in addressing addictions for decades (Leff & Warner, 2006), is described here. It is a strengths-based approach that elicits the subjective experience of optimism about outcomes from treatment and helps individuals to create value and appreciation for their own hard work and effort to stop using and abusing substances.

A program evaluation of a mental health and substance abuse treatment program that was conducted in a community-based agency for persons who are homeless and experiencing substance use disorders helps to explain the functions in a system of care that integrated ARM principles into a comprehensive social model recovery and rehabilitation delivery system (Fitzpatrick, 2014). In this care setting, decisions about treatment are made collaboratively with the individual and the identified support person (i.e., the sponsor), which essentially is an informal contract to succeed, such as what one might observe in a mentoring relationship. Furthermore, research scholars (Leff & Warner, 2006) have documented outcomes from this model, such as a renewed interest in educating oneself about illness management, addressing stigma and peer-led advocacy, mentoring, and support networks in community-led drop-in centers.

A competency-based education framework that seeks to improve psychosocial intervention and accessibility of the services, across groups, may find this community-capacity-building social movement useful. It is necessary for social workers to understand the dimensions of diversity as the intersectionality of multiple factors including, but not limited to, age, class, race, gender, orientation, religion, and a host of other variables (CSWE, 2015).

The IOM (2015) defines psychosocial interventions as interpersonal or informational activities, techniques, or strategies that target biological, behavioral, cognitive, emotional, interpersonal, social, or environmental factors with the aim of improving health functioning and well-being. The California Department of Alcohol and Drug Programs (2004) suggests that the effectiveness of these programs is derived from their ability to assist individuals with building and leveraging strong indigenous and social support systems during treatment and posttreatment.

Social workers are uniquely prepared to integrate these program attributes into practice paradigms. Education and practice are guided by a person-in-environment framework, global perspectives, respect for human diversity, and knowledge based on scientific inquiry (CSWE, 2015).

Relevant Theories or Frameworks

Addiction Recovery Management

Much of the recent attention focused on treatment in an ARM has emphasized its underpinning of long-term treatment sustainability and continuity of care for chronic disorder (Kelly & White, 2011; White, 2008). Proponents of ARM suggest that short-term treatments have helped many people but, if decision makers truly believe that substance abuse is a chronic disorder, then a move toward a long-term treatment and continuing care should be implemented. The ARM framework recommends the necessary components of monitoring, leveraging, and coordinating an interdisciplinary process of engaging providers. ARM is comprehensive in its delivery approach and systems of care. A key difference between the short-term, acute treatment framework and the ARM framework is the length of treatment and/or observation. While the ARM framework is excellent for organizing and implementing roles and functions within the care system, it is necessary to have a good theoretical understanding of the implications of cultural differences when engaging diversity in practice.

Critical Race Theory

Analytic concepts in forensic social work can enhance the capacity of educators to prepare practitioners to be effective in closing the gap that exists for racial disparities in treatment approaches and programs. Critical Race Theory (CRT) explains why diversity is not simply a collection of group differences and it provides a model for understanding and evaluation of the outcomes of this study. CRT posits that the possession and demonstration of positive and accepting attitudes and the avoidance of racial stereotypes and stereotypical thinking are almost universally prescribed for effective multicultural practice. Although these attitudinal predispositions will not necessarily result in effective service outcomes for people of color (Abrams & Mojo, 2009; Delgado & Stefanic, 2001), the current research suggests that CRT can be used to develop guiding principles for competency-based education and outcomes that address the gaps in existing systems of care. According to Kirmayer (2012), the nature of clinical encounters and mental health services, in general, are challenged by cultural diversity because individual and group experiences, expressions, and treatment outcomes are all influenced by culture. Therefore, practitioner preparation and training that seeks to eliminate disparities and promote social justice necessitate a framework that goes beyond race as an explanatory variable (Bullock & Hall, 2015). Knowledge, values, skills, and cognitive processes must be observable behaviors, that denote competency in social work practice and policies areas.

Relevant Ethical, Legal, and Policy Issues

Despite challenges inherent in homelessness, a forensic social work intervention can successfully integrate the social recovery model for homeless individuals. Furthermore, CRT combined with the ARM framework of practice helps to inform policy planning and development for effective practice with homeless individuals in recovery. A particular distinction is that these recovery programs rely on the ethical and legal practices of incorporating "networks of indigenous and professional supports designed to initiate, sustain and enhance the quality of long-term addiction recovery for individuals and families" (Kelly & White, 2011). This approach creates value-latent policies that are viable and sustainable in the larger cultural and policy environments that are the driving forces of the recovery processes.

Relevant Assessment, Prevention, and Intervention Strategies

A model for integrating ARM principles into a comprehensive recovery and rehabilitation delivery system relied on the elements that Scott and Dennis (2011) describe as comprehensive ARM features in their acronym "TALER": (a) Tracking, (b) Assessing, (c) Linking, (d) Engaging, and (d) Retaining. Using this framework, the Recovery Shelter shows that 70% of participants are still sober and living productive lives at the one-year postcompletion checkup. Retention tools are essential, and one of the most powerful tools is secure housing (Kaskutas, 1999; Stahler & Stimmel, 1995). This also provides individuals with a reprieve from external environmental issues that could lead to a potential relapse. The evidence-based social engagement intervention is facilitated by peer-led recovery staff members, which seems to be particularly appealing to persons who have experienced episodic and/or chronic homelessness because peer counselors tend to share common experiences of substance abuse and recovery, mental illness, oppression, and/or discrimination. Case management is provided throughout the program and during transition to outside housing and employment.

Methods

Retrospective data were gathered upon entry to the recovery program between the years 2007 and 2010. During this period, there were 1,758 admissions, 1,084 men and 674 women. The data represent 1,394 individuals.[1] This is the most recent data for those individuals who have completed the program. All cases represent individuals who have either completed the program in compliance or left the program before completion. Except for the dependent variable, all data were collected by participant self-reports, at the time of admission to the recovery program at the shelter.

Data on gender, age, race, drug of choice, veteran status, and age of first use were collected from individual self-reports. Gender, age, race, and veteran status could be, but were not necessarily, corroborated through public records or presentation of official identification. Years of use was calculated by subtracting the age of first use from the age of the client at admission. Whether the client was a new client or returning client was determined from a review of previous records. Completion in good standing was determined by a professional staff. Age, age of first use, and length of use are continuous variables. In order to determine if group differences exist, these variables have been divided into categories. The categories were determined by the researcher based on knowledge of previous research and a review of the data to determine if any logical breaks in the data existed.

Forensic Practice Skill Set

One of the greatest challenges for social workers is figuring out what (if any) role does race play in forensic practice. While we may understand that generalizations based on race should be avoided, race is a component of culture that is known to predict health-related outcomes (Abrams & Moio, 2009; Delgado & Stefanic, 2001; North & Smith, 1994). Therefore, race and culture become important factors to attend to in developing practice skills. Moreover, individuals seeking treatment are likely to present culturally variant care preferences, attitudes, and behaviors that are not explained by a generalized category of race (Hall & Bullock, 2015).

While significant gains have been made in the detection and treatment of mental health and substance misuse, these advances have not eliminated the risk of homelessness in the lives of individuals and families faced with these problems. The data generated from the present research suggests that distress screening (Kayser, 2012), which has been effectively applied in social work practice with other populations, can prove to be a promising mechanism for identifying individuals with high levels of psychosocial morbidity so as to subsequently assess and deliver culturally competent care. Furthermore, the use of psychosocial screening instruments can lead to a reduction in emotional distress, better quality of life, and improved patient–provider communication (Kayser, 2012).

It is essential to establish cultural competence standards of treatments and interventions that are derived from evidence-based practice approaches. The research, reported in this chapter, supports the argument that practice approaches and assessment tools should include the dissemination of information in multiple formats and from multiple points of view, giving participants some time to think through and understand the information and to discuss it with others. Also, the communication mechanisms should be culturally sensitive and inclusive. An example of the latter would be creating and/or using visual and auditory messages that are familiar and welcomed in Latino, African American, and other racially diverse communities to increase the likelihood that individuals and family members will

---

[1] There are cases of individuals who entered the program, did not complete, and returned on a subsequent admission.

utilize the resources. Furthermore, social workers should engage members of the lesbian, gay, bisexual, transgender, and queer (LGBTQ) community in partnerships to explore culturally sensitive and appropriated practice skills and interventions.

In conclusion, social workers should tailor community-based outreach that incorporates informal helpers and advocate for patients' rights to self-determine in health care so that these patients can have a meaningful quality of life. The lack of culturally appropriate resources will perpetuate the burden currently experienced by this population:

1. Excluding trusted members of the patient's social support networks will sustain existing barriers to care.
2. When conflicts arise between the patient/family cultural values, beliefs, and attitudes and those of the treatment team, failure to address these through culturally appropriate strategies may result in the patient receiving no care at all.

Case Example and Application

Dennis is a 59-year-old, divorced African American male diagnosed with schizoaffective disorder. He was admitted to the inpatient unit after being found wandering the streets, believing he was a disciple of Jesus. He experienced his first psychotic break at age 19 when he was a student at Brown University and spent several months in the hospital.

Dennis was first incarcerated at age 16 for "petty theft" after "breaking and entering" a local high school with a group of friends one night. Since then, Dennis has had several hospitalizations for delusional and grandiose thinking and has continued to smoke marijuana daily.

Dennis has been misusing drugs and alcohol since his first incarceration at age 16. His driver's license has been revoked for "driving while impaired." Before admission to your agency's outpatient program, his behaviors were becoming increasingly out of control and he was homeless. He was verbally abusive toward his girlfriend who was also homeless and, when under the influence of drugs and alcohol, had pushed her down a set of stairs, from which she survived without injury.

Dennis has not eaten in three days; he says he is fasting to cleanse his spirit. Both his brother and sister are with him for the appointment. When meeting with you, Dennis tries to debate the validity of various psychoanalytic references made to him, about him, by the social worker. He turns to his brother and says, "There is no need for me to be here. I have seen too many therapists and none have been able to help me. Why don't you all just leave me to the streets?"

Two theoretical and practice frameworks that are helpful in forensic social work to address the very complicated individual and family dynamics presented in this case are CRT (Delgado & Stefanic, 2001) and a cultural competence perspective (Delgado & Stefanic, 2001). Practitioners should assess the cultural background of each individual and family using appropriate assessment tools that allow for the inclusion of values that may affect care at the end of life. We need to continuously educate ourselves about culturally specific beliefs and practices of the groups that we serve and assess the degree to which the person and/or family adheres to the specific cultural beliefs and norms. The attention to cultural difference increases the likelihood that all people will receive comprehensive and compassionate care.

It is important to note that when working with people of marginalized groups, the psychosocial needs of the individual and family may have an historical basis, keeping in mind that research (Le Cook & Alegria, 2015) has documented the higher rates of criminal history and socioeconomic factors associated with substance misuse and treatment. Their views of human rights and justice may be inconsistent with those of our U.S. health care system.

Conclusion

When working with incarcerated persons, the psychosocial needs of the individual and his or her family members may be intersectional. Regardless of how careful we are to be inclusive of differences, treatment decisions occur in a social context and there is a risk that inequality, bias, and unequal access to health care services may prevail. People who have felt discriminated against over the life course and denied equal social, economic, and health care access may refuse to participate in programs and services that are not culturally congruent and when historical and sociological influences such as race, gender, and/or socioeconomic status are not considered in the treatment planning. The knowledge, skills, and values of forensic social workers in the areas of human rights and social justice are imperative to effect change in health care and criminal justice systems across populations.

CHAPTER EXERCISES

Exercise 1. Two persons are identified for a role-play. One person will play the role of the person seeking services and one will play the role of the practitioner/provider of services. Demonstrate your knowledge and the usefulness of assessment techniques and tools that incorporate collective decision making about the treatment plan. What types of questions would you ask? Whom would you include in the assessment interview and why? Apply self-awareness and self-regulation to manage the influences of personal bias and values in working with diverse groups.

Exercise 2. Refer to Competency 2 and Competency 3 of the Social Work Educational Policy and Standards (EPAS). Write a brief treatment plan for this individual/family. Demonstrate how you would gather the necessary information, apply the information, and communicate understanding of the importance of diversity and differences that have shaped the life experiences of the individual/family in this case. Incorporate strategies designed to eliminate oppressive structural barriers.

Additional Resources

The Huffington Post. (2014). Women's health behind bars: Not so black and orange. Retrieved from http://www.huffingtonpost.com/jaimie-meyer/womens-health-behind-bars-not-so-black-and-orange_b_6308892.html

The Nation's Health: A Publication of the American Public Health Association. *This monthly online newsletter provides the latest health news, public health professionals, legislators, and decision makers.* The Nation's Health focuses on the news that public health professionals need to know, whether it is happening in their state legislatures, the nation's capital or on a global scale. Retrieved from http://thenationshealth.aphapublications.org

National Consensus Project for Quality Palliative Care. (2013). *Clinical practice guidelines for quality palliative care* (3rd ed.). Retrieved from https://www.hpna.org/multimedia/NCP_Clinical_Practice_Guidelines_3rd_Edition.pdf

Peterson Center on Healthcare. Transforming Healthcare. Improving care for high-need patients, providing best practices and tools to states, charting healthcare performances, and fostering patient engagement. Retrieved from http://www.petersonhealthcare.org

Substance Abuse and Mental Health Services Administration. *The agency within the U.S. Department of Health and Human Services that leads public health efforts to advance the behavioral health of the nation.* SAMHSA's mission is to reduce the impact of substance abuse and mental illness on America's communities. Retrieved from http://www.samhsa.gov

References

Abrams, L. S., & Moio, J. A. (2009). Critical race theory and the cultural competence dilemma in social work education. *Journal of Social Work Education, 45*(2), 245–267.

California Department of Alcohol and Drug Programs. (2004). *Social model recovery: Fact sheet.* Sacramento, CA: Author.

Clemmens, M. C. (2016). *Getting beyond sobriety: Clinical approaches to long-term recovery.* Cleveland, OH: Gestalt Press.

Council on Social Work Education. (2015). *Educational policy and accreditation standards for baccalaureate and master's social work programs.* Alexandria, VA: Author.

Delgado, R., & Stefanic, J. (2001). *Critical race theory: An introduction.* New York: New York University Press.

Dietz, T. L. (2007). Predictors of reported current and lifetime substance abuse problems among a national sample of U.S. homeless. *Substance Use & Misuse, 42,* 1745–1766. doi:10.1080/10826080701212360

Fitzpatrick, D. C. (2014). Hope for underserved populations. *Addiction Professional Magazine.* Retrieved from http://www.addictionpro.com/article/hope-underserved-populations

Hahm, H. C., LeCook, B., Ault-Brutus, A., & Alegria, M. (2015). Intersection of race-ethnicity and gender in depression care: Screening, access, and minimally adequate treatment. *Psychiatric Services, 66*(3), 258–264.

Hall, J. K., & Bullock, K. (2015). A practicum partnership approach to addressing barriers to mental health among racially diverse older adults. *International Journal of Humanities & Social Sciences, 5*(8), 10–19.

Institute of Medicine. (2015). Psychosocial intervention for mental and substance use disorder. Retrieved from http://nationalacademies.org/hmd/~/media/Files/Report%20Files/2015/Psychosocial-Report-in-Brief.pdf

Kaskutas, L. (1999). The social model approach to substance abuse recovery: A program of research and evaluation. Retrieved from http://numerons.files.wordpress.com

Kayser, K. (2012). No patients left behind: A systematic review of the cultural equivalence of distress screening instruments. *Journal of Psychosocial Oncology, 30*(6), 679–693.

Kelly, J. F., & White, W. L. (Eds.). (2011). *Addiction recovery management: Theory, research and practice.* New York, NY: Springer/Humana Press.

Kirmayer, L. J. (2012). Cultural competence and evidence-based practice in mental health: Epistemic communication and the politics of pluralism. *Social Science & Medicine, 75,* 249–256.

Le Cook, B., & Alegria, M. (2015). Racial-ethnic disparities in substance abuse treatment: The role of criminal history and socioeconomic status. *Psychiatric Services, 62*(11), 1273–1281.

Leff, J., & Warner, R. (2006). *Social inclusion of people with mental illness.* Cambridge, UK: Cambridge University Press.

Maguire, M., Sheahan, T. M., & White, W. L. (2012). Innovations in recovery management for people experiencing prolonged homelessness in the city of Philadelphia "I want a new beginning." *Alcoholism Treatment Quarterly, 30,* 3–21. doi:10.1080/07347324. 2012.635548

Maschi, T. M., & Killian, M. L. (2011). The evolution of forensic social work in the United States: Implications for the 21st century practice. *Journal of Forensic Social Work, 1,* 8–36.

North, C. S., & Smith, E. M. (1994). Comparison of White and non-White homeless men and women. *Social Work, 39*(6), 639–647. doi:10.1093/sw/39.6.639

Robbins, S. P., Vaughan-Eden, V., & Maschi, T. M. (2014). It's not CSI: The importance of forensics for social work education. *Journal of Forensic Social Work, 4*, 171–175.

Scott, C., & Dennis, M. (2011). Recovery management checkups with adult chronic substance users. In J. F. Kelly & W. White (Eds.), *Addiction recovery management: Theory, research and practice* (pp. 87–102). New York, NY: Springer/Humana Press.

Stahler, G., & Stimmel, B. (Eds.). (1995). Editorial: Social interventions for homeless substance abusers: Evaluating treatment outcomes. *The effectiveness of social interventions for homeless substance abusers* (pp. xiii–xxiv). Binghamton, NY: Haworth Medical Press.

Substance Abuse and Mental Health Services Administration. (2006). The DASIS report: Homeless admissions to substance abuse treatment: 2004. Retrieved from http://www.samhsa.gov

Townsend, M. S., Peerson, J., Love, B., Achterberg, C., & Murphy, S. P. (2001). Food insecurity is positively related to overweight in women. *The Journal of Nutrition, 131*(6), 1738–1745.

Tucker, J. S., Wenzel, S. L., Golinelli, D., Zhou, A., & Green, Jr., H. D. (2011). Predictors of substance abuse treatment need and receipt among homeless women. *Journal of Substance Abuse Treatment, 4*, 287–294. doi:10.1016/j.jsat.2010.11.006

White, W. L. (2008). *Recovery management and recovery oriented systems of care: Scientific rationale and promising practices*. Rockville, MD: Substance Abuse and Mental Health Services Administration's Center for Substance Abuse Treatment.

Zerger, S. (2002). *Substance abuse treatment: What works for homeless people? A review of the literature* [Research Report]. Nashville, TN: National Health Care for the Homeless Council and Health Care for the Homeless Clinicians Network.

VOICES FROM THE FIELD

Dierdra Oretade-Branch, MSW, LCSW

Social Worker, Federal Bureau of Prisons,
Federal Correctional Complex, Federal Medical Center

Practice Responsibilities

I provide case management and clinical services to a wide range of male inmates, all ages, some acutely psychotic, some very assaultive, and some terminally ill. My duties include providing individual counseling and group psychotherapy, providing family therapy when needed, providing information and assistance regarding advance directives and compassionate release, and maintaining security of the institution. Additionally, my duties include assessing inmates for Residential Reentry Centers (RRC) and home detention, and providing written and/or telephonic communications to court personnel, probation officers, Bureau of Prisons personnel/executive staff, and/or other agencies. When necessary, I testify on behalf of the facility and the Bureau of Prisons regarding the handling of inmates and medical/mental health treatment. Upon an inmate's projected release date from custody, my responsibilities include coordinating all discharge planning needs, which may involve community treatment placement, state hospital placement, medical hospital placement, nursing facility placement, and other aftercare services/ resources across the United States. I collaborate with a wide variety of individuals and agencies such as attorneys, federal probation officers, physicians/hospital personnel, Department of Mental Health and/or correctional offices, other social workers, public health officers, nursing home directors, Veterans Administration officials, and other Bureau of Prisons staff. As a member of a multidisciplinary team, I meet regularly with the inmates to review their treatment plans during treatment team meetings, resolve complaints, address issues of mutual concern, and act as liaison between the inmate and community resources. I participate in Risk Assessment Panel and Compassionate Release Panel meetings, Improving Operational Performance meetings, and The Joint Commission (JCAHO) accreditation tours; present at national social work conferences; and, when needed, provide social work consultation regarding inmates' treatment needs in order to facilitate optimal care.

Expertise Required

- Master of Social Work degree
- Clinical Social Work licensure at the independent level

Ethical, Legal, Practice, Diversity, and/or Advocacy Issues Addressed

- Compassionate release/reduction in sentence
- Advocacy regarding civil commitment
- Treatment to meet the special needs of the population (e.g., deaf/blind inmates, Native American inmates, Spanish-speaking inmates)
- Limited treatment provider diversity
- Privacy/confidentiality issues

Interprofessional and Intersectoral Collaboration

My associations include release planning collaboration with U.S. probation offices, U.S. parole offices, U.S. attorneys, interstate compact coordinators, other correctional staff (e.g., unit team case managers, medical providers/staff, psychologists), and community providers (e.g., outpatient clinics, hospital staff, Social Security Administration staff, state Departments of Mental Health, nursing facilities, dialysis centers).

PART III

CORE SKILLS: PRACTICE, RESEARCH AND EVALUATION, POLICY, AND ADVOCACY

CHAPTER 20

Empirically Informed Forensic Social Work Practice

Melissa D. Grady

Jill Levenson

David S. Prescott

CHAPTER OBJECTIVES

The major objectives of this chapter are to:

- Describe how forensic social workers (FSWs) can utilize research in their practices.
- Introduce FSWs to three different approaches to include research in their practice.

CHAPTER COMPETENCIES HIGHLIGHTED

- Competency 1: Demonstrate Ethical and Professional Behavior
- Competency 4: Engage in Practice Informed Research and Research Informed Practice
- Competencies 6, 7, and 8: Engage, Assess, and Intervene With Individuals, Families, Organizations, and Communities

This chapter is aimed at helping FSWs understand how to incorporate research into their practices. FSWs, like all social workers, are practicing in an age where evidence-based practice (EBP) is the latest buzzword. Yet, within the social work profession, continued confusion exists about what EBP actually means (Wike et al., 2014). With this confusion comes avoidance and a lack of implementation of EBP in practice (Grady et al., in press). This chapter's aim is to clarify the terms associated with EBP and demonstrate three different approaches that FSWs can use in their practice settings. While research should be used in all levels of social work practice, the focus of this chapter is on clinical interventions within forensic settings. As part of this discussion, we provide a brief summary and overview of some of the intervention models used in forensic settings with established empirical support, along with a discussion of their strengths and limitations. Some of these models are discussed more fully in other sections of this book. We conclude the chapter with a case example that illustrates how to use EBP in order to ensure that FSWs are providing interventions that are the best combination of art and science.

Defining Evidence-Based Practice

The definition of EBP stems from the definition of evidence-based medicine (EBM), which is defined as "the integration of best research evidence with clinical expertise and patient values" (Sackett, Straus, Richardson, Rosenberg, & Haynes, 2000). In social work, Rubin (2008) states similarly that "EBP is a process for making practice decisions in which practitioners integrate the best research evidence available with their professional expertise and with client attributes, values, preferences and circumstances." Although these definitions are consistently used by other core health professionals (Academy of Medical-Surgical Nurses, 2014; American Psychological Association, 2015; American Speech-Language-Hearing Association, 2015; Guyatt et al., 1992; National Association of Social Workers, 2010; Sackett et al., 2000), within social work there is a great deal of confusion (described in what follows) regarding the definition of EBP and how to use it (Drisko & Grady, 2015; Grady et al., in press; Rubin, 2008; Simmons, 2013).

The current and most consistently utilized definition of the EBP process is broader than many social workers believe. It includes four distinct and equally weighted parts: (a) current client characteristics, needs, and situation; (b) the best relevant research evidence; (c) client values and preferences; and (d) the clinician's expertise (Haynes, Devereaux, & Guyatt, 2002). It appears that in most social work settings, although "the definition of EBP is actually very clear; it is just not well taught, nor well understood" (Drisko & Grady, 2015).

Confusion Surrounding EBP

One aspect of the definition that is most often misunderstood is the critical role of the practitioner in EBP. It is the expertise of the practitioner that integrates client needs, client characteristics, client preferences, and research knowledge (Drisko & Grady, 2012). Too often, practitioners perceive that EBP devalues the role and expertise of the practitioner (Manuel, Mullen, Fang, Bellamy, & Bledsoe, 2009) when in actuality the practitioner serves as the lynchpin for EBP. The practitioner expertise is essential in EBP from the first step that requires a thorough assessment through the subsequent steps of implementing and evaluating the intervention.

Another area of confusion is the role of research. In EBP, research is one of the pieces of information considered and does not trump or override the other domains. The role of research includes not just outcome or effectiveness studies, but also the use of the interdisciplinary and theoretical knowledge base to inform assessments and treatment plan choices. For instance, it has been difficult to "test" trauma-informed care (TIC), but research about the prevalence and impact of early adversity, along with the literature about therapeutic alliance, the common factors of psychotherapy, maladaptive schema, and empowerment, all shape our understanding of the importance of trauma-informed practice and essential components of its implementation. Practitioners must consider the best available research *along with* the client circumstances and preferences when planning for an intervention. Considered in this manner, EBP is a critical thinking *process* and *not* a product (Drisko & Grady, 2015).

Steps of EBP

In practice, EBP uses the following steps to guide practitioners in this critical thinking decision-making process:

- Draw upon client characteristics, strengths, needs, and circumstances learned in a thorough assessment to identify service goals and related research information
- Efficiently locate relevant research knowledge
- Critically appraise the quality and applicability of this knowledge to the client's characteristics, strengths, needs, and situation
- Discuss the research results with the client to determine how likely effective options fit with the client's characteristics, strengths, values, and goals
- Synthesize the client's clinical needs and circumstances with the relevant research, and develop a shared plan of intervention collaboratively with the client
- Implement the intervention (Drisko & Grady, 2012)

Using these steps, the practitioner's main goal is to integrate the relevant information about the client, his or her context, *and* the research.

Empirically Supported Interventions

All too often, EBP is defined as a *product* rather than a process (Grady et al., in press). Based on this confusion, when practitioners hear that their supervisors, agencies, third-party payers, and/or government agencies require them to use EBP, they assume this to mean "a model of intervention" (Grady et al., in press; Graybeal, 2014). They may react defensively to this request as they do not want to be told what to do with clients, and they may equate this request with being told to use a manualized or standardized implementation of practice (Graybeal, 2014; Wike et al., 2014). It is important to distinguish between EBP and an intervention model that has gained empirical support, which is referred to as an empirically supported intervention or treatment (ESI/EST; Chambless & Hollon, 1998). Almost two decades ago, Chambless and Hollon defined an EST as a treatment demonstrated to be better than no treatment in at least two experimental studies. In other words, ESIs/ESTs are discrete models of intervention that have been operationalized and tested using an experimental design. As a result of this experimental empirical evaluation, these ESIs often have manuals or other guidelines associated with them in order to ensure fidelity to the model and to facilitate replication.

It is important to note that there have been a number of critiques associated with the process for establishing support for an intervention as an ESI (see Drisko & Grady, 2012 for a thorough review). For instance, questions regarding generalizability arise when considering whether a treatment developed and tested under one set of circumstances will work as well under other circumstances (Littell, 2005). An excellent research methodology may not reflect the reality of the FSW's practice landscape (e.g., many studies exclude clients with various comorbid conditions, even as comorbidity is the norm at the front lines of practice).

It is also important to note that the absence in the literature of an ESI does not mean that there is nothing out there that works. Indeed, the research literature on psychotherapy in general is very encouraging (Wampold & Imel, 2015). Further, it is possible that practitioners are currently using effective interventions, but that these interventions have not been tested *and* the results published. What is often clear from reviewing the literature is that more research is needed in forensic settings and with a variety of populations.

Empirical Evidence of Effectiveness With Forensic Populations and Settings

Although there has been limited experimental empirical testing of social work practices with forensic populations, there are several interventions that have demonstrated empirical support in other interdisciplinary settings. In this section we provide a summary of these interventions that includes a brief overview of each model, with what population and in which settings it has been used, and its strengths (including empirical support) as well as its limitations. As stated previously, several of these models are presented more in-depth in other chapters of this book. We also provide resource links at the end of the chapter where readers can research more about the evidence-based process and the following commonly used forensic intervention models that are highlighted in this chapter: risk-needs-responsivity (RNR) models, motivational interviewing (MI), trauma-informed care, trauma-focused cognitive behavioral therapy (TFCBT), schema-focused therapy, dialectical behavioral therapy (DBT), and common/therapeutic factors.

There is a large overlap between crime and other types of social problems more familiar to social workers, and thus FSWs are well-positioned to provide assessment, treatment, and case-management services to offenders (Epperson, Roberts, Ivanoff, Tripodi, & Gilmer, 2013; Grady & Abramson, 2011; Robbins, Vaughan-Eden, & Maschi, 2015). Within the strengths-based and integrative environmental context of social work practice, we aim to promote social justice and protection of human rights for all individuals, including those who have committed crimes (Maschi & Killian, 2011; Saleebey, 2011; Sheehan, 2012). Social workers are trained to avoid overpathologizing behavior and to appreciate the complex nexus between poverty, oppression, and trauma.

Rehabilitation is a core goal of the criminal justice system, and thus treatment programs for justice-involved individuals are not uncommon. For instance, individuals charged with crimes involving substance abuse, domestic violence, anger issues, sexual assault, and child abuse are often mandated to attend treatment as part of their criminal sentence. As well, individuals with mental illness are often arrested for crimes that occur during an episode of acute psychiatric symptoms (for instance, mania, psychosis, or substance intoxication). Though many manualized programs for specific presenting problems like domestic violence or anger management have been developed, there are other empirically based models that can be woven through problem-specific programs in order to increase effectiveness. These practices incorporate knowledge about the biological, psychological, and social factors that contribute to behavioral and emotional dysregulation as well as distorted thinking, which, in turn, increase risk for crime.

Risk-Needs-Responsivity Models

Because criminal behavior is often related to general self-regulation deficits, social work services should aim to improve behavioral management skills. Punitive measures alone demonstrate little success in helping to alter self-control in ways that reduce long-term recidivism risk. RNR principles are based on the premise that treatment interventions should be applied according to the unique reoffense risks and criminogenic needs of each offender, and provided in a fashion that considers individual characteristics. Correctional programs that conform to the RNR principles have been found to be more effective in reducing recidivism than traditional cognitive behavioral treatments (Andrews & Bonta, 2007, 2010; Hanson, Bourgon, Helmus, & Hodgson, 2009).

The RNR paradigm argues that higher risk offenders require the most intensive services and that lower risk offenders should receive a lower dose of treatment, that treatment plans should be designed to address criminogenic needs (specific risk factors), and that interventions should be culturally relevant and tailored to the individual offender's motivation, cognitive abilities, and strengths (responsivity)—increasing the likelihood that a person will respond favorably to the intervention (Andrews & Bonta, 2010).

The risk principle states that the level of service should be concordant with the level of risk. Risk can be assessed by using various instruments that estimate the likelihood of reoffending based on factors that have a correlation with recidivism outcomes. Social workers should familiarize themselves with risk assessment protocols that are relevant for the problem or population with which they work. The need principle states that the treatment itself should target those risk factors most salient for the individual offender. Risk factors can include antisocial thinking, aggression or combativeness, association with criminal peers, substance abuse, negative moods, chaotic family dynamics, school failure, unemployment, lifestyle instability, substance abuse, and mental disorders. The responsivity principle requires consideration of the client's cultural background, gender, trauma history, learning style, motivation, and intellectual ability in order to maximize the offender's responsiveness.

A strength of RNR is that it has received empirical support in research studies (Andrews & Bonta, 2010; Hanson et al., 2009), and it conserves agency resources by administering treatment dosage according to risks and needs. One-size-fits-all approaches are rarely effective in promoting change, and therefore individualized case-management approaches help to deliver services in a fashion that feels relevant and personalized to the offender. A limitation of RNR is that it may focus too much on risk management and not enough on the personality or relational factors that contribute to criminal behavior.

Motivational Interviewing

MI is a style of interacting with clients that is client-centered and nonthreatening. Using a goal-oriented approach, MI seeks to uncover the unique and intrinsic incentives and obstacles to change that impact the ability to accomplish desired objectives (Miller & Rollnick, 2002; Prescott & Wilson, 2013). Recognizing that behavioral modification is difficult and that most people are ambivalent about change allows social workers to depersonalize resistance and maintain a positive and supportive therapeutic alliance. MI seeks to help clients identify the pros and cons of change, to mitigate the often overwhelming and frightening prospect of transforming one's life, and to reduce barriers that preclude achievement toward goals.

The acronym OARS has been used to capture the basic client-centered strategies of MI: (a) Open-ended questions, (b) Affirmations, (c) Reflective listening, and (d) Summaries. By keeping this acronym in mind, social workers can practice the skills that are effective in helping clients move in positive directions. Ask *open-ended questions* that allow clients to formulate their own narrative and elaborate on the ideas and topics that are salient to the treatment goals. Use *affirmations* that are positive, strengths-focused comments that highlight client assets and reframe discouragement, challenges, or negative behavior into a positive and empowering light. *Reflective listening* is a way of conveying to the client that you understand his or her experience, by paraphrasing content and labeling feelings based on statements made by the client. Finally, *summaries* provide a way for the social worker to expand reflective listening by consolidating a variety of material brought to the session by the client and identifying salient themes.

The goal of the OARS approach to MI is to elicit change talk, or self-motivational statements that indicate a desire to consider the possibility of growth and change. Miller and Rollnick (2002) identify four categories of change talk: problem recognition, concern about the problem, commitment to change, and a belief that change is possible. It is with this last part that social workers can play a prominent role in promoting hope. A strength of MI is that it is individualized and client-centered. A limitation is that because it is designed to be short term, follow-up may be limited and clients may not receive the ongoing support required to sustain change over long periods of time.

Trauma-Informed Care

Social workers taking psychosocial histories in justice-involved settings should seek to explore the role of child maltreatment and chaotic family environments on later criminal behavior. The person-in-environment (PIE) perspective (Kondrat, 2008) held by social workers helps us to recognize the role that adversity might play in the formation of maladaptive coping strategies, including criminal behavior (Robbins et al., 2015; Sheehan, 2012; D. S. Young, 2014). Child maltreatment has been correlated with the development of criminal behavior, and a survey of inmates reported that before age 16, 48% had witnessed family violence, more than one-third had been emotionally abused, 34% reported physical abuse, 19% had been sexually assaulted, and 18% felt they had been neglected (Courtney & Maschi, 2013). Prisoners also frequently report witnessing violence in childhood and many experienced the death of a family member, parental separation or abandonment, foster care placement, or parental substance abuse (Courtney & Maschi, 2013; Haugebrook, Zgoba, Maschi, Morgen, & Brown, 2010; Maschi, Gibson, Zgoba, & Morgen, 2011).

It is well-established that traumatic stress in childhood creates hyperarousal, increasing the production of hormones associated with fight-or-flight responses and inhibiting the growth and connection of neurons (Anda et al., 2006; van der Kolk, 2006). Over time, these changes in the brain can alter the capacity for emotional regulation, social attachment, impulse control, and cognitive processing (Anda et al., 2006; Anda, Butchart, Felitti, & Brown, 2010; Whitfield, 1998).

TIC seeks to create a safe, trustworthy service delivery setting in which client choice, collaboration, and empowerment are emphasized (Elliott, Bjelajac, Fallot, Markoff, &

Reed, 2005; Harris & Fallot, 2001). Social workers who utilize a trauma-informed practice framework recognize the prevalence of early adversity and the impact that violence and victimization can have on psychosocial development and relational skills (Elliott et al., 2005; Harris & Fallot, 2001). TIC emphasizes strengths over pathology and skills building over symptom reduction. It delivers services in an empowering and nonjudgmental manner that views presenting problems as symptoms of interrelated emotional wounds, which manifest in intimacy deficits, maladaptive coping, and self-destructive behaviors. Above all, TIC ensures that the dynamics of abusive relationships, which are characterized by invalidation and oppression, are not unintentionally repeated in the helping relationship (Elliott et al., 2005; Harris & Fallot, 2001).

A TIC approach assesses for a history of trauma and views it not as a discrete event but as a defining and organizing experience that deeply influences the core of an individual's identity (Harris & Fallot, 2001). Understanding how traumatic events impacted the client's fundamental assumptions about the world, the social worker can understand the meanings attached to traumatic events and early relationships, and reframe the role of coping strategies that were once adaptive in the abusive childhood environment but which prove to be unhealthy or harmful across various domains of adult functioning. A strength of TIC is its strong evidence foundation in research related to neurobiological impacts of trauma, and its use of client-centered social work skills using the environment context of social work practice. Limitations include the challenges in shifting organizational culture to become more trauma-informed, the loosely defined practices that comprise implementation of TIC, and the lack of experimental studies testing the effectiveness of TIC in improving long-term client outcomes.

Trauma-Focused Cognitive Behavioral Therapy

TFCBT differs from TIC by helping clients to discuss and process painful memories, reduce anxiety to a more tolerable level, and increase the ability to modulate emotion and behavior (Cohen, Mannarino, Kliethermes, & Murray, 2012; Harris & Fallot, 2001). TFCBT is a relatively short-term (12–16 weeks) rigorously researched treatment protocol that meets the criteria for an ESI/EST for children who have been abused and traumatized; usually it is implemented with a caretaker component to help increase positive parenting practices that support the child in his or her recovery. The strengths of TFCBT include very strong research evidence in multiple experimental studies that have found TFCBT to reduce the symptoms of posttraumatic stress disorder (PTSD), depression, and anxiety, and help children to decrease externalizing behaviors, sexualized behaviors, feelings of shame, and mistrust. Limitations include feasibility of implementation in some agencies, concerns about long-term lasting impact, and that most of the empirical studies have been conducted on sexually abused children, with few studies testing the effectiveness of the intervention with older youth, adults, or other types of traumas.

TFCBT is a validated approach to working with children, but its primary components can be adapted for traumatized adults as well. The key modules are reflected in the acronym PRACTICE, which stands for: *Psycho-education* about childhood trauma and PTSD along with a *Parenting* management skills component; *Relaxation skills* individualized to the child and parent; *Affective modulation skills* adapted to the child, family, and culture; *Cognitive coping* for thoughts, feelings, and behaviors related to the trauma; *Trauma narrative*: assisting the child in sharing a verbal, written, or artistic narrative about the trauma(s) and related experiences, and cognitive and affective processing of those events; *In vivo exposure* and mastery of trauma triggers, if appropriate; *Conjoint parent–child sessions* to practice skills and encourage trauma-related discussions; and *Enhancing future personal safety* through family safety planning and social skills training as needed. There is a free online training program that practitioners can explore. The link is located in the Additional Resources section.

Schema-Focused Therapy

Schema therapy (Unger & Young, 1994; J. E. Young & Brown, 1994; J. E. Young, Klosko, & Weishaar, 2003) is a cognitive intervention that focuses on identifying early maladaptive schemas (EMS), which reflect deeply held beliefs that guide an individual's feelings and behavior. A total of 18 schemas in five domains have been validated through research (disconnection and rejection, impaired autonomy and performance, impaired limits, other-directedness, and overvigilance and inhibition; J. E. Young & Brown, 1994; J. E. Young et al., 2003). For example, some individuals have a pervasive fear of being neglected or deserted by others (abandonment schema) or a conviction that they are fundamentally flawed or inadequate (failure schema). Maladaptive schemas are associated with depressive symptoms (Trincas et al., 2014), and are commonly present in individuals with personality pathology (Jovev & Jackson, 2004).

EMS are believed to arise from unmet core emotional needs in childhood. The time-limited therapy relationship in this intervention seeks to repair schemas by rescripting them under the therapist's guidance as interpersonal situations are reexperienced by the client. Schema therapy proceeds in three stages. First, the common core schemas are discussed with the client, who identifies the ones most pertinent to his or her own life. Then, there is an exploration of from where the schemas originate in early relational experiences with parents and others, and the connections between thoughts and emotions. Finally, the social worker will help the client to repair and reframe schema by identifying maladaptive schemas as they occur in the present, and infusing more healthy and correctional cognitions and relational strategies through practice and rehearsal with support from the therapist.

A strength of schema therapy is its demonstration of promising outcomes in the treatment of severe depressive disorders and borderline personality disorder (Bamelis, Evers, Spinhoven, & Arntz, 2013; Sempértegui, Karreman, Arntz, & Bekker, 2013). Female offenders, especially those who have experienced severe and extensive physical or psychological mistreatment in childhood, are more likely to be diagnosed with *Diagnostic and statistical manual of mental disorders* (*DSM*) Cluster B personality traits (Loper, Mahmoodzadegan, & Warren, 2008). Chaotic households and child abuse or neglect seem to contribute to disorganized attachment and emotional regulation deficiencies that characterize Cluster B personality traits, making schema therapy a good choice for forensic clients with personality disorders (Loper et al., 2008). Thus, a focus on thematic belief systems might be particularly beneficial for criminal offenders. A potential challenge is that it requires a good deal of flexibility on the part of the therapist, to be able to constantly adapt the intervention based on how the client is responding.

Dialectical Behavioral Therapy

DBT was developed to treat borderline personality disorder and, in particular, clients who present with suicidality, self-harm, chaotic relationships, and pervasive affective dysregulation (Linehan, 1993). DBT focuses on helping clients to develop, rehearse, and refine a number of core skills: mindfulness, distress tolerance, interpersonal effectiveness, and emotional regulation. The term *dialectical* refers to the convergence of two opposing ideas—in this case, acceptance and change. Treatment is delivered in a combination of group and individual modalities, and focuses not only on skills building, but on the identification and recognition of negative emotions that are believed to be connected to an invalidating childhood environment. Treatment groups provide opportunities for rehearsal of new relational skills, role-plays, and cross validation among clients.

DBT prioritizes the targeting of presenting problems by focusing first on those behaviors that are life-threatening or a danger to others, followed by behaviors that interfere with treatment engagement, quality of life, and skills acquisition. It has proven effective in reducing suicidal behavior, self-harming behavior, psychiatric hospitalizations, treatment dropout, substance use, anger, and depression. A strength is that it is a well-established ESI/EST, and randomized controlled studies have found the structured delivery of DBT to add effectiveness in reducing symptoms and improving functioning beyond the essential ingredients of a warm and empathic psychotherapy relationship (Linehan et al., 2006). DBT can be a good option for forensic clients, especially those with volatile and chaotic lifestyles or with behaviors that pose a threat to self or others. A limitation is that effects may fade with time, and follow-up, along with adjunct therapies like medication, might be necessary to maintain treatment gains.

Research on Common/Therapeutic Factors

In addition to discrete models of intervention, there is also a robust body of literature on the importance of factors that are common to all forms of bona fide psychotherapies (aka "the common factors" and "therapeutic factors"; Wampold & Imel, 2015). Factors such as the quality of the therapeutic alliance (including agreement on the nature of the relationship and the goals and tasks of treatment), hope, positive expectation, and the warmth and genuineness of the therapist have all received ongoing support in psychotherapy research, such that these findings are not controversial (Norcross, 2009).

Surprisingly, research on these therapeutic factors is not without controversy. Advocates of specific approaches have argued that on their own, common factors such as therapist empathy, while vital, are not sufficient to be considered a bona fide treatment approach. At the center of much of this debate has been researchers such as Bruce Wampold and his colleagues (see Wampold & Imel, 2015, for an exhaustive review) who argue that all bona fide forms of psychotherapy appear to produce roughly equivalent results. Understandably, this conclusion does not sit well with many researchers, including those who have developed specific approaches.

While a complete review of the controversies is beyond the scope of this chapter, some takeaway messages for the evidence-based FSW are noteworthy:

- When setting a therapeutic course of action, careful attention to developing agreement on the nature of the relationship and the goals and tasks of treatment (in accordance with the client's personal values and preferences) is crucial. All too often in the authors' experience, when treatment goes off track, clinicians often seek out alternative models and techniques rather than revisiting these elements of the alliance with their clients (Prescott & Miller, 2015). This is especially true in forensic settings, where clients may present with resistance and even hostility due to the inherent oppressive features of mandated counseling.
- A reasonable place to start when treatment is not producing the desired results is in checking on the alliance. Given the robust literature supporting the importance of the therapeutic alliance, it is itself a key component of EBP.
- Although the specific ingredients of a given treatment approach are important, therapist features such as warmth, empathy, genuineness, and positive regard are vital.
- Research has shown that therapists who actively and routinely seek feedback on the outcomes of their services can improve their outcomes considerably (Prescott & Miller, 2015).
- The nature of one's therapeutic relationship will vary from client to client, in accordance with their characteristics, needs, and values. Just as there are treatments of choice for individual clients, there are relationships of choice. This point is important in considering EBP as well as the professional development of each FSW. While most social workers receive some instruction in the nature of concepts such as transference and countertransference, the complexities involved in interactions and relationships with criminal justice clients are well-established (Blanchard, 1995; Jenkins, 1990; Prescott & Miller, 2015).
- While all of the areas in the previous bullet points are important considerations, it is crucial to remember that the nature of the therapeutic alliance is best assessed from the client's perspective. Beech and Fordham (1997) observed that therapists working with sex offenders often overestimate their helpfulness compared to the ratings of clients. Even in the general psychotherapy literature, the average therapist, like other professionals, often views himself or herself as being more effective than the majority of their peers (Walfish, McAlister, O'Donnell, & Lambert, 2012).

Case Example and Application

In an effort to demonstrate how these varying approaches to using research actually work together, we offer a case example of Jarred, a 15-year-old Caucasian cisgender male adolescent client involved in the juvenile justice system. Jarred did not know his biological father and he was first removed from his biological mother's custody at the age of 3 due to child maltreatment (severe physical abuse and neglect), with the state finally terminating parental rights when he was 11 years old. He has been in either foster care or group settings for the past 10 years. He is currently living in a group home and the staff now believes that he may need a more secure environment due to his increasingly violent behavior.

Using EBP, the FSW assigned to work with Jarred in the role of case manager first conducts a thorough assessment. She concludes that his main symptoms and high-risk behaviors meet the criteria for conduct disorder. In speaking with Jarred, he does not provide any input as to what he wants or would prefer. He is bright but disengaged with the entire assessment process and offers little interest in participating in his own treatment planning. At the end of step one, the FSW develops the following searchable question: What are effective interventions for adolescent males with conduct disorder who have a history of childhood trauma?

The second step of EBP asks the FSW to take the searchable question and go to the literature. A quick search using scholar.google.com identifies several different interventions for conduct disorder, as well as a systematic review that identifies several specific interventions with empirical support (Eyberg, Nelson, & Boggs, 2008). The authors conclude that the most effective interventions are parent-training programs, such as multisystemic therapy (MST; Henggeler & Lee, 2003), that require high levels of family involvement. However, the interventions are only focused on addressing the behaviors associated with conduct disorders and not the history of trauma. The most cited effective intervention for adolescents with trauma histories is TFCBT (Cohen et al., 2012), which also requires the participation of a caregiver, but not necessarily a parent specifically.

In step three, a critical point becomes clear: Jarred does not have involved parents of any kind. His biological parents have no contact with him and he is not in a foster home where he might have surrogate parents. It is at this juncture where the practitioner's expertise and attention to the *other* domains of EBP are essential. In spite of the empirical support of MST, given Jarred's circumstances, his intervention plan should not include a model that relies so heavily on parental involvement. Thus, the FSW should consider alternative child/adolescent-based interventions, even though they may not demonstrate the same level of empirical support or address the myriad issues facing Jarred. Such an approach could include a curriculum such as *Aggression Replacement Training* (ART) coupled with TFCBT, asking the group home staff to participate in the treatment to address specific areas of Jarred's life, such as early loss, separation, and maltreatment. Given Jarred's maltreatment history, it is essential for the FSW to understand the role of childhood adversity in Jared's behavior and to factor that into the service plan by using a trauma-informed framework when applying the intervention. This would include creating a safe and strong therapeutic alliance by which the social worker can model and help Jarred practice new relational and coping skills. If Jarred can bond with a trustworthy adult (the FSW), he can reshape the expectations (developed through his traumatic experiences) that all adults/caregivers are unpredictable, unreliable, and potentially abusive. This example illustrates how all aspects of the EBP model must be considered in order to develop the most appropriate and client-centered intervention. The practitioner's expertise is critical in understanding and weighing all domains of the EBP model.

(*continued*)

Case Example and Application (*continued*)

The fourth step of EBP involves a conversation between the clients, their caregivers, and the social worker regarding the various intervention options in order to establish a collaborative decision-making process. This discussion should include what the FSW found in the literature search, as well as her own expertise that she brings to the relationship. Although the FSW attempts to process these options with Jarred, he continues to state that he does not have an opinion. Here the FSW may choose to use MI with Jarred to find some area in which he has some interest in working toward a change. In this particular case, the FSW is in the role of a case manager, and therefore, it would not be appropriate for her to provide therapeutic services to Jarred personally. Therefore a referral is more appropriate. She and the group home staff agree that she will contact another agency that provides both ART and TFCBT in her community.

Although Jarred has not expressed any interest in participating in his service planning, EBP emphasizes in the fifth step the importance of working with Jarred to develop a collaborative intervention plan that integrates the relevant research with the expertise of the practitioner, and Jarred's wishes, strengths, characteristics, circumstances, and life history. The sixth step in EBP is to implement this integrated plan.

Throughout the entirety of her relationship with Jarred, it is essential that the FSW attend to the key ingredients noted in the common factors literature in order to create a strong collaborative relationship that is essential in the EBP process. For example, she would need to attend to her own transference related to Jarred's "resistance" and his emotional distance, regularly check in with Jarred about their relationship, and consistently demonstrate warmth, empathy, kindness, and genuineness in the relationship with him. In doing so, the FSW will increase the likelihood that Jarred will experience his interactions with her as positive, and demonstrate stronger outcomes. By attending to all aspects of the EBP process, informing herself about potential relevant ESIs, while seeking to establish a relationship with Jarred that is consistent with the research on TIC and the common factors, the FSW can feel confident that she is providing services based on sound empirical support.

Conclusion

This chapter provides an overview of how FSWs can use the EBP process paired with the common factors research to develop research-informed intervention plans grounded in empirically sound relationships. While much more research is needed on effective approaches for the forensic population, this chapter also provides a brief overview of some of the most relevant models for working in forensic settings. Using these resources, social workers will be prepared to address the myriad of challenges and opportunities in forensic social work.

CHAPTER EXERCISES

Exercise 1. Individually or in small groups, choose a client and apply how you would use an evidence-based decision-making model with that client.

Exercise 2. With the list of resources provided at the end of the chapter, either individually or in small groups, research one of the ESIs. Present your findings to the class.

Exercise 3. Choose a common issue found among individuals involved in the criminal justice system, such as homelessness or substance abuse, and so on. . . . Research available ESIs for this population. Share your findings with the class.

Exercise 4. Visit the Substance Abuse and Mental Health Services Administration (SAMHSA) at: www.samhsa.gov/nrepp. Locate an EBP in their registry that would be helpful to use with a client who has both mental health and substance use issues. Work individually or in groups and share your findings with the class.

Additional Resources

Dialectical Behavioral Therapy: http://behavioraltech.org/index.cfm

Encyclopedia of Social Work: http://socialwork.oxfordre.com/view/10.1093/acrefore/9780199975839 .001.0001/acrefore-9780199975839-e-877

Free Online Training: https://tfcbt.musc.edu

The Heart and Soul of Change Project: www.heartandsoulofchange.com

Motivational Interviewing: www.youtube.com/watch?v=cj1BDPBE6Wk and www.youtube.com/ watch?v=s3MCJZ7OGRk

Motivational Interviewing Network of Trainers (MINT) website: www.motivationalinterviewing.org

The National Alliance on Mental Illness: www2.nami.org/factsheets/DBT_factsheet.pdf

National Center for Trauma Informed Care: www.nasmhpd.org/content/national-center-trauma -informed-care-nctic-0

Risk-Needs-Responsivity Models (RNR): www.smart.gov/SOMAPI/sec1/ch7_treatment.html and http://publications.gc.ca/collections/collection_2012/sp-ps/PS3-1-2007-6-eng.pdf

Schema Focused Therapy: www.schematherapy.com

The Social Work Policy Institute: www.socialworkpolicy.org/research/evidence-based-practice-2.html

Substance Abuse Mental Health Services Administration: www.samhsa.gov/nctic

Trauma-Focused Cognitive-Behavioral Therapy: www.nctsnet.org/nctsn_assets/pdfs/promising_ practices/TFCBT_General.pdf

The Trauma Informed Care Project: www.traumainformedcareproject.org

References

Academy of Medical-Surgical Nurses. (2014). Evidence-based practice. Retrieved from https://www .amsn.org/practice-resources/evidence-based-practice

American Psychological Association. (2015). Evidence-based practice in psychology. Retrieved from http://www.apa.org/practice/resources/evidence

American Speech-Language-Hearing Association. (2015). Introduction to evidence-based practice. Retrieved from http://www.asha.org/Research/EBP/Introduction-to-Evidence-Based-Practice

Anda, R. F., Butchart, A., Felitti, V. J., & Brown, D. W. (2010). Building a framework for global surveillance of the public health implications of adverse childhood experiences. *American Journal of Preventive Medicine, 39*(1), 93–98.

Anda, R. F., Felitti, V. J., Bremner, J. D., Walker, J. D., Whitfield, C., Perry, B. D., . . . Giles, W. H. (2006). The enduring effects of abuse and related adverse experiences in childhood. *European Archives of Psychiatry and Clinical Neuroscience, 256*(3), 174–186.

Andrews, D. A., & Bonta, J. (2007). *The psychology of criminal conduct* (4th ed.). Cincinnati, OH: Anderson Publishing.

Andrews, D. A., & Bonta, J. (2010). Rehabilitating criminal justice policy and practice. *Psychology, Public Policy, and Law, 16*(1), 39–55.

Bamelis, L. L., Evers, S. M., Spinhoven, P., & Arntz, A. (2013). Results of a multicenter randomized controlled trial of the clinical effectiveness of schema therapy for personality disorders. *American Journal of Psychiatry, 171*(3), 305–322.

Beech, A. R., & Fordham, A. S. (1997). Therapeutic climate of sexual offender treatment programs. *Sexual Abuse: A Journal of Research and Treatment, 9*, 219–237.

Blanchard, G. (1995). *The difficult connection: The therapeutic relationship in sex offender treatment.* Brandon, VT: Safer Society Press.

Chambless, D., & Hollon, S. (1998). Defining empirically supported therapies. *Journal of Clinical and Consulting Psychology, 66*(1), 7–18.

Cohen, J. A., Mannarino, A. P., Kliethermes, M., & Murray, L. A. (2012). Trauma-focused CBT for youth with complex trauma. *Child Abuse & Neglect, 36*(6), 528–541.

Courtney, D., & Maschi, T. (2013). Trauma and stress among older adults in prison breaking the cycle of silence. *Traumatology, 19*(1), 73–81.

Drisko, J. W., & Grady, M. D. (2012). *Evidence-based practice in clinical social work.* New York, NY: Springer Verlag.

Drisko, J. W., & Grady, M. D. (2015). Evidence-based practice in social work: A contemporary perspective. *Clinical Social Work Journal, 43*(3), 274–282. doi:10.1007/s10615-015-0548-z

Elliott, D. E., Bjelajac, P., Fallot, R. D., Markoff, L. S., & Reed, B. G. (2005). Trauma-informed or trauma-denied: Principles and implementation of trauma-informed services for women. *Journal of Community Psychology, 33*(4), 461–477.

Epperson, M. W., Roberts, L. E., Ivanoff, A., Tripodi, S. J., & Gilmer, C. N. (2013). To what extent is criminal justice content specifically addressed in MSW programs? *Journal of Social Work Education, 49*(1), 96–107.

Eyberg, S. M., Nelson, M. M., & Boggs, S. R. (2008). Evidence based psychosocial treatments for children and adolescents with disruptive behavior. *Journal of Clinical Child & Adolescent Psychology, 37*(1), 215–237. doi:10.1080/15374410701820117

Grady, M. D., & Abramson, J. M. (2011). Has social work heeded the call? Sex offender content in social work. *Social Work Education, 30*(4), 440–453.

Grady, M. D., Wike, T. L., Putzu, C., Field, S. E., Hill, J., Bellamy, J., . . . Massey, M. (in press). Recent social work practitioners' understanding and use of evidence-based practice and empirically supported treatments. *Journal of Social Work Education.* doi:10.1080/10437797.2017.1299063

Graybeal, C. (2014). The art of practicing with evidence. *Clinical Social Work Journal, 42*(2), 116–122. doi:10.1007/s10615-013-0462-1

Guyatt, G., Cairns, J., Churchill, D., Cook, D., Haynes, B., Hirsh, J., . . . Tugwell, P. (1992). Evidence-based medicine: A new approach to teaching the practice of medicine. *Journal of the American Medical Association, 268*(17), 2420–2425.

Hanson, R. K., Bourgon, G., Helmus, L., & Hodgson, S. (2009). The principles of effective correctional treatment also apply to sexual offenders: A meta-analysis. *Criminal Justice and Behavior, 36*(9), 865–891.

Harris, M. E., & Fallot, R. D. (2001). *Using trauma theory to design service systems.* San Francisco, CA: Jossey-Bass.

Haugebrook, S., Zgoba, K. M., Maschi, T., Morgen, K., & Brown, D. (2010). Trauma, stress, health, and mental health issues among ethnically diverse older adult prisoners. *Journal of Correctional Health Care, 16*(3), 220–229.

Haynes, R., Devereaux, P., & Guyatt, G. (2002). Clinical expertise in the era of evidence-based medicine and patient choice. *Evidence-Based Medicine, 83*(Suppl. 1), 383–386.

Henggeler, S. W., & Lee, T. (2003). Multisystemic treatment of serious clinical problems. In A. E. Kazdin & J. R. Weisz (Eds.), *Evidence based psychotherapies for children and adolescents* (pp. 301–322). New York, NY: Guilford Press.

Jenkins, A. (1990). *Invitations to responsibility*. Adelaide, Australia: Dulwich Centre Publications.

Jovev, M., & Jackson, H. J. (2004). Early maladaptive schemas in personality disordered individuals. *Journal of Personality Disorders, 18*(5), 467–478.

Kondrat, M. E. (2008). Person-in-environment. In T. M. L. E. Davis (Ed.), *Encyclopedia of social work* (20th ed.). Washington, DC and New York, NY: National Association of Social Workers Press and Oxford University Press.

Linehan, M. M. (1993). *Cognitive-behavioral treatment of borderline personality disorder*: New York, NY: Guilford Press.

Linehan, M. M., Comtois, K. A., Murray, A. M., Brown, M. Z., Gallop, R. J., Heard, H. L., . . . Lindenboim, N. (2006). Two-year randomized controlled trial and follow-up of dialectical behavior therapy vs therapy by experts for suicidal behaviors and borderline personality disorder. *Archives of General Psychiatry, 63*(7), 757–766.

Littell, J. H. (2005). Lessons from a systematic review of effects of multisystemic therapy. *Children and Youth Services Review, 27*(4), 445–463.

Loper, A. B., Mahmoodzadegan, N., & Warren, J. I. (2008). Childhood maltreatment and cluster B personality pathology in female serious offenders. *Sexual Abuse: A Journal of Research and Treatment, 20*(2), 139–160.

Manuel, J., Mullen, E., Fang, L., Bellamy, J., & Bledsoe, S. (2009). Preparing social work practitioners to use evidence-based practice: A comparison of experiences from an implementation project. *Research on Social Work Practice, 19*(5), 613–629.

Maschi, T., Gibson, S., Zgoba, K. M., & Morgen, K. (2011). Trauma and life event stressors among young and older adult prisoners. *Journal of Correctional Health Care, 17*(2), 160–172.

Maschi, T., & Killian, M. L. (2011). The evolution of forensic social work in the United States: Implications for 21st century practice. *Journal of Forensic Social Work, 1*(1), 8–36.

Miller, W., & Rollnick, S. (2002). *Motivational interviewing: Preparing people for change*. New York, NY: Guilford Press.

National Association of Social Workers. (2010). *Evidence-based practice for social workers*. Washington, DC: Author. Retrieved from http://www.socialworkers.org/practice/clinical/csw081605snapshot.asp

Norcross, J. (2009). The therapeutic relationship. In B. Duncan, S. Miller, B. Wampold, & M. Hubble (Eds.), *The heart and soul of change*. Washington, DC: APA Press.

Prescott, D. S., & Miller, S. D. (2015). Feedback-Informed Treatment (FIT) with people who have sexually abused. In B. Schwartz (Ed.), *The sex offender* (pp. 17-1–17-18). Kingston, NJ: Civic Research Press.

Prescott, D. S., & Wilson, R. J. (2013). *Awakening motivation for difficult changes*. Holyoke, MA: New England Adolescent Research Institute Press.

Robbins, S. P., Vaughan-Eden, V., & Maschi, T. (2015). From the editor—It's not CSI: The importance of forensics for social work education. *Journal of Social Work Education, 51*(3), 421–424.

Rubin, A. (2008). *Practitioner's guide to using research for evidence-based practice*. Hoboken, NJ: Wiley.

Sackett, D., Straus, S., Richardson, W., Rosenberg, W., & Haynes, R. (2000). *Evidence-based medicine: How to practice and teach EBM* (2nd ed.). Edinburgh, Scotland: Churchill Livingstone.

Saleebey, D. (2011). Some basic ideas about the strengths perspective. In F. J. Turner (Ed.), *Social work treatment: Interlocking theoretical approaches* (pp. 477–485). New York, NY: Oxford University Press.

Sempértegui, G. A., Karreman, A., Arntz, A., & Bekker, M. H. (2013). Schema therapy for borderline personality disorder: A comprehensive review of its empirical foundations, effectiveness and implementation possibilities. *Clinical Psychology Review, 33*(3), 426–447.

Sheehan, R. (2012). Forensic social work: A distinctive framework for intervention. *Social Work in Mental Health, 10*(5), 409–425.

Simmons, B. (2013). *Individual, agency and environmental factors impacting clinical social workers' involvement with evidence-based practice.* Unpublished doctoral dissertation, Smith College School for Social Work, Northampton, MA.

Trincas, R., Ottaviani, C., Couyoumdjian, A., Tenore, K., Spitoni, G., & Mancini, F. (2014). Specific dysphoric symptoms are predicted by early maladaptive schemas. *The Scientific World Journal, 2014,* 1–7. doi:10.1155/2014/231965

Unger, K. V., & Young, J. E. (1994). Cognitive therapy for personality disorders: A schema-focused approach. *Psychiatric Rehabilitation Journal, 17*(3), 143–145.

van der Kolk, B. (2006). Clinical implications of neuroscience research in PTSD. *Annals of the New York Academy of Sciences, 1071*(1), 277–293.

Walfish, S., McAlister, B., O'Donnell, P., & Lambert, M. J. (2012). An investigation of self-assessment bias in mental health providers. *Psychological Reports, 110*(2), 639–644. doi:10.2466/02.07.17 .PR0.110.2.639-644

Wampold, B. E., & Imel, Z. E. (2015). *The great psychotherapy debate: The evidence for what makes psychotherapy work* (2nd ed.). New York, NY: Routledge/Taylor & Francis.

Whitfield, C. L. (1998). Adverse childhood experiences and trauma. *American Journal of Preventive Medicine, 14*(4), 361–364.

Wike, T. L., Bledsoe, S. E., Manuel, J. I., Despard, M., Johnson, L. V., Bellamy, J. L., & Killian-Farrell, C. (2014). Evidence-based practice in social work: Challenges and opportunities for clinicians and organizations. *Clinical Social Work Journal, 42*(2), 161–170. doi:10.1007/s10615-014-0492-3

Young, D. S. (2014). Social workers' perspectives on effective practice in criminal justice settings. *Journal of Forensic Social Work, 4*(2), 104–122.

Young, J. E., & Brown, G. (1994). Young schema questionnaire. In J. E. Young (Ed.), *Cognitive therapy for personality disorders: A schema-focused approach* (Rev. ed., pp. 63–76). Sarasota, FL: Professional Resource Press/Professional Resource Exchange.

Young, J. E., Klosko, J. S., & Weishaar, M. E. (2003). *Schema therapy: A practitioner's guide.* New York, NY: Guilford Press.

VOICES FROM THE FIELD

Melissa D. Grady, PhD, MSW, LICSW

Associate Professor
Catholic University
Clinical Social Worker
Self-Employed

Agency Setting

I am an associate professor at the National Catholic School of Social Service at Catholic University in Washington DC where I teach practice, theory and research, and conduct research on sexual violence and evidence-based practice. I am also in private practice in Washington DC.

Practice Responsibilities

I provide individual psychotherapy to clients using a variety of different modalities. Primarily I use relational approaches that are based on psychodynamic and attachment theories, cognitive behavioral therapy with an emphasis on trauma, and solution-focused therapy.

Expertise Required

To have knowledge related to trauma recovery, evidence-based practice process, various empirically supported interventions, and to be fully licensed.

Ethical, Legal, Practice, Diversity, and/or Advocacy Issues Addressed

The majority of the challenging issues I face are related to trauma and the intersection with the criminal justice system, in terms of reporting laws. Many of my clients struggle with previous trauma histories. Given their background, we often discuss the challenges they face with reporting and managing how to address their recovery within the context of the legal/criminal justice system.

Interprofessional and Intersectoral Collaboration

In my work as a practitioner, I work with other practitioners in consultation and supervision. In my research that informs my practice, I work with many collaborators who are focused on criminal justice reforms that include prison programming, postrelease services, early intervention, and empirically based policies, as well as prevention and intervention programs.

CHAPTER 21

Motivational Interviewing

David S. Prescott

George S. Leibowitz

CHAPTER OBJECTIVES

The major objectives of this chapter are to:

- Explain the theoretical basis for motivational interviewing (MI).
- Review the empirical evidence for the use of MI with diverse populations in forensic settings.
- Identify the four key processes and understand how to apply MI skills.

CHAPTER COMPETENCIES HIGHLIGHTED

- Competency 4: Engage in Practice Informed Research and Research Informed Practice
- Competency 6: Engage With Individuals, Families, Organizations, and Communities
- Competency 8: Intervene With Individuals, Families, Organizations, and Communities

Core Skill Addressed

At its heart, MI is a person-centered counseling approach for addressing the common experience of ambivalence about change (Miller & Rollnick, 2013). MI involves attention to the language of change and is designed to strengthen personal motivation and commitment to a specific goal by eliciting and exploring the person's own reasons for change within an atmosphere of acceptance and compassion. Although Miller (1983) and Miller and Rollnick (1991) first coined the term, many others have helped to develop MI into its current form (e.g., Wagner & Ingersoll, 2013).

Theoretical Basis for MI

Many of the theoretical underpinnings of MI have an empirical basis. For example, self-determination theory (Bem, 1972) emphasized how people are often more convinced by what they hear themselves say than by what others say to them. This has received further confirmation from Amrhein and his colleagues (Amrhein, Miller, Yahne, Palmer, & Fulcher, 2003). They observed that client statements related to the desire, ability, reason, and need to change are related to the proportion of days abstinent from drug and alcohol abuse, suggesting a pathway from client language to behavior.

Similarly, Ryan and Deci (2000) found that change often begins with external pressures, and that clients tend to discover their own reasons for change during the course of treatment. Where Ryan and Deci have emphasized people's inherent motivations in the direction of competence, autonomy, and connectedness to others, Emmons (1999) also emphasized the importance of meaning and purpose in one's life, which can also be fundamental to people's commitment to change in forensic contexts (e.g., "I don't want to be the kind of person who keeps getting arrested like this; it is not who I am").

Perhaps the best known theoretical underpinning of MI is the stages of change, a component of the transtheoretical model (Prochaska & DiClemente, 1992). In brief, people who succeed in making changes in their lives often proceed through five stages of change: precontemplation (not considering making a change), contemplation, preparation, action, and maintenance. Movement through these stages is typically sequential and, ideally, progressive. However, clients in forensic settings, like anybody else, can move back and forth among these stages in their change process. Further, they may be ready to change in some areas and not others. Therapists must continually assess the stage at which their clients are functioning and adjust their approach accordingly. The stages-of-change model is not without critics. Some have observed that it does not adequately account for the range of internal, external, or situational factors and that its practical application in some situations can be limited (e.g., Burrowes & Needs, 2009; Sutton, 2001). For that reason, it is a guiding framework but not a stand-alone treatment model. Practitioners who utilize MI recognize that ambivalence can take place as a client moves back and forth between these stages.

Empirical Evidence of Effectiveness of MI With Forensic Populations and Settings

The body of research on MI has grown significantly over the past two decades (Hettema, Steele, & Miller, 2005; Lundahl, Kunz, Brownell, Tollefson, & Burke, 2010). However, while MI has been demonstrated to be effective in a number of areas of behavioral health, there are fewer empirical studies with forensic populations. As Bogue and Nandi (2012) note:

> As a formal intervention, MI is now internationally recognized as an evidence-based practice intervention for alcohol and drug problems and a wide variety of other health problems (e.g., obesity) identify some of the mechanisms or causal ingredients of MI that produce significant and positive effects, the research on MI applications in criminal justice is currently insufficient to qualify MI as an EBP for offender populations. Until more corrections-specific research on MI is conducted, it is not possible to draw conclusions comparing MI to cognitive-behavioral treatments (CBT) and other established criminal justice EBPs in terms of recidivism reduction. Additional research is also needed regarding the level of fidelity and quality assurance in MI implementation required to produce desired client outcomes. (p. 2)

Despite the inconclusive findings across studies and the need for empirical investigations in forensic settings, MI was found in a systematic review to be a promising intervention when applied with fidelity, and can improve treatment retention, enhance motivation to make behavioral change, and reduce recidivism among offenders (McMurran, 2009). Moreover, MI is consistent with the risk-needs-responsivity (RNR; Andrews, Bonta, & Wormith, 2006) principles of offender rehabilitation. Specifically, use of MI skills can promote responsivity to the learning styles, characteristics, motivations, and abilities of the highest risk offenders.

Applying MI Skills

MI Spirit

MI involves an underlying spirit made up of *partnership, acceptance, compassion, and evocation* (also known by the acronym PACE). *Partnership* means that professionals view their work as collaboration, a joint commitment to a better future. *Acceptance* includes four aspects of absolute worth, accurate empathy, autonomy support, and affirmation. *Compassion* involves actively promoting the client's welfare and placing a priority on his or her needs. *Evocation*, also described earlier, means eliciting the client's personally meaningful and relevant reasons and methods for change.

In many respects, this underlying spirit is the hardest element to teach and to master. It can be easy to develop what David Burns (personal communication, December 2009) has called "the clinician's illusion" that we believe we are more effective and connected to our clients than we really are. More recently, a study by Walfish, McAlister, O'Donnell, and Lambert (2012) found that the average therapist rated himself or herself as more effective than 80% of his or her peers. The MI spirit, ultimately, rests on a foundation of humility and being willing to abandon any pretense at expertise. Therapists may possess expertise in understanding sexual abuse, but only the client is the expert at his or her own self.

In some areas of the world, this underlying spirit of MI will run directly counter to how programs for sexual abuse define themselves. For example, the Texas Department of State Health Services (DSHS) defines sexual offender treatment, in part, as differing from more traditional forms of psychotherapy. The DSHS further makes clear that treatment should be "mandated, structured, victim centered, and the treatment provider imposes values and limits" (Texas Department of Health Services, 2012).

By definition, treatment providers who actively impose values and limits on their clients and provide treatment that prioritizes others over the client in treatment are not engaging in MI. Setting aside ethical questions of who the client actually is in treatment programs, all professionals need to examine their beliefs and readiness to act as genuine partners in change. Even outside of settings that define treatment as imposing values on clients, many professionals have had the experience of clients in the criminal justice world who seem to interact with professionals in a way that invites a harsh and confrontational style. The challenge in MI is to stick with the spirit; it is possible—even desirable—to provide feedback, information, and advice in a manner adherent with the spirit of MI.

Guiding Style

The concept of guiding is vital. Older definitions of MI described it as a directive approach. Why prefer the word *guiding* to *directive*? Many clients in forensic settings who are in treatment are very aware of the power differences between themselves and their therapists. *Guiding* implies a working relationship where the therapist, figuratively, walks alongside the client, exploring and offering ideas about the direction he or she can take rather than directing each client to take a predetermined route. A guiding style provides high support for the client's autonomy. This is very different from an overtly directive style that does not support the client's autonomy, or a following style, in which the therapist hands over control of the session to the client.

Four Processes

The most recent conceptualization of MI involves four key processes: *engaging, focusing, evoking,* and *planning*. Recognizing that therapist–client conversations do not always follow a planned or straightforward path, Miller and Rollnick (2013) describe these four processes as going beyond earlier descriptions of MI. The therapist and client first explore motivation and then commitment to change. Real-life conversations (that is, conversations that occur outside of therapeutic contexts) often shift focus and move forward and backward as people explore what is and is not important to them. For example, some clients in treatment may have a high level of motivation to build a better life for themselves and are easy to engage in treatment until they realize that part of change would mean reexamining behavior that has brought them states of happiness and pleasure, or reappraising the nature of their relationships. It can be a common human experience to desire change and then reappraise that change once it is actually being implemented. Conversely, many people desire the experience of having changed, but are ambivalent about the effort involved in changing.

In MI, *engaging* is the process of establishing a helpful connection and working relationship, both within a single session and across the course of an assessment or treatment. A helpful guideline can be to ensure that the therapist uses the first 20% of the total length of a contact to engage with the client (e.g., the first 12 minutes of an hour-long session). *Focusing* is the process by which the therapist develops and maintains a specific direction in the conversation about change. The process of *evocation* involves eliciting the client's own motivations for change and lies at the heart of MI. The *planning* process encompasses both committing to change and formulating a concrete plan of action.

Part of the skill of the therapist using MI will be to remain engaging throughout treatment, suggesting and exploring areas of conversational focus in a way that guides treatment forward and does not compromise the therapeutic alliance. Depending on the progression of this conversation, the next area of focus may be evoking the client's motivations for change. Should the conversation become unexpectedly difficult, the therapist may choose to return to a renewed focus on full engagement. The work of the therapist, then, is to act as a guide, all the while keeping in mind the possible areas of focus and assessing the client's readiness to explore them in treatment. Ultimately, the four processes of MI can be linear or reoccur during the life of a conversation or course of treatment.

The Language of Change

The concept of resistance as a single construct no longer exists in MI. Among others, Miller and Rollnick (2002, 2013) have been vocal about their discomfort with the concept of resistance, despite having no replacement. Many professionals have expressed concern that thinking in terms of "resistance" can label the client rather than processes within the client, or between the client and the therapist. Many professionals have had the experience of working collaboratively with clients previously described as resistant, or finding that their erstwhile resistant clients had gone on to work very well with someone else. Miller and Rollnick (2013) have described the broader category of resistance as containing two components:

1. *Sustain talk* involves statements that favor the status quo (e.g., "I'm not interested in treatment and I don't want to change; I'm happy with who I am").
2. *Discord* involves disagreement and not being connected with the client (e.g., "Your treatment program is a joke and you couldn't make me change if you tried").

It is crucial to understand that many clients' presentation in forensic practice has to do with discord more than unwillingness to change. Clients who are rude to therapists are often exerting their drive to independence much more than an unwillingness to change or participate in treatment under the right conditions. Possible topics for further exploration that can prevent discord might include what independence means to the client and how the therapist might be helpful in the context of the client's autonomy.

While sustain talk is language favoring the status quo, change talk includes any statement reflecting a *desire, ability, reason,* or *need* (often referred to by the acronym DARN) to make a positive change. As noted earlier, research has found that client statements indicating a willingness, intent, or commitment to make positive changes are particularly important for clinicians to explore and reinforce (Amrhein et al., 2003). This "change talk" signals that the client is at least thinking about the possibility of change.

Microskills

There are five key communication microskills used throughout MI (Miller & Rollnick, 2013). These are:

1. Asking open-ended questions (i.e., questions that do not lend themselves to single-word, yes–no answers)

2. Providing affirmations (i.e., affirming a client and/or his or her actions in a way that conveys deep understanding and appreciation and in line with the spirit factors described earlier)
3. Offering summarizing statements (in which the therapist summarizes the key points made by the client in order to ensure that they are understanding and to convey that they are trying to understand and appreciate the client)
4. Providing information and advice with permission: Critical to MI is that it is done on behalf of and in collaboration with clients. In the spirit of partnership and compassion, it is vital that therapists seek permission before sharing feedback with clients. On one hand, this can be a matter of simple respect, and on another seeking permission is another means of ensuring that the client is fully engaged with the therapist.
5. Making reflective statements, which require further explanation:
   a. Simple reflections consist of reflecting the client's statements with his or her exact words or closely related words.
   b. Complex reflections consist of reflecting the client's meaning and the client's emotions, together or separately. A helpful principle can be to reflect back to the client more than he or she said, but not more than he or she actually meant.
   c. Double-sided reflections reflect both sides of a client's ambivalence about an area of his or her life (e.g., "on one hand, you want to make some changes to your life, and on the other hand you don't want to appear weak to others").
   d. Amplified reflections, in which the therapist slightly exaggerates what the client says and allowing the client to agree or disagree with it. It is critical that the therapist take care not to exaggerate to the point that the client feels misunderstood or angry.

Clearly, each of the approaches and techniques in MI can take years to practice and learn and the reader is strongly encouraged to seek further education in order to practice MI effectively.

Case Example and Application

Ricky (a fictionalized composite of many clients seen across the authors' several years of practice) came into treatment following an intensive series of crimes in which he had set two fires (one was a duplex apartment building that was unoccupied at the time, but declared a total loss, and another was a vacant industrial building) and molested the children of the family with whom he was living (in the previously mentioned duplex apartment). The court convicted Ricky for these crimes via an Alford plea, in which Ricky asserted his innocence even as he acknowledged that the evidence available to the court would likely result in his conviction. These "Alford" cases can be frustrating for therapists, because they lend themselves to difficulty in forming a therapeutic alliance. The client, mandated to attend treatment, can easily point to the fact that it was the court that found him guilty over his or her assertions. In short, the very nature of the conviction presents a dilemma for therapists.

The therapist, Amy, chose to start at the point of this dilemma. Using a double-sided reflection, she took note of the fact that:

- On one hand, Ricky believed he was innocent and, on the other hand, he had acknowledged through his attorney that the evidence against him was very strong.
- On one hand, he appeared comfortable with who he was and on the other hand he appeared at least a little interested in preventing further allegations when he reentered the community (and the intensive supervision that would accompany release from prison).

(continued)

Case Example and Application (*continued*)

Ricky agreed with these points and acted in a manner that other professionals might have perceived as resistant ("I doubt you could understand my situation—you don't live in my world and get to go home every night while I'm here"). However, Amy felt that Ricky's presentation had more to do with discord and possible sustain talk.

As Amy used reflective listening with occasional open-ended questions, it became clear that Ricky had experienced considerable adversity in his 31-year life. She explored this as a means to understanding him more deeply, and appreciating the strengths that he brought to the table. Even as she did not accept sexual abuse and arson as acceptable behaviors, she was still able to accept Ricky as the human being he was in front of her, and understood his challenging responses as indications that she had a way to go to fully engage him in a fully functioning therapeutic alliance.

Following the principle that the slower one goes in a conversation the faster he or she might arrive at consensus, Amy worked to stay grounded in the MI spirit of partnership, acceptance, compassion, and evocation. She and Ricky arrived at a shared understanding that even as his past experiences did not excuse his behavior, they certainly had contributed to it. He was able to acknowledge that he had engaged in many of the behaviors that had led to his conviction, even as he bitterly disagreed with some of the details. Amy was less concerned with the details than she was with building his capacities for living a life in which hurting others was unnecessary and undesirable. They came to agree on a focus on treatment as helping him manage risks at the same time as he built on the many strengths he had in his life (e.g., his ability to maintain a job and his interest in furthering his education).

Amy found that through the MI spirit and skills—which included not following through on the urge to provide feedback without permission and not rushing to solve his problems for him or make demands on his treatment participation—Ricky was more easily engaged in treatment than he appeared at first. She found that occasionally telling Ricky what professionals in forensic settings often call "the hard truth" was not difficult when he understood the spirit in which she was offering it.

Amy checked in periodically to make sure that she understood where Ricky was coming from and that he was as engaged as he seemed. Because Amy worked within a broader correctional model, she also worked with Ricky to explore his ambivalence about the supervision he received and his participating in certain assessment methods related to his crimes. In the end, Amy was able to guide Ricky through an intensive and assessment-driven treatment process by adhering to principles and processes that can seem easy to learn at first but that are often challenging to practice in real life.

Conclusion

MI can be an effective, evidence-based skill for forensic practitioners when applied with integrity. While widely used in behavioral health, more outcome research is needed with forensic populations to investigate who are the most responsive to MI in terms of treatment engagement and readiness to change.

MI approaches can help the practitioner achieve a deeper level of understanding of client needs to move toward behavior change, at the same time as it helps them feel understood. This can help to prevent attrition, and alert therapists to when a client's situation or treatment participation is worsening. Further, whatever the circumstances that may have brought them to treatment, being in treatment in any forensic setting is almost always a uniquely challenging event.

CHAPTER EXERCISES

Exercise 1. Format: Have students take turns talking with each other about any topic they choose as long as it is not too personal (e.g., talking about coursework or social life matters is okay, but this is not the time to discuss serious life challenges). The topic should be something they feel two ways about. Activity: As one student talks (up to three minutes) the other responds using only the reflective listening skills described in this chapter and asks no closed-ended questions. Further, the listener must offer no advice.

Exercise 2. Same format as Exercise 1, except only the first student speaks, while the listener listens with the goal of completely understanding. The listener then asks, "Did I understand correctly?" and then listens with interest to the speaker.

Exercise 3. Same format as Exercise 1, except only the listener summarizes the speaker's "change talk": statements that reflect the speaker's desire, ability, reason, need, or commitment to make a change.

Exercise 4. Have one student make a change talk statement, and then have three other students formulate an open-ended question that would have resulted in the change talk statement as an answer (Note: This is akin to jeopardy, where the host gives the answer and the contestant has to offer the question for which the answer is correct).

Additional Resources

Motivational Interviewing in Corrections: http://static.nicic.gov/Library/025556.pdf

Motivational Interviewing Network of Trainers: www.motivationalinterviewing.org

Motivational Interviewing Network of Trainers: www.motivationalinterviewing.org/category/resource-tag/dvd

References

Amrhein, P. C., Miller, W. R., Yahne, C. E., Palmer, M., & Fulcher, L. (2003). Client commitment language during motivational interviewing predicts drug use outcomes. *Journal of Consulting and Clinical Psychology, 71*, 862–878.

Andrews, D. A., Bonta, J., & Wormith, J. S. (2006). The recent past and near future of risk and/or need assessment. *Crime and Delinquency, 52*, 7–27.

Bem, D. J. (1972). Self-perception theory. In L. Berkowitz (Ed.), *Advances in experimental social psychology* (Vol. 6, pp. 1–62). New York, NY: Academic Press.

Bogue, B., & Nandi, A. (2012). *Motivational interviewing: A comprehensive guide to implementing MI in corrections*. Washington, DC: U.S. Department of Justice, National Institute of Corrections. Retrieved from http://static.nicic.gov/Library/025556.pdf

Burrowes, N., & Needs, A. (2009). Time to contemplate change? A framework for assessing readiness to change with offenders. *Aggression and Violent Behavior, 14*(1), 39–49.

Emmons, R. A. (1999). *The psychology of ultimate concerns*. New York, NY: Guilford Press.

Hettema, J., Steele, J., & Miller, W. R. (2005). Motivational interviewing. *Annual Review of Clinical Psychology, 1*, 91–111.

Lundahl, B. W., Kunz, C., Brownell, C., Tollefson, D., & Burke, B. L. (2010). A meta-analysis of motivational interviewing: Twenty-five years of empirical studies. *Research on Social Work Practice, 20*, 137–160.

McMurran, M. (2009). Motivational interviewing with offenders: A systematic review. *Legal and Criminological Psychology, 14*(1), 83–100.

Miller, W. R. (1983). Motivational interviewing with problem drinkers. *Behavioural and Cognitive Psychotherapy, 11*, 147–172.

Miller, W. R., & Rollnick, S. (1991). *Motivational interviewing.* New York, NY: Guilford Press.

Miller W. R., & Rollnick, S. (2002). *Motivational interviewing: Preparing people to change.* New York, NY: Guilford Press.

Miller, W. R., & Rollnick, S. (2013). *Motivational interviewing: Helping people change* (3rd ed.,). New York, NY: Guilford Press.

Prochaska, J. O., & DiClemente, C. C. (1992). *Stages of change in the modification of problem behaviors.* Newbury Park, CA: Sage Publications.

Ryan, R. M., & Deci, E. L. (2000). Self-determination and the facilitation of intrinsic motivation, social development, and well-being. *American Psychologist, 55*, 68–78.

Sutton, S. (2001). Back to the drawing board? A review of applications of the transtheoretical model to substance use. *Addiction, 96*, 175–186.

Texas Department of State Health Services. (2012). Council on sex offender treatment treatment of sex offenders—Difference between sex offender treatment and psychotherapy. Retrieved from http://www.dshs.state.tx.us/csot/csot_tdifference.shtm

Wagner, C. C., & Ingersoll, K. S. (2013). *Motivational interviewing in groups.* New York, NY: Guilford Press.

Walfish, S., McAlister, B., O'Donnell, P., & Lambert, M. J. (2012). An investigation of self-assessment bias in mental health providers. *Psychological Reports, 110*(2), 639–644.

VOICES FROM THE FIELD

David S. Prescott, LICSW
Director of Professional Development
Becket Family of Services

Agency Setting

Becket Family of Services provides inpatient and community-based care to diverse populations, including people who have been traumatized, people who have abused, and a wide range of mental health challenges. The clients come from both urban and rural areas.

Practice Responsibilities

Mr. Prescott functions in the role of clinical director, supervisor, and consultant for various programs within the Becket Family of Services. This can involve a wide range of approaches toward working with others, often with varying forms of responsibility for outcome (for example, clinical supervision and consultation can involve different expectations, roles, and responsibilities of each player involved). In addition to these duties, he also collects data and conducts program assessments for Becket's board of directors. Mr. Prescott also keeps a small caseload of clients for whom he provides assessments and treatment.

Expertise Required

Mr. Prescott's role requires expertise in understanding the how and why of personal change in diverse circumstances and in response to different treatment approaches. Knowledge of the workings of the therapeutic alliance is vital. Interagency collaboration is the norm, and clinicians in these programs often have to be familiar with documentation requirements of numerous stakeholder agencies.

Ethical, Legal, Practice, Diversity, and/or Advocacy Issues Addressed

The nature of Mr. Prescott's clientele (people often marginalized both in society and occasionally within practice settings) requires considerable advocacy. Working with people who have abused can present a number of ethical considerations, often centered on balancing community safety and client beneficence. Promoting this balance can require a considerable focus on educating stakeholders and the community, who often hold numerous misconceptions about trauma and abuse. In some cases, Mr. Prescott consults to agencies whose clients are on probation and live in shelters.

Interprofessional and Intersectoral Collaboration

Many of Becket's programs function as players within multidisciplinary teams. For example, a case manager might refer a client for residential placement and continue to monitor his or her case over the course of that client's treatment. In many cases, the same client also has a supervising agent in the criminal justice system. Becket staff must then coordinate services with other professionals, funders, and licensing authorities who have or will work with this client and family.

CHAPTER 22

Forensic Interviewing

Susan P. Robbins*

CHAPTER OBJECTIVES

The major objectives of this chapter are to:

- Utilize interviewing techniques that have been empirically found to elicit the most detailed and accurate information when conducting a forensic interview.
- Describe at least three evidence-based best practices for forensic interviewing.
- Delineate the ways in which interviewer beliefs and expectations can bias the interview.

CHAPTER COMPETENCIES HIGHLIGHTED

- Competency 6: Engage With Individuals, Families, Organizations, and Communities
- Competency 7: Assess Individuals, Families, Organizations, and Communities

Throughout history, the ways in which both professionals and the general public have responded to allegations of child sexual abuse have been inconsistent and varied (Faller, 2015; Krason, 2013). In fact, public policy and our current system of child protection was only first implemented in 1974 with the passage of the Child Abuse Prevention and Treatment Act (CAPTA), which provided federal funds to states for prevention and research, contingent on states implementing specialized child protection agencies (Krason, 2013). In addition, the "rediscovery" of child maltreatment and sexual abuse in the 1970s has been widely credited to the groundbreaking research on child sexual abuse by David Finkelhor (1979) as well as social justice movements of the era including the women's movement (Faller, 2015).

Initially, mental health professionals were used to conduct interviews with children who were suspected of being sexually abused (Faller, 2015; Newlin et al., 2015). Having received little or no training in this area, these interviews were often coercive and highly suggestive and several high-profile cases in the 1980s received significant media attention, often involving bizarre allegations that arose in day-care settings (Robbins, 1998). Subsequent to these widely publicized day-care abuse cases, child protection professionals came under fire for the improper and suggestive techniques that were used to elicit allegations, particularly since many of the children initially denied having been abused. Over the past 30 years, there has been a substantial body of research on proper interviewing techniques as well as critical knowledge about children's developmental capabilities that now guide such interviews. The quality of the information gained in the interview is largely dependent on the training and skill of the person conducting the

---

interview. Currently, when children are interviewed about sexual abuse, it is done in the context of a forensic interview. Ideally, where available, these interviews are conducted in child advocacy centers (CACs), a child-friendly setting that brings together professionals in child protection and law enforcement. This avoids the child having to undergo multiple interviews and ensures that the person or persons conducting the interview are forensically trained. CACs are child centered and their primary focus is advocacy, collaboration, evaluation and assessment, and training.

The Forensic Interview

When an allegation of child sexual abuse is referred to Child Protective Services (CPS), the forensic interview is the first step in the investigation. The goal of the forensic interview is to determine whether or not abuse has occurred in an objective and legally defensible manner. Further, according to Newlin et al. (2015):

> A forensic interview of a child is a developmentally sensitive and legally sound method of gathering factual information regarding allegations of abuse or exposure to violence. This interview is conducted by a competently trained, neutral professional utilizing research and practice-informed techniques as part of a larger investigative process.

In addition, according to the Michigan model of child abuse protocol (Governor's Task Force on Children's Justice Subcommittee, 1998), two essential features of the forensic interview are hypothesis testing and using a child-centered approach.

Currently, there is a growing evidence-based literature on interviewing protocols that have been shown to elicit more detailed and more accurate responses from children (Anderson, 2013; Ceci & Bruck, 1995; Faller, 2007; Governor's Task Force on Children's Justice Subcommittee, 1998; Hershkowitz, Lamb, Katz, & Malloy, 2015; Lamb & Fauchier, 2001; Lamb & Garretson, 2003; Poole & Lamb, 1998). Although there are a number of forensic interviewing models, all consist of sequential phases or stages and include the following:

- Rapport building: In this initial stage, the interviewer typically covers introductions, explains the setting and the rules for the interview, assesses the child's level of development, determines the child's ability to distinguish between the truth and a lie, and asks general questions about the child's life and interests. The developmental assessment may also include learning the child's name for various body parts. Questions about the child's interests should be asked in a manner to elicit narrative responses. Eliciting narrative responses from the child in this initial stage is critical because it not only allows the interviewer to assess the child's developmental level, but also "teaches" the child to provide narrative answers.
- Substantive phase: Once rapport has been established, the interviewer uses open-ended questions to obtain a narrative description of what, if anything, has occurred and, when necessary, follows up with more specific questions based on what the child has said. During this stage the interviewer may also use hypothesis testing in order to attempt to rule out alternative explanations for the allegations or to help clarify what the child has said.
- Closure: In this final phase, the interviewer moves to nonsubstantive topics, asks if the child has any questions, and thanks the child for participating in the interview. The interviewer may also discuss issues related to safety and explain what will occur next.

Theory and Research Knowledge Necessary for Forensic Interviewers

Human memory plays a crucial role in cognitive development as well as being central to learning and having a sense of self (Robbins, Chatterjee, & Canda, 2012). When children are interviewed about sexual abuse, the accounts that they give are based on autobiographical memory and the ability to accurately recall events that occurred in their lives (Baur, 2006; Powell, Thompson, & Ceci, 2003). Interest in the development of children's memory was popularized with the theories and writings of Jean Piaget, but it is only recently that researchers have begun to investigate the ways in which maltreatment affects memory (Howe, Cicchetti, & Toth, 2006). Current research has also investigated the ways in which suggestibility can distort children's memory and the importance of this in the forensic context (Poole & Lindsay, 2002).

A child's age and moral development coincide developmentally with her or his cognitive ability and linguistic ability (Robbins, Chatterjee, & Canda, 2012). In fact, age is one of the most important factors in a child's capacity for memory (Lamb, 2015). As children age, their vocabulary improves and they begin to engage in fuller conversations. They also begin to store more information in long-term memory and are better able to discuss events that they remember (Newlin et al., 2015). Importantly, children's understanding of truth/lie as well as their ability to provide full narratives of things that they experience is dependent on the intersection of their moral development and cognitive development, as well as their linguistic understanding of the concepts. Table 22.1 shows the concordance in the development of memory and moral development at different ages and developmental stages based on theories and research by Jean Piaget (Piaget & Inhelder, 1969) and Lawrence Kohlberg (1984).

It is also critical that forensic interviewers have knowledge about normal childhood sexual development so that they can distinguish between sexual behaviors that are most likely indicative of abuse from those that are part of normal development. This is particularly important because research has shown that children exhibit a wide range of normal sexual behaviors that adults may perceive incorrectly as being related to abuse. In general, children under the age of 5 or 6 engage in a wide variety of sexual behaviors, and after age 6 the frequency of these behaviors decreases with age until puberty. The most unusual sexual behaviors for children of all ages tend to be more aggressive and imitative of adult sexual behavior (Friedrich et al., 1992; Friedrich & Trane, 2002).

Two other considerations that are important to consider are disability and culture. According to Hershkowitz, Lamb, and Horowitz (2007), there is a greater risk for abuse among children with disabilities than for those without disabilities. Since most forensic interviewers do not have specialized training in working with this population it may be necessary to adapt the interview to the child's specific needs in a forensically sound manner, as well as consult with disability specialists and the child's primary caretaker (Newlin et al., 2015). Further, culture is one of the many contextual factors in a child's life that can influence the child's understanding of abuse and the ability to discuss it with others. It is therefore important to account for the child and family's culture when conducting a forensic interview.

TABLE 22.1   Memory Development and Moral Development in Children

Approximate Age	Memory Development	Moral Development
Birth–1½–2	Recognition	Unknown
2–3 or 4	Beginning recall Beginning of autobiographical memory	Based on obedience and avoidance of punishment
3 or 4–9	Recall becomes stronger and infantile amnesia becomes apparent	Egoistic—based on egocentric needs and earning rewards or favors
9–early teens	Recall becomes stronger and infantile amnesia is more apparent	Based on gaining approval and avoiding disapproval
Early teens–early adulthood	Recall is strengthened through rehearsal of events	Based on conformity to rules

Evidence-Based Forensic Interview Practices

In an effort to correct the leading and suggestive techniques that were used in the past, researchers have examined studies on the disclosure process and forensic interviews in order to better understand the ways in which interviewer beliefs and expectations can potentially bias the interview (London, Bruck, Ceci, & Shuman 2005). In addition, current research has also demonstrated that specific types of interview techniques can elicit misinformation as well as false allegations (Ceci, Crossman, Scullin, Gilstrap, & Huffman, 2011; Saywitz, Goodman, & Lyon, 2002; Wood & Garven, 2000). There is a growing evidence-based literature on interviewing protocols that have been shown to elicit more detailed, and more accurate, responses from children (Faller, 2007; Lamb & Fauchier, 2001; Poole & Lamb, 1998). As Newlin et al. (2015) have noted, forensic interviewers may be trained in more than one model and may also combine techniques from various models. It is also important to recognize that the jurisdiction in which the case occurs, as well as specific state statutes and case law, may determine the model that is used.

In an effort to build consensus about best practices in forensic interviewing, representatives from The American Professional Society on the Abuse of Children (APSAC), the CornerHouse Interagency Child Abuse Evaluation and Training Center, the Gundersen National Child Protection Training Center, the National Children's Advocacy Center, and the National Institute of Child Health and Human Development (NICHD) met to examine the similarities and differences in their models. This resulted in a bulletin published by the U.S. Department of Justice, Office of Juvenile Justice and Delinquency Prevention, that summarizes current best practices for forensic interviews (Newlin et al., 2015). Although there are similarities among the various models, there are also important differences in their methods as well as the amount of empirical support that each has garnered.

The one model that was specifically designed to produce operational guidelines and also has been rigorously tested and used internationally is the NICHD Structured Interview Protocol (Lamb, Orbach, Hershkowitz, Esplin, & Horowitz, 2007; La Rooy et al., 2015). The Michigan Forensic Interviewing Protocol (State of Michigan Governor's Task Force on Child Abuse and Neglect and Department of Human Services, n.d.) is also closely based on this model and the supporting research (Poole & Lamb, 1998). However, as Brackmann (2013) has noted, one of the primary limitations of the NICHD Protocol is that the model was developed by the researchers and, thus, may contain bias due to a lack of critical analysis by the researchers. Nonetheless, it remains the most empirically tested protocol and has added greatly to our knowledge about best practices in forensic interviewing. According to Lamb, Orbach, Hershkowitz, Esplin, and Horowitz (2007, para. 7):

> The findings obtained in independent field studies in four different countries (Cyr, Lamb, Pelletier, Leduc, & Perron, 2006; Lamb, Orbach, Warren, Esplin, & Hershkowitz, 2006; Orbach et al., 2000; Sternberg, Lamb, Orbach, Esplin, & Mitchell, 2001) demonstrate convincingly that when forensic investigators employ recommended interview procedures by following the structured NICHD Protocol, they enhance the quality of information elicited from alleged victims.

It is generally accepted that forensic interviews should be video- or audio-recorded so that a clear record of the interview is preserved. In addition, some of the main points in the NICHD Protocol and the Michigan Protocol for best practices include the following, and are discussed in more detail in the following:

- Avoid bias; explore alternative hypotheses or explanations
- Build rapport at the beginning
- Have a practice interview
- Provide ground rules
- Ask open-ended questions and encourage a free narrative from the child
- Pair specific questions with open-ended prompts

- Avoid pressure, coercion, and suggestion through giving the child information, asking leading questions, and repeating questions
- Closing the interview without a report of abuse is an acceptable outcome

When preparing for the interview, it is important for the interviewer to use a child-friendly room and remove any distracting materials. At this time, prior to the interview, the interviewer should also consider questions that can be used to test alternative hypotheses. The first hypothesis, always, is that the abuse occurred as alleged, but in order to avoid bias other hypotheses should also be explored. For example, the allegation may be valid, but the child may have identified the wrong perpetrator. Another possibility is that some of the allegations are valid, but the child has either confabulated details that are not accurate or has been influenced to make up additional details that are not true. It is also possible that the child has been pressured by someone with ulterior motives to make a false allegation or the child herself or himself is freely making a false allegation for revenge. Another possibility is that the child has been questioned repeatedly by adults who honestly believe abuse has occurred and the child eventually assents to please the adults and, through repetition, comes to believe that the abuse occurred. It is important to note that when a child comes to believe that abuse occurred, even though it did not, the child is no longer lying because she or he believes that it occurred.

When the interview begins, the interviewer should introduce herself or himself to the child and include both her or his name and role. If recording equipment is used, the child should be informed of this as well as who else is watching the interview. If the child asks spontaneous questions, the interviewer should answer them. It is equally important for the interviewer to explain the ground rules for the interview and get agreement from the child that she or he will tell the truth and not guess at the answers and to only talk about things that actually happened. The child should also be told to correct the interviewer should something be said that is incorrect. In addition, the child should be told that it is okay to say "I don't know" or "I don't understand." The interviewer can use practice questions such as "What is my dog's name?" to determine if the child can differentiate between statements that are true or false.

As the interviewer begins to build rapport with the child, this creates a relaxed environment so that the child feels supported. It is particularly important that open-ended questions be used so that the child is "taught" early on to respond with narrative descriptions. This is used as a "practice" interview that demonstrates for the child how the interview will proceed. To accomplish this, the interviewer can ask the child about a neutral topic such as a recent event or holiday (such as a birthday or Christmas) or a daily event (such as what the child does to get ready for school in the morning or details about a favorite game that she or he plays). In this initial stage, it is important to emphasize that the child tell everything that she or he remembers about the event, from beginning to end, and also include everything that she or he remembers, including things that might not seem particularly important. By asking about a neutral topic, the way in which the child responds to these questions also allows the interviewer to assess the child's cognitive and linguistic levels and abilities. Both verbal and nonverbal reinforcement can be used to show the child that the interviewer is interested in what the child is saying.

As the interviewer moves to the substantive phase of the interview, a series of nonsuggestive questions should be used and the interviewer should introduce the topic using the least suggestive prompt possible. Some examples of nonsuggestive prompts are: "Do you know why you came here to talk to me today?" or "I want to talk about why you are here today. Tell me why you came to talk to me," or "I understand that you've had some problems in your family, please tell me about that." If the child fails to make an outcry, suggestive questions or focused questions based on something that the child has not said should never be used.

If the child does make an outcry, the interviewer should follow up with a series of free narrative questions such as "Tell me more about that," or "Tell me everything that happened," or "Then what happened?" A large body of research on best practices has shown that open-ended and less directive questions that elicit free narrative from the child produce better information and should be used throughout the interview. When additional information is needed about something that the child has said, and it has not been obtained through free narrative questions, the interviewer can get clarification by asking more directive questions based on what the child has said. For example, the interviewer can use the more focused "W" questions to get additional information such as who, what, where, and when. There are times, particularly with young children, that forensic interviewers may need to ask option-posing (multiple choice) questions in an attempt to gain necessary information that has not yet been obtained. An example of this includes questions such as "Did it happen in the bedroom, the living room, or someplace else?" or "Did he touch you over the pants or under the pants?" Although this form of question may be necessary, it is important to recognize that this is the least accurate way of gaining information because it is based on assumptions of the interviewer and should be avoided, when possible, in order to not contaminate the rest of the interview.

Importantly, questions should also be asked to clarify any inconsistent or ambiguous things that the child has said. In addition, questions to test alternative hypotheses should also be included. It is important to remember that the forensic interview should be based on hypothesis testing, rather than hypothesis confirming, and that it is acceptable to end an interview with no report of abuse.

As the interview comes to closure, the interviewer moves to neutral topics, asks if the child has any questions, and thanks the child for taking part in the interview. If an allegation of abuse does emerge during the interview, the interviewer can also talk to the child about safety.

Areas of Contention

Although there is wide consensus on the use of open-ended questions and free narrative, there are other areas related to forensic interviewing for which there is substantial disagreement among professionals. Two of these areas involve the use of paper, markers, dolls, drawings, and other aids that allow children to express themselves nonverbally (Vieth, 2008) and the use of the extended forensic interview (Faller, 2007). Due to the fact that there is little consensus, some contend that additional research is needed in these areas (Newlin et al., 2015).

The Importance of Training and Ongoing Supervision

Unfortunately, research has shown that even when interviewers are properly trained, they typically fail to use the methods learned in training and they revert to using questioning that is not supported by the research or best practices (Lamb et al., 2007). This underscores the importance of ongoing supervision in order to retain newly learned skills and the supports necessary for this to occur. Tragically, this rarely occurs and it is clear that this should be the necessary focus of all posttraining supervision.

Forensic Practice Skill Set

As discussed previously, there is an established and growing body of research evidence to support the following forensic skills:

- Open-ended questioning to elicit narrative responses
- Hypothesis testing to rule out alternative explanations
- Assessment of developmental and cultural factors that affect the child.

Case Example and Application

Emma is a 4-year-old girl. According to her mother, Michelle, Emma has been displaying unusual behavior over the past month. Usually an affectionate and friendly child, she now refuses to hug her uncle and her grandfather and her teenage cousin, Ryan. She has been visiting her father every weekend since the couple separated six months ago, and she has not displayed any fear of him or been reluctant to visit him. The separation has been amicable and both Michelle and her husband have agreed to an uncontested divorce. However, Michelle is concerned because Emma has been masturbating while watching TV and her day-care teacher reports that Emma has taken off her underwear on the playground to show the other children her genitals.

This behavior is so unusual for Emma, her mother takes her to the family pediatrician and expresses her concerns to him. He examines Emma and finds nothing more than a skin rash that he says may be due to soap or bubble baths. He says that although he's not an "expert," he sees no signs of abuse. He assures her that masturbation is normal for a child of Emma's age, but Michelle is not so sure and is concerned enough to report this to CPS.

When interviewed by the CPS worker, Emma is initially unwilling to talk. After repeated questioning about what she does when she visits her father, Emma reluctantly says that he hurt her, but does not give any additional details. The case is then referred to the CAC for a forensic interview.

Case-Related Issues for the Forensic Interviewer to Consider

In preparation for the forensic interview, the worker should consider the following issues:

- Given Emma's age, how should I phrase initial questions in order to determine her linguistic ability and level of cognitive and moral development?
- If Emma continues to be reluctant to talk, what nontopic questions can I ask in the initial stage that will elicit narrative responses and "teach" her to provide a narrative?
- What is the general context and cultural context of Emma's home life that might be affecting her behavior or reluctance to talk?
- What alternate hypotheses might be examined to determine what, if anything, occurred?
- Do the behaviors that Emma is exhibiting fall within the range of normal sexual behaviors for a 4-year-old child?

Conclusion

Forensic interviewing requires a specific knowledge and skill set that includes rapport building, open-ended questioning to elicit narrative responses, the proper use of closed-ended questioning to gain specific details, and hypothesis testing to rule out alternative explanations. It is critical that the interviewer be free from confirmation bias and have knowledge of children's cognitive, moral, and normal sexual development, as well as considerations related to culture and disability. Finally, forensic interviewers should be aware of evidence-based best practices and receive ongoing supervision in order to retain these skills.

CHAPTER EXERCISES

Exercise 1. Using the chapter vignette, role-play how a social worker may conduct a forensic interview with this client.

Exercise 2. Using a client from the caseload, role-play how a social worker may conduct a forensic interview with this client. This exercise can be done in dyads or small groups.

Exercise 3. Prior to class, watch the following YouTube video on forensic interviewing: www .youtube.com/watch?v=RQrHHRqrPG8

Discuss in small or large groups the skills required for the use of one or more of these interviewing techniques.

Exercise 4. In small groups, choose one of the best practices in forensic interviewing discussed in this publication: https://www.ojjdp.gov/pubs/248749.pdf. Discuss in small groups and present your findings to the group.

Additional Resources

The American Professional Society on the Abuse of Children: www.apsac.org/practice-guidelines

Michigan Forensic Interviewing Protocol: www.michigan.gov/documents/dhs/DHS-PUB-0779_ 211637_7.pdf

National Children's Advocacy Center: www.nationalcac.org

References

Anderson, J. N. (2013). The CornerHouse forensic interview protocol: An evolution in practice for almost 25 years. *APSAC Advisor, 4,* 2–7. Retrieved from https://www.cornerhousemn.org/images/ Anderson_2013_CornerHouse_Forensic_Interview_Protocol.pdf

Baur, P. J. (2006). *Remembering the times of our lives: Memory in infancy and beyond.* London, UK: Routledge.

Brackmann, N. (2013). Interviewing children with the National Institute of Child Health and Human Development Investigative Interviewing (NICHD) Protocol. In E. Hjelmsäter & S. Landström (Eds.), *Interviewing child witnesses: Proceedings of the Erasmus Mundus Joint PhD in legal psychology theoretical course interviewing child witnesses.* Retrieved from http://clip.org.gu.se/ digitalAssets/1471/1471694_interviewing-child-witnesses-fall-2013.pdf

Ceci, S. J., & Bruck, M. (1995). *Jeopardy in the courtroom: A scientific analysis of children's testimony.* Washington, DC: American Psychological Association.

Ceci, S. J., Crossman, A. L., Scullin, M., Gilstrap, L., & Huffman, M. (2011). Children's suggestibility research: Implications for the courtroom and the forensic interview. In H. L. Westcott, G. M. Davies, & R. Bull (Eds.), *Children's testimony: A handbook of psychological research and forensic practice* (2nd ed.). Chichester, UK: Wiley-Blackwell.

Cyr, M., Lamb, M. E., Pelletier, J., Leduc, P., & Perron, A. (2006). *Assessing the effectiveness of the NICHD Investigative Interview Protocol in Francophone Quebec.* Paper presented at the Second International Investigative Interviewing Conference; Portsmouth, UK.

Faller, K. C. (2007). *Interviewing children about sexual abuse: Controversies and best practices.* New York, NY: Oxford University Press.

Faller, K. C. (2015). Forty years of forensic interviewing of children suspected of sexual abuse, 1974– 2014: Historical benchmarks. *Social Sciences, 4*(1), 34–65. doi:10.3390/socsci4010034

Finkelhor, D. (1979). *Sexually victimized children.* New York, NY: The Free Press.

Friedrich, W. N., Grambsch, P., Damon, L., Hewitt, S., Koverola, C., . . . Broughton, D. (1992). Child sexual behavior inventory: Normative and clinical comparisons. *Psychological Assessment, 4*(3), 303–311.

Friedrich, W. N., & Trane, S. (2002). Sexual behaviors across multiple settings. *Child Abuse and Neglect, 26*(3), 243–246.

Governor's Task Force on Children's Justice Subcommittee. (1998). *A model child abuse protocol.* State of Michigan, Department of Human Services DHS-Publication number 794. Retrieved from https://www.michigan.gov/documents/dhs/DHS-PUB-0779_211637_7.pdf

Hershkowitz, I., Lamb, M., & Horowitz, D. (2007). Victimization of children with disabilities. *American Journal of Orthopsychiatry, 77*(4), 629–635.

Hershkowitz, I., Lamb, M. E., Katz, C., & Malloy, L. C. (2015). Does enhanced rapport-building alter the dynamics of investigative interviews with suspected victims of intra-familial abuse? *Journal of Police and Criminal Psychology, 30*(1), 6–14.

Howe, M. L., Cicchetti, D., & Toth, S. L. (2006). Children's basic memory processes, stress, and maltreatment. *Developmental Psychopathology, 18*(3), 759–769.

Kohlberg, L. (1984). *The psychology of moral development: The nature and validity of moral stages* (Essays on moral development, Vol. 2). New York, NY: Harper & Row.

Krason, S. M. (Ed.). (2013). The Mondale Act and its aftermath: An overview of forty years of American law, public policy, and governmental response to child abuse and neglect. In *Child abuse, family rights, and the child protective system: A critical analysis from law, ethics, and Catholic social teaching* (pp. 1–81). Lanham, MD: Scarecrow Press.

Lamb, M. E. (2015). Toward developmentally aware practices in the legal system: Progress, challenge, and promise. *American Psychologist, 70*(8), 686–693. doi:10.1037/a0039634

Lamb, M. E., & Fauchier, A. (2001). The effects of question type on self-contradictions by children in the course of forensic interviews. *Applied Cognitive Psychology, 15*(5), 483–491.

Lamb, M. E., & Garretson, M. E. (2003). The effects of interviewer gender and child gender on the informativeness of alleged child sexual abuse victims in forensic interviews. *Law and Human Behavior, 27*(2), 157–171.

Lamb, M. E., Orbach, Y., Hershkowitz, I., Esplin, P. W., & Horowitz, D. (2007). A structured forensic interview protocol improves the quality and informativeness of investigative interviews with children: A review of research using the NICHD Investigative Interview Protocol. *Child Abuse & Neglect, 31*(11–12), 1201–1231.

Lamb, M. E., Orbach, Y., Warren, A. R., Esplin, P. W., & Hershkowitz, I. (2006). Getting the most out of children: Factors affecting the informativeness of young witnesses. In M. P. Toglia, J. D. Read, D. F. Ross, & R. C. L. Lindsay (Eds.), *Handbook of eyewitness psychology* (Vol. 1: Memory for events, pp. 423–446). Mahwah, NJ: Erlbaum.

La Rooy, D., Brubacher, S. P., Aromäki-Stratos, A., Cyr, M., Hershkowitz, I., Korkman, J., . . . Lamb, M. E. (2015). The NICHD Protocol: A review of an internationally-used evidence-based tool for training child forensic interviewers. *Journal of Criminological Research, Policy and Practice, 1*(2), 76–89.

London, K., Bruck, M., Ceci, S. J., & Shuman, D. W. (2005). Disclosure of child sexual abuse: What does the research tell us about the ways that children tell? *Psychology, Public Policy, and the Law, 11*(1), 194–226.

Newlin, C., Steele, L. C., Chamberlin, A., Anderson, J., Kenniston, J., Russell, A. . . . Vaughan-Eden, V. (2015). Child forensic interviewing: Best practices. *Juvenile Justice Bulletin.* Washington, DC: Office of Juvenile Justice and Delinquency Prevention.

Orbach, Y., Hershkowitz, I., Lamb, M. E., Sternberg, K. J., Esplin, P. W., & Horowitz, D. (2000). Assessing the value of structured protocols for forensic interviews of alleged abuse victims. *Child Abuse & Neglect, 24,* 733–752.

Piaget, J., & Inhelder, B. (1969). *The psychology of the child.* New York, NY: Basic Books.

Poole, D. A., & Lamb, M. E. (1998). *Investigative interviews of children: A guide for helping professionals.* Washington, DC: American Psychological Association.

Poole, D. A., & Lindsay, D. S. (2002). Children's suggestibility in the forensic context. In M. L. Eisen, J. A. Quas, & G. S. Goodman (Eds.), *Memory and suggestibility in the forensic interview: Personality and clinical psychology series* (pp. 355–381). Mahwah, NJ: Erlbaum.

Powell, M. B., Thompson, D. M., & Ceci, S. J. (2003). Children's memory of recurring events: Is the first event always the best remembered? *Applied Cognitive Psychology, 17*(2), 127–146.

Robbins, S. P. (1998). The social and cultural context of satanic ritual abuse allegations. *Journal of Issues in Child Abuse Allegations, 10.* Retrieved from http://www.ipt-forensics.com/journal/volume10/j10_8.htm

Robbins, S. P., Chatterjee, P., & Canda, E. R. (2012). *Contemporary human behavior theory: A critical perspective for social work* (3rd ed.). Boston, MA: Allyn & Bacon.

Saywitz, K. J., Goodman, G. S., & Lyon, T. D. (2002). *Interviewing children in and out of court: Current research and practice implications.* In J. E. B. Myers, L. Berliner, J. Briere, C. T. Hendrix, C. Jenny, & T. A. Reid (Eds.), *The APSAC handbook on child maltreatment* (2nd ed.). Thousand Oaks, CA: Sage Publications.

State of Michigan Governor's Task Force on Child Abuse and Neglect and Department of Human Services. (n.d.). *Forensic interviewing protocol* (3rd ed.). Lansing, MI: Author. Retrieved from https://www.michigan.gov/documents/dhs/DHS-PUB-0779_211637_7.pdf

Sternberg, K. J., Lamb, M. E., Orbach, Y., Esplin, P. W., & Mitchell, S. (2001). Use of a structured investigative protocol enhances young children's responses to free-recall prompts in the course of forensic interviews. *Journal of Applied Psychology, 86*(5), 997–1005.

Vieth, V. (2008). Letter to the editor. The development of forensic interview training models: A reply to Lamb, Orbach, Hershkowitz, Esplin and Horowitz. *Child Abuse & Neglect, 32*(11), 1003–1006.

Wood, J. M., & Garven, S. (2000). How sexual abuse interviews go astray: Implications for prosecutors, police, and child protection services. *Child Maltreatment: Journal of the American Professional Society on the Abuse of Children, 5*(2), 109–118.

CHAPTER 23

Expert Witness Testimony in Forensic Practice and Justice Systems

Shreya Mandal

CHAPTER OBJECTIVES

The major objectives of this chapter are to:

- Describe how forensic social workers can develop their expert witness testimony skills.
- Explain how to advocate on behalf of vulnerable racial and ethnic populations generally underrepresented in the American legal system, to increase advocacy from a human rights perspective.
- Explore how to use expert testimony to highlight a range of social justice issues including those affecting individuals most at risk for human trafficking, death, and persecution.
- Introduce forensic social workers to integrating narrative methods with evidence-based trends that can best support any legal claim for hardship.

CHAPTER COMPETENCIES HIGHLIGHTED

- Competency 2: Engage Diversity and Difference in Practice
- Competency 3: Advance Human Rights and Social, Economic, and Environmental Justice
- Competency 4: Engage in Practice Informed Research and Research Informed Practice
- Competency 6: Engage With Individuals, Families, Organizations, and Communities
- Competency 7: Assess Individuals, Families, Organizations, and Communities

Social workers can shape their practice for expert witness testimony in any area of law that requires persuasive mitigation evidence and proof of hardship. Social work testimony often comprises two coexisting theories: (a) the legal theory of mitigation and (b) narrative theory. The legal theory of mitigation is a defining component for social work expert testimony. In practice, the origins and evolution of developing mitigation evidence was required under *Wiggins v. Smith* (2003) under U.S. constitutional law. In 2003, Wiggins stated that any individual facing capital punishment in the United States has the constitutional right to present mitigation evidence—life histories emphasizing social, economic, psychological, and medical hardships that may potentially persuade sentencing judges and capital juries from imposing the death penalty (*Wiggins v. Smith*, 2003). Social workers and mitigation experts involved in death penalty cases have historically shaped the model for foundational mitigation practices in other noncapital criminal cases and various areas of civil law. In general, the development of mitigation reduces the damage or ameliorates a particular outcome by a clear showing of hardship. The basis of mitigation is often an interplay of psychological theories, medical theories, and systems theory. Narrative theory is an overarching framework that is frequently used to identify various mitigation themes in a case (Bullis, 2013).

Evidence of Effectiveness With Forensic Populations and Settings

Mitigation is a relatively new field. The empirical evidence emphasizing the effectiveness of capital mitigation in death penalty jurisprudence still remains in controversy (Hughes, 2012). The debate in this arena, however, focuses on the arbitrary nature of capital punishment in the United States. The effectiveness of capital mitigation is in danger. Moral, ethical, and political challenges presented in the death penalty system have often overshadowed the scope of mitigation, calling for much needed mitigation reform within capital defense jurisprudence. Despite its historical limitations, the broader application of mitigation in noncapital criminal cases and other areas of law have shown effective and successful outcomes.

Civil practice areas such as immigration law, personal injury law, family law, and employment discrimination law have effectively used mitigation evidence for successful legal outcomes. A foundational mitigation model that can be used in civil practices should be acknowledged as a direct outgrowth of capital mitigation practice. The standard guidelines for mitigation have been set forth by the American Bar Association and further developed by a number of mitigation experts throughout the United States (Maurice A. Deane School of Law at Hofstra University, 2008).

Since 2003, the legal demonstration of hardship in civil law practice areas has evolved. For example, the U.S. Department of Justice recognizes the need for psychological assessments and hardship evaluations among those who seek asylum or cancellation of removal (Justice, 2016). In the immigration context, hardship evaluations are analogous to the concept of mitigation—emphasizing one's life history, mental health, socioeconomic background, country conditions, medical histories, hardship of dependent spouses and children, and future prospects. In this respect, the components of mitigation and a hardship evaluation are universal (Silver, 2015).

The successful outcomes of mitigation, showing proof of hardship, and the use of social work expert testimony have been empirically measured by projects focused on discrete populations. For example, the use of effective hardship evaluations and expert testimony within immigration courts have often prevented noncitizen individuals from being deported (Silver, 2015). These psycholegal evaluations have played a large role in determining the fate of those facing complex immigration issues and potential danger in their countries of origin.

How to Apply This Skill

Expert witness testimony as a professional social worker often comprises core mitigation components: (a) client interviews; (b) collateral interviewing; (c) obtaining institutional records, including school records, mental health records, and medical records; (d) identifying core themes of hardship that have directly impacted the individual or the family; (e) identifying intergenerational patterns of illness and/or systemic traumas that impact the family; (f) identifying environmental and country conditions; (g) writing a report; and (h) preparing for direct testimony and cross-examination. These elements are often integrated into a written report, aiming to inform the courts (Silver, 2015). Expert witness testimony is often a culmination of these practices and is ultimately translated into formal oral advocacy. Since mental health is a commonly identified mitigating factor in cases, it is important to have a solid foundation in clinical practice. Although it is not always required for every social work expert witness, a clinical background often raises the credibility of the expert who offers oral testimony in a case.

Client Interviewing

Depending on the timeline of a case, client interviewing is an essential starting point to developing a mitigating assessment. The techniques that can be utilized in mitigation interviewing are multifaceted and largely depend on the client's individual needs. For purposes of mitigation, a narrative approach is a good beginning, as it allows clients to frame their stories from their own perspectives (Bullis, 2013). A series of narrative interviews helps experts identify collateral family information, institutional histories, and obvious hardships that impact clients. They are the basis of identifying trauma histories and past or present mental illnesses.

Trust is an important feature between the expert and the client and this is ideally developed over a period of time. Oftentimes, resources may be limited for developing quality mitigation. In these instances, experts are compelled to identify the top priorities and work as best as they can under more limiting parameters.

As trust is developed, the client is likely to reveal more sensitive information to the expert that may be vital to the case. However, every individual is different. Some clients are relatively good at self-reporting and others may have issues that impact their ability to communicate and report their own histories. As experts, forensic social workers should be prepared for the diverse range of clients who experience acute mental illnesses, are impacted by complex trauma, or have other debilitating illnesses. In cases where there are identified mental health issues, the use of mental health screening instruments can be useful and an objective way to measure mental health symptoms. Some commonly used screening tools are the Patient Health Questionnaire-9 (PHQ-9; Patient Health Questionnaire-9, n.d.); the Beck Inventory for Depression (Beck Institute, n.d.); the Hopkins Symptom Checklist-25 (Parloff, Kelman, & Frank, 1954), measuring for depression and anxiety symptoms; the PTSD Checklist (PTSD Checklist—Civilian Version, n.d.), assessing trauma symptoms; the Life Events Checklist (Life Events Checklist, n.d.), detailing various traumatic events experienced by the individual; and the Adverse Childhood Experiences (ACE) Questionnaire (Adverse Childhood Experiences Questionnaire, n.d.). There are similar corresponding screening tools that assess for substance and alcohol use. The use of screening tools can be a way to render a more objective assessment when integrating them with narrative interviewing.

Collateral Interviewing

Collateral interviews are essential to building up a case for mitigating hardship. Experts can rely on interviews with families, friends, coworkers, employers, teachers, counselors, religious leaders, and other relevant members of the community (Hinton, 2016). Family and community interviewing usually offers tremendous insight about a person, and can expand legitimate proof of hardship within one's life.

Interviews with families and community members can increase or reduce the credibility of clients. They can offer information that fills in the client's memory gaps and usually offer tremendous insight from a familial and larger systemic viewpoint. In addition, extensive collateral interviews may lead to identifying institutional participation and important records.

Retrieving Institutional Records

Collecting important institutional records for individuals and families is critical to building mitigation evidence. Documented narratives in records from schools, hospitals, mental health facilities, treatment clinics, prisons, and religious institutions usually provide detailed information that can add to mitigation themes in a case (First Judicial District of Pennsylvania and Philadelphia Bar Association, Criminal Justice Section, 2002). They are often used as objective references in written reports and can be essential to supporting expert witness testimony. One of the salient questions that is presented to an expert witness is: "How did you come to that conclusion?" After records are collected, they should be thoroughly assessed and analyzed. In this analysis, the expert determines whether the information is relevant to the case. The information rendered in institutional records is relevant to both direct testimony and cross-examination in court.

Identifying Core Themes of Hardship and Mitigation

As the expert gathers information from interviewing and collecting records, she will begin to formulate the mitigation story. The mitigation themes depend on the interplay of facts and insights over a period of time. It is common to identify various traumas that have impacted the individual or families—such as poverty, racism, incarceration, violence, torture, sexual abuse, and so on. Often, it is not enough to conclusively determine these themes, but rather to present the facts and details that effectively demonstrate that these themes are bases for hardship (Silver, 2015).

Identifying Intergenerational Family Patterns

Frequently clients in a criminal or immigration law context may come from challenging environments that have impacted them throughout generations within the family. For example, studies have found that there are intergenerational patterns of alcohol use among those who have severe drinking problems. Clearly showing intergenerational trauma, substance abuse, mental illness, violence, or sexual abuse can potentially provide tremendous insight about an individual or family's life (Castelloe, 2012). Judges and lawyers can make more informed decisions when properly educated about the impact of various intergenerational traumas that may exist.

Assessing Environmental and Country Conditions

A systems approach to mitigation gives us a more holistic overview of an individual or family's life. Was the person born and raised in a culture of violence? What is the political and socioeconomic climate of one's home country? Was the family living in impoverished conditions in their home? These questions are some examples of the type of inquiries an expert will ideally make in a case. Often the job of the expert witness is to educate and inform the court about the systemic conditions the clients face and the type of impact they had on the client. This type of information requires investigative research and deeper assessment of cultures that differ from our own.

Writing the Report

Writing a report is one of the major parts of building expert witness testimony. This document ideally looks like written advocacy that conclusively mirrors what the expert says on the witness stand. There are many styles of writing a report, depending on the area of law and style of communication the legal team wants to present in court. In criminal law, written reports are often called prepleading memoranda or presentencing reports. In immigration law, a report is called a hardship evaluation, submitted in the form of a notarized affidavit. Each court may require different formatting, but the essential components of the reports are often the same.

Preparing for Expert Testimony and Cross-Examination

As the expert approaches testimony, he or she will be asked to read case notes and the file to preserve memory. Attorneys who have retained the expert may run mock trials to simulate what ideal expert testimony will look like in court. Experts generally should prepare for direct examination and be able to answer more open-ended questions that allow them to establish their testimony in full detail. Preparation for cross-examination usually requires knowing what types of questions to anticipate from the opposing counsel. Most questions asked during cross-examination require closed-ended answers such as yes or no. Experts are allowed to further elaborate on an issue only when the judge or opposing counsel explicitly asks for more details. If an expert feels he or she did not make an adequate presentation of an issue during cross-examination, he or she usually has the opportunity to clarify the position during a redirect line of questioning.

Case Example and Application

In 2005, a human rights organization retained me as a trauma expert to testify on behalf of a 45-year-old woman, originally from Bangladesh. Mrs. M sought asylum under the Violence Against Women Act (VAWA) with a spousal abuse claim. Later that year, I was qualified as a trauma expert by the federal immigration court in Elizabeth, New Jersey. Meeting Mrs. M was one of the first times I ever had to assess for hardship and conduct my assessment entirely in another language, Bengali. This case served as a gateway to over 150 individuals who later contacted me to conduct hardship evaluations in support of their immigration claims. Many among this group were originally from Bangladesh, India, Mexico, Guatemala, and Honduras.

Clients who are from Bangladesh and India came to me with hopes of establishing a familiar cultural and linguistic rapport. Many of these families sought I-601 Hardship Waivers for cancellation of removal, asylum under VAWA, and other immigration claims. Many experienced torture in Bangladesh or the threat of persecution, imprisonment, murder, and enforced disappearances. Human Rights Watch World Report 2016 on Bangladesh stated, "Bangladesh headed in an authoritarian direction in 2015." Serious human rights abuses continue to occur, including arbitrary arrests, killings, and persecution for expression. In addition, the lesbian, gay, bisexual, and transgender (LGBT) community within Bangladesh that exhibits same-sex behavior is particularly vulnerable in this part of the world (Human Rights Watch, 2016).

The U.S. noncitizen families that came to me for help had the double task of proving hardship abroad and domestically. This pool of immigrant families exhibited acute mental health issues, separation anxiety, disruption of employment and school, interference with educational growth and development among children, and medical and economic hardships. It can be typical for families to face uncertainty about their immigration status for years, adversely impacting their lives and placing them in a long-term state of limbo. In this regard, families have struggled with permanent feelings of geographical displacement and, for many, unresolved traumas.

The challenge in working with immigrants was being able to effectively translate their traumatic experiences from one language to a clinical context in English. There can be additional linguistic barriers as there are six forms of known dialects that fall under Bengali as a dominant language. Many immigrant families do not speak a uniform language.

Hardship evaluations rendered for this immigrant group so far have demonstrated a high success rate in outcomes despite policy challenges and a complex political climate. Approximately 95% of the families were granted relief, due to the use of effective mitigation and presentation of hardship evaluations. The success of these cases was largely contingent on effective collaboration between this expert and immigration law firms who understand the importance of mitigation and hardship evaluations. In addition, positive outcomes depended upon the expert engaging with an ethnically diverse community and working to understand cultural and religious differences. In many instances, engaging and assessing immigrant families compelled the expert to explain the cultural differences between legal systems in the United States and abroad.

Expert testimony in many of these cases was offered in court or telephonically. Judges and attorneys asked me to establish the basis for extreme hardship for clients and their families. This process often involved assessing how hardship has impacted each adult or child within each family, and the family as a whole.

Conclusion

Forensic social workers can develop their expert witness testimony skills. Expert testimony is a human rights strategy that forensic social workers can use to advocate on behalf of vulnerable racial and ethnic populations generally underrepresented in the American legal system. Forensic social workers now can use expert testimony to highlight issues of poverty, trauma, mental health, chronic medical conditions, offense histories, women, immigrants and refugees, undocumented workers, aging individuals, the lesbian, gay, bisexual, transgender, and queer (LGBTQ) community, incarcerated individuals, torture survivors, and those most at risk for human trafficking, death, and persecution. Forensic social workers can integrate narrative methods with evidence-based trends. An integrative mitigation method can best support any legal claim for hardship.

CHAPTER EXERCISES

Exercise 1. Michael is a 44-year-old man charged with first degree robbery. He has already been incarcerated five previous times. Two of his previous convictions were for assault, where Michael maintains that he was defending himself after he was provoked. Michael was evaluated by psychologists three times while he was imprisoned. Psychologists diagnosed Michael with bipolar disorder twice, and once with schizoaffective disorder. Despite having a lengthy psychiatric history, there is no mention of Michael's childhood from birth to age 7.

1. Based on what we do know about Michael, what questions would be relevant to ask regarding his childhood?
2. What records would we want to secure to understand Michael's life better?

Exercise 2. Alina is a 19-year-old woman from India. She entered the United States two years ago, after marrying Raja, a U.S. citizen. Shortly after coming to New York, Raja's behavior toward Alina became violent and abusive. Alina ran away from her husband and was able to reach safety with a domestic violence shelter. Several months later, Raja filed for a divorce. Alina is now applying for asylum under the VAWA.

1. What kind of assessment would you conduct with Alina?
2. What questions would be relevant to ask Alina for a compelling VAWA claim?

Exercise 3. You have been retained as an expert witness as a forensic social worker on a criminal defense case and are being asked to testify on the client's likelihood to reoffend. You have had a chance to spend five sessions with the client, and have met some of the client's friends and coworkers. However, the client's family members refuse to speak with you and provide you with key mitigation information for the case. You have access to the client's lengthy school records, teacher's notes, and most recent progress notes from counseling.

1. What sources do you rely upon the most in this case?
2. Please devise a plan for a holistic mitigation assessment in this case.
3. What questions do you think are relevant to answer on direct examination?
4. What questions would be important to anticipate for cross-examination?

Additional Resources

How to Prepare a Power Hardship Evaluation to Prove Extreme Hardship for the I-601 and I-601A Waiver: www.smartimmigrationlawyer.com/i-601-i-601a-psych-evaluation

Human Rights Watch Work Report 2016: Bangladesh: www.hrw.org/world-report/2016

Social Context of Capital Murder: Social Histories and the Logic of Mitigation: http://digitalcommons
.law.scu.edu/cgi/viewcontent.cgi?article=1572&context=lawreview

Social Workers as Expert Witnesses: www.socialworkers.org/ldf/lawnotes/expert.asp

References

Adverse Childhood Experiences Questionnaire. (n.d.). Retrieved from http://www.ncjfcj.org/sites/
default/files/Finding%20Your%20ACE%20Score.pdf

Beck Institute. (n.d.). Beck inventory. Retrieved from https://www.beckinstitute.org/get-informed/
tools-and-resources/professionals/patient-assessment-tools

Bullis, R. (2013). *The narrative edge in expert testimony: A guide for social workers.* Alexandria, VA: Council
on Social Work Education.

Castelloe, P. (2012). *How trauma is carried across generations. Psychology Today.* Retrieved from https://www
.psychologytoday.com/blog/the-me-in-we/201205/how-trauma-is-carried-across-generations

First Judicial District of Pennsylvania and Philadelphia Bar Association, Criminal Justice Section.
(2002). Mitigation protocol manual. Retrieved from https://www.courts.phila.gov/pdf/manuals/
mitigation_protocol_manual.pdf

Hinton, J. (2016). Developing mitigation evidence. Retrieved from https://moe.fd.org/Dev_Mitigation
.php

Hughes, E. (2012). Arbitrary death: An empirical study of mitigation. *Washington University Law Review,
89*, 581–637.

Human Rights Watch. (2016). World report 2016: Bangladesh. Retrieved from https://www.hrw.org/
world-report/2016/country-chapters/bangladesh

Justice, U. D. (2016). Immigration judge benchbook. Retrieved from https://www.justice.gov/eoir/
immigration-judge-benchbook-mental-health-issues

Life Events Checklist. (n.d.). Retrieved from http://www.integration.samhsa.gov/clinical-practice/
life-event-checklist-lec.pdf

Maurice A. Deane School of Law at Hofstra University (Ed). (2008). Supplementary guidelines for the
mitigation function of defense teams in death penalty cases. *Hofstra Law Review, 36*(3). Retrieved
from http://www.hofstralawreview.org/tag/volume-36-issue-3

Parloff, M., Kelman, H., & Frank, J. (1954). *Hopkins symptom checklist-25.* Baltimore, MD: Johns Hopkins
University.

Patient Health Questionnaire-9. (n.d.). Retrieved from http://www.agencymeddirectors.wa.gov/files/
AssessmentTools/14-PHQ-9%20overview.pdf

PTSD Checklist—Civilian Version. (n.d.). Retrieved from http://www.mirecc.va.gov/docs/visn6/3_
PTSD_CheckList_and_Scoring.pdf

Silver, M. (2015). *Handbook of mitigation in criminal and immigration forensics: Humanizing the client towards
a better legal outcome.* Self-published.

Wiggins v. Smith, 539 U.S. 510 (The Supreme Court 2003).

VOICES FROM THE FIELD

Shreya Mandal, JD, LCSW

Executive Director and Qualified Mitigation Expert
One World Mitigation and Forensic Services

Agency Setting

One World Mitigation and Forensic Services (OWMFS) is a forensic consulting firm that was informally established in 2005 through a series of freelance opportunities provided by private criminal defense attorneys, immigration lawyers, human rights organizations, public defender offices, and court systems throughout the northeast and southern regions of the United States. In July 2016, it went into full-time operation and was formally named. The mission of OWMFS is to provide quality forensic social work and mitigation services in both criminal and civil areas of law. Services include providing prepleading, presentencing memoranda, and mitigation reports for populations facing the full range of state or federal criminal and capital charges. Written advocacy may address preconviction to postconviction phases of criminal law.

In the immigration sector, OWMFS provides hardship evaluations, potentially preventing removal or deportation of immigrant clients. It also renders specialized trauma and torture assessments of individuals who have faced severe human rights abuses under harsh country conditions. Oral advocacy is also provided through informal court conferences or through more formal qualified expert testimony. The heart of OWMFS embodies transferable skills that are applied to any area of law requiring the proof of hardship.

In-court expert witness testimony may or may not be required, depending on the specific issues presented in a legal case. As a mitigation expert, preparation for potential testimony often comprises extensive client interviewing, clinical evaluation, administering specialized risk assessments, collateral interviewing of family and important community members, collaboration with psychiatric experts, retrieval and review of various institutional records, research, writing reports that detail the client's life history, and potentially coordinating with treatment providers that assist people with different types of rehabilitation.

Expertise Required

A qualified expert witness in the legal system is typically a licensed clinical social worker, and may have other advanced doctoral degrees and certifications that speak to a particular area of specialty. Judges are gatekeepers in determining who is a credible and reliable witness based on lifelong experience; technical training; and whether the expert is a practitioner, specialist, researcher, published in an academic area with his or her own peers, and whether he or she advances her field. Experts are also more likely to take the witness stand if they have testified previously and have established a track record on a case-by-case basis.

Ethical, Legal, Practice, Diversity, and Advocacy Issues Addressed

Two big challenges that are critical for me to address within forensic practice are using trauma-informed methods and cross-cultural competency. Both of these issues are enormous undertakings. While I have worked with a large number of specialized populations over the years, advocating on behalf of a broad group of incarcerated individuals ethically presents the need to assess the effects of torture, undiagnosed complex trauma, and harsh prison conditions that frequently impact clients. Immigrants also present unique issues that must be placed in cultural and linguistic context while balancing the demands of the American legal system in both criminal law and immigration law. As a mitigation expert interfacing with clients, lawyers, social workers, other treatment providers, and judges, my job is to educate the legal community about the significance of trauma-informed practices and cross-cultural competency on a wider level. I also integrate this education into written and oral advocacy as an expert witness on a case-by-case basis.

Interprofessional and Intersectoral Collaboration

The slow and gradual growth of OWMFS has been a collaborative effort of legal providers, human rights organizations, and professionals who recognize the dire need for quality mitigation services in defense-based legal advocacy. The model for OWMFS was born out of traditional capital mitigation teams that mitigate against the death penalty. Each team usually has defense attorneys, mitigation specialists, investigators, paralegals, and other experts involved on each case. As a mitigation expert, I consult for local and out-of-state public defender offices, private defense attorneys, and other public interest organizations that represent clients facing legal crisis.

Currently my client providers are Brooklyn Defender Services, the Legal Aid Society, and private practitioners throughout New York and New Jersey. I have also worked with public defender offices in New Jersey, Pennsylvania, North Carolina, and South Carolina. In 2007, I was appointed as a mitigation expert by the court system in Jacksonville, Florida, for state death penalty cases. These various examples highlight different sources of clients if they are unable to retain an expert themselves—public defender offices, private attorneys, state and federal court systems, and universities. In 2009, I was retained by Lincoln Square Legal Services, a student-run trial advocacy clinic at Fordham University School of Law.

CHAPTER 24

Restorative Justice and Community Well-Being: Visualizing Theories, Practices, and Research—Part 1

Johannes Wheeldon

CHAPTER OBJECTIVES

The major objectives of this chapter are to:

- Introduce the theoretical basis for restorative justice (RJ).
- Assess the empirical evidence for RJ programs.
- Explore the challenges and opportunities associated with applying core competencies.

CHAPTER COMPETENCIES HIGHLIGHTED

- Competency 2: Engage Diversity and Difference in Practice
- Competency 6: Engage With Individuals, Families, Organizations, and Communities

The value of RJ for forensic social work is explicated in Roberts and Brownell's (1999) focus on the knowledge and skills social workers need to serve victims and offenders, based on a definition of forensic social work as associated with the "policies, practices, and social work roles with juvenile and adult offenders and victims of crime" (1999, p. 360). However, the expansion of RJ as a concept in recent years is most relevant for those who define forensic social work more broadly (Barker & Branson, 2000). Maschi and Killian (2011), for example, have argued for a broader and more integrative definition that includes the commitment to both social justice and human rights, while stressing the collaborative nature of forensic social work. Competencies of specific interest in this chapter include: engaging diversity and difference in practice, and engaging with individuals, families, groups, organizations, and communities.

RJ is based on the premise that the formal justice system inadvertently causes harm as it attempts to respond to criminal acts. Based on the predominant (but widely discredited) view that punishment changes behavior, too often the question of why people do things (or do not) is ignored. For those caught up in the justice system, participation is often limited to hiring a lawyer to navigate a variety of complex procedural set pieces that invoke simplistic notions of law and order (Elliott, 2011).

At its most worrisome, this approach divorces individuals impacted by crime from meaningfully engaging with their fellow citizens on fundamental questions of justice. It robs communities of the opportunity to understand, empathize, and resolve actions that

Figure 24.1 Common Themes in Restorative Justice

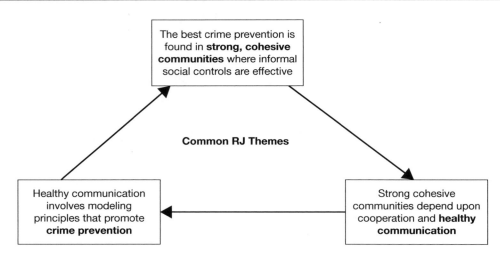

RJ, restorative justice.
Source: Wheeldon (2012, p. 220). Figure © Johannes Wheeldon.

impact everyone. Figure 24.1 outlines key themes and their interrelationship. In this way, RJ can serve as a means to expand community well-being because it offers a means to model principles associated with crime prevention, give voice to individuals who historically have been excluded from decision making, and explicitly support communities to get involved in crime prevention.

RJ is relevant for social workers because it requires engagement with diversity and difference in practice. Diversity includes—but is more than—factors such as age, class, color, culture, disability, ethnicity, gender, gender identity and expression, immigration status, political ideology, race, religion, sex, and sexual orientation. Engaging diversity also means understanding how traditional structures associated with the justice system create or enhance privilege for some while oppressing, marginalizing, or otherwise alienating others, and why various applications of RJ have emerged.

Core Skills Required for Restorative Justice

The skills essential to the success of RJ include supporting processes that value the experiences of people associated with a crime or harm including: victims, responsible parties, and communities. In addition, professional practice involves the dynamic and interactive processes of facilitating dialogue, responsive communication, active engagement, iterative assessment, and respectful intervention with individuals, families, groups, organizations, and communities. While many RJ programs are framed as evidence-based and evidence-informed, RJ approaches also suggest the importance of practical and context-specific knowledge and skills relevant when individuals, families, groups, organizations, and communities find themselves in conflict and require support. These skills will be revisited in the skills section of this chapter.

Theoretical Bases for Restorative Justice

Three books led practitioners to build on existent programs and design, develop, and participate in new forms of RJ processes. *Crime, Shame and Reintegration* (Braithwaite, 1989) offered a specific theory while *Changing Lenses* (Zehr, 1990) and *Criminology as Peacemaking* (Pepinsky & Quinney, 1991) combined a certain distrust of the state with community-centric models often informed by religious or spiritual values. Braithwaite has since suggested that the RJ paradigm has become the central feature of a number of new kinds of justice reform. Thus, RJ has consolidated a variety of other reform-oriented justice movements, integrating them within a common set of values. RJ, Braithwaite (2002) argues, includes numerous reform traditions including justice as redress, relational justice, and transformative justice.

Braithwaite's Reintegrative Shaming Theory (1989) is the leading theory for RJ. The theory distinguishes between two types of shaming: reintegrative shaming and disintegrative shaming (or stigmatization). Disintegrative shaming relates to labeling theory in which people, usually youth, begin to permanently adopt the behaviors for which they were initially ostracized (Heidt & Wheeldon, 2015). Disintegrative shaming takes place when society disgraces people to such a degree that they create a "society of outcasts" (Braithwaite, 1989, p. 55).

Braithwaite (1989) argued that the shame associated with the current justice system results in lower levels of informal social control because the offender loses his or her attachments to society. This makes it easier for those shamed in this way to justify taking part in the criminal subculture, which also happens to be a repository for knowledge and learning about deviant and criminal behaviors and skills.

In contrast to disintegrative shaming, which is disrespectful, unforgiving, and isolates the individual from groups, reintegrative shaming allows them to reenter society with no stigma or label. This occurs when disapproval for criminal behavior is partnered with respect for the individual, forgiveness, and acceptance back into the group. RJ practices and processes attempt to follow these principles in facilitating face-to-face meetings of affected parties but they also represent an opportunity to reform justice policy and inform legislation. The aim is to ensure any form of behavioral or social control is implemented in respectful ways that provide opportunities for repair and healing that have resulted from wrongful behavior and at the same time open spaces for the possibility of forgiving while attempting to maintain the person's prosocial bonds with primary groups, including family and community.

Empirical Evidence of Effectiveness With Forensic Populations and Settings

While the institutionalization of RJ has been a trend in many jurisdictions, it is important to note that there remains a tradition among RJ practitioners to resist efforts to define, measure, and professionalize its delivery. This is in part a result of the fact that for many in the RJ community, practice usurps theory as the leading mechanism of social transformation (McCold & Wachtel, 2002; Wood & Suzuki, 2016). Indeed, restorative programs and principles can be traced back to the work of either innovative practitioners, such as those involved with the Kitchener experiment, or approaches based on the perceived needs and practices of indigenous peoples in Canada, New Zealand, and the United States (Wheeldon, 2009).

Today, RJ is often framed as "evidence based" or "evidence informed" (Sherman & Strang, 2007; Umbreit, Coates, & Vos, 2007). While Hay (2001) found some support for Reintegrative Shaming Theory, including a durable negative effect of shaming on predatory delinquency, most research has focused on assessing practical programs that attempt to implement the theory. Sherman and Strang (2007), in their exhaustive review based on 36 direct comparisons to conventional criminal justice, found that when RJ programs involve face-to-face meetings among all parties connected to a crime—including victims, offenders, and their families and friends—they result in substantial and statistically significant outcomes. These findings included a reduction in repeat offending, reduced symptoms of posttraumatic stress, and reduced desire for revenge. In addition studies point to reduced costs for the justice system while participants report increased levels of satisfaction with the justice system (Sherman & Strang, 2007, p. 4).

One specific example is research on restorative justice conferences (RJCs). Designed to bring victims, offenders, and communities together, RJCs are face-to-face meetings among those involved in a crime to discuss and hopefully resolve the offense and its consequences. Conducted in the presence of a trained facilitator, RJCs often involve the families of the principal participants, friends, and others affected by the crime. For policy makers, there are two main concerns: (a) Do RJCs reduce future offending? (b) Do RJCs improve victim satisfaction? Published by the highly regarded Campbell Collaboration, a meta-analysis including a review of 10 eligible studies on three continents, including 1,879 responsible parties and 734 victims, furthered the suggestion RJ dramatically improves victim satisfaction and reduces future offending (Strang, Sherman, Mayo-Wilson, Woods, & Ariel, 2013).

How to Apply This Skill: Principles, Practices, and Paradoxes

The implications of RJ for social workers are numerous. Essential is the recognition of how three core principles continue to inform restorative programs. The first is that a broader definition of harm is required to understand crime and criminal acts. Harms can refer to those suffered by the victim of a particular incident; by an offender before, during, or after an incident; and even those suffered within communities. This expanded notion of harm provides an important shift in thinking about how best to respond to crime (Pepinsky & Quinney, 1991).

The second is a desire to root processes in the communities where the harm occurred. Elliott (2002) has argued this is important in at least two ways. First, the actual inclusion of the community in any process to address harm acknowledges the important role the community plays in crime prevention. Second, by specifically including the community in the process, there is the acceptance that even those not harmed in a particular case still have an interest in its successful resolution (Elliott, 2002, pp. 462–463).

The third principle is related to the moral potential for RJ to assist individuals to better understand themselves and take responsibility for their actions. This view of morality is rooted in attending to the real needs of actual individuals through processes, which are consistent with community values. This means that participating in problem solving itself can be a transformative experience for victims, responsible parties, and the communities in which they reside (Pepinsky, 1999).

Programs that rely upon restorative principles have been used at a variety of points in the criminal justice process. These uses include conflict resolution in schools and, among neighbors, precharge interventions aimed at diversion from court, presentencing victim impact, and family or community meetings. In addition, restorative programs can be used as a postconviction add-on to the sentencing process, as a supplement to a community sentence (probation), as an option within a custodial setting, as a preparation for release from a period of incarceration, or as part of reentry. Figure 24.2 outlines some examples of the use of RJ in criminal justice.

One practice that has involved social workers considerably is called a family group conference. Initially developed in New Zealand in large measure to balance out the decision-making power of the state in order to reduce disproportionate removal and placement of Maori and other Pacific Island young people, the family group conference is a meeting where a young person who has offended, as well as the person's family, victims, and other people like the police, a social worker, or youth advocate, make plans that:

- Help the young person own up to what he or she did wrong and learn from mistakes
- Find practical ways to put things right and make up for what he or she did
- Look at why he or she offended and find ways to help turn his or her life around

Family group conferencing was initially developed for use in both youth justice and child welfare. It has been adapted for situations that involve child abuse and domestic violence

Figure 24. 2 Restorative Justice Practices in Criminal Justice

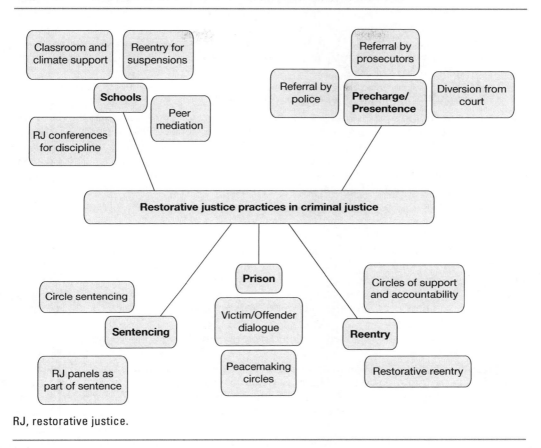

RJ, restorative justice.

(Burford & Pennell, 1998; Pennell & Burford, 2000), youth crime, school suspensions, juvenile delinquency, adult crime, reintegration of offenders, and neighborhood conflicts through a variety of hybrid approaches (Hudson, Morris, Maxwell, & Galaway, 1996; Merkel-Holguin, Winterfeld, Harper, Coburn, & Fluke, 1997; Nixon, 1998; O'Connell, 1998).

Another essential development of relevance for social workers is how RJ engages diversity and differences in individuals, families, groups, organizations, and communities. This involves confronting tensions within the movement itself. This tension is in part an outgrowth between a desire for more restorative programming on the one hand, and the fear of state co-optation on the other. It is an important consideration for forensic social workers as they understand their own role within human service systems. It also applies to definitional concerns (Wood & Suzuki, 2016).

While Braithwaite's detailed examination and integration of criminological theories and sociological concepts remains essential to understanding RJ, his explanation fails to include some of the other traditions organized through peacemaking criminology. For example, in the last chapter of *Criminology as Peacemaking*, Pepinsky suggests three traditions that form the basis of the book and of peacemaking criminology more generally: critical traditions, feminist traditions, and religious traditions (Pepinsky & Quinney, 1991).

Based on the critical traditions, there remains a distrust of the state as impartial arbiter and a desire to locate justice in individual communities (Gibbons, 1994) in which members of communities participate in the decision-making process (Einstadter & Henry, 1995).

One critique has focused a "paradoxical identity crisis," which ironically entrenches RJ's dependence on the system it purports to challenge by relying upon referrals and at least nominal cooperation. On this view, RJ programs may simply be another means to expand state control and promote victimhood without exposing the social factors that lead to crime (Wright, 2005). Pavlich (2005, p. 111) argues: "Restorative Justice as an alternative in this sense is unattainable because it constitutes its identity largely by deferring to the very institutions it seeks to replace reform or alter."

As state actors have increasingly taken on restorative practices, one concern has been a de-emphasis on the potential for communities to develop the capacity to solve their own problems (Elliott, 2011). Indeed, as Robbins, Vaughan-Eden, and Maschi (2014, p. 214) have noted, forensic social work requires interprofessional collaboration based on an appreciation of the roles and differences between lawyers, law enforcement, and social workers so that they can learn to navigate the legal arena and confront disparities within the criminal justice system. Without interdisciplinary collaboration led by informed and aware social workers, community-based reforms designed to replace the overuse of punitive criminal justice policies that have been the drivers of mass incarceration are unlikely to be successful.

Another paradox of relevance to the application of RJ in forensic social work can be connected to the underappreciated role of feminist traditions within the movement. Many from this tradition, including Kay Harris, have argued that restorative processes should allow those who have suffered harm to participate in the design of an appropriate response (Pepinsky, 1999). Yet, victim advocacy groups and others continue to suggest that RJ is offender focused and insufficiently concerned with victim experience (Acorn, 2004; Mika, Achilles, & Halbert 2004).

These concerns persist despite clear evidence that victims prefer RJ programs to the existing system (Sherman & Strang, 2007). Sometimes evidence is not enough. The potential for engaging with individuals, families, groups, organizations, and communities must contend not only with addressing definitional concerns and understanding how to use evidence to guide policy making. For some, conceptual differences and ideological resistance about how RJ programs can best be used will trump otherwise valuable applications (Heidt & Wheeldon, 2015).

Perhaps the promising consideration for forensic social workers keen to engage individuals and communities is to view RJ as part of a process to build social capital and empower communities to address harm themselves in prosocial ways. By creating a means by which people must confront real and difficult dilemmas, "social experiences can promote development . . . when they stimulate our mental processes" (Crain, 1985, p. 126). The idea is that when we are challenged, we develop through an increased competence in balancing conflicting value claims. By exposing individuals to morally formative experiences in which past behavior is called to account involving mutual conflict resolution, opportunities emerge for parties to understand and clarify community norms and values (Van Ness & Strong, 1997).

For social workers, this means rethinking obligations that communities and organizations have to individuals and families, whether they be victim, offenders, or others impacted by harm. It requires that interprofessional collaboration include community members in meaningful ways to ensure communities understand their responsibilities to support and help victims of crime to meet their needs and promote the welfare of its members by identifying for themselves the social conditions and relationships that promote both crime and community peace (Zehr, 1990).

RJ has been shown to play an essential social function when community members are actively involved and thus contribute to the strengthening of the community. While building and maintaining this concept of community has been difficult in the United States, few doubt the potential of models designed to involve communities and volunteers in the resolution of harm. When properly supported, restorative programs can further moral development among groups by emphasizing mutual problem solving, communication, negotiation, compromise, and responsibility among different people in a community (Minor & Morrison, 1996). In this way RJ offers a means to invigorate the sense of civic responsibility in people that many feel has been lost in an increasingly technocratic society.

Case Example and Application

For social workers interested in how the restorative process can engage communities, the development and sustainability of RJ in Vermont is a useful case study. In February 1995, the first case referred to a restorative process in Vermont was adjudicated in Newport, Vermont. District Judge Brian Burgess, who later became a justice of the Supreme Court, referred a young man convicted of possession of a malt beverage by a minor. Maggie Hawksworth was the intake probation officer and Jane Woodruff the state attorney. The young man was sent to the reparative board in Newport as a condition of a suspended sentence.

Building on the community-centered movement in Vermont in the 1980s and 1990s, research suggested Vermonters wanted more involvement with the justice system to allow communities to better respond to crime and conflict. They wanted repair, not vengeance; what was broken, fixed; what was stolen, returned; what was defaced, cleaned; what was destroyed, replaced. As a result of this research, in 1994, the Department of Corrections (DOC) received a Bureau of Justice Assistant grant to pilot Reparative Probation to allow volunteers to voice their concerns regarding harm to the community and facilitate a restorative agreement with those responsible. In 1998, based on the success of those programs, the DOC partnered with municipalities to develop the first community justice centers (CJCs).

While every case is different, in 1995 the young man sent to the reparative board in Newport was described as a "young rebel" in conflict with the law and disconnected from his single mother. Those who know the family describe that panel as a turning point for him. While sadly he passed away in 2015, he had more than 20 years with his mom, helping her and being part of her life. This was a trajectory he was not on before the reparative board. This case, like so many others, could not have occurred without volunteers who were supported, trained, and given the ability to work in their communities to prevent crime and harm and promote greater community understanding.

CJCs continue to advance RJ in Vermont. They are unique in that they provide the community-based infrastructure from which various programs and services can be delivered. In the past 20 years, they have developed new outreach protocols for victims of crime, piloted programming for fathers returning to the community from a period of incarceration, engaged in unique education programs, and created new forms of reentry support. One such program was developed in partnership with the DOC and adapted the Circles of Support and Accountability (COSA) model from Canada. This program allows individuals who would otherwise be incarcerated to be supported in their community by volunteers who meet every week to offer guidance, encouragement, and to hold these individuals accountable for the decisions they make as they transition to law abiding, contributing members of a community.

Based on just a few programs and volunteers in 1995, today there are 20 CJCs delivering services to youth at risk, victims, Vermont communities affected by crime, and those responsible for criminal offenses. In 2015, services included hundreds of hours of training and education on crime prevention, work in schools and among communities in conflict, and in-depth support to victims of crime. Together these efforts involved more than 700 community volunteers who together worked more than 22,000 hours.

Conclusion

In the past three decades RJ has captured the imagination of those interested in crime, society, and governance in ways that defy simplistic explanation (Wheeldon, 2009). Its appeal spans continents, peoples, traditions, religions, and even political ideologies. It can count on support from proponents of victim rights, prison abolitionists, and those who advocate for more local solutions to crime. It also has gained traction as a means to engage communities. As Elliott (2011) observed:

> . . . if we do not participate in the processes that affect our lives, we end up with a default society. The meaningful participation demanded by RJ affords us the opportunity to articulate our needs in contexts that are based on listening and affirmation and to act collectively to re-mediate the social conditions that generate these needs. (pp. 201–202)

Serious questions remain. These involve concerns about whether those interested in this work can ensure expanded notions of RJ and are committed to the foundational triad of supporting victims, responsible parties, and communities to participate in decision-making processes in meaningful ways. Likewise, RJ adherents must work to sustain support for trained practitioners to take on more serious crimes and not be limited to diversion or low-intervention justice practices for youth and less serious offenders. Finally, in terms of relevance, RJ must also contend with and be able to confront problems of divided justice whereby racial, ethnic, and indigenous identity shapes one's experience of social work interventions and sanctions within the criminal justice system (Wood & Suzuki, 2016, pp. 162–164).

Nevertheless, an enduring strength is the ability for restorative processes to fluidly connect disparate views by transforming competing interests into mutually agreed values. This requires engaging diversity and difference in a multitude of ways, and engaging with individuals, families, groups, organizations, and communities through processes that value their voices and views. Properly supported, restorative processes offer a means by which more detailed deliberation and decision making can occur. RJ offers a wide variety of mechanisms to address crime, harm, and criminality by respecting differences while providing opportunities for communities to grow together by creating a safe place for difficult conversations to occur.

As van Wormer (2003, pp. 445–446) notes, RJ is consistent with the mission of social workers to enhance human well-being, assist and empower those who are vulnerable, and respect the dignity of all people. While not all applications of RJ have proven sustainable, the Vermont model suggests the value for social workers involves not only successful programs but the importance of a community-based infrastructure where these programs can be delivered.

CHAPTER EXERCISES

Exercise 1. Discuss in small groups and then together as a large group: How are the three principles of RJ discussed in this chapter (expanded definition of harm, importance of community-based processes, and the transformative potential of RJ) relevant for social workers? What are some obstacles to integrating these principles into social work practice?

Exercise 2. Discuss in small groups and then together as a large group: What are some challenges for RJ as described in this chapter? Which seem particularly relevant to you? How could they be addressed?

Exercise 3. Find a short video on RJ on social media (Facebook, Twitter) or on YouTube. Consider the definition in this chapter of reintegrative shaming and write a short report. First, summarize reintegrative shaming in your own words. Next, describe the video you found, and finally connect the concepts in the video to your summary of reintegrative shaming.

Exercise 4. As a class, research and discuss what RJ programs exist in your state. How are clients referred? What types of RJ practices are being utilized? How do these programs support the work of social workers? What else would you like to know?

Additional Resources

Center for Restorative Justice and Peacemaking—University of Minnesota: www.rjp.umn.edu

Centre for Restorative Justice—Simon Fraser University, BC, Canada: www.sfu.ca/crj/index.html

Community Justice Network of Vermont: www.CJNVT.org

International Institute for Restorative Practices (IIRP)—Bethlehem, PA: www.iirp.edu

Restorative Justice Colorado: www.rjcolorado.org/restorative-justice/resources

Restorative Justice Online: www.restorativejustice.org

Safer Saner Schools: www.safersanerschools.org

References

Acorn, A. (2004). *Compulsory compassion: A critique of restorative justice*. Vancouver, BC, Canada: University of British Columbia Press.

Barker, R. L., & Branson, D. M. (2000). *Forensic social work: Legal aspects of professional practice*. Philadelphia, PA: Haworth Press.

Braithwaite, J. (1989). *Crime, shame and reintegration*. New York, NY: Cambridge University Press.

Braithwaite, J. (2002). *Restorative justice and responsive regulation*. New York, NY: Oxford University Press.

Burford, G., & Pennell, J. (1998). *Family group decision making: After the conference—progress in resolving violence and promoting well-being: Outcome report* (Vol. I & II). St. John's, Canada: Memorial University of Newfoundland, School of Social Work. Retrieved from http://faculty.chass.ncsu.edu/pennell/fgdm/OutcomeReport/index.html

Crain, W. C. (1985). *Theories of development* (2nd ed.). Upper Saddle River, NJ: Prentice Hall.

Einstadter, W., & Henry, S. (1995). *Criminological theory: An analysis of its underlying assumptions*. New York, NY: Harcourt Brace.

Elliott, E. (2002). Con game and restorative justice: Inventing the truth about Canada's prisons. *Canadian Journal of Criminology, 44*(4), 459–474.

Elliott, E. (2011). *Security, with care: Restorative justice and healthy societies*. Halifax, NS, Canada: Fernwood Publishing.

Gibbons, D. (1994). *Talking about crime and criminals: Problems and issues in theory development in criminology*. Newark, NJ: Prentice Hall.

Hay, C. (2001). An exploratory test of Braithwaite's reintegrative shaming theory. *Journal of Research in Crime and Delinquency, 38*(2), 132–153.

Heidt, J., & Wheeldon, J. (2015). *Introducing criminological thinking: Maps, theories, and understanding*. Thousand Oaks, CA: Sage Publications.

Hudson, J., Morris, A., Maxwell, G., & Galaway, B. (1996). *Family group conferences: Perspectives on policy and practice*. Monsey, NY: Willow Tree Press.

Maschi, T., & Killian, M. L. (2011). The evolution of forensic social work in the United States: Implications for 21st century practice. *Journal of Forensic Social Work, 1*, 8–36.

McCold, P., & Wachtel, T. (2002). Restorative justice theory validation. In E. Weitekamp & H.-J. Kerner (Eds.), *Restorative justice: Theoretical foundations* (pp. 110–142). Cullompton, UK: Willan Publishing.

Merkel-Holguin, L., Winterfeld, A. P., Harper, C. J., Coburn, N. A., & Fluke, J. D. (1997). *Innovations for children's services for the 21st century: Family group decision making and patch*. Englewood, CO: American Humane Association.

Mika, H., Achilles, M., & Halbert, E. (2004). Listening to victims: A critique of restorative justice policy and practice in the United States. *Federal Probation, 68*, 32–38.

Minor, K., & Morrison, J. T. (1996). A theoretical study and critique of restorative justice. In B. Galaway & J. Hudson (Eds.), *Restorative justice: International perspectives* (pp. 117–133). Monsey, NY: Criminal Justice Press.

Nixon, P. (1998). Exchanging practice: Some comparisons, contrasts, and lessons learned from the practice of family group conferences in Sweden and the United Kingdom. *Protecting Children, 14*, 13–18.

O'Connell, T. (1998). From Wagga Wagga to Minnesota. In the First North American Conference on Conferencing, *Conferencing: A new response to wrongdoing* (pp. 5–22). Pipersville, PA: Real Justice.

Pavlich, G. (2005). *Governing paradoxes of restorative justice.* London, UK: Glass House Press.

Pennell, J., & Burford, G. (2000). Family group decision making: Protecting children and women. *Child Welfare, 79*(2), 131–158.

Pepinsky, H. (1999). Peacemaking criminology and social justice. In B. Arrigo (Ed.), *Social justice. Criminal Justice* (pp. 57–70). Belmont, CA: Wadsworth.

Pepinsky, H., & Quinney, R. (1991). *Criminology as peacemaking.* Bloomington: Indiana University Press.

Roberts, A. R., & Brownell, P. (1999). A century of forensic social work: Bridging the past to the present. *Social Work, 44*(4), 359–369.

Robbins, S. P., Vaughan-Eden, V., & Maschi, T. M. (2014). It's not CSI: The importance of forensics for social work education. *Journal of Forensic Social Work, 4*, 171–175.

Sherman, L. W., & Strang, H. (2007). *Restorative justice: The evidence.* London, UK: Smith Institute.

Strang, H., Sherman, L. W., Mayo-Wilson, E., Woods, D., & Ariel, B. (2013). *Restorative justice conferencing (RJC) using face-to-face meetings of offenders and victims: Effects on offender recidivism and victim satisfaction—A systematic review.* Oslo, Norway: The Campbell Collaboration.

Umbreit, M. S., Coates, R. B., & Vos, B. (2007). Restorative justice dialogue: A multi-dimensional, evidence-based practice theory. *Contemporary Justice Review, 10*, 23–41.

Van Ness, D., & Strong, K. H. (1997). *Restoring justice.* Cincinnati, OH: Anderson Publishing.

van Wormer, K. (2003). Restorative justice: A model for social work practice with families. *Families in Society: The Journal of Contemporary Social Services, 84*(3), 441–448.

Wheeldon, J. (2009). Toward common ground: Restorative justice and its theoretical construction(s). *Contemporary Justice Review, 12*(1), 91–100.

Wheeldon, J. (2012). *After the spring: Probation, justice reform, and democratization from the Baltics to Beirut.* Den Haag, Netherlands: Eleven International Publishers.

Wood, W. R., & Suzuki, M. (2016). Four challenges in the future of restorative justice. *Victims & Offenders, 11*(1), 149–172.

Wright, M. (2005). Book review: Governing paradoxes of restorative justice. *Restorative Justice Online.* Retrieved from http://restorativejustice.org/rj-library/governing-paradoxes-of-restorative-justice/6190

Zehr, H. (1990). *Changing lenses: A new focus for crime and justice.* Scottdale, PA: Herald Press.

VOICES FROM THE FIELD

Johannes Wheeldon, PhD, LLM

Adjunct Professor
Norwich University
Northefield, Vermont

In February 2016 to celebrate 20 years of restorative justice in Vermont, Johannes Wheeldon collected quotes from community volunteers about their work involving restorative justice.

> I love working with such a diverse set of people . . . We're all connected to each other, want the best for one another, and provide an excellent example of grassroots community-building.

Montpelier Community Justice Volunteer

> Working with other people who live in the community and seeing them change through the restorative process is gratifying. They re-connect to the place they live in ways they never thought they would.

Hardwick Area Community Justice Volunteer

> We've seen people turn their lives around and become productive members of the community. For me, it has been a gratifying and fulfilling experience; it has significantly widened my perspective on life.

Rutland Community Justice Volunteer

> I believe that incarceration is unnecessary in many cases, but as long as people are going in they have to come out. This is where COSA is so important, community assistance is a crucial component to getting along in a successful life!

Randolph Community Justice Volunteer

> People want someone to own up to a mistake, and want to know that they are committed to fix the mess.

St. Johnsbury Community Justice Volunteer

> There is intrinsic value to helping others feel forgiven and returned to society. I honestly believe it will encourage those who go through the program to help others in the future.

Montpelier Community Justice Volunteer

> The vulnerability shared, as these who have been stripped of their dignity seek to become accepted, participating members of society once more, deeply fulfills my calling as a faith leader seeking to teach and model reconciliation and forgiveness.

Brattleboro Community Justice Volunteer

> My experience has made me more aware of the difficulties faced by some in our communities . . . restorative justice helps offenders see their own roots in a community and helps them understand their community's commitment to them.

Williston Community Justice Volunteer

CHAPTER 25

Restorative Justice: What Social Workers Need To Do—Part 2

Katherine van Wormer

CHAPTER OBJECTIVES

The major objectives of this chapter are to:

- Define restorative justice and discuss the various forms that this approach to wrongdoing and offending may take.
- Reveal the relevance of restorative interventions to social work practice.
- Recognize pioneers in the field of restorative justice with special emphasis on social work theorists.
- Describe the various forms of restorative justice from microlevel victim–offender conferencing to community-level healing circles to macrolevel reparative justice.
- Argue for greater social work involvement in shaping policies that include restorative justice options in situations of wrongdoing and social work involvement in facilitating victim–offender and antibullying conferencing.
- Describe aspects of restorative justice that address competencies related to advocacy for human rights and issues of spirituality.

CHAPTER COMPETENCIES HIGHLIGHTED

- Competency 2: Engage Diversity and Difference in Practice
- Competency 3: Advance Human Rights and Social, Economic, and Environmental Justice

Forensic social workers, like other social workers, often deal with the stresses and tragedies of life. In the juvenile and criminal justice systems, they may work as correctional officers and correctional counselors in prisons, with juvenile offenders, in programs for sexual offenders, and in victim assistance programs. And as indicated in the other chapters of this volume, forensic social work also relates to legal issues in traditional social work settings, such as child welfare. Although restorative justice is associated in the public mind more with the correctional arena than with child welfare, the principles of this philosophy cut across all areas of social work, wherever there is conflict caused by wrongdoing that needs to be resolved.

Unlike child welfare, the correctional arena has been largely overlooked by the social work profession as a major area of specialization and employment. This abandonment of the field, no doubt, was accelerated by the increasingly punitive nature of corrections (Gumz,

2004). A related factor may be the marginal status that social services hold throughout the criminal justice system (Orzech, 2006).

However, the role of social work within the legal system is changing significantly. Rehabilitation of adult and juvenile offenders has returned as a major focus. Innovative approaches under the rubric of restorative justice are changing the landscape of social work practice, particularly in the criminal justice system.

Let us start with some real-life examples:

- After several meetings with the facilitator counselor, a woman visits her grandson in prison; the grandson is serving time for the murder of his father (his grandmother's son). As the youth cries at the pain he has caused, grandmother and grandson express their love for each other in a deep embrace.
- A boy who had burglarized a friend's home sat with his family members in a circle that included the victim and the victim's family; after the victim told her story of fear and anguish and the offender apologized, arrangements were made for restitution.
- A big boy, "the school bully," listens to his victims tell of their misery caused by the threats and ridicule they have experienced from this classmate; shaken by what he has heard, the "bully" promises not to continue acting like that and to get help for his problems.
- In a Native American peacekeeping circle, members of the community open the session with a prayer and a reminder that the circle has been convened to discuss the behavior of a young man who assaulted his sister in a drunken rage; an eagle feather is passed around the circle, held by each speaker as he or she expresses feelings about the harmful behavior.

What Is Restorative Justice?

These examples are descriptions of actual cases in which restorative strategies were used to help repair a wrongdoing and bring about peace among parties in a dispute. The first two examples are known to me personally; the latter two are based on those found in the restorative justice literature. So what is restorative justice? As defined by the *Encyclopedia of Social Work* (National Association of Social Workers [NASW]):

> Restorative justice is an umbrella term for a method of handling disputes with its roots in the rituals of indigenous populations and traditional religious practices. A three-pronged system of justice, restorative justice is a non-adversarial approach usually monitored by a trained professional who seeks to offer justice to the individual victim, the offender, and the community, all of whom have been harmed by a crime or other form of wrongdoing. (van Wormer, 2013, p. 1)

Operationalizing Restorative Justice

Derived from indigenous and religious forms of justice, restorative justice is a concept that transcends national borders. Today, restorative initiatives are being introduced worldwide in their many varieties as forms of resolving conflict and of meting out justice to victims of wrongdoing. Along with members of the legal profession, child welfare workers, and school authorities, social workers have been actively involved in this movement.

Current trends in dispensing justice fall within three general areas—family group conferencing, victim–offender conferencing, and reparations. These trends in restorative justice are highly relevant to social work values and practice frameworks. At the intersection of policy and practice, restorative initiatives closely parallel the empowerment and strengths-based perspectives of social work.

Restorative justice not only refers to a number of strategies for resolving conflicts peacefully but also to a political campaign of sorts to advocate for the rights of victims and for compassionate treatment of offenders. Rather than emphasizing the rules that have been broken and the punishment that should be imposed, restorative approaches tend to focus primarily on the persons who have been harmed (United Nations, 2006). A restorative justice process does not necessarily rule out all forms of punishment (e.g., fine, incarceration, and probation), but its focus remains firmly on restorative, forward-looking, and least restrictive alternatives. Instead of incarceration, for example, the option of community service coupled with substance abuse treatment might be favored. Instead of the death penalty in homicide cases, a long prison term might be seen as more humane and reflective of the values of a just society.

A growing international movement, restorative justice neatly achieves the NASW ethical standard (NASW *Code of Ethics*, 2008, 6.04c), which states that "social workers should promote conditions that encourage respect for cultural and social diversity within the United States and globally." More specifically, the Council on Social Work Education (CSWE, 2015; Competency 3) urges that social workers "apply their understanding of social, economic, and environmental justice to advocate for human rights at the individual and system levels" (p. 8). The United Nations, in fact, has taken notice of alternative forms of justice, such as offender/victim conferencing and informal means of dealing with certain crimes, as a development consistent with human rights initiatives.

Worldwide, restorative justice has come a long way since two probation officers first pushed two tentative offenders toward their victim's homes in 1974 in Ontario (Zehr, 2001). Restorative justice has variously been called "a new model for a new century" (van Wormer, 2012), "a paradigm shift" (Zehr, 2002), and "an international social movement" (Beck, 2010, p. 3). This model originated in practice and experimentation; the concepts and the theory came later (Zehr, 2002).

The peacemaking powers of the restorative process are well recognized. Instituting such programs entails a new way of thinking about justice and change of heart as well as a change of mind. The best known restorative justice programs offer victims a carefully facilitated encounter with either their personal offender or offenders of other victims (Zehr, 2001). This vision of justice comes in many forms and shapes, as a visit to www .restorative.org will confirm. Restorative principles are seen in the settlement of school disputes, such as bullying on the playground, as well as in the formalized meeting of a murderer and the victim's family years after the crime for the purpose of enhancing healing. Sometimes forgiveness even occurs, although most often not. But research generally shows that the participants report a high level of satisfaction following encounters in which crime victims confront their offenders in victim–offender mediation (Umbreit & Armour, 2011).

Review of the Social Work Literature

For the earlier edition of this chapter, a search (as of August 16, 2008) of *Social Work Abstracts* listed nine articles and other writings under the heading "restorative justice" from 1998 to 2008. I compared the hundreds of listings contained in *Criminal Justice Abstracts*. Happily, at the present time (August 27, 2016) *Social Work Abstracts* lists 36 articles in refereed journals, many from international social work sources.

Compared to New Zealand, the United Kingdom, and Canada, the U.S. profession of social work has been slow to incorporate principles of restorative justice in social work research or in the social work curriculum. Turning to relevant sources from social work literature, restorative justice got its start within the field of U.S. social work through the work of Mark Umbreit, the Director of the Center for Restorative Justice and Peacemaking and Professor of Social Work at the University of Minnesota. His groundbreaking article on victim–offender mediation details the role played by two cofacilitators, both trained social workers, in a conference held between an offender and the victims he had burglarized (Umbreit, 1993). In his analysis of data from several Canadian community programs, Umbreit acknowledged the vital role that social workers play in victim–offender mediation as community organizers, program developers, trainers, and mediators. (As an aside, I have objected for over 20 years to the use of the term *mediation*, which is entirely inappropriate to denote the restorative process. In restorative justice, one person [or group or nation] has committed wrongdoing. There is nothing to negotiate or mediate in these situations; the victims/survivors are present for reconciliation and to receive compensation in some form such as an apology, not to give up something as is the practice in mediation [see van Wormer & Walker, 2013, preface]. Still today the term *victim offender mediation* is widely used in the literature).

Social work educators who got their training in Canada, Burt Galaway and Joe Hudson (2006), edited a definitive study on family group conferencing. Their text, *Family Group Conferencing: New Directions in Community-Centered Child and Family Practice*, described one model of which all social workers interested in child welfare innovation and juvenile justice should be aware.

Elsewhere, restorative justice has been presented as an antidote to oppressive judicial practices in *Confronting Oppression, Restoring Justice* (van Wormer, Kaplan, & Juby, 2012); see also Beck, Kropf, and Leonard (2010); Umbreit and Armour (2011); Walker, Johnson, and van Wormer (2013). These sources recognize the extent to which social work's strengths perspective is compatible with the principles of a form of justice that strives to bring forth the best in each person involved in the process. We can compare the paradigm used in these works with the goal of restoring peace with the assumptions of the standard retribution model, the goal of which is to punish. We can envision this paradigm as a table divided into three sections. Each section would correspond to each of the three components of restorative justice—victim, offender, and community—that are most strongly affected by crime or some other act that has generated harm. Whereas assumptions of the retribution model focus on wrongdoing as an act against the state, the strengths-based restorative model sees crime as an act against the person and the community as well as the state. The emphasis is on reparation and healing for all parties, rather than on retribution and isolation from the community. In contrast to the winner-takes-all concept of the adversarial system of justice, here the goals are: dialogue and truth-telling, prevention of further wrongdoing, and empowerment for all parties involved.

A major contribution to social work literature is the book by Mark Umbreit and Marilyn Armour (2011). They discuss the relevance of the family group conferencing process to the social work profession, and along with other aspects of restorative justice as something that should be included in the social work curriculum. Skills of group conferencing can be applied to dealing with concerns between the child welfare agency and family in parent–child conflict, for example. In interdisciplinary teams, social workers can advocate for culturally appropriate models and raise awareness of gender-based power imbalances in relationships and of the possibility of partner abuse. Similarly, in their edited books, van Wormer and Walker (2013) and Beck et al. (2010) include chapters on the controversial topics of use of restorative interventions in situations of domestic violence and acquaintance rape (Beck), and acquaintance rape, domestic violence, priest abuse, and environmental restoration (van Wormer & Walker).

The field of corrections is one in which treatment professionals such as social workers and correctional counselors have been less prominent since the 1970s, when the focus on punishment and mandatory sentencing replaced the focus on rehabilitation (Gumz, 2004; van Wormer et al., 2012). A clash between the values of members of the helping professions and correctional administrators in the criminal justice system became apparent. Correctional counselors were socialized into the predominant ideology of the Samenow school of treatment—an approach aimed at the errors shown in thinking that teaches that offenders have "a criminal mind" (Samenow, 1984; 2014). Although this one-size-fits-all approach continues to be taught to those working with male and female offenders, rehabilitation is making a comeback in hopes of reducing the very high recidivism rates that are associated with the present system. The introduction of restorative strategies, especially within prison walls, is a part of this new emphasis.

Varieties of Restorative Justice

All of the models discussed in this section—victim–offender conferencing, reparative boards, family group conferencing, and healing circles—are relevant to forensic social work and collaboration. Victim–offender conferencing is relevant to victim advocacy work; family group conferencing to child welfare work and to work with minority groups within extended-family structures; and healing circles to school social work, addiction treatment, and community organization. Policy advocates and lobbyists will want to keep abreast of treatment-evaluation findings so that they can conduct cost-effectiveness analyses. (The best U.S. resource for current data on treatment evaluation is found on the website of the University of Minnesota's Center for Restorative Justice and Peacemaking at: www.cehd .umn.edu/SSW/RJP/Resources/Research_Summaries/default.html).

At the *microlevel*, restorative justice is played out as conferencing between victims and offenders; the rituals take place in family groups and healing circles. At the *macro-* or societal level, where the wrongdoing has been on a global scale, restorative justice takes the form of reparations or truth commissions to compensate for the harm that has been done. Common to all these models is restoring justice. The magnitude of the situations ranges from interpersonal violence to school bullying to mass kidnappings to full-scale warfare. Of most relevance to social work practice are the following forms of restorative strategies: victim–offender conferencing, reparations, family conferencing, and healing circles.

Victim–Offender Conferencing

In its most familiar variation, victim–offender conferencing operates through the criminal justice system. In a court-referred process, victims and offenders meet in a circle to communicate their feelings and work out restitution agreements (Bazemore & Umbreit, 2001).

Social work professor Marilyn Armour (2002), Director of the Institute for Restorative Justice and Restorative Dialogue at The University of Texas at Austin, writes enthusiastically of the emerging initiative of victim–offender dialogue in cases of homicide. In her book coauthored with Umbreit, we learn from actual examples that because family victims often crave information about the crime that took their loved one, they sometimes request a meeting at the prison with the murderer (Umbreit & Armour, 2011). Such a process, when well-planned and monitored, accords the homicide survivors the recognition they were previously denied by the state's need to bring the murderer to justice. Moreover, such a process is affirming in offering the survivors the opportunity to tell the offender how the crime affected them.

Increasingly common are victim-impact panels in which victims/survivors give a presentation to reveal the impact of a crime on their lives. These panels, typically, are arranged by victim assistance programs, correctional staff, and trained volunteers. Sometimes following extensive preparation, victims/survivors meet with the very offenders who have so altered their lives. Within prison walls, members of victim-impact panels speak to inmates. The purpose of these panels is to enable offenders to empathize with victims or family members for their loss.

Social workers are actively involved in every area of victim–offender conferencing. As noted by Umbreit (2006), such conferencing, as an expression of restorative justice, is an emerging area of social work practice with youth in the justice system. Since the 1990s, as shown in a perusal of articles listed on *Social Work Abstracts,* steady progress has been made toward implementing a community restorative justice model in various parts of the United States. Forensic social workers are leading the way in expanding restorative programs nationwide.

Within the field of corrections, there are few better examples of evidence-based practices other than victim–offender conferencing, according to Umbreit (interviewed by Fred, 2005). In *Facing Violence*, which focuses on restorative programs in Texas and Ohio that handle cases involving severe violence, Umbreit, Vos, Coates, and Brown (2003) found that 8 out of

10 participants (victims and offenders) in the dialogue sessions reported major life changes occurring as a result of the program. The later section on research effectiveness describes additional program evaluation research.

Reparations

The traditional means of righting wrongs often occurs through a lawsuit followed by the threat of an adversarial trial. As described by Zehr (2001): "The adversarial setting of the court is a hostile environment, an organized battlefield in which the strategies of aggressive argument and psychological attack replace the physical force of the medieval duel" (p. 192).

One side wins and one side loses in such cases. Great legal expenses are involved in cases that make it to court, and sometimes huge winnings to the plaintiff and his or her representing law firm. But lawyers choose their personal injury cases carefully. Most situations do not qualify for economic reasons, mainly because the potential defendants do not have sufficient resources to make a lawsuit worth the effort and expense. The threat of a lawsuit serves some purposes in society in protecting the public from harm, but in most situations is not a practical means of resolving disputes and compensating victims.

Sometimes reparations do not involve money at all as in the Hawaiian ritual of *ho'oponopono*. Social workers in Hawaii have been quietly incorporating this Native Hawaiian culturally based tradition into their human service interventions. Hurdle (2002) chronicles how social workers in collaboration with Hawaiian elders worked to revitalize the use of *ho'oponopono*, an ancient Hawaiian conflict-resolution process. This model is embedded in the traditional Hawaiian value of extended family, respect of elders, need for harmonious relationships, and restoration of good will or *aloha*. The process is ritualistic and follows a definite protocol. With a facilitator in tight control of communication, the opening prayer leads to an open discussion of the problem at hand. The resolution phase begins with a confession of wrongdoing and the seeking of forgiveness. Uniquely, as Hurdle relates, all parties to the conflict ask forgiveness of each other; this equalizes the status of participants. This process effectively promotes spiritual healing and can be used in many contexts. In drawing on guidance of the *kupunas* (or wise elders) and a reliance on the family as a natural resource in relieving social problems, social workers are tapping into the community's natural resources, a cardinal principle of the strengths perspective (Heffernan, Johnson, & Vakalahi, 2002).

An example of reparations that involve monetary awards is described in one rare case of resolution following a proven complaint of sexual abuse perpetrated by a priest. This case, described in a newspaper article, involved an especially flagrant example of priest abuse from the diocese of Providence, Rhode Island (Carroll, 2002). This matter involved lawsuits filed by 36 people who were sexually abused. What is remarkable about this resolution is that it was arrived at not through adversarial procedures but through marathon conferencing sessions. Church representatives treated the survivors with empathy. Instead of attacking the victims' stories, church officials showed compassion; sincere apologies were offered. Final settlements varied in amounts proportionate to the severity of the abuse and the extent of pain and suffering. Consistent with the principles of restorative justice, the emphasis was on helping the victims, church, and community heal from the wrongs that had been done. Theo Gavrielides (2013), a consultant to the European Union on restorative justice practices, has found in his research on situations of clergy abuse that the use of restorative processes is successful in resolution of conflict between the church and the individual who has been victimized in a way that traditional adversarial approaches would not be.

Restorative initiatives are not limited to work with individuals and families, but also can be successfully applied to the unjust treatment of whole populations. At the macrolevel, reparation is the form of restorative justice that occurs outside of the criminal justice and child welfare context. In these scenarios the violator is the state: Wartime persecutions, rape of the land, slave labor, and mass murder are forms of crimes against humanity that demand some form of compensation for survivors and their families, even generations later, as long as the wounds are felt. The Truth Commission held in South Africa to address the wounds inflicted by Apartheid is one of the most powerful examples of restoration. Compensation came in the form of public testimony and apology (Green, 1998).

Reparations often involve monetary exchange in addition to public acknowledgment of responsibility for the crimes against humanity. Demands for compensation by African Americans for the cruelty inflicted on their ancestors through the slave trade and subsequent slavery have received much attention in recent years, but the wrongs have not been redressed. Similarly, the Australian government continues to deny reparations to the aboriginal people for their "stolen childhoods," a reference to the earlier policy of removing the children of mixed blood and placing them with White families. Reparations have also been denied to the South Korean relatives of innocent civilians slaughtered during the American–Korean war or women used as sex slaves by the Japanese in World War II.

Successful examples of reparations are U.S. compensation to families of Japanese Americans held in concentration camps during World War II, and German compensation to survivors of slave-labor camps. Although social workers have not been involved in any official way in the rewarding of reparations, the values represented in this peacemaking process are highly consistent with social work values, most particularly in regard to social justice, human rights, and empowerment of marginalized populations.

Family Group Conferencing

Developed from the Maori tradition in New Zealand, where it has become a state-sanctioned process, family group conferencing involves the community of people most affected by a situation in need of resolution. Child abuse is a typical example of a problem that can be resolved by a conference of caring and responsible members of the extended family. The similarities between restorative and aboriginal forms of justice coupled with the failure of the existing criminal justice system to deal with the problems of indigenous populations have enhanced its enthusiastic acceptance in New Zealand as in Northwest Canada. With the passage of the Sentencing Act of 2002, New Zealand enacted new legislation to make restorative justice processes that had formerly been used with juveniles and families in the child welfare system also available for adult offenders (Parker, 2002).

Actively involved in setting up the conference, social workers then take a back seat to allow the participants to come up with an appropriate sanction or solution. This process is empowering to the community and highly applicable not just for resolution in the criminal justice realm, but also in matters pertaining to child welfare as addressed by the child welfare system (Adams, 2002). Social workers help oversee and monitor the arrangements reached by extended-family members as to how the child's safety can be ensured.

Healing Circles

This innovative approach is relevant for work with victims/survivors who need family and/or community support following the trauma caused by a crime. The format is ideal for recovering alcoholics/addicts who wish to be reconciled with loved ones. The Toronto District School Board has adopted this approach for situations in which students have victimized others at school (Boesveld, 2013). All the people touched by the offense gather together, review the incident or incidents, try to make sense of it, and, they hope, reach a peaceful resolution.

Fania Davis, who had once been supportive of the Black Panthers, like her sister, Angela Davis, underwent "a life-changing epiphany, one that 'integrated the warrior and the healer in me'" upon learning of the power of restorative justice to change lives (Duxbury, 2013). With the help of judges, lawyers, social workers, and a member of the city council, she founded Restorative Justice for Oakland Youth. The results of her work have been extraordinary in terms of changes brought to the school system in Oakland and to the students in interrupting the school to prison pipeline (Davis, 2015). Today restorative justice strategies have been incorporated into programming in almost 30 schools in Oakland, a city infested with gang activity and drugs. Recently, the school district announced it would allocate over $2 million to further expand the program. School social workers have much to learn about the use of these healing circles for schools in high crime areas.

Common to all these examples of restorative strategies are an emphasis on face-to-face communication, truth-telling, personal empowerment, and healing by all parties to the wrongdoing. Relevant to social work innovators, all four of the strategies just outlined can be developed on a collaborative basis, involving, where appropriate, criminal justice agencies, social service agencies, and community associations (United Nations, 2006). In the absence of collaborative arrangements, it is likely that difficulties will be experienced in securing referrals from the courts, the prosecutor's office, victim assistance organizations, and other required supports.

Relevance to Social Work Values and Education

The mission of social work is rooted in a set of core values. According to the NASW *Code of Ethics* (2008, Preamble), the core values of social work are: service, social justice, dignity and worth of the person, importance of human relationships, integrity, and competence. Restorative justice clearly relates to all these values but most especially to *social justice* or fairness in treatment under the law and to integrity because of its emphasis on truth-telling in these person-centered proceedings (van Wormer & Walker, 2013).

The standards for social work education, which went into effect in July 2015, stress the necessity for social work programs to include appreciation of spirituality as a key dimension of diversity to be respected as a part of cultural humility (CSWE, 2015; Competency 2). This component of the Educational Policy and Accreditation Standards recognizes the key role that religion and spirituality play in the lives of many of our clients. This importance to clients is further stressed in the NASW (2015) standards for cultural competency. To build on client strengths, the social worker should consider the role of spirituality in enhancing client coping skills. Significantly, the rituals pertaining to healing circles often start and end with prayers, depending on the religious preferences of the participants.

Peacemaking circles, as Pranis (2001, 2013; Besthorn, 2013) indicates, engage the spiritual dimension of human experience in theory and practice. Enhancing empathy for another's pain, as Pranis (2001) further suggests, is a powerful force for social justice, and defining restorative justice in terms of empathy takes us out of the confines of religion into the realities of community living and decision making. Nevertheless, there is often a religious aspect to restorative practice as well. This aspect arises in much of the victim–offender work, religious devotion on the part of volunteers, religious conversion by the offenders in prison, and the whole forgiveness theme.

The teachings of restorative justice are consistent with those of the world's great religions, with the Jewish concept *tikkun*—to heal, repair, and transform the world—and with the Christian notion of forgiveness and belief in the duty to overcome evil with good. From the East, Confucianism supports the theory that human nature is basically good. Confucius taught his disciples the principle of *ren* or truthfulness and kindness. Confucianism, according to Walker, Johnson, and van Wormer (2013), advocates a restorative approach to matters of crime and justice. It assumes, first and foremost, that the first victim of any criminal offense is the offender, a victim of life and of himself or herself.

Research Findings Concerning Intervention Effectiveness

The best evidence for treatment effectiveness, as we know, is found in experiments that compare a group that received an intervention with a control group that did not on certain significant variables that can be measured. Such studies in the field of restorative justice have been rare. Most research in the field uses follow-up investigations of the extent to which participants are satisfied with the process; results have been consistently favorable. In the interests of obtaining more rigorous research results, Strang (2004) conducted a series of randomized controlled trials in Canberra, Australia, in which juveniles who had committed property or violent crimes were assigned to either restorative conferences or court hearings. The research involved over 5,000 participants and took place over several years. The findings on the whole were positive. Compared to victims who were involved in the conventional courtroom form of justice, participants in restorative justice processes expressed significantly reduced fear that the offender would harm them, far fewer of these victims expressed a wish to harm their offender if they had the chance, and the large majority of victims in the experiment received an apology compared to victims who went to court. Conference participants also experienced significant decreases in anger and increases in sympathy toward their offenders, as well as decreased anxiety. Results with the juvenile offenders, especially among aboriginal youth, were less positive. The fact that police officers head the conferencing is suggested as the reason for the poor outcomes.

The Jerry Lee Center of the University of Pennsylvania with funding by the British Home Office has focused for the first time on adult offenders, with conferences introducing both pre- and postsentencing for offenses including robbery, assault, and burglary (Sherman et al., 2015). Research results were measured in 12 experimental trials in Australia and the United Kingdom across the participants' lifetimes. Victims/survivors randomly assigned to attend restorative justice conferences with their offenders were found to be less fearful of repeat attack by the same person, more pleased with the way their case was handled, and less revenge-seeking, after receiving far more offender apologies and satisfaction with their justice than were their counterparts in the control group. Interestingly, London robbery and burglary victims suffered much less posttraumatic stress than did controls. As far as the offenders were concerned, the findings were mixed. Violent offenders in Australia had a reduced reoffending rate after 15 years, but offenders who had committed property crimes showed improvement after two years but not in the long term. The UK results are not complete at this time.

Case Example and Application

Sarah was only 14 years old when her father was killed. As an adult, consumed with anger, Sarah had spoken before a parole board, begging them not to release Jeff, her father's killer. Now, more than two decades later, she was plagued with memories and a sense of grief and loss. Her role in the restorative justice process is described in an article in *Social Work Today* by Orzech (2006). To guide the process, Mark Umbreit became Sarah's social worker; he spent one year working with Sarah as the family survivor to help prepare her for the journey she would make inside the gates of a maximum-security prison to spend five hours with the man who had brutally murdered her father. Umbreit also helped prepare the offender, Jeff, for the conferencing that would later take place. Following the meeting with Jeff, "Sarah spoke of how the encounter had been like going through a fire that burned away her pain and allowed the seeds of healing to take root in her life" (Orzech, 2006). The meeting had an equally powerful effect on Jeff as well.

Restorative justice processes within the criminal justice system, such as this one involving a case of homicide, inevitably are highly emotional experiences for both parties. This is an area that is ripe for forensic social worker involvement. Such innovations within the prison system are creating new professional roles for social workers, as Orzech suggests. In fact, hundreds of similar meetings between victims and offenders involved in violent crimes have taken place in recent years.

Conclusion

Restorative justice principles effectively bridge the gap between the formality of conventional criminal justice processes and the social work ethos. In its incorporation of activities related to community empowerment, spirituality, conflict resolution, healing of relationships through dialogue, and learning techniques of decision making inspired by indigenous people's traditions, restorative justice effectively links practice with policy.

Restorative justice programs are proliferating around the world and becoming established in this country through cultural transmission. Social work educators can play a major role through theory development and inspiring students to pursue application of restorative principles to a wide range of practice areas. To date, despite the work of a number of dedicated social work researchers, the social work profession, at least in the United States (though not in New Zealand or Canada), has failed to exert leadership in teaching about, writing about, or setting up restorative justice programs. There is evidence today, however, that social work is taking much more interest in the possibilities offered by these approaches.

The challenge to policy planners is to learn ways of making correctional strategies more consistent with social justice and to participate in the planning, research, policy making, and facilitation aspects of this more humanistic form of justice.

CHAPTER EXERCISES

Exercise 1. Check out www.restorativejustice.org and locate an article that describes a situation that could have been handled in a traditional way but which benefited from a restorative approach. Summarize your findings and discuss the advantages of the alternative approach.

Exercise 2. Imagine that it was your job to propose legislation to allocate a certain amount of money as reparative justice to African Americans who were descendants either of slaves or who survived the Jim Crow era under conditions of segregation and deprivation of resources. How would you go about this task? How much would be awarded and who would qualify? One historic example is the reparations rewarded to Japanese American survivors of detention in concentration camps in World War II. See the articles on this and the Korean case for reparations from Japan at www.restorativejustice.org.

Additional Resources

Center for Restorative Justice and Peacemaking: www.cehd.umn.edu/ssw/rjp

Lorenn Walker on Oprah Winfrey Network, case of homicide at Walla Walla prison: https://vimeo .com/45818900

Mark Umbeit's film, Being With the Energy of Forgiveness: www.youtube.com

Restorative Justice Consortium: www.restorativejustice.org.uk

Restorative Justice Online: www.restorativejustice.org

Restore Justice: www.cacatholic.org/restorejustice

References

Adams, P. (2002). *Learning from indigenous practices: A radical tradition.* Paper presented at the Council on Social Work Education Conference, Nashville, TN.

Armour, M. P. (2002). Journey of family members of homicide victims: A qualitative study of their posthomicide experience. *American Journal of Orthopsychiatry, 72,* 372–382.

Bazemore, G., & Umbreit, M. (2001). A comparison of four restorative conferencing models. *Juvenile Justice Bulletin.* Washington, DC: U.S. Department of Justice.

Beck, E. (2010). Introduction. In E. Beck, N. Kropf, & P. Leonard (Eds.), *Social work and restorative justice: Skills for dialogue, peacemaking and reconciliation* (pp. 3–14). New York, NY: Oxford University Press.

Beck, E., Kropf, N., & Leonard, P. (Eds.). (2010). *Social work and restorative justice: Skills for dialogue, peacemaking and reconciliation.* New York, NY: Oxford University Press.

Besthorn, F. H. (2013). Speaking earth: Environmental restoration and restorative justice. In K. van Wormer & L. Walker (Eds.), *Restorative justice today: Practical applications* (pp. 233–244). Thousand Oaks, CA: Sage Publications.

Boesveld, S. (2013). Detention is over: Schools trying out discussion first. *National Post.* Retrieved from http://www.news.nationalpost.com

Carroll, M. (2002). $13.5 million settlement in Rhode Island clergy abuse. *The Boston Globe.* Retrieved from http://www.boston.com/globe/spotlight/abuse

Council on Social Work Education. (2015). *Educational policy and accreditation standards.* Alexandria, VA: Author.

Davis, F. (2015). Interrupting the school to prison pipeline through restorative justice. *Huffington Post.* Retrieved from http://www.huffingtonpost.com

Duxbury, M. (2013). Box 5: Circles of change: Bringing a more compassionate justice system to troubled youth in Oakland. In K. van Wormer & L. Walker (Eds.), *Restorative justice today: Practical applications* (p. 107). Thousand Oaks, CA: Sage Publications.

Fred, S. (2005). Restorative justice: A model of healing. *NASW News, 50*(2), 4.

Galaway, B., & Hudson, J. (Eds.). (2006). *Family group conferencing: New directions in community-centered child and family practice.* Edison, NJ: Aldine.

Gavrielides, T. (2013). Clergy child sexual abuse: The restorative justice option. In K. van Wormer & L. Walker (Eds.), *Restorative justice today: Practical applications* (pp. 131–142). Thousand Oaks, CA: Sage Publications.

Green, C. (1998). Without memory there is not healing. *Parade,* 5–7.

Gumz, E. (2004). American social work, corrections and restorative justice: An appraisal. *International Journal of Offender Therapy and Comparative Criminology, 48*, 449–460.

Heffernan, K., Johnson, R., & Vakalahi, H. (2002). *A Pacific Island approach to aging.* Paper presented at the Baccalaureate Program Directors Conference, Pittsburgh, PA.

Hurdle, D. (2002). Native Hawaiian traditional healing: Culturally-based interventions for social work practice. *Social Work, 47*, 183–192.

National Association of Social Workers. (2008). *Code of ethics.* Washington, DC: Author.

National Association of Social Workers. (2015). *Social work speaks: NASW policy statements 2015–2017.* Washington, DC: Author.

Orzech, D. (2006). Criminal justice social work—New models, new opportunities. *Social Work Today, 6*(6), 34–37.

Parker, L. (2002). New Zealand expands official recognition of restorative justice. Retrieved from http://restorativejustice.org/rj-library/new-zealand-expands-official-recognition-of-restorative-justice/2373

Pranis, K. (2001). Restorative justice, social justice, and the empowerment of marginalized populations. In G. Bazemore & M. Schiff (Eds.), *Restoring community justice: Repairing harm and transforming communities* (pp. 287–306). Cincinnati, OH: Anderson.

Pranis, K. (2013). Reflections from a descendant of the Minnesota restitution centers. In K. van Wormer & L. Walker (Eds.), *Restorative justice today: Practical applications* (pp. 15–20). Thousand Oaks, CA: Sage Publications.

Samenow, S. (1984, 2014 updated and revised). *Inside the criminal mind*. New York, NY: Broadway Books.

Sherman, L., Strang, H., Barnes, G., Woods, D. J., Bennett, S., Inkpen, N., . . . Slothower, M. (2015). Twelve experiments in restorative justice: The Jerry Lee program of randomized trials of restorative justice conferences. *Journal of Experimental Criminology, 11*(4), 501–540.

Strang, H. (2004). *Repair or revenge: Victims and restorative justice*. New York, NY: Oxford University Press.

Umbreit, M. (1993). Crime victims and offenders in mediation: An emerging area of social work practice. *Social Work, 38*(1), 69–73.

Umbreit, M. (2006). Restorative justice through mediation: The impact of programs in four Canadian provinces. In B. Galaway & J. Hudson (Eds.), *Restorative justice: International perspectives* (pp. 373–385). Monsey, NY: Criminal Justice Press. (Original work published 1996.)

Umbreit, M., & Armour, M. (2011). *Restorative justice dialogue: An essential guide for research and practice*. New York, NY: Springer Publishing.

Umbreit, M., Vos, B., Coates, R., & Brown, K. (2003). *Facing violence: The path of restorative justice and dialogue*. Monsey, NY: Criminal Justice Press.

United Nations. (2006). *Handbook of restorative justice programmes*. Vienna, Austria: United Nations Office on Drugs and Crime.

van Wormer, K. (2012). *Working with female offenders: A gender-sensitive approach*. New York, NY: Wiley.

van Wormer, K. (2013). Restorative justice. In C. Franklin (Ed.), *NASW encyclopedia of social work* (20th ed., online publication). New York, NY: Oxford University Press.

van Wormer, K., Kaplan, L., & Juby, C. (2012). *Confronting oppression, restoring justice: From policy analysis to social action* (2nd ed.). Alexandria, VA: Council on Social Work Education.

van Wormer, K., & Walker, L. (2013). *Restorative justice today: Practical applications*. Thousand Oaks, CA: Sage Publications.

Walker, L., Johnson, A., & van Wormer, K. (2013). Brazil's prisons. In K. van Wormer & L. Walker (Eds.), *Restorative justice today: Practical applications* (pp. 151–162). Thousand Oaks, CA: Sage Publications.

Zehr, H. (2001). *Transcending: Reflections of crime victims*. Intercourse, PA: Good Books.

Zehr, H. (2002). *The little book of restorative justice*. Intercourse, PA: Good Books.

CHAPTER 26

Empowerment and Feminist Practice With Forensic Populations

Sandra Turner

CHAPTER OBJECTIVE

The major objective of this chapter is to:

- Disseminate theoretical and practice knowledge of practice using an empowerment and feminist perspective specifically when working with marginalized and oppressed forensic populations and in forensic settings.

CHAPTER COMPETENCIES HIGHLIGHTED

- Competency 2: Engage Diversity and Difference in Practice
- Competency 3: Advance Human Rights and Social, Economic, and Environmental Justice

Forensic social work focuses on both victims and offenders and strives to integrate the skills and knowledge of empowerment and feminist theory and practice with principles of social justice and human rights. This chapter discusses empowerment and feminist theories and their relevance to practice with forensic populations. Although first conceptualized and articulated in the 1970s by Paulo Freire, empowerment concepts have only quite recently been embraced by social work practitioners (Freire, 1973; Gutierrez, 1990; Lee, 2001). In the 1980s and 1990s, the social work profession shifted from a focus on deficits and problems to a strengths and resilience perspective (Saleeby, 1997). Empowerment practice then followed.

The embracing of empowerment as a theory and a process is an outgrowth of the strengths perspective work and it incorporates a human rights and social justice approach to both practice and a global perspective. Empowerment practice is also closely related to feminist theory and practice.

Feminist theory examines and emphasizes the importance of gender in any discussion of the effects of oppression and domination in our society and posits that women of all races and classes are oppressed and rendered powerless in ways that are different than men (Collins, 1991; DeBeauvoir, 1957; Kabeer, 2009).

Empowerment: History and Relevance

Freire (1973) originally developed his theory of empowerment as an educator working with poor and oppressed people in Brazil. He believed that what was being taught in schools in Brazil was largely irrelevant to the marginalized students as it did not acknowledge their oppression or the racism and discrimination they were living with. He developed the concept of "conscientization" or critical consciousness, which is learning and using the skills of reflection and action and then joining together with others who are experiencing similar oppressions (Carr, 2003). Freire believed that it is the joining with students in the classroom as well as in their lives in the community that is critical to both understanding them and their realities. This understanding and joining will lead to being able to teach them to become empowered.

Gutierrez (1990) drew on his understanding and writing as she developed her concept of empowerment from a social work perspective, which is working with those who are marginalized and oppressed to help them increase their personal, interpersonal, and political power. Both Freire and Gutierrez believed that this is the first step to helping people to become empowered and improving their lives. To work in this way, you must enter into the lives of the people you are working with and join them. Freire believed that a teacher cannot be effective and empowering without actually living among his or her students (Freire, 1973). An empowerment and feminist approach to practice is both clinical and community-oriented, and as such is ideal for working with forensic populations, some of whom have most likely been both victims and offenders. Carr stated that the ultimate goal of empowerment is the "sociopolitical liberation of marginalized communities" (Carr, 2003). There has been much discussion as to whether empowerment is a theory or a process. It is generally now thought to be a process that starts with the recognition of the oppression that is being experienced, which then leads to an increase in what Freire would term *conscientization* or an awakening of critical consciousness concerning one's powerlessness and oppression. Freire believed this has to be the first step in becoming empowered (Freire, 1973).

Core Skills Addressed

Empowerment and Feminist Practice

Feminist social work practice has a lot in common with empowerment practice. However feminist theory focuses on gender as it is related to power and status differences while empowerment practice tends to look more generally at the role of race and class (Turner & Maschi, 2015). Although both feminist and empowerment practice are relevant for both men and women who are oppressed and marginalized, it is important to recognize that women have been and continue to be oppressed and marginalized in ways that are different than men. Core skills that relate to both empowerment and feminist practice are joining and listening to the voices of the people you are working with.

Feminists such as Jordan, Kaplan, Miller, Stiver, and Surrey (1991) conceptualized the relational model of practice, where practitioners actually "join" with their clients as opposed to being outside observers of their lives. This skill is perhaps the most critical one to be able to call upon. As he developed the concept of empowerment, Freire was one of the first to advocate going out into the community to "join" with and listen to the people. Feminist practice also listens to and focuses on the "voices" that are outside the mainstream culture and patriarchal power. Those working from a feminist perspective tend to believe that it is the voices and perspectives of those who are often marginalized in our society that should be considered to be the "sources of greatest wisdom" (Brown, 2012).

Self in Relation Therapy was developed by practitioners and researchers at the Stone Center in Boston, Massachusetts. At the core of this practice is the desire and ability to acknowledge and value connection with others. Feminist and empowerment practitioners utilize other skills in addition to "joining" with and listening to their clients, some of which are the following:

- The practitioner establishes an equalitarian relationship, which is key to this work where the client is the expert, not the therapist.
- The practitioner teaches women to get in touch with and enhance their strengths and consequently their power.

- The practitioner uses the skill of making herself or himself "real" to the client and enters into a mutual relationship. The practitioner is not afraid to show her or his own emotions if they are to the benefit of the client. When self-disclosure is appropriate, it should be used.
- The practitioner communicates that the goal of the work together is change, not adjustment to a painful situation (Mahaney, 2007).
- Reframing is an important skill in feminist therapy. Helping a survivor of sexual abuse internalize that a crime has been committed against her and that what happened is not her fault is critical (Turner, 1993).

Feminist and Empowerment History and Theoretical Base

The first wave of feminism in the late 19th century was primarily a White middle class movement in England and the United States, and the focus was the fight to get women the right to vote (Kemp & Brandwein, 2010). Women of color also wanted the right to vote as Sojourner Truth demanded in 1851 at the Seneca Convention. After women succeeded in getting their voting rights and the country became involved in World War II, women in both the United States and United Kingdom took active roles in the war effort. "Rosie the Riveter" became a popular symbol of women's empowerment in the United States and the women of Bletchley Park in England were very influential in breaking the German Enigma code, which led to the sinking of the German warship, the *Bismarck*. This helped to begin to turn the tide of the war against Germany (Olson, 2010).

After the war, in the 1950s the second wave of feminists looked again at the patriarchal nature of our society and began to demand reproductive rights, equal pay for equal work, more equal power in general, and more access to resources (Friedan, 1963).

By the turn of the 20th century a third wave of U.S. feminists began to argue that debates over leadership and hierarchy were no longer relevant (Kabeer, 2009). Feminists were developing a new theory of women's psychological development that challenged traditional theories of human development. Feminists such as Miller (1976), Gilligan (1982), and Poorman (2003) articulated the value of connection with other people as essential to their survival and empowerment. Feminist principles state that women should have equal access to all forms of power (Turner & Maschi, 2015). Feminist practice takes into account the importance of economic and political structures that shape human societies and insists that gender must be acknowledged when looking at the effects of oppression and powerlessness in our society (Turner & Maschi, 2015).

Empowerment is the primary goal of feminist therapy (Mintz & Tager, 2012). Mintz and Tager (2012) argue that a feminist approach is excellent for men as well as women as it frames psychological and social distress as the result of living in an oppressive and patriarchal society. As discussed in an earlier article (Turner & Maschi, 2015), feminist theories focus on status and power differences as well as role expectations that are related to gender while empowerment theory looks at the role of race and culture and class and this effect on individuals and their problems. Empowerment practice is a partnership in which practitioners work side by side with clients to enable them to regenerate their strength and resilience and also work to help them access privileges that are theirs by right (Thompson, 2007). Thus, empowerment is a clinical, policy, and community-oriented approach.

Freire's concept of critical consciousness or conscientization signifies an awareness of the discrimination and oppression not only in our society but also the wider social and political implications of this oppression that marginalized people are dealing with (Freire, 1973). Arriving at a level of critical consciousness is an early step in the process of empowerment. Lee states that knowledge of the global nature of oppression is essential. "A global perspective moves us beyond ego and ethnocentrism to cross-cultural competence in empowerment work and building the beloved community" (Lee, 2001).

Freire believed that hope is critical in empowerment practice—hope gives people the strength to change. Hope is also the foundation of resilience practice, as Werner and Smith discovered in their study of the children of Kauai (Werner & Smith, 1982).

And so I went on a journey to answer for myself a few questions: What are our most human qualities? What sets us apart from animal and machine? From the masses and the monster? How can we believe in our infinite possibilities when our limitations are so conspicuous? And hope? What is this stubborn thing in man that keeps him forever picking the lock of time? The odds are against him, the odds have always been against him, and he knows it, but he has never believed it . . . (Werner & Smith, 1982).

Case Example and Application

Survivors of sexual abuse are perhaps among the most severely victimized members of our society. Small group work has long been considered an effective way of working with sexual abuse survivors. This is also an approach advocated by Carr (2003) for empowerment practice in general. Many feminist practitioners have been working with survivors in groups from a resilience or strengths perspective. They may not have framed this work in the 1980s and 1990s as being grounded in an empowerment perspective. This chapter highlights a case example of group work with women who were sexually abused that was first presented in the 1990s and told from a strengths-based approach, but could very much be considered both a feminist and empowerment process of working, although it was not named as such at the time (Turner, 1993). We reframe this sexual abuse group work from a feminist and empowerment perspective in this chapter.

Women who have been sexually abused experience an excruciating sense of powerlessness. They were unable to stop the abuse from happening, a fact for which they often blame themselves. If they were young at the time of the abuse, they may be incapable of seeing that what happened to them was not their fault. This is especially true if the abuser was a trusted adult. Women and girls often suffer long-lasting and devastating consequences such as loss of self-esteem, depression, sense of guilt and shame—and certainly a devastating sense of powerlessness (Turner, 1993). Lee (2001) suggests that the word *victor* should be used rather than *survivor*. Initially in the work with women who had been sexually abused the term *victim* was used; then, when a more strengths-based or resilience model of work was introduced, the term *survivor* was widely used. Thinking of oneself and fellow group members as victors is surely a sign of embracing the process of empowerment.

For women who have been sexually abused, the earlier the age at which the abuse occurred and if it was incest by a family member, the more pernicious and devastating are the effects. Most survivors of incest feel an enormous sense of alienation and isolation in addition to their feelings of worthlessness. Even women who might be considered to be in the mainstream of society by virtue of their race, class, or level of education feel alienated. Those who are marginalized and members of an oppressed group naturally feel even more alienated. In addition, girls and women are taught to internalize their anger and not express it. Those who do speak out about their abuse are often further victimized.

The most recent example of this is the case of the star swimmer from Stanford University who physically and sexually attacked a woman who was lying down passed out. The young woman initially did not tell anyone but dropped out of school and began to suffer severe depression, anxiety, and other symptoms of posttraumatic stress disorder (PTSD), which finally drove her to come forward about the abuse and go to the police. The judge presiding over the case only gave the swimmer a six-month sentence and then probation. His victim suffered severe emotional trauma for many months, actually three years. Fortunately, there was a tremendous outcry of protest (including a statement from U.S. Vice President Joseph Biden offering his support for the young woman), as well as other lawyers refusing to try cases in the judge's court. She wrote a long, moving description of the ordeal she had gone through for the three years since the abuse happened, which went viral.

(continued)

Case Example and Application (*continued*)

However, to this day, the light sentence for the swimmer has not been changed, and his father made the comment that six months was not too light a sentence "for only 20 minutes of action." (Stack, 2016).

The following are stories from a sexual abuse group of women. Some of them were abused as children by a family member, and some were raped as teens or adults. Because of the pervasive sense of guilt and shame, the women in this group had not been able to talk to anyone about what happened to them, except for mentioning the abuse when they first came for help to an outpatient clinic (Turner, 1993).

During the first several weeks of the group, survivors began to talk to each other about what happened to them. This does not happen for all right away. Girls who have been sexually abused are taught by their perpetrators and often by other adults in positions of authority, such as clergy men, not to mention their abuse. A woman in the group had been sexually abused by her father and for several years told no one. When a stranger forced her to touch his genitals, she went to her parish priest, who then told her father, who accused her of making it all up. She did not mention the abuse again for many more years. Another woman did not actually speak about her sexual abuse by her older brother for the first three months of group meetings. When she finally was able to talk about what happened, she was not able to return to the group for three weeks. When she did come back and realized that the other women understood her and shared similar feelings she began to feel a sense of connection and thus empowerment (Kammer, Turner, & Bowden, 2011).

As women begin to realize that other people can bear to hear—and often in fact share—an experience they think is intolerable, the process of healing and changing their self-images can begin (Turner, 1993). It is also important for the group leader to "join" with the members and let them know that what they are talking about has an impact on her. This helps to build a sense of mutual empowerment.

Another group member, when asked to think about the image she had of herself as a young girl, said that she had always pictured herself in a brown, stained dress sitting alone inside her house. After six months of participating in the group, another member asked her how she saw herself at that moment. She thought for a while and then said that she saw herself in a green field with lots of trees, and she was wearing a bright yellow dress (Kammer et al., 2011). She was empowered by the way the whole group, including the leader, was able to connect with her and empathize with her pain as they also shared theirs.

In addition to joining and creating an atmosphere of mutuality and empathy, other skills of an effective group leader are helping the members to set goals for themselves and each other (such as being able to sleep without a knife; wearing clothes they feel comfortable in; asking for promotions at work; writing letters to their abusers; and learning how to grieve for their lost childhoods (Turner, 1993).

Thompson (2007) states that for the social worker to be truly able to empower a client he or she must have empathy, mutual trust, openness, and the ability to work alongside clients to regenerate their potential rather than working for them. He further states that in our capitalist society that is institutionally segregationist and upholds and sustains inequality, maximizing clients' empowerment has many obstacles. East and Roll (2015) describe their 20 years of practice experience working with women who have experienced trauma, poverty, and multiple structural oppressions from an empowerment approach, which includes clinical interventions and community organizing strategies. They advocate three parts to helping women becoming empowered: engaging with each other through sharing stories, developing their voices, and going on to become community leaders and advocates. They also see personal empowerment development as integrated with working for community change. In promoting this, they helped to develop skills in

(continued)

Case Example and Application (*continued*)

team building, problem solving, advocacy, and leadership. East and Roll (2015) stress how important it is for social workers to recognize the pervasiveness of gender-based oppression. They advocate for group work with women who have been marginalized and traumatized. They encourage social workers to use group interventions that look at power, betrayal, and stigma.

This chapter also highlights applying an empowerment approach to working with female and male prisoners in London. There is a group of volunteers who are social workers, writers, and editors who encourage prisoners to write about their experience of being in prison. An organization called the Prison Reform Trust conducts research on the prison system and conditions and informs prisoners, staff, and the media about their findings. In doing this they advocate for reform of prisons among government officials. The Prison Reform Trust works to ensure that the conditions of prisons in England are just, humane, and effective. This organization is committed to advocating for and informing prisoners, staff, and the general public as well as government about needed reforms. One of their projects is a writing contest where monetary prizes are given to prisoners. The judges are writers and editors in the London area. A colleague who has been a judge of the writing contest shared some of the entries. This is a very creative and highly effective way of empowering the prisoners who choose to take part in this contest. The prisoners are given a choice of three topics to write about: (a) an essay on how to reform prisons; (b) a short story about the topic "Out for Good," which is not autobiographical; and (c) a rap/lyric on the topic of change.

Stories From a London Prison

One of the essays that won third prize was about "Time." It was written by the mother of three children who was serving time for selling drugs. She writes that the government is in control of her time in prison and that she is trying to create some time for herself to feel like she can take some of the control back. She writes:

> I don't have time, neither in the day nor in the night. I am middle aged and use the time I have to do education and voluntary work. I only watch the news on TV because I am hoping there may be some news about sentences being reduced.

> I wake up usually at 6:30, not because I want to wake up at this time but because I hear the keys or the officer's radio as they come in at that time every day. I don't know if that is to check on us or a way of telling us we are in prison and need to wake up.

She then goes on to say she washes, prays, and looks at her children's pictures and says good morning to them. She likes to go to education because when she is reading or learning something time passes quickly. When she is at work in prison, time passes very slowly.

> I wish a magician could change the time that I have to spend in prison and reduce the time. It has been a long time since I have been with my children. I wish my time in prison goes by quickly. . . . Once I get my freedom back I will get my time back, and with this I can use my time how I wish to.

Another prisoner writes on the topic of "How to Change Prisons":

> Why not send people that need help to a place where they can get the help to get clean, to face their addictions and be able to start a fresh life. And be able to understand what has happened in their lives and make better choices for their futures. Help them understand why they have committed the crime and what can they do to stop it happening again.

Prison should be there to help people to ensure that they won't re-offend and that people receive the help and support that they may need. Instead of judging them and thinking prison is the only way they will learn.

Instead many people are quick to judge others and just believe that individuals have committed a crime and should pay for it, without understanding what has led them to commit this crime and that they maybe want help to get away from the drug, alcohol or even domestic relationships but don't know how or have the strength to ask for it. There is a large amount of women (and also men), that have committed crimes due to domestic relationships and they don't know who to ask or where to go for help. So they end up in prison being punished, judged and not helped. How is this right?

There will always be different views but maybe they should listen to the pain and suffering so many people are experiencing. The need to try and understand why so many people are committing crimes and try to find a way that can help, provide more support, and help the people that need it instead of judging them and thinking prison is the only way they will learn.

Encouraging and enabling prisoners to write is a very effective way of empowering them to find their voices. Maschi and Killian (2011) discuss the importance of intervening with clients at both the individual and the policy level. They believe it is important for social workers to become familiar with laws and policies that influence their clients—in this case prisoners.

Livingston, Nijdam-Jones, and Brink (2012) studied patient-centered care in a forensic mental health hospital in Canada and found that those patients who had a higher level of recovery were those who felt the most empowered and had the lowest level of internalized sense of stigma. They also found that staff who are more concerned about their safety and less concerned about caring for their patients did not form empowering relationships.

The writings of these two prisoners reflect their feelings of powerlessness and sense of hopelessness that they can be understood and helped. The person writing about time desperately wants to be in charge of her life again. The story about prison life reads like a lament about being misunderstood and not helped.

The Prison Reform Project helps to empower people in several ways. It encourages those who enter to become more empowered in that they are asked to think about their lives in prison and in a way reflect on themselves and their situation as a precursor to becoming more able to exercise or advocate for themselves. They are engaging in an active approach to problem solving and are increasing their level of self-awareness as they write. Getting a monetary prize for their efforts also contributes to an increasing sense of empowerment.

Conclusion

Maschi and Killian (2011) stress how important it is for social workers to practice at both the micro- and the macrolevel in working to empower forensic and oppressed populations. Whether working with survivors of sexual abuse or prison reform, practitioners who work from a position of "conscientization" or critical consciousness and are able to join with their constituents to work together to empower them will be working to promote human rights and social justice as they help people realize their power.

Women who have been sexually abused can find their voices as they begin to see what happened to them as a crime rather than as something that happened because something is wrong with them. For example, one of the members of the sexual abuse group became empowered when she was called for jury duty and the judge asked her if she had ever been the victim of a crime. For the first time since her abuse she was able to see and state that yes, she was the survivor of the crime of sexual abuse. She walked out of the courtroom a more empowered and powerful person (Turner, 1993).

The prisoners who participate in the writing project may not have their prison time reduced, but the process of writing their stories and opinions has helped them feel valued and heard, which leads to increased self-esteem and a sense of empowerment.

Empowerment and feminist work leads to a just and more humane world—something we all strive for.

CHAPTER EXERCISES

Exercise 1. Role-play that you are the leader of a group of women who have been sexually abused as children.

Exercise 2. As a class, design a feminist and empowerment-oriented intake assessment for a woman who is coming to treatment for sexual abuse.

Exercise 3. Volunteer and join a rape crisis program in your city or town, get training, and volunteer to help women who call or come in for help. Present or discuss your experience with your classmates.

Exercise 4. Attend conferences in your area on women who have been sexually trafficked. Come prepared to present or discuss your experience with your classmates.

Additional Resources

Mental Health of Women in Prison in UK: www.together-uk.org

Prison Reform Trust: www.prisonreformtrust.org.uk

References

Brown, L. S. (2012). Feminist therapy. Retrieved from http://drlaurabrown.com

Carr, E. S. (2003). Rethinking empowerment theory using a feminist lens: The importance of process. *Affilia, 18*(8), 8–20.

Collins, P. (1991). *Black feminist thought: Knowledge, consciousness, and the politics of empowerment*. New York, NY: Routledge.

DeBeauvoir, S. (1957). *The second sex*. New York, NY: Alfred A. Knopf.

East, J. F., & Roll, S. J. (2015). Women, poverty, and trauma: An empowerment practice approach. *Social Work, 66*(4), 279–286.

Freire, P. (1973). *Education for critical consciousness*. New York, NY: Seabury.

Friedan, B. (1963). *The feminine mystique*. New York, NY: W. W. Norton.

Gilligan, C. (1982). *In a different voice: Psychological theory and women's development*. Cambridge, MA: Harvard University Press.

Gutierrez, L. M. (1990). Working with women of color: An empowerment perspective. *Social Work, 35*, 1499–1553.

Jordan, J., Kaplan, A., Miller, J. B., Stiver, I., & Surrey, J. (1991). *Women's growth in connection: Writings from the stone center*. New York, NY: Guilford Press.

Kabeer, N. (2009). *World survey on the role of women in development*. Report of the UN Division for the Advancement of Women UN-DESA, New York, NY.

Kammer, R., Turner, S., & Bowden, K. (2011). Treating women right. *Affilia, 25*(1), 83–86.

Kemp, S. P., & Brandwein, R. (2010). Feminisms and social work in the United States: An intertwined history, *Affilia, 24*(4), 341–364.

Lee, J. (2001). *The empowerment approach to social work practice.* New York, NY: Columbia University Press.

Livingston, J. D., Nijdam-Jones, A., & Brink, J. (2012). A tale of two cultures: Examining patient-centered care in a forensic mental health hospital. *The Journal of Forensic Psychiatry & Psychology, 23*(3), 345–360.

Mahaney, E. (2007). Theory and techniques of feminist therapy. Retrieved from http://www.goodtherapy.org/blog

Maschi, T., & Killian, M. L. (2011). The evolution of forensic social work in the United States: Implications for 21st century practice. *Journal of Forensic Social Work, 1*, 8–36.

Miller, J. B. (1976). *Toward a new psychology of women.* Boston, MA: Beacon Press.

Mintz, L. B., & Tager, D. (2012). Feminist therapy with male clients: Empowering men to be their whole selves. In C. Z. Enns & E. N. Williams (Eds.), *The Oxford handbook of feminist multicultural counseling psychology.* New York, NY: Oxford University Press. doi:10.1093/oxfordhb/9780199744220.013.0017

Olson, L. (2010). *Citizens of London.* New York, NY: Random House.

Poorman, P. B. (2003). *Microskills ad theoretical foundations for professional helpers.* Boston, MA: Allyn & Bacon.

Saleeby, D. (1997). *The strengths perspective in social work practice.* New York, NY: Longman.

Stack, L. (2016, June 6). Light sentence for Brock Turner in Stanford rape case draws outrage. *The New York Times.* Retrieved from https://www.nytimes.com/2016/06/07/us/outrage-in-stanford-rape-case-over-dueling-statements-of-victim-and-attackers-father.html?_r=0

Thompson, N. (2007). *Power and empowerment.* London, UK: Russell House Publishing.

Turner, S. (1993). Talking about sexual abuse: The value of short-term groups for women survivors. *Journal of Group Psychotherapy, Psychodrama and Sociometry, 46*, 110–121.

Turner, S. G., & Maschi, T. M. (2015). Feminist and empowerment theory and social work practice. *Journal of Social Work Practice, 29*(2), 151–162.

Werner, E., & Smith, R. S. (1982). *Vulnerable but invincible.* New York, NY: McGraw-Hill.

VOICES FROM THE FIELD

Keila Zapata-Kelly, MSW, CASAC-T
Administrator of Continuing Education and Social Work Licensure
Fordham University Graduate School of Social Service

Agency Setting

I currently work for the Fordham University Graduate School of Social Service (GSS) in the Continuing Education Department. Our university is committed to excellence in education and scholarship and is built on professional social work values and the Jesuit educational tradition with its focus on social justice. It is located in the New York City metropolitan region. Fordham GSS Continuing Education continues to prepare the social worker in the field to strive for excellence, assisting and enhancing him or her through diverse areas of social justice, palliative care, and clinical and mental health skills.

Practice Responsibilities

I serve as the school's expert on New York State (NYS), New Jersey (NJ), and Connecticut (CT) Continuing Education Hours (CEH) requirements for licensure, including renewal requirements and processes. As the Fordham Liaison with the State Education Department for all professional social work continuing education (CE) initiatives on all campuses, I develop administrative procedures and protocols for the management of CE requirements and educational events that include: (a) documenting CE procedures and distribution of NYS-approved CE certificates; (b) creating individualized CE certificates for all Fordham NYS-approved CE courses; (c) providing oversight and administrative support to all GSS events. I plan, develop, and implement all CE events for alumni and the extended social work community, which include educational and networking events and webinars. I recruit speakers and submit CE program plans to NYS within the required approval time frame for all GSS programs.

I also collaborate with GSS marketing and the university marketing team (as well as other related committees) to develop compelling content for CE event communications including website, print publications, advertising, and social media. I report to the Dean of Continuing Education and Extramural Programs and work closely with the Dean of Student Services, GSS Alumni Coordinator, and the Dean.

I serve as the school's expert on professional social work licensing requirements in the tristate area.

Also, I develop and implement professional licensure information sessions for all GSS students at all campuses. I am the key contact person for all LMSW/LCSW application/ process/preparation questions and prepare students at all campuses for the licensing examination, which includes review sessions on test taking strategies. I work with faculty on content review sessions both in class and online.

Expertise Required

Since receiving my Masters in Social Work, I have been working in the field for the past 11 years focusing on quality improvement, program evaluations, and staff development in the field of behavioral and mental health. It is important to have a diverse range of experience in order to understand the various areas of topics needed to provide skilled classes and courses to the social work profession.

Ethical, Legal, Practice, Diversity, and/or Advocacy Issues Addressed

For the past seven years I have been advocating and working closely with organizations to design and implement staff development as part of their business model. Staff development is normally at the bottom of the pyramid. Organizations are consistently worrying about numbers, making sure that they met the quota through patient visits, but unfortunately what suffers is the quality of service that is being provided. Very few supervisors sit in during individual sessions, observing to see if their social worker's techniques have been mastered in order to provide adequate counseling services. Many organizations focus their efforts on hiring directors of training to fulfill the required training from the state but fail to realize that the director is not skilled in all areas. Unfortunately, a large number of organizations were forced to close and merge with other organizations in the past several years. Training could have been implemented in the earlier stages in order to correct these difficult challenges. It is important to understand that CE is key in order to refine and build new skills to tackle the day-to-day challenges. Recently, in 2015 the State of New York made CE part of the requirements for renewal of licensure (Office of Professions). This was a shock to many social workers in the field, creating an eye opener effect to view and reflect on the quality of the social work practice.

Intraprofessional Collaboration

We are currently working to create partnerships with local nonprofit organizations that need CE for their social workers and provide ongoing courses that fulfill the need of their population.

CHAPTER 27

Family Engagement and Social Work in Statutory Settings

Gale Burford

CHAPTER OBJECTIVES

The major objectives of this chapter are to:

- Identify and discuss the concepts, underlying principles, benefits, and challenges of using "whole-family" approaches in social work.
- Articulate and critique the theory and skills associated with family engagement as part of a human rights and social justice framework for social work practice in forensic settings.
- Describe and critique the ethical imperatives and evidence base supporting the use of family group decision making (FGDM) in regulatory settings.
- Engage whole families as partners in the use of FGDM in child protection and youth justice.

CHAPTER COMPETENCIES HIGHLIGHTED

- Competency 2: Engage Diversity and Difference in Practice
- Competency 3: Advance Human Rights and Social, Economic, and Environmental Justice
- Competency 6: Engage With Individuals, Families, Organizations, and Communities
- Competency 7: Assess Individuals, Families, Organizations, and Communities
- Competency 8: Intervene With Individuals, Families, Organizations, and Communities

The following is used by permission of its author; after reading a news report about a local jurisdiction's intentions to use whole-family engagement approaches in their child protection and youth justice work, this individual was moved to contact the author of this chapter and share her own family's experience with the power of the state:

> If you ever want to talk to someone who was put "in the system" at a young age inappropriately, I would be happy to share my story with you. My end result was what many would consider a success story but the beginning of the story and the state involvement was not exactly something the state would want to highlight on their website. . . . I was put into child protective custody around the age of 1 and stayed in foster care until I was adopted a bit before my 5th birthday. It was based around suspected child abuse because I was found to have 21 fractures all at once which were either healed, healing or fresh. I was diagnosed at age 19 with osteogenesis imperfecta which is also known as brittle bone disease. My 16-year-old bio mom didn't have a chance against the state even though all of

my fractures likely occurred from normal handling and care. . . . The connective disorder should have been identified back then and a lot of heartache all around would have likely been averted but, unfortunately, the fact that my bio mom was a teen mother and from a very low socio-economic [area in the region], I don't believe a lot of investigation occurred around what was really happening. Assumptions were made based on the situation which was very unfortunate. I'm fine as an adult emotionally over this but I am sorry for what my biological family must have gone through. . . . Because of my very young age, I don't remember any of this really and have learned the background from my parents and info I later received from my bio mom. Like I said, I don't feel like I am terribly emotionally scarred over this but I like to share the story with people who are going to be working "in the system" so they can hear about how, while there are often good intentions when a child is removed from a home, the consequences can certainly be far reaching.

Core Skills Addressed

Whole-Family Approaches in Statutory Settings

Community-centered family work can, and probably should, underwrite all integrated approaches to service design and delivery, but the ethical imperatives and empirical supports for the use of whole-family approaches are strongest in statutory settings whenever decisions have resulted or may result in the displacement or dissolution of families through the removal of their children or young people. This chapter describes how social workers practicing in statutory settings where the potential consequences of the misuse of power and privilege, and failure to build in safeguards against a single or dominant explanation, are so high that their actions must be held in check by nonstate actors and institutions including families and community leaders. It is in these settings where the expectations for professional knowledge and skill in the exercise of regulatory authority must be exemplary and enabling of safe and beneficial engagement with the family group in the practice of forensic social work. Such practice is consistent with the United Nations (UN) Convention on the Rights of the Child (1989), the UN Economic and Social Council Declaration on Basic Principles on the Use of Restorative Justice in Criminal Matters (UN Economic and Social Council, 2002) and in practice (UN Office on Drugs and Crime, 2006), and with the National Association of Social Workers (NASW) *Code of Ethics* (n.d.) since 1996.

As an example of a whole-family approach that has been used extensively in child protection and youth justice, the chapter describes the theory, empirical support, and skills in the use of family group decision making (FGDM), or family group conferencing (FGC) as it is often called (Burford & Hudson, 2000; Pennell & Anderson, 2005). FGDM, when used in statutory settings, can be understood as a service to social workers that helps them fulfill their commitments to provide safety interventions while protecting the rights of individuals and supporting the well-being of families and communities. This is consistent with the human rights and social justice underpinnings of social work (Maschi & Killian, 2011) and at the same time consistent with the principles of restorative justice and responsive regulation (J. Braithwaite, 2002, 2010; V. Braithwaite, 2006; V. Braithwaite & Harris, 2009; Harris, 2011; Ivec, Braithwaite, & Harris, 2012; Parker & Braithwaite, 2003), that is, the practice is organized around the statutory worker's role in "steering the flow of events" in the service of safety, accountability, empowerment, and healing. In this view, regulation works to be responsive to the needs of persons affected, restorative of harms that have occurred, while at the same time regulating harmful behavior. The aims of engaging with the whole family is to help preserve and strengthen linkages between children and their families, halt abusive or neglectful behavior, and build confidence in the legitimacy of the state and in social workers. The family group is given the opportunity for concerned members to demonstrate their concern for and connections to the children or young people. This is best done early in the process before or with the family's full knowledge of assessments, investigations being carried out to inform the professionals' decision process, and with a view to strengthening the relationships among people with enduring connections to the child or young person.

Ethical and Competence Standards

The removal of a child or young person from his or her family is one of the most far-reaching, intrusive, least transparent, and underresearched of the state's powers (Burns, Pösö, & Skivenes, 2017a; Križ, Free, & Kuehl, 2017). Attempts to build knowledge that would aid in reforms are all too often dismantled in the wake of a child's death or in the aftermath of some other heinous crime that harms children or victimizes members of the community. The ethos of blaming, avoidance, and risk aversion that so often emanates from most child death reviews, along with the refractory effect of the public through the media, typically results in increased workload for social workers, and the unleashing of retributive impacts that are felt most heavily on parents who live in poverty and with those who also face racial discrimination (H. Buckley & O'Nolan, 2014; Connolly & Doolan, 2007; Featherstone, Morris, & White, 2014; Morris & Burford, 2017; Rawlings et al., 2014; Roberts, 2001). Mimi Kim points out the dangers of what she calls "the dance of the carceral creep," which could be applied to any setting where helpers become overidentified with judicial and police roles, in which the mechanisms of co-optation transform efforts toward reform and incorporate them into the very mechanisms that hold the criminal justice response in place (Kim, 2014, 2015). Social workers practicing at the interface of the state's mandate to protect children and other vulnerable persons and communities must, like others working in positions of public trust, demonstrate the highest standards for ethical and competent regulatory practice. Speaking to members of all regulatory disciplines, Coglianese (2015) says this requires practitioners to demonstrate utmost integrity, stellar competence, and empathic engagement.

Ethics, according to Dee and Braithwaite (2016),

> . . . must be the very soul of any profession or discipline legally charged with carrying compliance management responsibilities to prevent the use of deception by people in finding ways around the spirit of the law and of course around the Golden Rule of behaving towards other people in accordance with your own expectations.

In statutory settings, this means adopting principle-driven, holistic, risk- and evidence-informed approaches to "whole-family" engagement that take into consideration the usual child's or young person's developmental capacities, identity, cultural connections, education, health, and rights to safety. It includes additionally recognizing the child or young person's right to have current and potential linkages with members of his or her network of kith and kin preserved and nurtured while at the same time honoring the families' right to be understood, engaged, and supported in making decisions and planning for the future of their children (Morris et al., 2007; Pennell, Burford, Morris, & Connolly, 2011; Tew, Morris, White, Featherstone, & Fenton, 2016). Reconciling human rights and social justice in this way means not only holding social workers and other members of the forensic team to the highest standards of commitment to the public trust and confidence, but also to demonstrated standards of competence in their investigations, assessments, engagement, and interventions. The consequences of failing to do so are well-documented in rates of foster and congregate care and a history of too many children with bleak prospects aging out of systems facing the possibility of incarceration upon their entry into adulthood.

Theoretical Basis for This Skill

Any account of social work's history of practice in statutory settings is obliged to acknowledge that the profession's commitments to empowerment, human rights, and social justice have too often been compromised by a range of legal–criminogenic and pathologizing conceptualizations of parents and families that prescribe the worker's role (Cohen, 2000; Featherstone et al., 2014; Gallagher, 1999; Morris & Burford, 2017; Roberts, 2001; Silver, 2015). In statutory settings for children, youth, and families, this has meant that social work has too often been captured by the very same institutionalized processes that reproduce discrimination and alienation, and nearly always yields high pressure on social workers' time and professional autonomy. This has contributed to the disproportionate involvement of poor families and families of color being the targets of investigation, intervention, and dissolution.

Social workers in forensic settings have been both supported by and trapped by the profession's traditional construction of a duality between social treatment and social control. While this opened space for exploration of working with the "involuntary client" (Trotter, 2008), too often the separation has undermined engaging families and communities, while fueling discourses that separate people into "victims" versus "perpetrators," privileges individualized casework with clients, and promotes atomization and competition for resources, which undermines family, community, and culture. The resulting unbalanced investment of resources contributes to the segregation of forensic social workers from their colleagues, leaving no one in a position of engaging with families, groups, and communities around their own definitions of their problems and needs. In practical terms, this has led in child protection and youth justice to caseworkers working almost exclusively with a parent, most often mothers, to the exclusion of other significant people in the child's life, especially fathers (Brown, Callahan, Strega, Dominelli, & Walmsley, 2009; Holland & O'Neill, 2006; Strega, Fleet, Brown, Callahan, & Walmsley, 2008), and to investing in highly expensive and time-consuming court processes. Faced with domestic violence services aligned with a criminal justice response, and a child protection service aligned with investigative and adversarial approaches of the court, women have been especially impacted in the cross-currents of domestic violence and child maltreatment investigations where the pressure, especially for poor and minority women, too often means not being able to trust that forensic social workers can help (Coker, 2002; Goodmark, 2004/2005, 2010, 2012; Huntington, 2014; Kim, 2010, 2014). Under these circumstances, the categorization of disproportionality and social exclusion as "unintended" consequences of institutionalized laws, policies, and practices is a "soft" way of continuing to defend the practices that yield these results.

Girded with the knowledge, values, and skills of "whole-family" approaches as they have been used to foster responsivity in the social worker's carrying out of his or her regulatory responsibilities, the forensic social worker can fulfill the requirements of ethical, legal, and evidence-informed practice, while ensuring that both family strengths and vulnerabilities are fully explored and brought to bear on decisions that meet the tests of fairness, equity, safety, and the law.

Whole-Family Approaches

Whole-family approaches embrace the central tenets of social group work and family group work that aim to help develop the group's sense of social responsibility and work to build individual and collective well-being through advancing genuine partnerships and employing democratic decision making (J. Braithwaite, 2002; Burford & Pennell, 2004; Macgowan & Pennell, 2001). They use a broad and flexible definition of family as a relational network that includes significant kin, kith, and others who have become "like family." Cornford, Baines, and Wilson (2013) and Tew et al. (2016) contrast them with other family approaches that predominantly take either an individual focus, or focus on a particular subset of relationships centering on a primary caregiver, usually the parent. Individualized approaches to family typically consult with other family members at the discretion of the professionals who approach them, often without face-to-face contact. Approaches that focus on a subset of family relationships—or, as Cornford et al. (2013) refer to them, "axial relationships," such as parent–child dyads—usually engage the parent or caregiver in his or her designated role. Like individualized approaches, an axial approach is seen to reproduce the isolating processes that exclude people from their natural and informal sources of support, even to the point of undercutting their efforts to help, especially in legal processes like family court (Huntington, 2014). Practically speaking, this has meant the exclusion of fathers and a wider circle of persons in the child or young person's life who are or could be part of the young person's lifelong connections. Too often this puts all the demands on mothers to do all the "work" associated with healing and having to prove their capabilities and commitment as a parent often in the face of unclear and changing expectations placed on them (Brown et al., 2009; Strega et al., 2008) in what amounts to tests of endurance.

Importantly, whole-family approaches aim to foster the working together of members of these relational networks with members of the forensic and professional service team. Many variations of family engagement approaches in child and family welfare can be found, especially in the United States (Crampton & Yoon, 2016; Merkel-Holguin, 2007; Nixon, Burford, Quinn, & Edelbaum, 2005); while they share some things in common (Burford & Hudson, 2000; Ivec, 2013; Vandivere & Malm, 2015), the main divergences include the extent to which they widen the circle of family beyond the parent and the extent to which family members are given support to work together. Programs that support the inclusion of fathers have increased greatly in the past decade but many of these efforts run parallel to the individualized and "axial" approaches, increasing contact between fathers and their children but not focusing on enlisting cooperation and engagement with the whole family. Reviews of family engagement practices reveal that the word *family* typically means working mainly with a parent (Holland & O'Neill, 2006; Merkel-Holguin & Wilmot, 2005; Perry, Yoo, Spoliansky, & Edelman, 2013) and family teams or wraps consisting of more professionals than family.

Whole-family approaches share in common with some other family and community approaches the aim to support a relational network that mobilizes around shared concerns and supporting them to harness their capacities in realizing goals that are meaningful to them (e.g., Roose, Roets, Van Houte, Vandenhole, & Reynaert, 2013; Turnell & Edwards, 1997, 1999; van Wormer, 2013; Waldegrave, 2000; narrative approaches that emphasize community and family, e.g., E. Buckley & Decter, 2006). These approaches recognize that all family members need to be seen as people in their own right and that each has multiple roles and relationships inside and outside the family. They share the aim to be collaborative; to embrace nonpathologizing, strengths-based language in their approaches; and work to position people as having expertise on their own lives. This includes considerations of culture, gender, social, spiritual, economic, and psychological dynamics associated with capacity building within the relational network of the family and community. Whole-family approaches embrace the "no wrong door" principle, meaning that regardless of the source of the referral, the focus can better be maintained on solutions than on the interventions that any one agency or service would provide on their own. Coupled with the principles of responsive regulation (Adams & Chandler, 2004; J. Braithwaite, 2002, 2010; V. Braithwaite, 2006; V. Braithwaite & Harris, 2009; Burford & Adams, 2004; Crampton, 2004; Pennell, 2004), whole-family approaches in forensic settings are offered as an important way that social workers can stay true to their ethical obligations to honor the dignity and self-determination of their clients while fulfilling their obligations to use the full force of the law when necessary to protect children or the community.

Too often social workers in forensic settings are put in the position where they understand the work of assessment and engagement as only gathering information *from* the family in order to develop intervention plans *for* them and their individual members (Mezey & Sanford, 2009). Berrick (2011) and Berrick, Dickens, Pösö, and Skivenes (2016) point to this as an important difference in the conceptualization of assessment when comparing practice in countries with a strong tradition of family support where assessment more often connotes giving people information they need to make choices and decisions versus jurisdictions like the United States where assessment leans toward gathering information from the clients to enable the professionals to create a plan. Whole-family social work is aligned with an integrated family services model of delivery and requires a shift to partnership and interagency practice away from the traditional emphasis on isolated casework investigations and closed-door worker–supervisor decision making.

Forensic Social Work as Responsive Regulation

Family engagement in these settings focuses on key decision points and processes that can, without checks and balances, be one-way gates drawing families further into the system through professional and legally dominated investigations and assessments. Whether or not to substantiate an allegation of abuse or neglect, whether to place or hold a child or young person in a setting outside his or her family, who should be included or excluded in the decision-making processes, including in court, are all junctures at which the family can be engaged, along with other important assessments, to achieve better, more well-informed decisions. It is at these important junctures that systematic bias, especially by race and ethnicity and poverty, allows for judgments to exclude or subordinate the views and experiences of the people who are the subjects of the decisions. Whole-family approaches are designed to bring a balance of voices, considerations, and multiple viewpoints to the table.

Family Group Conferencing

FGC is an example of a whole-family approach that has been used extensively in child protection and youth justice matters including when domestic violence is involved. First legislated into practice in New Zealand in 1989 (Children Young Persons and Their Families Act, 1989), largely as a result of a renaissance among the indigenous people of New Zealand to reclaim language and assert land rights, FGC challenged the practices and impacts of national child protection and youth justice interventions on families (New Zealand Department of Social Welfare, 1989; Rangihau, 1986). One intention of the law was to reduce the disproportionate removal of Maori children and young people from their families by drawing from Maori traditions of *whanau*, or extended-family, decision making. Importantly, the law was implemented for use with all families involved with child protection and youth justice and not just Maori. Without diminishing the significance of Maori leadership, or the magnitude of the achievement, the acceptability of the effort to the New Zealand government at the time can also be understood as part of worldwide efforts including the mobilization of the International Children's Rights Movement that resulted in the 1989 signing of the UN Convention on the Rights of the Child (1989). Efforts to bring the family back to the foreground of decision making was being seeded at that time in many countries and jurisdictions along with acknowledgment of the genocidal impact of state interventionist policies, especially on indigenous populations. The New Zealand legislation and leadership has had a profound impact on practices worldwide, although in its movement to other countries, with important exceptions, the FGC has been used more often as a professional tool (Nixon et al., 2005), and compared in research with other treatment interventions, than as a set of principles aimed to empower families. The experience in New Zealand is both a beacon and a reminder that legislation alone is insufficient to counterbalance the creep of economic and professional intervention into the lives of families (Hyslop, 2016).

The law in New Zealand set out the principles and processes requiring that an independent coordinator be responsible for convening a meeting of the family group with agency personnel. The state was required to allow adequate authority and time, and to allocate resources to the family group, including giving the extended-family group an opportunity to work through allegations or concerns raised by the state, and to process information offered to them about why intervention was thought to be necessary. Moreover, the family was to be given the opportunity to caucus on their own in the creation of a plan without professionals in the room, and the state was obliged to give preference to the family's plan of action whenever that plan was seen to meet the concerns that had brought the state into their lives. The architects of the law were very aware of the way structural inequality adapts and reproduces itself, particularly in the form of discrimination. This led to efforts to build the design measures, such as careful and inclusive preparation, as well as the "private time," with the full knowledge that vigilance would be required to balance the "creep" professional and legal power. FGC does not downplay the crucial role of the state's responsibility to regulate the protection of children and communities nor does it turn decision making over to families without oversight as some critics of the approach have argued. The state holds the final say over the approval of plans and maintains its regulatory role. The practice and research on the use of FGC opens pathways for bridges to be built between forensic social workers and others involved with the families and communities of children and young people sharing as it does the principles of responsivity in carrying out regulatory obligations (J. Braithwaite, 2002; V. Braithwaite & Harris, 2009; Burford & Adams, 2004; Crampton, 2004; Pennell, 2004, 2017; Tyler, 2011). Responsive regulation is relational practice (Lewellyn & Downie, 2011), meaning that assessments, support, and enforcement are carried out though relationships of people who hold the person or persons most in need of protection or support, or in need of change, closest and draws on their influence and commitments to work together and with the regulator as allies. The notion of a regulatory pyramid (J. Braithwaite, 2002) puts both support and sanctions at the center of the partnership.

FGC involves engaging with multiple stakeholders to enlist cooperation in making the long-lasting choices that go along with the necessity of having to step into a family's life with the strength of the power of the state behind them.

Empirical Evidence of Effectiveness of FGC. There are few large, randomized trials or otherwise high-quality studies without serious flaws that compare FGDM with traditional approaches that do not incorporate some of the same principles as FGC. This means that most attempts to statistically aggregate findings across studies have found that including families shows no or few differences from approaches that do not include families. Instead of reporting this as a good reason to give families the right to participate, however, these researchers are concerned only with treatment outcomes (e.g., Dijkstra et al., 2016), and not with the outcomes for which family inclusion was intended, that is, to recognize the rights of families and young people to have a say in important matters that impact their lives. Other researchers acknowledge that there are as yet too few studies to complete such analysis (Shlonsky et al., 2009, Shlonsky & Mildon, 2017)) and have acknowledged at the same time the importance of taking into account qualitative research findings (Saini & Shlonsky, 2012) and at carefully looking to learn what works, the conditions under which they work (J. Braithwaite, 2002), and the model fidelity required to reproduce outcomes (Rauktis, Bishop-Fitzpatrick, Jung, & Pennell, 2013). A considerable body of literature on practice and numerous process and outcome studies have been carried out internationally. Importantly, the reasons given most often for not including families in decision making— that is, concerns that family will not come when invited, cannot meet and make plans in safety, and do not follow through—have been repeatedly shown as unfounded. No good reasons for excluding family have been substantiated, but the evidence of the consequences for their continued exclusion is considerable. The more important question is: Why is the research default in child welfare and youth justice set for exclusion? Studies, reviews of studies, and critiques of the studies are widely available on this highly researched practice (e.g., Crampton, 2007; Fisher & Marsh, 2015; Havnen & Christiansen, 2014; Holland & O'Neill, 2016; Kanyi, 2013; LaBrenz & Fong, 2016; McCrae & Fusco, 2010; Merkel-Holguin, Nixon, & Burford, 2003; Rogers & Cahn, 2010; Sheets et al., 2009; Weigensberg, Barth, & Guo, 2009). In general, international results are consistent that in most cases extended family and those "like family" can be located; are willing to come when invited or to ensure that their views are represented in some meaningful way; are willing to contribute ideas and shape the plans at meetings; engage constructively in the creation and approval of plans; meet with each other and the professionals in safety; contribute resources, including homes to the plans; develop positive family–agency working relationships; and result in greater trust in the family network and culture on the part of the public agency. Typical outcomes for children and young people include: reduce the use, and costs, of adversarial court hearings and out-of-family and congregate care; keep or quickly return children with family, siblings, or kin; and increased use of kin placement. Some studies show a decrease but not elimination in disproportional minority placements. Other studies have shown increased trust in the family network and culture on the part of statutory agencies, reduced child problems, improved parenting, improved child development, less anxiety, and better adjustment to care. While one study in Sweden showed an increase of reinvolvement of child protection for children after a family group conference, no other studies have shown this, and no studies indicate an increase in youthful offending after FGC; however, several studies show decreases in reoffending. Increased involvement of fathers and paternal relatives and high satisfaction from family and professionals are widely reported with indications that needed services are arranged faster when a family group conference has been held and children's connections to their families, communities, schools, and culture can be leveraged though this kind of engagement with the whole family. Protocols for use of FGC in situations involving child maltreatment and domestic violence have been developed and trialed extensively (Burford & Pennell, 1998; Pennell & Francis, 2005). Results of family, youth, and professional satisfaction reports show high levels of satisfaction with family group conferences on the part of young people, families, and professionals.

The role of the forensic social worker, and other members of the team representing the statutory interests of the state, work to help the family decide what needs to happen while taking reasonable measures consistent with the assessed best interests, risk, and needs assessments to work safely and appropriately while decisions are being made. The meeting facilitator or coordinator is usually from an independent service. This individual does the necessary preparations with the family and others who will attend—doing this as early as possible when it is first clear that a child or young person could be or has been taken into a care or custody arrangement. Other critical junctures where the offer of a family group conference should be made as a matter of right to the young person and family include when a child who has been taken into custody for his or her own protection is charged for an offense that arises when in custody and at each point in time when a case review is mandatory or a placement move is being contemplated. A great deal has been written in recent years about the so-called "cross-over" youth or dual jurisdiction youth (Burford, 2005; Pennell, Shapiro, & Spigner, 2011) and the particular challenges in accomplishing coordinated work under these circumstances where matters can rapidly escalate into higher and more punishing consequences for the young person and the family in the midst of jurisdictional disputes. A range of positive outcomes with youth in conflict with the law have been demonstrated with FGC including some studies that show reduced recidivism and high satisfaction with the process and outcomes on the part of crime victims, young people, and their families. Importantly, the practice is associated with greatly reduced use of court and congregate care for young people (Bergseth & Bouffard, 2007, 2012; Bradshaw & Roseborough, 2005; Jeong, McGarrell, & Hipple, 2012; Maxwell, Kingi, Robertson, & Morris, 2004).

The forensic worker and the coordinator need to develop a working alliance in which they sort out roles and responsibilities, as well as share information that is pertinent to helping the family come together and to communicate important information about the coordinator's own safety that may be pertinent to their setting up a positive meeting. These conversations must attend to the "nothing about them without them" ethic to avoid triangulating the coordinator into precooked ideas about the family that would undermine their ability to present themselves as genuinely open to helping the family put their best foot forward.

Among the challenges in the use of FGC is the need for social workers to be skilled and comfortable with: (a) working in settings where they have a statutory responsibility to represent the state in both regulating and helping their clients, and (b) working in settings with the family group, and in being undermined, as is much social work practice in statutory settings, by economic pressures (Featherstone et al., 2013).

How to Apply This Skill

Case Selection and Referral. The social worker's role revolves around engaging the family and setting out the reasons for a referral by clarifying the concerns and engaging with an independent coordinator who will help the family organize their meeting, work with the coordinator to set dates, work to put on pause any other proceedings that might usurp the family's confidence in the process, provide information at the conference to the family at the meeting about their concerns, and to be clear about anything that would have to be addressed in the plan to gain approval. When a family group conference is being organized around child protection issues including safety, permanency, and well-being issues, it is most often the social worker who introduces the idea of a family group conference to the family, usually to the parents or other primary caretaker, and explains what a family group conference is and why he or she thinks it would be a good idea. This need not be so in systems where FGC is offered universally and as a matter of right, in which case families or others involved with the family might initiate the referral. In any case, if any significant members of the child's family agree that the state's concerns are valid and they are willing to work together to keep the child safe, then a referral can be made to an independent coordinator or facilitator. This may not always be the parent. Sometimes a parent is incapacitated or so opposed to his or her family being involved that the social worker, in consultation, may choose to go around the parent to find out who in the family is willing to work. This is especially important if a child has been or is possibly going to be removed. It is in the best interest of the child, or in places where the child's rights are acknowledged, for these connections to be fully explored before decisions are taken. Sometimes when the tensions are so high between the family and the state, a coordinator can be asked to contact them to explain the benefits of an FGC in their situation and to help them understand the options and possible consequences for the child if there is no one able or willing to work with the state. Social workers do not give up their forensic/ statutory responsibilities in this moment; they are allowing for a third party to help the family understand that the state is serious in wanting the family to be involved. These can be particularly stressful moments for families, especially when their child has been put into protective custody or other immediate measures have been taken because the state has reason to believe the parent or caretaker is not doing a good enough job at the moment. In many systems, mediation can be offered to bring people together who are able to put the interests of the child at the center and avoid unnecessary delays that often cause children to languish in care with all the known challenges that accumulate when professionals and family members harden up their positions while not talking with each other.

The social workers' skills in communicating these concerns to families is intricately bound up with their ability to be respectful and clear and to weave into their assessment plenty of opportunity for the parent and other family members to acknowledge their view of the problem(s), to talk about what they have already done, and to determine what has proven to help—and what has not helped—without losing sight of the reasons that brought them into involvement on behalf of the child.

The forensic social worker will offer and sustain offers of working alongside families with the message that he or she is willing to listen and learn from them, to understand their hopes for their whole family and their ideas about what needs to be done to realize positive outcomes. This typically means beginning with the generous use of open, genuinely curious questions that help the family to be understood in their context as a family by asking what they hope for as an outcome for their child or young person. The forensic social worker is adept at spotting and sidestepping provocations and power struggles whenever possible, knowing that referral to a third party, such as the use of an FGC, is often the best way to stay focused on the issues. This means developing a keen sense of knowing when to push, when to persuade, and when to go around the edges.

The worker needs to learn about and be sensitive to other legal processes that may sabotage the family's full engagement and, whenever possible, find out if these other processes can be put on "hold" to give them the time to organize around the people they think are most important to be part of the process. The worker will normally consult with at least one family member about the referral and what this means, and often will meet with that family member and the person who will help the family plan the family group conference to introduce them and hand over the work of taking the planning forward.

Attending the Conference. The social worker comes to the meeting with a straightforward, clear, nonjargonized statement that he or she will present near the opening of the meeting describing the purpose of the referral. Even though the worker has already said this to some family members during the referral, and the reasons have been repeated by the coordinator, the impact of the worker giving this statement to the assembled group is based on a principle well understood in group and family work. Done well, this brings into the open, in the group, the shared purpose and invites members to engage face to face. The skilled worker will take care to be clear, positive, and work to ensure that he or she is not putting any "surprises" out that would undermine confidence and trust building with family and nonfamily who will need to work cooperatively. At the same time, the worker leaves room for questions and clarification. It requires considerable skill and practice on the part of the social worker to be clear without going into more detail than necessary, as well as to leave people wondering what has really happened. The following is lifted from a social worker's presentation at the opening of an FGC meeting for 15-year-old Julie, who had been taken into foster care. Importantly, it was the social worker's first attendance at a family meeting and he was understandably nervous, so he wrote out his message but with practice was able to deliver it at the meeting without sounding like he was reading or talking "at" the group. Also important was the fact that he had rehearsed his statement with Julie so that she would know what was going to be said and what she wanted to say. The meeting facilitator, Julie, and the other family members and professionals present later reported they thought that the way the worker spoke and the messages he gave were crucial to them being able to work together to come up with a plan:

> Julie was removed from the family home when it was alleged that her step-father, Don, raped and physically abused her. Don is accused of punishing Julie for coming home late by whipping her with a length of garden hose, forcing her to strip off her clothing so he could examine the bruises, and forcing her to have sexual intercourse with him. The investigators believe this is true and we have substantiated the allegation. The police and prosecutor have filed criminal charges which Don has denied. Julie wants to leave the foster home and live with her family. We find Julie to be a resilient and courageous teenager and we want to respect her wishes. However, we would not approve of any placement in which Don, or his brother Jim, who is a convicted pedophile, would have unsupervised access to Julie. Julie is afraid that her family will blame her for breaking up the family by telling the police and social workers what was happening. We need to know from the family whether Julie can be kept safe within the family, and if so how, and at the same time get the help she needs to deal with the abuse she has experienced.

Youth Justice Family Group Conferences. In cases where the FGC is being held for a young person who has violated the law, the conference is attended by the:

- Young person
- Young person's family and other invited community members
- The person or persons who have been harmed by the young person's behavior
- The meeting coordinator or facilitator
- Police or other investigative personnel
- Young person's lawyer and/or guardian ad litem
- A social worker
- Other professionals, for example, health and education

The purposes of the FGC in youth justice include involving the persons who have been harmed in shaping outcomes that will address the harms that have occurred to them, to hold the young person accountable for his or her behavior, and to support the family in managing the young person's behavior and get needed services. The young person must be willing to admit to the offense and to describe what he or she did and was thinking at the time, and to respectfully listen to what others have to say. The persons who have been harmed and the young person and their family members are given considerable preparation for the meeting. If the person who has been harmed is willing to attend, he or she is asked to tell others what happened, how he or she has been affected, and to ask questions of or confront the young person. For those who have been harmed, attendance is entirely voluntary, but whether they attend or not, they are asked to say what they want, if anything, by way of reparation or repair for the harm caused, and if they do not attend they are asked whether they want to be kept informed about what happens.

Making the Plan and Reporting Out the Results For Follow-Up

After the family has been given an opportunity to have time on their own to consider what has been said and to come up with a plan, the social worker or others who have been involved in making the referral are invited back into the meeting to hear, negotiate, and approve the details of the plan. In the case of a youth justice FGC, the persons who have been harmed, if they have been willing to wait while the family came up with the plan, are invited into the meeting. Since transparency, clarity, and respect guide the entire process, the worker's written report must be jargon-free, clear and understandable, and available in the family's first language. It should contain no surprises or new information that had not been introduced. It should include a summary of the reason for the referral for a family conference, the main concerns or allegations, and center on the needs of the child or young person, identify substantive strengths that have been demonstrated over time, and focus on what has been agreed to and the specifics of what the family says they need to fully realize the plan. Final approval of the plans come from referring workers and the persons harmed in the case of a youth justice FGC.

Case Example and Application

Fifteen-year-old Bradley was turned in to police by a couple who picked him up hitchhiking in a rural part of the state. Bradley had run away from a residential group placement some 150 miles to the south, thereby violating a placement order and the terms of a probation order for a charge of damage to property at a foster home. He was headed to visit his aunt and uncle. A nearby abandoned and wrecked car was later revealed to be stolen in another state. Bradley admitted to having received the car from two men who picked him up near the residential group placement and dropped him and the car off in a city some 80 miles away, saying that Bradley would be doing them a favor to get the car out of the city. Bradley admitted to knowing the car was probably stolen, driving without a license, causing damage to the vehicle, and leaving the residential group placement without permission.

A review of the case indicated that Bradley had been taken into state's custody for his own protection at the age of 12 when neighbors reported seeing his father assault him. Bradley established a pattern of leaving foster homes without permission, refusing to go to school, and recently uttering threats to a mental health worker. This was the first time Bradley had incurred charges other than violating the terms of his probation. Bradley's mother's parental rights had been terminated when he was 13 as she had been substantiated for failure to protect her son from his abusive father. She left the family home for her own protection just prior to the incident that brought Bradley into care despite the existence of a restraining order that her husband was not to be living in the house. There was a large extended family in the state and it was to a particular paternal aunt and uncle's farm in a northerly rural part of the state that Bradley always ran.

Investigation revealed that Bradley's version of events was consistent with the facts. He could not have been present when the car had been stolen and Bradley cooperated with police in describing the two men who had left him and the car at an all-night coffee shop, making him wait in the car while they unloaded the trunk. Bradley said one of the men told him that if he knew what was good for him he would either drive the car away or walk in the other direction.

The owner of the car in a neighboring state was willing to engage in a restorative family group conference to try and settle the matter of the damages to the car, though it was clear from the beginning that she hoped Bradley knew more about the laptop, camera, cell phone, and papers that were in the car at the time it was stolen.

(continued)

Case Example and Application (*continued*)

Bradley's probation worker and the arresting officer referred the matter to a community-based restorative justice center. The owner of the car volunteered to come from out of state and a family group conference was held near Bradley's aunt and uncle's home. The conference consisted of two parts. In the first, the allegations were read out by the arresting officer and by Bradley's probation worker, after which he acknowledged what he had done, what he was thinking at the time, and how he thought it impacted the owner of the car and everyone else involved. The owner of the car, her grown daughter, and her daughter-in law who accompanied her to the meeting were given time to describe the impact on them and to ask Bradley questions. The owner of the car was particularly interested in what Bradley had seen in the car that might indicate the fate of her missing items, in particular, a stack of manila-type folders. Bradley's revelation at the meeting that he saw one of the men reading through something in the front of the car that looked like what the owner was describing was described later as an important moment in the conference. It was then the owner of the car revealed that the laptop, camera, and folders contained photos and personal identifying information of people she had photographed in her work as a photographer, including children, and said how afraid she was for their safety and for her reputation as a photographer. It was then that the true extent of the impact settled over the group. She blamed herself for leaving the keys in the ignition of her car while running into the house to get something. She admitted to feeling used by the prosecutor in her home jurisdiction for what she thought was more about publicity than her incident, and she was afraid of having to give testimony now that one of the men had been arrested and identified by Bradley. Bradley admitted that he was certain the car was stolen when he was first picked up and that there had been opportunities for him to alert police without danger to himself. Aside from Bradley, the car owner and her two family members, the arresting officer, and the probation worker, this part of the family group conference was attended by Bradley's aunt and uncle, an older half-sibling, two grown cousins (one of whom brought along his wife), and the couple who had picked Bradley up while hitchhiking. They had offered to help since they lived in the same area and knew the family by name. The plan included that Bradley was to pay the insurance deductible on the damage to the car, a plan made possible by the couple who had picked Bradley up hitchhiking, offering him a part-time job on their farm when he could return to the area. A payment schedule was set in place. Bradley's cooperation in identifying the car thieves was noted but his having accepted stolen property, having driven without a license, and having driven under the influence—as one of the men had given him a joint of marijuana as they left the car—and his failure to take timely action that might have helped the owner get her property back were all identified as contributing to the harm and potential harm of himself and others. One of Bradley's cousins and the car owner's daughter-in-law thought Bradley should be forced to go back to the residential center to "do time for the crime" and his counselor wanted him to be required to attend counseling sessions regularly. The matter was closed when the car owner said she would like Bradley to write a regular diary of what he is doing to take responsibility for his life and to send the entries in letters to her once a month for the next year. She said she did not think more punishment or keeping him away from his family was going to help. She said to Bradley "You are not a criminal. You are a boy. And you did something really stupid. When you have a chance to help someone you should do that." She wanted him to write an anonymous letter to her local newspaper where fear over the car theft and recent drug dealing had given her a celebrity status that she did not want. An article had appeared saying a "teen" from Bradley's state had allegedly stolen the car and was involved in drug dealing. She asked him to tell the prosecutor what had really happened.

(*continued*)

Case Example and Application (*continued*)

The second part of the family group conference was to review Bradley's case plan and make revisions that would create placement stability, get him reengaged with school, and strengthen his relationships with family. Ordinarily, nonfamily victims of crime do not stay for a family group conference, but the car owner said she knew the group was going to continue to meet and wanted to know if she could help. Bradley asked her and her family members to stay. In addition, the preparation by the coordinator with Bradley's and the probation worker's assistance resulted in Bradley's mother and his maternal grandmother, at Bradley's request, joining the group, along with the vice principal of the school that Bradley would have been attending if he had not been moved away from the area when he was first placed in foster care and in subsequent placements, a supervisor from child protection services, a counselor from the residential group center, and two other half-siblings who had both aged out of foster care. What surfaced during the preparation for this meeting and during the meeting was a long history of the family's unhappiness and anger at the state for having shut them out of discussions when Bradley was first taken into care. Postconference interviews with Bradley's aunt and with Bradley and postmeeting evaluation documents are well summarized in the aunt's interview: "You're saying that you took him [into custody of the state] because he needed to be protected and cared for but yet you're keeping him from family that loves him and actually disconnecting him from our family."

And that had been going on since he had first been taken into custody:

We lost contact with Bradley because every time his mother or father would do something wrong that would keep him . . . they would end visits and then none of us got to see him . . . and we felt like we were being punished, that he was literally ripped out of the family and you know . . . because even if there is a dangerous situation with one of the parents it doesn't mean that the outside family doesn't want to be a part of that child's life. . . . It was hard when he would come visit because it was just like he was a stranger in the home and he didn't feel comfortable, you know. You'd see him . . . you know, we'd be lucky to see him at Christmastime or something like that, and then we wouldn't see him again for a year. You know? . . . Because a lot of these kids are taken into protective custody for their own protection but they don't realize that when you rip them from their whole roots their whole family system that feels like they're being punished for something again over. . . . It tore my heart out to watch Bradley being totally detached from the family and there was nothing I could do about it personally . . . they were bouncing him from one place to another . . . the thing that upset me the most is that he was taken into custody because [of what his father did] and yet it was like he was being punished this whole time for it . . . any time I would hear that he was acting out would be when they would punish him from coming up to see us . . . so I would rebel too . . . felt terrible when I'd see him so withdrawn from family he doesn't understand where he fits any more . . . there was other family out there that wanted him and was willing to open their doors . . . [they] are saying that [they] took him because he needed to be protected and cared for but yet you're keeping him from family that loves him and actually disconnecting him from our family.

Bradley wanted to move from the residential center but he knew it was a great stress on space and finances for his aunt and uncle to take him in despite their saying they wanted him. A plan was developed that called for Bradley to move in with his aunt and uncle and spend two weekends per month, starting with a weekend with the couple who had picked him up hitchhiking who had been vetted as possible foster parents during the preparation time for the conference, and another weekend with a cousin and his wife who were both at the conference. Bradley wanted the family to help his mother find adequate housing, and he wanted to be able to visit with her whenever he wanted. No one was agreeable to the idea of Bradley seeing his mother whenever and wherever he wanted and asked him to start off more slowly with a family member organizing and being present for the meetings, at least until his

(*continued*)

Case Example and Application (*continued*)

mother's situation was more stable. No one in the family was in a position to take his mother in to live unless she would agree to regular involvement in a mental health support group and would let someone from the family be involved in regular communications with helping her to manage her medications. Bradley and his mother agreed and an initial schedule of regular visits was set up. His mother was grateful and agreeable and thanked her own mother and other family members for offering to help. She wanted to help "undo" some of the damage she had caused for Bradley and the family. Bradley said he would attend school and agreed that he would need to spend time with two teachers who had raised concerns about his return to the school. Family members offered to take part in a meeting at the school to show that they were willing to help. The vice principal's recommendation that it would be good to follow up the family group conference with a meeting to update an individualized education plan was taken as a positive signal that the school would work with Bradley. The owner of the car and her daughter offered to be part of follow-up discussions that would support Bradley in succeeding to reengage with family and school life.

Conclusion

Social work jobs in statutory settings have traditionally exposed social workers to a great deal of talking "about" families, far less often engaging with the family group or other groups comprising mainly service users as an ongoing part of their assessments and interventions. Research has shown that while giving high approval to the concept of empowerment and to the human rights and social justice underpinnings of family and group work, practices of social workers have tended to be far more aligned to whatever dominant legal, policy, and organizational drivers prevail at any given time.

When workers are able and supported to use strategies that put the problem at the center of the circle, and resourced to engage the relational network of family, assessments and interventions are more fully informed and, as so many evaluations reveal, feel more like the kind of social work that social workers signed on for when they came into the profession. The argument that family and relational engagement in regulation is too high of an investment to make when the stakes are as high as the removal of a child from a family is untenable in the face of evidence of the consequences. There is every reason to engage the family early and persistently in the process, backed up with robust and responsive regulatory engagement. Of course, the argument that every delay in creating safety and permanence in a child's life, or that delays in holding young people accountable for their illegal behavior, has consequences needs to be taken seriously. Waiting to engage the family after a child has languished in foster care or has moved through multiple settings is too often used by professionals as giving things "time to cool off" with the family. Such arguments should be seen as a violation of the child's and family's rights to timely conclusion of matters. There is no reason not to invite legal counsel into the process as long as they are committed to seeing that the family has a genuine opportunity to step up to the plate; it may be the only way in the long run to bring in support from the legal community for such practices. The role of the court and other legal counsel is to help safeguard the principles of engaging the family including working together to help put on "pause" other proceedings that may undermine the legitimacy and timeliness of the engagement, including being clear on how matters of new disclosures of abuses and crimes will be handled so that the family can be encouraged to engage in truth-telling, trust building, and given space to nurture their hopes for the child or young person. Social workers must be skilled at helping calm knee-jerk reactions from other professionals who do not have experience or are uncomfortable participating in family meetings, circles, and other restorative approaches. Research indicates that participating in group and family processes is one of the best, if not the best, ways to help people build their own emotional intelligence and prepare for careers where group and family engagement is the norm.

Decision-making approaches in statutory settings must be weighed carefully against the well-known consequences of allowing short-term, risk averse, legal, economic, and discipline-specific imperatives to drive the time frames and protocols without widening the circle to include affected and concerned persons in the deliberations. Given the state of the "evidence" of the known consequences, it seems disingenuous at best to defend taking short cuts at the forensic stage of the process. The biggest and most costly delays in these matters occur once the legal processes kick in. Given the ethical and competency obligations that professional social workers have, along with the growing evidence of positive practice outcomes, forensic social workers are best positioned to ensure access for families to be involved while demonstrating high levels of skill in aligning with the laws of the land.

At the same time, family and group work, especially in forensic settings, may not be every social worker's cup of tea, yet it is clear that the profession's commitment to human rights and social justice means recommitting ourselves to working with families at "all levels" when a balance between the power of the state and the power of the citizenry is called for.

This chapter closes with an example of how alert forensic social workers must be to the potential for their best intentions to collide with the tenets of responsive practice and a quote from a child protection social worker who worked closely with the author on a pilot project using FGC. The vigilance needed on the part of social workers in any setting where oversight and safeguarding of people's rights is required by law is evidenced in the following excerpt from an interview with a tribal consultant who was invited to a meeting with professionals, the purpose of which was to plan for a "whole-family meeting" for a teen. Without any family members present, his worst fears were confirmed that the outcomes for the meeting, and the way the family was perceived, were being prefigured while they talked "about" the family without them:

> It was never more apparent to me than when I sat down at a planning meeting for [restorative session for a teen with local tribal connections]. I acted as the liaison between tribal council, [the treatment service], and [state social worker]. This was supposed to be progressive, right? When [representatives from the treatment service] identified who the parents were, I watched [the state social worker] draw a family tree [genogram] FROM MEMORY back to the great grandparents. FROM MEMORY, four generations of her [tribal] family tree. One would not acquire that skill without great exposure to the topic. That one act, that one thing I witnessed [explained to me the tribe's] over representation [of children taken into state custody]. I didn't need to see any more as a sign. It was supposed to be progressive. And I'm not casting judgment on their intent. They may have the best of intentions. That said, how many OTHER, non- [tribal] families could [the worker] have done that same thing with? Know what I'm getting at?

And finally, a quote from a child protection caseworker reflecting with researchers (Burford & Pennell, 1998) on his experiences with engaging families in FGC: "You know, if this was going to be the way we worked in the future, I'd have to become some kind of community worker." Practicing social work in statutory settings puts to the test social work's commitment to empowerment, human rights, and social justice. Rather than stepping back from those commitments, social work would do well to recommit to the principles of group, family, and community work, and reimagine its role in settings where the power of the state is so formidable as in child protection and youth justice.

CHAPTER EXERCISES

Exercise 1. This exercise requires preparation by the instructor to let the students know the example involves domestic violence. Instructions: Imagine that a close friend or relative of yours has asked you to attend a meeting with her and a social worker. You are being invited as part of her (choose a role that best fits for you) family or close friend network to help decide what is best for her child. Your friend/family member's child was removed to a foster home a few days ago because your friend/family member has continued to have contact with someone who has assaulted her repeatedly in front of the child. In groups of 3, each of you please address the following questions: Would you be likely to attend such a meeting? Why or why not? What are your first thoughts? What preparation do you think you, or most people, would need to attend such a meeting? Finally, what skills would you expect the social worker in such a meeting to demonstrate? What would you be looking for in that person? What other questions would be useful for your group to address or ask the rest of the class?

Exercise 2. Thinking about the quote by Mimi Kim in the chapter, about carceral creep, what do you imagine are the main implications for educating social workers for practice in using FGC in a forensic setting? What would be the implication for law, policy, and the allocation of resources?

Additional Resources

California Evidence-based Clearinghouse for Child Welfare, Family Group Decision Making: www .cebc4cw.org/program/family-group-decision-making

Child Welfare Information Gateway, Family engagement: Partnering with families to improve child welfare outcomes: www.childwelfare.gov/pubs/f-fam-engagement

Child Welfare Information Gateway, Working with families involved with child protective services: www.childwelfare.gov/topics/responding/child-protection/working-with-families-involved -with-child-protective-services

Family Group Decision Making Manual for Coordinators and Communities: www.ucdenver.edu/ academics/colleges/medicalschool/departments/pediatrics/subs/can/FGDM/Documents/ FGDM%20Web%20Pages/Resources/Tools/FGDM%20Coordinators%20Manual%20frnt.pdf

Handbook on Restorative Justice Programs: www.unodc.org/pdf/criminal_justice/06-56290_Ebook .pdf

National Center on Family Group Decision Making: www.ucdenver.edu/academics/colleges/ medicalschool/departments/pediatrics/subs/can/FGDM/Pages/FGDM.aspx

U.S. Department of Health and Human Services, Administration for Children & Families, Children's Bureau, Child Welfare Information Gateway: www.childwelfare.gov/FEI/program-strategies

References

Adams, P., & Chandler, S. M. (2004). Responsive regulation in child welfare: Systematic challenges to mainstreaming the family group conference. *Journal of Sociology and Social Welfare, 31*(1), 93–116.

Bergseth, K. J., & Bouffard, J. A. (2007). The long-term impact of restorative justice programming for juvenile offenders. *Journal of Criminal Justice, 35,* 433–451.

Bergseth, K. J., & Bouffard, J. A. (2012). Examining the effectiveness of a restorative justice program for various types of juvenile offenders. *International Journal of Offender Therapy and Comparative Criminology, 57,* 1054–1075.

Berrick, J. (2011). *Trends in the U.S. Child Welfare System.* In N. Gilbert, N. Parton, & M. Skivenes (Eds.), *Child protection systems: International trends and orientations* (pp. 17–36). New York, NY: Oxford University Press.

Berrick, J., Dickens, J., Pösö, T., & Skivenes, M. (2016). Parents' involvement in care order decisions: A cross-country study of front-line practice. *Child & Family Social Work.* doi:10.1111/cfs.12277

Bradshaw, W., & Roseborough, D. (2005). An empirical review of family group conferencing in juvenile offenses. *Juvenile and Family Court Journal, 56*(4), 21–28.

Braithwaite, J. (2002). *Restorative justice and responsive regulation.* New York, NY: Oxford University Press.

Braithwaite, J. (2010). *The essence of responsive regulation.* University of British Columbia, Fasken Lecture. Retrieved from https://www.anu.edu.au/fellows/jbraithwaite/_documents/Articles/essence _responsive_regulation.pdf

Braithwaite, V. (2006). *Ten things you need to know about regulation but never wanted to ask.* Canberra, Australia: Regulatory Institutions Network, Australian National University, Occasional Paper #10. Retrieved from http://regnet.anu.edu.au/sites/default/files/publications/attachments/2015 -07/10thingswhole.pdf

Braithwaite, V., & Harris, N. (2009). Seeking to clarify child protection's regulatory principles. *Communities, Children and Families Australia, 41*(1), 5–21.

Brown, L., Callahan, M., Strega, S., Dominelli, L., & Walmsley, C. (2009). Manufacturing ghost fathers: The paradox of father presence and absence in child welfare. *Child and Family Social Work, 141*(1), 25–34.

Buckley, E., & Decter, P. (2006). From isolation to community: Collaborating with children and families in times of crisis. *International Journal of Narrative Therapy & Community Work, 2006*(2), 3–12.

Buckley, H., & O'Nolan, C. (2014). Child death reviews: Developing clear recommendations. *Child Abuse Review, 23*(2), 89–103.

Burford, G. (2005). Family group conferences in the youth justice and the child welfare systems. In J. Pennell & G. Anderson (Eds.), *Widening the circle: The practice and evaluation of family group conferencing with children, young persons and their families* (pp. 203–220). Washington, DC: National Association of Social Workers Press.

Burford, G., & Adams, P. (2004). Restorative justice, responsive regulation and social work. *The Journal of Sociology & Social Welfare, 31*(1), 7–26.

Burford, G., & Gallagher, S. (2015). Teen experiences of exclusion, inclusion, and participation in child protection and youth justice in Vermont. In T. Gal & B. Duramy (Eds.), *International perspectives and empirical findings on child participation: From social exclusion to child-inclusive policies.* New York, NY: Oxford University Press.

Burford, G., & Hudson, J. (2000). *New directions in community-centered child and family practice.* Piscataway, NJ: Aldine de Gruyter/Transaction.

Burford, G., & Pennell, J. (1998). *Family group decision making: After the conference—Progress in resolving violence and promoting well-being: Outcome report* (Vol. I, II). St. John's, Canada: Memorial University of Newfoundland, School of Social Work. Retrieved from https://faculty.chass.ncsu.edu/pennell/ fgdm/OutcomeReport/index.html

Burford, G., & Pennell, J. (2004). From agency client to community-based consumer: The family group conference as a consumer-led group in child welfare. In C. Garvin, L. Gutierrez, & M. Galinsky (Eds.), *Handbook of social work with groups* (pp. 415–431). New York, NY: Guilford Press.

Burford, G., & Pennell, J. (2014). Taking a fresh look: Fathers and family violence. In A. Hayden, L. Gelsthorpe, V. Kingi, & A. Morris (Eds.), *A restorative approach to family violence: Changing tack* (pp. 169–183). Surrey, UK: Ashgate.

Burns, K., Pösö, T., & Skivenes, M. (2017a). Child welfare removals by the state—Complex and controversial decisions. In K. Burns, T. Pösö, & M. Skivenes (Eds.), *Child welfare removals by the state: A cross-country analysis of decision-making systems* (pp. 1–17). New York, NY: Oxford University Press.

Burns, K., Pösö, T., & Skivenes, M. (2017b). Removals of children by the child welfare system—Variations and differences across countries. In K. Burns, T. Pösö, & M. Skivenes (Eds.), *Child welfare removals by the state: A cross-country analysis of decision-making systems* (pp. 223–243). New York, NY: Oxford University Press.

Children Young Persons and Their Families Act. (1989). Ministry of Children, Youth, and Families, Wellington, NZ.

Coglianese, C. (2015). *Listening, learning, leading: A framework for regulatory excellence.* Penn Program on Regulation. Retrieved from https://www.law.upenn.edu/live/files/4946-pprfinalconveners report.pdf

Cohen, N. (2000). *Child welfare: A multicultural focus* (2nd ed.). Boston, MA: Allyn & Bacon.

Coker, D. (2002). Transformative justice: Anti-subordination processes in cases of domestic violence. In H. Strang & J. Braithwaite (Eds.), *Restorative justice and family violence* (pp. 128–152). New York, NY: Cambridge University Press.

Connolly, M., & Doolan, M. (2007). *Lives cut short: Child death by maltreatment.* Auckland, New Zealand: Dunmore Publishing.

Cornford, J., Baines, S., & Wilson, R. (2013). Representing the family: How does the state 'think family'? *Policy & Politics, 41*(1), 1–18.

Crampton, D. (2004). Family involvement interventions in child protection: Learning from contextual integrated strategies. *Journal of Sociology & Social Welfare, 31*(1), 175–198.

Crampton, D. (2007). Research review: Family group decision making: A promising practice in need of more program theory and research. *Child & Family Social Work, 12*(2), 202–209.

Crampton, D., & Yoon, S. (2016). Family group decision making. In R. J. R. Levesque (Ed.), *Encyclopedia of Adolescence* [online version]. doi:10.1007/978-1-4419-1695-2_193

Dee, B., & Braithwaite, J. (2016). Ethical compliance management [blog post]. *John Braithwaite: War, Crime, Regulation.* Retrieved from http://johnbraithwaite.com/2016/08/24/ethical-compliance -management

Dijkstra, S. M., Creemers, H. E., Asscher, J. J., Deković, M., Geert, J., & Stams, J. M. (2016). The effectiveness of family group conferencing in youth care: A meta-analysis. *Child Abuse & Neglect, 62,* 100–110. doi:10.1016/j.chiabu.2016.10.017

Featherstone, B., Morris, K., & White, S. (2013). A marriage made in hell: Early intervention meets child protection. *British Journal of Social Work, 44,* 1735–1749. doi:10.1093/bjsw/bct052

Featherstone, B., Morris, K., & White, S. (2014). *Re-imagining child protection: Towards humane social work with families.* Clifton, NJ: Policy Press.

Fisher, M., & Marsh, P. (2015). The research-practice relationship and the work of Edward Mullen. In H. Soydan & W. Lorenz (Eds.), *Social work practice to the benefit of our clients: Scholarly legacy of Edward J. Mullen* (pp. 47–64). Bozen-Bolzano, Italy: Bozen-Bolzano University Press.

Gallagher, N. (1999). *Breeding better Vermonters: The Eugenics project in the Green Mountain State.* Lebanon, NH: University Press of New England.

Goodmark, L. (2004/2005). Achieving batterer accountability in the child protection system. *Kentucky Law Journal, 93*(3), 613.

Goodmark, L. (2010). Mothers, domestic violence, and child protection: An American legal perspective. *Violence Against Women, 16*(5), 524–529.

Goodmark, L. (2012). *A troubled marriage: Domestic violence and the legal system.* New York, NY: Oxford University Press.

Harris, N. (2011). Does responsive regulation offer an alternative? Questioning the role of assessment in child protection investigations. *British Journal of Social Work, 41*(7), 1383–1403.

Havnen, K. J. S., & Christiansen, Ø. (2014). *Knowledge review on family group conferencing: Experiences and outcomes.* Bergen, Norway: Regional Centre for Child and Youth Mental Health and Child Welfare (RKBU West) University Research Health, Norwegian Directorate for Children, Youth and Family Affairs (Bufdir). Retrieved from http://www.fgcnetwork.eu/user/file/20140000_knowledge_ review_on_family_group_conferencing_uni_research.pdf

Holland, S., & O'Neill, S. (2006). "We had to be there to make sure it was what we wanted." Enabling children's participation in family decision-making through the family group conference. *Childhood, 13*(1), 91–111.

Huntington, C. (2014). *Failure to flourish: How law undermines family relationships*. New York, NY: Oxford University Press.

Hyslop, I. (2016). Where to social work in a brave new neoliberal Aotearoa? *Aotearoa New Zealand Social Work, 28*(1), 5–12.

Ivec, M. (2013). *A necessary engagement: An international review of parent and family engagement in child protection*. Hobart, Australia: The Social Action and Research Centre Anglicare Tasmania. Retrieved from http://regnet.anu.edu.au/sites/default/files/publications/attachments/2015-10/Ivec_A%20necessary%20engagement%20-%20An%20international%20review%20of%20parent%20and%20family%20engagement%20in%20child%20protection.pdf

Ivec, M., Braithwaite, V., & Harris, N. (2012). "Resetting the relationship" in indigenous child protection: Public hope and private reality. *Law and Policy, 34*(1), 80–103.

Jeong, S., McGarrell, E. F., & Hipple, N. K. (2012). Long-term impact of family group conferences on re-offending: The Indianapolis Restorative Justice Experiment. *Journal of Experimental Criminology, 8*(4), 369–385.

Kanyi, T. (2013). Lack of outcome research on New Zealand care and protection family group conference. *Aotearoa New Zealand Social Work, 21*(1), 35–42. Retrieved from http://anzasw.nz/wp-content/uploads/SWR-Issue-XXV-Number-1-Articles-Kanyi.pdf

Kim, M. (2010). Alternative interventions to intimate violence: Defining political and pragmatic challenges. In J. Ptacek (Ed.), *Restorative justice and violence against women* (pp. 193–217). New York, NY: Oxford University Press.

Kim, M. (2014). VAWA @ 20: The mainstreaming of the criminalization critique: Reflections on VAWA 20 years later. *CUNY Law Journal* [Online publication]. Retrieved from www.cunylawreview.org/vawa-20-the-mainstreaming-of-the-criminalization-critique-reflections-on-vawa-20-years-later-by-mimi-kim

Kim, M. (2015). *Dancing the carceral creep: The anti-domestic violence movement and the paradoxical pursuit of criminalization, 1973–1986*. Berkeley: University of California, Berkeley Institute for the Study of Societal Issues. Retrieved from: http://eprints.cdlib.org/uc/item/804227k6

Križ, K., Free, J., & Kuehl, G. (2017). How children are removed from home in the United States. In K. Burns, T. Pösö, & M. Skivenes (Eds.), *Child welfare removals by the state: A cross-country analysis of decision-making systems* (pp. 197–222). New York, NY: Oxford University Press.

LaBrenz, C. A., & Fong, R. (2016). Outcomes of family centered meetings referred to child protective services. *Children and Youth Services Review, 71*, 93–102. doi:10.1016/j.childyouth.2016.10.032

Lewellyn, J., & Downie, J. (Eds.). (2011). *Being relational: Reflections on relational theory & health law*. Vancouver, Canada: University of British Columbia Press.

Macgowan, M., & Pennell, J. (2001). Building social responsibility through family group conferencing. *Social Work With Groups, 24*(3/4), 67–87.

Maschi, T., & Killian, M. (2011). The evolution of forensic social work in the United States: Implications for 21st century practice. *Journal of Forensic Social Work, 1*(1), 8–36.

Maxwell, G., Kingi, V., Robertson, J., & Morris, A. (2004). *Achieving effective outcomes in youth justice: Final report to the Ministry of Social Development*. Wellington, New Zealand: Ministry of Social Development.

McCrae, J. S., & Fusco, R. A. (2010). A racial comparison of family group decision making in the USA. *Child & Family Social Work, 15*(1), 41–55.

Merkel-Holguin, L. (2007). Questions about implementation, research and practice: Patterns in the United States. In G. Ashley & P. Nixon (Eds.), *Family group conference—where next? Policies and practices for the future* (pp. 59–80). London, UK: Family Rights Group.

Merkel-Holguin, L., Nixon, P., & Burford, G. (2003). Learning with families: A synopsis of FGDM research and evaluation in child welfare. *Protecting Children, 18*(1–2), 2–11.

Merkel-Holguin, L., & Wilmot, L. (2005). Analyzing family involvement approaches and reviewing trends in FGDM. In J. Pennell & G. Anderson (Eds.), *Widening the circle: The practice and evaluation of family group conferencing with children, youth and their families* (pp. 183–201). Washington, DC: National Association of Social Workers.

Mezey, N., & Sanford, R. (2009). Family: Youth and adults. In T. Maschi, C. Bradley, & K. Ward (Eds.), *Forensic social work: Psychosocial and legal issues in diverse practice settings* (pp. 63–79). New York, NY: Springer Publishing.

Morris, K., & Burford, G. (2017). Engaging families and managing risk in practice. In M. Connolly (Ed.), *Beyond the risk paradigm: Current debates and new directions in child protection* (pp. 91–108). Basingstoke, Hampshire, UK: Palgrave MacMillan.

Morris, K., Hughes, N., Clarke, H., Mason, P., Burford, G., Galvani, S., . . . Becker, S. (2007). *Whole family approaches: A literature review*. London, UK: Social Exclusion Task Force. Retrieved from http://dera.ioe.ac.uk/7373/1/think_family_report%20pdf.ashx

National Association of Social Workers. (n.d.). History of the NASW *Code of Ethics*. Retrieved from https://www.socialworkers.org/nasw/ethics/ethicshistory.asp

New Zealand Department of Social Welfare. Children, Young Persons, and Their Families Act 1989. Public Act 1989 No, 24. Retrieved from http://www.legislation.govt.nz/act/public/1989/0024/latest/DLM147088.html

Nixon, P., Burford, G., Quinn, A., & Edelbaum, J. (2005). A survey of international practices, policy & research on family group conferencing and related practices. Retrieved from http://www.und.edu/dept/aquinn/fgdcreports.pdf

Parker, C., & Braithwaite, J. (2003). Regulation. In P. Cane & M. Tushnet (Eds.), *The Oxford handbook of legal studies* (pp. 119–145). Oxford, UK: Oxford University Press.

Pennell, J. (2004). Family group conferencing in child welfare: Responsive and regulatory interfaces. *Journal of Sociology and Social Welfare, 31*(1), 117–135.

Pennell, J. (2017). Family risk and responsive regulation. In M. Connelly (Ed.), *Beyond the risk paradigm: Current debates and new directions in child protection* (pp. 161–175). Basingstoke, Hampshire, UK: Palgrave MacMillan.

Pennell, J., & Anderson, G. (2005). *Widening the circle: The practice and evaluation of family group conferencing with children, youths and their families*. Washington, DC: National Association of Social Workers Press.

Pennell, J., Burford, G., Morris, K., & Connolly, M. (2011). Introduction—Taking child and family rights seriously: Family engagement and its evidence in child welfare. *Child Welfare, 90*(4), 9–18.

Pennell, J., & Francis, S. (2005). Safety conferencing: Toward a coordinated and inclusive response to safeguard women and children. *Violence Against Women, 11*(5), 666–692. doi:10.1177/1077801205274569

Pennell, J., Shapiro, C., & Spigner, C. (2011). *Safety, fairness, stability: Repositioning juvenile justice and child welfare to engage families and communities*. Washington, DC: Center for Juvenile Justice Reform, Georgetown University.

Perry, R., Yoo, J., Spoliansky, T., & Edelman, P. (2013). Family team conferencing: Results and implications from an experimental study in Florida. *Child Welfare, 92*(6), 63–96.

Rangihau, J. (1986). *Puao-Te-Ata-Tu (Daybreak): The report of the Ministerial Advisory Committee on a Maori perspective for the Department of Social Welfare*. Wellington, New Zealand: Department of Social Welfare.

Rauktis, M. E., Bishop-Fitzpatrick, L., Jung, N., & Pennell, J. (2013). Family group decision making: Measuring fidelity to practice principles in public child welfare. *Children and Youth Services Review, 35*(2), 287–295.

Rawlings, A., Paliokosta, P., Maisey, D., Johnson, J., Capstick, J., & Jones, R. (2014). *A study to investigate the barriers to learning from serious case reviews and identify ways of overcoming these barriers.* Kingston upon Thames, UK: Department of Education, Kingston University.

Roberts, D. (2001). *Shattered bonds: The color of child welfare.* New York, NY: Basic Books/Civitas.

Rogers, A., & Cahn, K. (2010). *Involving families in decision making in child welfare: A review of the literature.* Portland, OR: Center for Improvement of Child and Family Services, Portland State University. Retrieved from https://www.pdx.edu/ccf/sites/www.pdx.edu.ccf/files/Involving %20Familiesin%20DecisionMaking-4-12-10.pdf

Roose, R., Roets, G., Van Houte, S., Vandenhole, W., & Reynaert, D. (2013). From parental engagement to the engagement of social work services: Discussing reductionist and democratic forms of partnership with families. *Child & Family Social Work, 18*(4), 449–457.

Saini, M., & Shlonsky, A. (2012). *Systematic synthesis of qualitative research.* New York, NY: Oxford University Press. doi:10.1093/acprof:oso/9780195387216.001.0001

Sheets, J., Wittenstrom, K., Fong, R., James, J., Tecci, M., Baumann, D. J., & Rodriguez, C. (2009). Evidence-based practice in family group decision-making for Anglo, African American and Hispanic families. *Children and Youth Services Review, 31*(11), 1187–1191.

Shlonsky, A., & Mildon, R. (2017). Assessment and decision making to improve outcomes in child protection. In M. Connolly (Ed.), *Beyond the risk paradigm in child protection: Current debates and new directions* (pp. 111–129). Basingstroke, UK: Palgrave MacMillian.

Shlonsky, A., Schumaker, K., Cook, C., Crampton, D., Saini, M., Backe-Hansen, E., & Kowalski, K. (2009). Family group decision making for children at risk of abuse and neglect (Protocol). *Cochrane Database of Systematic Reviews, 2009*(3), CD007984. doi:10.1002/14651858.CD007984

Silver, L. (2015). *System kids: Adolescent mothers and the politics of regulation.* Chapel Hill: University of North Carolina Press.

Strega, S., Fleet, C., Brown, L., Callahan, M., & Walmsley, C. (2008). Connecting father absence and mother blame in child welfare policies and practice. *Children and Youth Services Review, 30*(7), 705–716.

Tew, J., Morris, K., White, S., Featherstone, B., & Fenton, S. J. (2016). What has happened to "Think Family"?—Challenges and achievements in implementing family inclusive practice. In M. Diggins (Ed.), *Pavilion annual parental mental health and child welfare work* (Vol. 1, pp. 59–64). Retrieved from http://www.familypotential.org/wp-content/uploads/2015/03/What-happened-to-Think -Family-Pavillion-Yearbook.pdf

Trotter, C. (2008). Involuntary clients: A review of the literature. In M. C. Calder (Ed.), *The carrot or the stick: Towards effective practice with involuntary clients in safeguarding children work* (pp. 3–11). Lyme Regis, Dorset, UK: Russell House Publishing.

Turnell, A., & Edwards, S. (1997). Aspiring to partnership: The signs of safety approach to child protection casework. *Child Abuse Review, 6,* 179–190.

Turnell, A., & Edwards, S. (1999). *Signs of safety: A solution and safety oriented approach to child protection casework.* New York, NY: W. W. Norton.

Tyler, T. R. (2011). *Why people cooperate: The role of social motivations.* Princeton, NJ: Princeton University Press. Retrieved from http://press.princeton.edu/chapters/p8230.pdf

United Nations Convention on the Rights of the Child. (1989). Adopted and opened for signature, ratification and accession by General Assembly resolution 44/25 of 20 November 1989 entry into force 2 September 1990, in accordance with article 49. Retrieved from http://www.ohchr.org/en/ professionalinterest/pages/crc.aspx

United Nations Economic and Social Council. (2002). Declaration of basic principles on the use of restorative justice programs in criminal matters. Retrieved from http://www.un.org/en/ecosoc/ docs/2002/resolution%202002-12.pdf

United Nations Office on Drugs and Crime. (2006). *Handbook on restorative justice* programs (Criminal Justice Handbook Series). Retrieved from http://www.unodc.org/pdf/criminal_justice/06-56290_Ebook.pdf

van Wormer, K. (2013). Restorative justice: A model for social work practice with families. Families in society. *The Journal of Contemporary Human Services, 84*(3), 441–449.

Vandivere, S., & Malm, K. (2015). Family finding evaluations: A summary of recent findings. Retrieved from http://www.childtrends.org/wp-content/uploads/2015/01/2015-01Family_Finding_Eval_Summary.pdf

Waldegrave, C. (2000). Just therapy with families and communities. In G. Burford & J. Hudson (Eds.), *Family group conferencing: New directions in community-centered child and family practice* (pp. 153–163). Hawthorne, NY: Transaction/Aldine de Gruyter.

Weigensberg, E. C., Barth, R. R., & Guo, S. (2009). Family group decision making: A propensity score analysis to evaluate child and family services at baseline and after 36–months. *Children and Youth Services Review, 31*, 383–390.

VOICES FROM THE FIELD

Louise Vandenbosch, MS
Private Practitioner

Degrees

Masters of Social Work (Community Development), Registered Social Worker, Registered Family Group Conferencing Coordinator and Trainer, Accredited Family Mediator, Certified Wraparound Coordinator and Trainer.

Agency Setting

I am a private practitioner, Province of Ontario, Canada, providing primarily an alternative dispute resolution (ADR) service to families involved with child welfare services; receive referrals from central point of access—ADR-Link, a brokering service that connects Children's Aid Societies with qualified ADR practitioners in the South West Region of Ontario. In the past I worked for an agency, which also received ADR referrals from the same central point of access. I practice family group conferencing (FGC), child protection mediation (CPmed), and family mediation.

Expertise Required

A postsecondary educational qualification in human services from an accredited college, university, or equivalent.

A minimum of 5 years of experience and demonstrated ability in working with families and children.

Either registered with or ability to be registered with the regulatory body governing their profession, where applicable.

An understanding of and experience interfacing with the child welfare system in order to sufficiently inform families about how the system functions.

An understanding of domestic violence risk assessment and management and/or experience of domestic violence dynamics and best practice.

Knowledge or experience in working with marginalized populations.

Experience in facilitating large groups and creating an environment of trust, collaboration and safety.

Ability to be flexible and adjust to changing, challenging environments.

Willingness and ability to work daytime, evenings and weekends to maintain service delivery.

Strong organizational competency and self-directive abilities.

Strong computer literacy skills, as well as strong oral and written communication skills.

Commitment to continuing personal and professional development.

Practice Responsibilities

One must be trained and mentored in the practice of FGC as a prerequisite to be registered as an Ontario Family Group Conferencing Coordinator. Emphasis is on collaborative engagement and facilitation skills, creating a platform for families to experience authorship and ownership of any plan of care, service, or "intervention" agreed upon.

Ethical, Legal, Practice, Diversity, and/or Advocacy Issues Addressed

Families have the right to have the "first kick at the can" in being able to plan for their own; if they are unable to come up with a plan, then the system should assist in a very respectful, collaborative family-centered approach. For me I think that nothing is more central to being a human being than the ability to procreate and care for our young—the human species depends on this very basic premise. We must remember that we are interfering with this very fundamental human building block and right.

Treatment requires close collaboration with the child's counsel. ADR practitioners need to remember that FGC and CPmed nearly always have a legal context. One needs to understand that context and contribute toward the resolution, if possible.

This is the most exciting and engaging work that I have been involved in as a social worker. I have been a social worker for more than 30 years. It is a privilege and an honor to work with families who are facing such obstacles. Many families struggle with issues of poverty, mental health, intellectual disability, or a combination of the former, often accompanied by a sense of disenfranchisement.

I also work in the background ensuring that the practice evolves in a way that meets the needs of our two client groups—child welfare and families. This allows me to put my community social work skills to good use.

FGC allows the coordinator to work with all families regardless of ethnicity, color, sexual orientation, or make up. It is a practice that uniquely customizes itself to the family who is directly in front of you. There is no cookie-cutter approach.

The ADR practitioners (FGC or CPmed) need to ensure that they are acting and functioning in an impartial manner. They need to focus on the process and make sure that it is completely unbiased; there should be no investment in the outcome. New coordinators, and sometimes some not so new coordinators, struggle with this concept. They need to identify when they fall off the perch and become advocates, name it, and then get back on the perch. Advocate for the practice and the right of access to the practice, not for the individual family. An important aspect of the advocacy role of the FGC coordinator: Coordinator advocates solely for the *family's voice* to be central in decision making and steers away from advocating on behalf of the family, which often risks making the professional's voice more central.

Interprofessional and Intersectoral Collaboration

As a social worker working with the referring child welfare worker and his or her supervisor, who nearly always are social workers, there is a great comfort in that we all are speaking the same language. They will often speak about their desire to do my job, as that is what they went to school for. . . . Child welfare is a tough job and I acknowledge that. I believe that is very tough on the psyche.

There is a great deal of collaboration among professionals from all sectors—public health, mental health, developmental services, counseling services, and legal professionals. I am continually working with others to ensure that their professional expertise is respected and tapped into and at the same time not boxed in within their own sectorial biases. Building cross-sectorial bridges is an important aspect of the work.

VOICES FROM THE FIELD

Michele Sneed, BSW, MSW, LGSW
Assistant Professor of Social Work
The College of St. Scholastica

Agency Setting

I completed a Bachelor of Social Work degree at Winona State University in 2007 and a Master of Social Work degree at the University of New England. I also completed an infant early childhood mental health certificate program through the University of Minnesota. My place of employment had a very rich in-service training program where I completed training in, among other things, Signs of Safety, Stages of Change, and a range of skills related to individual, group, family, and community practice. Training in family group conferencing (FGC) was provided by staff from Olmsted County. I have had the opportunity to present at a national conference for family group decision making on facilitation skills. Supervision required for all these degrees and programs has included one-on-one supervision, observing, weekly team consultations, and so on.

I have just taken on a new position as site coordinator/assistant professor, Social Work Department, with The College of St. Scholastica, Duluth, Minnesota. Prior to starting this position, I practiced social work as a child protection social worker in Olmsted County, Rochester, Minnesota, for 8 years where my responsibilities included case management of ongoing child protection cases. I moved into that position after working for Family Service of Rochester coordinating and facilitating family involvement meetings including family group decision making, rapid case planning conferences, and case planning meetings. Olmsted County has a somewhat unique and well-developed partnership with Family Service Rochester, which allows for all staff in Child and Family Services and the families they work with to have access to independent facilitators who have been trained to pull families together and facilitate a range of types of meetings. Olmsted County utilizes this service as one of the key ways to engage families, aimed at being transparent with all family members, decreasing fragmentation, always keeping with the families a sense that things are moving forward, and making sure that all families/kin that want to be involved for the children have that right to do so. While I am excited about moving into my new position, which I see as a wonderful opportunity to bring what I have learned about reflective practice and engaging with families into teaching and learning with students, I am at the same time humbled with the rich learning experiences I have had as a practitioner that were well beyond what I expected coming into the profession.

Practice Responsibilities

My practice responsibilities while at Olmsted County included: conducting random case record reviews; providing individual, group, and family counseling to explore, identify, resolve, prevent, or manage problems; develop and write individual and family service plans to treat identified problems; analyze and recommend on child welfare processes and procedures and draft improvements as needed; collaborate with referral agencies to provide information on clients and oversee statutory requirements related to child and community safety; carry out specially assigned studies of issues related to the Adoption and Safe Families Act; and conduct ongoing reviews of the match between client needs and services being provided.

Expertise Required

- Knowledge of federal and state laws, regulations, policies and procedures, and relevant welfare programs
- Skill in the use of motivational strategies and techniques and the knowledge of social work principles related to child protection and family engagement
- Knowledge and appreciation for impact of secondary stress and coping strategies as it applies to families and to social workers who work with them
- Ongoing participation in reflective individual and group supervision to further develop good judgment in conflict resolution and the ability to think critically while working alongside clients
- Participation in collaborative teams with a view to maintaining positive working relationships with peers at all levels of the system and across government and nongovernment partnerships
- Attending to efficiency, organization, and high quality in documenting and maintaining professional records
- Facilitation of ongoing and time-limited groups and teams and regular engagement with family groups
- Keeping on top of best-practice literature and research in child welfare
- Participation in regular and ongoing training and mentoring in family involvement strategies

Ethical, Legal, Practice, Diversity, and/or Advocacy Issues Addressed

Partnering with families during some of the most difficult times in their lives can be rewarding and terrifying all at the same time. The skills and patience of walking alongside families while recognizing their strengths and vulnerabilities, assessing them through cultural, trauma, and multisystem lenses, take years to learn. Every family is unique and presents a new opportunity for learning. During my time as a social worker in ongoing child protection, one of the biggest rewards was being able to offer the family the opportunity to have their own family group decision-making conference.

Parents typically come into the child protection system with the expectation that the system is unforgiving, that their children will be taken away, and that they will have no opportunities to make choices. Engaging the family with respect and understanding and offering them an opportunity to have an independent person help them bring their family group together to make a plan gives the opposite message. The social worker needs to stick closely to the fidelity of the process, including ensuring that they have the time and supports to have their voices heard and to play important roles in making decisions based on what they believe is in the best interests of their children. I have utilized FGC for a variety of reasons that include alternative permanency planning and the development of support plans including those that touch on youth justice issues. Plans often have many steps including pieces like "How can a family support a parent/child relationship that has been damaged?" "How can a family add in safety plans if there are concerns around domestic violence, or physical altercations between child and parent?" or "What are the hopes of parents/extended family for contact if a child is being adopted or a transfer of custody is occurring?" I have witnessed firsthand the benefit in contacting as many families/kin as possible to reunify connections that have long been broken, establish new boundaries among family members for the future, show an unconditional love and acceptance to those they have been hurt by, or show a united front to their children that they will stand together for their safety and well-being.

The responsibility of the social worker starts with first ensuring the safety of children and engagement with the family in the referral process. Speaking with parents, children, and extended family/kin about the family group conference takes compassion, requires the workers to be willing to respectfully and often repeatedly clarify the purpose, articulate the options, and help support the family in believing they will be listened to and have a say. It also requires having a sense of understanding around a family's cultural identity. I have been part of meetings that have occurred in homes, hotels, and churches. I have been fortunate to be part of FGCs where family members have made these meetings their own by saying a prayer before the meeting starts or bringing in pictures of deceased family members to give them strength. The facilitators and coordinators who prepare these meetings must walk into preparation with family members with open minds and make this process as individual to the particular family as they can. They need the backing of the social worker to support them in helping the family put their best foot forward. The diversity among families is such that no meetings should ever be exactly the same.

Assisting the entire family system in understanding that the child protection system respects their opinion, right down to the family having choices in planning the meeting, and that the system is listening to their ideas, thoughts, and worries is critical for success. I have had great achievement with always bringing the focus back to the children and reminding the family why they are coming together. Follow-through after the social worker has accepted the family's plan is crucial. Going into the family group conference as a social worker can be overwhelming. Social workers often do not know what to expect, what questions will be asked, or what the family will come up with in regard to a plan. Walking into the process with trust in the family and in the coordinator of these conferences is essential. The end result, from my experience, is generally a well-detailed plan that shows the hard work and effort on the family's part. It shows sometimes years of heartache that for a few hours is set aside by the family members to plan for their most vulnerable members. As the social worker in these meetings, one of the expectations I have for myself is to support a family's plan if that plan meets any nonnegotiable or bottom-line issue that I have set out. This does not always mean it feels right to me as a social worker. I have sometimes felt that there would be a "better" option at times but for me ethically it is about believing in families and understanding they know better than the system. When nonnegotiables are met in a plan it leaves me with no excuses as to why a plan should not be approved and moved ahead. As the social worker it is then my ethical duty to support this plan.

The preparation for families to get to the point of being able to be present for these meetings, participate in meaningful planning, be their own advocates, and feel comfortable with the outcomes can be long. The end result of giving families choices when it feels as though they have no control is beautiful.

Interprofessional and Intersectoral Collaboration

Collaboration for the FGC needs support and reinforcement from all levels of systems. The microlevel of the collaboration lies within the family system and the relationship with the social worker. This collaboration is essential to positive outcomes of the conference. The mezzo level of the system includes having community and agency support and commitment for this process. I have invited all professionals involved with families to these meetings. They have included school teachers, day-care providers, guardian ad litems, probation officers, mental health workers, clergy, and so on. These professionals all have expectations and knowledge to contribute during the information sharing portion of the meeting. This provides the family time to ask questions and have all of the information they need to do meaningful planning. The social worker must be willing to be clear and respectful in giving information to the family and the professionals. Everyone should be aware beforehand of the agencies' "bottom lines" or the things that are not negotiable within the plan. These "bottom lines" provide a framework for families to create their plan and support other professionals in working collaboratively to support the family in satisfying the statutory reasons for the child protection or youth justice involvement in their family.

CHAPTER 28

Collaboration and Care Coordination

Ida Dickie

Tina Maschi

CHAPTER OBJECTIVES

The major objectives of this chapter are to:

- Describe the importance and need for interdisciplinary collaboration in forensic settings.
- Discuss how the evidence-based principles of the risk, need, and responsivity (RNR) model can guide interdisciplinary collaboration with justice-involved individuals.
- Highlight a treatment program for high-risk justice-involved males demonstrating interdisciplinary collaboration and specifically the role of the forensic social worker.

CHAPTER COMPETENCIES HIGHLIGHTED

- Competency 1: Demonstrate Ethical and Professional Behavior
- Competency 6: Engage With Individuals, Families, Organizations, and Communities
- Competency 7: Assess Individuals, Families, Organizations, and Communities
- Competency 8: Intervene With Individuals, Families, Organizations, and Communities

Justice-involved clients regularly need services from social workers, psychologists, nurses, and medical professionals. Therefore, social workers who can collaborate in interdisciplinary teams will contribute to more effective and competent care of justice-involved clients. In fact, it can be argued interdisciplinary collaboration is an essential core skill in evidence-based forensic social work practice.

Kelly, Smith, and Gibson (2009) identify negotiating, sharing power, knowing your role, using strengths-based perspective, client empowerment, advocacy, and communication as essential microskills required for forensic social workers to be successful at using a macroskill of interdisciplinary collaboration. Interdisciplinary collaboration has been defined as "multidimensional, interactional, and developmental" and the following strategies have been identified as most important in achieving a best practice: (a) preplanning, (b) commitment, (c) communication, (d) strong leadership, (e) understanding the cultures of collaborating agencies, and (f) structural supports and adequate resources for collaboration (Bronstein, 2003). Within forensic settings, using these strategies must include efforts at both the individual forensic social worker level and organizational levels of the forensic interdisciplinary team.

The ethical codes of social workers, psychology, and nurses clearly mention the importance of collaborating with other professions as ethical practice that can improve client or patient outcomes (American Nurses Association, 2001; American Psychological Association, 2002; National Association of Social Workers, 2008; National Social Workers Code of Ethics, 2008; Public Health Leadership Society, 2002). Formal academic training programs often include interdisciplinary or interprofessional collaboration and students are required to demonstrate competency collaboration skills (Graham & Barter, 1999).

A growing body of evidence suggests interdisciplinary or interprofessional practice is common in social work practice, especially as it relates to settings involving justice-involved individuals, families, or communities. For example, in a sample of 78 U.S. social work academic programs, Bronstein, Mizrahi, Korazim-Ko Rosy, and McPhee (2010) reported interdisciplinary collaboration was most likely to happen in mental health settings (87%), followed by medical settings (83%), schools (73%), and children and family services (72.4%). Furthermore, research also has shown the benefits of interdisciplinary collaboration; when students have experience with interdisciplinary training while completing coursework, upon graduation, they are more likely to be receptive and open to working in interdisciplinary teams (Amundson, Moulton, Zimmerman, & Johnson, 2008).

However, it is important to note a key forensic interdisciplinary team member, the medical field, does not always recognize the need for collaboration (American Medical Association, 2001; D'Amour, Sicotte, & Levy, 1999). Although social workers may find collaboration helpful in managing the patient's case, medical doctors do not find reciprocal benefits (Mizrahi & Abramson, 2000). This viewpoint may be changing because integrated services, an interdisciplinary model of primary care, is becoming more mainstream (Weiss, Tilin, & Morgan, 2014).

Research examining the benefits of interdisciplinary collaboration from a social worker's perspective consistently reports positive outcomes. The one exception is the feeling of being forced to work in and navigate nonsocial work paradigms; advocacy versus adversarial (Chan, Chi, Ching, & Lam, 2010; Mizrahi & Abramson, 2000; Parker-Oliver & Peck, 2006). This is a key concern for social workers when working in forensic interdisciplinary teams because the justice system is built on an adversarial punitive framework. The dilemma between advocacy and the adversarial justice system can contribute to distress for social workers without proper training about how to work in a forensic interdisciplinary team. Therefore, it is necessary to articulate a definition of forensic interdisciplinary collaboration identifying the needs, goals, and core skills required of each forensic interdisciplinary team member—a definition in which social workers and other mental health team members can find a voice. It is critical that the definition provide clarity as to what contributes to and influences successful forensic interdisciplinary collaboration among professionals and with justice-involved individuals.

Interdisciplinary, Interprofessional, and Collaborative Practice

Interdisciplinary Collaboration

Interdisciplinary collaboration is based on the philosophy that clients are best served with better care coordination and collaboration with other disciplines. The term *interdisciplinary*, whether referring to practitioners or researchers, often refers to the process of analyzing, synthesizing, and harmonizing the links among different disciplines to create coordinated and coherent care responses to clients and their family's needs. However, there are issues with the use of the term *interdisciplinary* in social work; because it has not been recognized as a discipline, it has lacked the recognition as a hard or soft science, such as biology, psychology, and medicine. Yet, social work has been recognized as a profession. The term *interdisciplinary* also lacks the true collaboration and parity of roles inferred by the term *interprofessional* (Choi & Pak, 2006; Maschi & Youdin, 2010). Please note: For the purposes of this chapter, we use the term *interdisciplinary* to refer to team-based forensic practice arrangements, knowing the limitations of the use of this term in reference to social work.

Interprofessional Practice

In contrast, interprofessional practice refers to a practice situation where all members of a practice team participate in the team's activities. All members cooperate with one another and count on each other to work toward common goals and improve services to clients and client satisfaction. Overall, there is a positive interdependence among forensic professionals, such as law enforcement, social workers, psychologists, and other professionals on their team (Atwal & Caldwell, 2006).

Collaborative Practice

Collaborative practice is another term that might be used by some forensic professional teams. In collaborative practice, the process of collaboration involves individuals from diverse backgrounds and perspectives who are engaged in active and ongoing partnership to solve problems or provide services in a supportive environment (Freeth, Hammick, Reeves, Koppel, & Barr, 2005). In collaborative practice different professionals are involved in communication and decision making by sharing their separate but shared knowledge and skills to provide holistic services to their clients (Graham & Barter, 1999).

Interprofessional Education Collaborative Expert Panel (IECEP) Competencies

The IECEP (2011) have developed four core competency domains for interprofessional practice that are useful when conceptualize forensic interdisciplinary practice: values and ethics, roles/responsibilities, interprofessional communication, and teamwork. In the first domain of interprofessional practice, values/ethics for interprofessional practice, professionals work with other professionals to maintain a climate of mutual respect and shared values. In the second domain, roles/responsibilities, professionals use the knowledge of one's own role and those of other professionals to appropriately assess and address the care needs of the client and client populations served. In the third domain, interprofessional communication, professionals communicate with patients, families, communities, and other professionals in a respectful and responsible manner that supports a team approach, respect for the client and client population, and their care. In the fourth domain, teams and teamwork, professionals apply relationship-building values and the principles of team dynamics to perform effectively in different team roles to plan and deliver client- and population-centered care that is safe, time sensitive, efficient, effective, and equitable (IECEP, 2011). These principles can be infused in forensic settings or situations in which there is more than one profession involved or to evaluate how an existing interdisciplinary team is operating based on these principles.

Theoretical Base for Forensic Interdisciplinary Collaboration

Although interacting with other disciplines has always been a function of the social workers' case-management role, historically, a dearth of models existed to guide the interdisciplinary work. Bronstein (2003) reviewed the social work multidisciplinary, ecological, role theory to develop a two-part interdisciplinary model of collaboration. Part 1 involves (a) interdisciplinary collaboration; (b) interdependence of newly created activities; (c) flexibility; (d) collective ownership of goals; and (e) reflection on interdisciplinary process. Part 2 involves factors influencing collaboration: (a) professional role; (b) structural characteristics; and (c) personal characteristics and history of collaboration. At the most basic level, interdisciplinary collaboration is defined as "an **interpersonal** process through which members of different disciplines contribute to a common product or goal" (Berg-Weger & Schnedier, 1998). Bronstein (2003) augments the definition and states interdisciplinary collaboration is an "**effective** interpersonal process which facilitates the achievement of goals that cannot be reached without the collaboration of individual professionals from different disciplines." It could be argued the collaboration of individual professionals from different disciplines is absolutely necessary when dealing with justice-involved individuals. However, to function interdependently, each discipline has to know what the common goal is and how to incorporate evidence-based principles guiding effective practice with justice-involved individuals. Fortunately, this body of knowledge exists and provides the overarching framework for forensic social workers and other members of the interdisciplinary team when working with justice-involved individuals.

All interdisciplinary interventions with justice-involved individuals need to focus on the reduction of recidivism and enhancement of overall well-being. These common goals can be guided by *The Psychology of Criminal Conduct* (PCC; Andrews & Bonta, 2010). The PCC integrates the genetic, temperamental, and environmental covariates most predictive of engagement in criminal behavior (Andrews & Bonta, 2010). It is based on the General Personality and Cognitive Social Learning (GPCSL) theory (Andrews & Bonta, 2010). The evidence-based assessment and treatment principles of RNR originate from PCC.

The risk principle states justice-involved individuals vary in their risk to recidivate; the higher the risk, the more needs the individual has and the greater need for intervention. An important aspect of the risk principle pertains to the dosage of treatment required for various risk levels. For example, providing a low-risk individual with an incorrect dosage of treatment can increase his or her risk for recidivism and harm the individual (Gendreau & Andrews, 1990). Research suggests high-risk individuals require 200 to 400 hours of treatment to reduce risk for recidivism and address criminogenic needs (Sperber, Latessa, & Makarios, 2013).

Needs within the RNR framework are conceptualized as criminogenic (predictive of criminal recidivism) and noncriminogenic (related to subjective well-being of the offender, but not predictive of recidivism), such as self-esteem and anxiety (Andrews & Bonta, 2010). RNR posits the most effective model for facilitating desistance in offenders is by targeting the central eight risk factors, or criminogenic needs (Andrews & Bonta, 2010), for criminal behavior, which are shown in Table 28.1: history of antisocial behavior, antisocial personality pattern, antisocial attitudes and values, antisocial associates, family/marital circumstances, school/work, leisure/recreation, and substance abuse (Andrews & Bonta, 2010). A variety of these needs must be addressed in order to decrease the risk of the

TABLE 28.1   Central Eight Factors Predictive of Criminal Behavior

Central Eight
"Big Four"
1. Antisocial attitudes and values
2. Antisocial associates
3. Antisocial personality pattern
4. History of antisocial behavior
"Moderate Four"
5. Family/marital circumstances
6. School/work
7. Leisure/recreation
8. Substance abuse

offender to recidivate. A sole focus is not effective. In addition, these needs make up an important part of the individual's identity, and many of the offender's core emotional needs such as safety, relatedness, and self-determination are addressed by providing case management and treatment services targeting the aforementioned need areas, which assist individuals in meeting their emotional needs in prosocial ways (Andrews & Bonta, 2010).

The responsivity principle identifies the many factors influencing a client's ability to enter into, engage, and complete an assessment, case management, or treatment plan. There are two types of responsivity factors: specific and general. Specific responsivity refers to factors such as mental health concerns, motivation level, or personality characteristics (hostility). General responsivity refers to the importance of matching client characteristics to a social worker's characteristics to ensure a successful outcome. For example, if a social worker has a sexual trauma history, it may not be wise to work with sexual offenders or if a client has a low IQ, placement in a cognitive behavioral therapy (CBT) program may not be overly effective without accommodations. Social work concepts of autonomy, self-determination, and human rights are important aspects of how the RNR principles, specifically the responsivity principle, would be implemented by a social worker in an interdisciplinary team.

To summarize, the risk principle helps identify *who* should receive treatment, the criminogenic need principle focuses on *what* should be treated, and the responsivity principle underscores the importance of *how* treatment should be delivered (Andrews & Bonta, 2010). Any service provided by a forensic social worker working within an interdisciplinary team can be guided by the RNR principles. There are other evidence-based principles that are important to address but RNR is most essential to follow when working with justice-involved clients. The list of principles in Table 28.2 appears in the Report to the California State Legislature: *A Roadmap for Effective Offender Programming in California* (California Department of Corrections and Rehabilitation Expert Panel on Adult Offender and Recidivism Reduction Programming, 2007).

TABLE 28.2   Evidence-Based Principles and Practices

1. Target Highest Risk Offenders. Correctional agencies should provide rehabilitation treatment programming to their highest-risk-to-reoffend prisoners and parolees first. Provide other types of programs to low-risk-to-reoffend prisoners or parolees.
2. Assess Offenders' Needs. Correctional agencies should assess the criminogenic needs (dynamic risk factors) of their offenders using research-based instruments. The goal of programming should be to diminish needs.
3. Design Responsivity Into Programming. Programming should account for individual offender characteristics that interfere with or facilitate an offender's ability and motivation to learn.
4. Develop Behavior Management Plans. Individual programming should occur in the context of a larger behavior management plan developed for each offender, which will include the priority and sequence of treatment programs, the means for measuring treatment gains, and the goals for a crime-free lifestyle.
5. Deliver Treatment Programs Using Cognitive-Based Strategies. Research has consistently determined that cognitive behavioral treatments are more effective than any other form of correctional intervention because these treatment types address criminal thinking and behaviors in offenders. The therapeutic community treatment model, which uses cognitive-based treatment strategies, is a highly effective method for treating alcohol and other drug dependencies.
6. Motivate and Shape Offender Behaviors. Programming should include structure or capacity for rewarding positive behavior in addition to punishing negative behavior.
7. Engender the Community as a Protective Factor Against Recidivism and Use the Community to Support Offender Reentry and Reintegration. Programming should involve the offender's immediate family members and the social service agencies in the community to which the offender will be returning. The state should empower the community—families, neighborhoods, religious and cultural institutions, businesses—to reduce crime through deliberate efforts that assist offenders under correctional control and provide support to reduce criminal behavior.
8. Identify Outcomes and Measure Progress. All programs should have identified outcomes and integrated methods for measuring progress toward objectives. The system should use performance measures to evaluate progress and inform improvements.

Source: California Department of Corrections and Rehabilitation Expert Panel on Adult Offender and Recidivism Reduction Programming (2007).

Empirical Evidence of Effectiveness With Forensic Populations and Settings

The theory of PCC has produced a body of research called the "what works." This literature which has identified certain characteristics of successful interventions with justice-involved individuals. Indeed, recidivism can be reduced up to 50% if interventions with justice-involved individuals employ all three RNR principles (Andrews & Bonta, 2010). An additional PCC principle called the fidelity principle primarily focuses on how interventions effectively incorporate the RNR principles and subsequent outcomes.

For example, Barnoski (2004) examined the proper and improper implementations of functional family therapy (FFT) and aggression replacement therapy (ART) in juvenile/youthful populations. Results indicated when FFT was delivered according to the program model, recidivism was reduced by 38% for the treatment group. Similarly, the proper implementation of ART resulted in a 24% reduction in recidivism for participant youth in comparison to nonparticipants. However, when these programs were not implemented following the evidence-based principles of RNR, recidivism rates increased by 17% for FFT and 10% for ART.

Other research examining individuals who are a high risk for justice involvement indicates interventions with high-risk groups need to be multimodal and target multiple criminogenic needs (Dowden & Andrews, 1999a, 1999b). Results from a meta-analysis conducted by French and Gendreau (2006) involving 68 studies indicated a 29% reduction in recidivism for programs targeting between three and eight criminogenic needs whereas programs targeting between one and two criminogenic needs reported a 16% reduction in recidivism. Programs with no focus on criminogenic needs either saw no effect or a 0.06% reduction in high-risk behaviors.

Ample research exists to support the aforementioned evidence-based principles. The Washington Institute for Public Policy (www.wsipp.wa.gov/pub.asp?docid=06-10-1201) provides a comprehensive overview of well-designed studies presenting evidence-based programs for justice-involved clients.

Unfortunately, there are many barriers to implementing evidence-based practices with justice-involved clients. An important role for forensic social workers is advocating for their clients to receive evidence-based assessment and treatment. Reppucci and Saunders (1974) identified several barriers but noted the list is not definitive or mutually exhaustive: (a) lack of a clear vocabulary or language to describe each stakeholder's goal with the justice-involved client; (b) limited resources in terms of economics, staffing, time, and programming space; (c) lack of organizational commitment; and (d) maintaining the basic integrity of the treatment program without becoming unrealistically rigid.

Addressing the previously discussed barriers and successfully implementing evidence-based practices following PCC principles requires change at many levels and necessitates a greater than normal degree of collaboration among social workers, psychologists, and other community stakeholder groups. However, interdisciplinary collaboration can result in the development of new skill sets and knowledge bases; adjustments to organizational structures, policies, procedures, and work practices; and the establishment of new cultural values supportive of evidence-based practice (Sachwald & Tesluk, 2005). Bogue et al. (2004) presented a strategy called an integrated model with three overlapping areas: evidence-based principles, organizational development, and collaboration. This model can be improved by highlighting organizational commitment and interdisciplinary collaboration.

The integrated model of removing barriers to implementation of evidence-based forensic practice provides further support for using PCC as the framework to guide the interdisciplinary collaboration. The model is a reflection of core evidence-based PCC practices and "what works" literature: (a) Interventions are supported by community and policy-maker partnerships, as well as organizational commitment; (b) interventions are supported by qualified and involved leadership that understands the program objectives; (c) treatment plans are designed and implemented using proven theoretical treatment and case-management models, beginning with assessment of an individual's risk and need factors; the risk need assessment guides all services through aftercare; (d) interventions are delivered considering factors interfering with an individual's ability to enter into, engage in, and complete the intervention being suggested: learning style, cognitive ability, and personality characteristics. This is called the responsivity principle.

Clearly the research identifies interdisciplinary collaboration as a core forensic social worker skill and is essential in the implementation of evidence-based forensic practice with justice-involved individuals.

Case Example and Application

Healthy Lifestyles Program: Developing a New Identity

The mission of the Healthy Lifestyles Program (HLP) is to promote safer communities and the well-being of human beings by assisting individuals who have a high risk of engaging in criminal behavior to manage their risk to reoffend by developing a meaningful and purposeful lifestyle identity (Dickie, 2009).

The HLP is a manualized 14-month high-intensity, interdisciplinary, transitional reentry program designed for high-risk male offenders between 18 and 35 years of age who meet the criteria for antisocial personality disorder. The treatment program is delivered using an integrative system of psychotherapy that incorporates cognitive behavioral treatment and motivational interviewing (MI), as well as schema therapy techniques, and incorporates a strong case-management component. The interdisciplinary program staff includes licensed psychologists, social workers, occupational therapists, and a nurse practitioner. The treatment will address several areas found to be critical in changing criminal behavior, including: treatment readiness, identity development, self-management, relapse prevention, and social support. The program involves several treatment modalities: individual, group, and milieu therapy, as well as case management. Pre- and posttreatment psychological assessment, weekly case-management meetings, and program evaluation are also aspects of the HLP. There are three phases of treatment in the HLP. Prior to the start of treatment, the interdisciplinary team completes a comprehensive evaluation with the client preceding his release from incarceration.

The HLP focuses on identity because research suggests people generally behave in accord with the meanings of their identity standards.

However, identity change takes time; often individuals who are chronically involved with the law and have an antisocial personality may not realize the benefits of changing their antisocial lifestyle. Therefore, the HLP starts out with focusing on treatment readiness using motivational interviewing (MI) to create the possible prosocial identity based on the central eight. Motivation is targeted in the HLP because it fits with the responsivity principle of the RNR model. It increases the likelihood that the client will enter into, engage in, and complete treatment.

The HLP targets a global prosocial identity. However, it is possible clients may be willing to work on one of the central eight areas more than another. Even so, it is hoped using CBT techniques to modify core beliefs and schemas supportive of antisocial attitudes and values, which contribute to poor perspective taking, immediate gratification, selfishness, manipulation, and violence, will lead to global identity change. The HLP realizes that change is a process. Therefore, the program is voluntary, accepts relapse as a part of the change process, and builds in an aftercare phase. Upon release, clients' change may begin because of external pressure (e.g., conditions of supervision), but if autonomy is supported, engagement in the treatment process may be continued for internal reasons (e.g., the offender sees personal benefits).

Intervention Summary

Target group. Male repeat offenders between the ages of 18 and 35 who meet the criteria for antisocial personality disorder who are of medium or minimum/community level of security classification and applying for parole within eight to nine months of starting treatment. Individuals can be in the precontemplation/contemplation stage of change.

Exclusionary criteria. Psychotic, IQ below 75, no sexual offenses

Setting. Prison and community

Interdisciplinary team members. Psychology, social work, occupational therapy, nursing

Role of assessment. Pre- and posttreatment assessment will be completed and is interdisciplinary in scope. An individual assessment report will be written by a psychologist, a social worker, an occupational therapist, and a nurse and will be incorporated into an overall interdisciplinary treatment report.

Treatment format. Eight to ten clients, group, individual, milieu, peer support, case management.

Treatment theoretical model. Manualized CBT incorporating MI and schema therapy techniques using PCC and RNR principles of intervention.

Intervention length (three phases and aftercare):

- 14 months = 868 total intervention hours
- 240 hours psychological treatment (184 hours group therapy and 56 individual therapy hours)
- 232 occupational therapy hours
- 208 hours of case management/social work
- 44 hours (and as needed) with a nurse practitioner
- 24 hours peer support groups
- 120 hours—aftercare/milieu therapy

The interdisciplinary team will focus on the following goals during all phases of treatment:

- Increasing readiness to change
- Improved self-control/self-management
- Increased support network, increased contact with prosocial "faces and places," and reconnection to primary/healthy relationships
- Development and increase of prosocial value attitudes/identity in various areas of life, leisure, employment, school, and relationships, leading to change in overall self-concept
- Decrease in antisocial values
- Relapse prevention plans
- Improved overall well-being

How to Apply This Skill

Healthy Lifestyles Program and Forensic Social Workers' Interdisciplinary Collaboration Skills

The case example of the HLP described earlier incorporates an interdisciplinary team working with high-risk justice-involved males and focuses on the aforementioned "what works" areas. The team consisted of psychologists, social workers, occupational therapists, and nurses. The program and the interdisciplinary team were directed by a forensic psychologist. The first step in forming the interdisciplinary team was to have every member of the team discuss how they perceived their roles and responsibilities in relation to the six evidence-based practices listed in the following.

Due to the perception that psychology, occupational therapy, and social work engage in similar activities, it was important to establish what discipline was going to be responsible for what in the delivery of the HLP. It was very clear skills of negotiating and sharing power and knowing your role were essential in determining how social workers would collaborate with psychology, nursing, and occupational therapy to: (a) assess offenders' needs; (b) address responsivity factors in programming; (c) develop behavior management plans; (d) motivate and shape offender behaviors; (e) engender the community as a protective factor against recidivism and use the community to support offender reentry and reintegration; and (f) identify outcomes and measure progress. Similar to other team members, it was very clear from the team meetings that the social workers were invested in using strengths-based perspectives, client empowerment, and advocacy skills in their role on the team and to accomplish the following responsibilities.

Assessment of Offenders' Needs

Within the HLP, the overall assessment of risk for recidivism was completed by the forensic psychologists. The tool used is called the Level of Supervision/Case Management Inventory. However, the forensic social workers were responsible for developing the case-management or lifestyle plan based on the clients' risk/need areas. To further gather information for case-management planning, the forensic social workers would complete the Adult Needs and Strengths Assessment: An Information Integration Tool for Adults With Behavioral Health Challenges (www.in.gov/fssa/dmha/files/ANSA_Manual.pdf). They would also gather additional information about clients' substance abuse problems including treatment readiness. It was very important for the forensic social worker to share power in regard to assuming the case-management role rather than the risk assessor role in the HLP. Furthermore, commitment to balancing the rights of the clients and the communities' right for public safety reflected the social workers' understanding of the culture of the HLP.

Addressing Responsivity Factors in Programming

Using the information provided by the forensic psychologists and the information gathered about what stage of change the clients were in regarding their substance abuse problems, the forensic social workers would use MI techniques to address the responsivity issue of motivation. The team would also rely on the social worker to assist the client with homework for the treatment groups if accommodations were made to address cognitive responsivity factors. The clients appreciated the forensic social workers' focus on empowerment when using MI to increase treatment readiness. The team appreciated the strong communication skills demonstrated during weekly staff meetings when discussing the clients' responsivity factors and how they were impacting treatment. The forensic social workers were able to recognize the personality responsivity factors that contribute to attempts to split staff and communicate clearly to the client the team environment of HLP without decreasing safety for the client.

Develop Behavior Management Plans

The forensic social workers were responsible for developing and monitoring the case-management or lifestyle plan based on the clients' risk/need areas. As the team lead of the weekly staff meetings, the social worker was responsible for identifying resources to secure case-management goals related to risk areas. For example, occupational therapy worked with clients on developing skills needed to achieve educational and family-related goals. Often, case-management activities were required to assist clients in achieving their goals with other members of the team such as occupational therapists and assisting clients with obtaining information about education goals, conducting family reunification sessions, or helping clients implement relapse prevention plans developed in psychological treatment. The forensic social worker skill of preplanning and commitment to the mission of the HLP was evident during weekly team meetings.

Motivate and Shape Offender Behaviors

The forensic social workers met weekly to review goals and progress in the eight areas of their life plan and would use MI techniques reflective of the clients' stage of change in each of the areas. The social workers would use their advocacy skills and focus on empowerment to motivate the clients. These skills complemented the psychological and occupational therapy the clients were receiving and increased safety for the client in the HLP.

Engender the Community as a Protective Factor Against Recidivism and Use the Community to Support Offender Reentry and Reintegration

The forensic social workers, based on the clients' risk areas, would identify and connect clients to support groups and leisure activities necessary in the development of prosocial networks. The opportunities to meet prosocial people and engage in prosocial activities allowed the client to build a community to meet emotional needs of connectedness, belongingness, and creativity in healthy ways.

Identify Outcomes and Measure Progress

The forensic social workers met weekly with the clients to review progress in achieving their goals. They were responsible for leading the weekly team meeting discussing client progress and incorporating updates into the client's case-management plan. The forensic social worker was the central hub for information management and charting client progress. This role required strong leadership and communication skills as a member of the interdisciplinary team.

Conclusion

Forensic interdisciplinary collaboration needs to be considered as an integral aspect of evidence-based practice with justice-involved clients. Collaboration guided by the evidence-based principles articulated by PCC with a focus on human rights will contribute to effective advocacy, case management, and treatment services delivered by forensic social workers and provide clarity about the role of the forensic social worker as a member of a forensic interdisciplinary team.

CHAPTER EXERCISES

Exercise 1. Discuss in a small and then a large group: What are the obstacles and facilitators to successful interdisciplinary collaboration?

Exercise 2. After reviewing the IECEP (2011) competencies, discuss in at least four small groups the importance of: (a) values and ethics, (b) role responsibilities, (c) interprofessional communication, and (d) teams and teamwork.

Exercise 3. Prior to class, watch the following webinar on mental health and criminal justice collaboration: https://www.youtube.com/watch?v=8VLeWdKgOtU. Come to class prepared to discuss.

Additional Resources

CJ-MH COLLABORATION: www.youtube.com/watch?v=8VLeWdKgOtU

Forensic Case Management: http://static.nicic.gov/Library/021814.pdf

Forensic Case Management: www.ct.gov/opm/lib/opm/cjppd/cjcjpac/ct_wocmm_outcomes_pres_-_cj_pac-handout.pdf

Juvenile Justice: www.youtube.com/watch?v=tbFZzGIjHRU

References

American Medical Association. (2001). Code of medical ethics. Retrieved from http://www.ama-assn.org/ama/pub/physician-resources/medical-ethics/codemedical-ethics.page

American Nurses Association. (2001). *Code of ethics for nurses.* Retrieved from http://www
.nursingworld.org/mainmenucategories/ethicsstandards/codeofethicsfornurses/code-of-ethics
.pdf

American Psychological Association. (2002). Ethical principles of psychologists and code of conduct.
American Psychologist, 57, 1060–1073.

Amundson, M. L., Moulton, P. L., Zimmerman, S. S., & Johnson, B. J. (2008). An innovative approach to
student internships on American Indian reservations. *Journal of Interdisciplinary Care, 22*(1), 93–101.

Andrews, D. A., & Bonta, J. (2010). *The psychology of criminal conduct* (5th ed.). New Providence, NJ:
LexisNexis.

Atwal, A., & Caldwell, K. (2006). Nurses' perceptions of multidisciplinary team work in acute healthcare. *International Journal of Nursing Practice, 12*(6), 359–360.

Barnoski, R. (2004). *Outcome evaluation of Washington State's research-based programs for juvenile offenders.*
Olympia: Washington State Institute for Public Policy.

Berg-Weger, M., & Schnedier, F. D. (1998). Interdisciplinary collaboration in social work education.
Journal of Social Work Education, 34, 97–107.

Bogue, B., Campbell, N., Carey, M., Clawson, E., Faust, D., Florio, K., . . . Woodward, W. (2004).
Implementing evidence-based practices in community corrections: Leading organizational change
and development. Retrieved from http://www.nicic.org/Library/019344

Bronstein, L. R. (2003). A model for interdisciplinary collaboration. *Social Work, 48,* 297–306. Retrieved
from http://www.psychrights.org/Research/Digest/CriticalThinkRxCites/bronstein.pdf

Bronstein, L. R., Mizrahi, T., Korazim-Ko Rosy, Y., & McPhee, D. (2010). *Interdisciplinary collaboration
in social work education in the USA, Israel and Canada: Deans' and directors' perspectives.* London, UK:
Sage Publications.

California Department of Corrections and Rehabilitation Expert Panel on Adult Offender and Recidivism
Reduction Programming. (2007). *A roadmap for effective offender programming in California.* Retrieved
from https://www.prisonlegalnews.org/media/publications/roadmap_for_effective_offender_
programming_ca_panel_recommendations_2007.pdf

Chan, A. C., Chi, S. P. M., Ching, S., & Lam, S. (2010). Inter-professional education: The interface of
nursing and social work. *Journal of Clinical Nursing, 19*(1–2), 168–176.

Choi, B. C., & Pak, A. W. (2006). Multidisciplinarity, interdisciplinarity and transdisciplinarity in health
research, services, education and policy: 1. Definitions, objectives, and evidence of effectiveness.
Clinical Investigative Medicine, 29(6), 351–364.

D'Amour, D., Sicotte, C., & Levy, R. (1999). L'action collective au sein d'équipesinterprofessionnelles
dans les services de santé. *Sciences Sociales et Santé, 17*(3), 67–94.

Dowden, C., & Andrews, D. A. (1999a). What works for female offenders: A metaanalytic review. *Crime
& Delinquency, 45,* 438–452.

Dowden, C., & Andrews, D. A. (1999b). What works in young offender treatment: A meta-analysis.
Forum on Corrections Research, 11, 21–24.

Ethical Principles of Public Health. (2002). Retrieved from http://ethics.iit.edu/ecodes/node/4734

Freeth, D., Hammick, M., Reeves, S., Koppel, I., & Barr, H. (2005). *Effective interprofessional education:
Development, delivery & evaluation.* Oxford, UK: Blackwell Publishing.

French, S., & Gendreau, P. (2006). Reducing prison misconducts: What works! *Criminal Justice and
Behavior, 33,* 185–218.

Graham, J. R., & Barter, K. (1999). Collaboration: A social work practice method. *Families in Society, 80*(1),
6–13.

Gendreau, P., & Andrews, D. A. (1990). Tertiary prevention: What the meta-analysis of the offender treatment literature tells us about "what works." *Canadian Journal of Criminology, 32*, 173–184.

Interprofessional Education Collaborative Expert Panel. (2011). *Core competencies for interprofessional collaborative practice: Report of an expert panel.* Washington, DC: Interprofessional Education Collaborative.

Kelly, L., Smith, N., & Gibson, S. (2009). From intervention roles to multidisciplinary practice. In T. Maschi, C. Bradley, & K. Ward (Eds.), *Forensic social work: Psychosocial and legal issues in diverse practice settings* (pp. 51–60). New York, NY: Springer Publishing.

Maschi, T., & Youdin, R. (2010). *Social worker as researcher: Integrating research with advocacy.* Boston, MA: Pearson.

Mizrahi, T., & Abramson, J. (2000). Collaboration between social workers and physicians: Perspectives on a shared case. *Social Work in Health Care, 31*(3), 1–24.

National Association of Social Workers. (2008). *Code of Ethics of the National Association of Social Workers.* Washington, DC: Author. Retrieved from http://www.naswdc.org/pubs/code/code.asp

National Social Workers Code of Ethics. (2008). Retrieved from https://socialwork.utexas.edu/dl/files/academic-programs/other/nasw-code-of-ethics.pdf

Parker-Oliver, D., & Peck, M. (2006). Inside the interdisciplinary team experiences of hospice social workers. *Journal of Social Work in End of Life and Palliative Care, 2*(3), 7–21.

Reppucci, N., & Saunders, J. (1974). Social psychology of behavior modification: Problems of implementation in natural settings. *American Psychologist, 29*(9), 649–660.

Sachwald, J., & Tesluk, P. (2005). Leading change in community corrections: Embracing transformational leadership (*Topics in community corrections, 2005*). Washington, DC: National Institute of Corrections.

Sperber, K. G., Latessa, E. J., & Makarios, M. D. (2013). Examining the interaction between level of risk and dosage of treatment. *Criminal Justice and Behavior, 40*(3), 338–348.

Weiss, D., Tilin, F., & Morgan, M. J. (2014). *The inter-professional health care team: Leadership and development.* Burlington, MA: Jones & Bartlett.

VOICES FROM THE FIELD

Deana "Dee" McDonald, BS
Circuit Court Judge, Family Division
Juris Doctor, University of Louisville, Brandeis School of Law
Bachelor of Science, Western KY University, 1974, double major in Psychology and
Physical Education

Agency Setting

The premise of family court is "one family–one judge." It was developed, in the early 1990s in Kentucky, with the hope that having one judge for all the issues arising for one family would provide a much more accurate and more consistent handling of each situation, as well as making it easier on the family members. This court handles divorce, custody, parenting time, relocations (one parent moving away from Louisville with the child(ren)), domestic violence, determining the paternity of children born out of wedlock, child support issues, dependency, abuse, neglect, termination of parental rights, and many other family-related areas.

From January 1, 2011, to December 31, 2014, I served as a District Court judge, handling all juvenile delinquency cases within Jefferson County. In this capacity I touched the vast majority of juvenile cases that were not eligible for diversion outside of the court system. I left this seat when I was elected to the Circuit Court, Family Division Eight (8).

Background

Following graduation from Western Kentucky University I began a career as a social worker for the present Cabinet for Health and Family Services, the Kentucky state agency responsible for, among other things, the protection and welfare of the state's children. While holding that job, I was accepted into law school and graduated from the Louisville Brandeis School of Law, Night Division, in 1994. Since graduation from law school, I have worked as a prosecutor in the Domestic Violence, Juvenile and Child Support Divisions of the Jefferson County Attorney's Office, under three different county attorneys. I also spent four years with the Cabinet for Health and Family Services, as an attorney, handling termination of parental rights cases and dependency, abuse, and neglect cases in Jefferson County Family Court.

Observations

I first entered the Hall of Justice as a young, inexperienced social worker in 1979. I had never seen the inside of a courtroom, much less testified in one. Nevertheless, I began working with adolescents and found myself in a courtroom, almost daily. I learned quickly that the judges had little time to truly become involved in each case as there were simply too many of them. They and the attorneys working with the children, prosecutors, and defense counsel depended greatly on the information provided to them by the case managers (i.e., the social workers, i.e., me).

If my client were lucky, a skilled therapist had been working with them and was able to provide me with suggestions for continued treatment. The feedback and help I received from these professionals made my recommendations to the court much more credible and apt to morph them into some form of a court order, thereby giving me something stronger with which to work. Adolescents can sometimes be a bit contrary. Then, by my following through and advising those therapists of the workings within the courtroom, we were able to provide more of a "continuum of care," if you will, for the children. Having a form of support group in place for each client, and having the professional on the same page, allowed for consistency, which is something that my clients rarely had in their young lives. This was the beginning of what we now call "interdisciplinary collaboration." Little did we know, all those many years ago, that what we were trying to do was such a good thing that it actually would get its own name!

As time went on I eventually moved into the delinquency realm of the court system. The clients grew older and presented with far more difficult issues and I found myself dealing with residential programs that provided 24/7 care for the children. Again, the professionals with whom I dealt made all the difference in the world for these kids, especially when I was planning on transitioning them back into the community. Connecting the children with appropriate professionals back at home, to keep a support system in place, was of utmost importance to me. I was not having much luck being able to change the home environment and while I knew the kids would return with new problem-solving skills, those new skills would probably have little impact on the old problems at home. Affording the professionals a chance to communicate as the client returned home made the transition much less difficult. Luckily, many of the therapists from the residential programs were willing to continue to have contact with the clients and were also willing to communicate, on a continuing basis, with the local therapist. As a case manager, it was very important for me to have other professionals with whom to work, to problem-solve, and to make sure I was not missing something that could adversely affect the client. I repeat, the communication between myself and these skilled professionals routinely made it into the ears of the judges, prosecutors, and defense counsel.

Challenges

Ultimately, after many years and further education, I found myself wearing a black robe and sitting on a bench making decisions regarding children, just like I, as a young social worker, had worked with years before. I rarely took that social work hat off my head. I rarely do today. Many times the first question I ask is: "Are the children in therapy?" If not, why? If so, with whom? How often do they attend? Do you, as the case manager, meet with the therapist? If not, why? If so, how do they help you help your clients? More often than not, I fail to see much connection between the field workers and the therapists. I know that there are many more clients now to serve and fewer field workers to help them. I also know the turnover is great within the field services area. The seasoned workers are burning out as the caseloads increase and the support to and for them diminishes. So, to whom is that gauntlet passed? It appears to me, it has been thrown to those that provide the therapy, to and for the clients, to surround them with that ring of support to give them the boost they need to achieve the goals they have set for themselves. Oftentimes, this is an unmanageable request.

Today, as I sit as a family court judge, I see the need for therapeutic services on so many levels: individual therapy, family therapy, marital therapy, reunification therapy, parenting assistance, therapeutic visitation sessions, sexual behavioral therapy, alcohol/drug intervention, and I could go on and on. Without the support and assistance of highly trained, motivated, and skilled professionals, the children with whom I deal have little hope of developing into well-rounded adults who can be of benefit to our community and themselves. Their parents are left unto their own devices, which is why we must remove so many children from their homes, thus beginning the cycle again.

Collaboration between professionals who are tasked with providing services to the families and children of our community is even more important today than it was 30 years ago. The additional stresses present in today's society take a toll, not only on the clients, but on the service providers as well. The present introduction of the justice partners to this communication opens even more possibilities for the clients. The justice system can be a strange and confusing place, even for those of us with many years of experience working within it. Explanations from those of us responsible for making the difficult decisions, regarding our shared clients, hopefully can provide insight for those working on the ground level with them. When we share our knowledge, through communication, we can better serve our clients and thus our community. Together, we can continue to make this a wonderful place to be.

CHAPTER 29

Human Rights Issues and Research With Prisoners and Other Vulnerable Populations: Where Does Evidence-Based Practice Go From Here?

Sandy Gibson

CHAPTER OBJECTIVES

The major objectives of this chapter are to:

- Discuss the history of forensic research atrocities.
- Promote the use of National Association of Social Workers (NASW) *Code of Ethics* as a foundation for forensic research.
- Describe national and international responses to historic forensic research.
- Build awareness of the need for new research to serve forensic populations.
- Increase familiarity with forensic research methodologies.

CHAPTER COMPETENCIES HIGHLIGHTED

- Competency 1: Demonstrate Ethical and Professional Behavior
- Competency 3: Advance Human Rights and Social, Economic, and Environmental Justice
- Competency 4: Engage in Practice Informed Research and Research Informed Practice
- Competency 7: Assess Individuals, Families, Organizations, and Communities
- Competency 9: Evaluate Practice With Individuals, Families, Organizations, and Communities

Research in correctional settings has transitioned from one of exploitation of a vulnerable population, to one of restrictions during a time when there has been an explosion of inmate populations with significant mental health needs (Veeh, Tripodi, Pettus-Davis, & Scheyett, 2016; Wakai, Shelton, Trestman, & Kesten, 2009). A substantial challenge facing forensic social workers, especially in correctional settings, is providing effective treatment when security and custodial concerns are emphasized over treatment concerns (Ward & Willis, 2010), creating conflicts between the law and professional ethics codes (Birgden & Perlin, 2009; Wakai et al., 2009), and the challenge of conducting research to evaluate the translation of evidence-based clinical practices to correctional settings (Gee & Bertrand-Godfrey, 2014; Sampl, Wakai, & Trestman, 2010). One such challenge is that random assignment is often not a realistic option in criminal justice settings (DeMatteo, Filone, & LaDuke, 2011). Rubin and Bellamy (2012) argued that the evidence-based-practice (EBP) process allows social workers to identify which interventions, programs, policies, and assessment tools are supported by the best evidence; find and critically review research studies in seeking evidence to answer clinical questions; and measure treatment progress and outcomes. However, increased efforts at integrating EBPs in correctional settings have significantly grown over the past two decades, with correctional administrations realizing the cost-effectiveness of evidence-based treatment services (Sampl et al., 2010).

Ethics, Human Rights, and Research and Evaluation

The NASW *Code of Ethics* (2008, 5.02) purports that social workers should promote and facilitate evaluation and research to contribute to the development of knowledge. This underscores both an ethical and a human rights obligation for the need for more prevention and intervention studies with incarcerated individuals.

There is also a need to research services for individuals with legal problems who are not incarcerated. Existing research identifies that a clear link with aftercare services is vital to ensuring continuity of care after release from jail, and that prerelease planning, referral, and community service engagement ensures the forensic client a connection to treatment and support (Hunter, Lanza, Lawlor, Dyson, & Gordon, 2016; Solomon & Draine, 1995). Forensic research focusing on the strengthening of this link could serve to strengthen the services received postrelease, enhance multiservice communication and collaboration, and ultimately serve to reduce recidivism.

The substantially high rate of recidivism for incarcerated individuals with mental health diagnoses (Veeh et al., 2016), coupled with the costs associated with incarceration, also demonstrate the need for treatment research associated with forensic clients to move away from penalty only and move toward a more rehabilitation-oriented incarceration and probation/parole.

History of Human Rights and Ethical Violations in Research With Prisoners

History is fraught with human rights violations in research conducted with prisoners. For centuries, prisoners, a population of disadvantaged and vulnerable persons, have been used as subjects of research. Prisoners were considered expendable research subjects (Arboleda-Florez, 2005; Wakai et al., 2009). The abuses were such that authors would refer to prisoners as "human guinea pigs" (Adams & Cowan, 1971), who were "cheaper than chimpanzees" (Mitford, 1973).

In the mid-19th and 20th centuries, the dominant ideology was that the common good—either for social benefit or the development of science—justified the performance of experiments in humans without respect for their autonomy (Arboleda-Florez, 2005), as exemplified by the following forensic research studies.

Sexually Transmitted Infection Research

From 1946 to 1948, U.S. researcher John Cutler, an investigator from the Tuskegee Study, was also the lead investigator on another study that targeted prison inmates in Guatemala. This study intentionally infected subjects with sexually transmitted infections (STIs) through a grant that was approved and funded by the National Institutes of Health (NIH; Frieden & Collins, 2010). Initially subjects were unknowingly introduced to an STI through the introduction of sex workers into the prisons; however, when this proved to offer low transmission rates, prisoners were then directly inoculated with the disease. Although the majority of subjects were later treated with penicillin, some received only partial treatment.

Statesville Penitentiary Malaria Study (1945)

The Statesville Penitentiary Malaria Study was conducted by the University of Chicago and the U.S. Army and State Department. Malaria, an infectious disease, which results in extreme illness and death if left untreated, was hindering the military as they fought battles in the Pacific region. Experimental research was needed to quickly develop drugs to fight malaria, and prisoners were used to test these drugs. During World War II, in Illinois, hundreds of prisoners were inoculated with malaria to research effective methods for disease prevention and intervention (Advisory Committee on Human Radiation Experiments, 1995; Arboleda-Florez, 2005; Paulsen, 1973). An unknown number of inmates became ill or died, and a commutation of sentence or parole was later granted to 317 of the 432 research subjects.

Trends in Phase 1 Research (Until the Mid-1970s)

During the postwar years it was common practice for researchers to employ prisoners as research subjects for studies ranging from identifying the causes of cancer to testing new cosmetics. By the early 1970s, the Food and Drug Administration estimated that more than 90% of phase 1 research in new drugs was first conducted on prisoners (Adams & Cowan, 1971; Arboleda-Florez, 2005). Over the past two decades there has been a substantial reduction in the use of prisoners for research. As a result, phase 1 projects now use nonincarcerated subjects, although these individuals are still typically underprivileged.

University of Washington Radiation Study (1963–1973)

From 1963 to 1973, the University of Washington, Seattle, conducted studies on the effect of radiation on human testicular function using inmates at Washington State prison. The effects of the radiation were unknown, and vasectomies were suggested for the inmates on completion of the study as it was unknown what effect such radiation would have on future offspring. Initially, research subjects were not informed of potential risks associated with participation, although there was a vague reference to the possibility of tumors. In 1976, subjects filed a lawsuit alleging a lack of informed consent. During a deposition, the lead researcher, Dr. Heller, indicated "I didn't want to frighten them so I said 'tumor' . . . I may have, on occasion, said cancer" (Deposition of Heller, 1976). The suit (*Robert Case v. State of Oregon*) was settled out of court in 1979 for $2,215 in damages, which was shared by nine individuals. In 1994, President Clinton charged an advisory committee to uncover the history of human radiation experiments. The committee ultimately discovered that over 4,000 federal government-sponsored human radiation experiments were conducted between 1944 and 1974 (Advisory Committee on Human Radiation Experiments, 1995).

Human Rights? Responses to Historic Forensic Research Atrocities

There were many national and international responses to these tragic forensic research studies. These documents include the Nuremberg Code, Declaration of Helsinki, the National Research Act, Title 45 Code of Federal Regulations Part 46, and the Belmont Report (NIH, 1979).

The Nuremberg Code is a set of principles for human experimentation established as a result of the Nuremberg Trials at the end of World War II. Specifically, the code was created in response to the inhumane Nazi human experimentation carried out during the war, such as bone transplantation; sterilization methods; and exposure to extreme cold, high altitudes, and mustard gas (Marrus, 1999; Temme, 2003). The code includes principles such as informed consent and the absence of coercion. As horrific as these research efforts were, it is important to acknowledge that during the Nuremberg Medical Trial, defense attorneys argued that there was no difference between research conducted in American prisons and the experiments that took place in the Nazi concentration camps (Arboleda-Florez, 2005).

Another response to these historic forensic research atrocities was the Declaration of Helsinki, developed by the World Medical Association (WMA) in 1964 and currently operating in its ninth revision. It was and is a statement of ethical principles that provides guidance to professionals conducting research involving human subjects (WMA, 2013).

On July 12, 1974, the National Research Act (Pub. L. 93-348) was signed into law, thereby creating the National Commission for the Protection of Human Subjects of Biomedical and Behavioral Research. In 1979, the National Commission for the Protection of Human Subjects of Biomedical and Behavioral Research, a subsidiary of the Department of Health, Education and Welfare, published the Belmont Report, a set of ethical principles and guidelines for the protection of human subjects of research. The basic ethical principles of this report are respect for persons, beneficence, and justice, and the basic applications are informed consent, assessment of risk and benefits, and the selection of subjects (NIH, Office of Human Subjects Research, 1979).

Furthermore, Title 45 Code of Federal Regulations Part 46, Protection of Human Subjects, scripted in 1991, revised in 1995 and again in 2009, is a document that embodies the ethical principles of the Belmont Report, providing a framework in which researchers can ensure that serious efforts have been made to protect the rights and welfare of research subjects (United States Department of Health and Human Services [USDHHS], 2009).

The vulnerabilities experienced by forensic research subjects are recognized and addressed by the United Nations in principle 22 of the Body of Principles for the Protection of All Persons Under Any Form of Detention or Imprisonment (1988), which indicates: "No detained or imprisoned person shall, even with his consent, be subjected to any medical or scientific experimentation, which may be detrimental to his health."

Despite this international response for the protection of research subjects, Rawlinson and Yadavendu (2015) argue that clinical trials continue today that result in death and injury by targeting vulnerable populations with medical research outsourced to the private sector that targets human subjects in developing countries.

Institutional Review Boards

One protective factor for forensic research subjects is the requirement that researchers obtain Institutional Review Board (IRB) approval of their projects prior to implementation. In 1974, the U.S. Congress passed the National Research Act of 1974, which defined IRBs and required them to be used for all research involving human subjects. This was done primarily in response to the many aforementioned research abuses. IRBs are independent committees that approve, monitor, and review research proposals and protocols with the purpose of protecting the rights, safety, and well-being of the research subjects. IRBs are regulated by the Office of Human Research Protections, which is overseen by the Department of Health and Human Services (DHHS).

Information obtained from forensic research may be considered valuable to the criminal justice system administration, as it may do things such as help to identify previously unknown criminal behaviors or may help to identify those who are more or less likely to qualify for parole. If criminal justice administration is associated with the IRB process, it may cause the IRB to weaken the protections afforded to research subjects for the administration to gain the insights it feels would enhance its own system. To provide the protections necessary for ethical forensic research, including the absence or appearance of coercion, the knowledgeable and competent assent or consent of the subject, and the subjects' knowledge that they may quit the study at any time, forensic research IRBs must be free from criminal justice administration oversight (Hillbrand, 2005). Many departments of corrections (DOCs) maintain their own separate IRB, requiring all studies to obtain DOC IRB approval, in addition to the researchers' own institutional IRB approval. Non-DOC IRBs typically (and should) require DOC IRB approval first, as part of their own application process, in order to assess for any possible weakening of protections proposed.

Many of the documents that arose in response to the forensic research atrocities reference the rights of "prisoners." If this is strictly applied to research studies that are prison-based only, it will not afford the same protections to other research subjects who are involved with the criminal justice system, even though they too experience limited freedoms and liberties and are also subject to the possibility of coercion. In fact, in 2014, of the 6.85 million individuals involved in the U.S. criminal justice system, only 2.2 million were actually incarcerated, with the remainder being on either probation or parole (Kaeble, Glaze, Tsoutis, & Minton, 2016).

Need for Forensic Research

As these necessary safeguards were added to protect forensic research subjects, they had the unintended consequences of reducing research that could benefit this population. Out of concern that an IRB may deny a proposal that involves subjects who are involved with the criminal justice system, many studies exclude such potential subjects in their research design. This not only refers to prison-based research, but also to research studies at community mental health or substance abuse treatment centers, where individuals on probation or parole are often excluded from samples. Not only does this diminish the value of the research, particularly for understanding outcomes as they relate to forensic clients, but it also excludes forensic clients from enjoying the enhancement of self-esteem that comes from having a share in a project aimed at making a contribution on behalf of society (Sampl et al., 2010; Wakai et al., 2009). Everyone loses in the process. Subjects lose the benefits of innovation and improved services, and forensic social workers lose the improvement of knowledge on how best to serve this population.

"The American Academy of Psychiatry and the Law Committee on Institutional and Correctional Forensic Psychiatry takes the position that forensic mental health research is far too important to be allowed to sink into a sea of oversight requirements" (Young, 2005). Thus, there is a great need for forensic research. As forensic subjects are a captive population, they are vulnerable subjects in need of special protective measures. However, excessive protection can bring harm to those who it intended to protect. For example, if researchers avoid conducting forensic research because of the extensive protections required of subjects, then they are doing forensic populations a disservice by not developing knowledge on how to best serve them.

As protections to prisoners emerged in the 1970s, the amount of forensic research decreased immensely. This is mostly a result of the fact that much existing research was of no direct benefit to prisoners, but instead was likely to have been convenience research. Stringent oversight requirements, coupled with a lack of societal interest in investing in services to specifically treat forensic clients, resulted in a rather limited field of experimental research in forensic settings.

The rise of mass incarceration, attributed to drug offenses during the *War on Drugs* (Institute of Medicine [IOM], 2006), co-occurred with this reduction in research (Myers, 2015). However, because of the multiple needs, including high rates of substance abuse and mental health problems, among this population, there is a great need for prisoners to receive evidence-based mental health and substance abuse services (Sampl et al., 2010; Veeh et al., 2016). As Harner, Budescu, Gillihan, Riley, and Foa (2015) identify prisons as a "mental health safety net" (p. 58) for some of the most vulnerable people, without evidence-based research on how to best serve this population, we are not only failing prisoners, but also society, as 98% of incarcerated individuals will eventually return to the community (Hickey, Kerber, Astroth, Kim, & Schlenker, 2015).

Risks

As, one hopes, the past atrocities of forensic research have ended as a result of new protections of subjects, there is now a more common risk concerning emotional distress as a result of research participation. Social risks of research participation are largely related to confidentiality and the damage to one's reputation that can directly result from participation in the study, even if just as a control member (Cloyes, 2006; Elger, Handtke, & Wangmo, 2015). For example, in a treatment study for sex offenders, individuals who are known participants, even those nonsex offenders who are in the control group, are likely to be viewed by fellow inmates as sex offenders. In the prison-established hierarchy among inmates, sex offenders exist on one of the lowest levels and are viewed quite negatively; they are often subjected to extensive verbal and physical abuses from other inmates.

In addition, some studies elicit information of a highly personal and sensitive nature, and are often audiotaped (Cloyes, 2006; Overholser, 1987). This can be a cause of great concern for forensic clients as information disclosed to researchers, if discovered by the criminal justice system, could result in convictions for additional crimes committed, a denial of parole, or reincarceration of those on probation or parole. For these reasons, the importance of confidentiality and the trust that forensic clients must have for the forensic researcher are imperative; even more so, researchers must be very clear on the limits of their confidentiality (Elger, Handtke, & Wangmo, 2015).

Recognizing the importance of such protections to the completion of valid research, the federal government, through the NIH, offers a Certificate of Confidentiality (COC), which allows researchers to protect the identities and any identifying characteristics of research subjects in response to any legal demands, such as a subpoena for information. Without a COC, researchers could be required by law to disclose data collected that might reflect criminal behaviors, and that could ultimately be used against the subjects in the legal system. IRBs should, and many do, require a COC for any studies that will collect information in an identifying way that involves disclosure of illegal behaviors.

A different type of social risk entails the potential for coercion or undue influence often found in forensic settings. As forensic subjects lack the freedom and liberties of nonforensic individuals, it has not been uncommon to use incentives associated with greater freedoms or that someway manipulate their quality of life, such as better prison jobs or extended outdoor time (Cloyes, 2006). When subjects receive benefits such as these, the benefits can serve as coercion to participate in exchange for the desirable enhanced freedom. These types of incentives create resentments among nonparticipants, promoting a negative environment and possibly putting subjects at risk of physical harm. The American Psychological Association recommends that parole boards not take into account research participation when reviewing parole eligibility to avoid the possibility of coercion. Although Federal Regulations Code 46.306(a) mandates safeguards for prisoners who participate in research, there is no published standard of acceptable incentives with forensic clients to serve as a guide for researchers and IRBs when searching for a balance of incentive without coercion (Wakai et al., 2009). Recognizing this barrier to human subject protection, Brown and Merritt (2013) call for a global public database for human subject research.

To avoid coercion when conducting forensic research, it is essential that economic benefits are limited because of the impoverished nature of prisons. The Code of Federal Regulations (28 C.F.R., section 512.16) recommends that only concrete reinforcers, such as soft drinks and snacks, be used for reimbursement. If at all possible, external awards as incentives for study participation should be avoided altogether. If subjects are to be paid for their participation, the amount should never be more than the hourly wage they earn, which is typically much less than the federal minimum wage, and participation should be in lieu of work time (Arboleda-Florez, 2005; Wettstein, 2005).

Dugosh, Festinger, Marlowe, and Clements (2014) developed an instrument to measure perceived coercion for criminally involved subjects being recruited into research. Preliminary testing of this measure revealed that 51% of forensic subjects (drug court) reported they chose to participate in the research study of their drug court experience because they thought doing so would help their court case, and that they believed the judge would like it (Dugosh, Festinger, Croft, & Marlowe, 2010).

Benefits

There are also benefits to subjects of forensic research, such as the provision of access to treatment not otherwise available, as the Bureau of Justice Statistics Survey of prison inmates (James & Glaze, 2006) indicates more than half of prison and jail inmates had a mental health diagnosis, with less than half receiving treatment (34% state, 24% federal, and 17% jail) while incarcerated. Other potential benefits include immediate personal health gains, knowledge from classes, an opportunity to engage in altruistic behavior not commonly available in prisons, and an enhanced sense of purpose and usefulness (Arboleda-Florez, 2005; Childress, 2006). A qualitative study that specifically investigated perceived benefits of research participation among prison inmates reflected that such research offered a welcome respite from boredom, psychological satisfaction, and monetary gains, and that they did not feel coerced to participate or believe that they experienced any harm (Copes, Hochstetler, & Brown, 2013).

Forensic Research Methodologies

The National Commission for the Protection of Human Subjects identifies three categories of research in prison settings: convenience research, prison-oriented research, and treatment-oriented research. In convenience research, the accessibility of a large group is the main, if not sole, reason for using prisons for research. This differs from convenience sampling, which indicates that the researcher has intentions of studying forensic populations and simply took the easiest sampling route of studying this intended population. Convenience research means the forensic population is used solely because the entire population is convenient, but the purpose of the research is not intended to serve primarily (or even at all) this population. Forensic populations are simply a convenient population because of their captivity. This research typically has no direct benefit to the prisoners, and therefore nonincarcerated subjects should be used to reduce the likelihood of coercion or manipulation of the vulnerable incarcerated population (Overholser, 1987). An example of convenience research can be found in the pharmaceutical and cosmetic drug research that once was prevalent in prison populations. Because of the many protections now afforded to forensic populations, convenience research is unlikely to be approved by an IRB.

Prison-oriented research typically studies the effects of incarceration on areas such as psychological functioning, predicting adjustment to prison life, or identifying characteristics of participants in a riot. Prison-oriented research can be beneficial to prisoners when it involves direct, practical benefits to the prisoners, such as strategies for strengthening families for children of inmates. When this research serves the interests of prisoners and their families, it has value for both the subjects and the greater society (Overholser, 1987). Studies such as inmate abuse during incarceration (Dierkhising, Lane, & Natsuaki, 2014) and a study of effects of world assumptions on the mental health of older adults (Maschi & Baer, 2013) are examples of prison-oriented research.

Treatment-oriented research involves the development and evaluation of treatment programs designed specifically to benefit the subjects. This type of research is the most ethically justifiable of the three as it attempts to improve the welfare of incarcerated subjects. Such research should have direct implications for the later development or refinement of prison services or treatment programs. Studies of the evaluation of a prison-based music project (Caulfield, Wilkinson, & Wilson, 2016) and an evidence-based HIV prevention program for incarcerated women (Fasula et al., 2013) are examples of treatment-oriented research.

Mental health problems are more common among prison inmates than the general population (Fazel & Seewald, 2012), with more than half of all jail and prison inmates having a mental health problem (James & Glaze, 2006). The consolidation of such a large group of individuals meeting diagnostic criteria for a variety of psychological disorders facilitates the recruitment, sampling, and retention process of treatment studies (Metzner & Dvoskin, 2006). However, research reveals that although those with preexisting mental health challenges are at greatest risk for arrest (Fisher et al., 2011), the negative influence of the prison climate can also promote the development of mental health problems (Goomany & Dickinson, 2015). So, although it is common to find prison inmates with diagnoses, it is important to separate those disorders potentially capable of affecting or producing the criminal behavior from those that are apparently a consequence of the incarceration (Overholser, 1987), and to recognize that research on prevalence varies greatly based on the facility, type of research, and field/orientation of the researcher (Prins, 2014). In prison studies, it is extremely difficult, without baseline measures, to control for the effects of incarceration on the outcomes under study, which further supports the need to avoid the use of prisoners as research subjects in studies other than prison/treatment-oriented research.

Whether a research study will directly benefit the prison population is not adequate ethical justification to conduct a study with incarcerated subjects. It is also important to consider the degree of relationship between the subject of research and the offenders' crime. If there is no relationship between the subject and the subject under study, then the use of such a prisoner is again merely convenient and should be avoided.

Qualitative Research Methodologies

Qualitative research methodologies lend themselves well to forensic research, particularly because of the lack of existing research, which creates a need for more exploratory methods. Research subjects themselves can be more involved in the research through techniques such as member checks, follow-up interviews, and co-identification of themes in the data, and other forms of feedback and collaboration (Cloyes, 2006). This can enhance trust between the forensic subjects and the researchers, strengthening the outcomes of the study. Drake and Harvey (2014) reflect on their extensive experience with qualitative research in prison environments, which often necessitates contact with multiple discrete divisions within prisons requiring extensive negotiations for access. Such research also typically occurs over a much longer period of time than quantitative research, creating challenges with building new relationships due to high levels of prison staff turnover. Although qualitative research is time-consuming, and faces barriers beyond that typically associated with quantitative research, Myers (2015) encourages continued qualitative research in prisons, as such insights are crucial for crafting effective criminal justice and social policy.

Forensic Research With Juvenile Populations

Inclusion of children in forensic research is important. As social workers, it is essential for us to know the best proven interventions to use with this population. This importance is exemplified by NIH's requirement that all of its funded research include children, unless the investigator can provide a valid reason as to why they should not be included. There are special review requirements for IRBs (Inclusion of Children, 45 CFR 46, Subpart D, Sec. 401-409; USDHHS, 2009) that include various protections for child research, varying by the degree of risk involved in the research. These protections vary from simple parental consent, when the research has no greater than minimal risk, to requiring the permission of both the child and the parents, indicating the likelihood that the research is generalizable and specifically related to the child's disorder. In addition, the risk may only be slightly higher than minimal. Reed (1999) indicates the forensic juveniles who are imprisoned become regulatory orphans for purposes of guiding IRBs in their review process. This means that the IRB shall require appointment of an advocate for each child who is a ward, an advocate who is capable of acting in the best interests of the child for the duration of the child's participation in the research and who is not associated in any way with the research, the investigators, or the guardian organization (USDHHS, 2009).

Lane, Goldstein, Heilbrun, Cruise, and Pennacchia (2012) also highlight the challenge associated with research with juveniles associated with disclosures of abuse and harm to self or others. Mandatory reporting of such abuse can create conflicts with parents and facilities, both of whom control researchers' access to this population. Although there is no challenge in terms of knowing what to do (always make reports if abuse is disclosed), researchers should understand that making these mandatory reports may result in reduced or terminated access to this population.

As previously discussed, forensic populations require additional protections when participating in research, but it is still critical that forensic research move forward. For the same reasons that we must remain committed to conducting forensic research, we must also remain committed to including children, who do indeed require additional protections beyond that of adult forensic subjects, in our sample populations when appropriate.

Collaboration in Forensic Research

As research with criminal justice populations, especially prisoners, is conducted by various professionals such as psychologists, criminologists, social workers, psychiatrists, and others, as well as within various venues of the legal system, such as prisons, probation and social service departments, and court systems, interdisciplinary collaboration is essential. Apa et al. (2012) suggest that being familiar with the criminal justice system and all of its parts, along with highlighting mutual goals, serves to build the relationships necessary for such collaboration to occur. Wakai et al. (2009) lay out a formal strategy for such research that includes working with stakeholders, including experienced forensic researchers, proposing research that supports the mission, and offering a small pilot to start.

Data Collection

Forensic research is likely to require data collection from various sources within the criminal justice system, such as attendance records with probation and parole officers, drug-screen results, school records for youths, and criminal histories (i.e., past offenses). It is very important to include these systems in the development of any research proposal. Simply approaching these organizations with a fully developed proposal and asking for their participation is unlikely to result in a productive or open collaboration. Their inclusion in proposal development will also facilitate the identification of accessible and available data opportunities. In the case of prison collaboration, prison administration will understand the safety concerns involved with an outside researcher gaining access to the inmate population, whether there is space available to meet research needs, and the determination of who will pay for the additional security that will be required (IOM, 2006).

Conclusion

It is encouraging that there is a recent increase in forensic research. The massive prison population growth, known as mass incarceration, is an effect of the U.S. *War on Drugs*. As we know these individuals are significantly more likely to have a trauma history and mental health or substance use disorder than the general population, it is imperative that we learn best practices for effective interventions to increase their well-being that are tested on these very populations they are intended to serve. Although there are clearly barriers to moving forward with such research, they are by no means insurmountable, and the potential benefits of such work have the potential to not only increase prisoner well-being, but also their future success with reintegration.

CHAPTER EXERCISES

These exercises can be done individually or in a group as a short written paper, class presentation, or small and large group discussion, or as a discussion group thread in a course management system.

Exercise 1. Although phase 1 studies now use nonincarcerated subjects, most of these subjects are still typically underprivileged. Discuss why you think this population is specifically targeted from a social justice perspective, and develop advocacy proposals that could work toward reducing the targeting of this population for phase 1 study participation.

Exercise 2. The American Academy of Psychiatry and the law highlights that forensic mental health research is far too important to be allowed to sink into a sea of oversight requirements now associated with conducting forensic research. If you were to meet collectively with the DOC IRB and the administrator for your state prisons, what would you place on the agenda for your meeting to discuss in order to promote a relationship that values forensic research while maintaining the appropriate protection of subjects?

Exercise 3. Identify some of the potential social risks associated with participating in research for prisoners, and how you, as a researcher, can work to protect subjects from these social risks.

Additional Resources

Belmont Report: www.hhs.gov/ohrp/regulations-and-policy/belmont-report

Certificates of Confidentiality: https://humansubjects.nih.gov/coc/index

Children as Research Subjects HHS 45 CFR 46.407: www.hhs.gov/ohrp/regulations-and-policy/guidance/guidance-on-407-review-process/index.html

Declaration of Helsinki: www.wma.net/policies-post/wma-declaration-of-helsinki-ethical-principles-for-medical-research-involving-human-subjects

National Research Act: https://history.nih.gov/research/downloads/PL93-348.pdf

Nuremberg Code: https://history.nih.gov/research/downloads/nuremberg.pdf

Nuremberg Trials: https://history.nih.gov/research/downloads/nuremberg.pdf

Statesville Penitentiary Study of Malaria: www.gwu.edu/~nsarchiv/radiation/dir/mstreet/commeet/meet10/brief10/br10g1.txt

Title 45 Code of Federal Regulations, Part 46: www.hhs.gov/ohrp/regulations-and-policy/regulations/45-cfr-46

UN Principle 22: www.un.org/documents/ga/res/43/a43r173.htm

Washington State Prison Study: https://bioethicsarchive.georgetown.edu/achre/final/chap9_2.html

References

Adams, A., & Cowan, G. (1971). The human guinea pig: How we test new drugs, *World*, *5*, 20.

Advisory Committee on Human Radiation Experiments. (1995). *Final report of the Advisory Committee on Human Radiation Experiments 061-000-00-848-9*. Washington, DC: U.S. Government Printing Office.

Apa, Z. L., Bai, R., Mukherejee, D. V., Herzig, C. A., Koenigsmann, C., Lowy, F. D., & Larson, E. L. (2012). Challenges and strategies for research in prisons. *Public Health Nursing, 29*(5), 467–472. doi:10.1111/j.1525-1446.2012.01027.x

Arboleda-Florez, J. (2005). The ethics of biomedical research on prisoners. *Forensic Psychiatry, 18,* 514–517.

Birgden, A., & Perlin, M. L. (2009). "Where the home in the valley meets the damp dirty prison": A human rights perspective on therapeutic jurisprudence and the role of forensic psychologists in correctional settings. *Aggression and Violent Behavior, 14*(4), 256–263. doi:10.1016/j.avb.2009.04.002

Body of Principles for the Protection of All Persons Under Any Form of Detention or Imprisonment. (1988). G.A. res. 43/173, annex, 43 U.N. GAOR Supp. (No. 49) at 298, U.N. Doc. A/43/49. Retrieved from http://www.un.org/documents/ga/res/43/a43r173.htm

Brown, B., & Merritt, M. W. (2013). A global public incentive database for human subjects research. *IRB: Ethics & Human Research, 35*(2), 14–17.

Caulfield, L. S., Wilkinson, D. J., & Wilson, D. (2016). Exploring alternative terrain in the rehabilitation and treatment of offenders: Findings from a prison-based music project. *Journal of Offender Rehabilitation, 55*(6), 396–418. doi:10.1080/10509674.2016.1194943

Childress, H. (2006). The anthropologist and the crayons: Changing our focus from avoiding harm to doing good. *Journal of Empirical Research on Human Research Ethics, 1,* 79–87.

Cloyes, K. G. (2006). An ethic of analysis: An argument for critical analysis of research interviews as ethical practice. *Advances in Nursing Science, 29,* 84–97.

Copes, H., Hochstetler, A., & Brown, A. (2013). Inmates' perceptions of the benefits and harm of prison interviews. *Field Methods, 25*(2), 182–196. doi:10.1177/1525822X12465798

DeMatteo, D., Filone, S., & LaDuke, C. (2011). Methodological, ethical, and legal considerations in drug court research. *Behavioral Sciences & The Law, 29*(6), 806–820. doi:10.1002/bsl.1011

Dierkhising, C. B., Lane, A., & Natsuaki, M. N. (2014). Victims behind bars: A preliminary study of abuse during juvenile incarceration and post-release social and emotional functioning. *Psychology, Public Policy, and Law, 20*(2), 181–190. doi:10.1037/law0000002

Drake, D. H., & Harvey, J. (2014). Performing the role of ethnographer: Processing and managing the emotional dimensions of prison research. *International Journal of Social Research Methodology: Theory & Practice, 17*(5), 489–501. doi:10.1080/13645579.2013.769702

Dugosh, K. L., Festinger, D. S., Croft, J. R., & Marlowe, D. B. (2010). Measuring coercion to participate in research within a doubly vulnerable population: Initial development of the Coercion Assessment Scale. *Journal of Empirical Research on Human Research Ethics, 5*(1), 93–102. doi:10.1525/jer.2010.5.1.93

Dugosh, K. L., Festinger, D. S., Marlowe, D. B., & Clements, N. T. (2014). Developing an index to measure the voluntariness of consent to research. *Journal of Empirical Research on Human Research Ethics, 9*(4), 60–70. doi:10.1177/1556264614544100

Elger, B. S., Handtke, V., & Wangmo, T. (2015). Informing patients about limits to confidentiality: A qualitative study in prisons. *International Journal of Law and Psychiatry, 41,* 50–57. doi:10.1016/j.ijlp.2015.03.007

Fasula, A. M., Fogel, C. I., Gelaude, D., Carry, M., Gaiter, J., & Parker, S. (2013). Project POWER: Adapting an evidence-based HIV/STI prevention intervention for incarcerated women. *AIDS Education and Prevention, 25*(3), 203–215. doi:10.1521/aeap.2013.25.3.203

Fazel, S., & Seewald, K. (2012). Serious mental illness in 33,588 prisoners worldwide: Systematic review and meta-regression analysis. *The British Journal of Psychiatry, 200,* 364–373. doi:10.1192/bjp.bp.111.096370

Fisher, W. H., Simon, L., Roy-Bujnowski, K., Grudzinskas, A. J., Wolff, N., Crockett, E., & Banks, S. (2011). Risk of arrest among public mental health services recipients and the general public. *Psychiatric Services, 62*(1), 67–72. doi:10.1176/appi.ps.62.1.67

Frieden, T. R., & Collins, F. S. (2010). Intentional infection of vulnerable populations in 1946–1948: Another tragic history lesson. *Journal of the American Medical Association, 304*(18), 2063–2064. doi:10.1001/jama.2010.1554

Gee, J., & Bertrand-Godfrey, B. (2014). Researching the psychological therapies in prison: Considerations and future recommendations. *International Journal of Prisoner Health, 10*(2), 118–131. doi:10.1108/IJPH-06-2013-0030

Goomany, A., & Dickinson, T. (2015). The influence of prison climate on the mental health of adult prisoners: A literature review. *Journal of Psychiatric and Mental Health Nursing, 22*(6), 413–422. doi:10.1111/jpm.12231

Harner, H. M., Budescu, M., Gillihan, S. J., Riley, S., & Foa, E. B. (2015). Posttraumatic stress disorder in incarcerated women: A call for evidence-based treatment. *Psychological Trauma: Theory, Research, Practice, and Policy, 7*(1), 58–66. doi:10.1037/a0032508

Hickey, K. L., Kerber, C., Astroth, K. S., Kim, M., & Schlenker, E. (2015). Behind bars: Experiences conducting behavioral addictions research in a county jail. *Journal of Psychosocial Nursing and Mental Health Services, 53*(10), 1. doi:10.3928/02793695-20150923-05

Hillbrand, M. (2005). Obstacles to research in forensic psychiatry. *Journal of the American Academy of Psychiatry and the Law, 33*, 295–298.

Hunter, B. A., Lanza, A. S., Lawlor, M., Dyson, W., & Gordon, D. M. (2016). A strengths-based approach to prisoner reentry: The Fresh Start Prisoner Reentry Program. *International Journal of Offender Therapy and Comparative Criminology, 60*(11), 1298–1314. doi:10.1177/0306624X15576501

Institute of Medicine. (2006). *Ethical considerations for research involving prisoners*. Washington, DC: National Academies Press.

James, D., & Glaze, L. (2006). *Mental health problems of prison and jail inmates*. Bureau of Justice Statistics. NCJ 213600 US Dept. of Justice Office of Justice Programs. Washington, DC: U.S. Government Printing Office.

Kaeble, D., Glaze, L., Tsoutis, A., & Minton, T. (2016). Correctional populations in the United States, 2014. Bureau of Justice Statistics. Retrieved from https://www.bjs.gov/index.cfm?ty=pbdetail&iid=5519

Lane, C., Goldstein, N. S., Heilbrun, K., Cruise, K. R., & Pennacchia, D. (2012). Obstacles to research in residential juvenile justice facilities: Recommendations for researchers. *Behavioral Sciences & The Law, 30*(1), 49–68. doi:10.1002/bsl.1991

Marrus, M. (1999). The Nuremberg doctors' trial in historical context. *Bulletin of the History of Medicine, 73*, 106–123.

Maschi, T., & Baer, J. (2013). The heterogeneity of the world assumptions of older adults in prison: Do differing worldviews have a mental health effect? *Traumatology, 19*(1), 65–72. doi:10.1177/1534765612443294

Metzner, J., & Dvoskin, J. (2006). An overview of correctional psychiatry. *Psychiatric Clinics of North America, 29*, 761–772.

Mitford, J. (1973). *Kind and unusual punishment: The prison business*. New York, NY: Alfred A. Knopf.

Myers, R. R. (2015). Barriers, blinders, and unbeknownst experts: Overcoming access barriers to conduct qualitative studies of juvenile justice. *The Prison Journal, 95*(1), 66–83. doi:10.1177/0032885514563279

National Association of Social Workers. (2008). *Code of Ethics*. Washington, DC: Author.

National Institutes of Health. (1979) *Regulations and ethical guidelines*. Retrieved from https://humansubjects.nih.gov/ethical-guidelines-regulations

National Institutes of Health, Office of Human Subjects Research. (1979). *The Belmont report: Ethical principles and guidelines for the protection of human subjects of research*. Washington, DC: U.S. Government Printing Office. Retrieved from https://www.hhs.gov/ohrp/regulations-and-policy/belmont-report/index.html

National Research Act of 1974. (1974). (Pub. L. No. 93-348), 93rd Cong., 2nd Sess.

Office of the United Nations High Commissioner for Human Rights. (1988). *Body of principles for the protection of all persons under any form of detention or imprisonment.* Adopted by General Assembly (Resolution 43/173). New York, NY: Author.

Overholser, J. C. (1987). Ethical issues in prison research: A risk/benefit analysis. *Behavioral Sciences & the Law, 5,* 187–202.

Paulsen, C. A. (1973). *The study of irradiation effects on the human testes: Including histologic, chromosomal and hormonal aspects.* Terminal report, AEC Contract #AT(45B1)B2225. Seattle: University of Washington School of Medicine.

Prins, S. J. (2014). Prevalence of mental illnesses in U.S. state prisons: A systematic review. *Psychiatric Services, 65*(7), 862–872. doi:10.1176/appi.ps.201300166

Rawlinson, P., & Yadavendu, V. K. (2015). Foreign bodies: The new victims of unethical experimentation. *Howard Journal of Criminal Justice, 54*(1), 8–24. doi:10.1111/hojo.12111

Reed, J. (1999). Regulatory orphans: Juvenile prisoners as transvulnerable research subjects. *IRB: Ethics and Human Research, 21,* 9–14.

Robert Case v. State of Oregon et al., Civil no. 76-500; Paul Tyrell v. State of Oregon et al., Civil no. 76-499.

Rubin, A., & Bellamy, J. (2012). *Practitioner's guide to using research for evidence-based practice.* Hoboken, NJ: Wiley.

Sampl, S., Wakai, S., & Trestman, R. L. (2010). Translating evidence-based practices from community to corrections: An example of implementing DBT-CM. *The Journal of Behavior Analysis of Offender and Victim Treatment and Prevention, 2*(2), 114–123. doi:10.1037/h0100463

Solomon, P., & Draine, J. (1995). Issues in serving the forensic client. *Social Work, 40,* 25–33.

Temme, L. A. (2003). Ethics in human experimentation: The two military physicians who helped develop the Nuremberg Code. *Aviation, Space, and Environmental Medicine, 74*(12), 1297–1300.

United States Department of Health and Human Services. (2009). Code of federal regulations. Retrieved from http://www.hhs.gov/ohrp/regulations-and-policy/regulations/45-cfr-46

Veeh, C. A., Tripodi, S. J., Pettus-Davis, C., & Scheyett, A. M. (2016). The interaction of serious mental disorder and race on time to reincarceration. *American Journal of Orthopsychiatry.* doi:10.1037/ort0000183

Wakai, S., Shelton, D., Trestman, R. L., & Kesten, K. (2009). Conducting research in corrections: Challenges and solutions. *Behavioral Sciences & The Law, 27*(5), 743–752. doi:10.1002/bsl.894

Ward, T., & Willis, G. (2010). Ethical issues in forensic and correctional research. *Aggression and Violent Behavior, 15*(6), 399–409. doi:10.1016/j.avb.2010.07.002

Wettstein, R. M. (2005). Quality and quality improvement in forensic mental health evaluations. *Journal of the American Academy of Psychiatry and the Law, 33,* 368–370.

World Medical Association Declaration of Helsinki ethical principles for medical research involving human subjects. (2013). *Journal of the American Medical Association, 310*(20), 2191–2194. doi:10.1001/jama.2013.281053

Young, J. L. (2005). Commentary: Refusing to give up on forensic research. *Journal of the American Academy of Psychiatry and the Law, 33,* 368–370.

VOICES FROM THE FIELD

Sandy Gibson, PhD, LCSW
Associate Professor, Program Evaluator
for the Trenton Violence Reduction Strategy
The College of New Jersey

Agency Setting

The Trenton Violence Reduction Strategy (TVRS) is a comprehensive, evidence-based model built on elements of Boston Ceasefire, Project Safe Neighborhoods, Chicago Ceasefire (CURE), and Federal Prisoner Reentry programs, and also offers an alternative to these traditional models. It synthesizes the most effective components of these programs to address the underlying individual risk factors associated with reoffending by offering the targeted population of violent offenders, gang members, and their families with peer mentoring through outreach workers and case management, including job training, job placement assistance, life skills training, counseling, transportation, and assistance in negotiating the bureaucracies necessary to be a functional member of society.

Practice Responsibilities

As the program evaluator, I am responsible for monitoring that subjects referred for TVRS participation meet the selection criteria. I also develop the battery of instruments used to evaluate each component of the program, and the collection of baseline, 6-, 12-, and 24-month follow-up data on every subject recruited to participate in TVRS. As some subjects participate in baseline, but leave TVRS soon thereafter, I am also responsible for tracking subjects in order to complete follow-ups, which can be challenging as this population is rather transitory. Additionally I conduct qualitative interviews with both subjects and mentors in the community as well as in prisons for those who have reoffended.

Expertise Required

There is not a specific degree required for a forensic researcher; in fact, it is this diversity in disciplines that are involved with the criminal justice system that helps to strengthen many such evaluation designs. A graduate degree in a mental health field, with a subspecialty in forensic studies, is a strong background for conducting forensic research as it brings not only an understanding of the unique aspects of the criminal justice field, but also a clinical understanding that allows for much needed treatment-related research. Social workers new to the criminal justice field should initially partner with others who have extensive experience conducting forensic research to assist in negotiating the barriers commonly associated with forensic research, and to help to build new collaborative relationships with key gatekeepers within the system.

Ethical, Legal, Practice, Diversity, and/or Advocacy Issues Addressed

As the vast majority of subjects are currently on probation or parole, and were referred to TVRS through such programming, it can be a challenge to be grateful for the referrals, while simultaneously cutting such programming off from receiving updates to progress, and/or not disclosing relapses or continued criminal behavior. Such referral sources may at times expect a quid pro quo through such updates to assist in their own monitoring of these individuals. In addition to the extensive work involved with educating these systems about the research design and rationale for the subsequent disconnect, I also obtained a federal Certificate of Confidentiality, to further protect research subjects from any legally based requests for data disclosure. A personal challenge is not getting involved clinically with the research subjects, particularly if I do not agree with a diagnosis given or intervention being used by a provider. My role in this project is to record and evaluate the services provided, not to clinically supervise those services. Any such involvement would create a bias in my ability to effectively and independently evaluate the programming.

Interprofessional and Intersectoral Collaboration

TVRS subjects are recruited through referrals from the Trenton Police Department and the Departments of Probation and Parole. Out of benevolence, probation and parole will at times try to submit names of people greatly in need of services who do not meet the recruitment criteria. As the evaluator I need to communicate clearly our recruitment criteria, and diplomatically decline those who do not meet it without harming this interdepartmental relationship. The provision of services occurs through both ex-offender mentors and local social service agencies. I must partner with all involved to collect what is referred to as *dosage data* so that all are recording what services are provided, to who, and for how long. At times, providers may not prioritize the collection of data, as their main goal is service provision. Negotiating with all members of the collaboration to help create an evaluation design that everyone can buy into will go a long way toward data collection compliance throughout the course of the evaluation. I also completed the Department of Corrections (DOC) Institutional Review Board (IRB) application process in addition to that of my own institution to gain access to interviewing subjects who have reoffended. This requires a partnership with the DOC IRB, as well as gatekeepers from within several different prisons across the state. It is important to remember that the extensive paperwork and time involved in gaining such access is not intended to serve as a barrier, but rather a protection of inmates, making this a process to treat with understanding and respect.

CHAPTER 30

Forensic Research and Evaluation: Program and Policy Interventions That Promote Human Rights and Social Justice

Tina Maschi

George S. Leibowitz

Joanne Rees

CHAPTER OBJECTIVES

The major objectives of this chapter are to:

- Describe how forensic social workers can use the knowledge and skills of intervention development to design or evaluate existing interventions with forensic populations or settings, and about funding for their cause.
- Articulate the language of program and proposal development to prepare forensic social workers to be the creators of programs needed for forensic populations.

CHAPTER COMPETENCIES HIGHLIGHTED

- Competency 3: Advance Human Rights and Social, Economic, and Environmental Justice
- Competency 4: Engage in Practice Informed Research and Research Informed Practice
- Competency 5: Engage in Policy Practice
- Competencies 6, 7, 8, and 9: Engage, Assess, Intervene, and Evaluate Practice With Individuals, Families, Organizations, and Communities

Organizations that are forensic settings or serve forensic populations have historically used social interventions for individual and social change (Maschi, Bradley, & Ward, 2009; Maschi & Youdin, 2012; Mullen, Dumpson, & Associates, 1972). Similar to most programs, laws, or policies developed, forensic interventions are commonly based on a "theory of change" which hypothesizes that a targeted program or intervention will prevent or remediate the social problem or problems, such as recidivism, racial health, and justice disparities in education, employment, and disproportionate justice involvement (Rossi, Freeman, & Lipsey, 2004). For example, a community organization may offer both advocacy and support services to formerly incarcerated persons to improve their housing, education, and employment prospects, which in turn reduces their risk of recidivism. A state law may be passed to reduce the population of older incarcerated people by granting early release from detention or clemency. Another example is developing a countywide or statewide public awareness substance abuse prevention campaign with the goal of increasing community members' knowledge of addiction issues, such as alcohol or marijuana use among youth, or prescription drug overuse among the adults, which in turn are predicted to lead to a decrease in the risk of addiction issues and potential risk of criminal justice involvement among a targeted group of community members.

When considering the development or evaluation of a successful program or evidence-based program, the outcomes must be clearly identified and measurable (Chinman, Imm, & Wandersman, 2010). In an era of evidence-based interventions and accountability, everyone from case-level practitioners to agency administrators and political leaders are responsible to a host of stakeholders (Bamberger, Rugh, & Mabry, 2006). These stakeholders are clients of the program, executive board members, policy makers, public and private funders, and the general public. Clients may ask, "Can your agency provide us with services that will help us?" Executive board members may ask, "How did we do with the money that was invested? Did we have an impact?" Policy makers may ask, "Did your agency respond accordingly to legislative changes and mandates?" Public and private funders may ask, "How did you spend our money? Did the social benefits outweigh the financial cost?" The general public might ask, "Are our tax dollars worth the cost of funding this program over another program?" or "How will this program contribute to promoting the dual aim of public health and public safety?" Programs that work with forensic populations may have a more difficult time advocating for their programs because of the mixed views and stigmas of working with marginalized populations, including the formerly incarcerated. Forensic social workers, both frontline staff and administrators, can respond effectively to these questions with sound evidence generated from the field and/or available research studies. In this era of increased accountability and service effectiveness, programs with a human rights and social justice mission that serve marginalized groups, who also may be justice involved, must integrate their passion for justice with the use of sound evidence. For forensic programs that want to obtain funding, causes must be supported by some type of evidence of the effectiveness of their programs (Boulmetis & Dutwin, 2000).

The purpose of this chapter is to prepare forensic social workers with basic competencies in understanding the language and practice of program development and evaluation of forensic social work interventions. Emphasizing a human rights and social justice systems approach, it frames program development and evaluation in the context of a "theory of change" and "impact theory" using a logic model, that is, a visual depiction of the individual and social change process. Although this chapter focuses on programs, a theory of change framework can be applied to individual- and community-level forensic social work interventions with individuals, families, groups, programs, organizations, or communities at a local or global level. It reviews a variety of evaluation methods, such as needs assessments, process and outcome evaluations, and empowerment and culturally competent practice. It also provides some guidelines and recommendations on how to prepare for grants and obtain funding in a competitive funding world.

Applying a Human Social Justice Systems Approach to Forensic Interventions

Human Rights, Social Justice, and Social Problems

Using a human rights and social justice systems approach, social interventions are designed to advance (and hopefully achieve) human rights and social justice outcomes. If human rights and social justice are conceptualized as an ideal social condition in which every person has equal rights and opportunities (Barker, 2003; UN, 1948), programs or interventions should be designed with the outcome goals of human and community well-being. Societal conditions, such as mass incarceration, that create human rights violations or social problems are major obstacles to achieving human rights and social justice for many historically and emerging underrepresented and underserved groups, such as racial and ethnic minorities and low-income community members. Social problems often refer to adverse societal conditions that can cause emotional, social, or economic suffering among most often subordinate, as opposed to dominant, group members (Wronka, 2008). Examples of social problems include mass incarceration, crime and punishment, social inequality, poverty, racism, drug abuse, family problems, and unfair distribution of limited resources. Since the inception of forensic social work, social and justice interventions have attempted to combat these issues (Day, 2008). Despite progress, much more needs to be done by forensic social workers to combat adverse social conditions and reduce the stigma and discrimination experienced by the populations they serve.

Rights

The current trend that bodes well for forensic social workers is the social work profession's renewed emphasis on advancing human rights and social justice. Concurrent with this recommitment has been a shift from a social work *needs perspective* to a *rights perspective* (Reichert, 2003; United Nations [UN], 1994). Similar to Maslow's hierarchy of needs (see Table 30.1), the Universal Declaration of Human Rights (UN, 1948) espouses physical security, social esteem, and self-actualization, not just as needs but also as inalienable rights. These rights relate to economic, social, and cultural rights, such as the right to Social Security, shelter, education, work, social participation in community cultural life, scientific advancement, and the arts. Human rights also do not discriminate. These rights are guaranteed to all individuals regardless of age, race, gender, language, or religion.

More specifically, each individual is accorded basic civil rights (e.g., life and liberty), safety and security rights (e.g., personal security; freedom from arbitrary arrest, detention, or exile; and the right to a fair and public hearing by an impartial tribunal), self-esteem

TABLE 30.1   **Maslow's Hierarchy of Needs and Common Social Work Practice**

Level of Needs	Characteristics of Needs	Human Rights	Common Social Work Services That Address These Needs or Rights
5. Self-actualization	Self-awareness, personal growth, self-assertiveness, and fulfilling one's potential	Mental well-being rights, the right to education	Education, mental health services, politics, advocacy work
4. Esteem	Personal worth and recognition for achievements	Mental well-being rights, freedom of thought and conscience	Education, mental health services, community programs, politics
3. Social	Important social relationships (family, friends, and social groups)	Social and cultural rights, the right to relationships and freedom of associations	Community child and family agencies, mental health services, community prevention program
2. Safety and security	Freedom from violence in the home or community; shelter; access to health, education, and work	Safety and security rights; right to education and work; freedom from arbitrary arrest, detention, or exile; and the right to fair and public hearing by an impartial tribunal	Child welfare agencies, domestic violence shelters, medical hospitals, social services, education, correctional settings, family and community violence victims services, unemployment service, victim advocate programs, community organizing
1. Physical	Bodily needs, food, water, sleep	Economic rights; right to Social Security, shelter, life and liberty	Social services, homeless shelters, hospitals, case management agencies, advocacy organizations, legal aid

and self-actualization rights (e.g., the right to freedom of thought and conscience; the right to work and education), and social rights (e.g., the right to relationships and freedom of associations). Social workers and social service agencies are well positioned to engage in intervention efforts to improve people's economic and social conditions because of existing social service agency networks whose mission is to address issues related to Social Security, shelter, education, work, and social participation (UN, 1948, 1994; Wronka, 2008).

Conceptualizing Change

Historically, forensic social work interventions were designed with the distinct purpose of influencing change or having an impact in a desired direction, such as promoting public health and public safety (Addams, 1910; DuBois & Miley, 2010; Ely, 1895; Richmond, 1917). For example, programs or policies with a human rights and social justice mission have been created for purposes such as justice for juveniles, that is, the establishment of the juvenile court system or reducing incarceration, that is, alternatives to incarceration programs. Therefore, it is helpful to understand the change process using a lens of change or impact theory. As illustrated in these examples, a social intervention or program, or even law or policy, predicts that change will occur in a desired direction as a direct result of the impact of its intervention activities.

Intervention and Impact Theories

As illustrated in Figure 30.1, intervention and impact theories can be used to illustrate the change process and the cause-and-effect sequence of interventions. An intervention or program or policy theory can be described as a set of assumptions that clarify how a program or policy intervention will produce the expected level of individual and social benefits, and the strategies used to achieve their projected goals and objectives (Rossi et al., 2004). Similarly, impact theory is a causal theory for programs, policies, or other forensic social work interventions. Impact theory posits a cause-and-effect chain in which program or intervention activities facilitate a positive change in individual and social benefits and achieving human rights social justice. Therefore, similar to a theory of change, impact theory refers to the beliefs, assumptions, and expectations inherent in a program or policy

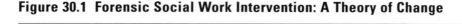

Figure 30.1 Forensic Social Work Intervention: A Theory of Change

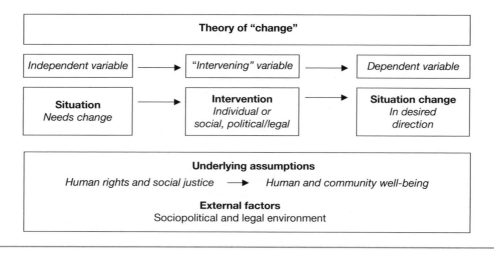

intervention and illustrates both the nature of the change brought about by program action and how it results in the intended improvement in social conditions (Rossi et al., 2004).

What Is a Program Intervention?

When considering developing a program intervention, it is helpful to understand what is meant by a community organization or agency. A social intervention often refers to an interception of, or intervening with, individuals, groups, communities, and events (Barker, 2003). In some cases, the term *intervention* has been viewed as similar to the term *treatment* in the medical profession. However, in forensic social work, the term *intervention* is much broader in scope than a medical prescription and includes an array of activities from case level (microlevel) to an agency or community level (macrolevel; Maschi & Youdin, 2012). In the case of law and policies, the development or amendment to a law is a type of intervention in which the laws are meant to promote improved public health and/or address public safety concerns.

Intervention Strategies

Similar to social work as usual, in forensic social work, intervention strategies may include, but are not limited to, individual, group, or family counseling, case management services, advocacy, mediation, social planning, community organizing, lobbying, policy practice, community development, finding and developing resources, media awareness programming, and psychoeducation (Council On Social Work Education, 2015; National Association of Social Workers, 1999). When developing a community program, policy, or advocacy campaign, these intervention strategies offer different options.

Despite the variety of methods for use in forensic social work intervention development or evaluation, choosing the program, policy, or advocacy strategy to develop is simply part of a problem-solving process. Problem solving involves a stepwise process that includes identifying assets and problem areas; developing an intervention plan; implementing the plan (which may include mobilizing resources); engaging community leaders, policy makers, and potential consumers; and encouraging collaborations (Marlow, 2010; Unrau, Gabor, & Grinnell, 2006). This common problem-solving process makes it feasible to apply a broad framework for developing a program or pitching a fundable grant proposal as to why such a program is needed (Maschi & Youdin, 2012).

Developing a Community Organization

The establishment of a forensic social work community organization or agency involves a large-scale organized and sustained intervention effort that uses collective action to help a community (i.e., people with a common interest and/or from the same geographic areas) to ameliorate social problems, enhance community well-being, and to create more socially just communities (Schram, 1997). A historical example is the establishment of Hull House in 1898. Perhaps the most well-known settlement house, it was founded in Chicago in 1889 by Jane Addams and Ellen Gates Starr. Hull House was designed to address poverty and the poor living and working conditions of the rapidly growing immigrant population. It was a community center for poor and disadvantaged people from the neighborhood. The agency also initiated various social reform efforts related to working conditions, poverty, immigration, and at-risk youth (Ehrenreich, 1985; Ely, 1895).

Organizational Types

Social services organizations or agencies are often part of the community. They can be public or private organizations that target the local, state, and/or federal level (Maschi & Youdin, 2012). Grassroots organizations, in which social justice may be involved, are citizen-led change efforts, such as Just Leadership USA (JLUSA), whose membership consists of formerly incarcerated people. Within that organization, there has been continual program development to serve the needs and rights of formerly incarcerated people and help to develop their leadership potential. Sources of funding for the organization can include any combination of public or private funding at the local, state, and/or federal level. In addition to governmental funding, other sources of revenue may include client or member fees, charity funds, and private donations (Schram, 1997; Unrau et al., 2006).

Activities and Change

The activities of the agency staff in collaboration with their clients or constituents foster an empowerment-based change process that works toward desired goals and objectives. These activities may include helping individuals become more self-sufficient, strengthening a mother-and-child bond, mobilizing community groups to increase community safety, and/or building a coalition to advocate for racial justice and a fairer criminal justice system. An essential first step is to create an organizational blueprint or plan that will address the problems that their service users experience accessing services and justice.

Intervention Development and Evaluation Planning: From Case- to Organizational-Level Intervention

Policies, organizations, programs, law, and policies or other types of forensic focused interventions can be designed and evaluated for their process and intended outcomes. Planning and implementing an evaluation refers to "the systematic collection of information about the activities, characteristics, and outcomes of a program or other intervention to make judgments about the intervention, improve intervention effectiveness, and/or inform decisions about future intervention efforts" (Patton, 2002). The purpose of a forensic intervention evaluation is to systematically determine whether an intervention works and the process by which it works. So the planning stages of program development are critical toward developing a sound plan or blueprint.

As described in an intervention change theory, a social organization's activities are designed so that they improve outcomes for those individuals and communities affected (Rossi et al., 2004). As illustrated in Figure 30.2, there is a direct connection between the case level (i.e., microlevel practice with individuals and families) and organizational level (i.e., macrolevel practice with organizations and communities; Smith, 2010; Unrau et al., 2006). Social workers conducting case-level evaluation assess services with one client at a time. These combined case-level evaluations contribute to initial and ongoing program development and evaluation. Similarly, program level decisions can influence social workers' case-level evaluation efforts. Therefore, no matter where a social worker is positioned in an agency, it is important to understand the connection between case-level and program-level intervention.

To be the most effective agents of change, agency staff would best be served by understanding how agencies are organized to bring about measurable change. Agencies are generally organized by an overarching mission statement from which their goals and objectives are established. Once a program is developed, agency staff carry out these goals and activities in their daily practices and activities.

Program Development Essentials: Mission, Goals, and Objectives of Social Organizations

When developing a program or seeking grant funding, it is essential to understand the agency and/or program mission and goals. In developing a social organization or program component within that agency, the vision, goals, and objectives help guide the development of an intervention and articulate to grant funders why a program or agency should be funded.

Figure 30.2 The Organization in the Environment: From Case-Level to Organizational Evaluation

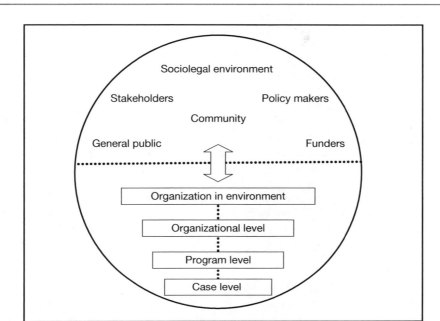

Mission Statements

An organization's mission statement, including the mission statement of a social service organization, articulates its vision. The mission statement serves as a declaration to the public about the organization's purpose and projected outcomes. It usually addresses the targeted clientele and services offered (Schram, 1997; York, 2009).

As a document, an organization's mission statement may vary in length from one paragraph to 10 to 20 pages. Its contents are used to help make planning decisions, and to provide a broad conceptual framework from which programs within that organization are constructed. The grand vision advanced in the mission statement influences the directive goals that flow from it (Schram, 1997; Unrau et al., 2006).

Goals

The mission statement guides how agency goals are formulated. Unrau et al. (2006) identified four components of goals: (a) the nature of the targeted social condition that the organization will address; (b) the targeted clientele for the services; (c) the direction of proposed change effort among clientele; and (d) the strategies used to bring about the desired change.

Goals can range from broad to narrow. This may depend on the geographical reach of an organization. The larger the organizational setting, such as at the national or state level, the broader the goal statements (Unrau et al., 2006). On a national level, a program goal may be to enhance the lives of youth and their families who have juvenile justice involvement by providing block funding to states that offer evidence-based programming related to reducing youth recidivism. More specific goals on a local level may include improving educational outcomes for county youth by providing remedial educational and/or mental health services for at-risk youth. These goals are further clarified or operationalized in the form of objectives that are observable and measurable (Neuman, 2002; Westerfelt & Dietz, 2010).

Objectives

Moving from goals to objectives in evaluation is similar to the process of moving from a conceptual to an operational definition in research. That is, an agency objective that is derived from a goal must be specific, measurable, and variable. The agency objective should clearly identify an activity or service that is directly linked to agency goals (Chinman et al., 2010; Coley & Scheinberg, 2008). For example, an agency offers an after-school tutoring program for middle- and high-school students who are at risk or who have failed a class to help improve academic performance.

Programs Inside Agencies

It is important to understand the structure of community organizations and the programs within them. An organization may offer one program, such as self-standing "Elder Abuse Services" for older adults. However, many organizations offer several programs housed under the umbrella of the organization. For example, the National Alliance on Mental Illness offers a host of programs, including one that provides support services for mental health consumers, and another program that provides support services for family members. Therefore, each program component must be directly related to the organization's mission statement, organizational goals, and at least one objective. Similarly, a program objective should be specific and measurable, and must clearly identify the desired direction of the change.

Program Goals

According to Unrau et al. (2006), the program goal must have four characteristics. A program goal must identify (a) a specific social problem, (b) the population affected by the target social problem area that the program will serve, (c) the projected change or desired state, and (d) the methods used to achieve the projected change or desired state. The next step is to derive program objectives from these goals.

Program Objectives

Program objectives offer a clearer direction for the specific, targeted changes or projected results for program participants or clientele. Program objectives generally relate to knowledge (thoughts), affect (values and feelings), and actions (behaviors) (Unrau et al., 2006). For example, a knowledge-based program objective often aims to increase knowledge about a specific content or topic area. For example, an anger management program objective may be to increase participants' knowledge of the physiological signs of anger by having them complete a 12-week anger management program. In contrast, an affect-based objective generally targets a change in feelings, values, and/or attitudes. For example, an anger management program may want to reduce participants' feelings of hostile anger upon completion of a 12-week program. Action-based objectives commonly aim to change the behavior or conduct of program participants. For example, a behavioral (action) objective may be to reduce the number of fights and/or hostile angry outbursts by participants to zero within three months of program completion.

SMART Objectives

Some evaluation projects use "SMART" objectives. SMART is an acronym that refers to specific (S), measurable (M), attainable (A), results oriented (R), and timed (T) objectives. SMART objectives must identify the person/s or situations that are the target of change (who/what?). They must also indicate the desired change (what change?) and the direction of the desired effect (what direction?), and be achievable (possibility to change), within a certain time frame (when?).

   Example 1. The Senior Center executive board will revise organizational policies designed to provide life skills programming to formerly incarcerated older adults and increase available programming for physical exercise, social activities, and peer supports services within two years.

Example 2. Justice-involved families participating in the parenting training program (who) will increase their knowledge of community resources (what directional change) by the completion of the four-week course (attainable and timed). Families participating in the parenting training-based program (who) will increase their use of community resources (what directional change) within six months of program completion (attainable and timed).

Logic Model for Program Development, Implementation, and Evaluation

Logic models are a useful tool for visualizing program planning, implementation, evaluation, and grant funding. As illustrated in Exhibit 30.1, a logic model tells the story of an organization and its theory of change. The logic model is commonly used in evaluation to plan decision making based on program development and refinement. It describes the situation that led to the creation of a program and inputs or resources that went into developing the organizations and the activities of staff and other stakeholders that are used to facilitate the projected desired outcomes (Taylor-Powell & Henert, 2008; W.K. Kellogg Foundation [WKKF], 2004). Exhibit 30.2 provides an example of a logic model for an after-school music program for at-risk youth aged 7 to 11 years.

The logic model is a versatile diagram that traces the change pathway to the intended program change. A logic model can be devised for just about any intervention, including a one-hour psychoeducation program or a longstanding complex organization that houses multiple programs. The logic model generally presents the most salient details that are essential to the change process and of interest to stakeholders. Different shapes, such as boxes, circles, and arrows, are used to indicate the direction of the change process and the outcomes. The diagram can be simple or complex, and can use nested models to illustrate multiple programs in context (Taylor-Powell & Henert, 2008; WKKF, 2004). This next section provides an overview of the different parts of the logic model and how it can be linked to program development and evaluation.

Exhibit 30.1 Logic Model Template

Agency/organization/program name:					
Brief situation statement:					
Assumptions:					
External factors:					
Inputs ⟹	**Process**		⟹	**Outcomes**	
	Activities	Participation	Short term	Medium term	Long term
What is invested?	What is done?	Who is reached?	Changes expected	Changes expected	Changes expected

Source: Based on W.K. Kellogg Foundation (2004).

Exhibit 30.2 Logic Model Example for Program and Grant Development and Implementation

Agency/organization/program name: After-School Music Program Delinquency Prevention Program for Local Youth (children aged 7 to 11 years)					
Brief situation statement: Low-income neighborhood comprised of mostly new immigrant Latino families with young children, who lack access to affordable arts training and after-school programs and prosocial activities that will reduce the risk of exposure to criminal and delinquent neighborhood activities.					
Assumptions: Positive youth development can be facilitated by participation in the arts.					
External factors: Lack of school and community access to music lessons and instruments					
Inputs	**Process**		**Outcomes**		
	Activities	Participation	Short term	Medium term	Long term
What is invested?	*What is done?*	*Who is reached?*	*Changes expected*	*Changes expected*	*Changes expected*
Financial resources (grants and donors) In-kind contributions Client fees Staff Volunteers Equipment Space for lessons and public performances Community support	Musical instruction Mentoring Community events	Students (children) Parents Teacher volunteers Parent volunteers Community members *Outputs*: Number of teacher volunteers recruited per month Number of children that attend 80% of lessons	• Music knowledge • Music appreciation • Musical skills	• Positive self-esteem • Creativity • Social competence • Prosocial behavior (non-delinquency)	• Academic achievement • Sustained music involvement

Source: Based on W.K. Kellogg Foundation (2004).

The Parts of the Logic Model

The logic model illustrates the change process from the initial problem to its projected intended results (see Exhibits 30.1 and 30.2). The first chain in the logic model often identifies the situation and needs, the target population, and key stakeholders. The next chain in the causal sequence illustrates intervention planning and implementation in the form of input or resources, activities, and output. The final chain in the causal sequence shows the outcomes of the intervention. Other influential factors are the underlying assumptions and external factors (Neuman, 2002; WKKF, 2004). These concepts in the context of the change process are described subsequently.

Problem or Situation

The problem or situation refers to an assessment of the adverse situations or problems and the priorities that need to be addressed. A short situation statement often includes a description of the problem (and assets) and the impact of social, economic, and/or environmental factors, how they impact the target population, and what might happen if it is not addressed.

Target Population

The target population refers to the population impacted by the problem, and who the agency and/or program were designed to serve. Organizations generally specify the target population they serve, such as lesbian, gay, bisexual, and transgender (LGBT) youth involved with the juvenile and/or criminal justice systems.

Stakeholders

Stakeholders involve the individuals, groups, organizations, or governmental agencies that have some interest in the target populations or intervention. These individuals may be members of the target population, staff, policy makers, and the general public. The organization is accountable to all of these stakeholders. Stakeholders are generally involved in the early stages of the process of identifying the situation (Neuman, 2002; Taylor-Powell & Henert, 2008; WKKF, 2004).

Inputs/Resources

Inputs commonly refer to what is invested or the resources that are put into the program. Inputs generally refer to assets, including human and material resources. Human resources generally refer to staff, volunteers, and community stakeholders. In contrast, material resources include such items as funding, training items, and equipment. Inputs are an essential investment that provide a mechanism for an agency to achieve desired outputs and outcomes.

Activities

Activities refer to what the program does to achieve its required outputs and outcomes. Activities of a program may include individual, group, and family counseling, intake assessment, discharge planning, psychoeducational classes, advocacy and lobbying, and staff meetings. Program clientele also engage in program activities. Participation refers to the individuals or groups reached by the program and how they participate. Examples might include mental health consumers who participate in individual and group counseling, or children who participate in play therapy services.

Outputs

Outputs generally refer to the concrete end products of agency activities and client participation. Outputs are activities conducted or products created that reach targeted participants/populations. For example, an output might be the number of individuals who completed the 12-week anger management program and workbook activities. Outputs also can be described as intermediate and final outputs. Examples of intermediate outputs can be the number of volunteers recruited per month. Final output could be the number of clients who attended 75% of scheduled anger management sessions.

Outcome or Impact Factors

Outcomes, or impact factors, are the projected results of a program. They represent the changes or benefits for individuals, families, or communities that are the target of the intervention. Outcomes are commonly described in terms of short-, medium-, or long-term outcomes (Neuman, 2002; Taylor-Powell & Henert, 2008; WKKF, 2004). For example, a group educational program for families teaches budgeting skills to increase their financial literacy, which, in turn, will assist families in controlling their spending, which, in turn, will assist them in maintaining long-term financial stability.

Assumptions

Assumptions are the fundamental beliefs as to why the problem exists and what the intervention is projected to achieve.

External Factors

External factors refer to environmental conditions that may impact the problem or the program intervention. Generally out of a program's direct control, these factors may influence the success level of a program. For example, public policies, economic factors, or community factors may have a positive or negative effect on the program.

Exercise—Logic Model Worksheet

One key value of a logic model is that it displays the chain of connections showing how a program is expected to work to achieve desired outcomes. A 30-minute online tutorial from the University of Wisconsin-Extension (www.uwex.edu/ces/lmcourse) serves as a useful resource to plan and develop logic models, and should be viewed before completing the following exercise.

Exhibit 30.1 can be used as a worksheet to complete a logic model for a planned or existing program. Working alone or as part of a group, choose a familiar agency program to complete the logic model worksheet. When finished, the logic model should explicitly illustrate the connection between the situation, input, activities, and outcomes.

Evaluation and the Logic Model

When planning a program, the methods for evaluation also should be preplanned. When applying for a grant, this evaluation plan should be based on sound scientific methods to measure program effectiveness. The research and evaluation process involves asking questions and answering them and can address the need for the program, its design, implementation, impact, and efficiency. Evaluation assists with accountability to central stakeholders, which is an important consideration for decision making in program development and evaluation (Unrau et al., 2006). The common types of evaluation include needs assessments and process, outcome, or efficiency evaluations. Exhibit 30.3 illustrates how these types of evaluations fit within the logic model sequence.

Assets and Needs Assessment

As a first step in program development, a needs and assets assessment is often conducted. An assets and needs assessment is an evaluation study that seeks to find answers about social and environmental conditions (Rossi et al., 2004). An assets and needs assessment is an evaluation study that attempts to determine the situation or problem, what individuals or groups are affected, and if there is a need to implement an intervention or to develop a program to ameliorate the problem and foster assets (Goldman & Schmalz, 2005). Often times, in the needs assessment phase, multiple stakeholders are involved in the process and information is obtained from all angles/perspectives to explain the problem (Percy-Smith, 1996; Soriani, 1995).

General questions that may be answered by a needs assessment might include the following: What are the characteristics of the problem (magnitude and severity)? What population segments does it impact? Of the identified problems, what are the priorities that need to be addressed? What are potential barriers to resolving the problem? What are the assets or facilitators that might help resolve the problem? Is there a need for a program to address this problem? What seems to work? What does not seem to work? (Rossi et al., 2004).

Exhibit 30.3 The Logic Model With Program Development Evaluation Plan and Implementation Stages

Assumptions and External Factors							

Situation/priorities	Inputs	Outputs			Outcomes-impact		
What is the problem? Who does it impact?	*What is invested?*	*What is done?*	*Who is reached?*		*What changes do we expect?*		
		Activities	Participation		Short term	Medium term	Long term
Needs	**Process**				**Outcomes**		**Impact**
Needs/asset assessment	*Process evaluation*				*Outcome evaluation*		
Common questions 1. What is the problem? 2. What are the target population characteristics, including assets? 3. What are the needs and priorities of the target population? 4. What are the potential barriers to resolving the problem? 5. What are the assets that can be used to solve the problem?	*Common questions* 1. How was the intervention implemented? 2. In what ways was it implemented as planned? 3. In what ways are activities delivered as intended? 4. Are participants being reached as intended? 5. What are participants' impressions, including satisfaction with intervention? 6. What are the program outputs? 7. How many participants were reached?				*Common questions* 1. What preferred changes are occurring? 2. To what extent have these preferred changes occurred? 3. What works? What does not work? 4. In what ways has the program made a positive difference? 5. What were, if any, unintended negative consequences of the program? If so, how did the program address them?		

Source: Based on W.K. Kellogg Foundation (2004).

Process Evaluation

Whether planning or implementing a program or seeking grant funding, a process evaluation is a necessary consideration. If a need is established, a blueprint or plan for a program is commonly developed and then implemented. A program must move from an idea on paper to an actual dynamic structure comprised of program activities that are expected to have an impact on improving outcomes for their program clientele. A process evaluation is a type of study that serves to examine the program's process, or course of action, that leads to its projected outcomes. It does so by examining program operations, implementation, and service delivery. A process evaluation is a useful evaluation to conduct when a program wants to know the degree in which the program being offered is consistent with the original program plan (i.e., program fidelity). It also often involves obtaining feedback from participants about their experience in the program. A satisfaction survey is a common tool used with consumers. A formative evaluation to a process evaluation goes one step further and actively applies the evaluation results to improve the program so that it can best reach projected outcomes (Maschi & MacMillan, 2009; Royse, Thyer, Padgett, & Logan, 2006; Unrau et al., 2006; York, 2009).

Some general questions that may be answered by a process evaluation include: What services or activities are delivered by the program? Does the program do what it was intended to do? To what extent are program participants satisfied with the program activities? To what extent was the program implemented according to the original program plan (i.e., fidelity)? Were the interventions delivered as planned (i.e., fidelity of the program implementation)? How many people attended? How many people completed the program (Rossi et al., 2004)?

An example of an agency satisfaction survey using both closed-ended and open-ended questions can be found in Exhibit 30.4. Similarly, Table 30.2 presents the descriptive results indicating how 17 juvenile correctional officers perceived how helpful services were for youth placed in detention. This survey also targeted areas for program improvement and development.

Exhibit 30.4 Satisfaction Survey Sample

After-School Music Delinquency Prevention Program for Youth Satisfaction Survey

Parent/Caretaker Survey

We are interested in knowing how satisfied you are with your child's (or children's) experience with the After-School Music Program for Youth. Note: Please respond to the following statements using the following scale. For each statement, please *circle* the response that *best represents* your views.

1=Strongly disagree
2=Disagree
3=Neutral
4=Agree
5=Strongly agree

How much do you agree or disagree with the following statements:	5	4	3	2	1
1. I am satisfied with the musical training provided for my child here.	SA	A	N	D	SD
2. This program makes good use of my child's time.	SA	A	N	D	SD
3. My child's musical skills have improved.	SA	A	N	D	SD
4. My child has improved at public performance because of this training.	SA	A	N	D	SD
5. The teacher always keeps me informed of my child's progress.	SA	A	N	D	SD
6. The teachers are well prepared and know what they are doing.	SA	A	N	D	SD
7. Overall, the teachers at this program are very helpful.	SA	A	N	D	SD
8. Other staff members are well prepared and know what they are doing.	SA	A	N	D	SD
9. The other staff members at this program are very helpful.	SA	A	N	D	SD
10. Everyone at the program treats each other with mutual respect.	SA	A	N	D	SD
11. My child received a lot of positive attention at this program.	SA	A	N	D	SD
12. My child is happy at this program.	SA	A	N	D	SD
13. My child feels a sense of belonging at this program.	SA	A	N	D	SD
14. This program has a calming environment.	SA	A	N	D	SD
15. This program teaches children about mutual respect of one another.	SA	A	N	D	SD
16. This program offers my child a strong sense of community.	SA	A	N	D	SD

(continued)

Exhibit 30.4 Satisfaction Survey Sample (*continued*)

17. Overall, this program has a positive influence on my child.	SA	A	N	D	SD
18. Overall, my child would love to come back to this program.	SA	A	N	D	SD
19. This program has many opportunities for me to see my child perform.	SA	A	N	D	SD
20. This program has many opportunities for me to volunteer.	SA	A	N	D	SD
21. I would recommend this program to my family and friends.	SA	A	N	D	SD
22. Overall, I am very satisfied with this program.	SA	A	N	D	SD
23. How would you describe the atmosphere here?					
24. How has your child changed as a result of participating in this program?					
25. Is there anything else you would like to share about your child's experience in the program?					
Thank you very much for sharing your views. Your opinions help make a difference toward improving our program.					

Source: Maschi and MacMillan (2009).

Outcome Evaluation

An outcome evaluation is conducted to determine if a program has met its specific goals and objectives. Also referred to as a summative evaluation or impact assessment, an outcome evaluation provides information on the extent to which change occurred among program participants (e.g., prosocial attitudes, reduced criminal activities) and the targeted larger/social environmental conditions (e.g., community crime reduction). Outcomes are often described in achievable increments that range from short-term (one year or less), medium-term (three years), or long-term (10 years) impact (Dudley, 2008; Engel & Schutt, 2010).

Generally, outcomes represent important milestones in the change process for individuals and communities. The end results often give rise to some type of improvement, such as improved mental well-being or reduced community crime, that are meaningful to key stakeholders. The progression of outcomes from short- to medium- and long-term outcomes must be directly connected to the program activities. Most of all, the outcomes must be achievable given the resources and the situation (Taylor-Powell & Henert, 2008; WKKF, 2004).

Some general questions that might guide an outcome evaluation are: To what extent are desired changes occurring (short term, medium term, long term)? For what individuals or groups does it work? Is the program making a difference in the intended direction? What are unintended outcomes or consequences of the program for participants, other stakeholders, and the community (Rossi et al., 2004)?

Efficiency Evaluation

As noted earlier, key stakeholders, particularly public officials, policy makers, and funders are most interested in fiscal issues related to community programming. Therefore, the costs of starting and maintaining an agency are an important area in which ongoing assessments are conducted. In order to address this concern, most programs conduct efficiency evaluations. An efficiency evaluation compares the effects of a program to its cost. It is an approach to making economic decisions of any kind and is often a requirement of program funding (Levin, 2001).

There are two types of efficiency evaluations commonly used in social program evaluation: a cost–benefit analysis or cost-effectiveness analysis. Cost–benefit analysis is an evaluation weighing the total expected costs against the total expected benefits of one or more actions, in order to choose the best financial option. A cost–benefit ratio is determined by dividing the projected benefits of a program by the projected costs. A wide range of projected benefits,

TABLE 30.2   Descriptive Statistics for Juvenile Correctional Officers' Perceptions of the Helpfulness of Detention Program Services for Detained Youth

Service kind	Percentage of services and their level of helpfulness				
	Not helpful	Kind of helpful	Helpful	Very helpful	N/A
Interaction time with staff	5.6 (n = 1)	5.6 (n = 4)	33.3 (n = 6)	27.8 (n = 5)	5.6 (n = 1)
Individual counseling	11.1 (n = 2)	27.8 (n = 5)	27.8 (n = 5)	22.2 (n = 4)	0.0 (n = 0)
Group counseling	16.7 (n = 3)	33.3 (n = 6)	27.8 (n = 5)	5.6 (n = 1)	11.1 (n = 2)
Family therapy	5.6 (n = 1)	5.6 (n = 1)	77.8 (n = 14)	88.9 (n = 16)	11.1 (n = 2)
Psychiatric help	22.2 (n = 4)	27.8 (n = 5)	5.6 (n = 1)	5.6 (n = 1)	22.2 (n = 4)
Medical services	0.0 (n = 0)	22.2 (n = 4)	44.4 (n = 8)	22.2 (n = 4)	5.6 (n = 1)
Psychiatric services	11.1 (n = 2)	11.1 (n = 2)	16.7 (n = 3)	5.6 (n = 1)	22.2 (n = 4)
Substance abuse counseling	22.2 (n = 4)	16.7 (n = 2)	27.8 (n = 5)	11.1 (n = 2)	16.7 (n = 3)
Case management services	16.7 (n = 3)	22.2 (n = 4)	33.3 (n = 6)	16.7 (n = 3)	5.6 (n = 1)
Classroom instruction	16.7 (n = 3)	16.7 (n = 3)	44.4 (n = 8)	11.1 (n = 2)	0.0 (n = 0)
Tutoring	5.6 (n = 1)	11.1 (n = 2)	11.1 (n = 2)	16.7 (n = 3)	50.0 (n = 9)
Gang training	22.2 (n = 4)	33.3 (n = 6)	11.1 (n = 2)	0.0 (n = 0)	27.8 (n = 5)
Job or vocational training	16.7 (n = 3)	5.6 (n = 1)	11.1 (n = 2)	5.6 (n = 1)	55.6 (n = 10)
Life skills training	22.2 (n = 4)	22.2 (n = 4)	27.8 (n = 5)	11.1 (n = 2)	11.1 (n = 2)
Social skills training	16.7 (n = 3)	22.2 (n = 4)	27.8 (n = 5)	11.1 (n = 2)	11.1 (n = 2)
Recreational activities	16.7 (n = 3)	22.2 (n = 4)	22.2 (n = 4)	22.2 (n = 4)	5.6 (n = 1)
Community service work	5.6 (n = 1)	16.7 (n = 3)	16.7 (n = 3)	0.0 (n = 0)	50.0 (n = 9)
Faith-based volunteers	5.6 (n = 1)	22.2 (n = 4)	38.9 (n = 7)	27.8 (n = 5)	0.0 (n = 0)
Mentors	5.6 (n = 1)	5.6 (n = 1)	44.4 (n = 8)	16.7 (n = 3)	22.2 (n = 4)
Transportation	0.0 (n = 0)	0.0 (n = 0)	38.9 (n = 7)	44.4 (n = 8)	5.6 (n = 1)
Aftercare services	22.2 (n = 4)	11.1 (n = 2)	5.6 (n = 1)	5.6 (n = 1)	44.4 (n = 8)

such as well-being or quality of life, are measured because of their potential indirect and long-term cost-saving benefits. In contrast, cost-effectiveness analysis analyzes costs related to a single, common effect (e.g., crime reduction), usually in terms of cost expended per outcome achieved (Levin, 2001).

General questions that an efficiency evaluation may answer about a program include the following: What are the program costs in comparison to the monetary value of its benefits? How much does it cost to run? Does the total cost exceed the budget? Do the social benefits outweigh the fiscal costs (Rossi et al., 2004)?

Stakeholder Collaboration

Engaging interested stakeholders who have direct or indirect interests in the formation of a program, its progress, and results is important. Social workers are well served before undertaking an evaluation project to have a general understanding of who the stakeholders are, and the motives for their interest, so that collaborative relationships can be fostered. For example, most often, policy makers are concerned about financial resources, community safety, or political ramifications in the decision-making process. Similarly, agency clientele, frontline social workers, program administrators, agency executives, and private and public funders often have a voice in the process.

Evaluation Exercise

It is recommended that readers complete the evaluation program information worksheet found in Exhibit 30.5. It provides questions related to the common types of evaluation, which include a needs assessment and process, outcome, or efficiency evaluations. Readers are encouraged to consult multiple data sources including a review of publicly available agency information, such as the program, county, or state websites, or agency report and interviews with agency administrators or other identified key stakeholders. If conducting an interview, request to record the interview or be prepared to write copious verbatim notes. If possible, create a logic model of at least one program. Based on your findings, write a five- to six-page report highlighting major findings and recommendations for the organization to incorporate to improve service provision. If requested, share a copy of the report with the interviewee/s.

Additional Evaluation Strategies

Additional program planning and evaluation strategies relevant to social justice include community asset mapping, empowerment evaluation, and action-oriented research. They are reviewed in that order, respectively.

Community Asset Mapping

Community asset mapping is another form of visual narrative of a neighborhood or community that can be used for social and economic development (Hillier, 2007). It can be used to document community assets, socioeconomic conditions, and housing patterns (Emery & Flora, 2006). Mapping is a user-friendly visual representation of sociodemographic data by geographical location.

Community maps can range from simple to complex, and display a few to multiple variables over a wide geographical area (context map). A context map is used to represent a few variables of interest over a wider geographic level to many variables over smaller geographic areas (e.g., display map), or a combination of both (analytical maps). Community mapping is a useful tool because it can visually map community well-being in an easy-to-understand manner (Jasek-Rysdahl, 2001). The understanding garnered from these maps can be used to support participatory decision making and program and intervention planning (Kretzmann & McNight, 1993).

Exhibit 30.5 Program Development and Evaluation Exercise

Directions: Please document the sources of data that were used to gather information for this exercise. They can include information obtained during interviews with agency supervisors, official agency reports, and/or agency official website, etc. . . . . *If information for any of the questions is not available, please document for that question that information is not available).*

Description of agency and organization
1. What is the history of the organization? What was the reason it was formed?
2. Who are the key stakeholders of the agency or organization?
3. What is the mission statement, goals, and objectives of the agency?
4. Is cultural competence, human rights, or social justice part of the mission statement?

Program services
1. What is the history of at least one program offered by the agency or organization?
2. What is the situation or "problem" that the program addresses?
3. What are the target population characteristics?
4. How were needs or rights assessed or identified for this target population?
5. What needs or rights are addressed by the current services?
6. What needs or rights are not addressed by the current services?
7. In what ways is cultural competence addressed in program services?

Program operations
1. Does the agency (or program) have a research and evaluation staff or unit?
2. How does administration or evaluation staff monitor how the program objectives are being met?
3. Does this agency monitor improvement in providing cultural competent services?
4. How are the program services being delivered to the target population?
5. Are there unserved individuals or groups that the program is not reaching? If so, why?
6. Do sufficient numbers of program participants successfully complete the program? Explain.
7. What is the program participants' level of satisfaction with the program? Explain.

Program outcomes
1. What are the stated goals and objectives of the program under investigation?
2. What, if any, are the beneficial effects of the program participation on its participants?
3. What, if any, are the adverse effects of program participation on the participants?
4. Are services distributed fairly among the subgroups that attend (age, race/ethnicity, gender, and/or other)?
5. Does it appear that the problem(s) targeted by the program are adequately addressed given the design of the services and interventions?

Program cost and efficiency
1. How is this program funded? Have the funding sources changed over time?
2. What is the cost of this program?
3. What is the yearly budget for this program? Does the cost exceed the budget?
4. What policies and procedures are there to ensure that agency resources are used efficiently?
5. Does the cost of the program outweigh its benefits to participants and the community?

Integration of social justice, ethical, and human rights principles
1. In what ways does the agency adhere to social justice or human rights principles?
2. What are common ethical issues that arise in this agency setting?
3. Overall, in what ways is the agency sensitive to issues of diversity, disparities, and cultural competence?

(continued)

Exhibit 30.5 Program Development and Evaluation Exercise (*continued*)

4. What articles of the Universal Declaration of Human Rights (UN, 1948) does this program directly address?

5 In general, in what ways does the agency support human rights and social justice in their program design and service delivery systems? And how can it be improved? Please explain.

Source: Based on Rossi, Freeman, and Lipsey (2004, pp. 87–88).

Program Planning and Empowerment Evaluation

Empowerment evaluation is an evidence-based evaluation strategy that uses an empowerment approach that fosters self-determination. Empowerment evaluation has been defined as an evaluation approach that aims to increase the probability of achieving program success by building the capacity of stakeholders to conduct evaluation from initial planning, implementation and evaluation, and by streamlining the process to make evaluation manageable. This involves mainstreaming evaluation as part of the planning and management of the program/organization (Fetterman & Wandersman, 2004).

There are 10 empowerment principles that guide the process: (a) improvement, (b) community ownership, (c) inclusion, (d) democratic participation, (e) social justice, (f) community knowledge, (g) evidence-based strategies, (h) capacity building, (i) organizational learning, and (j) accountability.

Empowerment evaluation shifts the traditional evaluation methods of the external expert to the "internal" program experts who know their program. It fosters internal expertise, self-determination, capacity building, and collaborative decision making. Empowerment evaluation has been used in a variety of settings from community-based programs to government agencies, business, and educational and religious organization settings. Populations include youth and adults and diverse racial ethnic groups, such as African Americans, Latinos, Caucasians, and Native Americans (Fetterman & Wandersman, 2004).

Action-Oriented Research

Action research, including participatory action research, is a collaborative research and evaluation framework in which creating positive social change and social justice are the driving forces. There are several common themes across action-oriented research methods. The methods used are highly rigorous and reflective, are characterized by actively engaging participants and contributors in the research process, offer the participants practical outcomes, and use a spiraling of steps comprised of collaborative planning, action, and evaluation (Stringer, 2007; Suarez-Balcazar & Harper, 2003).

Action research differs from traditional research and evaluation approaches in several ways. The action research approach is heavily reflective, experiential, and participatory. All individuals participating in the study, including research team members and participants alike, take part in the research process from formulating the problem, gathering data, analyzing the results, and taking action. An action research project also generates information directly for the individuals or agencies that need it. The strategies used often merge research, education, and sociopolitical action. It also educates and empowers the individuals involved in the project to use the information gained to take sociopolitical action (McIntyre, 2000, 2008).

Action research uses methods that suggest parity in the research process, consistent with human rights and social justice philosophies. An action-oriented research approach democratizes knowledge production and use. It is ethical in that the participants take part in the process and can reap the benefits of the knowledge gained. It uses an ecological and strengths perspective and assumes a holistic view of human beings' ability to reflect, learn, and transform (Stringer, 2007; Stringer & Dwyer, 2005).

Mixed Methods Designs and Evaluation

As the term *mixed methods* suggests, it mixes both quantitative and qualitative methods. This combination is commonly used in practice and program evaluation where gathering narrative and numeric data are a routine part of practice, for example, quantitative evidence in the form of test scores and census data, for the purposes of evaluation. Qualitative evidence, such as the use of participant interviews, may provide useful insights that can better explain how well the program worked (Creswell, 2009).

Creswell (2009) described two types of mixed methods designs that can be useful to consider for program planning and evaluation: sequential and concurrent designs. A sequential design is to use either one method first, such as quantitative, followed by the other method, such as qualitative. If quantitative methods are used, they can provide representative data in which results can be explored in more detail, especially if an unexpected result is found. If qualitative methods are used, they can explore an issue in which the information can be used to guide a quantitative study that would generate generalizable information useful to the target population. A concurrent design is a research design that uses both quantitative (e.g., sociodemographic characteristics, standardized measure scores on program outcomes, satisfaction surveys) and qualitative methods (e.g., open-ended interviews) to understand and explain a program's process or outcomes. It is able to capture both the breadth and depth of an issue under investigation.

The use of an experimental or quasi-experimental design for quantitative research in which an experimental and control group is used helps to increase confidence in the results that the program intervention has had a significant causal effect on the predicted outcomes and in the intended direction (e.g., increased self-esteem, decreased antisocial attitudes).

Data Sources

There are many data sources available for program development and evaluation. Test scores may be based on pretest and posttest knowledge quiz results; for example, comparing what such participants knew about the physiological signs of anger before and after 12 weeks of psychoeducational training. Standardized measuring scales often are used in evaluation because they represent a valid measurement instrument, especially for outcomes, such as self-esteem, anger, prosocial attitudes, and/or behaviors. Many standardized measures use a summative or additive score in which the individual scale items are added together for a total score. Standardized measures have benefits in that they are valid and reliable. Uniform administration and scoring generates normative data that can be used to compare results with different populations or with the same program participants to compare their scores before and after their participation. Common qualitative data sources include structured and semistructured interviewing of central stakeholders, including participants, program staff, public officials, policy makers, and community members (Creswell, 2009; Engel & Schutt, 2010). Review of program documents and observation also may be used.

Common case-level measures used include graphic rating scales, self-anchored rating scales, test scores, and standardized summative scales (Richards, Taylor, Ramasamy, & Richards, 1999). Graphic rating scales often represent an attribute on a numeric continuum, such as 0 to 10. Using an example of depression, 0 = not depressed at all, 5 = moderately depressed, and 10 = completely depressed. A self-anchored rating scale differs from a graphic rating scale in that participants use their own words to describe what makes sense to them about their experience on a continuum. Using a program participant's words to describe his/her depression, 0 = "feeling like frozen zombie," 5 = "cloudy thoughts but little chance of crying," and 10 = "feeling groovy!"

Advocacy and Research for Change

Another important avenue for the dissemination of research is for the purposes of advocacy efforts or policy debates. Mickelson (1995) defined advocacy as "the act of directly representing, defending, intervening, supporting, or recommending a course of action on behalf of one or more individuals, groups, or communities with the goal of securing or retaining social justice." Table 30.3 provides examples of different ways of disseminating research findings that involve advocacy.

The Relationship of Advocacy and Research

Social workers should be aware of two major types of advocacy, which are case-level and class advocacy. Case advocacy refers to social workers who work directly with the clients

TABLE 30.3   Possible Strategies and Venues to Present Forensic Research and Evaluation Projects and Results

Actions	Potential venues	Potential activities
Share research and/or practice		
Write	Publications, reports, testimony	Publish peer-reviewed research or practice journals
		Publish in e-journals
		Publish books or book chapters in area of expertise
Present	Professional research conferences—international, national, regional	Oral presentation
		Roundtable discussion
		Poster presentation
		Workshop
Broadcast	Internet	Your own or organization's website
	E-mail	E-mail newsletters
	Television or radio (local, national/international)	Press release, documentary, news item, interview
	Magazines, newspaper (local, national/international)	Editorial, press release
Events	Professional practice conferences—international, national, local	Do a workshop or presentation
Advocate	Political events	Use research to advocate
	Charity events	
	Legislature or courts	
	Policy makers—expert testimony	
	Internet and social media	Public awareness campaigns
Network	Community stakeholders	Build coalitions
	Internet and social media	Social movement building

and advocate on their behalf in the agency or immediate community environment. In contrast, class advocacy refers to intervention to change the environment through social policy (Mickelson, 1995).

Before taking action, social workers must understand the situation, policies, public perception, client–environment intervention, and issues related to the problem. Assessment of individual and community must occur (Mayer, 2009). These different positions may necessitate different advocacy responses. Case-level advocacy efforts may resemble case management, such as advocating for needed resources. In contrast, policy-level advocacy may be as a political advocate. However, there is also a critical communication that can occur between case-level advocates who are privy to information from the ground about a client population. This information can be shared with class advocates, who, in turn, can share this information with policy makers. The class advocate in return can provide the case advocate with critical information on laws, policies, and potential service loopholes to best help their clients (Mickelson, 1995).

Person-in-Environment Perspective

Use of the person-in-environment perspective allows the use of case advocacy because it connects individuals to their environment. The use of empowerment is to help increase individuals' ability to improve social justice outcomes. The use of this perspective also may assist agency administrators, public officials, and policy makers in learning how policies and laws can impact the individual (Mondros, 2009; Reisch, 2009).

Using the person-in-environment perspective, there are common steps in determining whether an advocacy approach or social action is needed. First, it is important to determine whether there is a condition in the environment or social injustice that is an obstacle to the self-determination of an individual or a group. Second, determine whether the individual/s, group/s, or community/communities affected can be empowered to address the social condition. Third, determine whether advancement has been made or could be advanced. If the individual or group cannot make or sustain the effort, the social worker or organization should advocate on their behalf. The social worker's knowledge of the existing empirical literature, the demographic statistics for the local population, and the common issues impacting this group would help legitimize the advocacy efforts (Humphries, 2008; Mickelson, 1995; Mondros, 2009).

Using Evidence to Facilitate Change

The use of research and evaluation can be a powerful advocacy tool, because it gives agency administrators and public policy makers evidence on which to base their decisions (Reisch, 2009). The use of research for advocacy purposes must move beyond the mere generation of findings to its application in community and policy practice arenas. This shift from conducting research to advocacy often lies with the social worker's ability to effectively communicate this information to key stakeholders using oral or written communication (Chataway, Joffe, & Mordaunt, 2009).

Lightbulb Effect

Research may serve as the light bulb that brings a social issue out of the closet. For example, child maltreatment was not always considered a social problem. However, research can be a very effective tool for change as a simple lack of data and knowledge about an issue may be the cause of government inaction. When presented with research, they may no longer be able to ignore an issue (Mayer, 2009).

For example, child maltreatment was not always considered a social problem. In fact, the "discovery" of child maltreatment in 1962 was the result of the "x-ray vision" of a team of radiologists and doctors to identify and document visual signs of physical abuse, such as the broken bones and fractures in infants and children. Dr. Kempe's naming of the "battered child syndrome" put a face to the once-hidden social problem of child abuse (Kempe, Silverman, Steele, Droegemueller, & Silver, 1962). The research that followed, and the work of child advocates, eventually made child maltreatment an illegal act with the 1974 federal passage of the Child Abuse Prevention Act (Finkelhor, Cross, & Cantor, 2005).

Empowerment Tool

Research can be used as an empowerment tool that bolsters a cause with administrators and policy makers. In fact, many policy makers are open to consulting with experts, including staff from a community organization that is familiar with the population and the problem. Therefore, organizational staff is best prepared to advocate for their population's causes when they know the empirical literature as well as the local population profile (Chataway et al., 2009; Mayer, 2009). Social workers can use sound evidence to influence politicians' political positions.

Mobilization Tool

Research also can be used to mobilize community members or groups (Humphries, 2008; McIntyre, 2008), as in the example of Alice McIntyre (2000) and a group of inner city youth, who used participatory action research to determine the problem of community violence in the form of trash in their neighborhood. This information helped this group of youth mobilize for change.

Action Steps

Thinking Beyond Results

Policy advocates generally discuss strategies for using research for policy purposes. Chataway et al. (2009) recommended thinking beyond results in policy research and engaging stakeholders in all phases of the process. It is recommended to meet with participants, funders, and other stakeholders to clarify issues, try out ideas, and determine what matters most to stakeholders. The research process is an iterative process and can deepen understanding and knowledge. Policy initiatives often may change, which may influence a research project. Therefore, if a reflexive dialogue occurs early in the process, it can help to refine the course of research to make it most relevant to all stakeholders involved (Mayer, 2009).

Communicating Results

Communicating results should be done strategically. Some options include formal or informal presentations to stakeholders, breakfast/lunch/dinner talks, and newspaper and popular journal articles. Public workshops with selected invitees from the policy world, experts, academics, and participants in the research also can be used (Chataway et al., 2009; Reisch, 2009).

The format to use for meetings and how to communicate results should be carefully weighed before deciding upon a choice. The scope of the project effects, the environmental context, and level of stakeholder involvement will influence the choice. The social worker also should be clear about the purpose of the meeting and the type of feedback that is desired, and when this meeting should be scheduled. Culture and context also can influence the communication of results (Chataway et al., 2009). For example, the language (e.g., formal versus informal) used for certain audiences, especially because research is often of a technical nature, should be carefully considered. Table 30.3 provides possible strategies and venues to present research and evaluation projects and results.

Global Evidence-Based Policy Making

Evidence-based policy is of growing interest among policy makers, including at an international level (Thomas & Mohan, 2007). Similar to evidence-based practice, evidence-based policy making draws on the best available evidence and knowledge to develop policies that help to improve health and well-being among individuals and communities and service provision (Mayer, 2009). However, Mayer (2009) noted some areas of concern. First, there is not always evidence available to make policy decisions. Second, there are serious issues of legitimacy and power relations on an international level if the western ways of knowing that revere logic, rationality, and the status of experts are the central frameworks used. Strategies should be employed to include alternative ways of knowing inclusive of and relevant to underserved populations in policy debates.

In reality, evidence-based policy making is complex when implemented in the field (Mayer, 2009). Mayer (2009) recommended strategies for improving the quality of one's research and its effectiveness in changing public policy and public action. Think critically about problems in advance and propose methods to use before acting. Careful reflection can assist with conceptualizing the central issues and with assessing the feasibility of the research and the data sources needed to provide evidence. As described earlier, strategies include involving stakeholders throughout the process.

There also are sober realities to consider when using evidence to take action or to make changes in public policy. Perhaps most important, using empirical evidence will not always result in a shift in other people's views. An important strategy is to talk about evidence realistically. That is, avoid talking about results as if they "prove" something. This assertion makes it easy for others to attack it because all research results are to some degree inconclusive (Mayer, 2009).

Increasing Awareness

In addition to field-based knowledge and skills in evaluation, scholars and practitioners often speak of the critical importance of self-awareness in evaluation (Singer, 2006). Reeser (2009) offered some strategies that help foster the activist and advocate within:

- **Awareness of the political nature of practice.** Forensic social workers should be aware that there is a political nature of social work practice, including research and evaluation. Garnering a vision of a just society will help promote social justice, human rights, and well-being among all individuals, both locally and globally.
- **Awareness of the *personal is political* connection**. Forensic social workers should be aware of the *personal is political* connection. This helps to remind social workers of the connection between the individual and the larger sociopolitical context.
- **Awareness of top-down strategies.** Forensic social workers should be aware of top-down strategies. That is, be aware of strategies used by the status quo (e.g., those that hold power) to maintain power and control, and strategies that advance equity and fairness.
- **Awareness of bottom-up change power**. Forensic social workers also should be aware of how power can be changed from the "bottom up." That is, the rank and file has the power to change unjust structures. Forensic social workers should be committed to helping empower people to recognize and use their resources. Frontline social workers also can realize the impact of building data from the ground up, which can help move the profession forward.
- **Engagement in reflection and action**. Forensic social workers should engage in thoughtful reflection and action. This involves engaging in critical self-reflection and reexamining one's position (e.g, race, sex, and class) and how it is linked to the larger environmental context (Reeser, 2009).

Grant Funding for a Developing or Existing Program or Research/ Advocacy Project

Grant Proposals

Funding is an important aspect of any intervention. The purpose of grant proposals is to obtain approval to start or fund a program and/or research or evaluation project. What distinguishes a proposal from an evaluation report is the plan to conduct a study, and it is written in future tense (Coley & Scheinberg, 2008). In contrast, an evaluation report documents a program evaluation that has been completed and is written in past tense (APA, 2009).

Proposal Sections

The common sections of a proposal are: (a) the introduction, (b) background, (c) specific aims/hypotheses, (d) research design and methods, (e) preliminary data, (f) references, (g) budget, and (h) appendices (Coley & Scheinberg, 2008; Yuen & Terao, 2003).

Similar to a research report, the introduction provides an overview of the problem and rationale and significance of the study. The background provides a succinct review of the relevant literature. The specific aims and hypotheses, research design, and methods are similar to the research report but are written in the future tense. The specific aims/hypotheses state exactly what the study will do, what the research team will do, and what they expect to find out. The methods section details the proposed steps to conduct the study (Gitlin & Lyons, 2008; Marshall & Rossman, 2010; Yuen & Terao, 2003).

The proposal also generally highlights the research team's preliminary findings that provide a rationale for the current study and demonstrates the research team's experience to carry out the project. The budget section documents the proposed expenses, including staff and supplies and a justification for these costs. The appendix or appendices generally include essential related documents, such as proposed timelines, sample measures, and informed consent forms. Length varies pending the purpose. The length of a grant proposal may range from 15 to 30 double-spaced pages (Gitlin & Lyons, 2008). Dissertation proposals are generally much more comprehensive (Locke, Spirduso, & Silverman, 2007).

Funding Pointers

For agency staff seeking grant funding, it is important to convey to funders that your program is important and the proposed program and evaluation plan will be completed. Therefore, a proposal should convey a compelling argument for the program, a feasible plan to conduct the evaluation plan, and clear indication that the proposed team can carry out the project (Gitlin & Lyons, 2008; Marshall & Rossman, 2010).

There are common pitfalls that can be avoided when writing a grant proposal. Many grant proposals are not funded because they do not follow the specific directions as to what is required (Gitlin & Lyons, 2008). Most grant seekers can avoid this pitfall by becoming familiar with potential federal and state funding sources and private foundations. Funding sources include the National Institute of Health, the National Institute of Mental Health, the Centers for Disease Control and Prevention, and the National Institute of Justice. Private foundations that provide funding for research projects and programs include the William E. Casey Foundation and the John D. and Catherine T. MacArthur Foundation. Becoming familiar with the list of their priorities is helpful. Additionally, carefully read the program announcement and consult with grant program officers about your project. Other important points relate to overall discipline. Be sure to strictly adhere to page limits, submission deadlines, and include all sections requested. The final submission should be flawless. Also ask colleagues to review the proposal and recommend revisions (Gitlin & Lyons, 2008). For programs specifically looking for social justice funding information please see the web links provided later in this chapter.

Conclusion

This chapter reviewed forensic intervention development using a human rights and social justice systems approach. The establishment of human and/or social service programs and agencies, or policy development, or public awareness and advocacy can help provide the advocacy and support services to achieve a fairer and just society for all underrepresented and underserved individuals and groups at risk of and/or involved with legal issues of the justice system. The logic model can serve as a blueprint and guide to plan, implement, and evaluate problem identification, the process of program implementation, and outcome evaluation. Knowledge of program evaluation can help in understanding program and grant development stages. It also reviewed aspects of using research for advocacy and evidence-based policy making. Many of the skills learned in program development can be applied to grant development but with an increased emphasis on skillful writing.

CHAPTER EXERCISES

Exercise 1. As an individual or group, identify a forensic population and/or social problem in your local area. The problem should be clear enough in which a program needs to be developed. Develop a logic model for the program.

Exercise 2. Identify a human rights and social justice issue in the local or global community. Identify a policy issue that affects this population; for example, the lack of legal protections for undocumented workers. Develop a petition at change.org or moveon.org to promote awareness and support for this issue.

Exercise 3. Identify a human rights and social justice issue you and/or your group feel most passionate about. Identify some potential funding sources to fund a program in development, an existing program, or a policy advocacy campaign.

Additional Resources

Program and Grant Development

ACLU-Campaign for Smart Justice: www.aclu.org/feature/campaign-smart-justice

OJJDP Program Database: www.ojjdp.gov/programs/ProgSearch.asp

Pew Charitable Trusts, Evidence-Based Policy Making: www.pewtrusts.org/~/media/assets/2014/11/evidencebasedpolicymakingaguideforeffectivegovernment.pdf

SAMHSA Evidence-Based Practice Registry: www.samhsa.gov/nrepp

University of Wisconsin Extension, Enhancing Program Performance with Logic Models: www.uwex.edu/ces/lmcourse/interface/coop_M1_Overview.htm

Human Rights, Social Justice Funding Resources for Forensic Research

- Edge Funders Alliance (funding social movements): http://edgefunders.org
- Ford Foundation: www.fordfoundation.org
- Funding Exchange: https://fex.org
- Interaction Institute for Social Change: http://interactioninstitute.org
- Social Justice Funders Network: www.justicefunders.org
- Social Justice Grantmaking: http://foundationcenter.org/gainknowledge/research/pdf/socialjustice.pdf
- Social Justice Infrastructure Funders: http://hillsnowdon.org/grantmaking/grantee-profile-pages/social-justice-infrastructure-funders

References

Addams, J. (1910). *Twenty years at Hull House*. New York, NY: Macmillan.

American Psychological Association. (2009). *Publication manual of the American Psychological Association* (6th ed.). Washington, DC: Author.

Bamberger, M., Rugh, J., & Mabry, L. (2006). *Real world evaluation*. Thousand Oaks, CA: Sage Publications.

Barker, R. L. (2003). *The social work dictionary* (5th ed.). Washington, DC: National Association of Social Workers Press.

Boulmetis, J., & Dutwin, P. (2000). *The ABCs of evaluation: Timeless techniques for program and project managers*. San Francisco, CA: Jossey-Bass.

Chataway, J., Joffe, A., & Mordaunt, J. (2009). Communicating results. In A. Thomas & G. Mohan (Eds.), *Research skills for policy and development: How to find out fast* (pp. 95–110). Thousand Oaks, CA: Sage Publications.

Chinman, M., Imm, P., & Wandersman, A. (2010). *Promoting accountability through methods and tools for planning, implementation, and evaluation*. Santa Monica, CA: Rand Corporation. Retrieved from http://www.rand.org/pubs/technical_reports/TR101

Coley, S. M., & Scheinberg, C. A. (2008). *Proposal writing: Effective grantsmanship* (3rd ed.). Thousand Oaks, CA: Sage Publications.

Council on Social Work Education. (2015). *2015 educational policy and accreditation standards*. Retrieved from https://www.cswe.org/getattachment/Accreditation/Accreditation-Process/2015-EPAS/2015EPAS_Web_FINAL.pdf.aspx

Creswell, J. W. (2009). *Research design: Qualitative, quantitative, and mixed methods approaches*. Thousand Oaks, CA: Sage Publications.

Day, P. J. (2008). *A new history of social welfare* (6th ed.). New York, NY: Allyn & Bacon.

DuBois, B., & Miley, K. K. (2010). *Social work: An empowering profession* (7th ed.). Boston, MA: Allyn & Bacon.

Dudley, J. (2008). *Social work evaluation: Enhancing what we do*. Chicago, IL: Lyceum Books.

Ehrenreich, J. H. (1985). *The altruistic imagination: A history of social work and social policy in the United States*. Ithaca, NY: Cornell University Press.

Ely, R. T. (1895). *Hull-House maps and papers. A presentation of nationalities and wages in a contested district of Chicago together with comments and essays growing out of the social conditions by residents of Hull-House*. New York, NY: Thomas Y. Crowell & Company.

Emery, M., & Flora, C. (2006). Spiraling-up: Mapping community transformation with community capitals framework. *Journal of Community Development, 37*(1), 19–35.

Engel, R., & Schutt, R. K. (2010). *The fundamentals of social work research*. Thousand Oaks, CA: Sage Publications.

Fetterman, D. M., & Wandserman, A. (2004). *Empowerment evaluation principles in practice*. New York, NY: Guilford Press.

Finkelhor, D., Cross, T. P., & Cantor, E. (2005). *How the justice system responds to juvenile victims: A comprehensive model*. Washington, DC: Office of Juvenile Justice and Delinquency Prevention.

Gitlin, L. N., & Lyons, K. J. (2008). *Successful grant writing: Strategies for health and human service professionals* (3rd ed.). New York, NY: Springer Publishing.

Goldman, K. D., & Schmalz, K. J. (2005). Accentuate the positive: Using an asset-mapping tool as part of a community health needs assessment. *Health Promotion Practice, 6*(2), 125–128.

Hillier, A. (2007). Why social work needs mapping. *Journal of Social Work Education, 43*(2), 205–221.

Humphries, B. (2008). *Social work research for social justice*. New York, NY: Palgrave MacMillan.

Jasek-Rysdahl, K. (2001). Applying Sen's capabilities framework to neighborhoods: Using local assets maps to deepen our understanding of well-being. *Review of Social Economy, 59*(3), 313–329.

Kempe, C. H., Silverman, F. N., Steele, B. F., Droegemueller, W., & Silver, H. K. (1962). The battered-child syndrome. *Journal of the American Medical Association, 181*, 17–24.

Kretzmann, J. P., & McKnight, J. L. (1993). *Building communities from the inside out: A path toward finding and mobilizing a community's assets*. Evanston, IL: Institute for Policy Research.

Levin, H. M. (2001). *Cost-effectiveness analysis* (2nd ed.). Thousand Oaks, CA: Sage Publications.

Locke, L. F., Spirduso, W. W., & Silverman, S. J. (2007). *Proposals that work: A guide for planning dissertations and grant proposals* (5th ed.). Thousand Oaks, CA: Sage Publications, Inc.

Marlow, C. R. (2010). *Research methods for generalist practice* (5th ed.). Pacific Grove, CA: Brooks/Cole.

Marshall, C., & Rossman, G. B. (2010). *Designing qualitative research* (5th ed.). Thousand Oaks, CA: Sage Publications.

Maschi, T., Bradley, C., & Ward, K. (Eds.). (2009). *Forensic social work: Psychosocial and legal issues in diverse practice settings*. New York, NY: Springer Publishing.

Maschi, T., & MacMillan, T. (2009). *After school music program for youth satisfaction survey: Parent/caretaker version*. Unpublished instrument.

Maschi, T., & Youdin, R. (2012). *Social worker as researcher: Integrating research with advocacy*. Boston, MA: Pearson.

Mayer, S. (2009). Using evidence in advocacy. In A. Thomas & G. Mohan (Eds.), *Research skills for policy and development: How to find out fast* (pp. 264–274). Thousand Oaks, CA: Sage Publications.

McIntyre, A. (2000). *Inner city kids: Adolescents confront life and violence in an urban community*. New York, NY: University Press.

McIntyre, A. (2008). *Participatory action research*. Thousand Oaks, CA: Sage Publications.

Mickelson, J. S. (1995). Advocacy. In R. L. Edwards (Ed.), *Encyclopedia of social work* (19th ed., Vol. 1, pp. 95–100). Washington, DC: National Association of Social Workers Press.

Mondros, J. B. (2009). Principles and practice guidelines for social action. In A. R. Roberts & G. L. Greene (Eds.), *Social workers desk reference* (2nd ed., pp. 534–544). New York, NY: Oxford University Press.

Mullen, E. J., Dumpson, J. R., & Associates. (1972). *Evaluation of social intervention*. San Francisco, CA: Jossey-Bass.

National Association of Social Workers. (1999). *Code of Ethics of the National Association of Social Workers*. Washington, DC: Author. Retrieved from http://www.naswdc.org/pubs/code/code.asp

Neuman, K. (2002). From practice evaluation to agency evaluation: Demonstrating outcomes to the United Way. *Social Work in Mental Health, 1*(2), 1–14.

Patton, M. Q. (2002). *Qualitative research and evaluation methods* (11th ed.). Thousand Oaks, CA: Sage Publications.

Percy-Smith, J. (1996). *Needs assessment in public policy*. Philadelphia, PA: Open University Press.

Reeser, L. C. (2009). Educating for social change in the human service profession. In E. Aldarando (Ed.), *Advancing social justice through clinical practice* (pp. 459–476). Mahwah, NJ: Lawrence Erlbaum.

Reichert, E. (2003). Move from social justice to human rights provides new perspective. *Professional Development, 4*(1), 5–13.

Reisch, M. (2009). Legislative advocacy to empower oppressed and vulnerable groups. In A. R. Roberts & G. L. Greene (Eds.), *Social workers desk reference* (2nd ed., pp. 545–550). New York, NY: Oxford University Press.

Richards, S., Taylor, R. L., Ramasamy, R., & Richards, R. Y. (1999). *Single subject research: Applications in educational and clinical settings*. Belmont, CA: Wadsworth/Thomson.

Richmond, M. (1917). *Social diagnosis*. Philadelphia, PA: Russell Sage Foundation.

Rossi, P. H., Freeman, H. E., & Lipsey, M. (2004). *Evaluation: A systematic approach* (7th ed.). Thousand Oaks, CA: Sage Publications.

Royse, D., Thyer, B. A., Padgett, D., & Logan, T. K. (2006). *Program evaluation: An introduction* (4th ed.). Belmont, CA: Brooks/Cole.

Schram, B. (1997). *Creating small scale social program: Planning, implementation, and evaluation*. Thousand Oaks, CA: Sage Publications.

Singer, J. (2006). *Stirring up justice: Writing and reading to change the world*. Portsmouth, NH: Heinenman.

Smith, M. J. (2010). *Handbook of program evaluation for social work health professionals*. New York, NY: Oxford University Press.

Soriani, F. I. (1995). *Conducting needs assessment: A multidisciplinary approach*. Thousand Oaks, CA: Sage Publications.

Stringer, E. T. (2007). *Action research* (3rd ed.). Thousand Oaks, CA: Sage Publications.

Stringer, E. T., & Dwyer, R. (2005). *Action research in human services*. Upper Saddle River, NJ: Pearson.

Suarez-Balcazar, Y., & Harper, G. W. (2003). *Empowerment and participatory evaluation of community interventions: Multiple benefits*. Binghamton, NY: Haworth Press.

Taylor-Powell, E., & Henert, E. (2008). *Developing a logic model: Teaching and training guide*. University of Wisconsin-Extension, Cooperative Extension, Program Development and Evaluation. Madison: Board of Regents of the University of Wisconsin System. Retrieved from http://www .uwex.edu/ces/pdande/evaluation/pdf/lmguidecomplete.pdf

Thomas, A., & Monan, G. (2007). *Research skills for policy and development: How to find out fast*. Thousand Oaks, CA: Sage Publications.

United Nations. (1948). The Universal Declaration of Human Rights. Retrieved from http://www .un.org/en/documents/udhr

United Nations. (1994). *Human rights and social work: A manual for schools of social work and the social work profession*. Geneva, Switzerland: United Nations Centre for Human Rights.

Unrau, Y. A., Gabor, P. A., & Grinnell, R. M. (2006). *Evaluation in social work: The art and science of practice* (4th ed.). New York, NY: Oxford University Press.

Westerfelt, A., & Dietz, T. J. (2010). *Planning and conducting agency-based research* (4th ed.). Boston, MA: Pearson.

W.K. Kellogg Foundation. (2004). *Logic model development guide*. Battle Creek, MI: Author.

Wronka, J. (2008). Human rights. In T. Mizrahi & L. E. Davis (Eds.), *Encyclopedia of social work* (20th ed., pp. 425–429). Washington, DC: National Association of Social Workers Press.

York, R. O. (2009). *Evaluating human services: A practical approach for the human service professional*. Boston, MA: Pearson.

Yuen, F., & Terao, K. L. (2003). *Practical grant writing and program evaluation*. Pacific Grove, CA: Brooks/Cole.

VOICES FROM THE FIELD

Tina Maschi, PhD, LCSW, ACSW
Associate Professor, Scholar, and Researcher
Fordham University Graduate School of Social Service
Founder and Director, The Justia Agenda
New York

Agency Setting

I am a professor at Fordham University Graduate School of Social Service (GSS), which is located in New York City. Fordham is a Jesuit University and the Graduate School of Social Service is one of the schools within the overall university. The school has a bachelor's, master's, and doctoral program. It is known as one of the largest social work schools in the world with over 2,000 students at any given time attending the program.

Practice Responsibilities

My responsibilities include teaching, scholarship, and service. I teach Bachelor's in Social Work (BSW), Master's in Social Work (MSW), and PhD students research and practice courses. I am also engaged in research and scholarship that is organized through the Justia Agenda Project (www.justiaagenda.com).

Expertise Required

A doctorate degree in social work or allied discipline is generally required for obtaining a tenure track faculty position at a university. Varying levels of practice experience along with a doctorate degree are generally required to teach practice courses. As for me, I have over 20 years of practice and research experience in the juvenile and criminal justice systems.

Ethical, Legal, Practice, Diversity, and/or Advocacy Issues Addressed

Just like any practice setting, ethical and legal diversity and advocacy issues may arise while teaching in the classroom or conducting research in the field. For example, there may be an instance where a student or students may voice their concerns over diversity issues (students of color, LGBT, and/or with a disability) in the classroom, such as bias and discrimination on the part of the administration or by teachers in the classroom. There may be instances in which I may play a role in advocating for students. In the field conducting research, especially related to my research on the aging-in-prison crisis, I have conducted research with a follow-up public awareness campaign to bring attention to the issue for policy or practice reform. Readers can review some of my public awareness and advocacy tools at my website (www.justiaagenda.com).

Interprofessional and Intersectoral Collaboration

It is quite common as an educator and researcher to work with other faculty or community service providers from different disciplines. This can be in the form of interprofessional team teaching or interdisciplinary research projects, which may include social workers, psychologists, medical doctors, nurses, and/or lawyers.

CHAPTER 31

Case Level and Policy Advocacy

Eileen Klein

CHAPTER OBJECTIVES

The major objectives of this chapter are to:

- Promote understanding of the intersection of social work case level practice skills and social welfare programs and policy.
- Describe the social work advocacy process.
- Explore how social and political values impact accessibility to social welfare programs.

CHAPTER COMPETENCIES HIGHLIGHTED

- Competency 5: Engage in Policy Practice
- Competency 8: Intervene With Individuals, Families, Organizations, and Communities

Casework, or microlevel practice, takes place when an individual requires an intervention to secure needed goods or services. A case level intervention may be required when a person has a problem related to his or her personal or family situation, or unmet needs. These may include needing help with financial, educational, interpersonal, housing, or employment issues. A client may seek the help of a social worker or social service agency to provide assistance or consultation about resolution of an unmet need. An individual may seek counseling or referral for issues related to health, mental health, substance abuse or social problems, or information on available services or entitlements. Individuals may also be referred by an outside agency, or system, to get a case level intervention. This may be the case when a person is referred by the legal or educational system.

Assisting a client with his or her presenting problem begins with taking a biopsychosocial history to determine eligibility and service requirements. While gathering this information, there is a simultaneous process of establishing a relationship, developing rapport, identifying goals, and gaining trust in the initial engagement. Case level assistance requires the social worker to use this information to assess the problem and determine the areas in need. This is a time when social workers ascertain if they will be able to obtain the necessary services, or if there are any barriers that must be overcome before the client is able to get what he or she is entitled to. The client may have personal hurdles to overcome, such as financial, language, or legal status, to obtain the necessary social services.

To provide comprehensive social services, the social worker also has to assess if there are any societal or political obstacles hindering getting services, such as discrimination or stigma. There are certain rights that extend to all, which should not impact accessing goods or services. At a minimum, the U.S. Bill of Rights entitles one to have freedom, feel secure in his or her home, and have the right to due process of law if accused of a crime. Casework includes not only problem evaluation, but assessing if clients are experiencing obstacles that interfere with safeguarding their rights.

Social justice is a core value in social work. John Rawls' (1971) theory of social justice concerns the right of individuals to have equal basic liberties and opportunities to be provided by the social and political systems that they interact with. Rawls postulated that a policy change is only an improvement if it improves the situation of the least advantaged person. Another popular view of social justice is described by David Miller (1999). Miller communicates justice as rights, goods, or advantages being distributed to individuals in society equally, with no one's capacity to obtain necessities obstructed.

Social workers have a responsibility to advocate for social justice on the individual, community, and societal level. They have a duty to recognize injustice and inequalities that impact their clients. A client's interaction with the environment locally and systemically may help or hinder the ability to obtain necessary services. Social workers have to ensure that they comprehend policy at the local, state, and federal level so that they can be active in employing effective practices that can effect change. In order to access services for a client one must understand the policies and regulations that control the benefit.

The intersection of one's gender, sexuality, race, ethnicity, culture, socioeconomic, and other social identities often interferes with an individual's ability for equality. The Council on Social Work Education (CSWE, 2008) requires social workers to understand policy formation and implementation so that they can recognize how they influence a client's social, environmental, and economic functioning. A social worker must be able to advocate for change if the policies are not equitable. CSWE also requires competence in a social worker's ability to think critically so that he or she can advocate for policies that progress social, economic, and environmental justice. This chapter assists social workers in developing competence in policy practice and in case and policy advocacy. It also helps social workers recognize when social welfare and economic policies are not fairly distributed, and become skilled in taking action at the micro-, mezzo, and/or macrolevel. Large institutions, such as the criminal justice and education systems, pose contradictions in equality and equal opportunity, which are discussed further in this chapter. There is a discussion of the interaction of direct practice with case advocacy to underscore the critical need to understand and interpret policy to achieve social justice.

History of Social Work Advocacy

Social workers have a long history of involvement in social reform. In the United States, social programs began based on the Elizabethan Poor Laws of the 1600s with an emphasis on work, individual responsibility, and self-sufficiency. This began the debate of conflicting ideologies of "worthy" and "unworthy," or "deserving" and "undeserving," which have influenced social welfare programs and policy for centuries. Taking care of those in need was primarily the responsibility of family members, and then became a duty of religious organizations. One's duty to help the less fortunate was often part of religious teachings. One felt a duty to help a neighbor when called upon for help. Members of communities, or parishes, looked out for each other.

The influx of immigrants and industrialization led to overcrowding in cities. As time went on, social conditions dictated a higher need for social services to be provided, which led to public awareness and involvement in care. In the mid-1800s, institutions were built to care for those who were orphaned, unemployed, or otherwise in need (Segal, 2016). While it was helpful to gather people in similar circumstances in a group setting, almshouses and work houses began to become places of abuse. As these settings became more common, so did poor conditions and mistreatment. Institutions that were run privately had to make a profit. This resulted in many of the residents working long hours to earn their stay. Many of these facilities housed people who were disenfranchised, or mentally or physically disabled, and became places to put them out of sight in a rural setting.

Early social workers were pioneers in studying social conditions such as overcrowding, unemployment, epidemics, and child labor. They began to understand that when an individual problem affects large numbers of people, it becomes a social problem. Social problems, as defined by the values of society, require a systemic and broad intervention to be properly addressed. In the 1880s, the settlement house movement began as a way to intervene in an individual's problems in a holistic way. Personal problems were seen as inseparable from environmental influences. Jane Addams, the founder of Hull House, lived among the people to help them participate in the community, feel ethnic pride, and gain skills in literacy and employment (Segal, 2016).

Staub-Bernasconi (2016) identifies the beginnings of social work advocacy for human rights in the texts of Jane Addams. She describes Addams using scientific research to invalidate prevailing public opinion when it fails to respond to social problems that violate social justice and individual freedom. Social workers began to be involved in many social and political causes as they began to understand more about living conditions. They began to share information and educate others about issues affecting vulnerable individuals. Jane Addams, and other social workers, took a lead role in advocating for child labor laws and women's rights. Their role expanded when the federal government became involved in social welfare policy with the Social Security Act in the 1930s. There were many initiatives that were developed to help people gain skills and employment. The need for social services grew with the number of orphans and widows affected by World War II.

The role of social workers in providing social welfare services was further extended in the 1960s with the Civil Rights Act and the War on Poverty (DiNitto & Johnson, 2012). The government developed programs to help individuals access health care through Medicaid and Medicare, food stamps, Head Start, and other antipoverty programs. It was a time when values emphasized social change and a just society. Civil rights and ethnic identities were important topics on the political and public agenda.

The cycle again shifted in the 1970s through the 1990s when social services were reduced. However, awareness of social problems became apparent with the increase in homelessness and the AIDS epidemic. While these issues affected large numbers of people, there was again a social value judgment on giving aid to those who brought these problems on themselves (Dolgoff & Feldstein, 2012). Social workers had to work closely with individuals on the case level to help them access services. They also had to understand funding streams, and the political process, to advocate for systemic change since many of those affected were stigmatized, oppressed, and highly vulnerable. It was difficult to get funding for programs as a result of societal views. This changed over time with more accurate information on the cause and spread of the disease.

The terrorist attack on the United States in 2001 again changed social services. Defense and homeland security were budget priorities for the federal government (DiNitto & Johnson, 2012). Unfortunately, the early 2000s brought forth other social issues that required attention. These included natural disasters, such as Hurricane Katrina, and the aging population needing access to health care and prescription drugs. Many social service agencies assisted individuals and communities to manage these competing priorities. Personal problems of unemployment, homelessness, and access to care were so widespread that they became social issues requiring large-scale intervention. Again, social workers were critical in helping those in need get their fair share of entitlements.

This brief historical account identifies the dynamic nature of social welfare problems, priorities, and policies. Interventions on the local, state, and federal levels require individuals to collaborate and form grassroots movements for change, coalitions, and educational campaigns to inform the public and policy makers of the need for services to be amended or created. This is an important role for social workers and mandated by the National Association of Social Workers *Code of Ethics* (NASW, 2008).

The NASW *Code of Ethics* was written in 1960 to identify the responsibilities of a social worker. It has since been revised several times and defines the profession's focus on helping individuals within their social environment and to attend to "forces that create, contribute to, and address problems in living" and "promote social justice and social change with and on behalf of clients" (NASW, 2008). This clearly corresponds to the CSWE core competencies to "advance human rights and social and economic justice" and to "engage in policy practice to advance social and economic well-being and to deliver effective social work" (CSWE, 2015).

Theory

Intervention and prevention cannot take place outside of social justice and public policy advocacy (Romano, 2015). The relationship between managing a client's case and understanding how it is impacted by societal values and constraints cannot be separated. Curry-Stevens (2012) asserts that social workers cannot be value-neutral in their position, but have to be strategic and persuasive in advancing social justice with policy makers. A social worker can use critical theory to understand how policy decisions are made. This informs who does and does not benefit from the implementation. This theory addresses power and privilege, as well as the influence of one's ethnicity, race, sexual orientation, class, and other personal attributes, in shaping social welfare policy (Segal, 2016).

Social workers are trained to see the "person in environment." It would be difficult to determine an appropriate intervention without understanding the problem, scope, meaning, and what barriers may be in place to impede its resolution. Staub-Bernasconi (2016) ascertains that social problems must be described scientifically when engaging in human rights work. She further states that this work requires action for social change to occur. This action will take the place in helping to develop new laws or changing the ones that currently exist.

Barnes, Green, and Hopton (2007) see the ability to view a person within society as a great strength in the social work method. They see that the intervention will be more effective if there is an understanding of how a problem interfaces with the social environment of the individual. The problem cannot be addressed at the case level without considering its social construction, or underlying assumptions, of the social reality that inform the understanding, rules, and norms of the interaction.

Social constructions are subject to change as values and conditions change. In society there are those with power, the dependents or powerless, and the deviants. All of these groups can have positive or negative images, and benefit or burden society (Schneider & Sidney, 2009). Roles transform as perceptions and conditions change. The social worker has to be cognizant of where one stands in society when determining a plan of action for an individual. While thinking of the action to assist the individual, the social worker may also begin to plan for a policy intervention or formulate an advocacy strategy for change. These have to be considered concurrently and cannot be separated if the intervention is to be successful.

Policy Practice: Framework

Almog-Bar, Weiss-Gal, and Gal (2015) state that policy practice is a central element of social work and the importance of understanding the process of policy decision making to access services on the microlevel, or case level. They discuss two frameworks for social workers to use to consider social welfare policies; John Kongdom's Multiple Streams Framework (MSF) and Paul Sabatier's Advocacy Coalition Framework (ACF).

MSF describes policy formation as having three parts: problems, policies, and politics. Problems are the issues requiring an intervention; policies are the proposals requiring change or proposed solutions; politics define public opinion on problems and prospective solutions (Almog-Bar et al., 2015). This formulation identifies ideas and continual change as important in policy decisions and highlights the nonlinear formulation in the policy-making process. ACF views the policy process as in continual movement based on coalitions, alliances, and competing systems and relationships. The process is an intersection of fundamental core beliefs, policy core beliefs, and secondary empirical beliefs employed by a group or coalition.

This includes societal norms, the movement of external forces, and subsystems interacting (Almog-Bar et al., 2015).

Both of these frameworks underscore the importance of individual understanding of the definition of the problem and how that is influenced by the societal values, beliefs, and processes that construct the policy. They also point to the changing nature of our beliefs based on current conditions, legislative mandates and media influence, or the social construction of social problems. Therefore, social policies can be framed as "collective responses to perceived social problems" (Jimenez, Pasztor, Chambers, & Fujii, 2015). The social worker has to take all of this into consideration when accessing a social welfare program or engaging in advocacy efforts to make changes in an existing program.

There are several steps to consider in accessing case level services. Are all services available to be distributed equally using the same parameters for all? How are the intended recipients of the services viewed by society or in the political climate? These questions may direct the ability to make case level interventions effectively, or indicate the necessity of beginning an advocacy process. In some cases it is important to get clients equal treatment and equal access to a program or benefit; in others, one must use different methods to get to the same end because of the diversity of the client (O'Brien, 2011). This is important when we consider access to education by diverse populations and the use of affirmative action programs to gain entrance to schools. It may also be a factor in accessing programs for citizens versus noncitizens, or health care for insured versus uninsured. Social workers are often trying to assist individuals not seen as deserving of assistance, or blamed for their situation. This was a factor in getting services for persons with AIDS at the onset of the epidemic. Were they afflicted with this illness because of their own transgressions or victims?

Applying Advocacy Skills

What is an advocate? One who advocates can also be called a champion, defender, supporter, proponent, crusader, or fighter. An advocate can have a negative connotation when engaging in a cause that is not uniformly seen as something positive. Social workers often work with vulnerable, disenfranchised, and oppressed populations. Clients may be viewed by society as deserving or undeserving of assistance. Therefore, social workers have to influence policy makers and agencies to improve the clients' circumstances through access or change in current practice. O'Brien (2011) refers to social workers as a bridge between the "included" and the "excluded." Their goal is to get clients across the bridge by reducing or removing barriers so that the client can have equal access to opportunities and services to promote social justice.

When engaging in the advocacy process it is critical for the social worker to have knowledge of who is in power. Power is often associated with money and political and social connections (Karger & Stoesz, 2005). Understanding who will be an ally or opponent is essential when beginning the change process. Engaging with allies that have a support base in the community or in the political arena will be an important step.

After understanding who may help or hinder the cause, a social worker has to gather information. This includes: clearly defining the social problem, determining what the current policy is for alleviating this problem, the target population and objectives, getting data on who is impacted by this policy, determining the effects of the problem on individuals or society, and possible alternatives to the current policy (DiNitto & Johnson, 2012). These facts have to be presented to those who will support the proposed change or policy. Once this is done, a group or coalition can be formed to determine a plan of action. Having a person with the "lived experience" as part of the group may help give a human face to the issue, as well as offer essential insights into the problem and its resolution.

Advocacy efforts can include providing education of the problem to the public or elected officials, writing letters to policy makers, writing an editorial in the local newspaper about the issue, and/or testifying at a public hearing or community meeting. All of these actions will direct attention to the issue. There are some issues facing the incarcerated that are not considered or well understood by the public. Solitary confinement, or restrictive housing, is an issue that has recently come to the fore. If an inmate violates a rule, is in a fight, or assaults another person, this may be used as punishment or as a way to protect the inmate from further harm. Grassian (2006) studied the psychiatric effects of solitary confinement and found that prisoners in long-term solitary confinement often had cognitive impairment, affective disturbances, or became psychotic with agitation and disorganization. Some of the confinement resulted in a permanent disability, which reduced an inmate's capacity to reintegrate into the community when released. As a result of public awareness of the deleterious effects of this type of punishment, there are movements to end this practice in several states. In January 2016, President Obama banned its use for juveniles held in federal prisons. Public campaigns and education are very effective forms of advocacy.

Another important component of effective advocacy is being aware of who is responsible for funding the program that they are trying to access. Social workers need a working knowledge of regulations for local, state, and federal programs, as well as how to contact representatives serving their client's community (DiNitto & Johnson, 2012). Contacting the appropriate source for assistance with a client's needs is essential for guidance in problem resolution. These contacts can be made via e-mail, the telephone, or in writing a policy to improve client outcomes. This can result in beginning a dialogue on finding a solution, or proposing a program. This is an area where social workers can use their skills at negotiation, engagement, rapport building, and group process. Perseverance and continuing the advocacy process over time is essential for a change to occur. Effective advocacy requires understanding program and policy functions, as well as their administration.

Social Work With Forensic Populations

Social workers are employed in many settings with a forensic population. They work in the criminal justice system, child abuse and neglect, corrections, probation, and domestic violence, to mention a few examples. They also may be involved in forensic issues when dealing with mental health or substance abuse treatment. These areas often require social workers to help clients to get access to housing, employment, entitlements, and/or treatment.

There are many barriers to accessing these necessary services for clients in or returning from the criminal justice system. In addition, these clients often experience discrimination and are stigmatized in the community. These are clients who may have participated in criminal acts of violence or abuse and are viewed negatively by the public. To access services, social workers often face legal challenges in securing housing and employment, as well as opposition from family or community. These clients require advocacy quite often to gain access to what they need to integrate into society and sustain them.

There are times when assisting a client to access essential needs and services conflicts with ideals of public safety. These issues often arise in community reentry. The social worker may have to enforce conditions that are not consistent with his or her right to self-determination, as stipulated in the NASW *Code of Ethics* (NASW, 2008). These are instances when clients have to respond to conditions of parole or probation by attending certain programs, or living in a structured setting, not of their choosing. Social workers have to consider their conflicting position of being responsible to both their client and to the broader society. They may have to negotiate for their client to pursue education or employment.

In some states, forensic clients are denied some of the basic rights of U.S. citizens, including the right to vote or live in public housing. According to the National Conference of State Legislators (2016), 38 states restore voting rights to felons, some states have a waiting period to vote after returning to the community, and some states require a pardon to restore voting rights. Public housing is restricted to those with a conviction of sexual offense or having a family member with a conviction. When a sentence is completed, not being able to vote or secure housing impedes a person's ability to reengage in society equally.

In addition, while the federal government does not allow discrimination for employment for those with a criminal history, they do not prohibit states from asking about your criminal history. Again, this adversely affects a person's chance of employment. Employment has been shown to improve one's quality of life, enhance self-esteem, increase social support, and provide a sense of achievement (Beck & Wernham, 2014). Besides the financial reward, having a job gives a person a place to go and helps to structure the day.

When clients reenter the community from a structured forensic program, they may not be prepared to independently plan for their day since this was not required during their incarceration. Roberts, Davies, and Maggs (2015) found that helping clients develop vocational skills was highly valued by forensic mental health clients as a way of helping them reengage in a community-based setting. Clients in their study also benefitted from participating in an exercise program to promote healthy living as a way for them to begin to plan for leisure activities on their own.

In order to have a fair chance to restore community life, clients with forensic histories have to be able to have a place to live that is affordable, secure job training or employment, and participate fully in society when they have completed their sentences. These are certainly areas for social workers to advocate for change. Networking with other forensic service providers to effect change is one step in this process. Working with others to educate the public about the benefits gained by this change is also an essential component.

In 2015, President Obama issued an executive order prohibiting the federal government from asking about criminal history on employment applications to assist reentry into the workforce of the formerly incarcerated. Some cities and states have implemented "Ban the Box," which prevents employers from asking about criminal history on employment applications. These initiatives are the result of advocates' efforts in seeking reform on discriminatory policies.

Case Example and Application

The New York Campaign for Alternatives to Isolated Confinement (CAIC) is an advocacy group that is made up of formerly incarcerated persons, family members of currently incarcerated persons, community members, lawyers, and individuals throughout New York State interested in human rights. This group engages schools of social work through educational programs, documentary movies, and panel discussions in an effort to involve social work professionals and students in their fight to end solitary confinement.

CAIC is a group that educates the public and policy makers about the facts of solitary confinement. They have a website with information on the number of men, women, and children placed in solitary confinement on a daily basis (approximately 4,000), the psychological damage incurred with use of solitary confinement, and its use on vulnerable populations, including the mentally ill, older adults, and pregnant women (CAIC, 2016). They raise awareness in community meetings, giving facts, as well as personal stories of the formerly incarcerated, on the abuse endured while in isolation. Their campaign to end this practice also includes contacting policy makers and their political representative through letters, postcards, e-mails, and peaceful demonstrations.

This is an advocacy group that is working to eliminate the policy of using solitary confinement to protect or punish in the prison system. They work at raising awareness about this method being unsafe and counterproductive. CAIC reaches out to individuals who have experienced solitary confinement and provides a forum where they can speak directly to the public and the legislators about their experience. This is a very powerful advocacy tool. Attaching a person and his or her story can deliver direct evidence on the devastating impact of solitary confinement. This will be an important addition to the 2008 New York State Law, which limits the use of solitary confinement for people with a mental illness.

(continued)

CAIC uses the Internet to contact people to join in their advocacy efforts. They use their e-mail list to contact others to inform them of upcoming legislation, suggest wording of letters to politicians, and provide information about public hearings and community meetings with legislators and other community leaders. They use local venues, like churches and public school auditoriums, to gather people. They often have family members of inmates speak out on how prison had a long-term negative effect on their family member. They provide actual narratives of real experiences that are very difficult to hear and often inspire their audience to join their fight for prison reform.

They also work on individual cases when they are brought to their attention. Again, when someone is brought to their attention as being unjustly treated, they will use their outreach of letters, phone calls, and public meetings to inform the public and policy makers. An important form of advocacy that they use is networking with other organizations that share a similar purpose related to prison mistreatment. They are affiliated with civic (Correction Association of New York), legal (Legal Aid Society's Prisoners' Rights Project), and religious groups (National Religious Campaign Against Torture) in their efforts, as well as local community organizations. CAIC also uses legislation from other states or entities to make their case. They note that the United Nations (UN) supports their efforts and has met with U.S. officials to discuss the UN Convention Against Torture and Other Cruel, Inhumane, or Degrading Treatment or Punishment (CAT). The UN has issued a Special Rapporteur on Torture.

The advocacy and outreach determination of CAIC have led them to be instrumental in getting the New York State legislature to consider the Humane Alternatives to Long Term (HALT) Solitary Confinement Act. They engaged several of the members of the New York State Assembly and Senate in proposing and sponsoring this bill. This act is designed to limit the use of solitary confinement by placing a 15-day limit on solitary confinement, and create new more rehabilitative housing options for inmates designated a safety risk to others. It will often limit the use of solitary confinement for minor "offenses" such as talking back to a guard or not finishing your meal (solitarywatch.com). There are 16 Senate cosponsors and two Assembly sponsors as of the 2015 to 2016 session (New York State Senate, 2016). It is currently in committee in both the New York State Assembly and the New York State Senate. The bill is aimed at restricting the use of segregated confinement for vulnerable populations and creating alternative therapeutic and rehabilitative confinement options.

CAIC is an example of how one person's horrific experience began a grassroots connection to others who have had the same experience to form a coalition of concerned individuals, legal experts, other organizations, and policy makers. Their efforts have raised public awareness about conditions in the prison system that require change.

Discussion

This chapter highlights the need for social workers to be educated and competent in political and policy issues to ensure the best results for their clients. This is essential when working on the microlevel, or case level, to ensure that all of the benefits a client is entitled to are received. Noting any programs or policies that do not apply to all clients equitably and equally calls for the social worker to engage in advocacy for policy reform or implementation.

Reaching out through social media has been an effective tool for educating the public about the need for policy reform, political action, and social service provisions. This will get the attention to initiate advocacy efforts, including letter writing, public service announcements, and attendance at public hearings to identify gaps and propose policy change to respond to arising need. It is essential that those suggesting legislation or policy are aware of budget constraints (DiNitto & Johnson, 2012). If the budget does not include funds for a policy to be implemented, or agency personnel are not in favor of the implementation, there can be no enactment of the policy or legislation.

Once you can gather support for the funds to implement any policy, it is important to carry out an evaluation as a way of defining what the policy has accomplished, who is benefitting from the change, and if there are any unintended consequences. It is essential to find out if the program goals are being achieved and if the resources put into the program are being used efficiently. Defining the positive impact of a program or policy will help in it being sustained and continued support.

Social workers are critical in all phases of policy and program evaluation. They will help to identify gaps in service provision or human rights, work for change to be implemented to close them, and advocate by assisting others in getting their needs met with all available entitlements. This is essential for anyone impacted by the criminal justice or legal system since they often face stigma and barriers to reentering their community.

Conclusion

Thoughtful consideration of how programs and policies are impacted by societal values is key to providing successful interventions and identifying allies and obstacles. This chapter highlights the importance of social workers engaging in case and policy advocacy to achieve a socially just outcome for any individual or group, especially those impacted by involvement in the criminal justice system.

CHAPTER EXERCISES

Exercise 1. Joanna will be released from prison after serving two years for drug possession. While in prison she learned that she is HIV+. She has to find a source of income to pay rent and other expenses and she needs assistance to pay for the medication she needs.

You are a social worker in an agency that provides services for prison reentry clients. How would you define Joanna's needs for returning to the community? What social services would you prioritize to obtain for her upon her release?

Exercise 2. You are working with a client recently released from prison. You find out that he served two years in the military and was honorably discharged. He is unable to find the paperwork he received upon discharge. You think he may be entitled to benefits from his service. Describe the process you would use for advocating for him to get veterans benefits.

Exercise 3. You find out that the area your agency is located in has had many young men subjected to "stop and frisk." These men were not informed why they were detained and 85% were not charged. How would you go about making the community aware of this and what would you do to advocate to reduce this practice?

Additional Resources

American Civil Liberties Union. End the Overuse of Solitary Confinement: www.aclu.org/files/assets/stop_solitary_-_two_pager.pdf

Council on Social Work Education. (2015). 2015 Educational Policy and Accreditation Standards: www.cswe.org

National Association of Social Workers *Code of Ethics* (2008).

National Conference of State Legislators (2016): www.ncsl.org/research/elections-and-campaigns/felon-voting-rights.aspx

New York Campaign for Alternatives to Isolated Confinement: http://nycaic.org/facts

New York State Assembly: http://assembly.state.ny.us/leg

United States Bill of Rights: www.billofrightsinstitute.org/founding-documents/bill-of-rights

References

Almog-Bar, M., Weiss-Gal, I., & Gal, J. (2015). Bringing public policy into policy practice. *Journal of Social Work, 15*(4), 390–408.

Barnes, H., Green, L., & Hopton, J. (2007). Guest editorial: Social work theory, research, policy and practice—Challenges and opportunities in health and social care integration in the UK. *Health and Social Care in the Community, 15*(3), 191–194.

Beck, C., & Wernham, C. (2014). Improving access to competitive employment for service users in forensic psychiatric units. *British Medical Journal Quality Improvement Reports, 3*(1), u204182.w1821. doi:10.1136/bmjquality.u204182.w1821

Campaign for Alternatives to Isolated Confinement. (2016). Website. Retrieved from http://nycaic.org

Council on Social Work Education. (2008). Council on Social Work Education accreditation standards and policies. Retrieved from https://cswe.org/getattachment/Accreditation/Standards-and -Policies/2008-EPAS/2008EDUCATIONALPOLICYANDACCREDITATIONSTANDARDS (EPAS)-08-24-2012.pdf.aspx

Curry-Stevens, A. (2012). Persuasion: Infusing advocacy practice with insights from anti-oppression practice. *Journal of Social Work, 12*(4), 345–363.

DiNitto, D. M., & Johnson, D. H. (2012). *Essentials of social welfare: Politics and public policy.* Cranbury, NJ: Pearson.

Dolgoff, R., & Feldstein, D. (2012). *Understanding social welfare: A search for social justice* (9th ed.). Boston, MA: Allyn & Bacon.

Grassian, S. (2006). Psychiatric effects of solitary confinement. *Washington University Journal of Law and Policy, 22*(1/24), 327–383.

Höfer, F. X. E., Habermeyer, E., Mokros, A., Lau, S., & Gairing, S. K. (2015). The impact of legal coercion on the therapeutic relationship in adult schizophrenia patients. *PLOS ONE, 10*(4), e0124043. doi:10.1371/journal.pone.0124043

Jimenez, J., Pasztor, E. M., Chambers, R. M., & Fujii, C. P. (2015). *Social policy and social change: Toward the creation of social and economic justice* (2nd ed.). Thousand Oaks, CA: Sage Publications.

Karger, H. J., & Stoesz, D. (2005). *American social welfare policy: A pluralist approach* (4th ed.). Boston, MA: Pearson.

Miller, D. (1999). *Principles of social justice.* Boston, MA: Harvard University Press.

National Association of Social Workers. (2008). *Code of Ethics of the National Association of Social Workers.* Retrieved from https://www.socialworkers.org/pubs/code/default.asp

National Conference of State Legislators. (2016). Felon voting rights. Retrieved from http://www.ncsl .org/research/elections-and-campaigns/felon-voting-rights.aspx

New York State Senate. (2016). Senate bill S2659. Retrieved from https://www.nysenate.gov/ legislation/bills/2015/s2659

O'Brien, M. (2011). Equality and fairness: Linking social justice and social work practice. *Journal of Social Work, 11*(2), 143–158. Retrieved from http://www.socialworkers.org/pubs/code/code.asp

Rawls, J. (1971). *A theory of justice.* Boston, MA: Harvard University Press.

Roberts, C., Davies, J., & Maggs, R. G. (2015). Structured community activity for forensic mental health—A feasibility study. *Journal of Forensic Practice, 17*(3), 180–191.

Romano, J. L. (2015). *Social justice and public policy advocacy*. Washington, DC: American Psychological Association.

Schneider, A., & Sidney, M. (2009). What is next for policy design and social construction theory? *The Policy Studies Journal, 37*(1), 103–119.

Segal, E. A. (2016). *Social welfare policy and social programs: A value perspective* (4th ed.). Boston, MA: Cengage.

Staub-Bernasconi, S. (2016). Social work and human rights—Linking two traditions of human rights in social work. *Journal of Human Rights in Social Work, 1*(1), 40. doi:10.1007/s41134-016-0005-0

VOICES FROM THE FIELD

MichaelTodd, LCSW

Psychiatric Social Worker-Forensic Committee Chairperson

Agency Setting

The South Beach Psychiatric Center is one of the New York State Office of Mental Health (OMH) facilities that deliver mental health services across New York State. South Beach provides intermediate inpatient services to persons living in sections of Staten Island, Brooklyn, and Manhattan south of 42nd Street. The inpatient facility, located in Staten Island, has 12 inpatient units with 280 beds and a transitional housing unit. While it is a civil mental health facility, it also admits forensic patients under New York State Criminal Procedure Law 330.20 (CPL). These patients fall under six forensic designations determined by the court because of being incapacitated, or not responsible for their crime because of a mental defect (OMH website).

Patients are designated as CPL 330.20 when they are deemed not responsible for their criminal conduct because of a mental defect. Typically, this is done as an agreement between the District Attorney and the court; it is rarely done by a trial. Patients who are designated as CPL 330.20 have committed a felony. (There is a separate category for people accused of misdemeanors; these get designated as CPL 730.40 and fall under a different process.) All patients admitted under CPL 330.20 are first evaluated in a secure facility since they have been determined to have a dangerous mental disorder. Once they are considered to be not dangerous, they are moved to a less secure site, such as South Beach. All 330.20 cases are reviewed by the Forensic Committee. Court orders are required for each movement to a less restrictive setting including off-grounds furloughs and release to the community. Once released, CPL 330.20 persons are subject to renewable five-year Outpatient Order of Conditions. In my role as Forensic Chairperson, it is my responsibility to ensure that their cases are appropriately reviewed, with documentation, to progress through the mental health system.

Practice Responsibilities

I work full time as the Director of Social Work at South Beach where I have responsibility for all of the inpatient and outpatient social workers. As Forensic Chairperson, I provide guidance to social workers for their work with CPL 330.20 patients. These patients have often committed a dangerous act and require a strict protocol after being admitted. I help them identify appropriate treatment interventions, including preparing them for their forensic interviews and court appearances. I guide them in terms of the requests that they are presenting to the Forensic Committee as well as recommending appropriate responses when a 330.20 patient has violated the terms of their treatment.

Although treated by an interdisciplinary team, these have their cases reviewed on an ongoing basis by the Hospital Forensic Committee. The multidisciplinary Forensic Committee consists of psychiatrists, psychologists, social workers, and other treatment staff, headed by a chairperson. I am responsible to schedule the committee meetings, ensure all of the proper documentation is submitted, and conduct the forensic interview with the patient at the meeting. After the committee meeting, I prepare the CPL 330.20 report and send it to the Clinical Director of South Beach for review and approval. Central OMH Forensic Services get involved when the request is for escorted off-grounds privileges, unescorted off-grounds privileges, conditional release from the inpatient hospital, or termination of the Order of Conditions. These privileges must also be reviewed by the District Attorney and the court

Expertise Required

Although I received many formal forensic trainings (including training in the HCR-20 violence risk assessment tool), much of my knowledge was attained as on-the-job training.

Ethical, Legal, Practice, Diversity, and/or Advocacy Issues Addressed

One very important challenge is balancing the rights of the CPL patient to move forward and progress into program areas, and community outing, with community safety. Before an individual can return to the community there have to be small steps toward conditional release. It is important to pay attention to detail but also be able to tolerate risk. These steps include having unescorted walks on the hospital grounds, visits into the community (escorted and unescorted), and eventually passes for longer periods of time. Each pass requires a specific plan approved by the Forensic Committee at South Beach, the OMH Bureau of Forensic Services, and the court. Upon return from all passes the patient is given a drug screen to ensure there is no alcohol or drug use when in the community. This can lead to issues of trust between the patient and the treatment staff and possible conflict. Höfer, Habermeyer, Mokros, Lau, and Gairing (2015) studied the quality of the relationship for forensic patients and found that the therapeutic relationship was adversely affected by the patient's hostility, not their legal status. I have seen this in my experience with this population and their treatment team. One of the main challenges is for the 330.20 patient to understand that his or her goal and the Forensic Committee's goal is the same: The patient is *safely* released into the community.

As written in the preceding paragraph, there are many considerations prior to risking any independent community reentry. Forensic patients may feel a lack of control over their treatment and get frustrated since every step must be overseen by individuals outside of their treatment team. Typically, they expect to proceed through the forensic process rather quickly whereas the reality is that they often spend more time in the hospital than they would have spent in a correctional facility if they were sentenced criminally for the offense. They may feel that many of the actions they have to take are coerced or mandated by outside forces and have resentment for the inability of staff to give them dates and time frames for their discharge. Many feel they have served their time, but cannot move forward. They may not feel that they are living in the "least restrictive environment," which is a right for civil patients. As the philosophy of recovery has progressed, it has become clearer that it is possible for a 330.20 patient to work in outside competitive employment if he or she is stable and has the skill.

Some common ethical challenges arise when the treatment team is not progressing the 330.20 patient fast enough. On many occasions, I have had to advocate for the teams to request privileges faster than they were doing. It can be ethically challenging to walk the fine line of helping the patient without overstepping the role of the treating social worker.

Interprofessional and Intersectional Collaboration

The goal of the 330.20 statute is to ensure safety to the community while not criminalizing the felony of the mentally ill individual who committed it. As such, there are multilayers of legal interactions. The 330.20 patients are usually represented by an attorney of the Mental Hygiene Legal service although they can also hire a private attorney at their own cost. The patients' attorney advocates for them. The District Attorney of the county where the original crime was committed weighs in on all requests where 330.20 patients are moving outside of the hospital; they can hire their own forensic evaluator and the District Attorney may oppose the request made by the hospital. The court makes the final decision. The local police precinct is notified whenever unescorted passes are authorized by the court. The police will also be contacted if the 330.20 patients fail to return from an unescorted pass.

Additional Information/Training

I rose to the position as chairperson by virtue of being a committee member while working as both an inpatient and an outpatient social worker. As mentioned previously, as the recovery philosophy has developed, it impacted the way in which I saw the 330.20 patient. Some could hold jobs or attain their bachelor's degrees while receiving inpatient treatment. Twenty years ago, I never would have thought that was possible.

CHAPTER 32

Victim Advocacy

Marie Mele

Working with victims of intimate partner violence can be both a rewarding and challenging job. The rewards come from helping people who are in need of information, assistance, and advocacy. The challenges come from navigating an unorganized, fragmented, and underfunded criminal justice system that often fails to meet the needs of crime victims. This chapter addresses the experiences and needs of female victims of intimate partner violence. It examines common practices used and issues faced by victim advocates—who are often trained social workers—who work with women who have been victimized by a male intimate partner. The firsthand experiences of a victim advocate for female victims of intimate partner violence are highlighted.

Scope of the Problem

Although men are victims of intimate partner violence and there are cases of mutual violence, women are much more likely than men to be victimized by an intimate partner. Women account for four out of five victims of intimate partner violence (Catalano, 2012). Each year, roughly 2 million women are physically assaulted by their intimate partners, and 52% of women report that they have been physically assaulted by an intimate partner at some point in their lives (Tjaden & Thoennes, 2000). Roughly, 9 out of 10 women who are assaulted by an intimate partner suffer a physical injury (Smith & Farole, 2009), with about 20% of victims requiring medical treatment for their injuries (Catalano, 2012). Victims of intimate partner violence also experience depression, substance use, poor physical health, and chronic mental illness as a result of their victimization (Coker et al., 2002).

Although women of all races, ethnicities, and income levels may suffer violence at the hands of their intimate partners, some women are at greater risk of victimization than others. African American and Native American Indian women have the greatest risk of victimization by an intimate partner (Rosay, 2016; Tjaden & Thoennes, 2000). Women of low income are also at an increased risk for intimate partner violence (Bonomi, Trabert, Anderson, Kernic, & Holt, 2014). The relationship between race and risk of victimization may be confounded by income, since African American women generally have lower incomes than non-African American women (DeNavas-Walt, Proctor, & Lee, 2005). Women of low income often have few resources to escape abusive relationships and may be financially dependent on their abusive partner. As a result, their risk of victimization (and revictimization) is higher than that of women who are financially independent. Research also suggests that Native American Indian women suffer the highest rates of intimate partner violence in the United States, and have the greatest need for medical, legal, and advocacy services as a result of their victimization (Rosay, 2016). Despite this need, there is a significant lack of services available to this population of victims.

Relevant Theoretical Frameworks

Intimate partner violence has been described as a pattern of coercive control (Pence & Paymar, 1986), in which the abusive partner asserts his power over the victim through the use of verbal threats and physical violence. Within this framework, violence and the threat of violence are seen as tools that the abusive partner uses to gain greater power in the relationship (Dobash, Dobash, Wilson, & Daly, 1992). Intimate partner violence has also been described as "instrumental aggression," whereby acts of aggression and violence are intended to control the victim's behavior and demonstrate dominance (Frieze & McHugh, 1992).

Johnson (1995) suggested that intimate partner violence could not be understood as a single phenomenon, and offered two typologies: *common couple violence,* which is characterized by mutual low-level physical aggression; and *patriarchal intimate terrorism,* in which men batter female partners to maintain coercive control. These typologies highlight the importance of understanding the context within which violent acts occur, because a single act of violence can take on different meanings in different contexts. Dutton and Goodman (2005) likewise suggested that social context gives meaning to the abuser's behavior and the victim's response, emphasizing the importance of examining the social context within which coercion, acts of aggression, and violence are used in intimate relationships. Although research suggests that women do use violence against their intimate partners (Archer, 2000), women's use of violence is often committed in response to male violence or in self-defense (Swan, Gambone, & Fields, 2005). In addition, women are more likely than men to experience severe violence at higher frequencies and to experience negative consequences (e.g., poor mental health) as a result of violence (Anderson, 2002; Archer, 2000).

Understanding intimate partner violence as a pattern of coercive control and instrumental aggression can help advocates and social service providers assist victims (and offenders) in understanding the complex dynamics of abusive intimate partner relationships. Interventions can be tailored to address the systemic use of coercion and control to help batterers reform their behavior, alter their way of thinking, and protect victims from further victimization. Knowledge of the dynamics of intimate partner violence can also assist criminal justice practitioners (e.g., police, prosecutors, judges) to understand the pattern of abuse within which individual acts of violence occur, and make more informed decisions about case disposition and victim safety.

The Rise of Victim Advocacy

For many years, social workers and activists have advocated for the rights of crime victims and assisted with their needs, especially during the criminal justice process. Efforts to help victims were formalized in the early 1970s, when the first victim assistance programs were established in San Francisco and Washington, DC (Wallace, 1998). Over the next two decades, victim assistance programs were created throughout the United States. These programs were designed to serve as a resource for crime victims and provided services, including support groups, counseling, and accompaniment to criminal justice proceedings.

Among the first adult victims to receive special attention from advocates were victims of sexual assault and intimate partner violence. This was largely due to the result of the efforts of the National Organization for Women (NOW), which formed a task force in 1976 to examine the problem of intimate partner violence, and the National Coalition Against Sexual Assault (NCASA), which was established in 1978 to promote services for sexual assault victims (Wallace, 1998).

As public knowledge of and attention to violence against women increased throughout the 1970s and 1980s, more programs and services were created to assist victims and help protect them from further victimization. During this time, police departments and prosecutor's offices began hiring victim advocates, also known as victim/witness coordinators, to assist victims of intimate partner violence whose cases were being processed in the criminal justice system. This assistance usually came in the form of trial preparation and referral to social services (e.g., victim compensation and counseling). Over time, the role of victim advocates for this population has remained largely the same, although the numbers of advocates working in the criminal justice system and the types of services available to victims have increased significantly. Today, advocates can offer victims of intimate partner violence a variety of services, including access to legal aid, short-term financial assistance, safe housing, individual and family counseling, and assistance in obtaining a restraining order.

The Role of Victim Advocates

Victim advocates are typically employed by a prosecutor's office or victim service agency, although some are employed by a police department. Advocates who work within a police department are usually counselors or social workers who are called to the scene of an incident of intimate partner violence by police to assist the victim and provide her with information on available social services (e.g., counseling and safe housing). Advocates who work within a prosecutor's office usually do not make contact with the victim until a criminal case has been filed by police and the case is transferred to the prosecutor's office (usually a day or two after the incident is reported to police). The first meeting between an advocate and a victim typically takes place at the courthouse where the defendant is being arraigned or the victim is filing for a restraining order against the defendant. Advocates who work for a victim service agency might not make contact with a victim until she contacts the agency for assistance.

Advocates who work with victims of intimate partner violence have numerous responsibilities and work with a number of other professionals, including police officers, prosecutors, judges, caseworkers, probation officers, and social service providers. The advocate's primary responsibility is to ensure that the victim's immediate needs are met. These needs often include information on her case (e.g., day, time, and location of the next court hearing) and the victim's role in the criminal justice process, as well as access to legal aid, financial assistance, and safe housing.

Legal aid is most often needed by victims who wish to file a petition in civil court (e.g., restraining order, child custody). Advocates can provide information on local attorneys who represent victims of intimate partner violence either pro bono or for reduced fees. Financial assistance usually comes in the form of victim compensation, which is allocated to victims by a state compensation board. Advocates usually make victims aware that these funds exist and help them fill out the paperwork to apply for needed assistance. Safe housing is mostly a concern for victims who believe they are in physical danger and cannot return home. Battered women's shelters and safe houses are usually able to accommodate short-term housing needs. Advocates can make victims aware of these services and arrange for transportation if victims cannot get to safe housing on their own.

Another common need among victims of intimate partner violence is professional counseling. Counselors help victims begin to process their experiences of abuse and understand that they are not to blame for their partner's actions. This is especially important for victims who have endured chronic or long-term abuse, because they are at the greatest risk of further victimization and are most likely to return to their abusive partner. Although some police officers provide counseling information to victims when they respond to a call for service, advocates are usually the first to disseminate this information to victims.

If a criminal case goes to trial, advocates often assist in preparing the victim for her role in the trial process. This role may entail testifying in court on behalf of the state, although most criminal cases are resolved through a plea bargain and do not result in a trial. In plea bargaining, advocates make the victim's wishes known to the prosecutor so that an appropriate resolution to the case can be decided. Advocates may also assist victims in writing a *victim-impact statement*, which is usually read to the court (or by the judge) at the defendant's sentencing hearing. A victim-impact statement can be a powerful tool for victims to express how their partner's abuse has personally affected them. It also allows the victim to express her opinion on how the defendant should be punished and/or how the case should be resolved. In some cases, a victim advocate may also serve as an expert witness to provide testimony on the dynamics and implications of intimate partner violence.

Depending on the outcome of the criminal case, the victim may decide to file a petition in civil court. Victims of intimate partner violence use civil courts to obtain restraining orders, seek child support and custody, and initiate divorce proceedings. It is common for victims to feel overwhelmed by the prospect of navigating the civil justice system, especially if they have never done so before. Victim advocates play a key role in helping victims understand and access the services available to them in civil court.

In my practice as a victim's advocate, the service most commonly sought has been obtaining a *civil restraining order*, also known as a *protection order* or *protection from abuse order*, which is a civil court order that instructs the defendant not to harm or have contact with the victim. A restraining order may also prohibit the defendant from having contact with the victim's children or family members. Advocates often explain to victims the process of obtaining a restraining order and assist them with the necessary paperwork. Advocates may also accompany victims to restraining order hearings and help them understand the outcome of proceedings, including the judge's final ruling and the provisions of the order.

Common Practice Settings

Although most victim advocates are employed by a prosecutor's office or victim service agency, a great deal of their time is spent in courthouses, where most criminal justice proceedings take place. Accompanying victims to court hearings and explaining the proceedings requires advocates to be familiar with the functions and operations of both the criminal and civil court systems. This also requires advocates to have close working relationships with court administrators, prosecutors, and judges, as well as caseworkers and social service providers.

These relationships can be fostered by the existence of multidisciplinary teams. Multidisciplinary teams are groups of professionals from diverse disciplines who come together to provide comprehensive assessment and consultation on specific cases. In cases of intimate partner violence, multidisciplinary teams usually consist of victim advocates, police officers, prosecutors, court administrators, probation officers, child protection workers, and victim service providers. Teams promote coordination and communication among agencies by bringing agency representatives together on a regular basis to share information and expertise. This coordination often helps to identify service gaps and ensure that the needs and interests of all parties involved, including victims, offenders, and children, are addressed. The primary purpose of a multidisciplinary team is typically to help resolve difficult cases, such as those that involve repeat victims and those with children at risk of harm. Because children witness intimate partner violence, and may also be victims of abuse themselves, cases involving children usually receive greater attention from team members. Cases that involve elderly victims may also be given priority.

Domain-Specific Legal and Ethical Issues

There are several laws that seek to protect victims of intimate partner violence from their abusive partners. Laws regarding mandatory (or presumptive) arrest are the most notable and perhaps most controversial. Mandatory-arrest laws were largely a result of academic research (Sherman & Berk, 1984) and civil liability lawsuits (e.g., *Thurman v. City of Torrington*, 1984), which called into question the widespread practice of nonarrest in cases of intimate partner violence and led to significant changes in public policy.

Mandatory Arrest

The single most influential piece of research regarding mandatory arrest was conducted by Sherman and Berk (1984), who found that arresting batterers was associated with a reduction in subsequent intimate partner violence. The results of their research led to the creation of mandatory-arrest policies by police agencies throughout the United States. These policies require officers to arrest a batterer when probable cause exists to believe that a crime occurred, regardless of the victim's consent or preference. Despite the lack of consensus on the utility (i.e., deterrent effect) of mandatory arrest, most police departments in the United States have a policy that mandates or encourages police officers to arrest in cases of intimate partner violence.

The civil court case of *Thurman v. City of Torrington* (1984) also had a significant impact on the police response to intimate partner violence. Tracy Thurman was a battered woman from the city of Torrington, Connecticut, who repeatedly sought and did not receive police protection from the violent attacks of her estranged husband. She subsequently filed a civil lawsuit against the City of Torrington, challenging policies that treated intimate partner violence differently from other assault cases as a denial of equal protection under the law. She won the lawsuit and was awarded $1.9 million in damages. This case was an important part of the momentum to change the way police respond to intimate partner violence, and challenged police administrators to create policies that would better protect victims from their abusive partners.

Restraining Orders

Laws regarding restraining orders also seek to protect victims of intimate partner violence from subsequent victimization. Although civil courts typically issue restraining orders, violating the conditions of a restraining order may result in criminal penalties. In most states, violation of a restraining order is considered a misdemeanor offense and is punishable by jail time and/or a monetary fine. The purpose of these penalties is to protect victims by deterring defendants from violating the conditions of the order.

Every state also has what are called "full faith and credit" laws. The full faith and credit provision of the Violence Against Women Act of 1994 requires that every restraining order issued by a state court be given full faith and credit by courts in other states. This means that the conditions of a restraining order should be enforced regardless of what state the victim is in, as long as the order is valid (i.e., has not expired).

When advocating for victims of intimate partner violence, the legal document that victim advocates work with most often is a restraining order. Although every state has a slightly different process for obtaining a restraining order, it usually starts with the victim (plaintiff) filing a petition in a civil court (e.g., Court of Common Pleas or Family Court) that describes the abuse she has suffered and the protection she is seeking. Next, an emergency or ex parte hearing is held, at which a judge will either grant the plaintiff a temporary restraining order and set a date for a final hearing (usually held within 10 days of the initial hearing) or deny the temporary order. At the final hearing, a judge decides whether to grant a final order and rules on the conditions of the order. Depending on state statute, a final restraining order can be effective for any length of time. In the state of New Jersey, for example, final restraining orders do not expire unless the victim requests a withdrawal hearing, at which time a judge will decide whether to vacate the order based on the victim's request.

The process of obtaining a restraining order can be confusing and overwhelming to victims, especially those who are reluctant to follow through with the process. Because the majority of victims who seek a restraining order do not have an attorney, many of them rely on advocates to explain the process and prepare them for court hearings. Advocates also help victims understand the protections offered by a restraining order and how the provisions of the order will affect their lives. Advocates may also have to convince victims of the importance of obtaining a restraining order and the importance of notifying the police if the defendant violates the order. This is especially true for victims whose partners pose a continuing threat to their safety.

Ethical Principles

The primary mission of victim advocates is to assist victims by protecting their rights, assessing their needs, and referring them to the appropriate social services. Although advocates are not necessarily bound by a formal set of ethical principles, they adhere to many of the principles set forth by the National Association of Social Workers' *Code of Ethics* (1999).

To assist victims of intimate partner violence, advocates must treat each person in a caring and respectful manner. This is especially true for victims who are reluctant to accept help or who may not recognize the potential danger their partner poses to them. Advocates often must convince victims of what is in their best interest while respecting their right to self-determination. If a victim refuses to accept necessary services (e.g., safe housing), the advocate must respect her decision. This requires advocates to walk a fine line between insisting on necessary help and honoring the victim's choices. Advocates must also respect a victim's right to privacy. Although there is no legal expectation of privacy between an advocate and a victim, advocates may refer victims to a professional (e.g., counselor) who can promise confidentiality if that is something the victim requests. As a general rule, however, advocates only disclose information shared by a victim if it is necessary to protect her safety or for the purpose of legal proceedings (i.e., to prosecute a criminal case).

Assessment, Prevention, and Intervention

To assess victims' needs and refer them to the appropriate social services, advocates typically complete an intake or screening form for each victim with whom they come in contact. These forms record the victim's personal and demographic information, including her name, age, race, sex, marital status, occupation, address, and phone number. Advocates may also collect information on the victim's experiences of abuse (e.g., type of abuse suffered) and the length and status of the victim/offender relationship. This information is collected and maintained by advocates for the purposes of needs assessment and service referral, but may also be shared with other professionals, including members of a multidisciplinary team.

Although biopsychosocial assessment tools, such as the Rapid Psychosocial Assessment Checklist for Juvenile and Criminal Justice Settings (Maschi, 2009), are not routinely used by victim advocates, elements of such tools may be used, including the reason for referral and relevant history. The psychosocial areas of family, medical/mental health, legal issues, and environmental conditions (e.g., safe housing) are often affected by intimate partner violence. For this reason, advocates may collect information on these areas to make appropriate decisions regarding service referral. The following is a list of questions and requests often asked by victim advocates to develop a better understanding of a victim's experiences and needs:

- Describe the most recent incidents of abuse or threats of abuse you have experienced.
- Were children involved in these incidents?
- Were there any witnesses or evidence (e.g., texts, phone messages)?
- Did you call the police? Did the police take any actions? What was the outcome?
- Has your partner used or threatened to use a firearm against you?
- Does your partner have access to a firearm?
- Do you have a safety plan?
- Do you feel safe returning to your home?
- What are your immediate needs (e.g., shelter, money, legal aid)?

Core Skills

Advocates who work with victims of intimate partner violence must draw on a number of professional and personal skills. Among the most important are oral and written communication, interpersonal skills, professionalism, networking, and collaboration. Advocates must be able to communicate with victims face to face and in writing. This requires an understanding of the victim's plight and knowledge that the victim may be overwhelmed by (or disappointed in) the amount of information she has received from criminal justice professionals and social service providers. Advocates often help victims sort through the information they have received and assist them in obtaining information they still need. Obtaining this information usually requires advocates to network with other actors in the criminal and civil justice systems. Thus, networking skills are crucial for advocates to do their job effectively. Equally important is the ability to collaborate with professionals from a wide range of agencies (e.g., law enforcement, social services, court administration) to help victims navigate the system. Collaborating with people of different backgrounds and expertise requires advocates to have a sense of professionalism. This includes properly addressing people of standing (e.g., judges) and behaving appropriately in situations that require reverence (e.g., courtroom). Professionalism also requires credibility and follow-through, as well as setting boundaries with victims who may ask more of advocates than the advocate can deliver.

For advocates who work with victims of intimate partner violence, communicating empowerment to victims is an important aspect of advocacy. Empowerment is communicated to victims not only by providing them with necessary information and referring them to appropriate services, but also by helping victims take control of their situation and giving them a sense of self-worth. This entails normalizing their feelings of shame or embarrassment and letting them know that they are not alone in their efforts to free themselves from abuse. Empowerment is especially important for victims who may feel powerless to escape abusive relationships. Advocates, in a sense, help victims find their voice and encourage them to do what is in their best interest and the interest of their children. This may entail helping a victim prepare a victim-impact statement to be read in court or to organize a safety plan for the next time she encounters violence at the hands of her abusive partner.

As a victim advocate who works primarily with victims of intimate partner violence, I have met many women who found themselves in terribly abusive relationships that were difficult for them to escape. Many of these women had children in common with their abusive partners, were financially dependent on their partners, and hoped that their partners would change. These characteristics applied to one woman in particular, who I met after her husband beat her so badly she needed to be hospitalized to receive medical treatment for her injuries. The day after her attack, I went to the hospital to try to convince her to come to a battered women's shelter, because her husband had still not been caught by the police and I was concerned about her safety. Despite her extensive physical and emotional trauma, she refused to go to a shelter and was convinced that her husband did not intend to harm her as badly as he did. She wished to return home once she was released from the hospital. Although I was disappointed in her decision not to seek shelter, I respected her decision and informed her of other options she could take to protect herself and her children, including obtaining a restraining order and pursuing criminal charges against her husband.

Ultimately, she did obtain a restraining order and assisted in the prosecution of her husband on charges of aggravated assault.

As an advocate, my job was to educate her on the services available and allow her to make her own decision as to what she believed she needed. Although I did not agree with all of her decisions, I respected her right to self-determination and I did my best to empower her to take control of her situation. It was also my responsibility to help her navigate the criminal justice system, which required me to collaborate with prosecutors, police officers, court personnel, and service providers. Collaborating with people of various backgrounds and disciplines called for professionalism and a commitment to protecting the rights and interests of a woman who was in desperate need of advocacy and support. Advocating for this woman taught me the importance of "starting where the client is" and viewing a complex situation from the client's perspective, which is often very different from the perspective of a professional seeking to help.

Conclusion

As the information provided in this chapter suggests, many women continue to be victims of intimate partner violence, and the work of victim advocates who serve these women is challenging. Advocates must be able to assess the needs of victims, refer them to appropriate services, protect their rights, empower them, and help them navigate the criminal and civil justice systems. These responsibilities require advocates to possess various personal and professional skills and to collaborate with many different professionals. Unfortunately, there is never a shortage of victims in need of assistance; however, advocates are often motivated by the knowledge that they have made a difference in someone's life and can effect change by helping one person at a time.

CHAPTER EXERCISES

Exercise 1. Using the chapter vignette, choose two learners to role-play the victim and advocate. Role-play a discussion between them.

Exercise 2. Watch the following short video on victim advocacy (or another of your choice): www.youtube.com/watch?v=Vx5jI4vwYhE. Discuss in small or large groups the skills you see that are needed in becoming a victim advocate and how an advocate might go about acquiring these skills.

Exercise 3. Watch the following short video on vicarious trauma and victim advocacy: www .youtube.com/watch?v=azeJ292FO3E. Discuss in small and then large groups what self-care strategies the group can engage in to minimize the impact of vicarious trauma.

Additional Resources

National Center for Victims of Crime: www.ncvc.org

National Coalition Against Domestic Violence: www.ncadv.org

National Crime Victims Research and Treatment Center: www.musc.edu/cvc

National Organization for Victim Assistance: www.try-nova.org

Office for Victims of Crime: www.ojp.usdoj.gov/ovc

Office on Violence Against Women: www.justice.gov/ovw

References

Anderson, K. (2002). Perpetrator or victim? Relationships between intimate partner violence and well-being. *Journal of Marriage & Family, 64,* 851–865.

Archer, J. (2000). Sex differences in physical aggression to partners: A reply to Frieze (2000), O'Leary (2000), and White, Smith, Koss, and Figueredo (2000). *Psychological Bulletin, 126*, 697–702.

Bonomi, A., Trabert, B., Anderson, M., Kernic, M., & Holt, V. (2014). Intimate partner violence and neighborhood income: A longitudinal analysis. *Violence Against Women, 20*(1), 42–58.

Catalano, S. (2012). *Intimate partner violence, 1993–2010.* Bureau of Justice Statistics. Washington, DC: U.S. Government Printing Office.

Coker, A., Davis, K., Arias, I., Desai, S., Sanderson, M., Brandt, H., & Smith, P. (2002). Physical and mental health effects of intimate partner violence for men and women. *American Journal of Preventive Medicine, 23*(4), 260–268.

DeNavas-Walt, C., Proctor, B., & Lee, C. (2005). *Income, poverty and health insurance coverage in the United States.* Washington, DC: U.S. Government Printing Office.

Dobash, R., Dobash, R., Wilson, M., & Daly, M. (1992). The myth of sexual symmetry in marital violence. *Social Problems, 39*, 71–91.

Dutton, M., & Goodman, L. (2005). Coercive control and intimate partner violence: Toward a new conceptualization. *Sex Roles, 52*, 743–756.

Frieze, I., & McHugh, M. (1992). Power and influence strategies in violent and non-violent marriages. *Psychology of Women Quarterly Special Issue: Women & Power, 16*, 449–465.

Johnson, M. (1995). Patriarchal terrorism and common couple violence: Two forms of violence against women. *Journal of Marriage & the Family, 57*, 283–294.

Maschi, T. (2009). Rapid psychosocial assessment checklist for juvenile and criminal justice settings. In T. Maschi, C. Bradley, & K. Ward (Eds.), *Forensic social work: Psychosocial and legal issues in diverse practice settings* (pp. 367–372). New York, NY: Springer Publishing.

National Association of Social Workers. (1999). *Code of Ethics.* Washington, DC: Author.

Pence, E., & Paymar, M. (1986). *Power and control: Tactics of men who batter.* Duluth: Minnesota Program Development.

Rosay, A. (2016). *Violence against American Indian and Alaska native women and men.* National Institute of Justice. Washington, DC: U.S. Government Printing Office.

Sherman, L., & Berk, R. (1984). The specific deterrent effects of arrest for domestic assault. *American Sociological Review, 49*, 261–272.

Smith, E., & Farole, D. (2009). *Profile of intimate partner violence cases in large urban counties.* Bureau of Justice Statistics. Washington, DC: U.S. Government Printing Office.

Swan, S., Gambone, L., & Fields, A. (2005). *An empirical examination of a theory of women's use of violence in intimate relationships.* United States Department of Justice. Washington, DC: U.S. Government Printing Office.

Thurman v. City of Torrington, 595 F. Supp. 1521 (United States District Court, D. Connecticut, Oct. 23, 1984).

Tjaden, P., & Thoennes, N. (2000). *Full report of the prevalence, incidence, and consequences of violence against women: Findings from the national violence against women survey.* National Institute of Justice. Washington, DC: U.S. Government Printing Office.

Violence Against Women Act of 1994, Pub. L. No. 103–322, Title IV, 108 Stat. 1902 (1994).

Wallace, H. (1998). *Victimology: Legal, psychological, and social perspectives.* Needham Heights, MA: Allyn & Bacon.

VOICES FROM THE FIELD

Marie Mele, PhD
Victim/Witness Advocate
Morris County Prosecutor's Office, Morristown, NJ

Agency Setting

The Morris County Prosecutor's Office is a county law enforcement agency located in suburban New Jersey. The agency is operated by a variety of criminal justice practitioners, including assistant county prosecutors, detectives, victim/witness advocates, case coordinators, and administrative personnel.

Practice Responsibilities

As a victim/witness advocate, I traveled to municipalities within the county to meet with victims of intimate partner violence. Typically, the victims I worked with were identified in criminal cases sent to the prosecutor's office by police departments within the county. I often met with victims at the defendant's arraignment or at the initial restraining order hearing (if the victim obtained a restraining order against the defendant). The purpose of my meeting with the victim was to assess her immediate and short-term needs, and make referrals to appropriate social service providers. I also provided courtroom assistance to victims during the prosecution of their case. In addition, I maintained follow-up with victims to assess their unmet needs and make additional referrals.

Expertise Required

Before becoming a victim/witness advocate, I earned a master's degree in law and justice. Some advocates have advanced degrees in social work or psychology. In addition to a degree in one of these fields, victim/witness advocacy requires knowledge of the criminal and civil justice systems, excellent communication skills, a strong sense of empathy, and the ability to foster interagency relationships.

Ethical, Legal, Practice, Diversity, and/or Advocacy Issues Addressed

The primary advocacy issue for a victim/witness advocate is the protection of a victim's rights throughout the criminal and civil justice process. Victims are often unaware that they are entitled to rights or the importance of their participation in the justice process. Informing victims what they are entitled to (i.e., victim compensation, victim-impact statement), and protecting victims' interests as they navigate through the court system is a vital aspect of victim advocacy.

Interprofessional and Intersectoral Collaboration

As a victim/witness advocate, I worked with a variety of other professionals through the establishment of multidisciplinary teams. Multidisciplinary teams are groups of professionals from diverse disciplines who come together to provide comprehensive assessment and consultation on specific cases. In cases of intimate partner violence, multidisciplinary teams usually consist of victim advocates, police officers, prosecutors, court administrators, probation officers, child protection workers, and victim service providers. Teams promote coordination and communication among agencies by bringing agency representatives together on a regular basis to share information and expertise. This coordination helps to identify service gaps and ensure that the needs and interests of all parties involved (e.g., victims, offenders, children) are addressed. The primary purpose of a multidisciplinary team is to resolve difficult or complex cases, including those that involve repeat victims and those with children at risk of harm.

CHAPTER 33

Family Televisiting: An Innovative Psychologist-Directed Program to Increase Resilience and Reduce Trauma Among Children With Incarcerated Parents

Frank J. Corigliano

CHAPTER OBJECTIVES

The major objectives of this chapter are to:

- Identify how psychological frameworks can be integrated into a cohesive, multigenerational intervention to connect children with their incarcerated parents.
- Describe scenarios through which televisiting develops resiliency in children.
- Delineate how geographic, financial, temporal, and intergenerational barriers can be reduced or removed via televisiting.

CHAPTER COMPETENCIES HIGHLIGHTED

- Competency 3: Advance Human Rights and Social, Economic, and Environmental Justice
- Competency 8: Intervene With Individuals, Families, Organizations, and Communities

Supportive televisiting services are innovative, psychologist-directed, multidisciplinary programs that connect children and teenagers with their incarcerated parents via secure, live, interactive video teleconferencing. Of the billions of dollars invested into the criminal justice system, televisiting is one of the very few programs that actually connect children, parents, and supports.

Collaborative parenting is essential to the functioning of televisiting. Caregivers and parents have complicated and sometimes strained relationships. Mental health and family experts such as psychologists and social workers are in a position to help parents focus on their commitment to the child even while facing the challenge of adults who may not get along.

The goal is to shift the primary focus on the best interests of the child and the child's needs. With this goal in mind, we are able to help families participate in supportive televisiting services. Creative solutions may include enlisting a neutral third party to escort the child to the televisit when there is a strained relationship between the parent and caregiver.

There are seven main pillars that make up the theoretical foundation of the televisiting program: being child-focused; the attachment theory; trauma-informed care; resilience and strengths-based perspective; mental health challenges; the developmental, life-span, and intergenerational approach; and "yellow flag not red flag" policy.

First, when the primary focus of televisiting is child-focused, the benefits of televisiting are clear for many of the incarcerated parents and caregivers involved. This often provides clarity and a focus around how a televisit can be structured. Parents (and caregivers) are often very willing to let go of their immediate concerns or challenges in service of being fully present and available for the child.

Second, with the Attachment Theory, we know that a strong positive attachment to a parent can provide a foundation for emotional, social, and academic success. Third, trauma-informed care processes allow us to recognize the historical and current trauma that parents and children may be facing. The specific context of incarceration and separation may exacerbate trauma, so it is important to be supportive, nonthreatening, and encourage choice and empowerment throughout the experience.

The fourth pillar, resilience and strengths-based perspective, is one of the key components of our program development. We understand that families have gifts, talents, and joys to offer each other. We also understand that although some families may have negative outcomes directly related to or connected to incarceration, many families do well in the face of adversity. It is important that we collaborate to identify and maintain this narrative of strength and resilience.

Mental health challenges are the fifth key factor in developing programs with people who are facing the challenges of incarceration. Issues such as depression, anxiety, ineffective problem solving, difficulty with impulse control, as well as multiple systems of societal and economic stressors are all part of what must be assessed and understood when working with children whose parent or parents are incarcerated. Given that these are prime areas for intervention, psychologists and social workers have a responsibility toward addressing the needs of children and families who are affected by incarceration.

The sixth factor is the developmental, life-span, and intergenerational approach. This approach necessitates the acknowledgment of the intergenerational traumas that may be transmitted from grandparent to parent to child. These approaches also recognize and gain support from the extended kinship networks and multigenerational family systems that care for children. Additionally, the life-span approach requires that the unique stages of each child must be taken into account when developing interventions and activities. For example, having a range of games, toys, and educational projects available contributes to a supportive environment.

Finally, the yellow flag not red flag policy can be used. Because supportive televisiting is directed by a licensed psychologist and is a social work internship, the program has the clinical and cultural competency to provide a high level of support and understanding to families. Rather than have immediate rule-outs or exclusions, we confront challenges as opportunities to provide support to families who televisit.

Instead of saying "No," we ask "How can we support this family to succeed?" For example, if a parent–child relationship is just getting reconnected, we may encourage more structured visits that are focused around an activity such as art or music.

Clinical Issues

Many incarcerated individuals are living with mental health challenges that existed prior and frequently contributed to their incarceration. These include difficulty managing emotions, impulse control, depression, anxiety, substance use problems, and psychosis. In defining the role of the parent in the context of incarceration, we identify the parent's strengths and provide coaching and support around challenges or areas of growth.

Our goal is to create a session that facilitates emotional connections by having a room that is child-friendly. The room must look and feel safe and welcoming to the caregiver, the parent, and the child. It is also important to ensure privacy without stigmatizing. Photos of families and children adorning the walls helps to normalize the experience and let children know they are not the only one with a parent who is incarcerated.

Talking about incarceration and why the parent is incarcerated in language that is appropriate for the age and stage of the child is also helpful. Parents with younger children may explain that incarceration is like a "time-out" for adults. Children readily understand the term and accept what it represents.

Sesame Workshop has developed a series of kits called Little Children, Big Challenges: Incarceration. These kits provide video clips and two stories about children who have a parent who is incarcerated. Often children are not told where the parent is, which creates a "missing father" or "missing mother" scenario. This approach is often not helpful. We attempt to find a way to the truth because while families have good intentions in telling the child a story that is not true such as "Dad is away at work" or "Mom is in the military" or "Dad is at school," secrecy may fuel feelings of shame and stigmatization.

Because children have active imaginations and see things in the media that may scare them, the truth that Mom or Dad is incarcerated, and being able to see that parent through televisit, is reassuring. Children can then see for themselves that their parent still loves them and that Mom or Dad is "OK." Although it is important to be truthful, a family reporting the reality of incarceration to a child or children but then requiring that a secret be kept from teachers, friends, or other family members places undue responsibility on the child.

With individual sessions and during the family sessions, we ensure that children know they have support, someone to talk with openly about their feelings, and that incarceration is "not their fault." Among children in foster care, there may be feelings of disorientation, abandonment, and anger, which can be discussed and worked out in a televisit.

Empirical Evidence of Effectiveness With Forensic Populations and Settings

Background and History

Incarceration in the United States is on the rise with a disproportionate number of citizens residing in jails or prisons compared to our historical rates and with other countries. According to the International Centre for Prison Studies, in 2000, some 1.9 million individuals were incarcerated in U.S. prisons or jails versus 2.2 million in 2002 (Walmsley, 2016).

That is compared to 6.8 million persons in 2014 who were under U.S. adult correctional systems supervision with 2.2 million incarcerated in a prison or local jail under the jurisdiction of the U.S. Department of Justice or Office of Justice Programs. To put this in perspective, per 100,000 citizens, the United States incarcerates 737 people, topping both Russia (615) and China (118), according to Prison Studies and the Bureau of Justice Statistics (Kaeble, Glaze, Tsoutis, & Minton, 2015).

In New York State alone, Rikers Island houses 11,400 people in 10 jails with an additional 3,000 people housed in borough jails in Manhattan, Queens, Brooklyn, and the Bronx (City of New York, 2016; New York State Department of Corrections and Community Supervision, 2016).

Employing 19,254 correction officers, sergeants, and lieutenants, some 52,000 people are housed in the New York City Department of Corrections' 54 facilities. When it comes to incarceration and mental illness, some 1.3 million of America's mentally ill live in jail or prison and more than 50% of prisoners suffer from mental health disorders, substance dependence, or both (Wilper et al., 2009).

Incarceration and Parenting

Parental incarceration disrupts communities, families, and the lives of children. Prior to incarceration, many parents have strong, supportive roles in the lives of their children. These positive influences are altered by incarceration. Some 60% of people who are incarcerated are parents, according to the Sentencing Project (Glaze & Marushcak, 2010; Porter, 2015).

Around 25% of incarcerated parents have a child under the age of 10. In 2007, 1.7 million children had a parent in prison, an 82% increase since 1991. One in 43 American children has a parent in prison. In the federal system, 74% of people between the ages of 25 and 34 and 72% of people between the ages of 35 and 44 reported being a parent. In state prisons alone, 34% of parents reported living at home with their child a month prior to incarceration and 54% were contributing financially. Finally, a family study revealed that of incarcerated parents, 10.9% who are mothers and 2.2% who are fathers have a child in foster care, indicating that incarceration of parents leads to foster care of their children.

Risks to Disrupted Family Life

Parental incarceration creates barriers to effective parenting by disrupting contact and communication between parent, child, and caregiver (Maschi, 2006). Inconsistent contact with a parent can contribute to anxiety and uncertainty in the child's life. Trips may be infrequent or nonexistent. Phone calls are often costly and limited in time and frequency. Letters may take a week or two to send and receive.

In addition, interaction with a child's medical providers, educators, and mental health professionals may be sparse or completely out of reach for parents who are incarcerated. This lack of interaction makes it almost impossible for a parent who is incarcerated to get basic information about his or her child and makes it even more difficult for the parent to play an active parenting role.

There are also geographic barriers to visit many correctional facilities, which are located hundreds of miles away from residential neighborhoods where children often reside. Fathers who are originally from New York City are housed far upstate with little affordable transportation available for families from the five boroughs of New York City. Unless privately financed, barriers to visits can be overwhelming on already financially challenged families. A flight to Albion Correctional Facility, one of the women's prisons in New York State, can cost several hundred dollars per family member.

Time constraints are also a barrier for some families to visit. For example, a child's visit to Rikers Island might require a caregiver to take off a full day of work for each visit. Children may have to take time off from school or miss out on afterschool sports or creative activities. Much of the time spent traveling includes hours of commuting and being processed into the facility.

Increasing Resilience and Decreasing Risk to Children: Parents as a Protective Factor

From our years of experience and well-established research (Gostin, Vanchieri, & Pope, 2007; Poehlmann, Dallaire, Loper, & Shear, 2010) and theory described previously, we know that children benefit from the consistent, positive, supportive presence of a parent. We also know that incarceration of a household member is on the list of Adverse Childhood Events, which are linked to negative health outcomes years later (Gjelsvik, Dumont, & Nunn, 2013).

Televisiting provides access in a protective environment, which can buffer against negative social and academic outcomes in children such as internalizing an externalizing behavior, substance abuse, truancy, and academic failure. Research has even shown that the presence of a parent can reduce dangerous cortisol levels in a child (Dozier, 2005).

Many parents who are incarcerated are talented, creative, loving, and seek to develop and maintain a positive healthy relationship with their children. As a result, providing an enriched and supportive environment allows the parent to demonstrate these positive parenting skills.

Despite the obstacles, children who have a parent who is incarcerated can maintain strong nurturing bonds with that parent and others can benefit from consistent supported interaction with the parent. Such strong early parent–child attachment can support positive social and emotional function later in life (Thompson, 2008).

How to Apply This Skill

As noted earlier and described in what follows, psychological theories inform every aspect of the supportive televisiting services.

Supportive televisiting services of the Social Service Board, at the New York Society for Ethical Culture (NYSEC), New York, New York.

Community-Based Televisiting at the New York Society for Ethical Culture

Televisiting started in 2011 at the NYSEC as a special project of the Social Service Board chaired by Dr. Phyllis Harrison-Ross, who is a physician and practicing child psychiatrist. Since its inception, this innovative, community-based program has served hundreds of families, connecting children and teens with their parent(s) or grandparent(s). The core service is connecting children and parents. However, televisiting has also connected parents and grandparents with their incarcerated youth or adult child. Beyond families, televisiting holds the promise of creating and maintaining critical connections between anyone who is separated from a critical community resource due to incarceration. For example, a person identified as transgender sought out and was connected with her priest who has been a support for her for years. However, it was difficult for the priest to take full days away to travel to the jail. Televisiting provided more acceptable communication and pastoral care.

Responding to a Crisis for Children

Our aim is to establish an ethical approach to effective parenting from prison. The Mission of the NYSEC is to "Elicit the Best" and thereby create a more ethical society. This mandate is embodied and brought to life by the Social Service Board's commitment to "Ethics Into Action" and to:

> selflessly serve the social needs and the empowerment of the lives of children, families and individuals who have been neglected, underserved and excluded by our modern life and to provide strength and support to others who also work with us to initiate progressive social change and build a more ethical culture in our society and a better future for tomorrow. (Social Service Board, n.d.)

Televisiting contributes to these manifestations of an ethical society by honoring the role of the parent in the life of a child and seeks to increase resilience in children, their parents, families, and communities. Through supportive televisiting services, the Social Service Board recognizes and responds to the trauma of separation and the history of trauma that may be present in the lives of the families they serve. Televisiting empowers parents who are incarcerated to fulfill their roles. Psychological constructs that inform the televisiting program include understanding the child's ages and stages. We seek to determine the developmental goals of the child, the role of the parent in supporting the child being able to reach these goals, how the parent fulfills his or her role while incarcerated, and how these goals translate into concrete actions and activities, which will occur during a televisit.

Nuts and Bolts of Televisiting

Televisiting is the use of secure, live, interactive video teleconferencing to connect children and teenagers with their incarcerated parent so that the children can see and hear their parent in real time while the parent can see and hear his or her child simultaneously. This provides an opportunity for interactions that are spontaneous, genuine, and emotionally rich. This is in stark contrast to what is often found in correctional facilities, which are highly controlled, highly restrictive, and not child-friendly or focused.

Televisits are provided in a convenient, safe, and child-friendly space at the NYSEC adjacent to Central Park on the Upper West Side of Manhattan. This location is readily accessible via public transportation for families throughout the greater New York City area.

For 45 minutes, parent and child spend time talking about things like homework, sports activities, creative pursuits, and also more emotional topics such as how they are coping with the separation or the unexpected changes in school or living arrangements that are often the result of a parent's incarceration. Most notably, all televisits are supported by a psychologist or social work intern who is in the room the entire time to offer support, guidance, and coaching.

What is helpful are large 56-inch television sets that display a full-size picture of the parent that is easy for the child to see. It allows the child to instantly recognize his or her parent and pick up on all the nuances of facial expressions and body language. Screens of smaller size create challenges to the attention that is needed during a televisit. Without large screen televisions and appropriate equipment for children and family interactions, the quality of the visit quickly disintegrates.

Comfortable couches and chairs provide places for children to bounce around during the visit so that the televisit with the incarcerated parent is associated with fun. Tables with construction material to create art, do homework, or meditate with Mom are also available to enrich the experience of visiting with Mom or Dad on TV.

Without a camera that zooms, pans, and tilts, the image displayed on the TV screen is far too "frozen" and cannot follow the child or provide different viewing angles. With state-of-the-art cameras, parent and child can zoom in on book titles so that they can choose a book together, for example. Microphones with noise-cancellation features can block out extraneous noise while still transmitting a clear signal of the parent and child's voice. A split screen, also known as Picture-in-Picture/Self-View, allows children to see themselves on the screen and at the same time as they see their parents. With this feature activated, the children can see themselves on the couch and the background. The backdrop of the room is typically reflective of the season or holiday if there is a special occasion. So, for example, if a child is celebrating a birthday, we may hang a birthday banner and the parent might have us write a special note that says, "Happy Birthday, Love Daddy" on a dry erase board behind the child. This then creates a memory and narrative of experiencing a wonderful birthday with the parent even though they are separated because the parent is incarcerated. Computer input is used to share videos, educational materials, and music to demonstrate parenting skills and manuals. For example, the social worker can play videos of a child's talent show or play music for the parent and child to sing together. Another opportunity for using a shared screen is to show learning materials such as Sesame Workshops' Little Children, Big Challenges video series on incarceration. Finally, cloud-based telepresence hosting and a "codex" encrypts and secures the video and audio signals for privacy.

Outreach for supportive televisiting services is conducted on-site at the Rikers Island jails and through the borough jails in Manhattan and Brooklyn. We also receive referrals from agencies who work with families who are incarcerated. Increasingly referrals are coming from family court judges who are committed to ensuring that the child's right to spend time with his or her parent is maintained even when a parent is incarcerated. Televisiting policy and procedure starts with an intake process and for all family members including the incarcerated parent, caregiver, and child. If needed, the foster care social worker or another agency is involved. These intake documents enable us to assess and understand the strengths and challenges of families with very complex stressors and dynamics. The intake form consists of approximately 13 questions. The first section is basic identifying information. The second section asks about family dynamics such as history of engagement between parent and child, and whether there are any additional issues that need to be known in order to support the family. Incarceration-related details are obtained such as the status or sentence of the detained parent, the next court date, earliest release date, and also the charge. The intake process is carefully designed to gather essential information about the family to determine the nature or types of support that may help the family have successful televisits. We do not have predetermined rule-outs based on mental status or charge. Each intake is conducted individually by a licensed clinical psychologist or social work intern. Because of our high level of psychologist—and social work—training and expertise, we are able to support positive outcomes for complicated family histories and dynamics. Scheduling is typically at least 72 hours in advance and involves coordinating with the Department of Corrections, the family, and the agency to find a time that works well for everyone. There are no restrictions on the frequency except that televisits are based on family availability, agency hours, and Department of Corrections facility capacity. A typical family will visit every two weeks, some families even have multiple visits a week, and some families have "special occasion televisits." At the beginning of each session, the televisit facilitator will check in with each family member, the incarcerated parent, the caregiver, and the child to see how they are doing that day, to see if any major changes have occurred since the last televisit, and to anticipate if any major changes or important events will be happening before the next televisit. This allows everyone to have a sense of what unexpected event might occur during a televisit that may require additional attention or support. Feedback forms are completed at the end of every session for all children. There are two versions: a version for children under 10 and one for children 10 and older. These feedback forms ask questions such as "How did your televisit go today with your parent?", "Would you like to televisit again?", and "What was the best part of your televisit session?"

Supportive Services

In the process of providing televisits for children and their incarcerated parents, it becomes apparent that many other supportive services would be helpful. For example, services can include integrating anger management, parenting and parent prep counseling sessions, and financial literacy skills. Additionally, psychological skills can be interwoven into activities and discussions. These psychological skills include emotional intelligence, cognitive behavioral therapy, and dialectical behavioral therapy (DBT) skills such as mindfulness, distress tolerance, interpersonal effectiveness, and emotion regulation.

Education and enrichment are integrated into televisits with opportunities for reading, writing, and creating and sharing art between and with children and their parents.

Because almost every person and parent who is currently incarcerated will return to the community, we have developed reentry services to support the transition back to home, work, and community such as mock job interviews and resume writing.

The Unique Challenges of Women Parenting From Prison

Although there are many variations and each family is unique, when Dad is incarcerated, children typically live with the mother. However, incarcerated mothers present unique challenges. If the child is not living with the mother, the next most common caregiver is the grandparent, typically the mother's mother, also known as the maternal grandparent. When Mom is incarcerated, children typically live with the maternal grandmother, the paternal grandmother, or another relative. Children who do not have a supportive family member to live with are often placed in foster care. When a child is in foster care and wishes to televisit, we require that the social worker participate in the first and every third televisit. This participation provides a unique opportunity for the caseworker to witness the parent and child interact in a supportive enriched environment.

Fathers Too Readily Unincluded in the Lives of Their Children

This is true in the community and perhaps even more true when a father is incarcerated. Family, educators, and even faith-based community supports all too often do not pursue more strongly the presence and role of the father for the child. Frequently, an assumption is made "if the father is not in contact then he does not want contact" and some have said, "perhaps it is better that way."

What we have learned from the televisiting program is that many fathers very much want contact and a meaningful relationship with their child. However, there are barriers such as lack of an advocate to help them negotiate the process of connecting with their child, a strained relationship with a child's other parent or family members, or a general feeling of discouragement due to their incarceration or from inconsistent or a lack of visits with their child.

Session Support

Before each session, a check-in is conducted with the child and caregiver to see how they are doing and help them transition into televisits. When children and families are coming straight from school or a busy life, it helps to give them a drink of water, a snack, and a kind word to help comfort them and get them ready to see their parent. A parent may be having a particularly difficult day before the televisit. If not addressed, the parent's stress can impact the quality of the televisit with the children. For example, the parent may be concerned about her next court hearing and feel "stressed out" because she has not heard back from her lawyer. The psychologist or social worker can work with the parent to refocus her attention away from the current stressors and consequences of incarceration and refocus on being present and emotionally available for the child.

Simple interventions and DBT skills such as a brief mindfulness exercise often help calm an incarcerated mother emotionally and physically. Overall, parents understand the impact of their well-being on the reaction of the child and are willing to try and relax through deep breathing. A moment or two spent with the parent prior to the visit can make a difference in the mom's mood.

When family members want to have a difficult conversation, they often seek guidance or language to do so. These difficult discussions can include experiences while living in foster care, the inability to attend a special event or birthday, or even something as critical as explaining where Mom or Dad is and why the parent is there.

The supportive aspects of the program offer resources and structure for families to have these difficult conversations. At the end of each session, a check-in is conducted with the parent, caregiver, and child to see how things went, find out if there were any unexpected surprises, and to schedule the next visit. Specific feedback is regularly offered to parents in a "coaching" format in order to reinforce the wonderful creativity and parenting skills that they already have and to offer suggestions to improve future visits. Scheduling the next visit at the end of the current visit promotes continuity and allows the child to look forward to the next televisit.

Reporting and evaluation is typically monthly especially for those with court ordered televisiting. The televisiting session report (TSR) lists the number of televisits that were scheduled that actually occurred. It is an outcome and tracking measure of televisits and parent–child interaction.

Effectively Engaging Stakeholders for Success

Expanding the televisiting program into the community will require the support of the executive director, a board of trustees, an information technology director, a clinical staff, a director of supportive televisiting, internship supervisor, and psychology interns from psychology, social work, marriage and family therapy, and art therapies.

Our community-based televisiting program is located at the NYSEC, an educational and religious organization. The setting is warm, welcoming, family-friendly, and enriched with a range of programming such as Ethics in Film, Ethics in Theater, and Ethics for Children, Youth, and Teens. Clinical expertise is required for cultural competency, working with children, working with people who are incarcerated, working in a correctional setting, and ability to engage families with complex histories, in complex settings, and embedded in complex systems (Minnesota Department of Corrections, 2011).

Administrative support is required from the Community Televisiting Center location as well as from the correctional facility. Leadership commitments from the executive director, board of trustees, warden, assistant commissioner of programs, and correctional officers all play critical roles to the success, or struggles, of a televisiting program. Financial and staffing resources are required to support staff and a correctional officer who will host the visit at the correctional facility. Correctional facility leadership, including the warden or superintendent, the deputy warden of programs, and the deputy warden of security, are required to provide the staffing, funding, and culture to ensure that the program is clearly supported and to address challenges directly.

We have found that participants are respectful of the equipment and there have been few, if any, incidences of damage when video units are secured and stored at the correctional facility. At its foundation, televisiting is a technology program for families. It is live, interactive, secure video and audio communication delivered via the Internet between a community-based televisiting room and a correctional facility. As a result, technical support is essential.

Paying specific attention to the needs of the caregiver and offering a heartfelt acknowledgment of his or her efforts will often go a long way toward gaining caregiver support because caregivers are often the source of stability, safety, and basic care and love for the child. This relationship is often the one that is most active in the child's day-to-day life. Caregivers also come with their own stresses and challenges and are frequently trying to make things work against significant challenges, such as creating the time, money, patience, and love to support the child in participating in the televisit with his or her incarcerated parents.

Because the televisiting program is child-focused, which is both ideological and strategic, keeping the focus on the child helps to inform the support, the structure, and the message of the program to participants, administrators, staff, and supporters.

Case Example and Application

We collaborate with the New York and Brooklyn Public Libraries' Daddy & Me and Mommy & Me early literacy programs because early literacy research highlights the clear benefits of parent–child reading. Early on, we realized that we would need to collaborate with experts on reading and learning. This led to an initial meeting with correctional services to learn what sort of resources parents may have while incarcerated at Rikers Island. We initially joined with the New York Public Library and the Brooklyn Public Library, which provide Daddy & Me and Mommy & Me programs; these programs engage parents at Rikers Island in reading with their child.

We began by offering televisiting to the parents who completed the libraries' Daddy/ Mommy & Me program. As the collaboration developed, the Social Service Board worked with the Brooklyn Public Library to launch the first Brooklyn Library-based televisiting program for children with incarcerated parents. The program has grown to include the Central Library at Grand Army Plaza and three Brooklyn branch libraries. The Social Service Board's investment in developing library-based televisiting has ignited an unprecedented wave of innovative social justice intervention throughout the system of New York City libraries.

Another collaborator is Carnegie Hall's Lullaby Project, which works with mothers in stressful situations. Carnegie Hall artists, musicians, vocalists, and composers meet with mothers to help them develop a very personal lullaby for their child. They then bring the lullaby to life with Carnegie Hall artists performing and recording the mother's lullaby. This lullaby is then hosted online in the cloud and made available for the child. A case study example is when the Social Service Board partnered with Carnegie Hall's lullaby project to provide a very special televisit in which the mother and child listened together to the lullaby that mom had created and Carnegie Hall produced. This unique series of lullaby televisits represent some of our most artistically enriched and emotionally expressive televisits. This mother and child then continued to televisit weekly as long as they liked.

(continued)

Case Example and Application (*continued*)

Training, consultations, and site visits have been provided to the National Association of Forensic Social Work (NAFSW), The Black Psychiatrists of Greater New York & Associates, and various foster care agencies.

Activities and Interventions

Televisits empower families to celebrate special moments and achievements. A particularly poignant example is the creation of a tele birthday party. For example, Alex, a child who had been televisiting with his mom for several months, walked into the televisiting room one day. Alex was confused because the room was dark. As he continued to enter the room, he noticed a light on the table. Just as the child saw the burning flame of a candle on top of a cupcake, he heard his mother's voice singing, "Happy Birthday to you. . . . Happy Birthday to you . . ." from the television screen on his left. This child was able to spend his birthday with his mother and experience the fact that he is loved, he is special, and that he is important to his mother.

These are the moments that can often make a difference in a child's life. When they have a wonderful special birthday, it increases resilience. When they do not, the children may be tempted to "feel sick" or get into trouble at school in order to avoid people asking if they celebrated their birthday with their mom.

A popular holiday televisiting tradition is the tele Easter egg hunt. Easter egg hunts are often a family tradition for many people. However, when Mom or Dad is incarcerated, often the joy is taken out of holidays, and traditions are forgotten or discarded. During televisits, parents are able to celebrate an acknowledged holiday or tradition and even create new traditions. One clever family suggested hiding plastic Easter eggs around the televisiting room. Because the camera pans, tilts, and zooms, the parent was able to tell the child when he or she was getting "warmer" or "colder" to guide the child to finding the hidden Easter eggs.

Another version of this is a televisiting hide and seek, which is a joy to watch because there are *not* a lot of places to hide in a television room. Talent shows are another event that provides opportunities to engage families during televisits. Our children are incredibly talented and often excel in talent shows, science fairs, and spelling bees.

Homework, study time, and practice are some of the greatest losses due to the lack of consistent contact between incarcerated parents and their children during their homework time. The time that children would spend with their parents going over math problems, developing science projects, or showing off their new dance move is lost. These moments can be recaptured during televisits. Children can bring in their homework, chat about science projects, or belt out a song that they are working on for a school talent show.

Future Directions, Next Steps, and Call to Action

We are expanding to the New York State Department of Corrections, which is responsible for the confinement and supervision of approximately 52,000 people under custody held at 54 state facilities. Furthermore, we are expanding to more community settings, foster care agencies, treatment facilities, libraries, and schools.

CHAPTER EXERCISES

Exercise 1. Role-play using the chapter vignette or a client from the field. Imagine what it might be like to be a child of an incarcerated parent televisiting with his or her parent in prison.

Exercise 2. Watch the following video clip from Sesame Street: www.youtube.com/watch?v=kDUdniEig38

How might a cartoon be helpful or not for children of incarcerated parents? Discuss in small and large groups.

Additional Resources

Child Welfare Information Gateway: www.childwelfare.gov/topics/supporting/support-services/prisoners

National Institute of Corrections: http://youth.gov/federal-links/national-institute-corrections-nic-children-incarcerated-parents-coip-project

Youth.gov: http://youth.gov/youth-topics/children-of-incarcerated-parents

References

City of New York. (2016). Facilities overview. Retrieved from http://www1.nyc.gov/site/doc/about/facilities.page

Dozier, M. (2005). Challenges of foster care. *Attachment and Human Development, 7*(1), 27–30. doi:10.1080/14616730500039747

Gjelsvik. A., Dumont D. M., & Nunn. A. (2013). Incarceration of a household member and Hispanic health disparities: Childhood exposure and adult chronic disease risk behaviors. *Preventing Chronic Disease, 10,* 120281. doi:10.5888/pcd10.120281

Glaze, L. E., & Maruschak, L. M. (2010). Parents in prison and their minor children. *Special Report.* Department of Justice, Office of Justice Programs, Bureau of Justice Statistics. Retrieved from http://www.bjs.gov/content/pub/pdf/pptmc.pdf

Gostin, L. O., Vanchieri, C., & Pope, A. (2007). *Ethical consideration for research involving prisoners.* Washington, DC: National Academies Press. doi:10.17226/11692

Kaeble, D., Glaze, L., Tsoutis, A., & Minton, T. (2015). *Correctional populations in the United States, 2014,* NCJ 249513 (Revised January 21, 2016). Washington, DC: United States Department of Justice, Office of Justice Programs, Bureau of Justice Statistics. Retrieved from http://www.bjs.gov/content/pub/pdf/cpus14.pdf

Maschi, T. (2006). Trauma and delinquent behavior among males: The moderating role of social support. *Stress, Trauma, and Crisis: An International Journal, 9*(1), 45–72.

Minnesota Department of Corrections. (2011, November). *The effects of prison visitation on offender recidivism.* Minnesota Department of Corrections. Retrieved from https://www.doc.state.mn.us/pages/files/large-files/Publications/11-11MNPrisonVisitationStudy.pdf

New York State Corrections and Community Supervision. (2016, September). DOCCS fact sheet. Retrieved from http://www.doccs.ny.gov/FactSheets/PDF/currentfactsheet.pdf

Poehlmann, J., Dallaire, D., Loper, A. B., & Shear, L. D. (2010). Children's contact with their incarcerated parents: Research findings and recommendations. *American Psychologist, 65*(6), 575–598. doi:10.1037/a0020279

Porter, N. D. (2015). *The state of sentencing 2015: Developments in policy and practice.* The Sentencing Project. Washington, DC. Retrieved from http://www.sentencingproject.org

Social Service Board. (n.d.). Ethics into Action. Retrieved from http://socialserviceboard.org

Thompson, R. A. (2008). Early attachment and later development: Familiar questions, new answers. In J. Cassidy & P. R. Shaver (Eds.), *Handbook of attachment* (2nd ed., pp. 348–365). New York, NY: Guilford Press

Walmsley, R. (2016). *World prison population list* (11th ed.). [World Prison Brief]. International Centre for Prison Studies. Retrieved from http://www.prisonstudies.org

Wilper, A. P., Woolhandler, S., Boyd, J. W., Lasser, K. E., McCormick, D., Bor, D. H., & Himmelstein, D. U. (2009). The health and health care of US prisoners: Results of a nationwide survey. Research and Practice. *American Journal of Public Health, 99*(4), 666–672.

VOICES FROM THE FIELD

Eileen Price-Farbman

Social Work Master's Program
Fordham University
Social Work Intern
Supportive Televisiting Program
The New York Society for Ethical Culture

Agency Setting

The New York Society for Ethical Culture is a nonprofit organization in Manhattan dedicated to advancing social justice, environmental causes, and ethical living, with humanism as its guiding philosophy. The New York Society for Ethical Culture provides a range of community services such as social services, including homeless shelters, an elder empowerment program, the supportive televisiting program for children of incarcerated parents, and a social work internship program in collaboration with local universities, as well as lectures and arts activities.

The televisiting program is run by Dr. Frank Corigliano, PhD, and a social work intern. Its aims are to facilitate connections between parents at Rikers Island with their children via televisits. Televisits are held at the New York Society for Ethical Culture and coordinated with Rikers Island Prison. Televisits allow incarcerated parents to see and talk to their child(ren) in real time.

Practice Responsibilities

As a social work intern I am responsible for facilitating operations and growing the televisiting program. My duties include conducting intake evaluations, scheduling televisits, coordinating with families and the criminal justice system as well as other agencies, recruiting participants for the program, and administrative documentation and record keeping. Importantly, I am directly present during the televisit and engage with the participants if appropriate.

I ensure that during the intake process I stress that this is a child-centered program. Our policy is as follows: *A caregiver may be present during the televisit **only if** the child has special needs or is under 5 and needs the caregiver there for the first few minutes to help him or her feel comfortable.* One way we support the child is to help him or her understand that the parent is incarcerated. Providing supportive, therapeutic communication to parents and children before and after televisits is a fundamental and highly important responsibility. I am also responsible for scheduling the visits with the caregiver and providing the necessary information to all of the parties in the justice system prior to the visit. I work with the criminal justice system to determine which parents and caregivers are eligible for our program. Understanding the best practices of the criminal justice system as well as how to complete important necessary paperwork is a key element to a successful televisit.

My practice responsibilities also include recruitment for the supportive televisiting program. When recruiting for the program, I visit correctional facilities to screen and select participants, and contact the child's caregiver to determine eligibility before scheduling visits. I look for children through foster care agencies and other agencies. I want families to know that during televisits, they can reassure and comfort the child(ren) during this separation. A major goal of my work is to strengthen and maintain a healthy parent–child relationship. We find that having a strong connection with and support from a parent may help to prevent, address, or reduce a child's behavioral, emotional, or school problems. Additional responsibilities include coordinating with other professionals, such as lawyers, clinicians, and correctional officers, as well as other agencies.

Ethical, Legal, Practice, Diversity, and/or Advocacy Issues Addressed

Several legal and ethical issues are salient in facilitating supportive televisiting. Often, the court has mandated that a child regularly visits with his or her incarcerated parent in accordance with state laws, which hold that family court rulings must be based on "the best interest of the child." When a visit is court mandated, scheduling, documenting, and ensuring that these visits consist of the child(ren)'s caregiver as well as the child(ren) is essential. The stakes are very high as noncompliance with a court order can jeopardize the caregiver(s) custody of their child(ren). Accordingly, my role also involves documenting no shows and the absence of televisits, something which carries tangible legal implications.

Many of the legal issues arise prior to any televisit. In the intake process, I address some of the following community-based issues: Is the child in foster care? Is there a permanency goal? Are there legal or other restrictions that may prevent the child from having contact with the parent? For example, is there an order of protection? These questions are samples from a formal intake evaluation form provided by the New York Society for Ethical Culture.

The fact that the parent is part of the criminal justice system and has limited rights poses challenges for the televisiting program. For example, the incarcerated parent may have scheduling limitations due to a variety of factors, such as prison/jail rules about when visits are allowed, as well as loss of phone privileges for whatever reason. The caregiver also has challenges with regard to what he or she feels may be best for the child. For instance, a caregiver may believe it is best for the child not to have contact with the incarcerated parent or wish to protect his or her child from the reality that he or she has a parent in prison. My job is to be objective, factual, and transparent, as well as to ensure consistency with the court mandate and build a healthy, supportive, secure parent–child relationship. It is crucial to stress in all of my communications that the goal of the program is doing what is best for the child and that the program is *for* the child.

Multicultural competence and awareness as well as an understanding of diversity issues are very important from an ethical and practical standpoint. My role requires culture competence as the criminal justice system in New York City has a disproportionate number of African Americans and Latinos. I need to ascertain if English is spoken or if Spanish speaking material, such as children's books, would enhance the visit.

There are ethical factors inherent in televisiting as there are several parties involved (e.g., the incarcerated parent, the nonincarcerated caregiver, and the child(ren)). For example, a parent or caregiver may want to vent excessively or get advice in areas that are not either relevant to televisiting or appropriate. There may be conflicts between parents and caregivers. Recently, an incarcerated parent reported that he no longer wanted to continue with televisits, and it is not my role to play either therapist or lawyer to either party even if I am tempted to. In order to navigate these issues, it is important to keep in mind the best interests of the child and the goals of the televisiting program.

In general, advocacy work on behalf of the supportive televisiting program is central and underlies a wide variety of my responsibilities. I interact with other professionals such as lawyers, public defenders, psychiatrists, other advocacy groups, and other social workers in order to advocate for the child, parent, or televisiting program. Collaborating with the criminal justice system and other professionals is key to help secure other services for the individuals involved in the televisit; I will advocate to find the best practitioner(s) to help the parent, child, or both, and will speak to anyone on behalf of a parent or the program.

In addition, advocacy involves fundraising and generating awareness of the supportive televisiting program. I help look for funding through grants and hope to expand upon this line of advocacy going forward. I plan to meet with members of the city council to raise money for the program. Furthermore, I engage in outreach to grow the program by contacting foster care agencies throughout the metropolitan area as well as other locations where there is a high prevalence of at-risk children.

Index